Fast Sailing Ships

Frontispiece: The three skysail-yarder *Morning Star* is here seen lying at Princess Wharf, Bristol, at 2.30pm on the afternoon of 4 June 1858. The photographer, Charles William Warren, has captured a splendid image of a large wooden sailing ship. The ship is probably the vessel built at Saint John in 1854 by F & J Ruddock with a tonnage of 1327. She is presumably equipped with Howes' double topsails, as the upper yard is lowered right down on top of the lower one. *Reece Winstone, Bristol*

DAVID R MACGREGOR

Fast Sailing Ships

THEIR DESIGN AND CONSTRUCTION, 1775-1875

Dedicated To Roger and Jill Hadlee who have stimulated my interest in marine art as well as providing good sailing experience.

BY THE SAME AUTHOR

The Tea Clippers (1952; reprinted 1972)
The Tea Clippers 1833-1875 (1983, enlarged and revised edition)
The China Bird (1961; enlarged and revised 1986)
Square Rigged Sailing Ships (1977)
Clipper Ships (1979)
Merchant Sailing Ships 1775-1815 (1980; second edition 1985)
Merchant Sailing Ships 1815-1850 (1984)
Merchant Sailing Ships 1850-1875 (1984)
Schooners in Four Centuries (1982)

First Edition published 1973
Second revised Edition published 1988 by
Conway Maritime Press Ltd
24 Bride Lane, Fleet Street
London EC4Y 8DR

ISBN 0-85177-452-0

Designed by Tony Garrett
Typeset by MJL Typesetters, Hitchin, Herts
Printed and bound by Butler and Tanner, Frome, Somerset

CONTENTS

Foreword 7

Introduction to First Edition 9

Introduction to Second Edition 11

Chapter One: SHIP DESIGN AND CONSTRUCTION 1775–1850 13
- Employment of fast ships 13
- Principles of naval architecture from English books 15
- Criteria for hull analysis 20
- Innovations in construction 20
- Tonnage measurement and registration 23

Chapter Two: EARLY FAST SHIPS 1775–1815 26
- Clipper terminology 26
- Cutters and cutter-build 26
- English privateers 32
- Swedish, French and American privateers and blockade runners 34
- Post Office packets 47
- The *Transit* and other long ships 50
- Some royal yachts 52
- Revenue cutters and smugglers 53
- Brigantine *St Helena* 55

Chapter Three: CLIPPER SHIP DEVELOPMENT 1815–1839 58
- Definitions 58
- Post Office packets 59
- A merchant ship and an East Indiaman 62
- Hilhouse schooners 66
- The brig *Neilson* 68
- The *Falcon* 71
- Outline specification of alterations to the *Falcon* 74
- T & J Brocklebank's brigantine *Dash* and barquentine *Bonanza* 75
- Leith smacks 79
- Clipper schooners 82
- A demand for clippers 86
- The Symondites 88
- Opium clippers 90
- Fast ships in eastern trades 95
- New measurement tonnage 97

Chapter Four: THE ABERDEEN BOW 1839–1850 99
- The *Scottish Maid* 99
- Development of Aberdeen bow 105
- Some of Hall's clippers compared 109
- Other clippers of the 1840s 121
- Early American clipper ship development 123
- The *Camertonian* 126

Chapter Five: PROGRESS OF SHIPBUILDING 1850–1875 130
- Iron as a shipbuilding material 130
- Rules for iron ships 132
- Spread of iron shipbuilding 134
- Steel shipbuilding 135
- Review of wood shipbuilding 135

Diagonal and experimental construction in wood 140
Composite construction 141
Improvements to deck fittings and rigging 146
Tonnage measurement by 1854 rule 151

Chapter Six: THE CLIPPER SHIP BOOM 1850–1859 153
Introduction 153
The *Three Bells* 155
The Australian gold rush 157
Alexander Duthie and Walter Hood 158
The *Hurricane* and other iron clippers 159
The 'Gauntlet' clipper ship 162
William Rennie 165
Alexander Stephen jnr and the *Storm Cloud* 167
Benjamin Nicholson and the *Annandale* 172
Alexander Hall's tea clippers 175
John and William Pile 182
American and Canadian clippers 183
The *Schomberg* 193
Sarah Neumann and the clippers of southern England 196
Charles Tayleur & Co, Warrington 198
Clippers of north-west England 201
Clippers of the late 1850s 202
Clipper schooners and brigs 206
Conclusions 214

Chapter Seven: THE LATER CLIPPERS 1860–1875 216
Introduction 216
The *Fiery Cross* and *Black Prince* 219
The auxiliary steamer *Sea King* 221
Other clippers of 1860–68 225
William Pile and the *Maitland* 231
Robert Steele & Co's tea clippers 234
Charles Connell and the *Spindrift* 239
Bernard Waymouth and the *Thermopylae* 242
Some of Alexander Hall's clippers 249
Clippers of 1869–70 253
The *Mermerus* and other iron clippers of the 1870s 258
Clippers, brigs and schooners 263

Conclusions 270

Appendix 1: Definitions of tonnage measurements and registration 271

Appendix 2: Ships built by Alexander Hall & Sons, Aberdeen, 1811–1875 274

Appendix 3: Spar dimensions of *Thermopylae* 280

Appendix 4: Specification of iron sailing ship *Sarah Palmer* 281

Sources and Bibliography 283

Acknowledgements 290

References 292

Index 302

FOREWORD

English Maritime History is noted for its high standards of excellence. It has examined its naval history in depth, the growth of its national merchant marine and of its important trades, including the national fisheries. Operations, economic effects, and social relations of many trades have been studied.

It has recorded the lives of great English navigators and explorers, described the lives of seamen in commercial and naval services. It has discussed the national maritime policies in various periods and many other matters.

English maritime history had the support of active nautical research studies by members of the Society for Nautical Research, much of which has been published in the *Mariner's Mirror*, journal of the society.

However, in spite of all this, there has been an important area of neglect; the history of the evolution of the fast-sailing vessels in the English merchant marine and in their naval service, utilizing contemporary ship plans as evidence.

This is different from American practice, in which the evolution of American naval architecture is an important historical factor. As a result, ship plans are employed in America as technical evidence; these are the foundations for many historical conclusions. For example, a claim that a vessel was a clipper is accepted only if a plan, half-model, or a surviving technical description verify the claim. The plans or half-models are visible evidence of the shape of the hull of the vessels in both cases and sometimes of the rig in plans. Usually the lines of a ship, for which a half-model exists, are 'taken off' and converted to a plan of the hull, as a convenience. There are instances where extensive technical descriptions of individual ships are in existence, adequate to justify acceptance as evidence of hull-form, but these are relatively rare.

The criterion of excellence of sailing ship design has been speed, by common consent, therefore the fastest ship of a type would be the 'best design'. However, the suitability of a ship for her trade would undoubtedly be a more realistic evaluation for such a judgement, but it is very difficult to assess.

The apparent neglect of the history of English naval architecture by English marine historians has been puzzling, particularly so because of the immense collections of ship plans preserved in England. The greatest of these and probably the largest in the world is the *Admiralty Collection of Draughts* preserved in the National Maritime Museum at Greenwich. This collection contains contemporary plans of sailing ships built between 1675 and 1875, or later. Predominantly the plans are of men-of-war built for, or captured by, the Royal Navy. However, there are also many merchant ship plans in the collection, English and foreign. In addition there are surviving plans in some of the Old English shipyards and in private hands, which are large and important collections.

The *Admiralty Collection of Draughts* contains the most complete and valuable plans of American sailing vessels between 1745 and 1845 so this collection of plans has been a very valuable source to American students, if to few English historians.

The excuse for the neglect of the history of English naval architecture has been that ship plans and professional data are 'too technical' for English readers.

The American practice of utilizing numerical factors in the analysis of a ship design gives some support to this excuse. These factors did not prove very decisive in analysis, however, and visual comparison was found adequate. Experience and publication showed that plans were understood to far greater extent than had previously been thought to be the case. It should be acknowledged that ship-model builders have been of great assistance in this; their need for an understanding of plans is obvious.

In view of what has been said about the state of the history of English naval architecture this work is a great departure. Through its use of plans, as historical evidence, the true evolution of English fast-sailing ship designs becomes well-defined. In addition, the development of English vessel types such as the cutter and three-masted lugger, are brought to attention.

It will be found that the history of English sailing merchant ship design is outlined, showing ships of various classes — in the eighteenth and nineteenth centuries. The history of iron ship design and construction in England, the leader in this, is traced. Also, the development of composite construction is examined.

The ubiquitous clipper ship receives attention and all classes of these that were developed in England, are shown, with liberal use of plans. Ships that have not been previously introduced, in English clipper ship history, are brought to light. It will now appear that English construction and evolution of clipper ship design paralleled American development and construction of the extreme clipper ship model. The part played by iron construction in the evolution of extreme clipper ship in England is particularly interesting. The claims that English designs were influenced by American principles are completely exploded. The comparative developments can now be explored and the history of the clipper revised and corrected.

Howard I Chapelle

13th March 1973

INTRODUCTION TO FIRST EDITION

The word 'clipper' has probably been subjected to more misuse than any other word in the maritime vocabulary, but today we desire to give it the more distinct title it deserves, namely to denote a hull that is formed for speed rather than for the carriage of cargo. The precise shape of this hull is not important, and indeed the plans reproduced here demonstrate an infinite variety of patterns which competent naval architects over the years have considered would provide a ship of incontestable and undisputed speed, although such convictions have frequently proved too sanguine.

At no single period did clipper ships form anything but a small minority of the thousands of vessels in trade throughout the world, but their exploits did capture the imagination and provide headlines in the press, just as the attainment of higher speeds has always done. Fast ships have always been in demand for various purposes and their development can be traced from the earliest times, thus proving that there can never have been a 'first clipper'. Such a term is a misnomer and denigrates the capabilities of naval architects during the seventeenth and eighteenth centuries.

This myth of a 'first clipper' has been created by the custom of reserving the title of 'clipper' exclusively for ships built in the years 1840–75, and of calling previous vessels by such terms as 'fast-sailing ship' or 'early clipper'.The words 'extreme' and 'medium' are frequently prefixed to clipper to denote a ship of ultra-sharp form or of relatively full hull, but the latter variety does not figure to any large extent in this book. In any case, the word 'clipper' or 'fast ship' is always a comparative one and the hull-form so described in 1775 will be found totally different to that of later decades. The use of the word 'clipper' for later full-bodied nineteenth-and twentieth-century ships is to be deplored and its continued use indicates an ignorance of the facts behind the development of the sailing ship.

Clipper ship building was at its peak in the years 1853–55 and at this period there was a wider range of experimentation in ships built on fine lines and a greater change in hull-form in every type of craft than was ever to occur again. Ten years later when there was a minor boom in the building of clippers, principally for the China trade, most classes of vessels had already abandoned their short bluff hulls for slightly longer and fractionally sharper versions—like Kipling's 'Elephant's Child' they had all got new noses—and this second clipper ship boom did not therefore affect them.

The clipper ship development here described is mainly that of British ships but there were so many close links with America that it is natural to compare ships of the two countries whenever a suitable opportunity occurs, and several plans of American ships are included.

The choice of plan material certainly has been the dominant factor in this book, coupled with the intention of describing the ships in those very terms usually lacking in other works—hull-form, deck arrangements, sail and rigging plans—and to employ these descriptions as the central theme. Throughout, the emphasis is on the development of the ships and the factors that brought this about and not on the careers of the ships, nor their passages and owners. The shipbuilders have received too little attention in the past and correspondingly any detailed analysis of ship design and construction has been neglected.

The prime consideration in presenting these plans has been to offer examples which are as complete as possible and which have not been reproduced before. With one or two exceptions this has been attained. It seemed desirable that as a minimum standard each selected ship should have a lines plan and a sail plan, together with a deck layout if it existed. In certain cases, missing sail plans have been reconstructed from existing spar dimensions or rules for mast-making. When this has sometimes been impracticable, the lines plan is nevertheless included if considered important enough. In addition, there are some sail plans illustrating interesting ship types for which no hull lines exist. Most of the plans are newly drawn as accurately as possible, being worked up from old shipyard drawings or from lines taken off models, but a few examples of old plans are submitted to show the style of draughtsmanship.

This study is confined primarily to ships whose principal purpose was the carrying of cargo, passengers and mail. Within this definition it is limited to sailing ships, although there are references to auxiliary steamers and indeed plans of the *Sea King* are included. Fishing boats are omitted altogether, and yachts are only included to describe the development of the fast-sailing ship; sometimes yachts were purchased for specialised cargo carrying where speed was of primary importance. There are also examples of privateers, slavers and naval craft because in the years before 1815 there was often little to distinguish between them and purely fast merchantmen.

Clipper ship design was a very personal affair, and the naval architects and shipbuilders responsible for these splendid creations must have possessed more than ordinary vision and design ability, as well as the art of persuading reluctant owners to risk their capital in a ship whose insufficient carrying capacity could result in lower profits when freight rates fell. The economic factors involved with fast sailing ships are frequently referred to, because they form such an important part of the whole story.

DRM , Barnes, London, 1972

INTRODUCTION TO SECOND EDITION

In the Author's Preface to *Merchant Sailing Ships 1850–1875*, I recounted how the project called 'Heyday of Sail' was finally completed with the publication of that volume. At that time, *Fast Sailing Ships* was out of print and the contents of the three volumes in the Merchant Sailing Ships series was really confined to cargo carrying vessels or, in some cases, to medium clippers, with a few selected examples of sailing ships added where appropriate. The three volumes in this series together with *Fast Sailing Ships* cover a hundred years between 1775 and 1875.

The first edition of the present work was well received because the clipper ship story had always possessed many devoted admirers and the work then provided an in-depth study of many famous ships to which were added other forgotten examples that were of no lesser calibre. However, although it is not possible to state whether every extreme clipper built in Great Britain has been included in this work, yet no additional contenders for a place in the ranks have been found. As previously emphasised, the claim of clipper status has only been accorded to vessels when plans or models have been examined. It will be noted that this rule has been broken in a few instances when sufficient documentary evidence has been assembled, but I have normally explained my reasons for so doing.

In this new edition of *Fast Sailing Ships*, all the detailed ship studies have been retained and some of those in Chapter 7 have been expanded. This has been possible because this chapter now represents the original manuscript, whereas that in the first edition was much curtailed and partially re-written. Some alterations have also been made in Chapter 2 with the insertion of more examples of merchant ships and revision of the material on privateers. Other additions consist of more illustrations of brigs, barquentines and schooners in Chapters 6 and 7, although the text has not been greatly expanded.

The award of a gold medal by the *Daily Mail* for the first edition and with it the title of 'Best Book of the Sea for 1973' was much appreciated.

The acknowledgements to the first edition remain as evidence of the great help I received from many individuals, some of whom are no longer alive, and also from numerous museums and institutions. For additional work to the new edition, I am grateful to David Lyon of the National Maritime Museum, Greenwich, for drawing my attention to new material relating to ship plans. For permission to use photographs of paintings or prints from their files, I am grateful to Bertram Newbury of the Parker Gallery, to Paul Mason of the Paul Mason Gallery, and to Colin Denny. James Fairweather of Salcombe has also allowed me to reproduce photographs from his collection and David Clement has generously placed his collection at my disposal. I continue to be grateful to James Henderson for all his expertise on Aberdeen clippers and particularly for drawing a new set of lines of the *Cairngorm*. My thanks go also to Janette Rosing for making drawings and reconstructions of old ship plans. I should also like to thank my wife for her assistance with compiling a new index.

DRM, Barnes, London, 1987

One
SHIP DESIGN AND CONSTRUCTION 1775-1850

Employment of fast ships

The majority of merchant ships were built to carry cargo as safely and cheaply as possible for which only rudimentary sailing qualities were needed to reach the port of loading or discharge, and speed was of secondary importance except in a few limited cases. But there were always ships designed to outsail their competitors and whenever an owner required a fast ship, any builder could provide one to order. Admittedly, some builders achieved the result with greater success than others for it was only practice that ensured perfection in the art of naval architecture and the need for fast ships was always limited. In times of war, fast ships were greatly in demand for requisition by the Navy or for employment as privateers; but whether in peace or war, fast-sailing ships were regularly required as packets, pilot cutters, slavers, smugglers, revenue cutters and to carry fruit, fish and other perishable cargoes at maximum speed. There were many reasons why small vessels were essential for these occupations: to avoid risking too much capital in a single enterprise; to negotiate safely poorly-charted coastal waters; to spread the risk of damage to perishable cargoes caused by stress of weather; and to provide a well-found, weatherly vessel that was fast on all points of sailing. For these reasons the rudiments of fast-sailing were generally established and proved in small craft of under 200 tons, and during the eighteenth century the rigs of such vessels in Great Britain were generally those of cutter and brig, while in America the schooner or true brigantine were preferred. In Great Britain the schooner rig became increasingly popular about 1820.

Until 1815 all merchant ships had to be armed against attack, but whereas American ships relied principally on speed to escape, British ships had the advantages of a well-organised convoy system for protection in wartime. The continual reliance on this system tended to render many British merchantmen slow sailers with hulls designed to carry the maximum amount of cargo, although well-armed ships with greater pretentions to speed could secure licences to sail without convoy protection. These were known as 'running' ships and were sure of obtaining good freights because of their ability to outsail the slow convoys and capture the market on arrival. A ship such as the *Cupid* of 290 tons which was bought into the Navy in 1777, could have been a West Indiaman with her deep hold and low 'tween decks, but her moderately fine lines and nine gunports each side suggest that she could have been a 'runner' in time of war.[1] Had the ship's depth been measured in computing tonnage, rather than conveniently assuming it to have been half the breadth, a much better form of ship would have evolved.

The American War of Independence is considered to have begun in 1775 but it was not until two years later that the Navy seriously began buying merchant ships of about 300 tons for use as transports or sloops of war. Amongst these, according to the Admiralty plans, are some ships of undoubtedly finer form than the usual cargo carrier and the sharpest vessels were frequently fitted out as fireships. Perhaps it is hardly surprising to find that of the finer-lined ships several were American-built vessels. It was also not until 1777 that the Admiralty began issuing commissions for privateers, and the ports of Bristol and Liverpool were soon busy equipping suitable ships. Liverpool is stated to have fitted out 120 privateers between August 1778 and April 1779.[2] As the convoy system improved, so privateers had to be larger and faster ships capable of cutting out the better armed merchantmen which ran without convoy protection, and this in turn reduced the number of ships requesting letters of marque. A plan of a Lancaster ship is included here (figure 28) to show the type of ship in use in about 1780. When war was declared against France in 1793, fewer privateers were fitted out than in previous wars.

The slave trade was a highly organised and profitable business, and in the second half of

1: This painting by Robert Salmon shows the slaver *Kitty* off Liverpool, where she was built in 1784. Of 366 tons, she could carry 505 slaves. She was armed with 20 9-pounders and 218-pounder carronades. In 1795 she beat off a French privateer off Old Calabar. In 1805, she was almost rebuilt. She could undoubtedly cross royal yards, judging by the stays from the mast heads. She was still afloat in 1809. *Parker Gallery*

the eighteenth century many ships of about 300 tons were specially built for it, and were designed to sail fast in order to reduce the rate of mortality on board. In 1771, there were reported to be 190 British ships in this trade.[3] After 1806, when the carriage of slaves in British ships was prohibited, the importance of speed to a slaver increased as the British Navy policed the Atlantic in its efforts to stamp out this distasteful trade. The result was that, in the second quarter of the nineteenth century, foreign designers exerted themselves in producing slave ships of unprecedented sharpness of form to out-sail the steep-floored brigs and sloops which the Navy was building especially to capture them. Plans of one of these slave chasers, *Dolphin*, are given in figure 111.

All foreign-going ships were accustomed to carry passengers when space permitted, but where a faster passage was desired there were the Post Office packets which, at the beginning of the nineteenth century, sailed to such places as Lisbon, Brazil, the West Indies, New York and Halifax. They were frequently rigged as brigs although some three-masted vessels were employed, particularly after the Admiralty took over the service from the Post Office. In addition, there were many coastal packet companies which also served the Irish and Continental ports and for these the cutter was the most popular rig. Examples of each type are given here and the conditions affecting design are fully discussed.

Smuggling was a popular occupation which was carried out extensively both in peace and war, and many fast vessels were constructed, both to carry the goods and to intercept them. It is frequently recounted that a smuggler and a revenue cutter were built on adjacent slipways by a certain builder, but it is certainly true that much ingenuity was expended in designing craft of each type that would out-sail the other. Some idea of the extent of smuggling can be gained from the amount of legislation enacted to suppress it, and the effect of this on ship design is of like interest.

An Act of 1784 stated that to avoid seizure, cutters, luggers, shallops, wherries, smacks or yawls had to be 'square-rigged' or fitted with a standing bowsprit and a standing jib stay of reasonable size, and that no traveller on the bowsprit was allowed, nor a flying jib. Such vessels were not permitted to have a bowsprit which was greater in length than two-thirds of the distance between the fore side of the stem and the after side of the stern-post, measured along the deck. No vessels of any description, unless square-rigged or sloops with standing bowsprits, were allowed to be clinker built. As to armament, square-rigged vessels could carry two 4-pounders and some muskets, but the fore-and-aft rigs were prohibited from being armed. Licences could be obtained if a ship were likely to arouse suspicion. A final clause stated that no vessel was to have a beam-to-length ratio greater than three-and-a-half to one.[4]

This last was a very stultifying clause and in 1825 Colonel Beaufoy, of the Society for the Improvement of Naval Architecture, was complaining that it was 'detrimental to science' to fix a ship's ratio by Act of Parliament.[5] By 1833, the regulations about the standing bowsprit, jib stay and the clinker build had been dropped but not the ratio of beam to length which remained as before, although now it was only restricted to vessels under 200 tons which were not square-rigged. There were also the same restrictions on arming ships with carriage guns and manning and a table was now given, showing the maximum number of crew allowed for differing scales of tonnage. Luggers were allowed more men: for instance, craft of

2: One of Baugean's engravings which captures the mood of ships and sea so imaginatively. Here a schooner and a cutter are making sail out of a tidal harbour and, judging by the rocks along the base of the harbour wall on the left, they are not a moment too soon. The cutter has a deeply rouched topsail set, but her topgallant is still furled. The schooner has topsails and topgallants on each mast, and has loosed her fore topgallant sail ready for hoisting it. There is a man standing on the boom at the base of her foremast, on which a square sail is furled; this sail is capable of being set between this boom and the fore yard. *Reproduced from plate 56 in* Recueil de Petites Marines, *1817*

between 80 and 100 tons were allowed 12 men as opposed to 7 for sloops. Licences could again be obtained if the ship was outside these proportions and engaged in lawful trade.[6]

The requirements of the Smuggling Acts undoubtedly had widespread influence on basic design concepts for coastal craft — how to avoid detection or how to comply legally — and it is hardly surprising that vessels retained the large beam and short length generally associated with the eighteenth century for so long.

In the earlier Acts the square-rigged vessel and the sloop were exonerated from complicity in smuggling and the rigs so encouraged made great headway in numbers. Schooners were not mentioned, perhaps because they usually carried square topsails, although the exact description of the term 'square-rig' is not specified. Shallops were usually rigged like fore-and-aft schooners with pole masts. The definition of 'sloop' in Burney's edition of *Falconer's Dictionary* (1815 edition) states that 'it differs from a cutter by having a fixed steering bowsprit and a jib-stay; nor are the sails generally so large in proportion to the size of the vessel'. The same dictionary describes a 'smack' as 'a small vessel commonly rigged as a cutter and used in the coasting or fishing trade, or as a tender in the King's service'.

Although for British ships slaving and privateering were both officially dead by 1815, yachting and commercial competition gave renewed stimulus and financial reward to ships of sharp hull-form, and more efficient forms of transport at higher speeds came to be increasingly expected. The skills of the mechanical engineer were widely followed on land and eventually were demanded at sea, but the adoption of steam power for propulsion and iron for construction were slow in coming. Trade cycles affected a shipbuilder's orders and profits, but there was always a small demand for fast ships in highly specialised and competitive trades, and for the carriage of expensive and perishable commodities. The examples given here probably cover most of the prinicipal outlets for which sharp-bodied hulls were required.

Principles of naval architecture from English books

Like many branches of creative art, the design of ships remained a jealously guarded secret until the greater thirst for knowledge in the middle of the eighteenth century prised open the age-old mystery. From today's vantage point the so-called 'mystery' was based on a minimum of technical knowledge but relied greatly on practical experience. Once the designer had decided on the principal dimensions he could obtain precise directions on how to complete the plan if he was willing to follow the rules and proportions given, and the description of how to draw out a plan also represented the method of how to design a ship.

What must have been a real mystery to many ship-builders was how to determine in advance a ship's performance at sea under sail and her draught of water. Other uncertainties were stability, cargo capacity, weatherlines, and, in the case of a warship, her suitability as a gun platform in bad weather. With experience, a clever shipbuilder could vary a hull-form but the novice needed to follow the rules precisely to ensure that his ship floated upright and performed in the manner desired, and such information could be found in only a few printed books.

The first English book which really dealt with naval architecture was William Sutherland's *The Ship Builder's Assistant*, which was first published in 1711 and went through various amended editions throughout the eighteenth century before adopting its final form in 1784. But two further editions in identical form were issued in 1794 and 1840, together with proportions for spars and rigging taken from the first edition of 1711! Sutherland's other work, *Britain's Glory, or Ship-Building Unvail'd*, first appeared in 1717. Next came Mungo Murray's *Treatise on Ship-Building and Navigation* in 1754; the second edition of 1765 included an abridged translation from the French of Duhamel du Monceau's *Eléments de l'Architecture Navale* and part of Bouguer's *Traité du Navire*. The first edition of William Falconer's *Universal Dictionary of the Marine* was published in 1769 and included a 13-page entry on 'Naval Architecture'. There were numerous subsequent editions, culminating in that of 1815 which Dr William Burney revised and enlarged. But in none of these editions, including Burney's, were there entries for the terms 'displacement', 'centre of gravity' or 'stability', although under the definition of 'trim' the last two were mentioned. Falconer understood the relation of the height of the centre of gravity to the stability both in full-bodied and steep-floored ships and appreciated its effect longitudinally on the pitching and labouring motions.[7]

In his *Outline of Ship Building*, John Fincham

gives a résumé of the principles advocated by some of the above writers, illustrating his remarks with diagrams of how the various authorities formed the midship section, including Bouguer's rules for sharp ships. The method of design practised by Sir Thomas Slade about 1770 is briefly described and illustrated, which makes his midship section very similar to that of many contemporary merchant ships.[8]

In 1781 Marmaduke Stalkartt's *Naval Architecture* was published together with a selection of plans of various ship types — yacht, sloop, cutter and various warships — probably the first time such a range had appeared in an English book. Amongst them was the lines plan of a 1000-ton frigate with extremely steep deadrise and without any hollows in the straight, rising floors. This ship was designed by the American scientist, Benjamin Thompson (Count Rumford 1753–1814), but the design was never built by the Royal Navy.[9]

The anonymous *Shipbuilder's Repository*, which can be ascribed to the year 1788, refers to tank tests and how the centre of gravity affects stability. There are lengthy tables of proportions for every part of the ship and its structure, including the anticipated draught of water, so the prospective naval architect could be sure of moderate success if he followed these rules. For a ship to 'take the ground well, carry a good sail, quickly answer her helm, and . . . be fitly qualified to carry a large cargo',[10] the author listed the following requirements: '. . . let them have a long floor, and little rising, the lower futtocks very full, and upper futtocks near a straight. To have a good depth in the hold, wing transom to be carried pretty high, the fashion pieces formed lean below the water line, and very full above, and to have a raking bow. Also to give a good length and not too much breadth, the midship frame to be carried pretty forward, and to have no hollow water lines in the fore body, the upper works should be kept as low, and as snug as possible, and no roundhouse should be admitted in the smaller ships, or where it could be possibly done without.'[11]

Two important works appeared in 1805, both published in London by David Steel: the larger was entitled *The Elements and Practice of Naval Architecture* and had a separate folio of thirty-eight plans of naval and merchant ships; the smaller and shorter was *The Shipwright's Vade-Mecum* which repeated word-for-word much of the other, and there was a separate, thin volume of four folding plates. In 1822, the former was in its third edition and the other in its second, and their influence undoubtedly continued for another 20 or 30 years until they were gradually superseded by more modern and scientific books.

Amongst the plates in *The Elements and Practice of Naval Architecture* are several fine-lined vessels: the Royal yacht *Royal Sovereign* and a yacht for the Prince Royal of Denmark; an 18-gun brig; a cutter; a Virginia-built privateer; a 'fast-sailing' Bermudian schooner, now identified as *Ant*;[12] a Virginia pilot boat.

Unfortunately, much of the section on ship design in the above work is paraphrased or copied from *The Shipbuilder's Repository* or a late edition of Sutherland's *Ship Builder's Assistant*, including the description of how to form the midship section with arcs of circles. The author concludes that to sail fast a ship should be given a good length and not too much beam; that she should have no parallel body nor should the maximum breadth be carried too far aft; that she should have a big rise of floor, without any hollows in her entrance; and that 'as she will feel great resistance sideways, or on her broadside, with little resistance a-head, she will consequently, sail fast, and not fall much to leeward'.[13]

The 1822 edition of *The Elements and Practice of Naval Architecture*, as revised by John Knowles, refers to a ship's displacement and shows how it can be usefully employed in various calculations. The Swedish naval architect, F.H. af Chapman, based his calculations on displacement, but his book *Tractat om Skepps-Byggeriet* (1775) was not translated into English until 1820, although it was published in French in 1779.[14] Its influence in Great Britain prior to 1820 is difficult to assess, but his parabolic system of ship design received attention amongst theoretical naval architects. Examples of his ship design are given in Chapter 2. The *Shorter Oxford English Dictionary* (1959) assigns the first use of the word 'displacement', referring to hydrostatics, to the year 1802, but previously some English books had employed the term 'cavity' in a similar sense. Steel's *Elements of Naval Architecture* did not link displacement with any form of coefficient but used it to check the

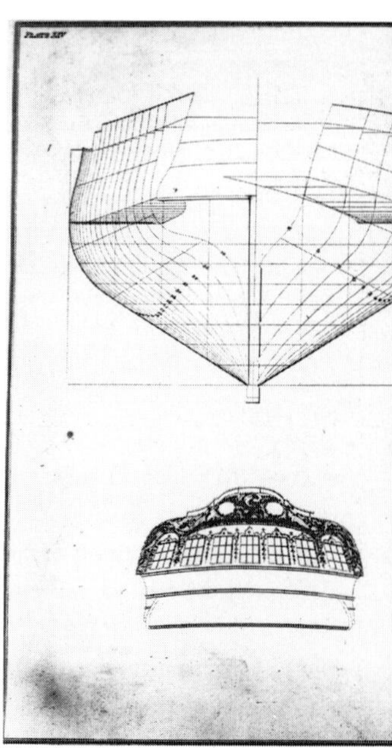

draught of water and to determine if the ship would float on an even keel.

In this book and his *Shipwright's Vade-Mecum*, Steel was anxious to encourage greater attention to theory although coupling many of his remarks with the value of experience. The shape of the hull was largely governed by the manner of forming the midship section which was still recommended to be based on arcs of circles for the floor sweep, and lower and upper breadth sweeps. The reconciling sweep, which joined the floor sweep to the lower breadth sweep, was to be a fair curve, but its precise shape was conveniently ignored, although the *Shipbuilder's Repository* said that a mould formed by the arc of a circle should be used. The rising lines and heights of breadth on the sheer elevation and half-breadth plans at which the centres of radii occurred and where the arcs terminated, remained of the utmost importance. Nevertheless, Steel admits that the designer had to decide the position of the rising line himself when he writes that 'the rising varies according to the ideas or judgement of the artist . . . as theory and experience dictate for the best'.[15] He adds that this line cannot be 'found by a regular proportional method' because warships, cargo-carrying merchant ships and fine-lined vessels are all of differing hull-form, and he is sufficiently broad-minded to state that some builders do not employ a rising line or a narrowing line in their designs.

So without any of the paraphernalia of modern mathematical techniques or the

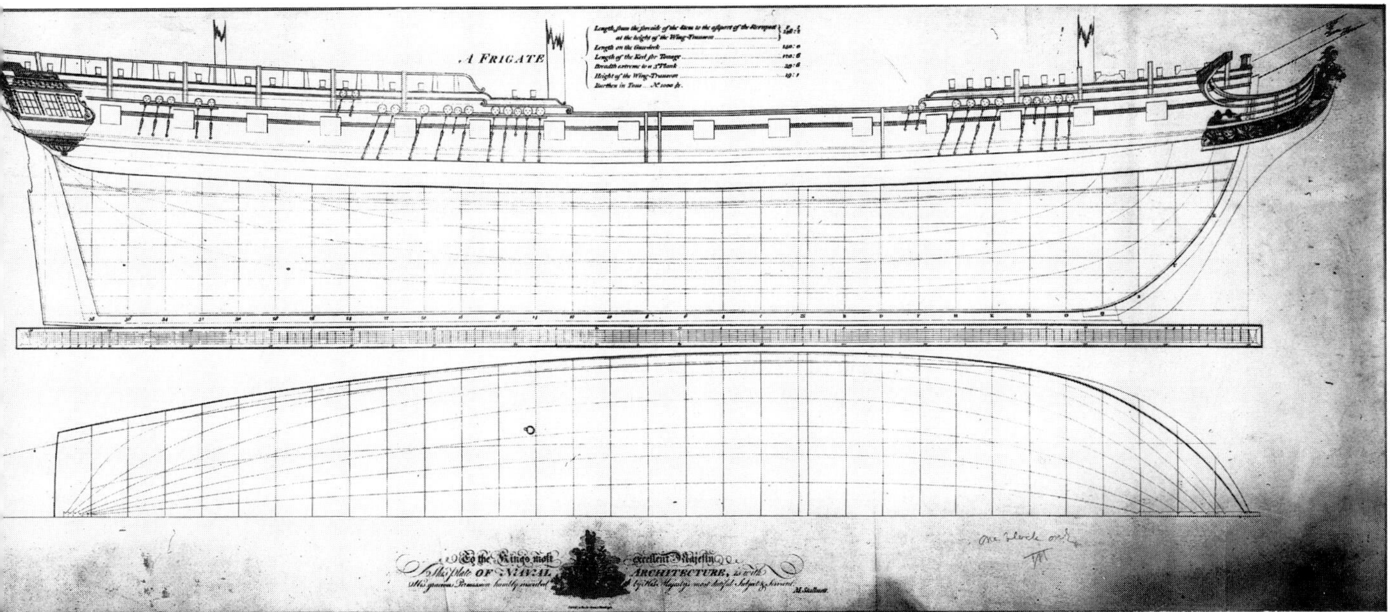

advantages of sophisticated tank tests, shipbuilders were expected to produce sound examples of naval architecture after sifting through archaic text books. Nor does it take much skill to follow in the period 1770–1850 the identical plates and sketches which are repeated through one encyclopaedia and book after another with the quality of the engraving gradually deteriorating. No wonder the development of new ship types was restrained.

The *Present Imperfect State of British Naval Architecture* was one of the typical titles given to anonymous pamphlets that were published towards the end of the eighteenth century and indicates the concern felt in certain quarters. The formation in 1791 of the Society for the Improvement of Naval Architecture focussed public attention on the subject, and various experiments were conducted by it on the forms of least resistance. A School of Naval Architecture was established in Portsmouth Dockyard in 1810, but it never obtained the high station it deserved and the men trained there rarely received the promotion they anticipated. Much of this controversy was centred on the Navy but merchant shipbuilders felt the backwash of it sufficiently for the Ipswich shipbuilder, George Bayley, to write to the *Mechanic's Magazine* in 1827, complaining that merchant shipyards were usually ahead of the naval yards, but that the latter always received credit for what had been in common usage for many years in merchant yards. 'I wish to vindicate my

3: Stalkartt's frigate, Projected design by the American scientist, Benjamin Thompson (Count Rumford). Reproduced from plate XIV in Marmaduke Stalkartt's *Naval Architecture* (1781). Dimensions on plan: 148ft-2in (length from foreside of stem to aft part of sternpost at height of wing transom), 39ft-6in (breadth extreme to a 3in plank), 19ft-1in (height of wing transom); 1000³/94 tons. This design was never built by the Royal Navy.

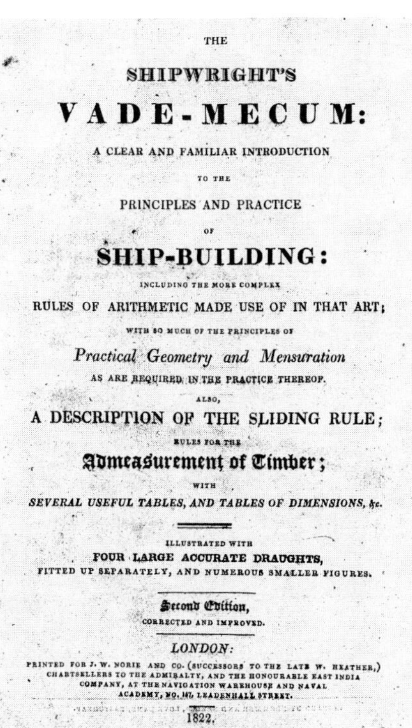

THE

SHIPWRIGHT'S

VADE-MECUM:

A CLEAR AND FAMILIAR INTRODUCTION

TO THE

PRINCIPLES AND PRACTICE

OF

SHIP-BUILDING:

INCLUDING THE MORE COMPLEX

RULES OF ARITHMETIC MADE USE OF IN THAT ART;

WITH SO MUCH OF THE PRINCIPLES OF

Practical Geometry and Mensuration

AS ARE REQUIRED IN THE PRACTICE THEREOF.

ALSO,

A DESCRIPTION OF THE SLIDING RULE;

RULES FOR THE

Admeasurement of Timber;

WITH

SEVERAL USEFUL TABLES, AND TABLES OF DIMENSIONS, &c.

ILLUSTRATED WITH

FOUR LARGE ACCURATE DRAUGHTS,

FITTED UP SEPARATELY, AND NUMEROUS SMALLER FIGURES.

Second Edition,

CORRECTED AND IMPROVED.

LONDON:

PRINTED FOR J. W. NORIE AND CO. (SUCCESSORS TO THE LATE W. HEATHER,) CHARTSELLERS TO THE ADMIRALTY, AND THE HONOURABLE EAST INDIA COMPANY, AT THE NAVIGATION WAREHOUSE AND NAVAL ACADEMY, NO. 157, LEADENHALL STREET.

1822.

4: This is the title page of a useful book on shipbuilding, which is referred to in the text.

brother shipbuilders', he wrote, 'from the imputation which is so frequently cast upon us by some of the gentlemen connected with HM dockyards, of not being able to make any improvement in naval architecture without their aid.'[16]

But even if the School of Naval Architecture did not achieve the station it deserved, it stimulated the production of numerous books on the subject which exerted a wide influence. John Fincham's book on shipbuilding was in its third edition by 1852, and was originally published in 1825 for use at the School; he later produced such works as *A Treatise on Masting Ships and Mast Making* (editions of 1829, 1843 and 1854), *Directions for Laying Off Ships* (2nd edition 1840 and 1859), and *A History of Naval Architecture* (1851). Two former students, William Morgan and Augustin Creuze, edited four volumes of *Papers on Naval Architecture* (1826, 1828, 1830 and 1832–65) which contained many articles on the subject of a scientific quality not seen before. Augustin Creuze later wrote the article on 'Ship-Building' for the seventh edition of the *Encyclopaedia Britannica* which was published separately in 1841. Various other authors wrote similar articles for encyclopaedias.

In *An Outline of Ship Building*, John Fincham described his method of designing a ship, and although this account is taken from the third edition of 1852 it is thought unlikely to be much different to the first edition of 1825. First to be decided were the length, breadth and mean draught of water and he suggested adherence to the following proportions to determine these:

	Frigates and Large Ships	Brigs
Ratio of breadth to length	3.65:1	3.23 or 3.44:1
Ratio of draught of water to breadth	.41:1	.442:1

This gave a very broad vessel, because his conclusions are all based on the results of measuring existing ships, some of which date back to 1719.

The next thing was to draw the ship's profile or sheer plan and the half-breadth plan, and mark on them the 'intended draught of water', the waterlines and sections of the body plan. 'Balance sections' at bow and stern, situated at one-sixth of the length of the load line from stem and sternpost, were then marked, and their shape drawn on the body plan together with that of the midship section 'according to the views of the constructor'. To assist the designer, Fincham lists areas of each balance section in proportion to the midship section for four classes of warships. Based on the sections obtained, the fairing-in of the half-breadth plan and remainder of the sections in the body plan could proceed.[17]

An important point to notice is that there are no precise rules for forming the shape of the midship section, unlike earlier authorities, and absolutely no reference to drawing the body plan by arcs of circles, which was one important result achieved by the School of Naval Architecture.

'Having thus determined the form of the body below the load-water line,' continues Fincham, 'we proceed next to calculate it, ascertaining first, whether we have the required displacement: if we have, the position of the centre of gravity may be calculated; this point should be a definite proportion of the length of the water-line before the middle of that line; in fast sailing ships this proportion varies between .01:1 and .015:1.'[18]

By adjusting the height of the load line, or by reducing or filling out the hull, the displacement and position of the centre of gravity could be altered. Fincham devotes much space to explaining the various calculations involved. Later in the book he gives rudimentary plans of a brig, a clipper schooner with a raking stem rabbet, and three merchant ships, as well as plans of four steamers.

Another important work was *A Treatise on Marine Architecture* by Peter Hedderwick which was published by the author in 1830, together with 21 plates in a separate folio. A unique feature of this work is that the text and plates are wholly devoted to merchant ships; in addition many of the plans are of sloops, schooners and brigs, while there are actually three detailed sail plans drawn to scale. Of the plans, only two attempt to illustrate fast vessels: one is of a 'Fast-sailing Brig or Yacht of 223 tons'; the other is of a Leith Smack and is reproduced here (figure 94). Hedderwick comments at some length on a ship's motion at sea, discusses stability, lists properties and measurements of a series of craft, and finally describes how to draw a ship's plan with which is combined his method of design. The midship section is formed first and then, as in Fincham, 'balance-frames' are formed, but positioned closer amidships. This is a combination of old and new methods because parts of the sections are drawn as arcs of circles which are related to the rising line for the floors. Although the position of the centre of gravity is discussed

5: Parts of a ship. This page, from an eighteenth century encyclopaedia, was reproduced in many combinations in differing publications. The vessel appears to be a 74-gun ship which was a popular subject. In the centre, the structural timbers are laid out; on the bottom line, the body plan is drawn to a much larger scale, and there are two stern views—one shows the wing transoms, the other the planking.

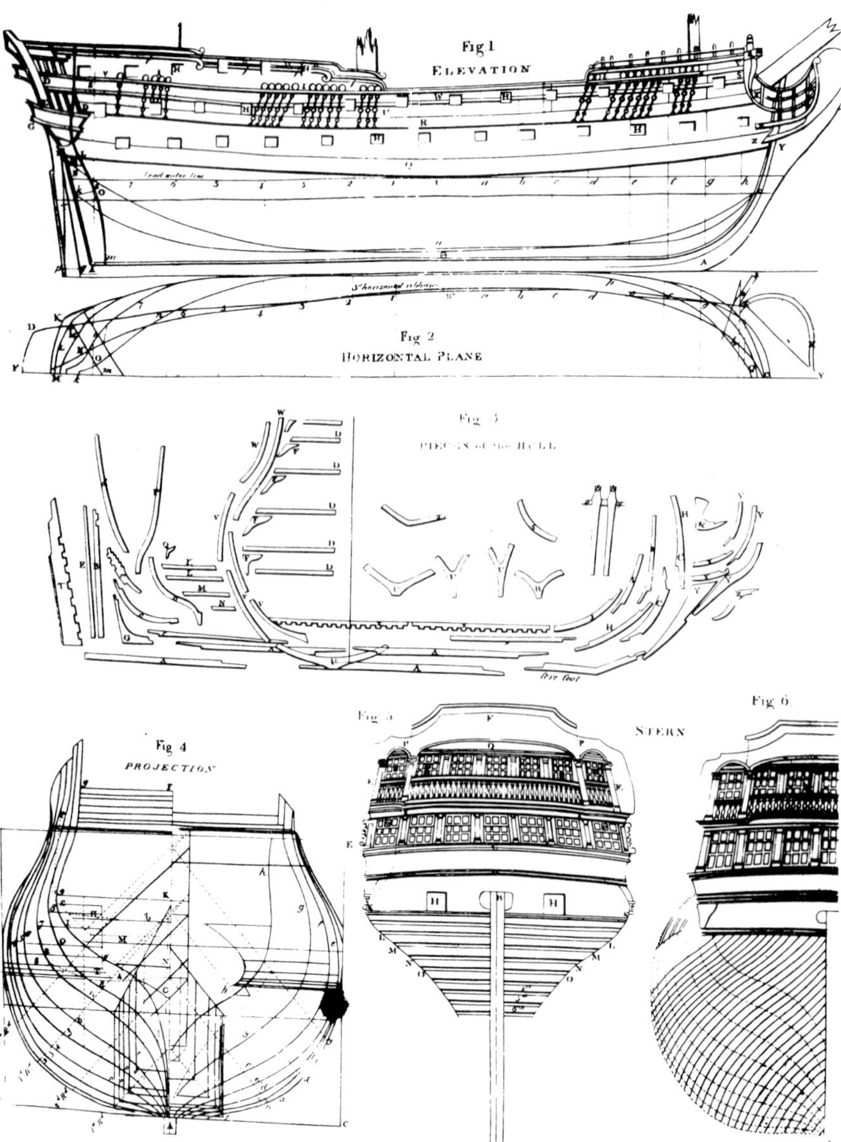

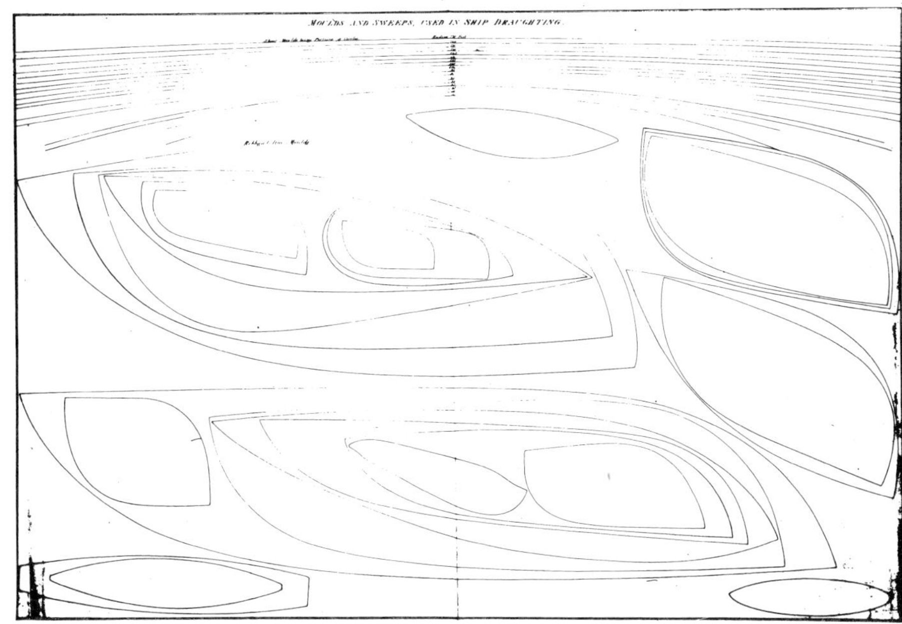

6: Moulds and sweeps used in ship draughting. Reproduced from a plate in Peter Hedderwick's *Treatise on Marine Architecture* (1830).

and its relation to stability, displacement receives only a brief mention, and there is no attempt at describing how it should be calculated.

All published works led the reader through the intricacies of drawing a plan, but how many builders could follow the calculations? The majority found it easier to make a model, which was also the habit of many sophisticated naval architects, and in any case, a prospective owner was probably unable to understand a plan. Occasionally, a model of the whole hull was made, but more often only half—hence the half-model. The earliest kind was carved from a solid block of wood and was probably introduced into England prior to 1700.[19] In the first half of the eighteenth century the bracket type of half-model appeared; it was also known as 'bird's nest' in England, but 'hawk's nest' or 'crow's nest' in America. In this model, an example of which appears in figure 7, the base board is shaped to the profile of the sheer elevation, and quarter to half-inch thick sections of 'brackets' attached to it, each moulded to the shape of specific frames and stiffened on their outer edges by ribbands. This type permitted the dead-wood, transomes, knightheads and cant frames to be clearly indicated. Nineteenth-century examples of the bracket model in Great Britain have been traced to Robert Steele & Co.'s yard at Greenock (1800–35); to Joseph White of Cowes who used such a model for his yacht *Waterwitch* (1834); to Uphams yard at Brixham, where they were in use for about ten years from the mid-fifties; to William Ferris on Restronguet Creek, near Truro, who designed with them from 1867 to 1877; and to Aldous of Brightlingsea who used them for his smacks and yachts. They were also used in Holland.

The lift model, composed of horizontal laminated planks or 'lifts', which were pegged together to form a solid block, does not appear to have been introduced until late in

8: A lift half-model which was in common use in Great Britain and other countries in the nineteenth and twentieth centuries. Sometimes, alternate lifts are composed of different timbers to accentuate the beauty of the hull-form. This photograph is of a modern model in my collection representing the clipper *Storm Cloud* which was made by Ralph Bird. *MacGregor Collection*

7: A bracket-type of half-model from the yard of J W & A Upham of Brixham, dating from the mid-1850s. I photographed this model when it was still in their possession. *MacGregor Collection*

the eighteenth century although it was the most commonly used version in both Great Britain and America during the nineteenth century. Measurements could be taken back to the centre line by taking the laminations apart and so dimensions could be transferred to the mould loft floor or to the drawing board. In nearly all models, the convention was to show the starboard side, although Alexander Hall & Sons and other builders occasionally varied this practice (figure 8).

None of the books on naval architecture gave any clear directions on how to design a fast-sailing ship, and it is obvious that designers were obliged to bend the rules to meet a particular situation. It is also fairly certain that all sharp ships were either experimental in design or were improved copies of another vessel, but it is unreasonable to suppose that every fast ship was derived from a French or American craft, particularly when there were so many examples of the fast English cutter hull to study. This question of foreign influence is considered in more detail under specific ships.

Criteria for hull analysis

Various methods of comparison are commonly adopted to determine the relative speed of different ships: their performance in company with other ships, the distance sailed in 24 hours, their speed in knots, or the time taken between two ports. These measurements are subject to many over-riding factors such as the sizes of the ships, wind and weather conditions, amount of cargo carried and so forth. More constant factors are desirable which indicate the relative type of hull-form and intrinsic speed capabilities. Sometimes the proportions of beams to length or depths to length are used as ratios to compare two separate vessels in order to examine changes in hull proportions over the years.

A more positive factor is the 'speed-length ratio' found by dividing the highest speed of a ship (in knots) by the square root of the load line length (in feet). This will give a factor enabling vessels of different length and size to be compared on the same basis. It has been shown that any ship whose ratio exceeds 1.25 is a fast vessel.[20] In the case of Brocklebank's ship *Jupiter*, it is recorded that she sailed between 11 and 12 knots. Her load line scales 77ft–0in. At 11 knots, her speed-length ratio is 1.25; at 12 knots the ratio increases to 1.37, indicating that she was an exceptionally fast vessel. This ratio will be referred to in future cases where the speed and length are known.

There are coefficients also available where the displacement is known, such as the block coefficient and the prismatic coefficient, but as in this work the plans submitted are not subjected to such close analytical study as to render the calculation of displacement essential, so the use of these coefficients is not necessary. Howard Chapelle in his work, *The Search for Speed under Sail*, examines in considerable detail the value of these ratios and states that the prismatic coefficient best indicates speed potential in a hull. This ratio is the proportion of the hull displacement to the 'prism' formed by the midship section area below the load line multiplied by the length of the load line. The smaller the ratio, the higher the speed potential, although a figure of .57 is probably the lowest for any merchant sailing vessel. On this basis and for some ships mentioned here he gives values of prismatic coefficients of .65 for HMS *Sea Lark* ex *Fly*, .59 for the extreme Baltimore clipper *Nonpareil*, .65 for the ship *Ann McKim* (1832), and .61 for the clipper ship *Lightning*.[21]

The block coefficient is the ratio of the displacement to the product of the load line length, breadth and draught, using moulded dimensions. It permits the comparison of hull volume below the load line between vessels of varying size. An approximation of this coefficient was outlined in *The Tea Clippers*, where I suggested that the displacement could be substituted by under deck tonnage and the moulded dimensions by the register dimensions. This ratio was called the 'Coefficient of Under Deck Tonnage'.[22] Under deck tonnage only appears in tonnage calculations after 1854, so that this coefficient is only applicable after that year.

Between 1836 and 1854 a comparison of old and new measurement tonnages will be found helpful, a considerably smaller figure by the new measurement being indicative of sharp hull-form. (See Chapter Four.) Opportunities will be taken of employing the methods of comparison outlined above, where the figures for such calculations are available.

A full study of the forms of least resistance cannot be attempted here, although certain features will be commented on when describing the hull-form of individual vessels, particularly the intersection of the load line and the quarter-beam buttock in the afterbody, the amount of deadrise, the shape of the entrance and run.

Innovations in construction

By the middle of the eighteenth century, the forests of the world were beng scoured for timber to build naval and merchant ships, and every means was taken to reduce wastage in converting it into the timbers needed to build a ship, and ways were studied of supplementing it with iron. Oak was, by tradition and experience, the best wood for shipbuilding but the forests in England were so denuded that, by the end of the century, oak was being imported from Canada and the Adriatic. Other woods to be introduced included teak from Burma, larch from the Baltic, pitch pine from central America, mahogany from Honduras, while politics played its part in securing an uninterrupted supply.

The amount of timber in a ship was considerable and it has been calculated that at the end of the eighteenth century merchant ships consumed just over one load of timber, equal to about one ton, for every ton of shipping. In the Navy the quantity was one-and-a-half to two loads per ton.[23] There was enormous wastage in converting the trunks or branches to the shape of the finished timbers, and about one half of the wood was lost. It is estimated that in 1805 the hull of a 74-gun ship – completely equipped for sea with guns and stores aboard – accounted for 55% of the total weight, that is to say, 1672 tons out of a total of 3040 tons.[24] In merchant sailing ships, the weight of the wooden hull was proportionally less, owing to the smaller scantlings used, and the hull was usually considered to be one-third of the total displacement.[25]

In all wooden ships built according to normal practice, the frames formed an almost solid wall or palisade when seen broadside on, such as the framed hull of a model at the Science Museum, London, reproduced in figure 14. The bottom is almost solid in the floors and lower futtocks, and it is only in the topsides that the frames become distinctly separate. This was common practice in all sizes of vessels.

In an attempt to improve constructional methods and minimise timber wastage, Gabriel Snodgrass, surveyor to the Honourable East India Company from 1757, made some useful suggestions on three occasions between 1771 and 1796. He considered that timber should be converted where it was felled in order to obtain better wood and to assist in transport; and that to deter rot setting in, a roof should be built over the slipways where the ships were built, a practice which had been used for many years in Venice. As regards constructional matters, he recommended that the excessive tumblehome be reduced, to give greater room on deck, and to alleviate the heavy demands for 'grown' timber for the topside framing; that staple knees and hanging knees be made of iron instead of wood, which would save space and weight, and remove the difficulties of obtaining suitable 'compass' timber; and that diagonal struts be placed in the hold from the keelson to the shelf of the gun deck beams to stiffen the hull. This last suggestion was found impracticable and was only tried in a few ships.[26]

Another of his improvements was the 'round-headed' rudder, which he introduced into East Indiamen in 1779, and which was widely adopted. (This, and his other improvements are discussed in more detail in my book *Merchant Sailing Ships 1775–1815*, Chapter 4.)

Another person to make worthwhile improvements was Sir Samuel Benthan (1757–1831) who had once been a shipwright's apprentice, gained the rank of general in Russian service, and finally became a Com-

9: This model of the midship section of a 74-gun ship of c1795 illustrates the enormous amount of timber consumed in wood construction. The scantlings did not have to be quite so heavy in a merchant ship, but stowing cargo in such a forest of structural timbers was quite a problem. *Science Museum, London*

10: This model shows a vessel complete in frame, but without any planking, and demonstrates the massive quality of the construction. As ships grew longer in proportion to breadth, the necessary longitudinal strength required the addition of enormous timbers in the form of sister keelsons and bilge stringers. *Science Museum, London*

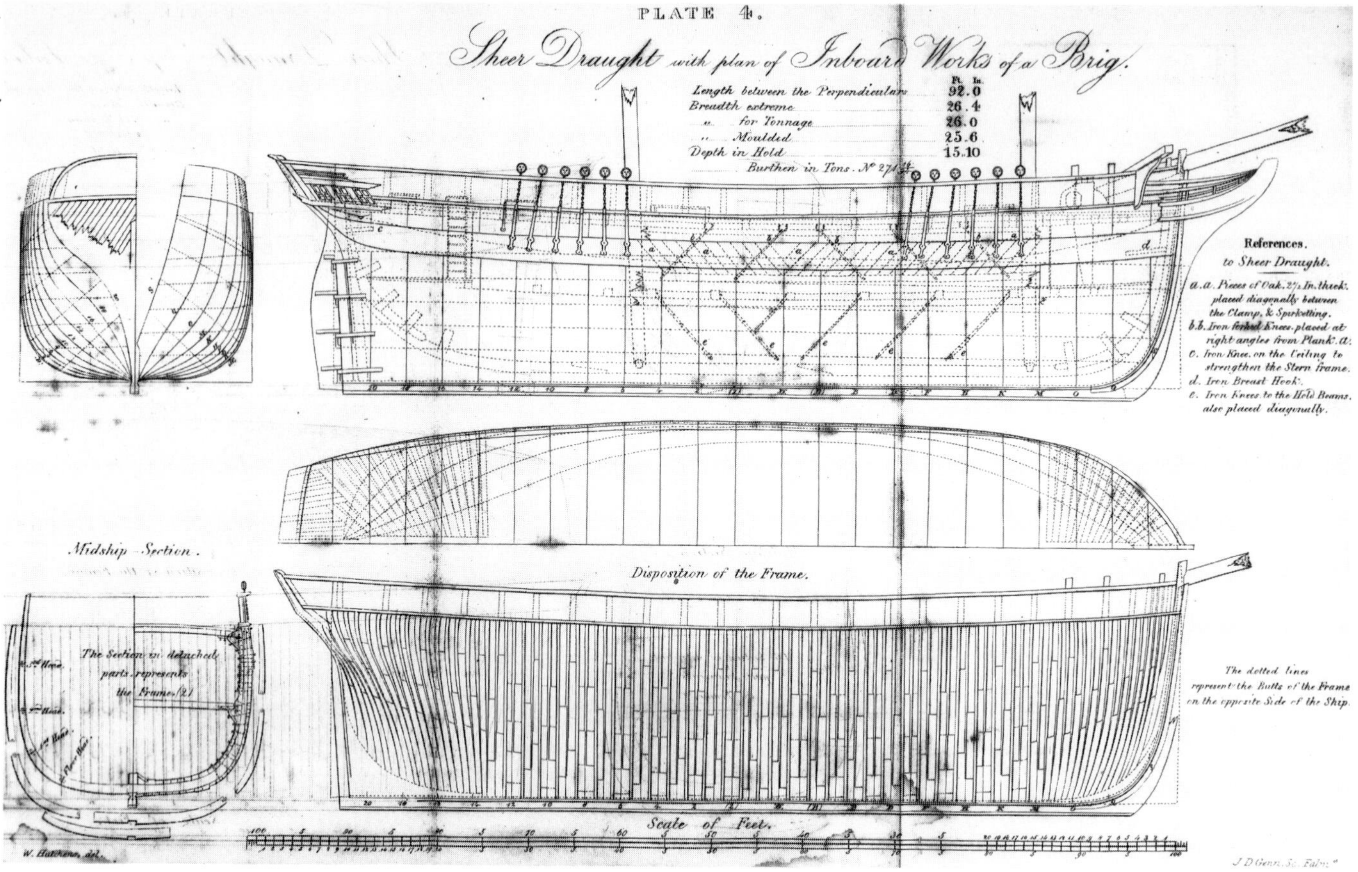

12: *Brig.* Lines, midsection and frame elevations reproduced from the 10th Annual Report of the Royal Cornwall Polytechnic Society, 1842, plate 4, as submitted by William Hutchins. Brig not identified. Accompanying text given here in full.

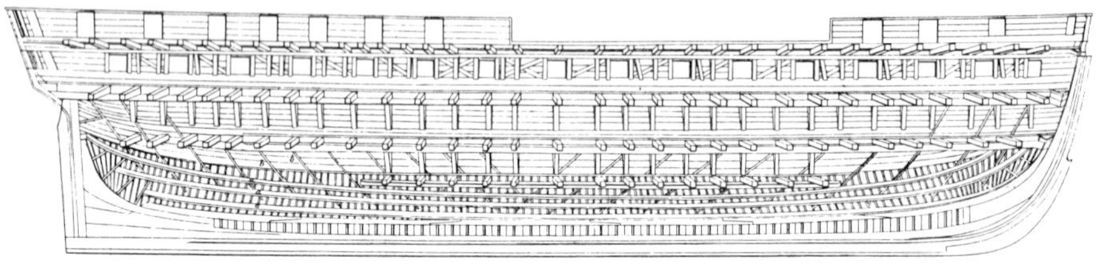

11: Seppings' Diagonal Construction. The plate normally reproduced applies to the trussed frame for a ship-of-the-line, but for a frigate or large merchant ship Seppings proposed the introduction of diagonal iron trussing as illustrated here. *John Fincham,* A History of Naval Architecture *[1851] p 202*

missioner of the Navy. He had saw mills and other machinery shops erected in the naval dockyards, and recommended that Sir Marc Brunel's block-making machinery be installed at Portsmouth. This was the first mass production plant ever built. In the years 1796–98, Bentham also designed two brigs and four schooners on a new system by which smaller timbers could be used.

Wooden shipbuilding methods remained very conservative and little change may be discerned before the general introduction of iron in the form of knees, diagonal braces or riders, hooks and crutches, hold pillars and beams. Towards the end of the Napoleonic Wars the great shortage of grown timber for members of maximum curvature accelerated the use of iron and also brought changes in the shape of the hull. In particular, wall sides began replacing tumblehome and attempts were made to utilise shorter lengths of timber. Sir Robert Seppings (1767–1840) substituted diagonal riders that were fixed across the inside of the timbers instead of the ceiling, a practice that was adopted in the Royal Navy in 1810. Various applications of diagonal framing and ceiling were advocated by French writers and naval architects in the eighteenth century.[27]

Sir Robert Seppings, who was Surveyor to the Royal Navy in the years 1813–32, also put forward suggestions regarding the construction of merchant ships, which recommended the jointing of the frames end-to-end with circular dowels rather than use of chocks; the use of shorter members for each frame; filling the space between the frames solid to a certain height above the bilge; and inserting diagonal iron trusses or braces across the frames. These remarks were delivered to the Royal Society in 1820.[28] Basically triangular in shape, chocks accentuated the weakness in the jointing of frames and were introduced in the eighteenth century, perhaps before, to overcome the shortage of grown timber bends. The first edition of *The Shipwright's Vade-Mecum* in 1805 shows the timbers of a 330-ton merchantman to be joined with chocks; but had Seppings' proposals appeared in print earlier, it is likely that this drawing would have incorporated his recommendations. However, it must be observed that the text of the 1822 editon of the *Vade-Mecum* still referred to the use of chocks.

Yet Seppings' remarks seem to have borne fruit immediately in some circles, as John Knowles reported in 1822 that some shipbuilders, both on the Thames and at Scarborough, had employed diagonal timbering in the hold.[29] William Fearnall and Joseph Fletcher, at whose Limehouse yard several ships were so built, also constructed eight steamers between 1826 and 1831 according to Seppings' diagonal system. One of these, the *Shannon*, measured 513 tons and cost £2 per ton more than vessels of usual construction; but against this, she had been ashore several times and sustained no injury.[30] Sir

Robert Seppings himself designed some opium clippers and two of these, *Sylph* (1831) and *Cowasjee Family* (1835) were built on his principle of diagonal trussing; the former survived a severe stranding.[31] Further evidence as to the employment of Seppings' principles in named vessels is lacking, but his recommendations were disseminated through a wide range of technical literature during the first half of the nineteenth century, which could not have failed to leave its mark. But the additional labour involved in effecting these improvements was reflected in higher costs which prevented their widespread adoption, and chocks continued in use for many years. The doubling of timbers and use of iron or yellow-metal bolts was preferred by most shipbuilders to the use of dowels.

An attempt to obviate the difficulties of obtaining suitable grown timber and simultaneously to impart greater longitudinal strength was made by William Annesley, who patented a system to build vessels with laminated skins. His patent was dated April 1818. The process was to set up temporary frames or formers around which the planking was laid athwartships and longitudinally in anything up to seven layers; in the latter case the total thickness was 5⅝in. The planking was held together with treenails, and tarred paper was inserted between each skin. Finally the formers were removed. (His method is illustrated and described in *Merchant Sailing Ships 1815–1850*, page 41.) By 1822, 11 vessels had been built on this plan.[32]

Diagonal construction was employed intermittently for first class work where money was no object, such as in the Royal yachts *Victoria and Albert* (1834) and *Elfin* (1849);[33] and Oliver Lang employed a single diagonal layer under longitudinal planking on some vessels built with solid frames.[34] In the 'fifties it was employed extensively by John White at Cowes and Alexander Hall & Sons at Aberdeen.

Following on from Annesley's laminated skins, a writer to the *Mechanics' Magazine* in 1832 observed:

'I have seen somewhere a proposition for building vessels entirely of plank, without any scantling, by arranging four thickness to cross each other diagonally, so that all the joints might break each other, tarred canvas or paper being introduced between the layers, and the whole bolted together. The planks were to be bent by steam, to form the shape of the bow, stern and bottom. The afterwards to be bolted in and the deck to be fixed by knees to the sides, after the hull had been finished.

'I have heard that such a vessel was built in America; but the objection to her was, that she was too firm and immovable in her build, and would not sail well. But such a complaint would be rather an advantage to a steam-vessel. After all, sheet-iron seems to me the substance to which we must come. It is found effective for canal boats; what then should be the objection to it for the sea? It will, probably, be found to form a more buoyant boat than oak, and for the resistance of a shock, I should imagine a sheet of malleable iron much more effective than timber.'[35]

The second part of this letter was strangely prophetic.

A limited number of first class shipbuilders were building entirely in iron by the beginning of the 1830s, and ten years later such construction was well established, but it is impossible to determine which was the first sharp-hulled ship of this new material. Amongst the Lloyd's Register survey reports at the National Maritime Museum, Greenwich, are those of several schooners, launched in the 'forties, which probably merit a 'clipper' distinction, such as the *Flash* and *Foig a Ballagh* built in 1843 and 1844 by John Coutts at Newcastle and designed with big deadrise and sharp ends. Another was the *Dove* of 73 tons, built in 1844 by John Laird at Birkenhead, with very steep deadrise and described as 'a vessel of small capacity, very sharp forward and aft'. During the 'fifties, iron was employed with outstanding success to furnish some of the most splendid clippers ever built.

Tonnage measurement and registration

When describing a ship, the tonnage figure often takes precedence over any other information but it is incredible that until 1836 the complex curved structure of a ship was only measured in two places in order to compute the tonnage. Two measurements make a flat, two-dimensional object not a solid, three-dimensional one, trembling and vibrant like a ship. The length was indeed measured and so was the breadth. Those were the only two actual measurements that had to be taken. Various assumptions were made, the chief of which was that the depth equalled half the breadth. How convenient for the surveyors and for everyone involved! A simple multiplication sum of the length, breadth and the assumed depth was followed by the division of the product by 94 and the quotient was the ship's tonnage.

Between 1775 and 1875 three distinct and different systems of tonnage measurement were in operation: the one outlined above and latterly known as the 'Old Measurement' was in force until the end of 1835; from 1836 to 1854 the 'New Measurement' rule was employed; from 1855, and still in current use today, the system as suggested by George Moorsom and specified in the Merchant Shipping Act of 1854.

The first English rule for measuring tonnage is probably that of 1582, and during the next two centuries it underwent various amendments, but in 1773 an Act was passed to prevent smuggling in which was embodied a more precise method of tonnage measurement than in previous regulations.[36] This system was similar to the instructions issued by the Customs in 1719. At first the new tonnage rule only applied to vessels carrying spirits or hovering off the coast or to cases where tonnage had to be stated officially, and it did not apply to colliers or certain fishing boats. However, by the Registry Act of 1786 the tonnage rule of 1773 was adopted officially for every class of vessel and remained in force until the end of 1835.

The adjacent diagram shows between which points the length was measured for tonnage by the rule of 1773. No after perpendicular is required. The main stem continues up to the underside of the bowsprit while the stem and knee of the head rake forward in a large overhang.

Many ports and shipyards had their own personal tonnage rules. Alexander Hall at Aberdeen and John Brockbank at Lancaster both used the formula

$$\frac{K \times B\ (\text{moulded}) \times \tfrac{1}{2}B}{94}.$$

Hall termed this 'carpenter's measure'; it produced a slightly larger figure than with the official method, or about 3% higher in the case of his schooner *Plough* (1811).

The Registry Act of 1786 fell within the

range of the Navigation Acts because intended for the 'increase and encouragement of shipping'. In addition to consolidating the method of tonnage measurement and stating what constituted British ships, it also extended the scope of the 1696 Plantation Registration Act, by establishing a permanent registry of all British ships of 15 tons and upwards. The Custom House Registers of shipping, often referred to here and of immense value, date from the year 1786.

In Appendix I there is a detailed description of the points between which dimensions were taken both for registration and for tonnage measurement, and a description of the terms used.

After the termination of the Napoleonic Wars it was soon realised that the mode of tonnage measurement then operating was detrimental to the proper form of ships, and in 1821 a Commission was appointed by the Government to hold an inquiry. It was conceded by the Commission that the tonnage figure often varied from the capacity of the ship, and recommendations for a new system of internal measurement were submitted in which the depth and breadth were to be measured at three separate positions, the result of which was to produce three crude cross-sectional areas, as illustrated by figure 27. This was the first time that a ship's depth of hold was considered for measurement. The Commission was hampered by its desire to make the rule workable by uneducated men; a desire which limited the number of dimensions to be taken and thus the practicality of the scheme.[37] But it was the first step taken to obtain a more accurate measurement of the internal volume of the hull and it is obvious that the system adopted in 1835 was largely based on this rejected method.

'The mode recommended', commented

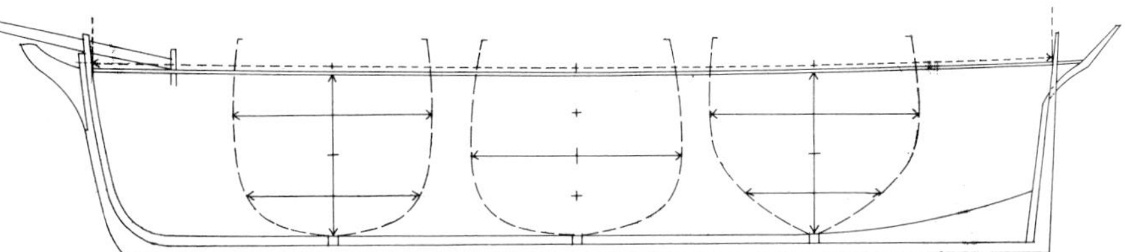

14: Old measurement tonnage. This diagram shows between which points the only two dimensions were taken.

15: Proposed 1821 tonnage. This diagram shows the first attempt at measuring the internal volume as proposed by the Committee convened in 1821

13: This photograph was taken in about 1845 near Swansea by Calvert Jones and depicts an unidentified ship with an enormously deep hull. A ship's depth was measured for tonnage calculations for the first time in 1836 and it may be that the ship pictured here was built prior to this data or at least before the significance of the new tonnage rule was fully comprehended. Her depth must be at least three-quarters of her breadth. This ship would have proved an excellent cargo carrier but her weatherly qualities at sea must have suffered, and she needed a tall sail plan to drive her along. The pair of spars projecting vertically above her forecastle are the whisker booms which have been topped up. When in position they rested in a boom iron at the outer end of the cathead

George Moorsom on the 1821 report, 'consisting only . . . of a few internal measurements, proved to be but an inadequate and distant approximation to true mensuration, and being, also, greatly open to evasion, no legislative results accrued from it; and, consequently, the original, or "Old Law", as it is designated, was still left, year after year, to its injurious operations; the several Acts relating to it being, finally, consolidated into one, by 3 & 4 Will. IV c. 55.

'At length, however, in the year 1833, the attention of Government was again called to the question, and a second Commission was appointed, "To consider the best mode of Measuring the Tonnage of Ships." '[38]

This Commission reported the following year and its recommendation became law from the beginning of 1836. It was known as the New Measurement Rule, and a description of it appears at the end of Chapter three.

Two
EARLY FAST SHIPS 1775-1815

Clipper terminology

The clipper ship era is generally considered to have occupied the years 1840–70, and during this period the term 'clipper' is applied to all vessels of proven sharp hull-form. Prior to this, ships of the years 1815–39 which were of fine lines are generally referred to as 'early clippers', but use of the world 'clipper' is rarely employed before this date. Instead, ships of sharp form are called 'early fast ships', sometimes with the corollary that 'forty years later they would have been called clippers'. Such terminology has been adopted throughout this book.

Cutters and cutter-build

By 1760 the cutter must have been a well-tried combination of rig and hull as 31 such craft were listed by Charnock as being bought into the Navy in 1763.[1] One of these, the *Pitt*, closely resembles the English cutter whose lines Chapman gives.[2] The *Pitt* measured 61ft-6in from foreside of stem to afterside of taffrail, 20ft-8in extreme beam, 9ft-1½in depth of hold and $99\frac{90}{94}$ tons, according to figures given on a lines plan at the National Maritime Museum, Greenwich.[3] These cutters had fine waterlines and steep deadrise but were very broad in proportion to their length, the ratio of beam to length being only 2½ or 3 to 1. They were fast, weatherly craft and well able to carry the enormous sail area of square and fore-and-aft canvas given them. Numerous examples of these cutters in the Admiralty draughts at the National Maritime Museum reveal that throughout the eighteenth and well into the ninteenth centuries these vessels possessed similar characteristics to those seen in the plans of the cutter *Fly*, reproduced in figure 16, which was purchased in 1763 for the Navy.

The *Fly* measures 51ft-6in overall, 20ft-10½in extreme breadth, 8ft-1¼in depth of hold, and $78\frac{34}{94}$ tons. She has considerable rise of floor above hollow garboards and the greatest beam occurs above the load line. There is a square tuck below the counter and an acute angle in the last four stations along the top line of the deadwood. The excessive beam is necessary to provide sufficient stability for the enormous spread of sail which she carries. There is a drag of about 1ft-3in aft, but it should be noticed that the keel is somewhat deeper at the forefoot than at the heel of the sternpost.

The arrangement of the sails in the *Fly* is typical of heavily-rigged cutters of the eighteenth century, particularly the cut of the deeply roached topsail and the manner of setting the head of the square sail on the crossjack yard. The topsail was sheeted to a 'spread yard' or 'spreading yard' and the square sail passed over the fore side of it. The principal sails and spars were extended from the lower mast alone which thus left little for the topgallant mast to do. In cutters and early schooners the word 'topgallant mast' was generally substituted for that of 'topmast'. Sometimes the topgallant mast was fidded on the forward side of the lower masthead, sometimes abaft it; there are also variations on the fidding of the jibboom. By 1800, the crossjack yard and spread yard had become a single yard.

The sail plan of the *Fly*, figure 17, has been

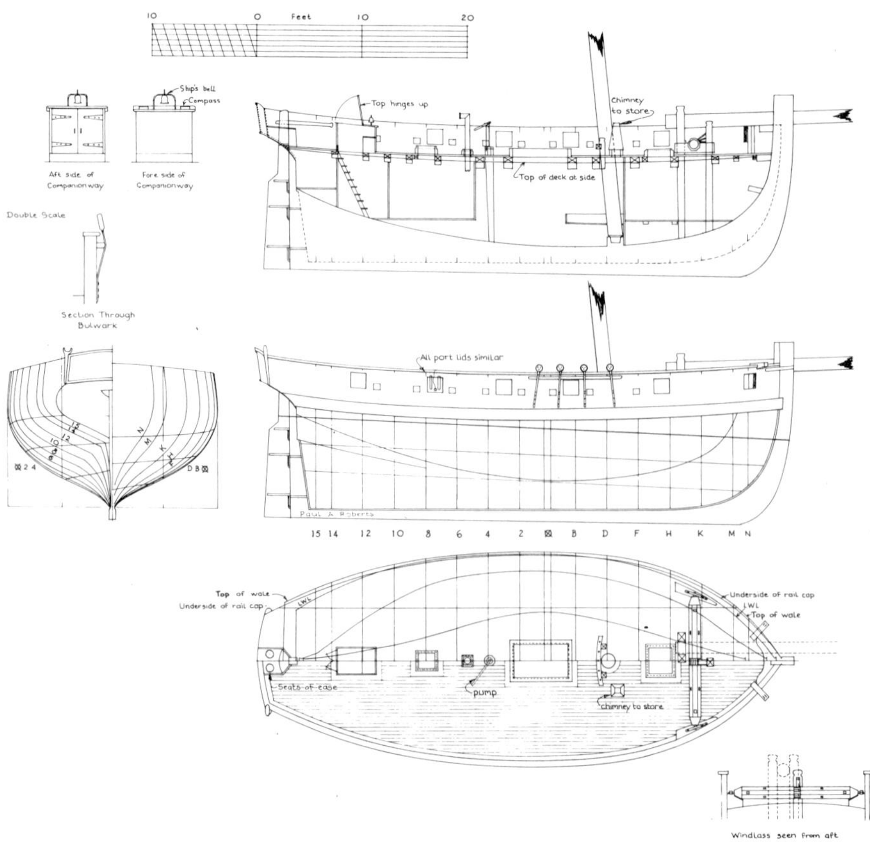

16: HMS *Fly*. Lines plan. Redrawn by Paul A Roberts from Admiralty draughts at the National Maritime Museum, Greenwich. Dimensions on plan: 46ft-0in (length on range of deck), 33ft-10½in (length of keel for tonnage), 20ft-10½in (breadth extreme), 8ft-1¼in (depth of hold); $78\frac{34}{94}$ tons. Other sources for reconstruction: sketch book of Thomas Lung at National Maritime Museum, with drawings of cutter *Hector;* rigged mould at Science Museum, London.

reconstructed from the spar dimensions given on the Admiralty draught of her lines and deck layout. The sail plan of an English cutter dated 1787, found by Howard I Chapelle in the Danish Royal Archives, has been closely followed for the shape of the square sail and the stunsails, as these sails rarely appear on sail plans of cutters.[4] The lower stunsail boom of the *Fly* would project about ten feet beyond the outer leech of the stunsail, if the boom was fitted to a goose-neck on the channel, but if the boom was secured to the mast, its length would be just right.

The continuance of these fine-lined cutter hulls was as important to the development of fast-sailing ships in Great Britain as the Baltimore clipper was to fast ships in America.

In *The National Watercraft Collection* — a detailed account of the merchant ship models at the Smithsonian Institution — Howard I Chapelle gives the plans of the sloop *Mediator*, built on the Chesapeake in 1741–42 and bought into the Royal Navy in 1745.[5] He

17: HMS *Fly* Sail plan: Reconstructed from sheer elevation and from spar dimensions listed on lines plan. Arrangement of yards and square sails conforms to practice of heavily-rigged cutters of this date, as illustrated in contemporary books and illustrations, and particularly to plan of English cutter of 1787 in *Search for Speed under Sail by H I Chapelle.*

18: This model of the cutter *Hawke*, dating from 1777, has the same arrangement of sails as the *Fly*, although no stunsails are fitted. The running backstay with a big tackle was a feature of these vessels; there was one on each side. *National Maritime Museum, Greenwich.*

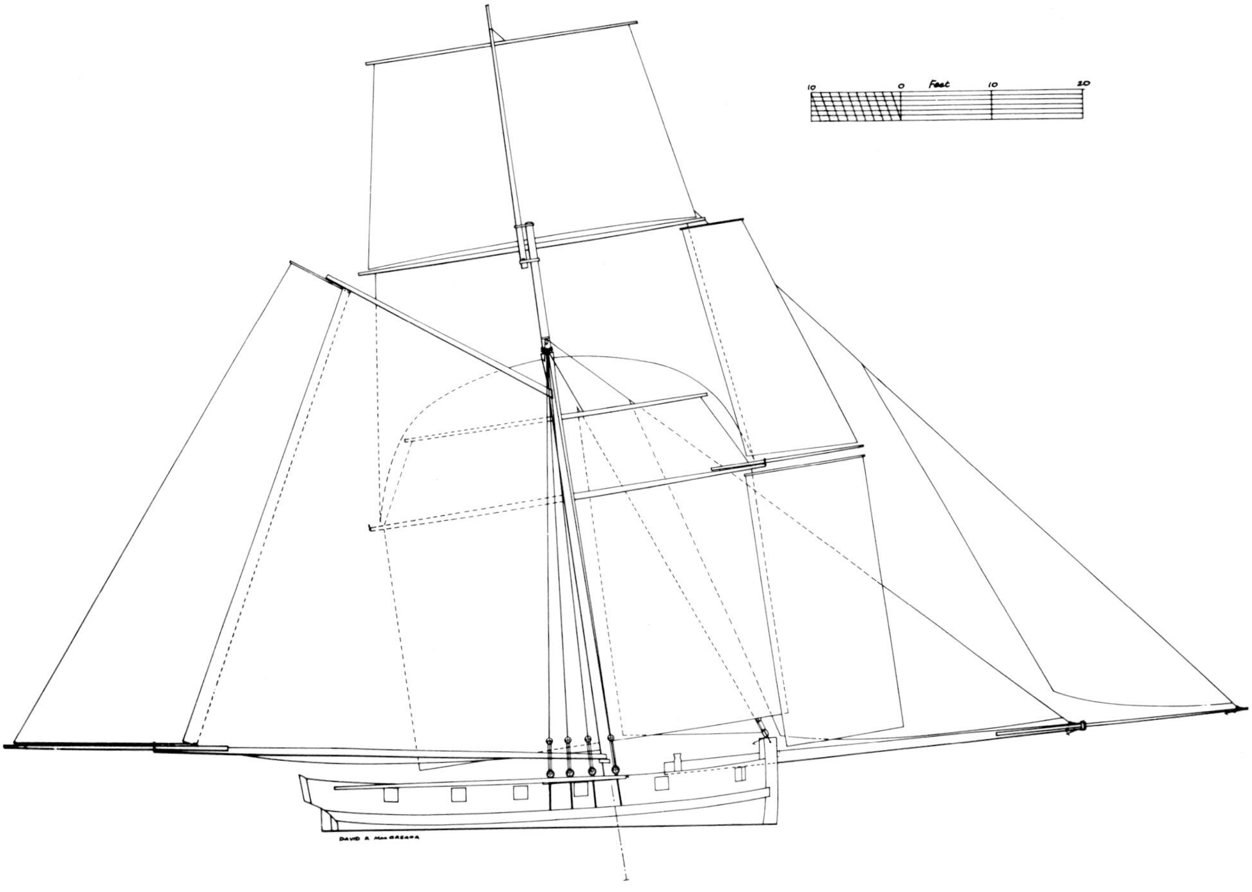

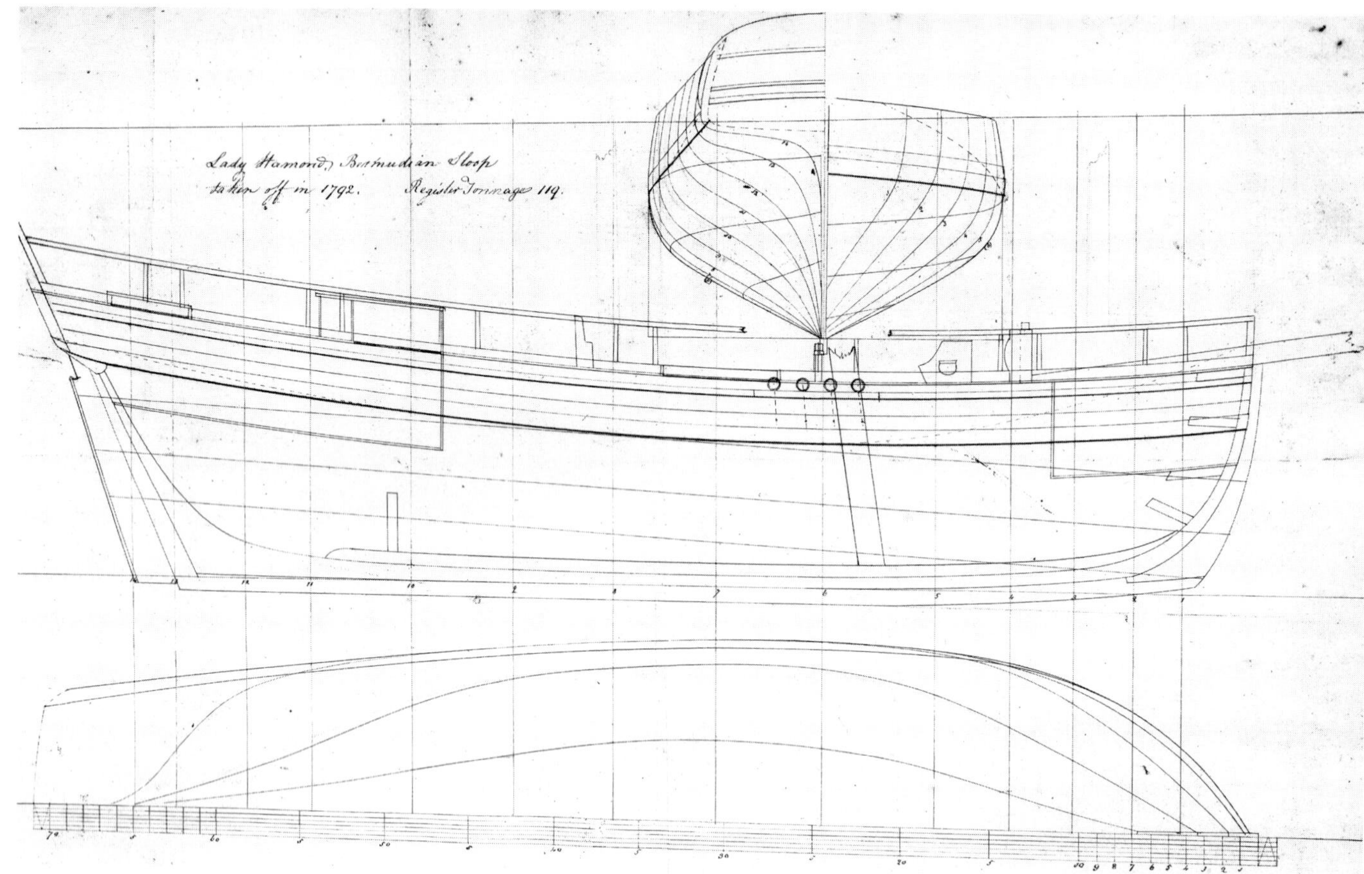

19: *Lady Hamond.* Lines taken off 1792. Probably built in Bermuda. Reproduced from plan in Hilhouse Collection and photographed through the courtesy of John C G Hill. Dimensions scaled off plan: 68ft-0in (length overall), 20ft-0in (beam); 119 tons. Two mast positions in pencil can be discerned.

shows that it was the Bermudian sloop which was used as a model for a sharp vessel and not the French luggers which tradition said had visited America and had their lines taken off during the Revolution. The *Mediator*'s combined length of bowsprit and jibboom is equivalent to that of her main boom and gives her a large area of fore-and-aft canvas with only a tall, narrow area of square canvas. With a tonnage of 105, she is a short and deep vessel and has a breadth to length ratio of 3 to 1, but she has quite sharp lines, only a small drag, a high stern and big sheer, and considerable deadrise. The Bermudian model was employed to construct the 24-gun ship *Lyme* which was built on the Thames in 1739–40 and whose plans are preserved in the Admiralty draughts.[6] 'It is obvious', writes Howard Chapelle, 'that this model for fast-sailing hulls was known in the colonies and in England long before the American Revolution.'[7] The English cutter design may well have made use of the Bermudian model.

Amongst the plans in the Hilhouse Collection at the National Maritime Museum are to be found lines of two Bermudian sloops: one, signed 'G Hilhouse', is a copy of the plan published in 1768–69 by the Swedish naval architect Chapman;[8] the other shows the *Lady Hamond* whose lines were taken off in 1792. (Reconstructed sail plans are available for both these sloops: the first by William A Baker;[10] the second by Howard I Chapelle.[11]) The *Lady Hamond* has steep deadrise with straight floors and the turn of the bilge set below the load line; also fine waterlines, a dray aft, a raking sternpost and a rockered keel. Although plans for reference were collected by J M Hilhouse from varying sources, it is significant to find such plans in this collection and confirms the high regard held by many shipbuilders for the Bermudian model. Whether Hilhouse was influenced or inspired by such plans when formulating his own designs for fast sailing vessels is a matter for speculation. Plans of French privateers and English smugglers are also to be found in the Hilhouse Collection.

Whereas the Americans lengthened the sharp hulls to add a second mast for a schooner rig, thereby increasing the breadth to length ratio by as much as 4 to 1 and simultaneously improving the sailing qualities, the British, with one or two exceptions, retained the single-masted cutter rig and the inevitably shorter, broader and deeper hull-form which one mast imposed. The cutters attempted to solve the problem of only one mast by hoisting three square sails with additional stunsails, as shown in the reconstructed sail plan of the *Fly*. In *The Sailor's Word-Book*, Admiral Smyth, in defining a 'cutter', wrote that 'the name is derived from their fast sailing. The cutter (as HMS *Dwarf*) has been made to set every sail, even royal studding-sails, sky-scrapers, moon-rakers, star-gazers, water and below-water sails, that could be set by any vessel on one mast. One of the largest which has answered effectually, was the *Viper*, of 460 tons and 28 guns;. . .'[12] The *Viper* appears to have been employed during the American revolution of 1775–83 and particularly in breaking the blockade of Gibraltar.

When a vessel was bought into the Navy it was customary for the draughtsman to inscribe the spar dimensions on the lines plan,

20: A Naval cutter of about 1800 which shows the large amount of square canvas carried. One interesting feature is that each yard had braces led to the bowsprit end, which meant that a large quantity of gear was clustered in a single position, and this resulted in a massive spar. When in a chase, cutters were accustomed to set a variety of flying kites. *National Maritime Museum.*

and several of the larger cutters have a mizen mast and yard listed among their spar dimensions. A lug sail would be set from this yard and sheeted to an outrigger, giving the cutter a 'dandy' rig; but as the main boom projected well beyond the stern, the mizen must undoubtedly have been stepped only temporarily, when on a long reach. A few of these big cutters were rerigged as brigs or schooners when bought into the Navy and there are plans of such vessels among the Admiralty draughts at the National Maritime Museum, Grenwich. For instance, the *Rambler*'s lines plan bears the inscription: '28 Oct 1796 Draught of Mr. King's Cutter'; and at the top of the sheet it states: 'The Works. . . in fitting the Vessel for a Brig. . .' It seems logical to apply the definition 'cutter brig' to such a craft, a term which describes both hull form and rig.

Discussion in the *Mariner's Mirror* showed that this term was in use in England in the years 1781–1807 and that it was employed by David Steel in 1805 as part of his brief definition of a brig: 'In the Royal Navy, when cutter-built vessels are thus rigged, they are called Cutter-brigs.'[13] Further confirmation is supplied by plans found in Sweden by John Lyman which are inscribed: 'Drawing of the cutter brig *Alexander*, built in London 1785 . . . Measured during the cutter brig's repair at. . . Stockholm, May 1794.' From the tracings he made it is obvious that this vessel is built on the lines of a cutter with large beam, big drag and steep deadrise, but rigged as a brig with no square mainsail.[14] Incidentally, it is unlikely that the term 'cutter built' implied that the vessel so described was either clinker built, as some cutters were, or that she had to have a running bowsprit, but rather that her hull form was that of a cutter.

Many of the plans of fast or fine-lined ships which were built during the eighteenth century have a hull form in which the characteristics of steep deadrise, slack bilges and maximum beam at load line height are prominent. These features were integral parts of the design of a cutter and as this form of hull was proved as being capable of high speed, it is probable that designers looked to this hull-form for inspiration when commissioned to build a fine-lined vessel. Thus it becomes increasingly difficult to separate the cutter's design from that of other sharp-built ships and the term 'cutter build' or 'cutter built' becomes the accepted form for describing a fine-lined vessel. Between the figures of 100 and 250 tons can be found many craft of basically cutter hull form while the rig can vary considerably with one, two or three masts. John Lyman confirms this point of view by suggesting 'that "cutter-built" in 1790 meant about the same as "clipper-built" in 1835'.[15] This is a significant statement for clipper ship development in Great Britain.

During the American War of Independence, several vessels with hulls of cutter build found their way into the Navy, such as the *Busy, Camelion* and *Helena*. These three were all clinker built up to the wales and carvel above, and they had great beam but were fairly long for their depth. Their measurements are compared below:

Name	*Lines taken off*	*Dimensions length on deck, extreme breadth, depth of hold*	*Tons*	*Rig*	*Guns*
Busy	1778	73ft-6½in x 25ft-8in x 9ft-7in	188	Cutter + mizen	12
Camelion	1781	85ft-0in x 29ft-3½in x 12ft-0in	268	Brig	14
Helena	1778	76ft-1½in x 26ft-9in x 10ft-8in	215	Schooner with square sails on each mast	14

The *Busy* was bought at Folkestone in 1778. According to dimensions on her plan, her mainmast was 78ft-0in long, and although her boom projected about 12ft-0in beyond the taffrail, she had a mizen mast 42ft-4in long with a yard 36ft-6in. The mizen must have set a dipping lug and was sheeted to an outrigger 48ft-0in long.[16]

The *Camelion* was bought in 1781 and had slightly less deadrise than the other two but there was considerable sheer aft. The drag aft was approximately four feet. She also had a head with trail boards, and the bowsprit was fitted between knightheads.[17]

The *Helena* was built in 1778, for what purpose has not been established, but presumably to obtain a letter of marque; however, she

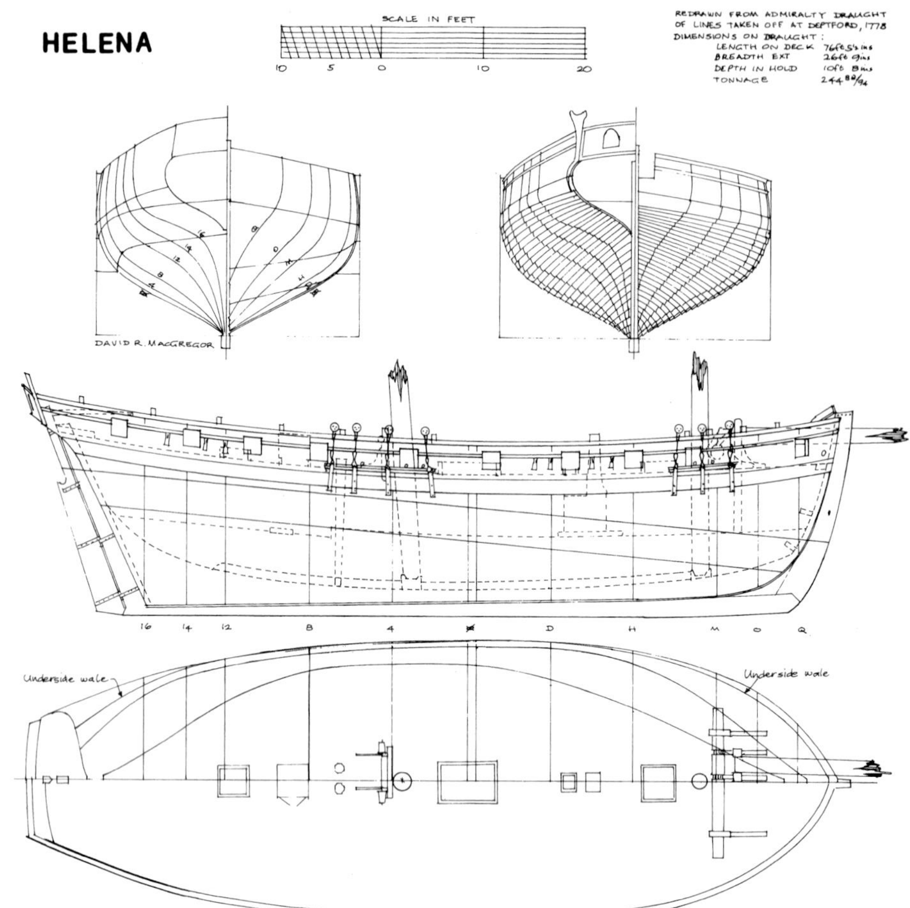

21: *Helena.* Lines plan, general arrangement and planking, redrawn from an Admiralty draught at the National Maritime Museum, Greenwich. She was built in 1778. Dimensions on the plan: 76ft-1½in (length on deck), 56ft-5½in (length of keel for tonnage), 26ft-9in (extreme breadth), 10ft-8in (depth of hold), and 215 tons. Reconstruction: deck plan combined here from a separate drawing and plan layout re-arranged. See text for the history of this schooner.

22: *Helena.* Sail plan, entirely reconstructed from spar dimensions listed on an Admiralty draught, as tabulated in the text; mast positions and rake of masts taken from original. Not given in spar list: head yard to square fore sail, doublings of masts and jibboom. See text for further comments on reconstruction.

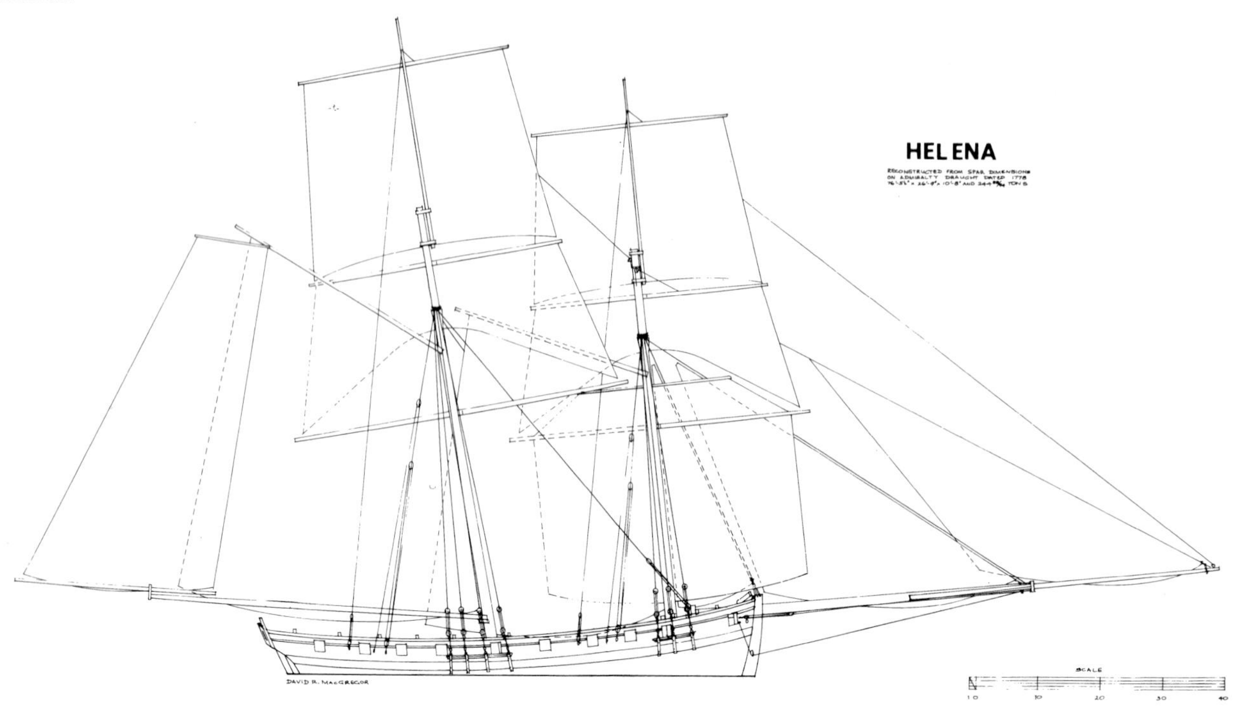

was captured by the French the same year, re-taken in 1779 and added to the Navy in that year under her original name. Her dimensions were 76ft-1½in length on deck, 56ft-5½in length on the keel for tonnage, 26ft-9in extreme breadth and 10ft-8in depth in hold. These measurements resulted in a tonnage of 214⁸⁸⁄₉₄. She has steeply rising floors with the maximum beam just above the load waterline and is really outside the scope of this book but for the fact that it is rare at this date to find the spar dimensions of a named schooner with an accompanying lines plan. The keel is slightly rockered forward, where it is also deeper below the rabbet than it is at the heel of the sternpost. There are end elevations drawn on the plan showing the run of the clinker planking, a style employed on several Admiralty draughts at this date.[98] She drew 13ft-9in aft and 7ft forward, was pierced for ten guns on the starboard side, and was fitted with a windlass. The deck layout and internal layout shown on the longitudinal section depict the manner in which she was fitted out, presumably at the time she was taken into the Navy.[18] The spar dimensions, given below, must be her original ones. The lower masts are certainly massive sticks; it is instructive to read that the lower yards are termed 'spread yards' and that there are no topmasts, only 'topgallants'. The base of this sail plan is of immense length, and the full suit of sails can have been set only in moderately light breezes. Sometimes the term 'topgallant' mast indicates one fidded abaft the lower mast, but this is more likely in cutters or schooners with smaller spars, and so it has not been done here.

Reconstructing the sail plan of the *Helena* has proved something of a problem as there were so few contemporary examples of schooners but, after trying various arrangements of spars and sails, the only logical solution appeared to be that of a cutter's rig on each mast, which makes the result look like Edward Gwyn's schooner. The deeply-roached topsails set on spread yards halfway down the mast are certainly peculiar to one variety of cutter. This rig set a square sail whose head fitted into the roach of the fore topsail, and so it has been drawn here. Compare this with the sail plan of HMS *Fly* in figure 17. A variation was to have the head laced not to a short yard but to a longer crossjack yard which was slung on the after side of the topsail. However, as no crossjack yard

Spar dimensions of schooner *Helena* inscribed on Admiralty Draught (No 4523 Box 64) at National Maritime Museum, Greenwich

	Length	*Diameter*
Mainmast	81ft 0in	22½in
Main topgallant mast	36ft 0in	7⅞in
Main topgallant yard	35ft 0in	6¾in
Main topsail yard	42ft 0in	8½in
Main spread yard	55ft 6in	9¼in
Main gaff	38ft 0in	10in
Main boom	54ft 5in	12⅞in
Foremast	71ft 0in	19½in
Fore topgallant mast	32ft 0in	7½in
Fore topgallant yard	32ft 0in	6½in
Fore topsail yard	38ft 4in	6¾in
Fore spread yard	49ft 0in	8¾in
Fore gaff	32ft 0in	8in
Bowsprit	56ft 5in	19in
Jibboom	50ft 0in	9in
Ringtail	33ft 9in	8in

Ringtail dimension refers to the boom.
Not given in above list: lengths of stunsail booms; length of crossjack yard or head yard to spread head of square sails; lengths of doublings or head of lower masts; length of jibboom inside bowsprit.

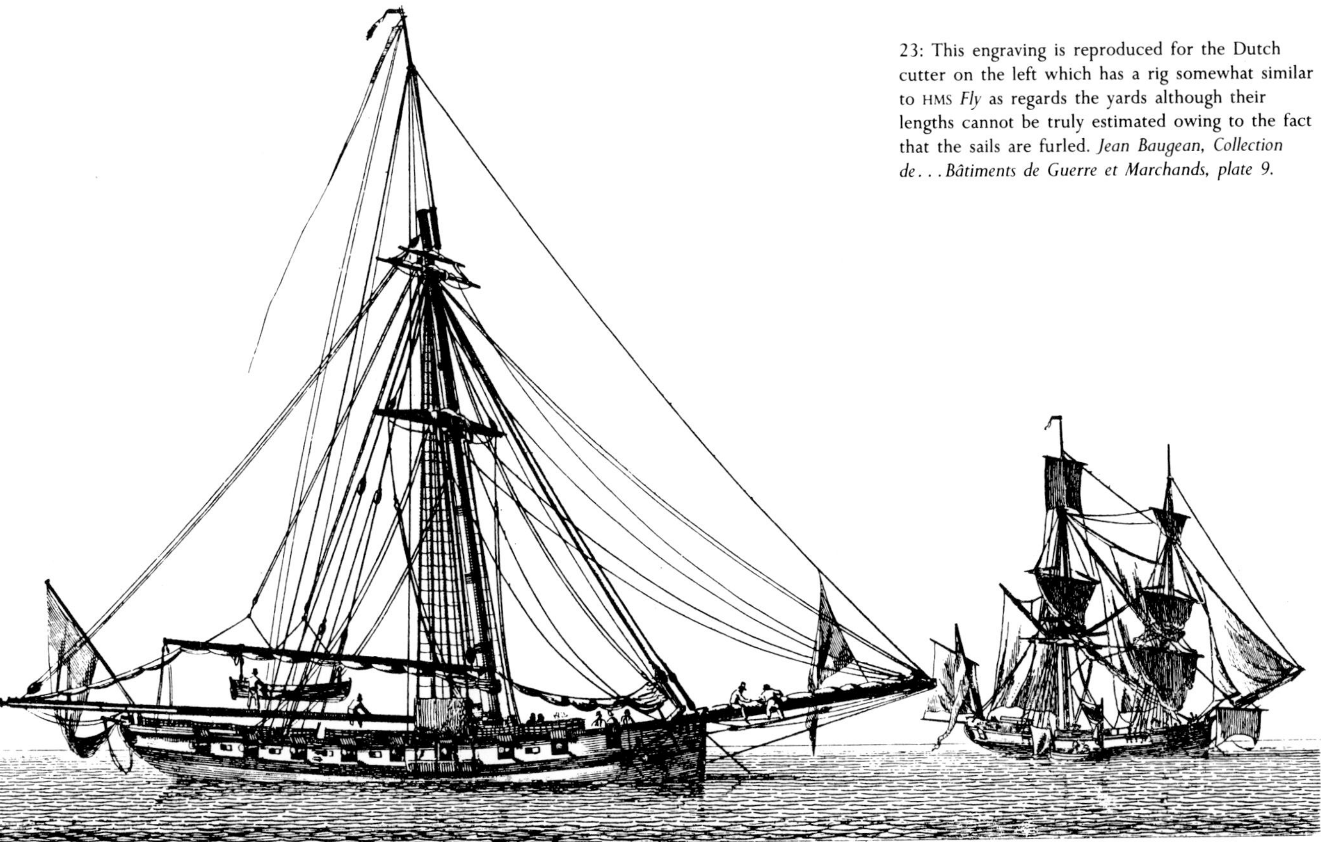

23: This engraving is reproduced for the Dutch cutter on the left which has a rig somewhat similar to HMS *Fly* as regards the yards although their lengths cannot be truly estimated owing to the fact that the sails are furled. *Jean Baugean, Collection de... Bâtiments de Guerre et Marchands, plate 9.*

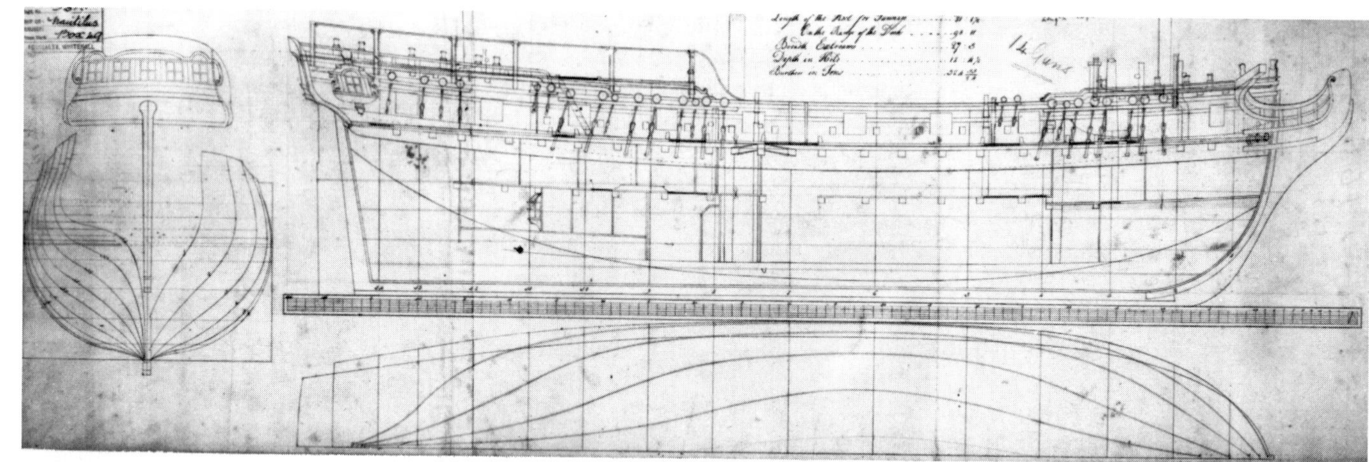

24: *Nautilus.* Built 1762 by Thomas Dodgson at Hull. Lines taken off at Portsmouth in 1763. Reproduced from Admiralty plan in National Maritime Museum. Dimensions on plan: 98ft-11in (length on deck) × 27ft-5in (extreme beam) × 12ft-4½in (depth in hold); 324 tons. Probably built as a privateer.

is listed amongst the *Helena*'s spar dimensions, it was decided not to employ this form. The stem head is drawn with holes bored through it to take the fantail end of a stay and so the fore stay is set up at this point, thus making it difficult to decide on the sizes of staysails between the foremast and the outer end of the bowsprit. The jib — or flying jib — is hoisted to the head of the lower mast, so that no headsail goes to the 'topgallant' mast. At this date, fore-and-aft topsails do not appear to have been carried by cutters and so none has been drawn above the main gaff, but a main topmast staysail could have been carried.

American schooners of this period had more rake to their stems and less beam, and the bowsprit was stepped on top of the stem. In their hull-forms, there was greater fineness in the waterlines, particularly in the run, which was longer and more concave. The American hulls were designed for a schooner rig, whereas the British hull was of the traditional cutter form with a two-masted rig.

English privateers

Prior to 1775, a number of fine-lined ships were purchased by the Admiralty in time of war for use as fireships, sloops and transports, and the *Nautilus*, whose lines were taken off at Portsmouth in 1763, forms a good example. She was built in 1762 at Hull by Thomas Dodgson and measured 98ft-11in on deck, 27ft-5in extreme beam, 12ft-4½in depth of hold and 324 tons. Her plan shows her to have considerable deadrise with a very rounded midsection and extremely long, sharp ends. In the body plan, radii for the topsides are drawn, but below this the Admiralty draughtsman was presumably unable to ascertain any centres for arcs. There is some similarity to certain body plans in Chapman's famous *Architectura Navalis Mercatoria* (1768) which were designed by the Swedish naval architect on a parabolic system. The *Nautilus* was probably built as a privateer during the Seven Years' War 1756–63, and her plan is evidence that fine-lined ships were produced in England prior to 1775.

In the Science Museum, London, is a half-model of a steep-floored ship bearing the name *Alexander* on her stern and pierced with nine gun ports each side. This indicates a well-armed ship, and the fitting of a windlass establishes a connection with a merchant ship, whereas a capstan would have indicated a naval vessel. The lines, taken off by William Salisbury, indicate by the form of her midship section that she is not of the orthodox naval hull form with a body plan shaped like a pear, but her straight rising floors and slack bilges suggest that her designer was influenced by the cutter's hull-form. Her hull proportions of depth to length are common for many West Indiamen of her date, although a sharp-built American ship would have been of shallower draught. Her lines and proportions are broadly similar to the privateer illustrated in figure 25. The *Alexander*'s entrance is moderately full and convex, but the run is finer and concave. There is a full height poop and the wheel is positioned close abaft the mizen; the windlass is on the afterside of the foremast. The hatchways are much longer than would be found in a purely cargo-carrying ship but would be common in a privateer or even a slaver. Dimensions taken from the model give an overall length of 106ft-0in and maximum breadth of 28ft-0in, and the tonnage has been calculated to measure 280 tons.

It has been suggested that she may be the Bristol privateer *Alexander* which made two cruises in 1778. This ship measured 250 tons, was armed with 14 6-pounders and six swivels, and carried 80 men. An advertisement described her as 'a remarkable fast sailer', but in order to attract seamen, could it really have done otherwise? The previous year she had been rebuilt from the keel upwards and in 1779 she was sold. On the second cruise, she and the *Tartar* captured the French ship *Ferme* whose cargo was insured for £100,000. This was a good reason for having a model of the ship made.[19]

Privateers were of all rigs and the *Tartar* referred to above could set the sails of either schooner or lugger, being fitted with three masts and measuring 110 tons. Several sloops and cutters were fitted out at Bristol between 1775–83, but their size was often larger than a full-rigged ship. Nicholas Pocock sketched a number of Bristol privateers some of which are reproduced in Damer Powell's book. One of the most splendid of his drawings shows the ship *Old England* running before the wind with skysails set on fore and main masts, stunsails set on both sides up to the royals, and two spritsails set. This ship was commissioned in 1778 with 120 men; she mounted 20 6-pounders and 20 swivels, and measured 280 tons.[20]

A larger ship was the *Mars* which J M

25: This half-model in the Science Museum bears the name *Alexander* on her stern. She has fine lines and is well-armed, and the long hatchways suggest she could have been a privateer or a slaver.

Hilhouse built in 1779 at Bristol on the lines of a fast naval sloop, with a fine, convex entrance and a longer, concave run. The sections of the body plan are developed by arcs of circles, with short floors and rounded sides, to judge from lines which William Salisbury took off the half-model in Charles Hill & Sons' possession. Dimensions measured off this half-model give 108ft-6in (afterside of sternpost to foreside of stem), 27ft-9in (moulded beam), 13 to 14ft-0in (approximate depth of hold). She mounted 22 12-pounders on her main deck, with eight other carriage guns, and carried 150 men, which made her one of the largest privateers built during the American War of Independence. There is a rigged model in the Bristol Museum which shows that she carried royals on all three masts, with a long mizen gaff and driver boom. Unfortunately she went missing on her first cruise.

Another probable Hilhouse-built privateer is depicted on an incomplete plan in the Hilhouse Collection, but sufficient has been drawn to indicate a ship with extreme rise of floor and a sharp run. This plan, folio 104,

26: The privateer *Ranger* is here seen as the large ship in the centre with her prizes taken in 1779, from a print by Nicholas Pocock dated 1780. She was built in America and does not look particularly lofty.

is unnamed and undated, and the dimensions are listed in the section on 'Post Office Packets' in this Chapter.

In the Lancaster Museum is a model bearing the name *Thetis* which suggests that it is intended to represent a ship of that name which John Brockbank built at Lancaster in 1801 of 290 tons and ten guns, but the builder's contract indicates that the model had larger dimensions than the actual vessel. The *Thetis* was renowned for beating off a French privateer in the West Indies. Her contract, in the Lancaster Museum archives, gives dimensions of 77ft-0in keel for tonnage, 25ft-0in moulded beam, and 16ft-2in depth of hold; whereas the model scales 92ft-0in keel and fore rake, 30ft-6in beam, and 16ft-0in depth of hold (approx). William Salisbury has taken lines off this model (figure 28) and transcribed the contract, which has permitted such an analysis to be made. He considers that it probably represents a design for a heavily armed letter of marque of *c*1780, such as Brockbank might have thought of building and that her midship section could very well fit his conception of drawing midship sections with a single sweep.

The hull has the same straight floors and steep deadrise as in the *Alexander*, but there is greater tumblehome and the entrance is somewhat sharper, yet the run less concave; otherwise the proportions are somewhat similar. She is pierced for 24 guns with a poop and forecastle, but instead of a windlass she has two capstans on deck.

Swedish, French and American privateers and blockade runners

In the magnificent work by Fredrik af Chapman, which was published in 1768 at Stockholm under the title of *Architectura Navalis Mercatoria*, are to be found a large number of plans of fine-lined ships.[21] Chapman's father was an Englishman who had emigrated to Sweden and the son had studied at many shipyards both in England and on the Continent where he must undoubtedly have acquired numerous plans of ships in addition to much valuable knowledge on methods of design. He was 47 years old when his book was published, at which time he held the post of Chief Shipbuilder to the Swedish Navy at Karlskrona and Stockholm. In his work, plans of fine-lined vessels are given for the categories or 'classes' of 'Privateers' (13 plans), 'Packet Boats' (five plans) and 'Pleasure Vessels for Sailing (ten plans). The yachts are all of broad, shallow-draught hull form with very hollow garboards and great tumblehome; the hulls are decorated with extensive carving as well as elaborate bows and sterns. One of his two plates of packet boats is reproduced later in this chapter and shows his liking for

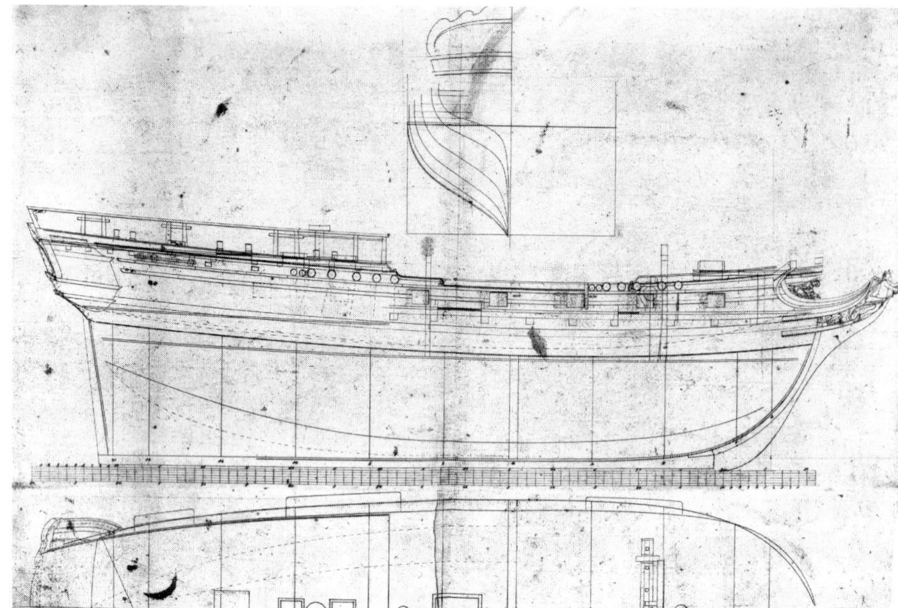

27: Unnamed ship in Hilhouse Collection. Incomplete, with forward stations in bodyplan not drawn. Dimensions: 84ft-0in (keel and fore rake) × 24ft-9in (moulded) × 17ft-6in (approx). Photographed from folio 104 through the courtesy of John C G Hill.

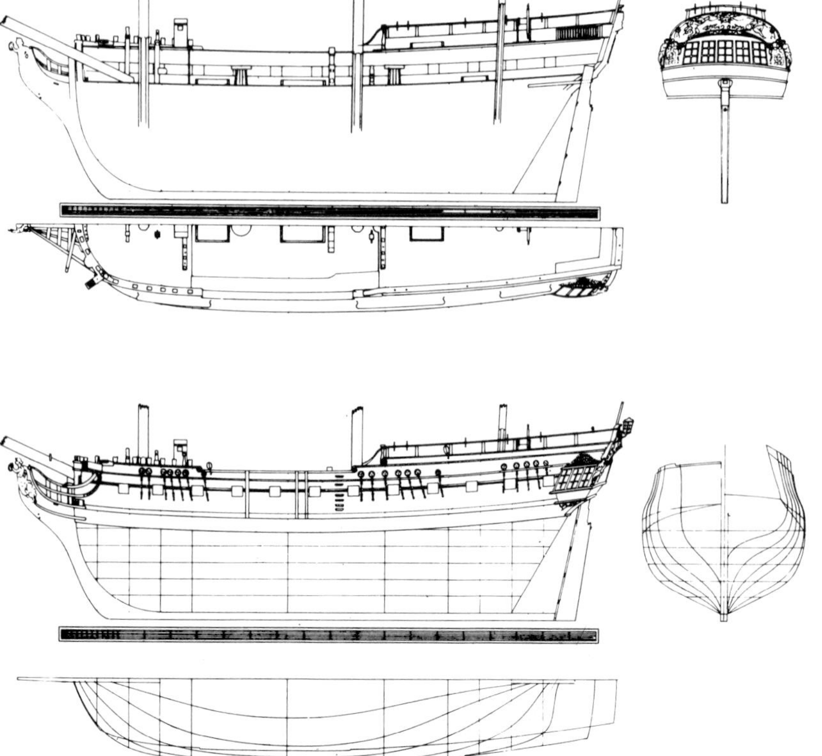

28: *Thetis*. Unidentified privateer c1780, possibly designed by John Brocklebank at Lancaster (see text). Reproduced from lines taken off model in Lancaster Museum and drawn out by W Salisbury. Dimensions of model: 92ft-0in (length of keel and fore rake) × 30ft-6in (beam) × 16ft-0in (approx depth in hold). Reconstruction: unknown.

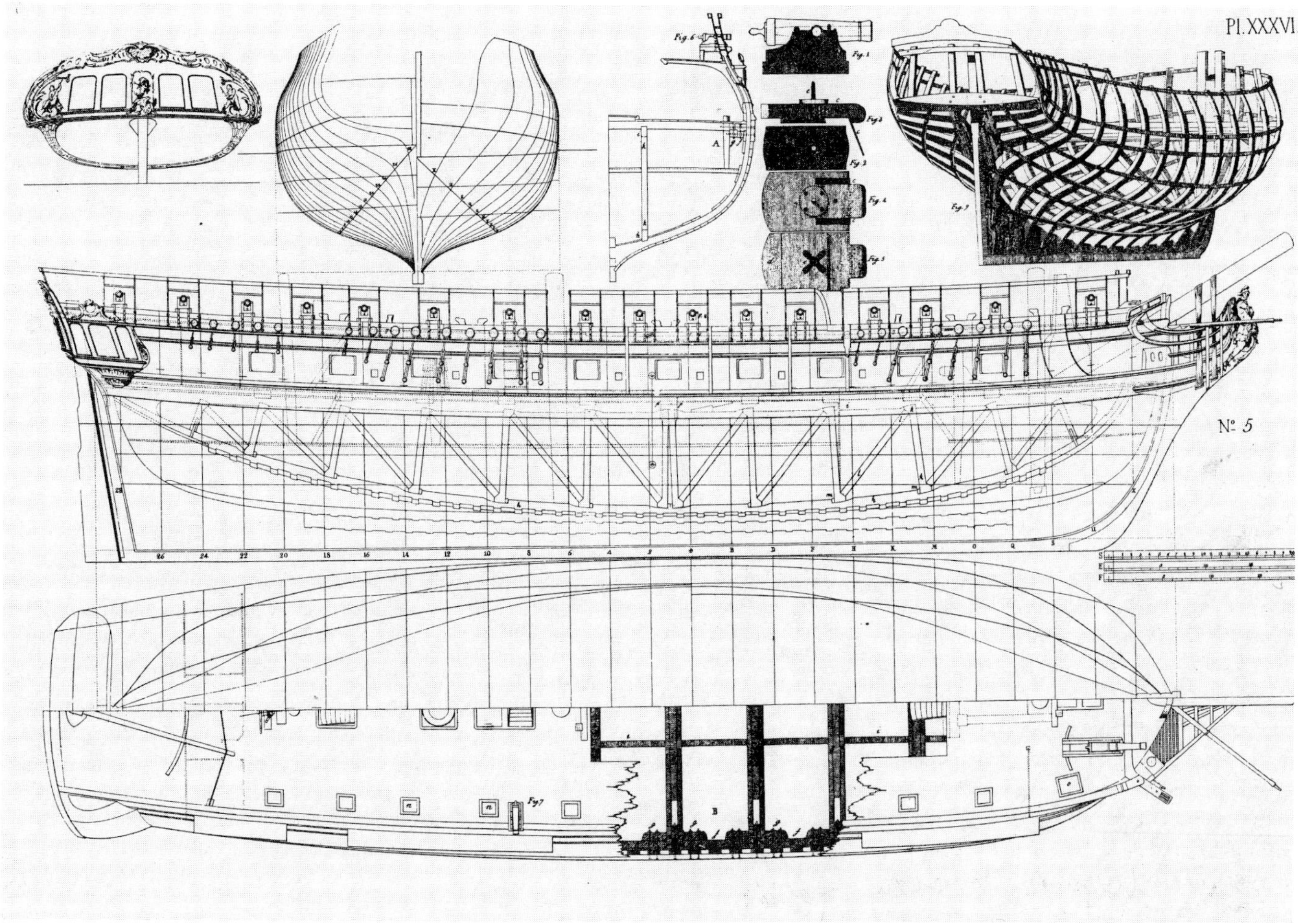

the same form of hull to be found in the privateers.

Of the 13 privateers, one is a sloop, two are schooners, two are ketches, one a snow and the rest ships. All possess the type of hull form to be found in the ship on plate XXXVI, reproduced here as figure 29. The great deadrise, hollow garboards, rounded bilges and marked tumblehome resulted in a fine-lined entrance and run, the lower part of which was hollow but the upper part was convex. Her dimensions, which are listed in the table of contents, give 116ft-6in length between perpendiculars, 30ft-6in moulded breadth, 14ft-9in draught of water 'abaft'; she also mounted 22 guns, was equipped with seven pairs of oars and had a complement of 220 officers and men. On the sheer elevation is drawn a form of diagonal bracing which ran the full length of the vessel, one on each side of the centre line. The half midship section also shows the bracing.

29: *Privateer.* Lines plan, deck layout and constructional details from plate XXXVI in *Architectura Navalis Mercatoria* by Fredrik af Chapman (1768). Dimensions: 116ft-6in (length between perpendiculars), 30ft-6in (breadth moulded), 14ft-9in (draught of water 'abaft'). Note that the perspective of the vessel in frame does not apply to this privateer but to the ketch in plate XXXIX fig 9 of the same work. See text for further details.

30: *Joly.* Lines plan. Three-masted slaver built in 1776 at La Rochelle. No dimensions are inscribed on the plan and no scale is drawn. Photographed from original in Guibert Collection of plans at the Mariners' Museum, Newport News.

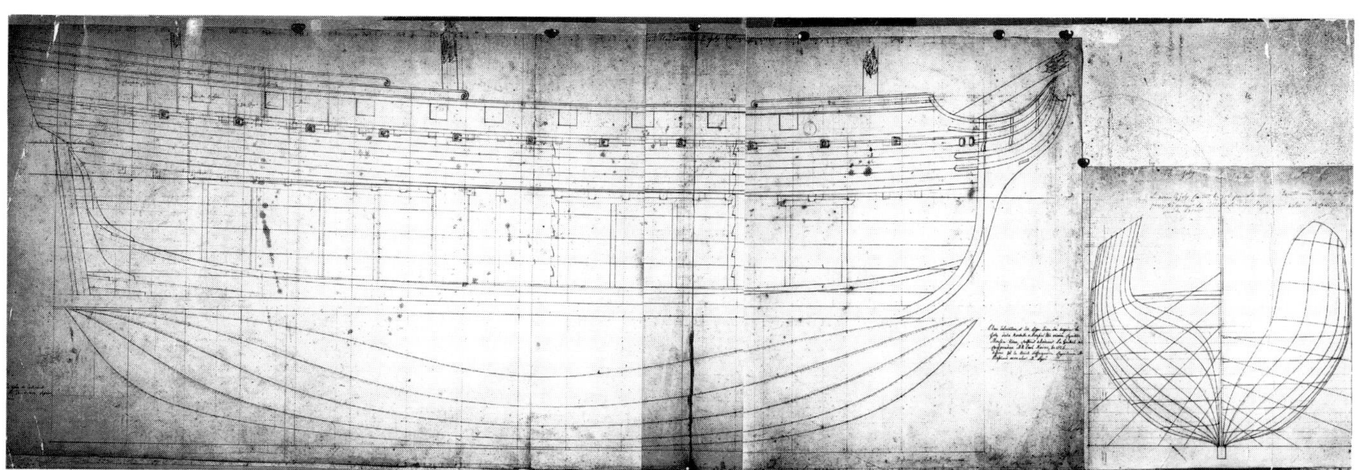

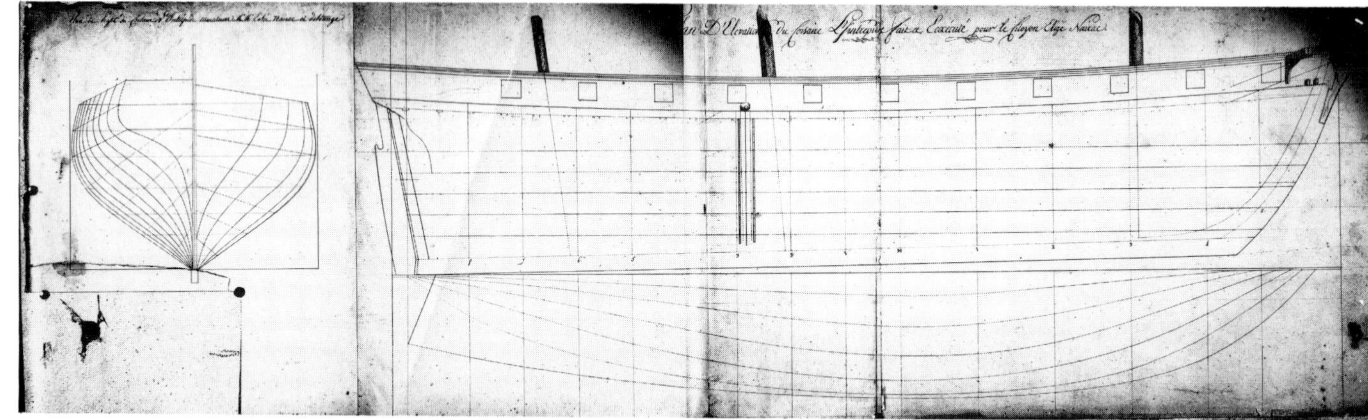

31: *L'Intrepide.* Lines plan. Three-masted French privateer designed for Citizen Nairac and drawn by Guibert Snr in about the years 1790-1810. No dimensions are written on plan and no scale is drawn. Photographed from original in the Guibert Collection of plans at the Mariner's Museum, Newport News.

The much-reproduced perspective of a vessel in frame, seen from the starboard quarter, does not apply to this privateer but to a smaller ketch-rigged privateer whose lines appear on Chapman's plate XXXIX (figure 9). This ketch had a length of 83ft between perpendiculars and possessed a somewhat similar hull form to the larger privateer described above. This style of midship section later appeared in a few clippers in the 1850s and 1860s.

Another designer of fine-lined hulls was a Frenchman named Guibert who drew many plans in the period 1770–1815; he was latterly aided by his son. Many of the drawings bear the names of actual vessels which adds to their importance as being indicative of the types of hull-form then being contemplated in France. The traditional midship section of French ships was pear-shaped, and although a number of the fine-lined hulls do possess such a shape in the body plan, others represent a radical departure from this with steeply rising floors. Compare this pear-shaped cross-sections of the slaver *Joly*, dated Rochelle 1776, with the very steep deadrise of the privateer *L'Intrepide*. The *Joly* (figure 30) has generally convex waterlines with slight concavity near the stem and some more hollow is worked into the run. The maximum beam is placed above the load waterline along the main wale. Below the gunports are small black ports which are probably intended to give ventilation to the slave deck rather than for the use of sweeps.

The draught of the French privateer, reproduced in figure 31, is inscribed 'Sheer Plan of the Corsair *L'Intrepide* drawn out for

32: *Rackoon.* French Corvette. Plan signed and dated: John H Beale, Bristol, 1801. Lines probably taken off in that year, presumably after her capture. Reproduced from plan in National Maritime Museum. Dimensions on plan: 75ft-6in (length on range of deck), 61ft-0in (length of keel for tonnage), 20ft-8in (moulded breadth), 9ft-8in (depth in hold from skin to skin); 141 tons. Style of rig not stated.

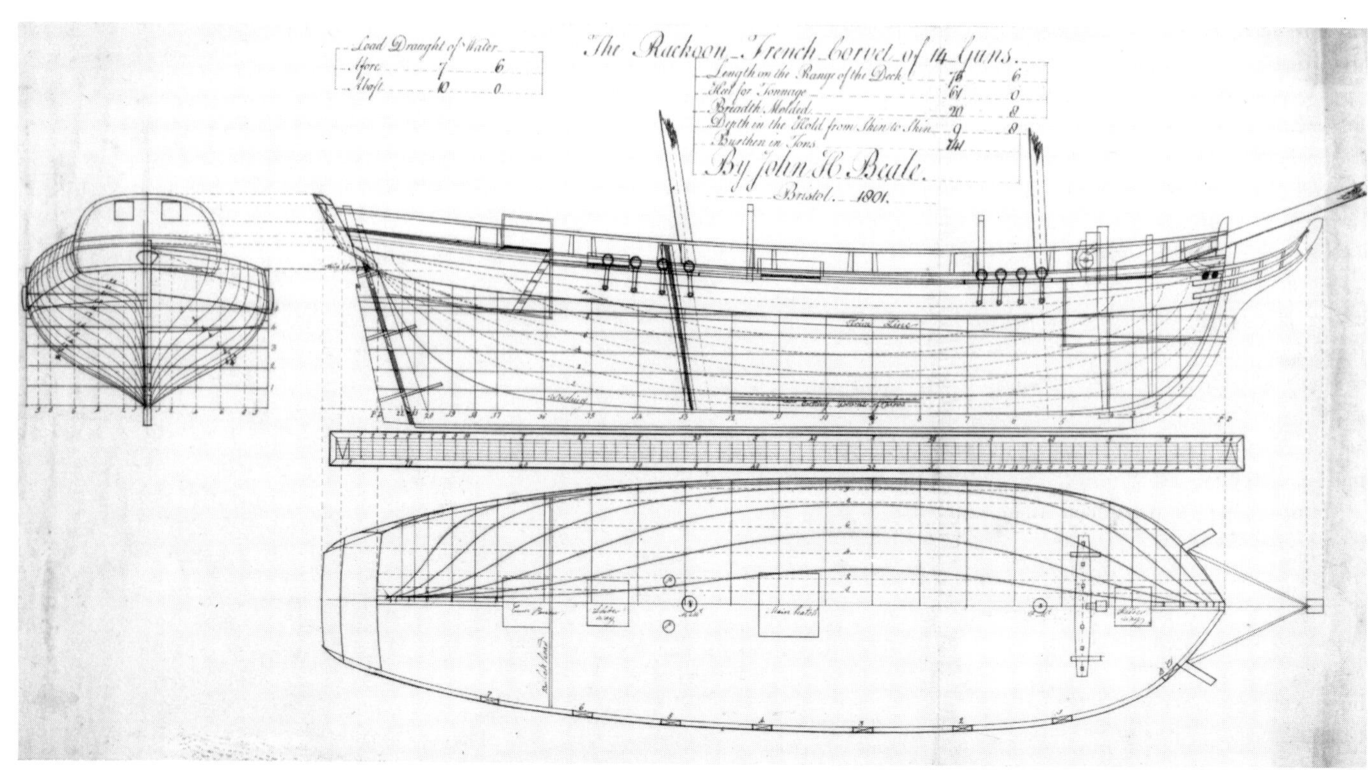

Citizen Elizé Nairac'. She is a flush-decked ship with a plain stem surmounted by only a fiddle-head, and a shallow counter at her stern. She has more concavity in her waterlines than the *Joly* although they are mostly convex in shape. A pump well is drawn on the sheer elevation amidships. There are no deck plans or spar dimensions for either ship.

Thanks to the British Admiralty's policy of getting lines taken off all ships of more than ordinary interest which were taken into the Navy and the preservation of such plans at the National Maritime Museum, Greenwich, it is possible to study some magnificent examples of foreign naval architecture. In this collection the Baltimore clipper and the French privateer are well represented and show the type of sharp ship which British men-of-war, packets, privateers, cutters or merchantmen had to elude or capture.

The French privateer *Les Huits Amis*, captured in 1798 and taken into the Royal Navy as the *Bonetta*, was an exceedingly fine-lined clipper to judge from the lines plan, and was similar to *L'Intrepide* in hull form but without quite such steep deadrise. She had a finely modelled entrance and run, and few hollows are to be found in her waterlines. Indeed many of the sharpest ships at the turn of the century had convex lines at bow and stern. Her tonnage is given as 347 with measurements of 103ft-1in on deck, 27ft-8in extreme breadth and 13ft-0½in depth of hold beside the keelson. At least seven other French privateers, which were captured by the British Navy between 1795 and 1803, display similar characteristics of steep deadrise, fine lines and flush decks — characteristics which are to be found in the Chesapeake model and confirm reports that American shipbuilders were active in France during this period.[22] Prior to this, plans in the Admiralty draughts of captured French ships built on fine lines show the body plan to be of the traditional pear-shape, in which the floors, bilges and topsides are all arcs of circles, but these later privateers indicate a fresh influence at work. A ship such as *L'Intrepide* was finer-lined than many clippers of half a century later and it was only the additional length that gave these later clippers that extra turn of speed.

The *Les Huits Amis* had a fine figurehead of a warrior with a scimitar in his right hand, but another example of these privateers is *La Vengeance* which had a plain bow and fiddle head. She had the reputation of being a very fast sailer but also of being considerably wet when diving into a head sea. She was added to the Navy in 1800 under the name of HMS *Scout*.[23]

33: *L'Invention.* A painting of the ship was done by an Italian artist at Naples in 1803 and it was reproduced in *Sea Breezes* in No 73, Vol VIII, December 1925 (page 101). The drawing reproduced here has been copied from it as accurately as possible. Of course, the painting was executed after the ship was captured and was trading under Guernsey ownership. In the lines plan, there are 14 gunports; here there are 13, and the bulwarks appear to have been raised. The ex-privateer was put up for sale at Plymouth in 1801 and was purchased by Guernsey merchants, who placed here in the North Atlantic and Mediterranean trades with a crew of a master, two mates and 29 seamen and boys. Her armament was reduced to four guns. After a change of ownership, she was lost off the River Plate. The particulars given of the *Invention* in the bill of sale at Plymouth in 1801, were communicated by the correspondent G G Tardif to *Sea Breezes* as follows:

'To be sold on Friday, October 9th, by ten o'clock in the forenoon, the handsome ship *L'Invention*, of the following dimensions: — Length on lower deck, 185 feet 5 inches; ditto of Keel, 121 feet 3 inches; Breadth, extreme, 27 feet 5 inches; Moulded, 27 feet 1 inch; Height between decks, 4 feet 9 inches; Depth in the hold, 9 feet 4 inches, and admeasures 486 tons.

'She is quite new, and was built at Bordeaux, under the immediate care and inspection of Citizen Thibault, a celebrated member of the Society of Arts and Sciences and Belles Lettres; and fitted with four masts, which have been found to answer extremely well, in here sailing even before the wind; she is allowed by the first Master Builders, by whom she has been examined, to be an exceedingly well and fine build Vesssel, of a beautiful Form and Model; her Superiority of Sailing had enabled her to elude the Vigilance of our best Frigates, and she was only taken after a Chase of Ten hours, and the loss of Top Masts in a Fog and heavy Sea, which also prevented her Escape by her Sweeps, worked by an entire new and novel Machine of singular Simplicity and Effect; she abounds in Stores, which are all new and of the best Materials; has a neat Figure Head; a deep Waist; and is full Coppered to the Wals. Mounts 24 guns . . .

A quite exceptional vessel was built in France in 1801. This was the four-masted, full-rigged ship *L'Invention* which was almost certainly the first of this type of rig to be constructed. In addition, she was built on extremely sharp lines, and what really equated her with the clippers of 50 years later was not so much her raking stem but rather her great length in proportion to breadth which resulted in a ratio of 5.44 beams to length. The following quotation from James' *Naval History* describes the circumstances surrounding her capture, and provides some pertinent details of her design and rig.

> On the 27th of July [1801] at 1 A.M., in latitude 43°34′ north, and longitude 11°42′ west, the British 18-pounder, 36-gun frigate *Immortalité,* Captain Henry Hotham, fell in with an enemy's cruiser of a very extraordinary appearance, a ship with four masts, which the former immediately chased, and at 7 h. 30m. A.M., the 38-gun frigate, *Arethusa,* Captain Thomas Wolley, in sight, captured. The prize proved to be the *Invention,* French privateer, nine days from Bordeaux, on her first cruise, having only been launched since the beginning of the month.
>
> The *Invention* had been designed by her commander, M. Thibaut, and was peculiar in more respects than her masts, her length being 147 feet, with

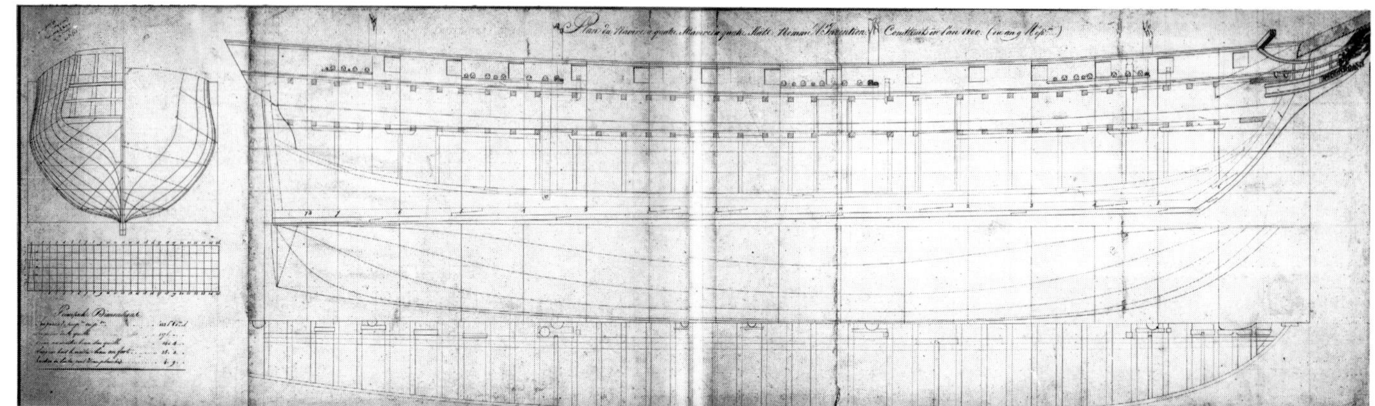

34: *L'Invention.* Lines plan and plan of deck beams. No spar dimensions listed, but dimensions inscribed and scale is drawn. Photographed from original plan in Guibert Collection at the Mariners' Museum, Newport News. Plan photographed in two halves without overlap.

> only 27 feet in breadth of beam. Her force consisted of 24 long 6-pounders on a single deck, and two 12-pounder carronades, either on her poop or top-gallant forecastle, with a crew of 210 men and boys. Her four masts were nearly at equal distances apart, the first and third of the same height, the second stouter and higher, and the fourth much smaller. She had four top-gallant yards rigged aloft, and was accounted a good sea-boat and sailer.[24]

Later in 1801, *L'Invention* had lines taken off at Plymouth but the only surviving plan amongst the Admiralty draughts at the National Maritime Museum, Greenwich, is one of the sheer elevation as far down as the load waterline and a deck plan drawn to the centre line. The lines plan reproduced here in figure 25 is from the Guibert collection at the Mariners' Museum, and shows the acquisitive nature of ship designers in collecting plans. J M Hilhouse of Bristol also had a similar habit.

The lines plan of *L'Invention* shows her to have had the traditional pear-shaped body plan with slack bilges and steep deadrise, so that the maximum beam occurs at about the level of the load waterline. The entrance and run are long and tapering with some concavity in the lower body; the stem is remarkable for its long raking line. On the sheer elevation, the deck beams indicate a flush main deck and below it a continuous lower deck; other items appearing on this part of the drawing are the hold pillars, keelson, and the fore and after deadwoods. At the bottom of the sheet is a plan of the deck beams. The channels are drawn on the sheer elevation with the appropriate number of deadeyes secured to each, and this information would permit a correct reconstruction of the shrouds and backstays on each of the four masts. From such particulars, it may be judged that the jigger mast was shorter than the other three masts and so would have carried shorter yards and smaller sails.

In addition to the fine-lined ships being built at Baltimore, sharp vessels were being constructed in many areas of America as the result of the War of American Independence 1775–83 and the Naval War of 1812–15; both of these demanded fast ships as blockade runners to elude the British naval squadrons or as privateers to prey on British merchant shipping. The Royal Navy early evinced an interest in these sharp schooners by building two at New York in 1767,[26] and from time to time adding others by capture. Gradually the term 'Baltimore clipper' was applied to any schooner of sharp build, irrespective of where she was constructed.

The design of these ships was not restricted by any rules to which European naval architects were in bondage, but they were generally built with long, straight or slightly curved floors with bilges kept high, convex waterlines, and frequently without any concavity in the run. The head was often plain with a scroll fiddle head, but no knee, figurehead or trail boards, and it raked forward boldly. The sternpost raked aft and there was

35: The *Challenge* exhibits the limits of square canvas that could be set on a schooner. The yards on the mainmast appear to be shorter than those on the fore; the square sail from the fore yard has been clewed up; and only one stunsail is set. *Peabody Museum, Salem*

considerable drag to the keel. The decks were flush. The rig was usually that of a heavily-rigged schooner with square sails on one or both masts, but sometimes the rig was that of true brigantine, brig, or ship.

The Baltimore clipper selected here as an example is the schooner *Fly*, which was captured in 1811, 50 miles off the Scillies, and taken into the Navy the following year under the name of *Sea Lark*. The plan in figure 36 shows he is not such an extreme model as the *Nonpareil* or *Musquidobit* but is typical of the fine-lined model under construction in the early years of the nineteeth century.[27] Another reason for her choice is the interesting comparison she affords with the East India Company's brigantine *St Helena* (figure 36) which possesses several similarities: the length on deck and along the keel, the amount of drag, and the curvature of the sheer. Here the similarities end as the *Sea Lark* has steeper deadrise, finer waterlines, and a shallower hull. She measures 81ft-3in length on deck, 22ft-8in extreme breadth, 9ft-10in depth of hold and 178 27/94 tons. She has no windlass, but riding bitts abaft the foremast and a capstan abaft the mainmast. The sail and rigging plan (figure 37) has been reconstructed from her spar dimensions given on the draught, and from a reconstruction kindly furnished by Howard I Chapelle, which has been followed for the rigging and sails. The great height of the lower masts and large hoist given to the gaff sails was a very prominent feature in the Baltimore clipper and provides a striking contrast to the sail plan of the *St Helena*. The American schooner often spread her square sail on a boom, and many of the schooners were rigged with a square topsail and topgallant on the main as well. The fitting of the *Sea Lark*'s main topsail jack yard is also different to British practice at this date.

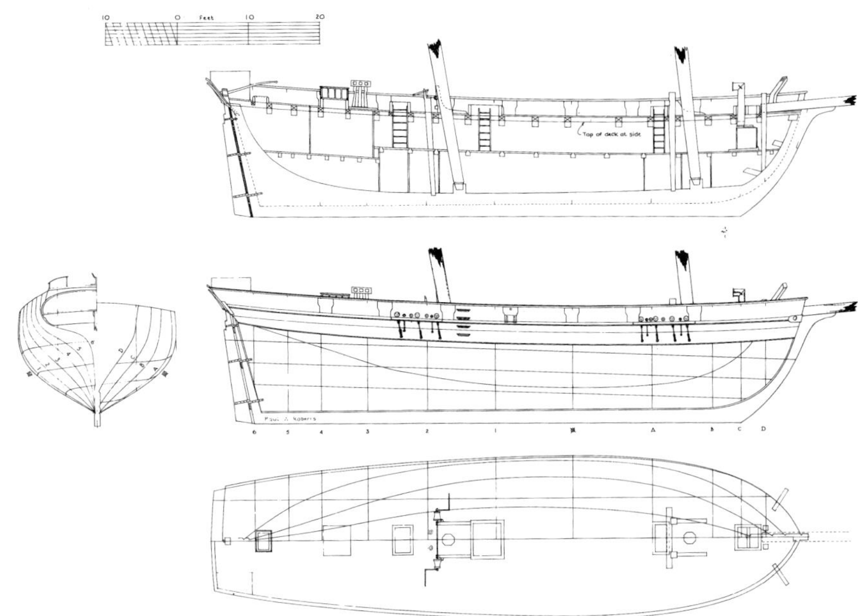

36: HMS *Sea Lark*, ex *Fly*. Lines, deck plan and longitudinal section, redrawn by Paul A Roberts from Admiralty draughts in the National Maritime Museum, Greenwich. Dimensions on plan: 81ft-3in (length on deck), 22ft-8in (extreme breadth), 9ft-10in (depth of hold), and 178 tons. Reconstruction: particulars on longitudinal section were obtained from the original lines plan, where they were overdrawn in a different coloured ink; deck plan from a separate drawing.

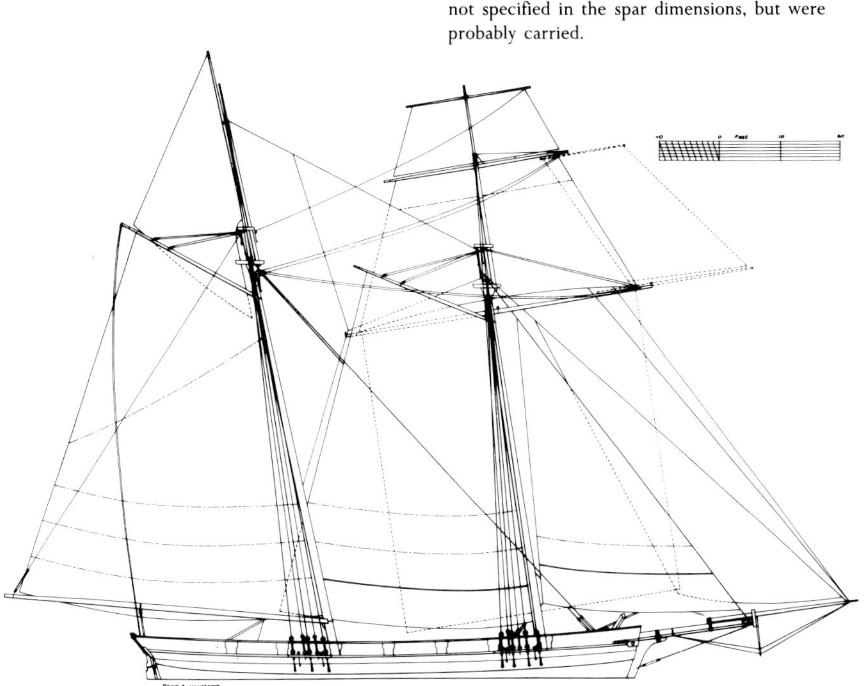

37: HMS *Sea Lark* Sail plan: Reconstructed from sheer elevation and from spar dimensions listed on lines plan. Also from reconstructed sail plan loaded by Howard I Chapelle. The stunsail and the square sail below the fore yard are dotted because they are not specified in the spar dimensions, but were probably carried.

The presence of so many fast sailing predators caused a number of fine-lined sloops and gun-brigs to be built in the Navy and in this manner exerted an influence in forcing shipbuilders to design vessels that would outsail their enemies. But the continual wars and the necessity to be ever on the alert against privateers and smugglers produced naval architects who could design a fast vessel when required. In the matter of steep deadrise, the ten-gun brigs of the *Rolla* class, designed by Sir Henry Peake in 1807, were quite up to the standard of the American schooners, and Sir William Symonds was later to continue this trend in the 1830s, as discussed in chapter three. James A Sharp, Sir William Symond's biographer, refers to the 'strong family likeness in the three fastest classes of vessels – the English cutter, French lugger and American clipper'.[28]

Some direct influence of the Baltimore

clipper trend is claimed by Basil Lubbock for the design of the opium clipper *Red Rover* which was built in 1829 on the lines of the American brigantine *Prince de Neuchâtel* and was in turn the model for several other opium ships.[29] But many analogies are too swiftly drawn between any British fine-lined ship and the first Baltimore clipper that comes to mind and great care must be exercised in such judgements, especially when there is such excellent native British fast-sailing tradition at hand.

Of merchant ships bought into the Navy in the years 1775–83, plans in the Admiralty collection of draughts at the National Maritime Museum, Greenwich, indicate that many were built on moderately fine lines, such as the *Cupid* (bought 1777 of 290 tons) or the *Britannia* (bought 1781 of 537 tons). Both these ships, and others like them, had two decks, a poop and a forecastle; they were fitted with a windlass and were pierced with a fair number of gun ports. In the ends, there was generally some concavity in the lower part of the entrance and particularly so in the run where it was carried all the way up. In American-built ships which were added to the Navy in these years, the upper deck was usually flush and sometimes more rake was given to stem and sternpost. They were of markedly sharper form than the West Indiamen being built in Europe.

An example of a North American ship of this date is the *Cupid*, which was built in Newfoundland in 1777, placed in the Leghorn trade by a London owner, purchased in the same year by the Admiralty for use as an armed ship, and fitted out at Deptford at a cost of £2970 8s 6d. She foundered the following year. Her plan, dated August 1777, gives dimensions of 92ft-1in length on lower deck, 27ft-0in breadth extreme, 12ft-2in depth in hold, and 290 tons. The lines plan is redrawn in figure 40 and the deck plan is added, but the alterations made in Deptford Dockyard have been omitted.

Compared with those of the sharp-ended *Grasshopper* (ex *London* 1770), the measurements of length and breadth are almost identical, but she is 1ft-4in deeper in the hold. This appearance of greater depth is accen-

38: In this watercolour sketch by Admiral Philip Brown, entitled 'The *Midas* of Baltimore bound to Bordeaux', the schooner is drawn stern-on with the masts in line; the lower crosstrees are those on the foremast. She has a great variety of flying kites set, and the triangular area between the sailor in the rigging and the mainmast could be the lowered peak of the fore gaff sail or else the head yard of some other fancy sail about to be set. *MacGregor Collection.*

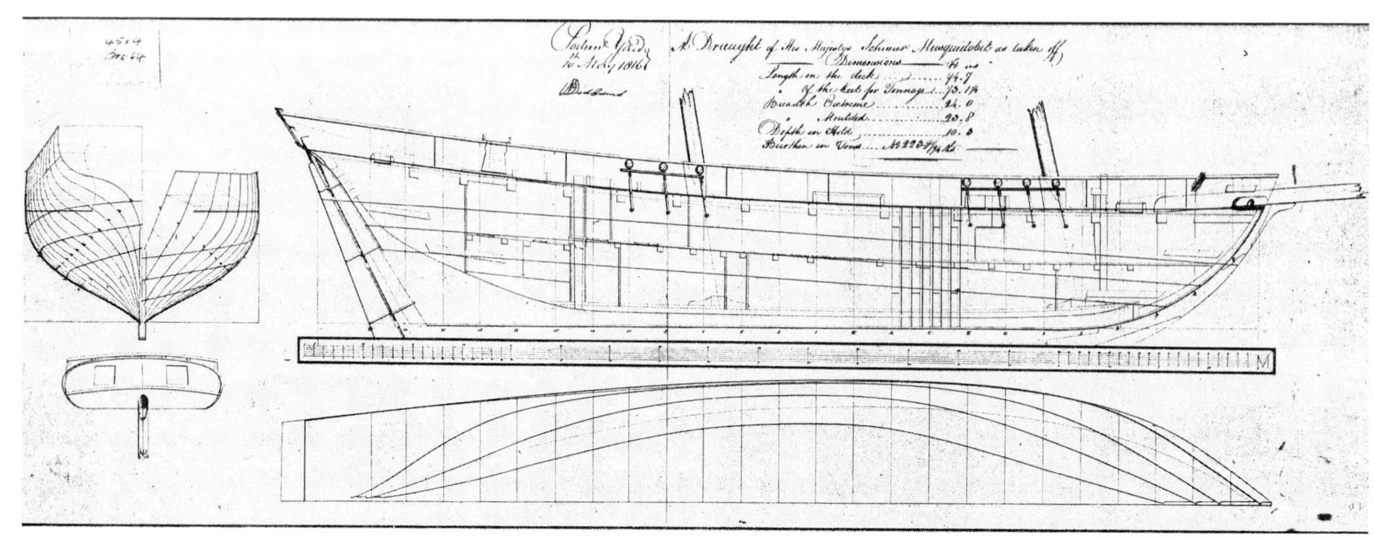

39: HMS *Musquidobit*. Built 1812 at Baltimore as the *Lynx*. Captured in 1813 and taken into the Royal Navy under the name of *Musquidobit*. Reproduced from Admiralty plan dated 1816 in the National Maritime Museum. Dimensions on plan: 94ft-7in (length on deck) × 24ft-0in (extreme breadth) × 10ft-3in (depth in hold); 223 91/94 tons. Six guns.

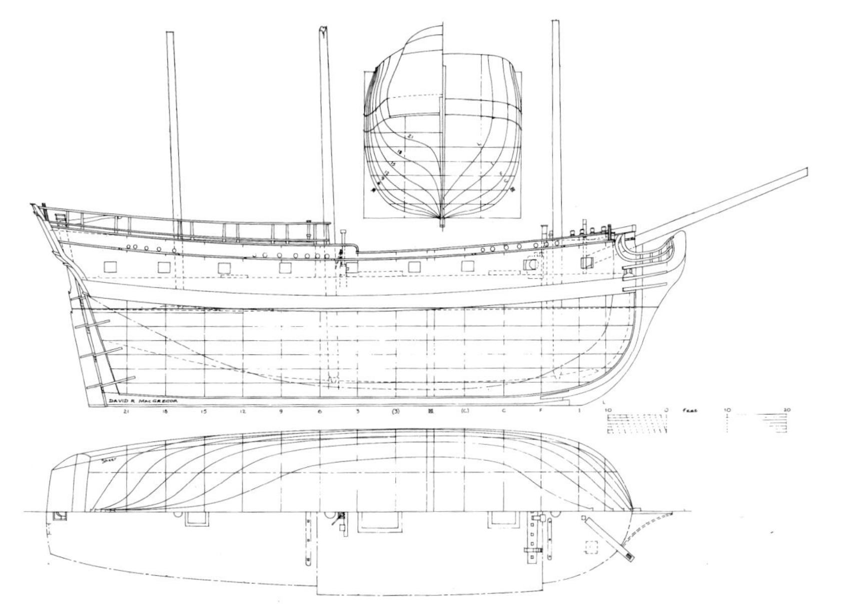

40: *Cupid*. Lines plan. The *Cupid* was built in Newfoundland 1777 and bought by the Royal Navy in the same year. The plan has been redrawn from Admiralty draughts at the National Maritime Museum. Reconstruction: elevation of stern; omission of alterations proposed by Royal Navy; addition of deck fittings from a second plan. Dimensions on plan: 92ft-1in (length on lower deck), 74ft-9¾in (keel for tonnage), 27ft-0in (extreme breadth), 12ft-2in (depth in hold) and 290 tons. Note that the mizen mast steps on the lower deck. Chain plates are drawn on the sail plan.

tuated by the high solid bulwarks in the waist, which are 4ft high at their lowest point. There is a good sheer at the rail, but the two decks are almost straight with practically no sheer whatsoever, which was unusual by this date. The height in the 'tween decks is 5ft at the stern and 5ft-6in in the bows. There is a short forecastle up to the foremast, and the poop extends to the mainmast; nine gunports are pierced in her side; there is no decoration at bow or stern; there is a windlass on the main deck; and she has tiller steering. In hull form, she has a short, sharp entrance, and a longer, more hollow run; the quarter beam buttock is straight where it crosses the load line; the floors are slightly concave, but the bilges and side round up to give a deep midsection. Above lower deck level, her stem rabbet is plumb vertical. *Lloyd's Register* of 1778 gives her armament as four 9-pounders, four 6-pounders and ten 4-pounders.

One point of interest is that her mizen mast is stepped on the lower deck, not on the keelson. Her lower masts and topmasts are as long as or longer than those of *Grasshopper*, but her topgallant masts are much shorter, and no long pole heads are indicated, which has been taken as meaning that there was just a short head above the topgallant rigging. *Grasshopper*'s yards, mizen gaff, bowsprit and jibboom are all from 1 ft to 2ft longer than those of the *Cupid*. Here is a comparison of their mast lengths, together with those of Steel's ship, whose sail plan appears in figure 47.

The spar dimensions from the Admiralty draught have been utilised to reconstruct the sail plan in figure 41, from which it will be noticed that the *Cupid* is much squarer aloft than Steel's ship and confirms the large sail areas commonly given to ships built in North

Comparison of mast lengths of three ships

	Cupid 290 tons	*Grasshopper* 282 tons	*Steel's ship of 330 tons*
	(fig 77)		(fig 126)
Main lower mast	65ft 6in	65ft 2in	66ft 0in
Main topmast	38ft 8in	36ft 9in	38ft 0in
Main topgallant mast	25ft 0in	37ft 0in	32ft 0inb
Fore lower mast	58ft 6in	57ft 5in	61ft 0in
Fore topmast	38ft 2in	33ft 10in	37ft 0in
Fore topgallant mast	23ft 3in	33ft 5in	30ft 0inb
Mizen lower mast	44ft 11ina	56ft 0in	58ft 0in
Mizen topmast	30ft 0in	25ft 10in	28ft 0in
Mizen topmast pole	—	11ft 0in	—
Mizen topgallant mast	—	15ft 0in	

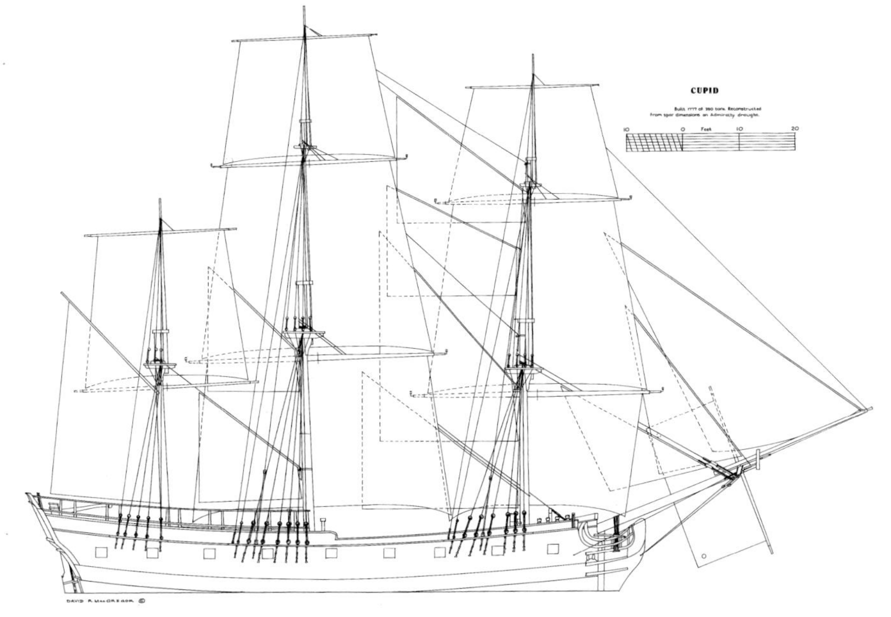

41: *Cupid*. Sail plan, entirely reconstructed from the sheer elevation on the lines plan and from spar dimensions on an Admiralty draught dated 27 August 1777. Rigging, sails and spar details are from contemporary text books and paintings.

42: A ship getting under way in Pegwell Bay near Deal, as painted by Thomas Whitcombe in 1810. The ship is coming from the right, and in the centre of the painting she has got the royals loosed and ready for hoisting; the stunsail booms are being run out and men are aloft overhauling the gear; many of the staysails are set. On the left of the painting, she is seen under a cloud of canvas. She carries a broadside of six guns. It is interesting to note that there is a bobstay above and below the spritsail yard, thus making it impossible to set a sail here.

America. The staysails are typical of ships at this date. There is a dearth of books on rigging prior to the 1790s, which adds to the problems of reconstruction work; but unrestored paintings and models provide vital evidence.

In British merchant shipping there were no noticeable effects of the Baltimore clipper model because the full-bodied, deep ships were protected by the convoy system and those that were issued with 'passes' and ran outside the convoys had always been built to sail fast and protect themselves. Perhaps the press reports of massive captures and sinkings by American or French privateers had the intangible effect of making better known these fast-sailing ships and possibly some owners may have tried to emulate or improve on them. Naming ships *Experiment*, *Fly* or *Dash* suggests that the owner had built a fast sailing craft, or it may just be wishful thinking on our part. The degree of sharpness and fine lines in a ship had not then been subjected to such scrutiny in every shipyard as became the case half a century later, and the terms 'sharp', 'hollow', 'rake' had a different meaning to a merchant shipbuilder, owner or captain at the end of the eighteenth century than they had in the clipper ship era.

Take the case of the ship *Jupiter* which Daniel Brocklebank built at Whitehaven in 1793 for his own use. He had some very positive remarks to make about her performance and hull form which, when compared with her lines plan, provide a useful commentary on late eighteenth-century design concepts, and he commented thus on her in his notebook:

'The bow was made very sharp and thin with considerable hollow below five or six feet of water. When in ballast the *Jupiter* is represented to sail remarkably fast by the wind or with the wind on the beam. Going before the

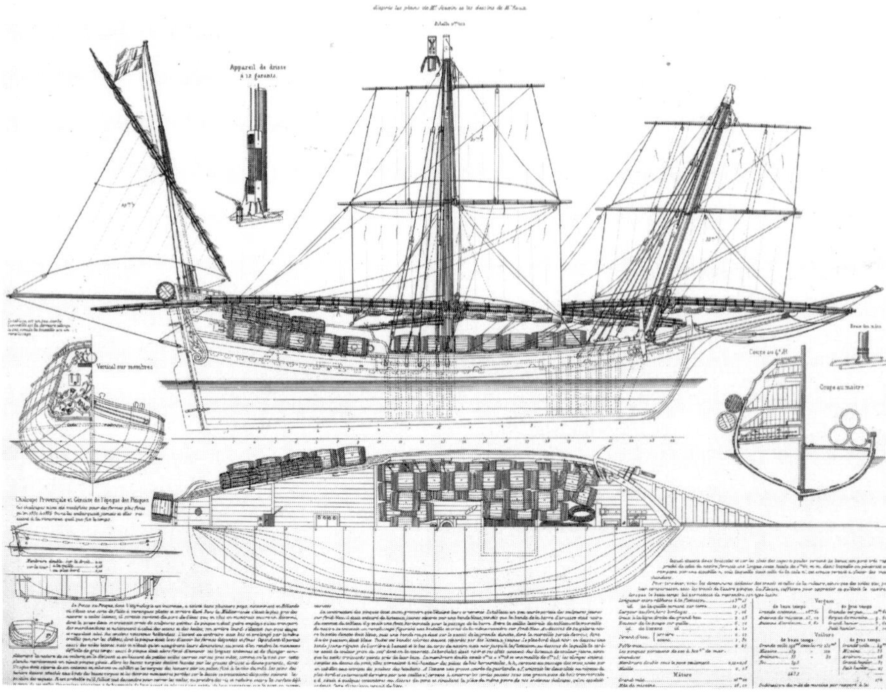

43: Genose Pink of 1800. Plan of lines, sails and rigging, cargo stowage and cross sections reproduced from *Souvenirs de Marine* by Admiral Paris (plate 120). She is a broad, shallow draught craft with short, sharp ends and slack bilges. The long lateen yards are lowered and the square sail rig is shown set. The masts are single sticks without tops.

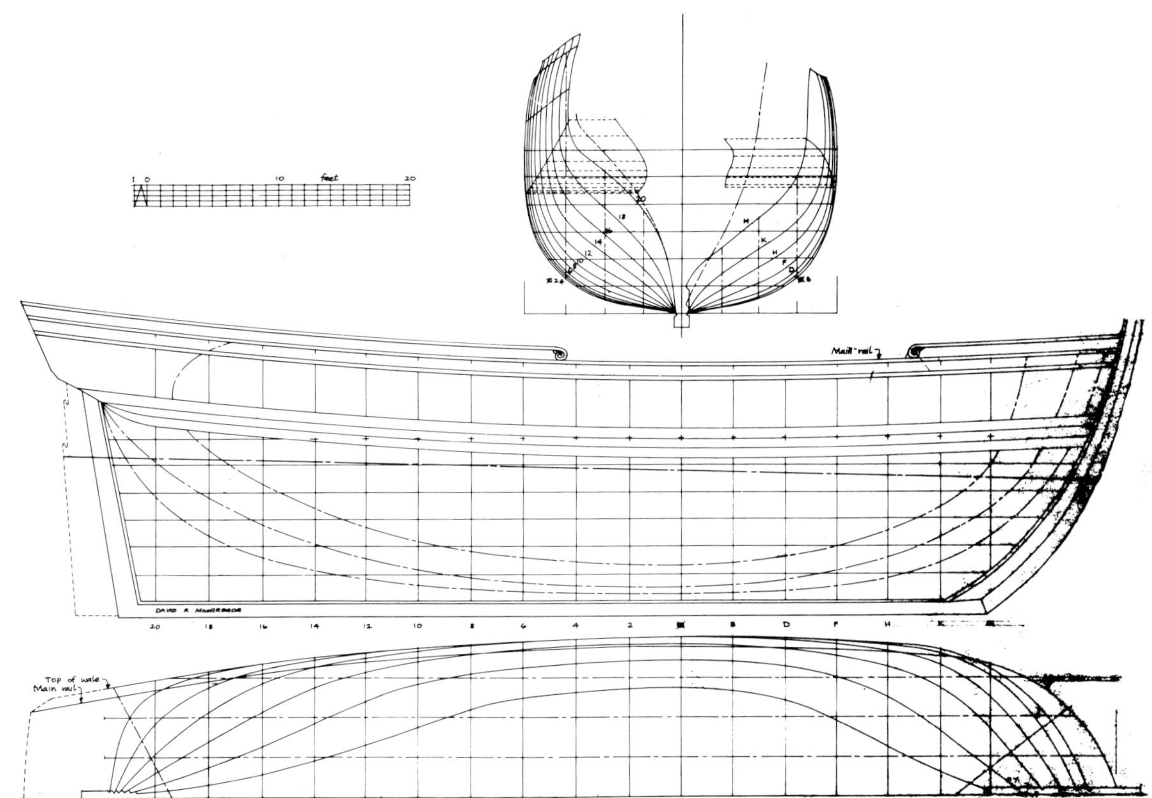

44: *Jupiter*. Built 1793 by Daniel Brocklebank at Whitehaven. Redrawn from plan in possession of T & J Brocklebank, Liverpool, Dimensions on plan: 84ft-0in (length aloft) × 24ft-0in (moulded breadth) × 16ft-3in; tonnage 207. Reconstruction: load waterline from *Lloyd's Register* (1797); suggested shape of rudder dotted; buttock lines added.

wind not so fast in proportion. Her sailing fast by the wind must be attributed more to the fine bow than the after end; her great rake forward prevents her from plunging deep in the sea tho' I believe she pitches rather more than usual. When on her first passage out to St. Petersburg in ballast and with a clean bottom she passed nearly 70 sail of merchantmen. With the wind upon the beam and smooth water near Bornholm she sailed from 11 to 12 knots. Her great disadvantage is not laying well upon the ground and requiring 10 to 15 tons of ballast to steady her with masts and yards aloft but when loaded or in ballast she is perfectly stiff.'[31]

First a comment is needed about the *Jupiter*'s dimensions before discussing her design and its implications. It is stated on her plan: 'Length aloft as built 84 feet, one flooring being added amidships; length on the ground 69 feet; breadth moulded 24 feet; depth in the hold 16ft-3ins; admeasures 207 tons.'[32] Dimensions scaled off the plan give 81ft-6in length aloft (foreside of the stem head to afterside of the sternpost at assumed deck level) and 66ft-6in length of keel on the ground. The plan is thus a design drawing and it was common practice to inscribe on such drawings the dimensions of the vessel 'as built'. Sometimes the design dimensions are also added by the builder as in the Adams' plans of ships built at Buckler's Hard. The frame inserted amidships apparently added 2ft-6in to the length of the hull, which is the difference between the design length and the length as built; this suggests that the room and space was 2ft-6in, even though the stations of the body plan are spaced at 4ft-0in centres. However, stations and frames do not always coincide and the discrepancy of six inches may also be ascribed to inaccuracies in scale and to paper movement. Indeed, differences between scaled and written dimensions are frequently much larger.

The lines of the *Jupiter* are given in figure 44, being developed from a tracing made of the original. Buttock links have been added to assess the hull-form by modern standards, and they assist in showing that the *Jupiter* had very easy lines. The entrance and run are moderately full above the light waterline level, but are sharp below. The second waterline, 5ft-6in above the keel, runs into the stem in a straight line; below that it is hollow. The hull possesses the big sheer in vogue before the nineteenth century, but no gun ports, deck levels, or mast positions are shown. A plain bow is drawn, but the *Jupiter* would probably have been constructed with the normal head knee, trail boards and figurehead, although as a Baltic trader it is just possible that she did actually look like the drawing. The load line is reconstructed from the 14ft-0in draught given in *Lloyd's Register* for 1797, and utilised here as the average draught amidships; but a drag of 2ft-0in is suggested by her form and run of planking on the wales.

Although the lower part of the *Jupiter*'s entrance is much sharper than in some eighteenth-century merchantmen, it certainly does not strike the modern eye as 'very sharp and thin with considerable hollow' when one examines some of the extreme clippers of the

45: A typical flamboyant painting of the eighteenth century to extol the owners' pride in a successful ship. The *St Helena* was built in 1776 in South Carolina of 240 tons. *Parker Gallery, London.*

nineteenth century; and compared with some of Guibert's designs and of other French privateers, it looks positively bluff. The hull proportions are similar to the *Alexander*, referred to above, with the exception of the latter's steep deadrise.

The *Jupiter*'s floors commence straight and with little rise, but they soon sweep up gradually as arcs of circles to the load line, above which there are vertical sides and a sharp tumblehome. The radii for these arcs are given on the body plan. This form of body would induce considerable heel when the *Jupiter* took the ground on a falling tide, but this was not an important factor in the Baltic where the rise and fall of tide is minimal; however, it would have serious repercussions in British waters, unless she could be laid alongside a quay, in a wet dock as at Liverpool, or in deep water. When sailing in ballast on her maiden passage, she would have had a hull of quite sharp proportions compared with many other merchantmen. She was sold by Brocklebank's in 1796 to owners in Newcastle who employed her in the Atlantic trade; she was captured in 1800.

The matter of steep deadrise in American ships and flatter floors in British ones can probably be attributed, as Robert Craig has pointed out, to the fact that British ships had to stand moderately upright when they took the ground, whereas the American clippers which sailed out of ports between Boston and Chesapeake Bay rarely had to take the ground as the rise and fall of the tide in their home ports was negligible. Hence steep deadrise was no embarrassment to a vessel permanently afloat. It will be noticed that British sources make frequent reference to the necessity of giving ships flat floors so as to take the ground in as upright a position as possible.

Another contemporary example of a master mariner's expressed opinions is to be found in the description published by William Hutchinson in his book entitled *A Treatise on Naval Architecture*, and dated 1794. The vessel concerned was the *Hall* which was a West Indiaman and occasionally a slaver. She is referred to extensively in the text and her lines appear in plate I of his book, and are reproduced here as figure 46. Hutchinson fancied himself as an adviser on the best forms of ships and the following is his story of how they were translated into the design of the *Hall*. Of course, for his word 'sheet' one should read 'sheer':

> After the peace 1783, a nephew of mine, William Ward, was going to have a ship built for the Jamaica trade; I gave him a manuscript that I had wrote for the best form, and proportional dimensions, in length, breadth and depth of merchant ships in general, he shewed it to his owners, who approved so much of it as to say, that they wondered that I not published it before. They gave it to an ingenious drafter of ships, Mr Joseph Elliot, who served his time at the King's yard, Deptford, who approved of the plan, and drew a sheet draft, that the ship *Hall*, of 362 tons, carpenters' measure, was built by, which answering so well, that I got Mr Elliot to draw a draft in miniature from the sheet draft, and got a plate engraved, (as represented at the bottom of plate the first) in order to illustrate and help our ideas to fix the best rule for the shape and rake of the stem and stern-post, that makes so essential a part for the best form of ships, which I hope will be perceived by professional men that are concerned in shipping, by

PLATE 1st

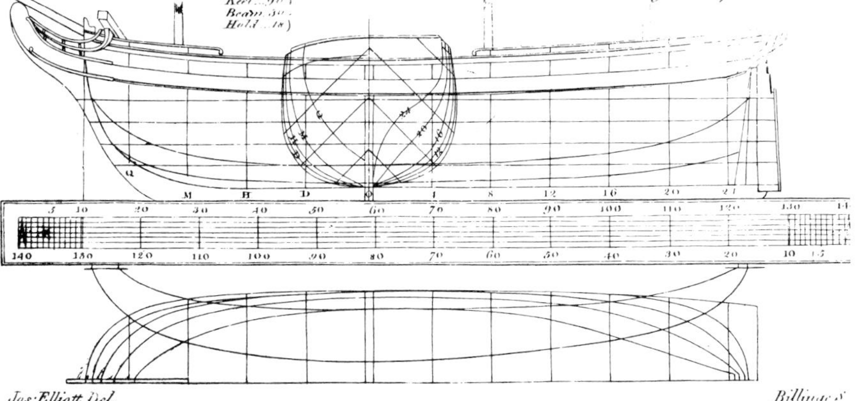

46: *Hall.* A remarkable composite drawing of sheer elevation, sails and lines plan, reproduced from *A Treatise on Naval Architecture* by William Hutchinson (1794). The *Hall* was built at Liverpool in 1785. Customs House dimension; 103ft-0in (length), but plan scales 113ft; 29ft-7in (breadth); 5ft-0in (depth of hold below lower deck); 5ft-7in (height between decks); 375 tons. Dimensions printed on the drawing: 90ft keel [probably straight rabbet], 30ft beam, 18ft hold [perhaps from deck at side to keel rabbet].

> this small draft of the ship *Hall*, which will be detailed hereafter, the rule I took for this important purpose.
>
> The curve for the water-line of the harpen forward, and the load-mark aft, was formed by a sweep of half a circle toward the main frame, the three fourths of the main breadth; and from there with a regular convex curve to the midship or main frame: And that the shape and rake of the stem be justly so as to admit the rabbit for the huddens of the bows, from the keel upward, to be exactly in the same form as the water-line from the stem.[33]

I have interpreted the description of her design in his last paragraph above to mean that the loadline in the entrance and run was formed by an arc of a circle, taking the radius as three-quarters of the main breadth, and the rabbet of the stem from keel to load line was an identical curve. The 'harpen' or hairpin refers to the forward end of the wale by the bows; 'rabbit' is now spelt rabbet; the 'huddens' is presumably a corruption of hood ends, or the ends of the planking which fit into the stem rabbet.

Joseph Elliot who drew the plan was draughtsman to John Fisher who built the *Hall* at Liverpool in 1785; the Custom House register gives her dimensions of 103ft-0in length, 29ft-7in breadth above the main wales, 5ft-0in depth of hold below the lower deck, 5ft-7in depth between upper and lower decks, and 375 tons. William Ward was her first master and Hutchinson himself eventually got command in 1792. When fully loaded she drew 14ft-9in forward and 16ft-0in aft.

Some further dimensions are given below, prefaced by Hutchinson's opening comments:[34]

> As this ship *Hall*, answers her designed purpose so well as to give satisfaction both to the owners and crew, it may be well to repeat my proposed rules in figures, that they may be the easier and readier understood by inspection.

Extreme length or tread, of the keel from the forefoot to the keel at the after part of the stern-post that stands upright	90ft-0in
The keel to be made and laid upon concave blocks with a curve downward at the rate of 2in for every 30ft, that the curve or sheer of their bottom may be equalled to that of their top.	0ft-6in
The bottom of the keel to be made straight, but put upon blocks laid with a concave curve, an inch for every 30 ft, to make it lie with a convex curve exactly under the main frame for an allowance for the tendency of all ships to hog.	0ft-6in
Extreme breadth at the main frame, one third of the length of the keel.	30ft-0in
Depth of the hollow at ditto from the ceiling to the main deck, 6 tenths of the extreme breadth.	18ft-0in
The main frame to be between the two lower midship floor-timbers, 7 twelfths from the after part of the sternpost.	52ft-6in
The main transom to be three fourths of the main breadth.	22ft-6in
Height of main transom from the upper part of the keel at the main frame to the upper part of the main deck.	19ft-0in

The *Hall*'s lines plan reproduced in figure 46 is a copy of that in plate I of Hutchinson's book. We should describe her as a ship with a full entrance and run, with rounded floors and bilges, but without much tumblehome. The rockered keel is not drawn on the lines

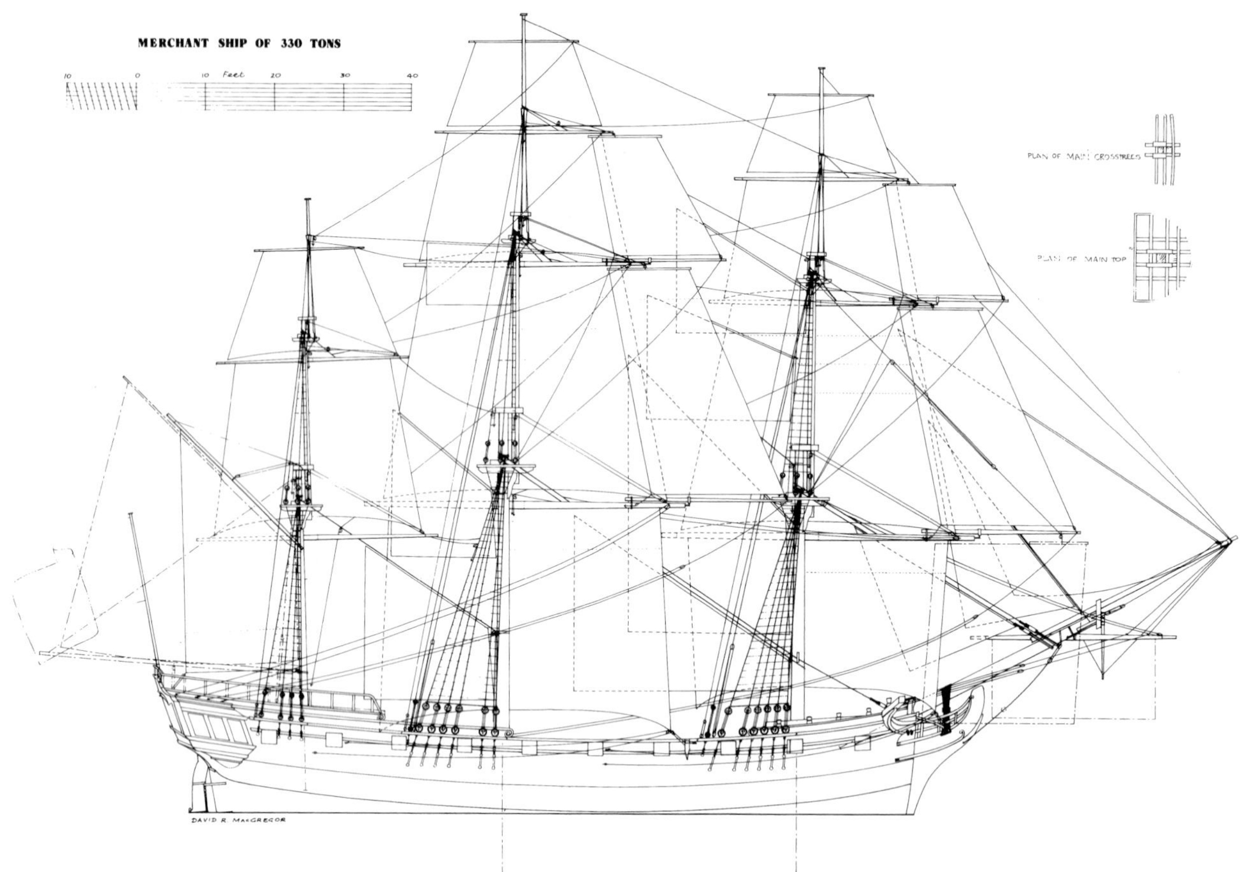

47: *Three Sisters* Sail plan: This is a reconstructed sail plan for the ship identified as *Three Sisters* which was built in 1788 at the Blackwall Yard, London. The hull is taken from the lines plan but the remainder of the plan is reconstructed to show a typical merchant ship at the end of the eighteenth century. Length of spars from *Rigging and Seamanship* (1794 and 1816) by David Steel; sails and rigging from same source, contemporary illustrations and books, and *Young Sea Officer's Sheet Anchor* (1806) by Darcy Lever.

plan but does appear in a sheer elevation on plate XII, which also depicts the fitting of a jury rudder. No centres are given for the arcs of circles to construct either the sections in the body plan or the entrance and stem profile. Hutchinson added several novel features, such as a rockered keel fore and aft, which rose at the rate of 2in in every 30ft; also a spar deck built over the waist to avoid shipping water and to give her a flush deck.[35]

The sail plan of the *Cupid*, which is reproduced here, depicts a full-rigged ship, but only the basic standing and running rigging has

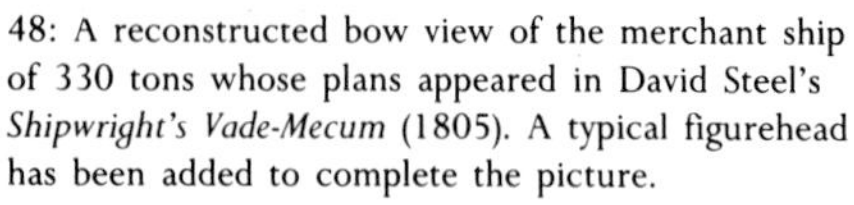
48: A reconstructed bow view of the merchant ship of 330 tons whose plans appeared in David Steel's *Shipwright's Vade-Mecum* (1805). A typical figurehead has been added to complete the picture.

been drawn on the plan, and so in order to provide a more detailed sail plan, I have decided to include that of the ship *Three Sisters*. A full description of this West Indiaman and the attribution of her name can be found in my book *Merchant Sailing Ships 1775–1815*. This plan, reproduced as figure 48, is reconstructed for the merchantman of 330 tons, whose lines appear in David Steel's *Shipwright's Vade-Mecum* (1805). Dimensions on her plan give 103ft-3¾in between perpendiculars, 27ft-6in extreme breadth, 12ft-0in depth of hold. Lengths of masts and spars are taken from Steel's tables dated 1794, for a merchant ship of 300 to 330 tons and much of the data on rigging, sails and spars comes from the same work,[37] and also from Darcy Lever's *The Young Sea-Officer's Sheet Anchor* (1808). In these tables, no mizen royal yard or mast is listed and so the topgallant mast is drawn with a common pole head.

At this date, the mizen course was always the gaff sail, but the driver boom is listed by Steel and so this sail has been drawn dotted. The yards were comparatively short in length, but without stunsails on each side, a sail plan was tall and narrow. The size of the bowsprit is worthy of comment as it was a massive stick and remained so until well into the second quarter of the nineteenth century, both in large ships and in brigs and schooners. In 1794, Steel showed a dolphin striker in one of his engravings which suggests it had been in use for several years as he is unlikely to have included any fittings on his plans that were not well-proven in practical usage. The standing jib was the principal headsail and hooked on to a traveller on the jibboom. On the mainmast, the topgallant and topmast staysails were set up on spring stays, and between them was the middle staysail which had a timble at the nock that could be hoisted or lowered on a tricing line from the fore cap to the topmast trestle trees. On many ships there was no fidded mizen topgallant mast and probably no mizen topgallant was set, but the topmast had a long pole. Trysails on fore and mainmasts which sometimes hoisted on separate trysail masts, began to appear about the turn of the century and soon became popular. In a full-rigged ship, the lengths of all the masts are based on the length of the main lower mast, and all the yards on the length of the mainyard.

From the north-east coast of England comes a variation on the *Jupiter*'s hull-form in the plan of the *Venus* of Hull. When I visited the exhibition in the Maritime Museum at Pickering Park, Hull, the lines plan of the *Venus* were displayed, and the curator allowed me to trace it. The original plan is signed by James Spencer and dated 31 May 1807. As the plan is named, the ship was presumably built, but as she was not deep in proportion to length it is unlikely that she was a whaler. In 1807, Spencer was a shipwright foreman in Hull and later that year went to live at Paull; three years later he was foreman and manager of the yard which built HMS *Anson*, but by 1811 he had returned to Hull. He was still living at Hull in 1854. He also signed a plan dated 1805 of a brig of 226 tons pierced with nine ports each side, and of similar hull form to the *Venus*.[38]

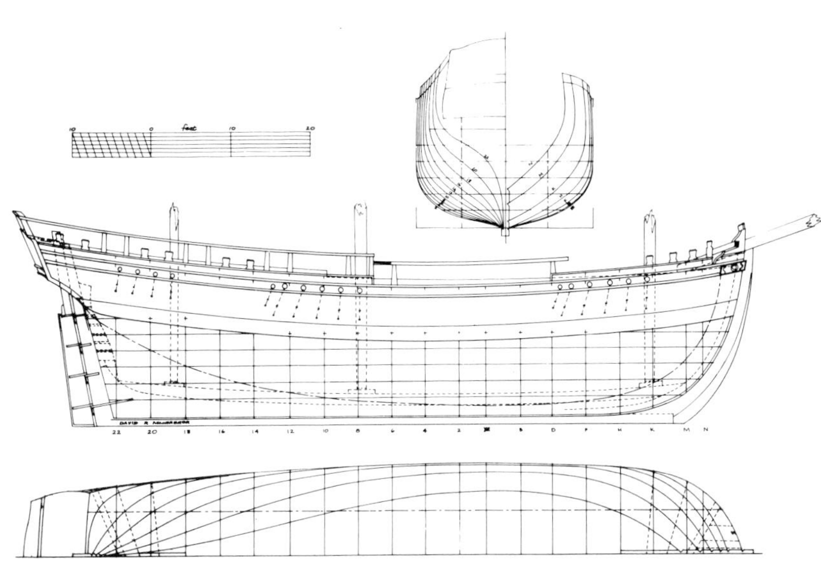

49: *Venus*. Plan signed and dated: 'James Spencer, Hull, 31 May 1807', but no actual vessel has so far been identified with her measurements. Redrawn from plan in Maritime Museum, Pickering Park, Hull. Dimensions given on plan: 83ft-2in (keel and fore rake) × 23ft-5in (extreme breadth) × 9ft-0in (depth in hold from ceiling to under side of lower deck beams), 5ft-0in (height in 'tween decks from beam to deck); 201⁵⁵/₉₄ tons. No reconstruction.

The interesting point about this ship is that she has wall sides and virtually no tumblehome, but there is appreciable deadrise and slack bilges. Her hull is somewhat after the 'cod's head and mackerel tail' shape with a long, fine run but fuller convex entrance. There is a plain bow with no vestige of a knee, which was common enough in many ports, and there is a good sheer aft which suggests she drew about two or three feet more aft than forward. The deck is almost flush and there are no solid bulwarks but only an open rail. Dimensions on the plan give length on keel 73ft-0in, rake of stem 10ft-2in, breadth extreme 23ft-5in, depth in hold from ceiling to underside of lower deck beam 9ft-0in, and height in 'tween decks from beam to deck 5ft-0in; tonnage is 201⁵⁵/₉₄.

If James Spencer designed the *Venus* it was an original design created without much reference to text books, and the shape of the midship section was much more in the style of the following century than some of those examined so far in this chapter.

Post Office packets

For a collection of merchant ship plans of this period it would be hard to find a better selection than those of vessels built at Bristol by James Martin Hilhouse (1748–1822) who in 1772, with the aid of his father's fortune — acquired from privateering ventures — purchased a drydock and adjacent land just below Bristol at Hotwells. Three years after his death, his son George took Charles Hill into partnership under the name of Hilhouse, Hill & Co.[39]

Two types of ships were built in this yard: full-bodied, flat-floored cargo carriers for the West Indies trade, many of which were owned by the firm; and fine-lined, steep-floored ships, brigs and cutters built where

50: The Post Office Packet *Windsor Castle* (left) capturing the French privateer *Jeune Richard* off Barbados in 1807. The packet carried a crew of 29 all told while the privateer had 92 men and boys. The latter was a schooner with square topsails on each mast. This aquatint was by J B Harraden after T Whitcombe in 1808. *Parker Gallery.*

speed was required. To judge from surviving plans, there seems to have been no attempts at producing a compromise design. Of the vessels with steep deadrise, six schooners are listed in chapter three and the others, of varying rigs, are summarized as follows:

Hilhouse plans of steep-floored vessels (schooners excluded)[40]

folio	
50	*Rebecca* (1791); cutter; 50ft-6in (aloft × 16ft-0in 8ft-0in (approx.). Three perspective views, folios 56, 57, 58, probably of her.
46	*Flying Fish* (1802); pilot cutter; 41ft-0in (aloft) × 14ft-3in (moulded) × 8ft-0in (approx.).
41	*Charlotte* (1808); pilot cutter; 38ft-0in ('extreme aloft') × 11ft-8in × 6ft-4½in ('skin to skin'); 19 tons; for John Berry.
61	Unidentified; two masts; *c* 1790; similar in style with fo. 104; 79ft-0in (aloft) × 22ft-0in (extreme) × 12ft-6in; 152 tons; flush deck, no gun ports.
15	(Men-of-War list) unidentified; two masts; nine gun ports each side; 79ft-5in (keel for tonnage) × 26ft-0in × 12ft-8in; 260 tons.
16	(Men-of-War list) 'Cunningham Schooner'; nine gun ports each side; identical body plan to fo. 15, but rail about 9in lower; flush deck.
64	Unidentified; three masts; *c* 1780; fore body incomplete; possibly a yacht; flush deck with windlass; 75ft-0in (keel for tonnage); figurehead.
104	Unidentified; three masts; *c* 1780; fore body incomplete; possibly a privateer; poop and forecastle with windlass; said to have figurehead of Orpheus; 84ft-0in (keel and fore rake) × 24ft-9in (moulded) × 16ft-6in (approx.) Reproduced in figure 27.
113	Post Office Packet, described below; 179 tons.

The only three-masted ship to be complete as to the lines plan is unnamed, but her tonnage figure of 179 suggests that she was a Post Office packet and was built about 1795 to conform to the new regulations issued in 1793.[41] These fixed the size of the packets at 179 tons and by specifically reducing the armament, obliged the packets to flee from their enemies rather than to risk the mails in attempting to make prizes. 'The most patient thought had been given to the selection of the model', wrote Arthur H. Norway. 'It was believed that vessels built on the new design would out-sail most things afloat.'[42] Events showed that the Post Office had been too sanguine as to the speed of the new model and was obliged to authorise an increase in the armament to protect the packets. A lines plan that was at one time in the Post Office archives and is entitled 'Packets built 1790'[43] may possibly embody the salient features of the projected model, even though the tonnage of 173 is fractionally below the stipulation of 1793; alternatively, it may record improvements in design. This plan, dated 1790, has considerable deadrise with straight floors and slack bilges; there is a long, fine run but a rather full entrance for an intended fast vessel, thus making her of the 'cod's head and mackerel tail' variety. British designers were apparently reluctant to incorporate a sharper entrance into their models, but relied on steep deadrise, a fairly fine after body, and a large sail area to secure the necessary speed. Men-of-war, on the other hand, displayed rather more balanced lines.

Referring to the matter of size in the Post Office packets at the turn of the century, a short, privately printed history of the service comments:

> 'Up till 1823 the packets sailed under contract between the General Post Office and the Commander (of the packet) who received his appointment from that establishment and engaged to provide, equip and man a proper ship for the purpose, at a hire of £1800 per annum. These vessels were from 180 to 210 tons register. The shares in them were generally taken up in sixteenths by private individuals as a speculation, the owners receiving one-third of the freights and the profits arising from passengers being retained by the commander.
>
> 'After this period the above system of providing vessels for the service was changed, by their being placed under the orders of the Admiralty instead of the Post Office, and as vessels were wanted they were supplied by men-of-war, 10 guns rated.'[44]

The ship in the Hilhouse plan measures 83ft-0in along the deck, 23ft-6in extreme breadth, 14ft-0in depth of hold (approx) including a 'tween deck clear height of 5ft-1in. She has three masts, flush decks and open bulwarks; deadrise is very steep with hollow floors, and there is a fairly fine after body but a comparatively full entrance. No buttock lines are drawn on the original plan but those projected here have very easy curves, particularly in the after body. The original draught shows two body plans: the left-hand one, as first designed, has flaring topsides reminiscent of the *Transit*; in the other, labelled 'no 2', the topsides have been altered to introduce a slight tumblehome. By superimposing tracings of the two body plans, it is evident that the only differences lie above the lower edge of the wales, as the form of the sections below are identical. The plan in figure 52 has been redrawn from the original at Bristol, through the courtesy of John C G Hill, and the lines have been developed in accordance with 'no 2' body plan. It is not known how closely Hilhouse's design resembled the official Post Office model, if indeed there was one.

Robert Salmon's beautiful painting, dated 1807, of 'A Mail Packet off Liverpool' (figure 52) shows a fairly small ship to judge by the stature of persons aboard. It is not suggested that she bears any connection with the Hilhouse plan, but she does provide an example of another small, full-rigged ship that carried mail. If the man standing on the rail by the mizen mast was 5ft-9in tall, the length on deck would be approximately 98ft-0in. She appears to be well armed and the separately fidded royal masts seem odd for so small a ship.

Of slightly finer lines is the packet brig drawn by William Salisbury from the offsets and dimensions in David Steel's *Naval Architecture*, and reproduced here in figure 45 through his courtesy.[45] This brig measures 201 tons and represents a packet built about 1800 at a Thames-side shipyard. She has dimensions of 79ft-0in on deck, 25ft-0in extreme breadth and 11ft-2in depth of hold. There is considerable deadrise and the body plan is very similar to Hilhouse's ship of 179 tons described above, but the waterlines are finer, particularly in the entrance which is altogether sharper.[46] The brig has a drag of about 3ft-6in, a single deck with solid bulwarks, and forms a further variation of the cutter-brig.

Many of the packet brigs were built at Falmouth, and during the first decade of the nineteenth century the yards of Blight and of Symons launched a number of these packets. A well known brig, such as the *Duke of Marlborough*, built at Falmouth in 1806 of 180 tons, was making fast passages in 1821 such as: Lisbon to Falmouth, 21–31 January, nine

52: *A Mail Packet off Liverpool* by Robert Salmon, dated 1807. Unfortunately no name is assigned to this ship. She is a small full-rigged vessel but well-armed, and has fiddled royal masts. *Parker Gallery.*

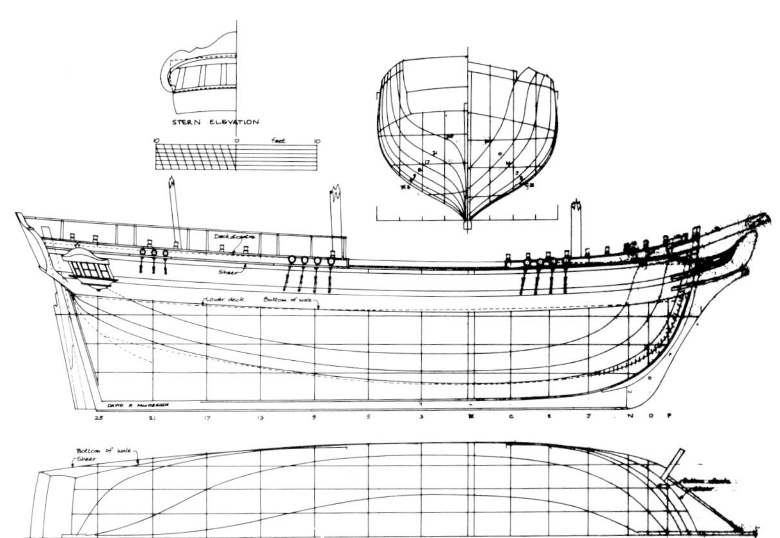

51: Post Office Packet. This unnamed ship has been identified as a Post Office Packet because of her tonnage figure and her fine lines. Redrawn from a plan in the Hilhouse Collection, folio 113. Plan probably dates from about 1795. No. 2 body plan used to plot lines. Dimensions on plan: 61ft-0in (keel for tonnage) × 23ft-6in (maximum beam) × 14ft-3in; tonnage $179^{12}/_{94}$. No reconstruction.

days; Falmouth to Lisbon, 9–19 February, ten days; Lisbon to Falmouth, 25 February–2 March, five days.[47]

Reference was made earlier in the chapter to Chapman's plans of packets, and lines of a cutter and a brig are given in figure 54. The midship section has the prominent hollow garboards to be seen in his plans of privateers, and there is an elaborate head to each vessel. The half-breadth plans have diagonals plotted, which make the waterlines harder to follow.

An example of a later Falmouth Post Office packet, the *Marchioness of Salisbury*, is discussed in chapter three.

53: Post Office Packet. Lines plan drawn by William Salisbury from offsets in David Steel's *Elements and Practice of Naval Architecture*. In the third edition of this work (1822), the table of offsets is listed on page 25 among a series of such tables which together follow on after page 438 of the main work. See text for dimensions.

The *Transit* and other long ships

There have always been experimental vessels, some enjoying success because of a combination of inherent good qualities and patronage, and others being failures for opposite reasons. But failures of good designs through lack of patronage or some quality of the promoter have always been tragic to relate. In this category fall the designs of Richard Hall Gower and the four ships he designed, three of which received the name of *Transit*.[48] They were unusual vessels, particularly in their great length in proportion to breadth and in their barquentine rig. The following table lists their date of build and other particulars. The dimensions have been scaled off the plans.

1. *Transit*; launched 1800; 195 tons; 102ft-6in length for tonnage, 22ft-0in extreme breadth, 12ft-6in depth in hold (approx.), rigged as a five-masted barquentine. In 1801 reduced to four masts. 4.6 beams to length.
2. *Transit*; launched 1809; 261 tons; 134ft-0in length for tonnage, 22ft-6in breadth, 12ft-0in depth in hold; rigged as a four-masted barquentine. 5.9 beams to length. In 1810 shortened by some 20ft-0in and topsides and deck lowered between 1ft-0in and 1ft-3in.
3. *Transit*; launched 1819; 232 tons; 103ft-9in length for tonnage, 22ft-6in extreme breadth, 12ft-6in depth in hold (approx.), rigged as a three-masted barquentine.
4. Probably named *Gower*; launched 1824; 125 tons; rigged as a ketch with a square-rigged mainmast and a gaff and boom mainsail and mizen. No plans of her are known.

A modified copy of No. 1 was built at Constantinople by the Turks in 1803–4.

The most successful of these four was

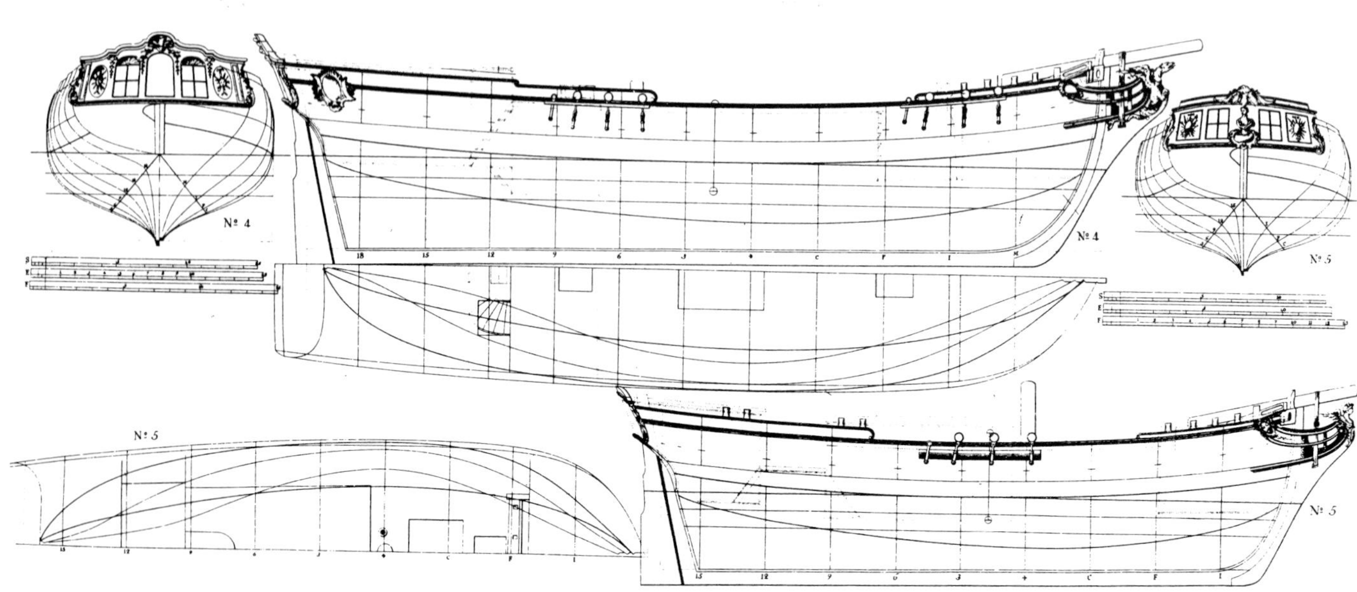

54: Schooner and Sloop. Lines plans with deck plan superimposed and inboard works dotted. Reproduced from *Architectura Navalis Mercatoria* by Fredrik af Chapman (1768) plate XLII nos 4 and 5. Dimensions of no 4 (from table on contents' page): 54ft-7in (length between perpendiculars), 15ft-7in (breadth moulded), 7ft-1in (draught of water). Dimension of no 5 (at similar points): 38ft-3in; 13ft-3in; 5ft-6in.

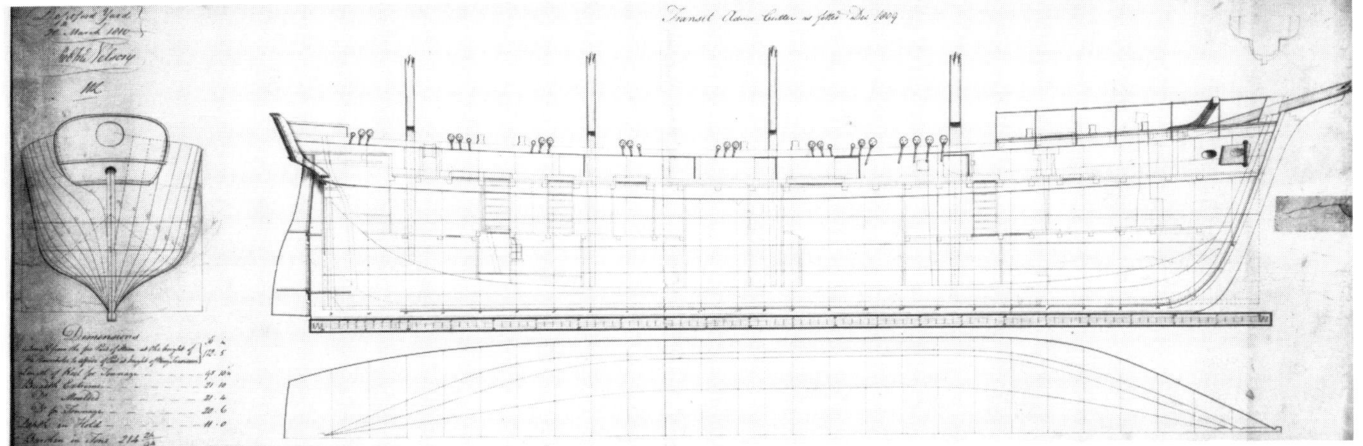

56: *Transit* [no 2]. Lines plan with inboard works. Built in 1809 at Deptford by W H Gower. Reproduced from Admiralty draught dated 1808 at National Maritime Museum. Dimensions: 134ft-0in (foreside of stem to after side of sternpost, scaled off the plan), 22ft-6in (extreme breadth), 12ft-0in (depth of hold); 260 61/94 tons.

undoubtedly the very first one to be built, and in her performance she fulfilled her designer's ambitions although, to his regret, she was never bought or hired by the Admiralty, the East India Company or the Post Office, in spite of several trials of speed to the detriment of her selected antagonist. Richard Gower, her designer, was a master mariner in the East India Company's service and his design was the result of a personal conviction of the poor weatherly qualities in ships and the unnecessarily heavy masts and rigging. It is not known what experiments Gower made before he arrived at the hull form employed in the *Transit*, but in 1799 he exhibited a model embodying his ideas, and having obtained sufficient subscribers, constructed the ship at Itchenor during that winter, at a cost of £6900.[49] There is a very crude engraving of her lines in one of Gower's books but a clearer plan in Fincham's *History of Naval Architecture*.[50]

In this first hull, the high proportion of beams to length which is approaching 5 to 1 gives her an intrinsic advantage in speed, and the long parallel middle body which extends for about 55ft-0in gives excellent stowage capacity and good stability. Simultaneously, her ends are reasonably sharp, although not excessively so. Gower's engraving of the half-breadth plan shows the waterlines to have a slight curve the entire way, but this was probably a fault of the engraver as all other plans show a straight parallel body, which was one of the features of the design. The bottom half of the hull was designed by arcs of circles of the same radius and as Captain Gower had no experience as a naval architect, such a design could have appealed to him as being easy to construct and develop. The resulting plan gives very steep deadrise, firm bilges and flaring sides. Gower wrote that 'the *Transit* was built for a packet, to be sailed at a light draught of water, with empty extremities;'[51] and elsewhere stated that she was not built to take the ground. The same style of design in the midsection below the load line can be seen in Alexander Hall's extreme clipper *The Caliph*, built in 1869.[52]

Captain Gower took out a patent in 1800 for the design of hull and rigging, and this document describes the masts and sails. The foot of the fore course was bent or sheeted to a boom, which was the equivalent of a bentinck boom, and the sails on the after masts were extended by sprits. She sported five masts during her first year at sea, but these were reduced to four in 1801, as shown in Gower's own published plans, which also omit the sprit that had proved a constant source of anxiety in bad weather. But the rig was still unique. No attempt was made to describe the rig, although the second *Transit* was described as a 'cutter' by the Admiralty! The important features of the rig are that the masts were stayed independently of each other; that the sails were small in area and could be taken in easily; and because they were divided amongst several masts, the masts and rigging could be light in weight. The *Transit* traded to the Mediterranean for several years, beating all her competitors by a large margin and was wrecked in 1810.

The second *Transit* was commissioned by the Admiralty and the design, after much discussion, followed the same model as for the first ship, except that the entrance and run were finer and the proportion of beams to length was as high as 5.9 to 1 (figure 56). She had a short, chequered career. When contributing an article and plan of the first *Transit* to the *Mechanics' Magazine* in 1828, the Ipswich shipbuilder, George Bayley, remarked on the foolish act of the Admiralty to reduce the length of the second *Transit* by some 20 feet and concluded by saying:

> 'After this, as might be expected, we hear nothing more of the *Transit*; but Mr. Gower has at least the satisfaction of knowing that his principle of construction is adopted, to a limited extent, with great advantage, in some of the fastest merchant schooners that navigate the North Sea.'[53]

Corroborative evidence of this last state-

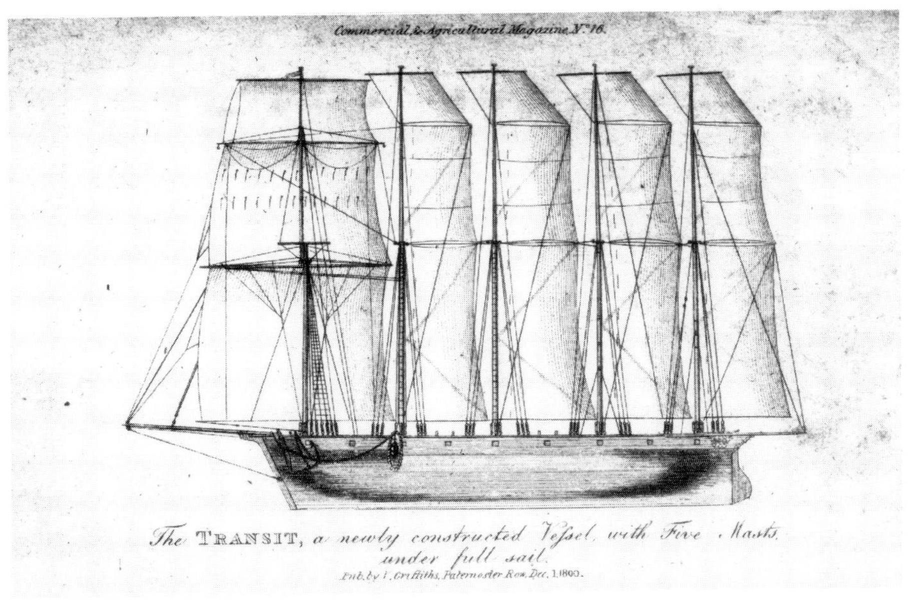

55: The *Transit* as first rigged with five masts in 1800-01. She was an early form of baraventine. *MacGregor Collection.*

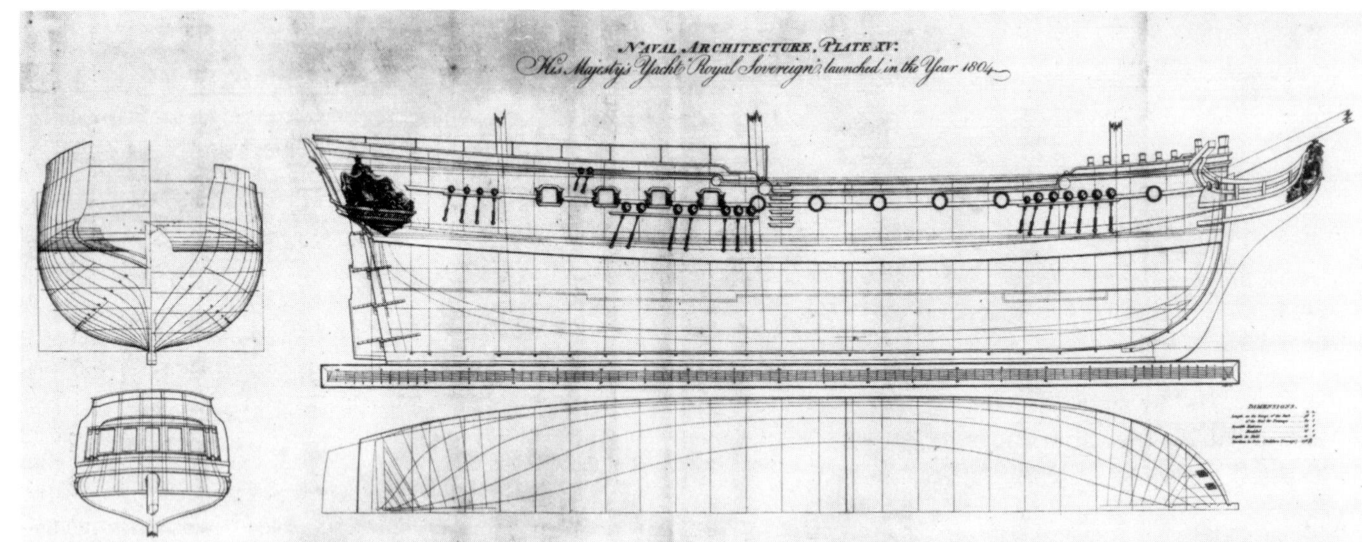

57: *Royal Sovereign*. Lines: Built in 1804 at Deptford from design by Sir John Henslowe. Reproduced from plate 15 in *Elements and Practice of Naval Architecture* by David Steel (3rd ed. 1822). Dimensions on plan: 96ft-0in (length along deck) × 25ft-6in (extreme breadth × 17ft-0in (approx. depth in hold, scaled off plan), $278\frac{13}{94}$ tons.

ment has so far not been traced, nor the vessels to which he refers.

The third *Transit* was built at Ipswich in 1819 as a yacht for the Hon G Vernon on the same model as the first of this name, but 'to effect greater simplicity, and to be more in accordance with the preconceived notions of seamen, she was rigged with three masts instead of four'.[54] A waterman who boarded her when she was under sail in the Thames in 1819 exclaimed with surprise, 'My God, what a clipper!'[55]

Other long, narrow vessels had been the subject of experimental building at the turn of the century, such as the three-masted lugger built by Charles Gore as a result of tank tests made both by the Society for the Improvement of Naval Architecture and himself.[56]

A contributor to the *Mechanics' Magazine* in 1826 who signed himself 'Noah', wrote the following, as part of a longer article:

> 'Prior to Mr Pitt's Act, so called, which confined vessels to one-third of their length for their breadth, vessels, particularly luggers, were generally as one is to four. I know a lugger, at this time, seventy feet long, with only ten feet beam; this vessel, in light winds, would sail faster than any vessel in Europe. She continued many years as a smuggler, sporting with every vessel that would attempt to give her chase, till she was lost in a gale of wind.
>
> 'A Dutch merchant, some years since, built a vessel of 200 tons on the principles of the ark; that is, one-sixth of her length for the breadth; this appears to be carrying things to an extreme, yet she answered fully his expectations, and proved a serviceable vessel.'[57]

Some Royal yachts

The increasingly popular pastime of yachting which appealed to the public imagination was responsible for producing many sharp-built craft. There had been Royal yachts from the middle of the seventeenth century and several yacht clubs pursued their cruises throughout the eighteenth century in sloops and cutters, such as the Cumberland Fleet which was founded in 1775 as the first English yacht club, of which the Royal Thames Yacht Club is the direct descendant. After 1815, the activities of these clubs increased rapidly and many large cutters of 150 tons and upwards were constructed, which were of quite a different type to the ketch-rigged Royal yachts of the eighteenth century with their square sails on two masts. In 1800, the newest Royal yacht was the small full-rigged ship *Princess Augusta* of 184 tons, which had been built at Deptford in 1771, but between 1804 and 1817, four ship-rigged Royal yachts were launched: the *Royal Sovereign* in 1804, the *William and Mary* in 1807, the *Prince Regent* in 1815, and the *Royal George* in 1817 (plans dated 1813). From plans of these yachts in the National Maritime Museum, Greenwich, some interesting comparisons can be drawn.

The *Royal Sovereign* measured 278 tons with dimensions of 96ft-0in along the deck, 25ft-6in extreme breath, and approximately 17ft-0in depth of hold. She was designed by Sir John Henslowe (1730–1815) who was surveyor to the Navy from 1784 to 1807 and who designed 156 naval vessels of all types. She has the fine lines of a yacht with the rounded bottom and sides to be found in the traditional form of body that was produced with arcs of circles. She was expensively decorated and throughout her life was celebrated for her speed, being described as 'beyond controversy, the best sailer of the British Navy'.[58] However, this was probably a rather over-optimistic estimate.

By contrast, the *Royal George* is of quite a different model with straight floors, steep deadrise, hard bilges, minimum tumblehome, and finer waterlines which are slighly hollow in the lower entrance. She was designed by Sir Henry Peake and is seven feet longer on deck but only one foot broader in beam. The hull form is much more nineteenth-century in character than is the *Royal Sovereign* and displays a further development of the English cutter style.

In sharp-built ships at the turn of the century lie some of the fundamental differences in design methods. The traditional midship section, put into the *Jupiter* or the *Royal Sovereign*, employs the rule advocated by such writers on naval architecture as Mungo Murray and William Sutherland, in which the shape of the body plan is constructed by arcs of circles. 'By this way', writes William

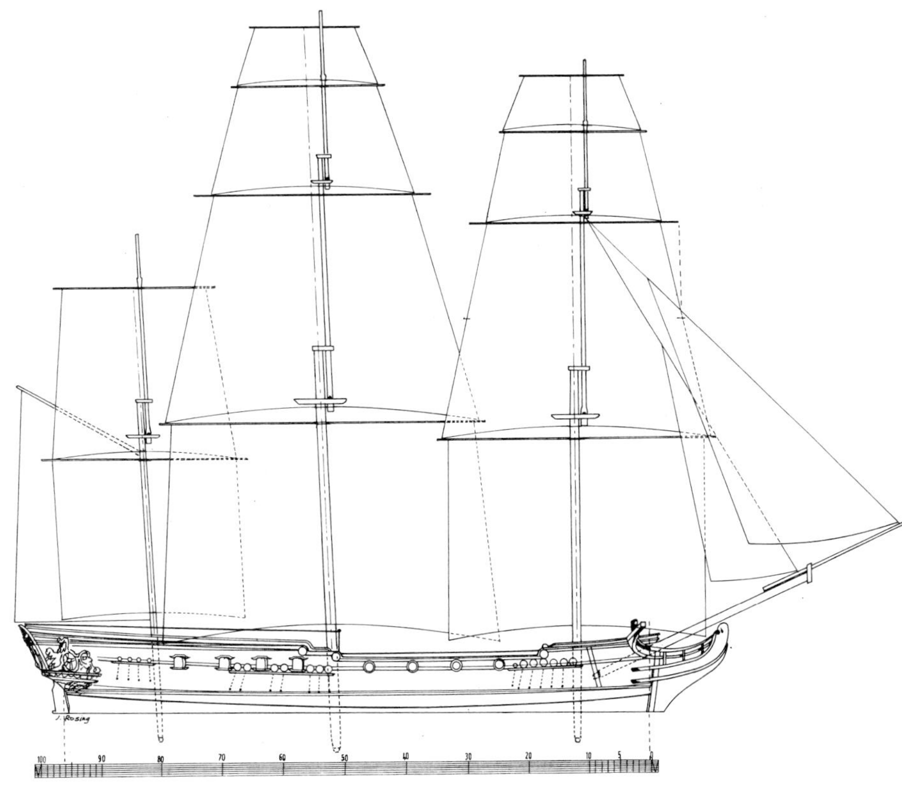

Sutherland, 'it is plain the Centers and Radii of the sweeps are arbitrary, but they must be determined . . . if by no other Means, by repeated Trials, till they are made to please the Fancy and Judgement of the Artist'.[59] The rounded form of the resultant body is quite different to that of *L'Intrepide* with its long, straight floors, steep deadrise, and maximum beam situated above the load line. The rounded body form was gradually being replaced early in the nineteenth century, although several vestigial examples can be observed in the plans reproduced here, such as in the brigantine *Dash* (1828). It also persisted in such passenger frigates as the *Seringapatam* (1837) and *Blenheim* (1848). The hull form exemplified in Hilhouse's mail packet and developed by the English cutters was increasingly adopted in sharp-built craft. In larger vessels, provided the beam was not excessive, the additional length permitted much finer waterlines to be employed.

58: *Royal Sovereign* Sail plan. Redrawn from plan in National Maritime Museum. Reconstruction: headsails, standing rigging. The crossjack was drawn on the original, and its presence is unusual at this date.

59: *Le Coureur.* Lines and sail plan, reproduced from *Souvenirs de Marine* by Admiral Pâris (plate 29).

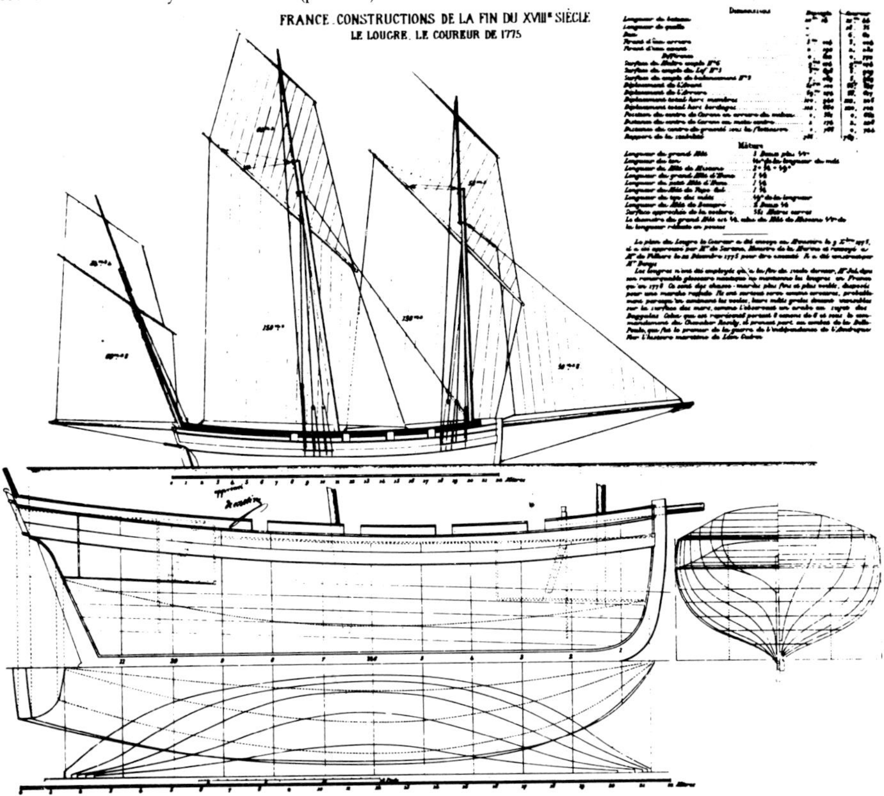

Revenue cutters and smugglers

The three-masted lugger was employed extensively by both England and France in smuggling and privateering ventures and the few lines plans in existence for this period indicate a hull form somewhat similar to a cutter but longer, with big deadrise and fine waterlines. A plan of the *Lark*, taken into the Danish Navy in 1790 as *Larken*, shows a longer hull than was usually found in a cutter, with some concavity in both entrance and run.[60] Such craft sailed very fast to windward. Although extensively used in fishing boats, the lug was rarely employed in legitimate merchant vessels.

Admiral Paris gives the lines and sail plan of a three-masted lugger in *Souvenirs de Marine*, reproduced here as figure 59. The proportion of breadth to length is 3:1, making her a broad vessel, and the midship section and lines are similar to those of a cutter, although the entrance is very sharp and hollow. The waterlines are projected as far up as the load line, but the line of deck and rail is plotted separately on a different centre line, and it is on this part of the plan that the diagonals are projected. On the sail plan, each mast has a fidded topmast. The vessel is named *Le Coureur* and dated 1775.[61]

Revenue cruisers, in addition to some smugglers, generally favoured the rig of cutter or sloop, in which capacity they set as many sails as are seen in the plan of HMS *Fly*, although by 1800 the topmast was more commonly fidded on the foreside of the lower mast, and

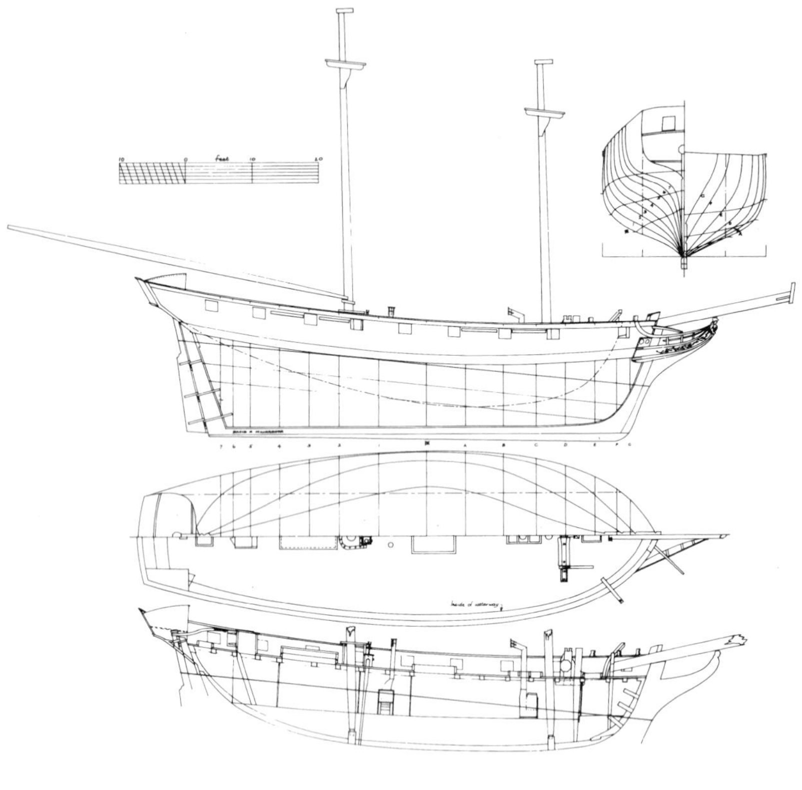

the lower yard was slung only a short distance below the hounds. The huge roach of the topsail was thereby omitted. It is no wonder that anti-smuggling regulations were enforced whenever possible when one reads about the widespread activities on every coastline which were carried out by ably-manned, skilfully-designed, fast vessels. Such a craft was the *Abeona* of Fowey, which in 1791 was decribed

60: *Shamrock*. Lines plan: Built 1805 in England as the *Resolution*, probably from a design by Mr Thomas. Redrawn from Admiralty plans dated, Plymouth 1817, in the National Maritime Museum. Dimensions on plan: 74ft-1in (length on deck) × 25ft-1in (extreme breadth) × 10ft-10in; tonnage 185$\frac{29}{94}$. Reconstruction: lines plan and deck plan combined. Employed as revenue cutter, Irish coast.

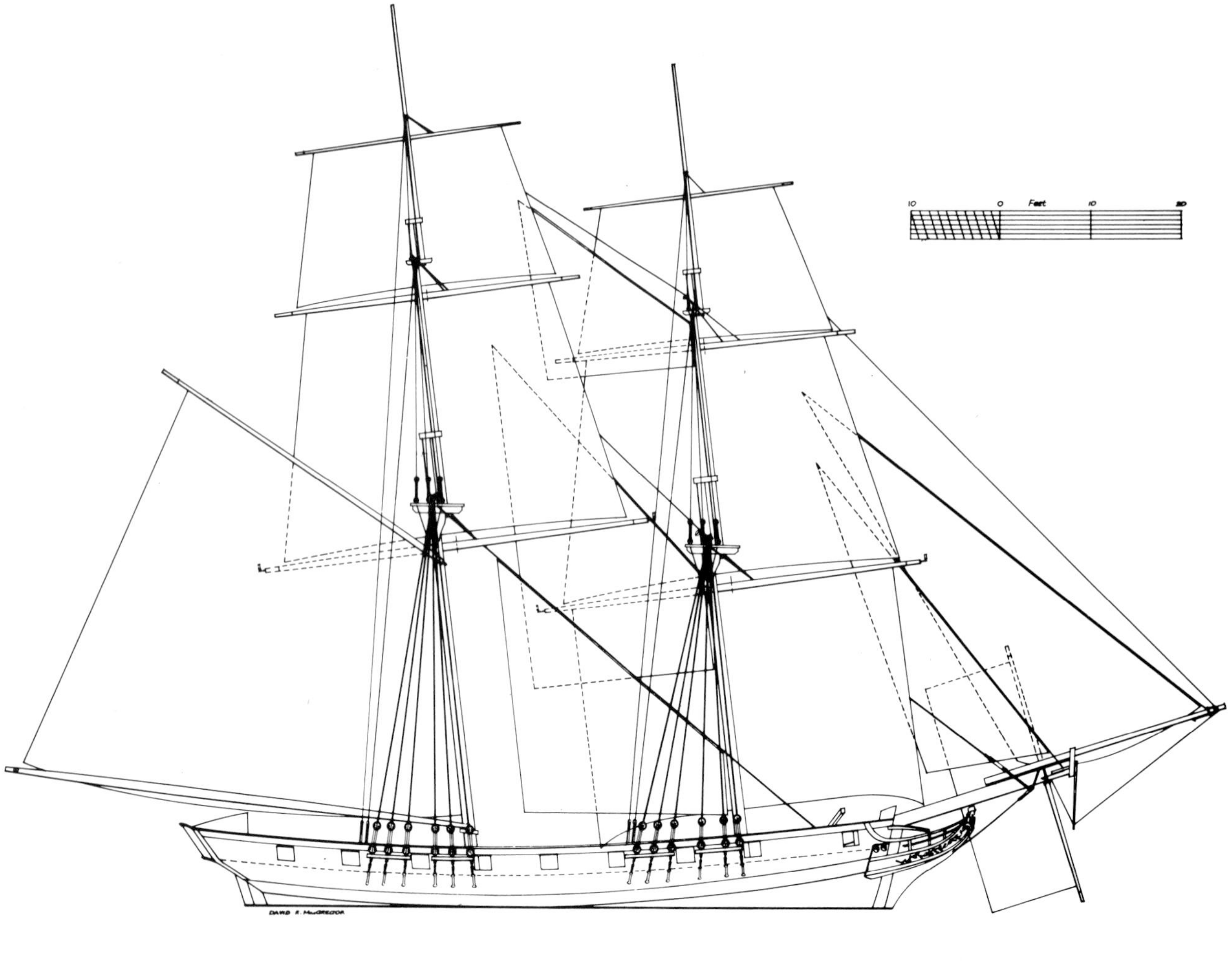

61: *Shamrock*. Sail plan: Reconstructed from sheer elevation and from spar dimensions listed on lines plan. Rigging and sail outlines from contemporary illustrations and books on rigging. The gun ports are drawn at right angles to the keel, but there is a big draft aft which gives them an apparent rake. As a true brig, no main course has been drawn. No royal yards are listed in the spar dimensions but she would undoubtedly have sent them aloft in fine weather, on which occasion rigging to the mastheads might have been rove.

as a new smuggling cutter of 100 tons which had been driven ashore near Appledore; her crew of 22 had time to throw overboard her armament of 16 6-pounders.[62] The employment of the cutter in such conditions ensured that the type was developed to the ultimate stage of perfection.

Examples of the cutter-build in vessels of more than one mast can be studied in several plans reproduced here and described in detail, such as Hilhouse's Post Office packet (*c* 1795), the schooner *Sappho* (1821), the ship-rigged yacht *Falcon* (1824), and the brig yacht *Anonyma* (1839), but so many diverse influences were making themselves felt that after about 1825 it becomes harder to trace the cutter-build with any degree of accuracy. All these four vessels have greater length in proportion to breadth than the single-masted cutter although the brig-cutters in use at the turn of the century usually possessed the large breadth peculiar to the cutter. Steel's Post Office packet, already referred to, and the Revenue brig *Shamrock* form good illustrations of brig-cutters.

There is a detailed lines plan of the *Shamrock* amongst the Admiralty draughts, reproduced here as figure 60, which shows all the cutter features: a big drag aft (6ft-3in), a big sheer, three beams to length, steep deadrise with hollow floors, and bilges kept high. She was built as the *Resolution*, probably in 1805, and her lines were taken off in 1817 and drawn out by John Marshall. In addition to this Admiralty plan at the National Maritime Museum, there is a plan in the United States National Archives drawn by Philip Inch and dated July 1820.[63] The latter plan states that the brig was 'Constructed by Mr. Thomas'. Regarding these two plans, both of which have the same hull dimensions, Howard Chapelle writes: 'There is no doubt in my mind that the two plans represent the same design and vessel. She was certainly a cutter-model brig of clipper form and purely British'.[64] He suggests that Mr Thomas was probably responsible for her design; also that he was a fellow apprentice at Portsmouth Dockyard with Henry Steers, whose son, George, designed the yacht *America*. Thomas later worked in the Washington Navy Yard and induced Henry Steers to go to America. It is interesting to compare the design of a fine-lined schooner which Henry Steers drew in 1805, whilst still an apprentice, with the plan of the *Shamrock*. The schooner plan exhibits strong American influences and Howard Chapelle published it in *Search for Speed Under Sail*.[65]

As stated on the Admiralty plan, the *Shamrock* measured 185 tons with dimensions of 74ft-1in length on deck, 24ft-1in extreme breadth, 10ft-10in depth of hold, and she carried 12 guns. The spar dimensions listed on the lines plan have been plotted in figure 61 to give a lofty rig, with closely spaced raking masts and long lower masts, and a huge fore-and-aft mainsail with the boom projecting 20ft-0in over the taffrail. The yards on the mainmast are a foot or two longer than those on the fore. She carries a spritsail yard 28ft-8in long and is fitted with a windlass but no capstan, which suggests merchant ship influence rather than naval. No deadeyes are indicated for topmast or topgallant backstays, and so these are shown set up with a tackle hooked to a ringbolt on deck. Royals would be set in light, favourable winds, but without lifts or braces, the yards being hoisted by use of halyards led through sheaves in the masts heads.

Brigantine *St Helena*

An example of a packet ship employed in the South Atlantic may be found in the decision of the Honourable East India Company to build for itself, almost at the termination of the Napoleonic Wars, the 'schooner packet *St Helena*', which was launched in August 1814. Her duties were to attend Indiamen calling at St Helena and to take provisions and supplies to the island. She was constructed by Wigram & Green at the Blackwall Yard at a cost of £21 per ton, her measurements being given on her draught as 75ft-0in length on deck, 20ft-7in beam and 13ft-0in depth in hold, and a tonnage of $135^{20}/_{94}$. But on her plan the deck length scales 81ft-3in as drawn here. Although no picture of the vessel has come to light, it is rare to come across the lines, spar dimensions and log-books of a schooner of such an early date, which is one of the reasons that makes her such an interesting study.

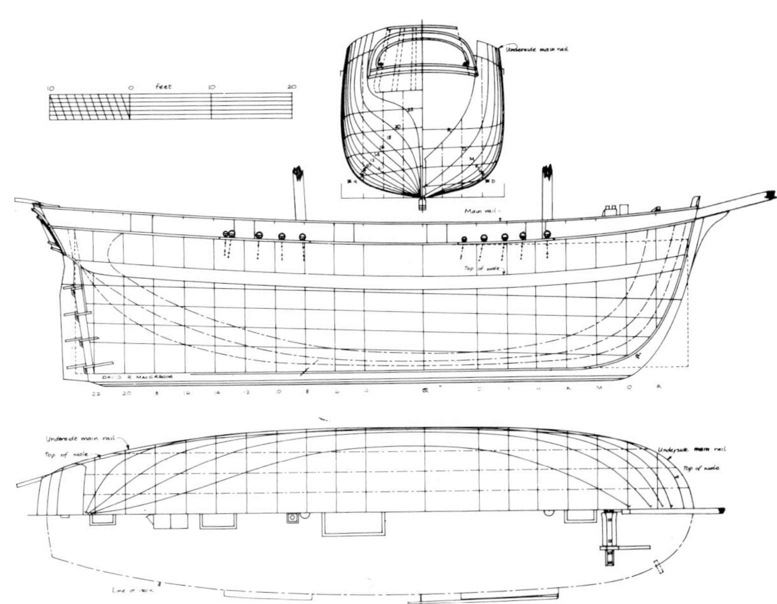

62: *St Helena.* Lines plan: Built 1814 by Wigram & Green at the Blackwall Yard, London. Redrawn from plan in National Maritime Museum. Dimensions given on plan: 75ft-0in (length on deck) [but scales 81ft-3in] × 20ft-7in (beam) × 13ft-0in (depth in hold); $135^{20}/_{94}$ tons. Reconstruction: plan view of deck fittings; also windlass, channels, quarter davits, stunsail boom.

The lines reproduced in figure 62 are redrawn from a plan in the National Maritime Museum, Greenwich.[66] The arrangement of deck fittings has been reconstructed from contemporary sources, and from the inboard profile superimposed on the sheer elevation. The carriage of provisions and good sea-keeping qualities were her essential elements, and she had a good shape for capacity in the hold although her waterlines were not too full. She drew about 2ft-6in more aft than forward. A plain bow and small head-knee make a welcome change from the over-elaborate heads usually seen on plans. Three boats were carried: a jolly boat, launch and gig; the launch would have stood in chocks on the deck abaft the fore mast, with the jolly boat inside it, and the gig would be slung from the stern davits. She makes an interesting comparison with the Baltimore clipper schooner *Fly* which was captured in 1812 and taken into the Navy as HMS *Sea Lark* (figure 36) as they are both about the same length on deck. The latter was built for speed, doubtless as a privateer, as her big deadrise indicates. Her sail plan is also worthy of comparison with the *St Helena,* as showing the differing ideas held by the designers and the purposes for which they were built. The reconstruction is fully detailed on the plan.

The sail plan of the *St Helena* provided some puzzles: in particular, the length of the fore topmast head above the rigging is not tated, although it is on the mainmast. The spar dimensions given on the original plan suggest that she was designed as a topgallant yard schooner, whereas the log-book refers unequivocally to a fidded topgallant mast such as the entry on 7 July 1819 which reads, in part: 'Fidded the foretop-g-mast got the flying jib boom out'.[67] On the sail plan, the fore topmast rigging terminates at the height given in the spar dimensions, but the fore topmast head and fore topgallant mast are reconstructed. So also are the flying jibboom, spritsail yard and royal yard, all of which are mentioned in the log-book. Indeed, with the exception of the rigging, all the spars and sails are those referred to in the log-book and portray the vessel as she might have looked in the years 1819–22. The fore lower mast is only four feet shorter than the mainmast which makes her a hybrid form of brigantine — more like a schooner-brigantine as sketched by numerous artists — and really exonerates anyone who, like her master, called her a schooner. Nautical terminology was not then so strict which, considering the many rig variations, was probably just as well and ships were not assigned to the rigid categories that became the case in the twentieth century.

The *St Helena*'s log-book leaves the impression that the master, at least, enjoyed his time aboard and that discipline was not so strict as in the regular Indiamen.[68] Between 1814 and 1819 she made eight return trips between St Helena and Cape Town, making the run down light and returning to St Helena with sheep, bullocks and supplies such as grain and wine. Between 1819 and 1822 she went once to Benguela returning with

63: *St Helena.* Sail plan: Reconstructed from lines plan, from spar dimensions listed on this plan, and from log-books of schooner in India Office Library. Length of fore topmast above rigging reconstructed, because not stated on lines plan. Probably designed as a topgallant yard schooner. Reconstruction: Length of fore topgallant mast, royal yard, spritsail yard and flying jibboom. Sails and rigging based on log-book descriptions, and contemporary illustrations and rigging books. The long fore lower mast offers other solutions for the lead of the stays and arrangement of head-sails.

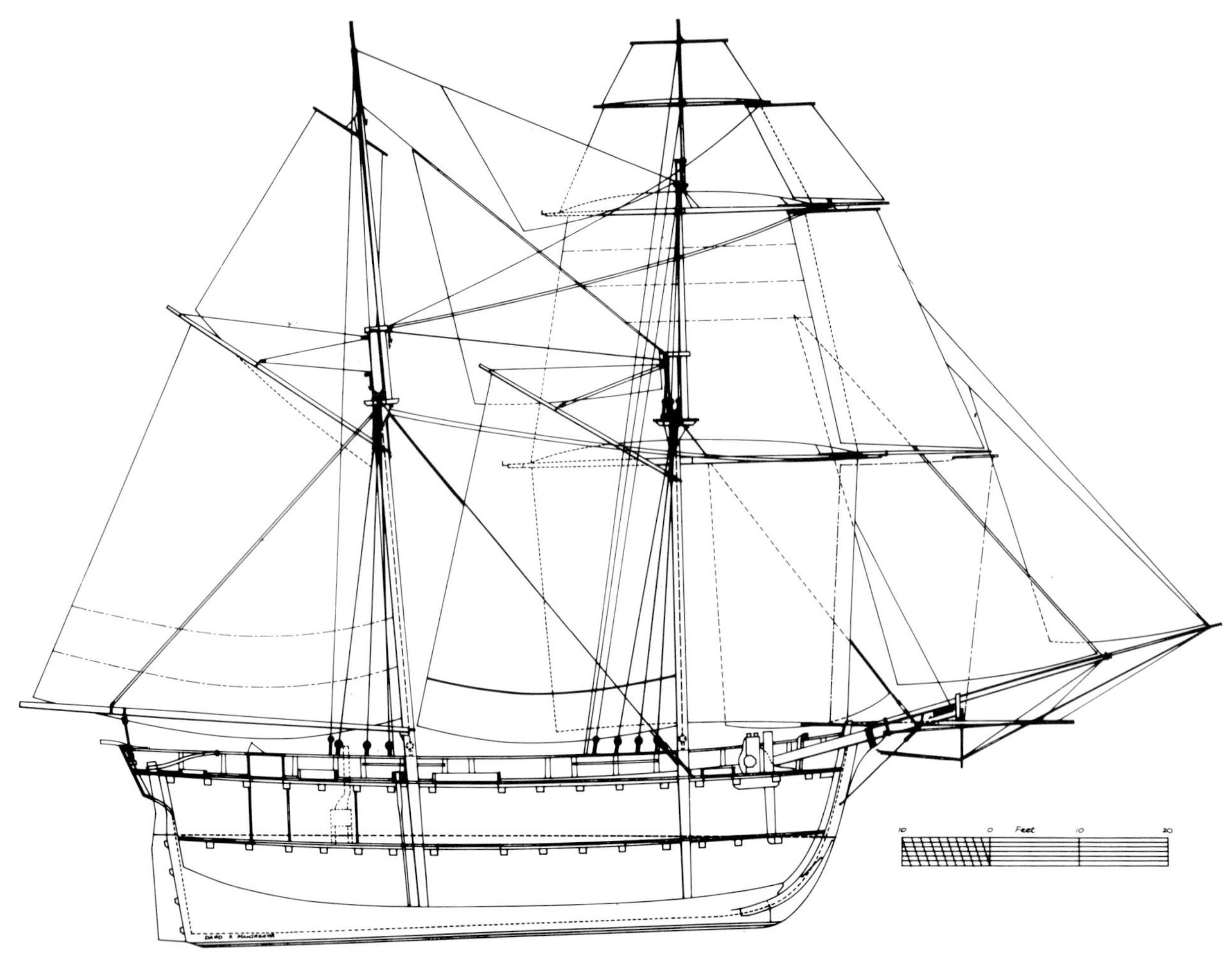

bullocks, and once to Angra Pequena. For much of 1821 she remained in the vicinity of St Helena attending upon visiting Indiamen. Her first return trip to England was in 1821–2 and she next returned in 1830 when she was sold by the Company.

When at St Helena she had to refit at sea and the log opens with her refitting there in 1819, stripping the lower masts of rigging and sending it ashore. The *Thalia* called at St Helena on 26 June, homeward bound from India on her maiden voyage, with James Ballingall in command. Her arrival was noted in the *St Helena*'s log-book. (*Thalia*'s maiden voyage and lines plan are described in chapter three.) After the topmasts were fidded again the *St Helena* was hove down – 'careened' – for the carpenter to repair the copper on the starboard side. Five days later the schooner-brigantine was righted. Meanwhile, the topsail yard was crossed and the rigging rattled down, and the log records on 7 July 1819 that the crew 'fidded the fore-top-g-mast and got the flying jib boom out'. It seems unlikely that she was intended to receive a fidded topgallant mast at the time the list of spars was tabulated, else the wording would have been different. But the log has frequent references to making new spars – 'received a spare jib boom for a new main boom', 'carpenter making a new main boom', 'carpenter making a sprit sail yard out of old main boom' – so that it was quite likely that the rig was changed somewhat, after the schooner took up her station in the South Atlantic.

The log only once mentions the royal yard: 'Bent flying jib and royal'. Obviously, a light weather sail, it probably had no braces as was the practice in many small vessels. There are frequent references to setting and taking off the bonnet from the foresail.

On 2 August 1819 in a hard squall, bound to Cape Town, she 'carried away fore and main topmasts, flying jibboom and fore top-g-mast, split the gaff foresail, main topmast staysail and top-g-sail'. After clearing away the wreck, the following day they 'carried away the main sheet boom and outer guy, repaired them and set the whole mainsail'. Two days after losing her topmasts, new ones were fidded and the topsail and square sail were set.

On this passage in 1819 she took 24 days to reach Cape Town and her best day's run was 183 miles, during which the highest speed was eight knots. With a load line of 77ft-0in, a speed of eight knots results in a speed-length ratio of 0.91. While beating in to her anchorage at Cape Town she grounded on a hard, sandy bottom but got off by throwing all sails aback and drifted off amongst the shipping. She immediately dropped her best bower anchor, but the cable parted. Then she let go her small bower anchor and brought up against the schooner *Uitenhague*, losing her starboard stern davit and lower stunsail boom; but quickly bending her best bower cable to the spare anchor she wore round and brought up in two-and-a-half fathoms. Later she drifted to deeper water and the harbour master's boat recovered the bower anchor next day.

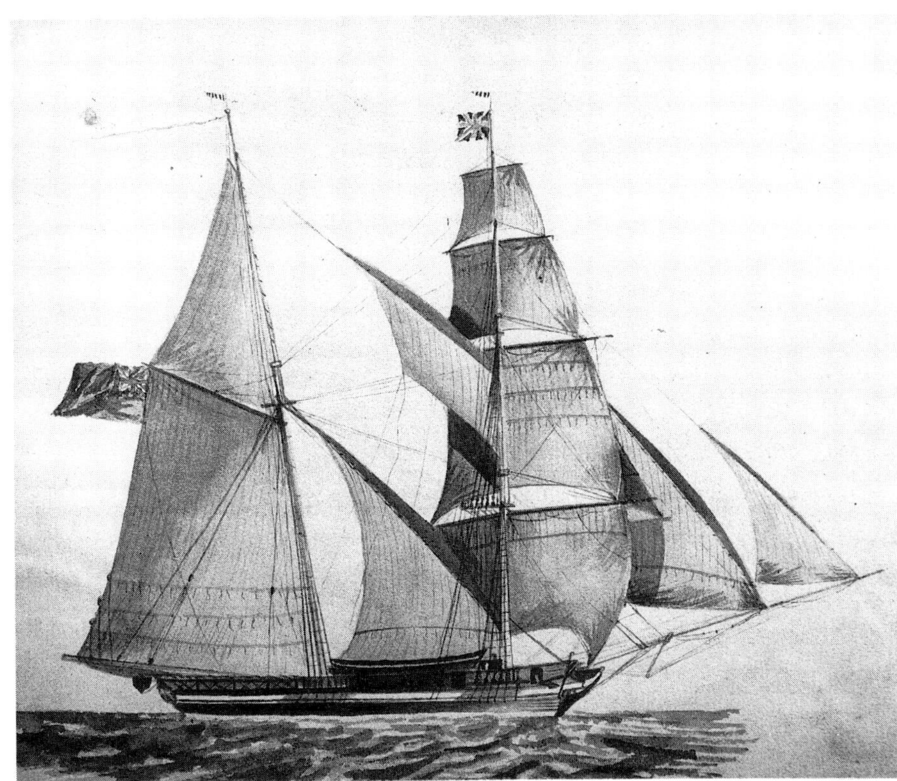

64: Hand-written inscription at bottom reads "*Hardy* Schooner Commanded by Lt George Lambert 1820 & 1821". The second half of the surname as well as the dates runs along the mount beyond the edge of the picture, and has been masked off the photograph. The foremast is a three-piece mast and she would today be called a brigantine. Without the fore trysail there are some similarities with the *St Helena*. *MacGregor Collection.*

On the return passage, partitions were erected in the 'tween decks to carry sheep. Some 134 were loaded and also four horses. She sailed back in 12 days making four consecutive runs of 158 miles, 172 miles, 180 miles and 139 miles. On a later voyage, after levelling the hold with sand, she loaded 128 sheep and 17 bullocks. The carpenter shaped new spars and fished sprung ones though he was 'sick from frequent intoxication'. The method used to destroy rats on board was to light four charcoal fires in the hold, batten down the hatches and wait for a day, after which the hatches could be opened and the bodies removed.

The brigantine left St Helena for London on 22 September 1821 with 23 soldiers, 8 women and 19 children, as well as a woman passenger and her child. The Lizard light was seen 38 days later and Dungeness was passed on 5 November, after a passage of 44 days.

Her master from 1819–21 was John Augustus Atkinson. Her crew and their wages for a new commission in 1822 was:

Master, James Fairfax	£30	per month
Chief mate	£15	per month
Second mate	£10	per month
Boatswain	£ 5	per month
Carpenter	£ 5	per month
8 seamen	£ 2.10	per month
Landsman	£ 2	per month

Unfortunately, no contemporary illustration has been found of the *St Helena*, although several views of the island have been examined in case she had been included amongst the shipping pictured there.

Three
CLIPPER SHIP DEVELOPMENT 1815-39

Definitions

The Thames waterman who employed the term 'clipper' when boarding the yacht *Transit* in 1819 was undoubtedly coining no new word, but using one which was acceptable for an exceptionally fast sailing ship. Many of the vessels described in chapter two might have been referred to in similar terms: indeed, with our present conception of the meaning of the word, many of these sharp, fast-sailing ships could be early clippers or at least the ancestors of them. By present usage, the clipper ship era lies between the years 1840 to 1870 and any sharp, fine-lined ship within that period merits the description 'clipper', while similar ships of earlier years are classified as 'early clippers'; eighteenth-century vessels on the other hand tend to be described as 'fine-lined' or 'sharp-built' with occasionally a qualification that they were the ancestor of the clipper.

Unfortunately, when it was realised that by describing a ship as a 'clipper' an extra high rate of freight could be obtained, agents and owners were not slow to employ the word for any full-built vessel that had made a fast passage, so that even before the advent of the true clippers of the late 1840s the word, in the light of present knowledge, was beginning to have suspect connotations. Many ships like the *Jupiter*, described in a contemporary account as having a sharp, hollow bow and sailing at 12 knots,[1] would have been taken up as a 'clipper' by the 1830s. The early clippers were mostly restricted to vessels engaged in limited specialised trades, such as the carriage of fruit, opium, tea, perishable goods, passengers and mails. The clipper model was also employed in privateers, slavers, smugglers and revenue cutters, small naval vessels and, of course, yachts.

The influence of the cutter model on fast sailing theory was discussed in chapter two and examples given of how a cutter's hull was rigged with two and three masts, in the brig *Shamrock* and the Hilhouse design for a ship-rigged Post Office packet. It was shown how the term 'cutter-brig' was employed in contemporary usage to embrace sharp-built hulls with cutter proportions which were given other mast combinations. In this chapter the process continues as the cutter hull becomes widely recognised as possessing great potentialities of combining speed and cargo capacity. Simultaneously, the hull length is undergoing an increase which produces a

65: A watercolour of an unknown schooner captured off Havana, Cuba, on 26 July 1858 by HMS *Lapwing* with 500 slaves aboard. The artist was Capt Montague Reilly RN who wrote the above details on the painting, adding that the schooner was built of mahogany. Each mast is a pole. *MacGregor Collection.*

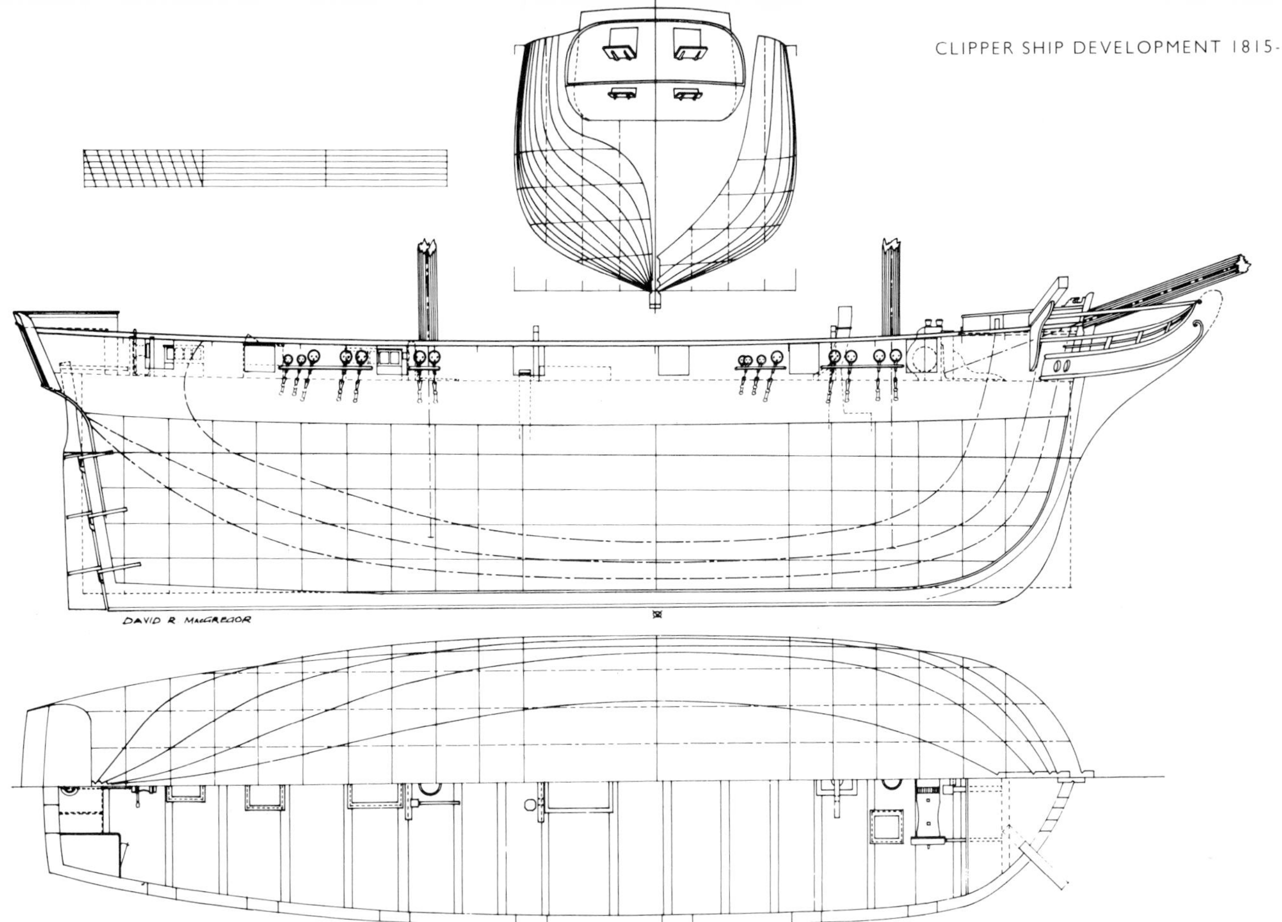

66: *Marchioness of Salisbury*. Built in 1816 on the Thames. Redrawn from Admiralty plan in National Maritime Museum dated 1838, when she was named *Nightingale*. Dimensions on plan: 82ft-1½in (length on waterline from main stem to afterside sternpost) × 23ft-10in (extreme breadth) × 14ft-11in (depth in hold); 198 tons. Reconstruction: chain plates, wheel, cathead on plan.

somewhat narrower version: the two-and-a-half to three beams to length of the cutters now becomes four beams to length in schooner and brigs. In these formative years there was little difference between fine-lined commercial vessels, and schooner or brig-rigged yachts. Examples given here show the development of the cutter hull in the fruit schooner *Sappho* and the brig *Anonyma*; later it will be shown how the Aberdeen schooner *Scottish Maid* fell under the same influence and the far-reaching results this produced.

Post Office packets

The design of Post Office packets at the turn of the century was described in chapter two, but an example of a later packet brig is provided by the *Marchioness of Salisbury* which was built on the Thames in 1816 and whose plan appears as figure 66. This plan has been redrawn from an original in the Admiralty Collection at the National Maritime Museum, Greenwich.[2] The chief feature of her design is the very steep deadrise, with straight floors, slack bilges and marked tumblehome; the run is quite fine but the entrance somewehat full; and like many contemporaries she is fairly deep for her length which, with a big outreach to the head, gives a somewhat ponderous and ungainly appearance. Compared with the *St Helena*, built two years earlier, she has a finer bottom and after body but is approximately the same shape in the entrance. The windlass marks her as a merchant ship but the rest of the deck layout suggests naval influence. The pumps are placed well forward of the mainmast; there are two gallows for spare spars to rest on, and a pair of pawl posts with a belfry above; it is interesting to note the iron knees running forward from the carrick bitts and from the bitts abaft the mainmast.

The *Marchioness of Salisbury* operated as a Falmouth packet, owned by her master, who chartered her to the Post Office in the time-honoured manner. After 1823 the Admiralty began to take control of the packets and contributed men-of-war when new ships were required. In 1829, the *Marchioness of Salisbury* was bought by the Navy and renamed *Nightingale*. Her lines plan is dated 1838 and her measurements are given as 82ft-1½in between perpendiculars (measured along load line from main stem to after tide of sternpost), 23ft-10in extreme breadth, 14ft-11in depth of hold and 198 tons. She was told out of the Navy in 1842 for £690. Examples of her passages are as below.

The distance sailed on the 1833 passage has been estimated as 4000 miles making an average speed of 5.21 knots.[3] The above passages are good average times. In the early 'twenties some packets sailed exclusively between Falmouth and Lisbon, a few went into the Mediterranean, and others sailed to the West Indies, Brazil and New York. The *Duke of York* in 1821 took 24 days between

1820 dep Lisbon	10 December bound for the Leeward Is.		
1820 dep St. Thomas	30 December	arr Falmouth 27 January	28 days
1821 dep Falmouth	25 March bound for the 'Brazils'.		
1821 dep Rio de Janeiro	22 May		
1821 dep Bahia	8 June		
1821 dep Pernambuco	16 June	arr Falmouth 25 July	39 days
1833 dep Falmouth	8 April	arr Barbados 10 May	32 days
1838 dep Vera Cruz	2 January		
1838 dep Tampico	17 January		
1838 dep Havana	6 February arr. Falmouth	5 March	27 days

67: Although this painting of the *Henry* shows a broadside of seven guns, she was a merchant brig engaged in trade between Liverpool and South America. She was built at Newcastle in 1827 of 314 tons and drew sixteen feet of water. The painting is signed 'Walters & Son 1830'. The father was Miles Walters, and the son Samuel. *Parker Gallery.*

New York and Falmouth, from 13 February to 9 March. She was a brig of 180 tons, built at Bideford in 1817. Only a few of the packets were ship-rigged. The three-masted naval schooner *Seagull* was a packet and both Sir Henry Peake and Sir William Symonds designed vessels especially for the service. In 1838, there were still 38 sailing men-of-war in the service and the last stronghold of sail was the run to Madeira and Brazil, steamers having taken over the remainder of the routes. By 1850 Falmouth had ceased to be a regular packet station.

The Post Office also employed cutters to carry the mails to the Continent and to Ireland, and thanks to a report in 1819 by a Select Committee of the House of Commons, four plans of packets for the Irish Sea route have been preserved.[4] These plans show the lines of the packet *Countess of Chichester*, and proposed designs by Peter Hedderwick, Philip Sainty and Sir Robert Seppings. The lines contributed by Sainty of Wivenhoe are in the tradition of sharp-built English cutters, and in 1821 the packet *Sylph* was built at Woolwich to these lines which are given in figure 68.[5] Dimensions on the plan give 49ft-3in length of keel for tonnage, 20ft-10in extreme breadth, and $110^{8}/_{94}$ tons; but the length from foreside of stem to afterside of sternpost or between the perpendiculars drawn on the plan is 63ft-4in.

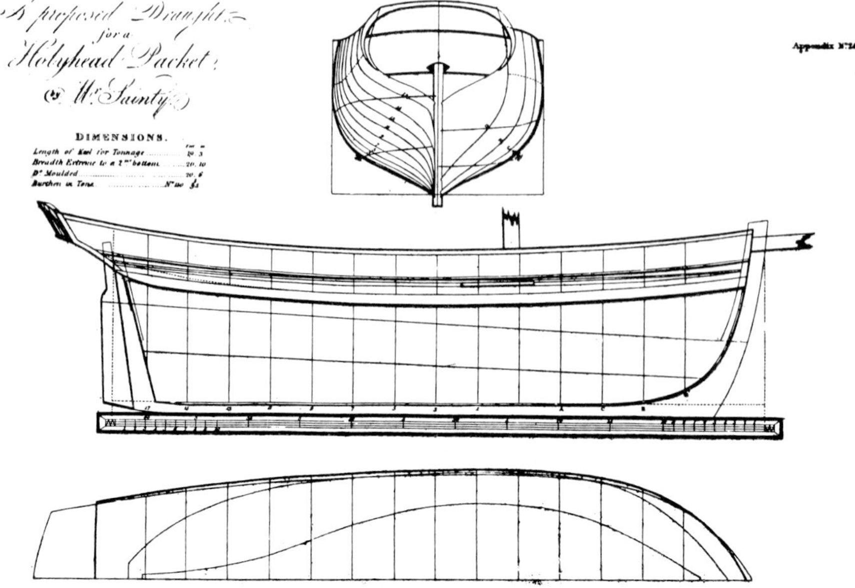

68 *Sylph.* Lines plan: Built in 1821 at Woolwich from a design by Philip Sainty. Reproduced from plan in Parliamentary Paper, 'Fifth Report from the Select Committee on the Road from London to Holyhead', printed July 1819. Dimensions: 49ft-3in (keel for tonnage) × 20ft-10in (extreme breadth); $110^{8}/_{94}$ tons.

69: *Sylph*. Sail plan: Reconstructed from lines plan and from spar dimensions listed on an Admiralty lines plan in the National Maritime Museum. Sails and rigging are from contemporary illustrations and rigging books. She probably set a square topsail and stunsails.

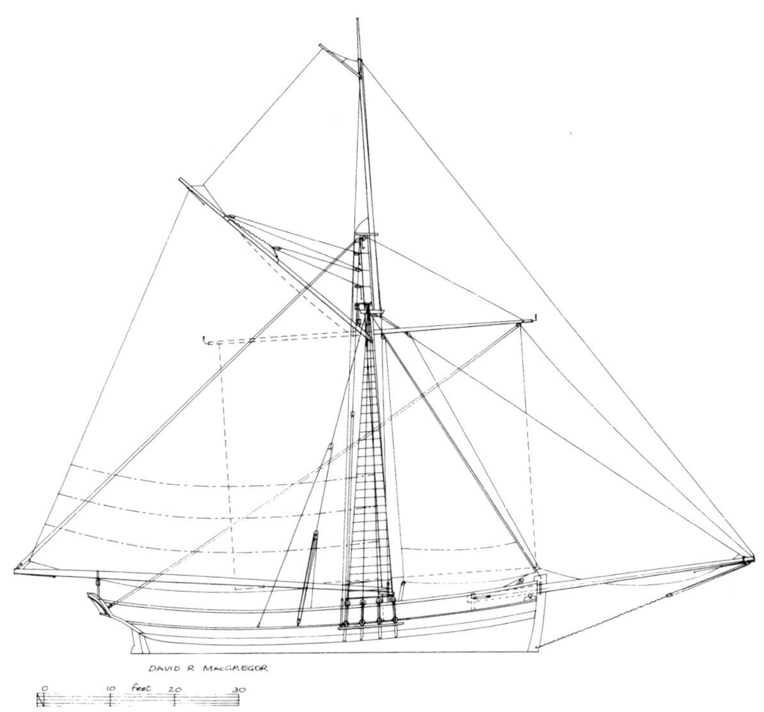

Inevitable amendments during her construction produced dimensions that varied slghtly from these and resulted in a tonnage of 112. She was a heavily-sparred cutter carrying a square sail yard and is a good example of the large sharp-built type of vessel that was suitable for various services, both official and illicit. In light winds she probably set a jib topsail, square topsail and stunsails.

Philip Sainty has been described as 'a notorious builder of smugglers'[6] but he simultaneously built revenue cutters, and in 1820 achieved fame with his design of the cutter yacht *Pearl*, of about the same tonnage as the *Sylph*. In his evidence in 1819 to the Parliamentary Select Committee, Sainty stated that for 30 years he had been building ships of all sizes up to 400 tons.[7] In 1828, he built the naval sloop *Pearl* of 558 tons, based on

70: A watercolour by William Joy showing a packet rigged as a cutter and running before the wind, with her big gaff sail boomed out to port and stunsails set to starboard. The crew and passengers are looking at another similar cutter which is close hauled on the port tack. *Private Collection.*

the lines of the yacht *Pearl*, and in 1832 his shipyard was taken on by Thomas Harvey who continued to build yachts and fruiters at the Wivenhoe Shipyard. Sainty himself died in 1844.[8]

It would be hard to find a more shapely-looking cutter than the *Sylph* and it was from models such as hers that the British clipper was developed.

A merchant ship and an East Indiaman

Before 1813 it had been illegal for a British ship to round the Cape of Good Hope without a licence from the Honourable East India Company, so that the lifting of regulations in this year for trade with India caused a minor boom. In 1820, *Lloyd's Register* listed 263 ships, none of which was chartered to the Company, as leaving Great Britain for India, and their average tonnage was approximately 485 tons. Simultaneously, the Honourable East India Company were dispatching chartered ships to India and China, of which four-fifths were of the 1200-ton class, and for ships in competition the great difference in size, design and tradition affords an interesting comparison.

While the boom was at its height, Balthazar and Edward Adams, sons of Henry Adams, built the full-rigged ship *Thalia* in 1818 at Buckler's Hard. Her plans, like those of nine other ships built there during the years 1778–1829, are preserved at the National Maritime Museum, Greenwich, and their brig *Neilson* is discussed later in this chapter. Another of their fine-lined ships was the *Australia*, built in 1826 of 373 tons, and she had more balanced ends than *Thalia*, but the latter has been chosen because she is the subject of a contemporary description.

The builder's drawing of *Thalia* is cruder in execution than some of his other plans, such as *Neilson* or *Australia*, and follows the style of the snow *Mary*, also built in 1818. The *Thalia* was a deep vessel with a full entrance and a very hollow run, and she drew 2ft-0in more water aft when loaded. During the nineteenth century this marked hollow in the run came to be associated principally with schooners and small vessels of under 150 tons. Figure 71 shows *Thalia*'s lines as redrawn from the builder's plan which indicates a flush deck, although a raised quarter-deck has been added in pencil. However, it is not clear whether this raised deck was an integral part of the ship when first built or a later addition; because of this doubt it is not included. The builder's plan gives positions for the deck beams, and it may be deduced, from the siting of the pawl post, that the windlass was abaft the foremast. Steps for two capstans are likewise given. The dimensions pencilled on the draught, 'as built', are:

Length from fore part of stem to after part of post on a range with rabbet of the keel [i.e. length for tonnage]	99ft-0in
Breadth extreme	28ft-8in
Breadth moulded	28ft-4in
Depth in hold (below lower deck)	13ft-0in
Height between decks	6ft-6in

Lloyd's Register (1818) gave her tonnage as 357 and stated that she had nine pairs of iron knees. It also gave the name of her first master as Ballingall, who must undoubtedly be the author, James Ballingall, who had a book published in 1832, *The Mercantile Navy Improved*. In it he refers to a ship he commanded that was newly built in 1818 and although he does not give her name the similarity to the *Thalia* is too great to be a coincidence, so that the following account by Ballingall undoubtedly describes this vessel's maiden voyage.

> 'A new ship in which I sailed to the East Indies in 1818, her first voyage off the stocks, was found, like many new vessels, to be leaky, and as she was coppered on the stocks, before she was launched, there was no getting at her bottom to caulk it, without stripping off the new copper, which, in addition to the expense, would have lost the voyage for which she was engaged, owing to the detention, as another vessel must have been got to supply her place. This ship being built very sharp aft, (she drew four feet more water by the stern than by the head, when launched, with a clean swept hold), and the pumps being put down by the mainmast in the common way, when she heeled over upon a wind, and there was water in her, not a drop of it remained at the foot of the main pumps, even although she was trimmed two feet by the stern, while it was considerably over the ceiling in the lee bilge, between the fore and main hatchways. In crossing the south-east trade winds, it being necessary to carry a press of sail upon a wind, to weather the coast of South America, it was found that the water did not come to

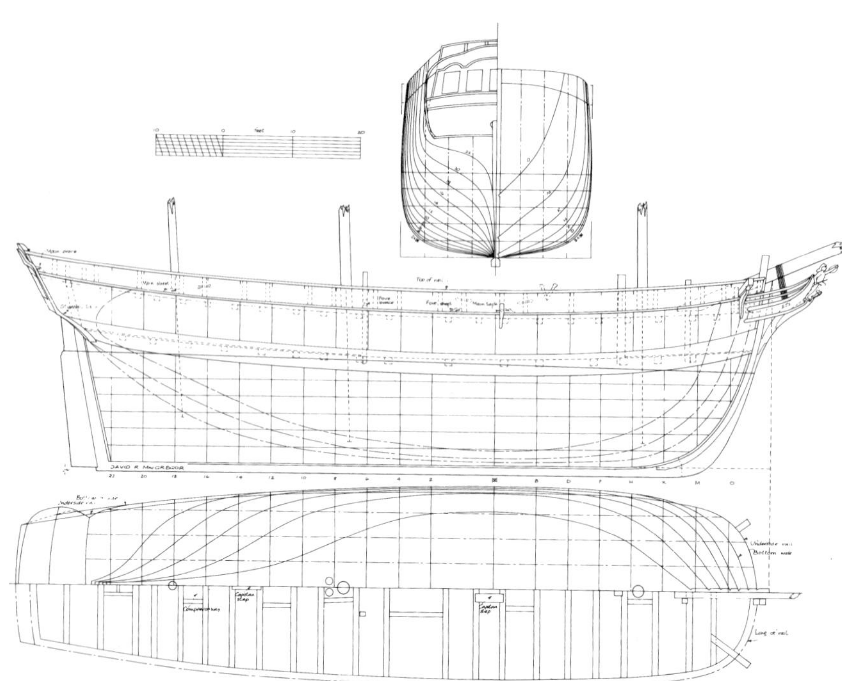

71: *Thalia*. Built in 1818 by Edward and Balthazar Adams at Buckler's Hard. Redrawn from builder's plan in National Maritime Museum. Dimensions: 99ft-0in (tonnage length) × 28ft-8in (extreme breadth) × 19ft-9in (approx. depth of hold); 357 tons. No reconstruction. A raised quarterdeck, drawn in pencil on original, is not included here.

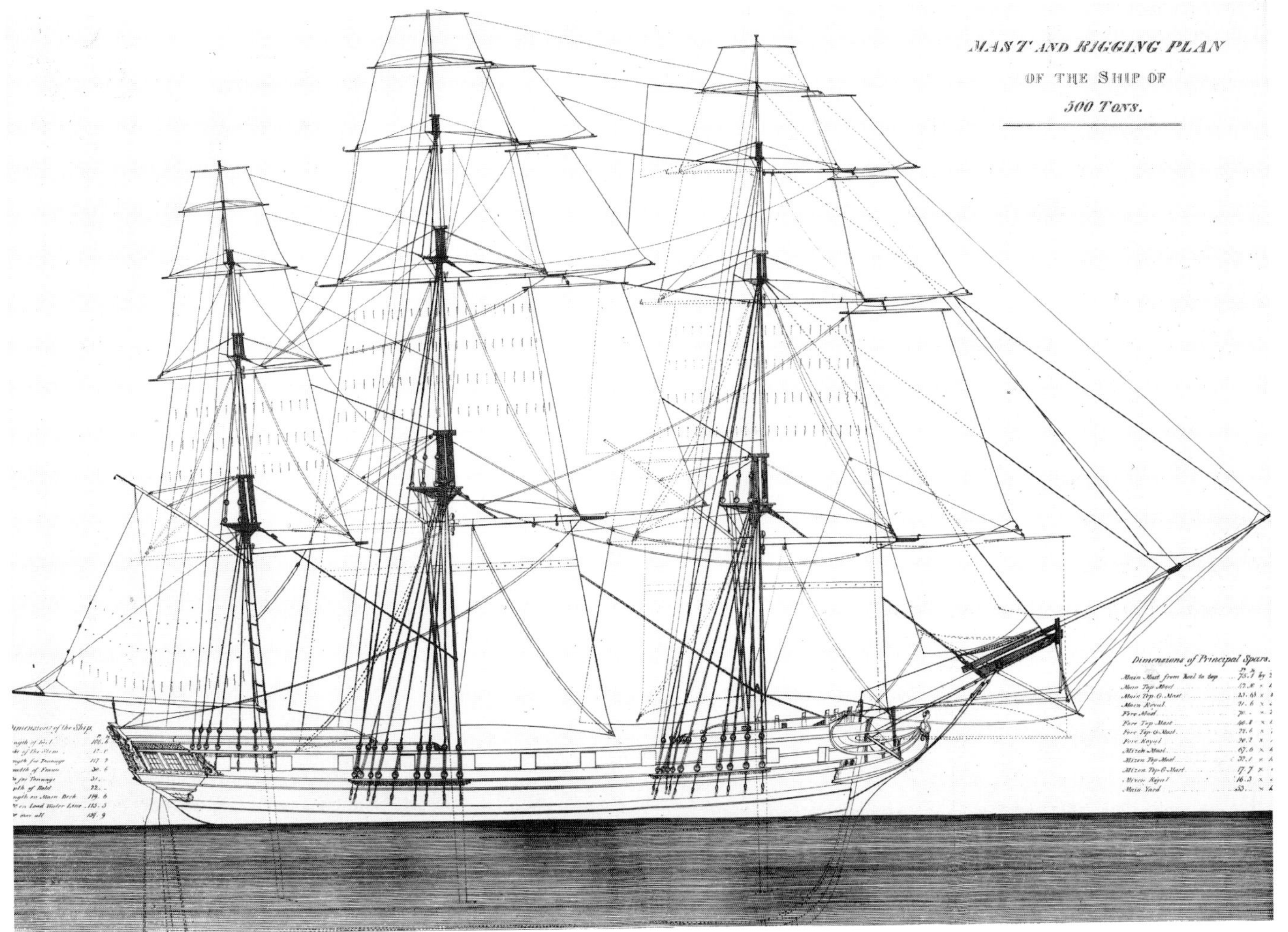

72: Hedderwick's ship of 500 tons. Unidentified ship but possibly designed by Peter Hedderwick in 1820-25. Reproduced from Plate XXVII in *Treatise on Marine Architecture* by Peter Hedderwick (1830). Dimensions: 117ft-2in (length for tonnage) × 31ft-0in (extreme breadth) × 22ft-0in (depth in hold); 500 tons. Plan drawn by P Hedderwick Jnr.

the pumps, and whenever it was practicable, she was put before the wind to pump her out. She had no bilge pumps. It was found, when the chalk she had in for ballast, was landed at Calcutta, that it was wet two feet above the ceiling in both bilges, having in course of the passage been obliged to carry a press of sail on either tack.

'. . . If this ship's ceiling had been caulked, it would have prevented the water getting within it, and consequently have preserved the cargo. New vessels are frequently leaky, and it is a common thing to take them into dry dock, and fill them with water, to find out the leak. By caulking the ceilings, the practice would be reversed, and it would only be necessary to float them, to find out a leak.'[9]

When he wrote this book, Ballingall was surveyor of shipping for the port of Kirkcaldy and manager of the Kirkcaldy & London Shipping Company. His book advocated the desirability of caulking the ceiling and building the bottoms solid as a safeguard against accidents. He only made one voyage in *Thalia*; on subsequent voyages the ship traded to India and the West Indies. James Ballingall appears to have settled in Australia because he was writing letters to the *Melbourne Argus* in 1855 on the subject of better ship construction.

An example of the 1200-ton class of East Indiaman, which has been selected to compare with *Thalia*, is the *Farquharson* of 1326 tons which was built in 1820 by Gordon at Deptford. She is almost four times *Thalia*'s size, and ships of her type, together with the passenger frigates that succeeded them, remained the largest merchant sailing ships afloat until the fifties. Although the Indiamen were not really built on clipper lines, the removal of the convoy system after the Napoleonic Wars and the spur of competition produced some fast passages, such as the 103 days which the *Lowther Castle* took in 1826 between Whampoa and Deal[10] and the 107 days which *Farquharson* took the same year from Lintin to Portland, Gravesend being reached three days later.

On this last passage, *Farquharson*'s log-book records speeds of ten and occasionally 11 knots, and with a load line length of 170ft-6in a speed of 11 knots results in a speed-length ratio of 0.84, which is moderately fast for a ship of her type, although under a skilful master and with good gear she could probably stand considerable driving. The biggest day's run that was found in her log-book was 244 miles during which the fore topmast stunsail was split. This was made in the above passage shortly after a series of big, consecutive runs when homeward-bound from China in the south-east trades, and between 24 January and 1 February 1826 these runs were: 208, 214, 242, 220, 171, 148, 197, 207 and 212 miles.

Like the majority of the East Indiamen, the *Farquharson* was built on the Thames and dimensions scaled off her plan give 171ft-0in foreside stem to after side sternpost, 42ft-9in moulded breadth, 31ft-6in top of floors to underside of upper deck; the height between decks was 6ft-6in to underside of the deck above. The tonnage given on the lines plan is 1326, although on her seventh voyage her log-book states it to be 1406, proving that she was of the largest class. Plans of East Indiamen are very scarce at this date which is surprising when the amount of money invested in these ships is considered. Plans of an East Indiaman of 1257 tons are given in Steel's *Naval Architecture* (1805),[11] and a very similar plate, engraved in 1816, appeared in Abraham Rees's *Cyclopaedia*.[12] At the National Maritime Museum, Greenwich, there are five plans of the *Farquharson* drawn to ¼-in scale by Charles Dandridge, but as

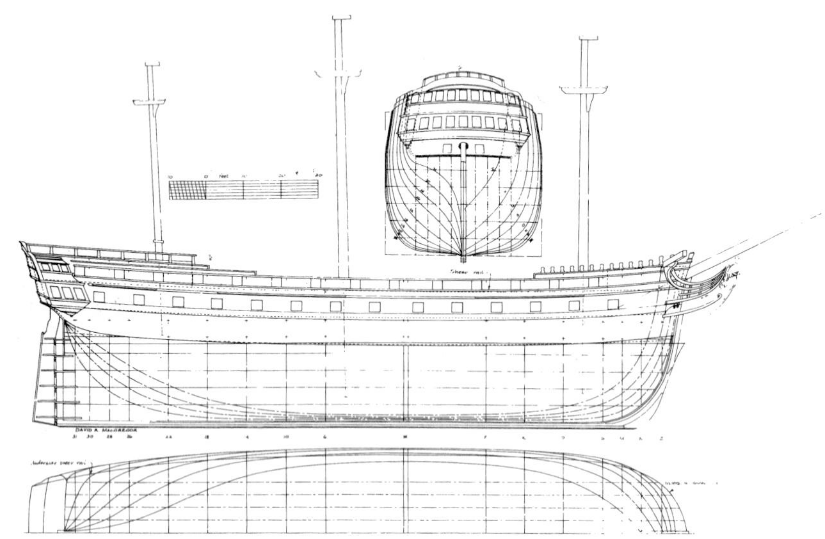

73: *Farquharson.* Lines plan: Built in 1820 by Gordon at Deptford. Redrawn from plan in the National Maritime Museum signed 'C Dandridge 1820'. Dimensions (scaled off plans): 171ft-0in (foreside stem to afterside sternpost) × 42ft-9in (moulded breadth) × 31ft-6in (top of floors to underside of upper deck); tonnage 1326 (log-book on seventh voyage gives 1406). Reconstruction: load waterline from log-book, 22ft-3in forward and 21ft-10in aft in 1823.

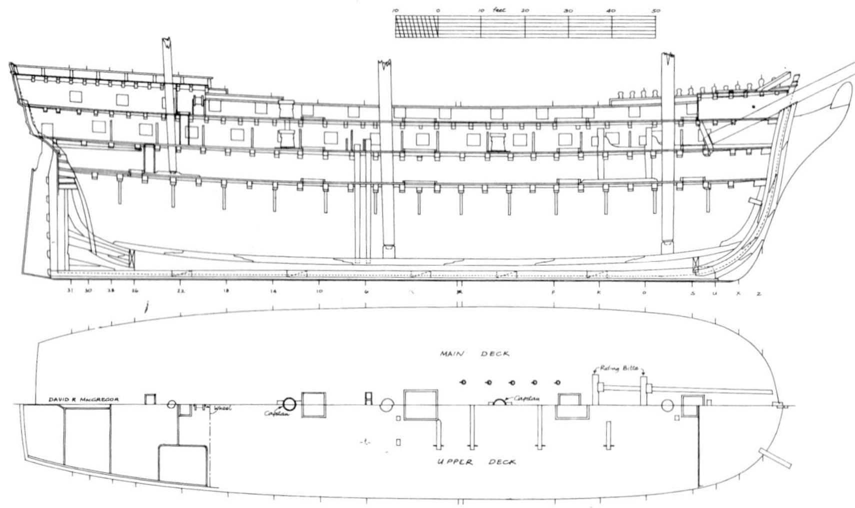

74: *Farquharson.* Section and decks: Compiled from plans dated 1820 and 1821. Reconstruction: capstans and hatch coamings both added.

the lines plan is dated 1820 it must be a copy of the original. Needless to say, none of these five plans comprises a sail plan, which has had to be reconstructed.

Comparing the *Farquharson* with other published plans, it is apparent that there was a fairly standard form of design and that, even if the ships could be mistaken for a frigate or a two-decked ship-of-the-line in profile, it was easy to tell from their almost flat floors, full rounded bilges and only small tumblehome that they were merchant ships. The *Farquharson* has a convex hull-form, but there are no dead flats amidships, and her great length at the load line derived from the huge hull gave her a large speed potential.

Features of an Indiaman were the heavy timber davits at each quarter, the double tier of stern windows without galleries, the square hances, high bulwarks and gun ports. *Farquharson*'s plans show that she was pierced for 56 guns divided equally between the upper and middle decks, but with a total crew of about 130 it was impossible to man such an armament and many of the upper deck ports would be empty. A painting of the ship by Thomas Whitcombe only indicates 38 guns — 12 on the upper deck and 26 on the middle deck.

The presence of a windlass on deck was the sure sign of a merchant ship, for the Navy did not employ this mechanism except in cutters and schooners. Indiamen followed the naval practice of heaving-in the anchor cable by means of an endless messenger taken to the capstan, a system to which the *Farquharson* conformed. On her middle deck are two capstans for this purpose and also two sets of massive riding bitts abaft the foremast, to which the cable could be made fast when riding to anchor. Internally, the chief difference between the Indiaman and a large warship lay in the deck arrangement. The warship still had an open waist, with the quarter-deck and forecastle merely connected at the sides with wide gangways, while in the Indiaman the waist was covered over and the quarter-deck and forecastle formed one continuous deck, called the upper deck; there was also a small topgallant forecastle for some of the crew placed right forward. The *Farquharson*'s wheel was positioned just under the break of the poop and the tiller ropes would have taken several turns on the barrel before leading down to the deck below and then aft to where the tiller was mounted. The capstan on the upper deck was used for hoisting the topsails and the lower yards, the fall from the tackles being led to the capstan through sheaves in bitts placed at the foot of the foremast and mainmast.

The only sail and rigging plan discovered for an Indiaman appeared in *Marine Models* in 1934 and is a reconstruction made by G W Munro who stated that the hull was taken from a lines plan engraved in 1816. This suggests that he used the lines appearing in Rees's *Cyclopaedia* which are dated 1816; he estimated the tonnage for this ship to be 955.[13]

The most reliable information on the *Farquharson*'s spars and rigging is to be found in her log-books, preserved in the India Office Library, which includes a list of the sails carried.[14] Unfortunately, no spar dimensions are listed, and accordingly those given by David Steel for a merchant ship of 1300 tons have been used for the purpose of reconstructing a sail and rigging plan that could accompany the lines plan and deck layout.[15]

75: *Farquharson.* Sail plan: This is a reconstructed sail plan. Apart from the sheer elevation, which gave the position and rake of lower masts and bowsprit, and of chain plates and lower deadeyes, everything else is reconstructed to show a typical East Indiaman of the largest class. The log-books of the ship in the India Office Library list the sails carried. The spar lengths are based on *Rigging and Seamanship* (1794 and 1816) by David Steel; sails and rigging are from the same source, contemporary illustrations and books.

As the *Farquharson*'s mizen steps on the lower deck, some adjustment to the length of Steel's lower mast was required, otherwise the mizen cap would be much too high. Conversely it would be too low if the dimension was taken from the keelson. Contemporary illustrations show that the crossjack yard and the fore yard were level, and the length of the mizen lower mast has accordingly been adjusted to bring this about.

The first reference to skysail does not occur until her fifth voyage which began in January 1829:

12 February 'Up royal masts and crossed yards'

20 February 'Got the skysail masts up and royal studding sail booms on the yards'.[16]

The log records the skysails and royal stunsails being set and taken in and the masts, yards and booms being sent down and re-stepped on several occasions. From the above extracts, it might be said that the sail plan reconstructed here shows the ship as she was in 1829.

There are a number of illustrations showing Indiamen and other vessels with separate royal masts fidded either abaft or on the fore side of the topgallant masts, but on the *Farquharson*'s reconstructed sail plan it seemed logical to step the royal masts on the fore-side to allow the skysail masts to be fidded abaft. These slide through a cranse iron fixed to the royal mast head and the heel steps on the topgallant mast cap, the arrangement being similar to the manner of rigging out a flying jibboom. Several other plans in this book show these sliding gunter masts rigged, such as the *Susanna* (figure 103) or the *Acasta* (figure 141).

David Steel's dimensions for the yards of a 1300-ton merchantmen are identical in the 1794 and 1816 editions of his book, but to avoid making the *Farquharson*'s spars like those of a ship 30 years earlier it was necessary to lengthen the upper yards somewhat to avoid a too-narrow sail plan. The lower yards listed by Steel are sufficiently long — the main yard measures 86ft-0in — but the length of the fore and main topsail yards is increased by four feet, and all the other upper yards by two feet each, with the exception of the mizen topgallant yard which is increased by only 18 inches. The spar dimensions that Edye gives for a 52-gun frigate form a useful comparison.[17] The increase in the length of the topsail yards has resulted in less curve to the leeches of the fore and and main topsails and yet the cringle of the lowest reef band still lies vertically under the sheave in the yard.

The sails drawn on the reconstructed plan are those referred to in the log-book, with the exception of a main moonsail which appears in a list of sails carried.[18] The staysail from the main royal stay was termed a 'spindle staysail'.

Farquharson's plan has ten chain plates for both the fore and main lower rigging, which is two more for each mast than is usually shown on paintings. The tops drawn here are to man-of-war proportions, namely one-third of the topmast length to give the breadth and

76: The *London* under sail with all her flying kites set, including three mizen stunsails. The only sail not set is a main moonsail. She was an East Indiaman of 1352 tons built in 1817 and carried a crew of 130 men. *Parker Gallery.*

three-quarters of this for the fore-and-aft length.[19] Thus the main top measures 18ft-8in across and 14ft-0in fore-and-aft.

A good illustration of the largest class of Indiamen under a press of sail may be seen in figure 76 which depicts the *London* on a broad reach with all her flying kites set. This ship measured 1332 tons and was constructed in 1817 by Pitcher's yard at Northfleet. In the painting, she has every square sail set up to skysails on each mast except for a moonsail on the main which, to judge by the distance apart of two stays above the main skysail yard, could be regularly set in light winds. Three large trysails are carried, each with its own mast, and there is a great variety of staysails; outside the square sails are topmast, topgallant and royal stunsails on fore, main and even the mizen. A fore lower stunsail was undoubtedly available when running before the wind. The lead of standing and running rigging is generally similar to that drawn on *Farquharson*'s sail plan.

Considerable expertise was displayed by the East India Company in transporting large numbers of troops about the world, and this knowledge must have proved of great benefit to the packet and emigrant ships. The passenger trade was an entirely new business as emigration from Great Britain and Europe to America and Australia got into its stride. In 1818 the Black Ball Line began regular sailings on scheduled dates from New York, which required fast trans-Atlantic passages throughout the year.[20] The packet ships designed for this gruelling service were deep, full-bodied ships with sharp ends, which could beat to windward well and withstand hard driving. Many American companies were formed to participate in this expanding traffic, but the British generally confined their activities to their West Indies possessions and the Australian emigrant trade.

Hilhouse schooners

It is undoubtedly a fallacy to suppose that every fine-lined British schooner built between 1815and 1875 was destined for the fruit trade because there were several other occupations available, some of which took them into deep water. Nevertheless, the fruit trade did prove a great stimulus for the development of fast schooner models and the plan of the Bristol-built *Sappho* provides an early example. This schooner was built by J M Hilhouse in 1821 and at the time of her launch measured 78ft-5in by 20ft-4in by 11ft-7in and 145 tons.[21] The original plan in the Hilhouse Collection bears the statement 'as altered in 1824' which may account for the fact that the tonnage length on the plan – foreside of stem to afterside of sternpost along the rabbet– scales 83ft-6in.

The chain-dotted lines on figure 77 show the extent of reconstruction needed for the *Sappho* in order to make the plan visually comparable with others. This schooner has very steep deadrise for a merchant vessel but an easy entrance and a fine run. The midship station is placed well forward; the maximum beam is slightly above the level of the load line; the profile of the keel, stern, sternpost, rudder and stem have been reconstructed from other plans in the Hilhouse Collection; likewise, the load line has been reconstructed from similar sources and on a figure of 12ft-0in loaded draught given in issues of *Lloyd's Register* between 1822 and 1826, and 10ft-0in in 1827. The ratio of four beams to length, together with a depth of hold that is only slightly more than half the breadth, result in a hull of long and shallow proportions that was infrequently seen in England at this date. The employment of the two-masted schooner rig permitted the lengthening of the hull given to the single-masted cutter and resulted in a finer entrance and run within the same

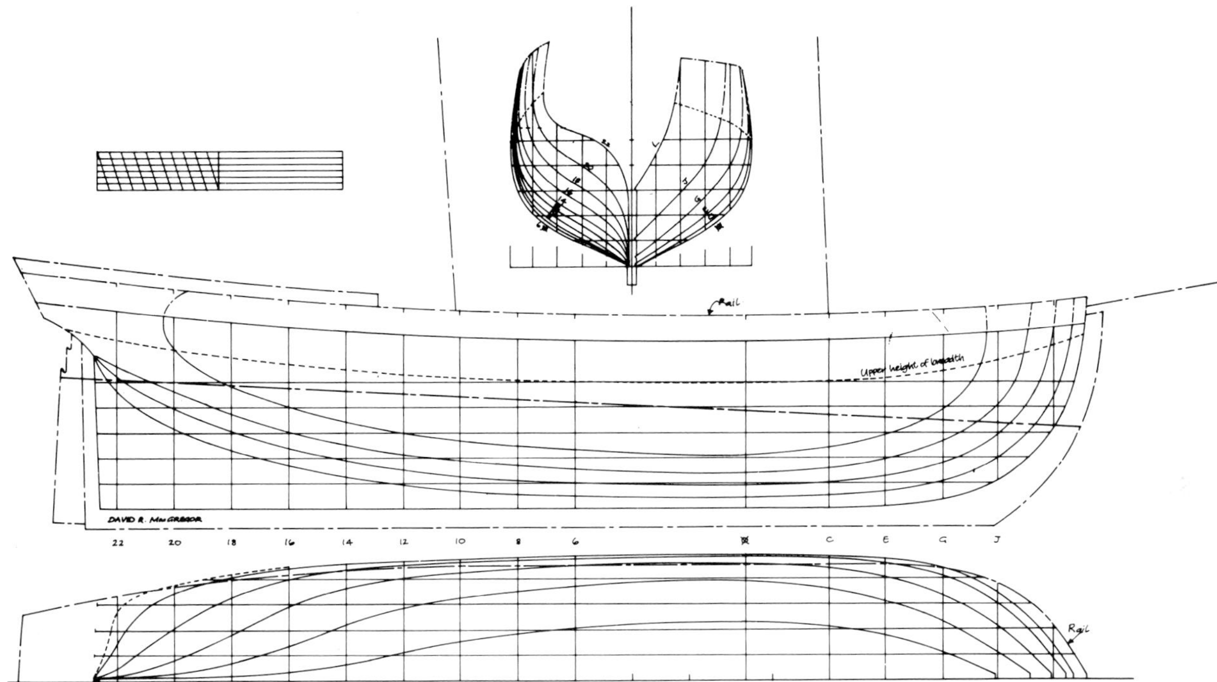

breadth. The *Sappho* could be said to possess several features similar to the cutter-rigged Post Office packet *Sylph*, built in the same year, and a comparison of their register dimensions reveals the extra length given to the *Sappho*'s schooner-rigged hull.

	length for tonnage	*maximum beam*	*depth of hold (approx.)*
Sylph	61ft-6in	20ft-10in	10ft-3in
Sappho	83ft-6in	20ft-4in	11ft-7in

The *Sappho* was owned in London by Llewellyn but was registered at Bristol. An advertisement in 1822 stated that she had 'made one voyage to Smyrna' and was a 'new and very fast sailing schooner'.[22] She appears to have spent all her life in the Mediterranean trade, making outward passages to Turkey, Malta and Smyrna, presumably for dried fruit. The only passage so far tracked down occupied 72 days between London and Smyrna in 1824–5, from 25 November to 5 February, and the length of this passage must be ascribed to the calls made at various ports *en route* to Smyrna. In 1827 she stranded in the Dardanelles and was presumably lost.

There is a note on the *Sappho*'s plan to the effect that the *Emma* had a moulded breadth of 19ft-8in, which suggests that her lines were similar to *Sappho*'s. There was a brig named *Emma*, built at Bristol in 1824 and trading

77: *Sappho* Built in 1821 by J M Hilhouse at Bristol. Redrawn from builder's plan by courtesy of Charles Hill & Sons, Bristol. Dimensions, as built: 78ft-5in × 20ft-4in × 11ft-7in; 145 tons. Length from foreside stem to aftside sternpost scaled off plan 83ft-6in, which may have been length after schooner was altered in 1824. Reconstruction: load waterline, profile, bowsprit and masts as shown by chain-dotted line.

78: A painting by Thomas Buttersworth (1768-1842) entitled 'Shipping in the Tagus' has in the foreground a heavily rigged schooner-brigantine, with a three-piece foremast on which there are four yards, but also a large gaff sail. This shows the amount of canvas which could be set and includes a ringtail, stunsails, square sail from the fore yard, and a fore royal that has been set flying, without any braces. *Parker Gallery.*

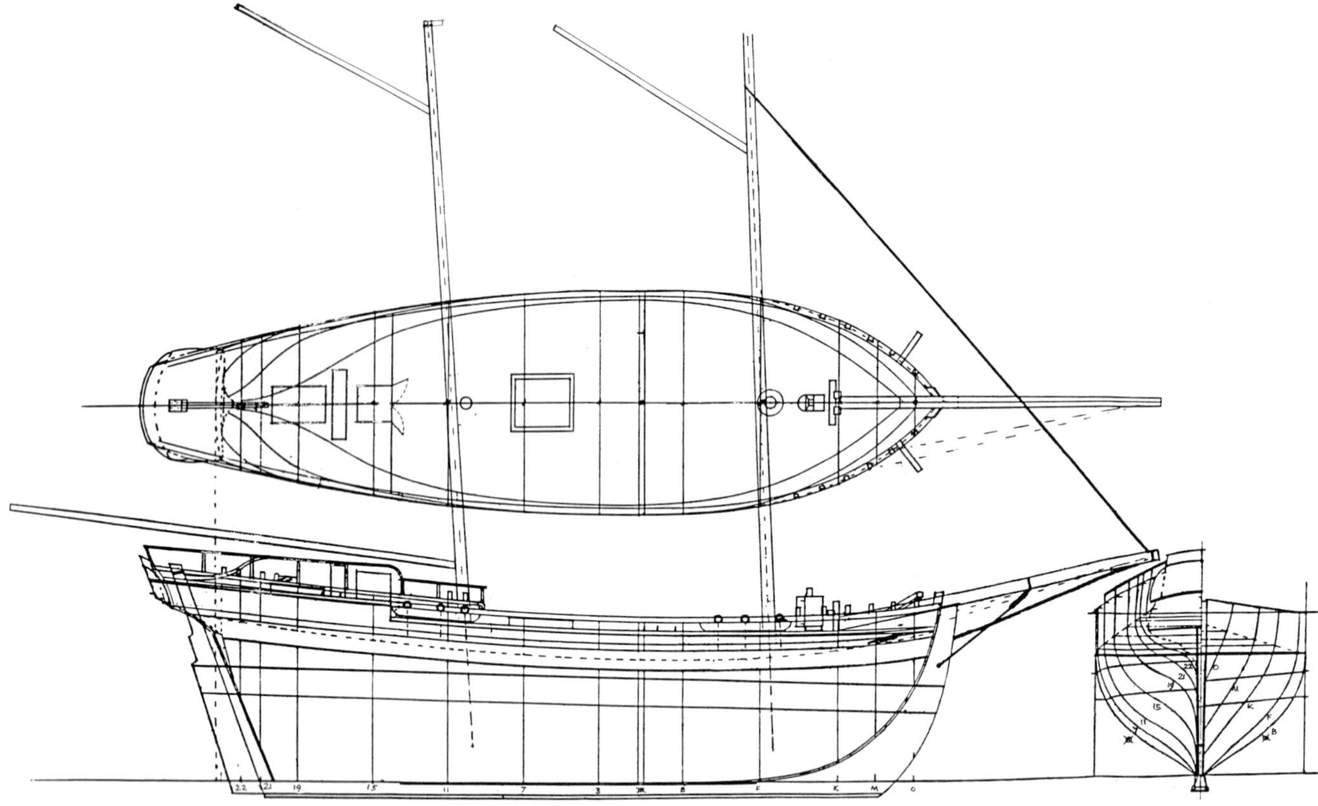

79: Plan of Hilhouse schooner. Unidentified. Photograph made of original plan through the courtesy of John C G Hill; it has had an alternative deck plan and part of a body plan masked out to make a clearer plan. The fore gaff has been reconstructed; only the peak was indicated previously. A cap is drawn on the head of the mainmast, but none is indicated on the foremast. No attempt has been made to draw in the sail outlines. No scale drawn on original.

to the West Indies, with measurements, according to the Custom House registers, of 80ft-3in by 21ft-7in (below wales) by 4ft-0in (height in cabin) and 167 tons; however it seems unlikely that J M Hilhouse built her, as the *Emma* built by him was launched in 1826 and measured 311 tons.[23]

It is interesting to note that the Hilhouse yard built or designed a number of steep-floored schooners in the ten years after 1815.

Plans of steep-floored schooners in Hilhouse collection

folio

37 *Harrier* (1816); 46ft-0in × 13ft-4in × 6ft-1in and 36 tons, probably a yacht for Mr Peach.

34 *Sappho* (1821); 78ft-5in × 20ft-4in × 11ft-7in and 145 tons; length altered in 1824 to 83ft-6in; fruit schooner.

43 'Beal's schooner'; unidentified, but possibly connected with John H. Beale of Bristol who put his name in 1801 to the lines plan of the French 14-gun corvette *Rackoon*;[24] 31ft-4in × 10ft-0in × 5ft-0in (approx.); a more raking stem overdrawn in pencil on plan increases length to 35ft-6in; two raking masts shown.

35 Unidentified; note infers lines are to build *Danion* [?] in 1825; 82ft-6in × 19ft-8in (moulded) × 11ft-0in (approx.).

42 Unidentified; 60ft-0in (along deck) × 16ft-8in × 7ft-0in; very similar to *Sappho*, but with more deadrise.

51 Unidentified; probably drawn to ⅛in-scale and used to make perspective drawings of three sloops.[25] (Figure 79).

The significance in the Hilhouse Collection of two plans of Bermudian sloops has already been discussed; there are also lines plans of two smugglers, the *Lattery* and the *Ferrett*. Nevertheless, it cannot be inferred that the presence of such plans means that Hilhouse actually based his designs of fast vessels on these craft or others like them; rather does it indicate an enquiring mind. In any case one can trace a greater family likeness between the hull-form of his Post Office packet of about 1795 and his clipper schooner *Sappho* of 1821 than between his own designs and those of other builder's plans in his collection.

At present, the Bristol-built *Sappho* is by far the earliest fruit schooner whose plans have been discovered, but one cannot speak with such authority about schooners built for the fruit trade at other shipyards; yet the rapid development of the fresh fruit trade with the Azores after the end of the Napoleonic Wars meant that schooners on equally fine lines must have been constructed elsewhere, particularly along the south coast of England.

The Brig *Neilson*

A good example of a brig built between 1815 and 1855, that was designed with good cargo capacity, accommodation for about six passengers and an above average turn of speed, may be found in the *Neilson* which Edward Adams (1768–1849) built at Buckler's Hard in 1824. Her lines plan is at the National Maritime Museum, Greenwich. This is the same yard that had produced the ship *Thalia*, and *Neilson* has several similarities in hull

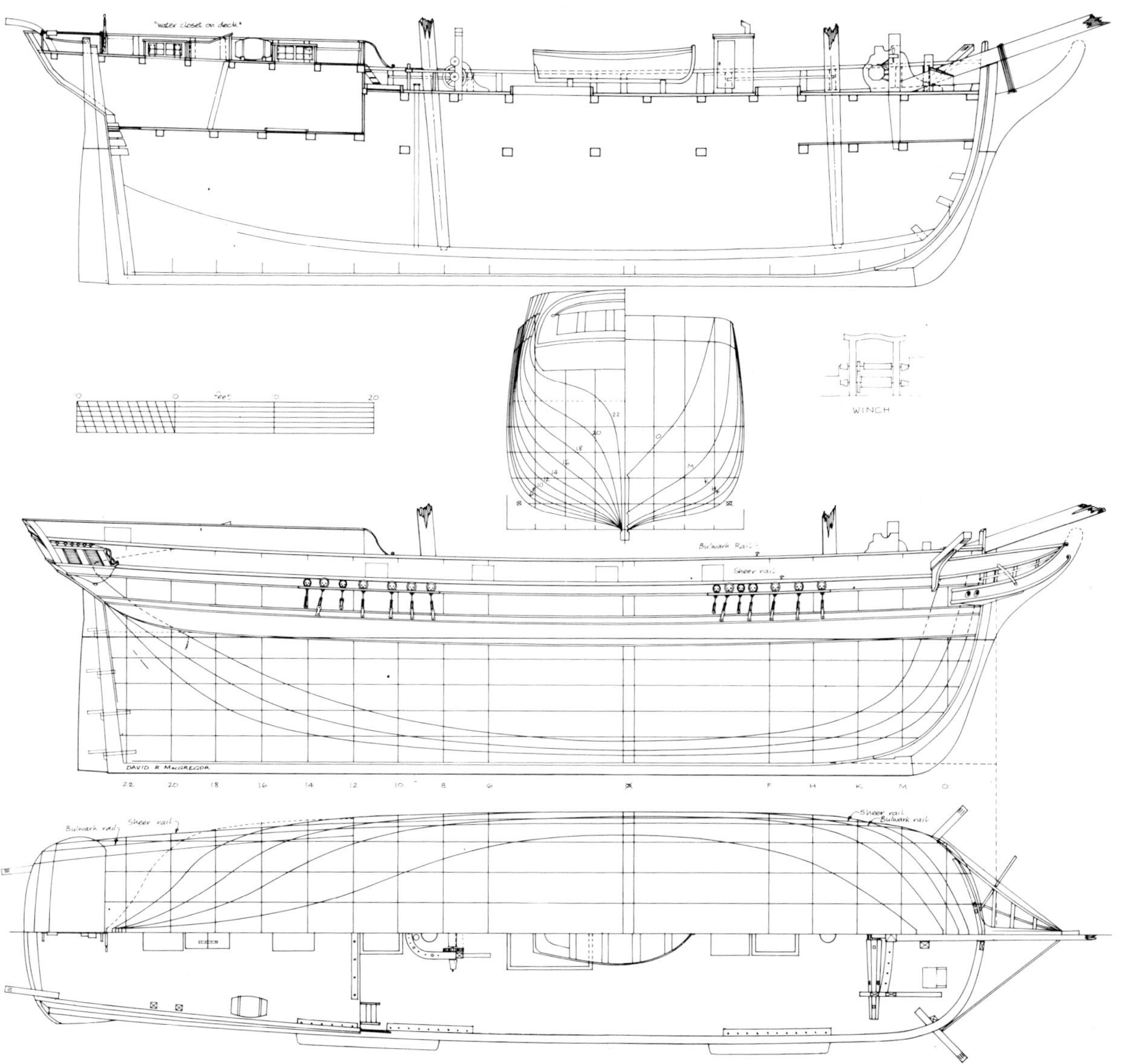

form, but neither their brig *Mary* (1818) nor their schooner *Friendship* (1824) are so fine-lined.

The *Neilson* has a moderately full entrance but the run is fairly long and concave, and even at the load line there is some hollow near the sternpost. An indication of good speed potential is the straightness of the quarter beam buttock where it crosses the load line aft. There is not much deadrise and the maximum beam is kept low with appreciable tumblehome above. Compared with the *Marchioness of Salisbury* (figure 66), she is about eight feet longer on the load line but of similar breadth and depth; she is also much fuller-bodied amidships with flatter floors. The *Neilson*'s dimensions given on the plan are: length aloft 91ft-4in; length of keel [and fore rake] 89ft-4in; breadth 24ft-1¾in, depth of hold 16ft-2in.

Most of her life was spent in the West Indies trade, and an example of her speed can be seen in a passage made in 1827 between Deal and Trinidad which took 44 days, from 15 September to 29 October; at the time of her departure, the winds in the Channel were northerly. She does not appear in *Lloyd's Register* after 1830, but during her career was owned by her master, Laughton.

These Adams' drawings repay close study, particularly in the case of the *Neilson*, on whose plan is a faintly-written list of spar dimensions. As a complete set of drawings for a merchant brig of this date was unknown, the discovery of *Neilson*'s spar dimensions was seized upon to work up a sail and rigging plan, and reconstruct a deck plan from basic information on the original draught. The original lines plan has been redrawn and a longitudinal section compiled from matter superimposed on the sheer elevation. The original plan bears various noted remarks, one of which is written above the raised quarter-deck and reads 'water closet on deck', but no attempt has been made to reconstruct this. Nevertheless, a galley, longboat, stern davits and cargo winch have been added, using contemporary sources. The winch has been sited at the deck beam on the foreside of the mainmast, with supporting knees along the deck,

80: *Neilson*. Lines plan: Built in 1824 by Edward Adams at Buckler's Hard. Redrawn from builder's plan in National Maritime Museum. Dimensions (given on plan): 91ft-4in (length aloft); 89ft-4in (length of keel [and fore rake]); 24ft-1¾in (breadth); 16ft-2in (depth of hold); 232 1/94 tons. Reconstruction: the following appeared on the original in elevation only: wheel and tiller, companionway and two skylights on poop, mooring bitts, windlass, cathead; sizes of hatches given. All other fitting reconstructed and the above fittings also in plan. Fife rail was in plan only.

bolted through to carlings. No fore scuttle is shown but access to the cramped crew's quarters could have been down a ladder at the fore hatch or more likely through a scuttle on the fore side of the windlass, to port or starboard of the bowsprit. In some plans this fore scuttle is placed between the heel of the bowsprit at the bitts and the pawl post. The height in the forecastle was about 4ft-6in maximum which meant that even the ship's boy could barely stand upright. The longitudinal section clearly shows the arrangement known as 'single deck with beams', the main deck being the only continuous deck and the lower row of beams being only decked-over

81: *Neilson* drawn by T W Ward. No painting or other illustration is known of this brig and this drawing is based entirely on the reconstructed plans. Some additional deck fittings have been added by William Ward, in consultation with the Author, and extra detail has been added to others.

where accommodation was required. The height in the *Mary*'s forecastle was 5ft-6in but in the schooner *Friendship* it was slightly less than in the *Neilson*. Comfort for seamen received no attention then: they were merely allotted so much length each for berths, and no account was taken of height.

A perspective of the *Neilson* has been drawn by William Ward to show a workmanlike sea-going craft, and it is reproduced in figure 81. The bust figurehead has been reconstructed; a fore scuttle is placed on the starboard side of the bowsprit bitts; a spider band is shown added to the foremast as no fife rail is marked on the plan; there is a rack for handspikes placed on the galley; the relationship of the hatchways to the other fittings is clearly shown; ring bolts are provided on the coamings for lashing down tarpaulins because no evidence has been found as to the existence of battens and ledges at this date; hen coops were probably carried on the quarter deck; and the arm and crutch for the lower stunsail boom are included.

Although the original plan is headed 'Brig *Neilson*', most two-masted square-rigged vessels are shown with a main trysail mast and accordingly this arrangement has been adopted here as representative of a typical sail plan of the period. The pictures of the Yarmouth-built brigs *Brazils Packet* (1828 of 173 tons) and *Preston* (1823 of 200 tons), reproduced in figure 83, portray very similar vessels, and these paintings have been employed extensively in the reconstruction of the sail plan which is typical of countless other brigs. The long, massive bowsprit is a feature of the period prior to 1840 and the

82: *Neilson*. Sail plan: Reconstructed from lines plan and from spar dimensions faintly written in pencil on original. Also reconstructed from contemporary sources; lengths of topgallant masts; sails, rigging and main trysail mast; also all stunsail booms, yards and sails.

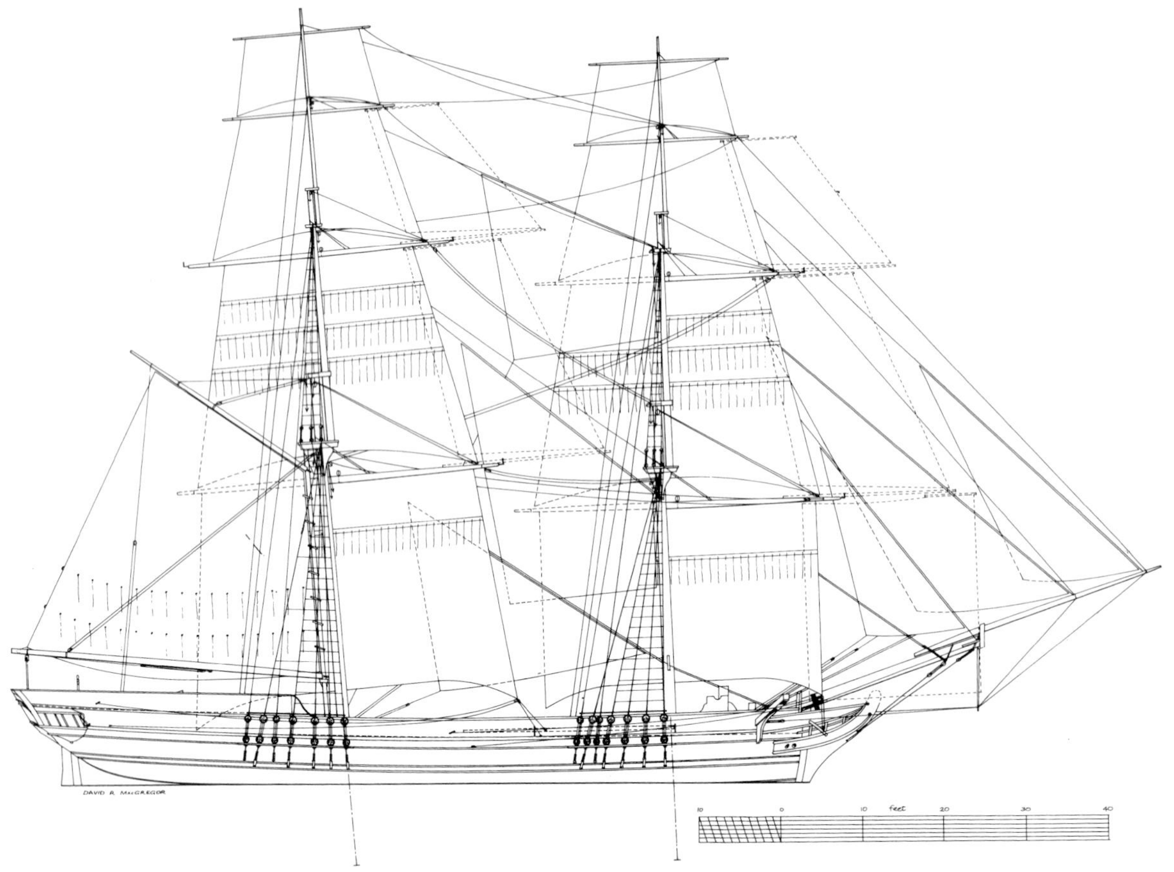

83: The Italian artist Guiseppi Fedi painted this broadside view of the *Preston* and a tiny quarter view of her below the jibboom, in which he has got the perspective wrong. The painting is entitled '*Preston* of Weymouth departing from Genoa'. This brig was probably built at Yarmouth in 1823 with a tonnage of 200. The flags are strange. *Private collection.*

chain plates are also of an old pattern. A spritsail yard was not always fitted in small vessels, but a bumpkin for bowsing down the fore tack was essential, especially when the foremast was stepped right in the eyes of the ship. The *Neilson*'s bumpkin is 6ft-6in long, canted downwards, the heel secured to the hull and the outer end stayed against the pull of the fore tack by two guys; additional support at its centre is given by the trail board through which it passes. The leeches of the fore course are at right angles with the head, to bring the fore tack vertically above the bumpkin; but if the tack is taken to the cathead, then the foot has frequently to be shorter than the head and the leeches slope inwards. Fincham said that if the bumpkin 'can be carried sufficiently forward to bring the tack properly down, it will be better to lessen the narrowing, not only on account of gaining sail, and for appearance, but the sail will, in general, stand better with parallel leeches'.[26]

The sail plan remains tall and narrow, and a number of features are worth special mention: the main course normally has a foot which is longer than the head by three to six feet per side, depending on the size of the ship; one row of reef points in the courses and three rows in the topsails were normal in merchant ships; the standing jib is still by far the largest of the headsails; the shape of the staysails on the mainmast was generally four-sided and Robert Salmon shows an interesting arrangement in his painting of a 'Snow off Greenock' in the Glasgow Museum and Art Gallery. In the case of the *Neilson*, no dimensions were given for stunstail booms and these are accordingly reconstructed from contemporary rules and proportions; from contemporary pictures it will be observed that the spanker was often brailed into the mast instead of being lowered to the deck. The lead of the running-rigging varied from ship to ship and might be changed, often in the course of a single voyage, so no solution drawn here can be absolutely perfect, nor suit all tastes. Some brigs in foreign trades used to set skysails on sliding gunter poles, fidded on the afterside of the royal masts.

In the home trade, the brig rig was a popular one for colliers and Baltic traders but the hull form tended to be fuller than *Neilson*, and many such craft set nothing above their topgallants.

The *Falcon*

An important example of an early clipper is the full-rigged ship *Falcon*, originally built as a yacht in 1824, later employed in carrying tea to England and finally operated as an opium clipper. Designed to replace a brig-rigged yacht of the same name, she was constructed by List at Wootton Bridge, Isle of Wight, for Lord Yarborough, the commodore of the Royal Yacht Squadron, and she remained the flagship of the squadron for 12 years.

In the first edition of this book I used a rigged model in the Science Museum, London, as the source for my claim that the *Falcon* was designed on clipper lines, and to substantiate this claim, I had to take off the lines from this hull and draw out a set of plans. The hull lines certainly revealed that this model had very steep deadrise and sharp tapering ends, but the identification of the model was open to doubt, and therefore its authenticity was not beyond question. Since then, however, a lines plan and a sail plan have been located in the archives at the Sjöhistoriska Museum, Stockholm.

The lines plan, reproduced as figure 84, has been re-drawn from the original to show a vessel with very steep deadrise above hollow garboards, but the turn of the bilge is much lower than in the French privateer *L'Intrepide*, illustrated in the previous chapter, and in some of the American Baltimore clippers. It is more in the style of cross-section employed by Sir Robert Seppings in the 1820s. This plan

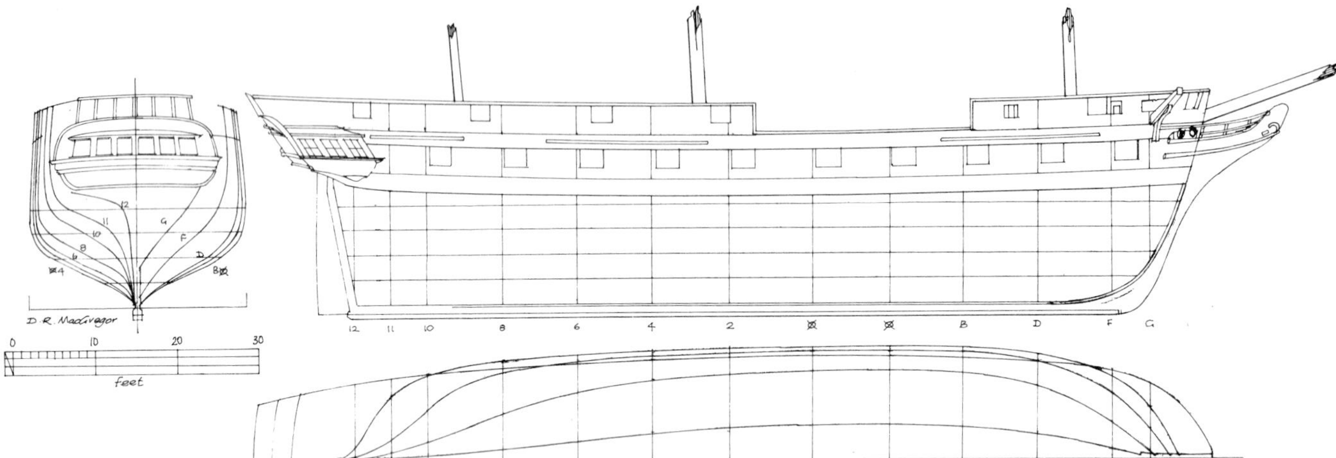

of *Falcon* shows an unexpectedly full entrance for a ship that was a yacht, although the run is reasonably fine. The topsides are taken up fairly high, presumably to provide staterooms in the 'tween decks, and the bulwarks to the long poop would have provided protection to passengers. There is no deck plan. Dimensions written on the lines plan state: length of deck 103ft-9½in; length of keel for tonnage 86ft-7½in; breadth extreme 27ft-0in; breadth moulded 26ft-6in; depth in hold 8ft-3½in; burthen [?] in tons 334$^{4}/_{94}$.

It is the purpose of this study to show the steady development of sharp ships and the care required before singling out one lone vessel as the precursor of a whole era. Thus the *Falcon* is an early example of a ship whose importance in the development of the clipper ship evolution has so far been overlooked. In the case of the American ship *Ann McKim*, wild assumptions have been made that she was the first clipper ship, whereas she was a ship-rigged clipper of extreme build, constructed at Baltimore in 1832 and another

84: *Falcon*. Lines plan: Redrawn from plan in Chapman Collection at the Sjöhistoriska Museum, Stockholm. Dimensions on plan (written in English): 103ft-9½in, (length of deck), 86ft-7½in (length of keel for tonnage), 27ft-0in (breadth extreme), 26ft-6in (breadth moulded), 8ft-3½in; tonnage 334$^{4}/_{94}$. Reconstruction: it was necessary to plot again the waterlines from the body plan, due to distortion of the paper, and only alternate stations were employed; some of the waterlines also omitted; deadeyes and chain plates omitted.

85: An engraving by E Duncan after W J Huggins of the *Falcon* under sail off Cowes. She appears to have an unbroken sheer, but the bulwarks in the waist are filled with hammocks. *Parker Gallery*.

vessel in the line of clipper ship development.[27]

No independent naval architect is named as the designer of the *Falcon*, but several interesting observations can be made respecting the influences and examples available to Mr List, her builder. In the first place, he must have been an established yacht builder of some eminence to be commissioned by Lord Yarborough and as such would have had the opportunity of seeing and designing many yachts of the day. Secondly, the yachtsmen themselves, such as the Hon. George Vernon, the Marquis of Anglesea, Lord Belfast, the Duke of Portland and others, had very definite ideas on naval architecture and insisted that their yachts were built in accordance with their wishes. Finally, the authors of *Memorials of the Royal Yacht Squadron* wrote that Captain Symonds, later surveyor to the Navy, 'designed some notable vessels which were built by List'.[28] As Captain William Symonds was primarily celebrated for steep deadrise, it is natural to wonder what contact he had with List while the *Falcon* was under construction, although Sharp's biography of Symonds does not record him as meeting Lord Yarborough until 1825, the year after the *Falcon* was launched.[29] However, Symonds' pamphlet, *Observations on Naval Architecture*, had appeared in 1824.

In the 1820s John Fincham, superintendent of the School of Naval Architecture at Portsmouth Dockyard, selected five notable yachts in the Royal Yacht Squadron as a subject for his inquiries and published his calculations and the yachts' spar dimensions in *Papers on Naval Architecture*.[30] The yachts selected were the *Falcon*, the brig *Coquette* and the cutters *Emerald, Nautilus* and *Pearl*. Fincham must have taken off the *Falcon*'s lines to calculate the displacement and other properties and it may be that the plans at Stockholm are the very ones he drew. Certainly his name is inscribed across the top of the sheer plan, but I have not been able to decipher the full wording to enable any conclusions to be drawn.

The sail plan found in the Sjöhistoriska Museum was very basic; no royals were drawn, nor staysails between the masts, and not even trysail gaffs; the flying jibboom and flying jib were omitted, and so also was all the standing and running rigging. The masts and spars on the plan were, in fact, those listed by Fincham in one of his tables on the properties of the yacht, as set out below. This sail plan has been re-drawn in figure 86 to include some of the obviously missing items, and their inclusion is corroborated by contemporary engravings of the *Falcon* under sail off the Isle of Wight.

The proportions of the spar dimensions

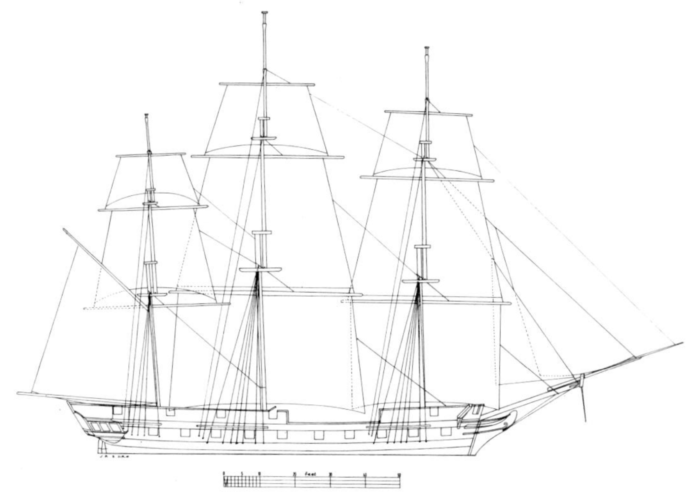

86: *Falcon*. Sail plan: Redrawn from plan in Chapman Collection at the Sjöhistoriska Museum, Stockholm, entitled: '*The Falcon*, Lord Yarborough's yacht'. The spars and sails drawn here are those on the original plan with the exception of the flying jibboom and dolphin striker, which have been added. The foot of the square sails has not been altered. Reconstruction: shrouds and backstays added according to position of deadeyes on the channels; lower, topmast and topgallant stays added. The trysail gaffs in figure 85 do not appear.

Masts of the *Falcon*

Dimensions of Falcon

	Ft	In
Length on water-line	102	8
Breadth	27	2

Dimensions of Masts and Gear, in Terms of known Quantities.

Species of Masts and Gear	*Known Quantities*	*Proportions*
Main-mast	Breadth	2.463
Main Top-mast	Main-mast	.612
Main Topgallant-mast	Main-mast Hounded	.283
	Hounded Length Pole	.634
Fore mast	Main-mast	.918
Fore Top-mast	Main Top-mast	.999
Fore Topgallant-mast	Main Topgallant-mast Hounded	.868
	Hounded Length Pole	.713
Mizen-mast	Main-mast	.865
Mizen Top-mast	Main Top-mast	.701
Mizen Topgallant-mast	Main Topgallant-mast Hounded	.737
	Hounded Length Pole	.65
Bowsprit	Length	.408
Jib-boom	Bowsprit	.714
Main-yard	Length	.544
Main Topsail-yard	Main-yard	.75
Main Topgallant-yard	Main-yard	.464
Fore-yard	Main-yard	.875
Fore Topsail-yard	Fore-yard	.775
Fore Topgallant-yard	Fore-yard	.5
Cross Jack-yard	Main Topsail-yard	.976
Mizen Topsail-yard	Main Topsail-yard	.666
Mizen Topgallant-yard	Main Topgallant-yard	.737
Driver-boom	Length	.392
Gaff	Boom	.743

	Feet	Ins.
Rake of Main-mast in 12 Feet		6
Rake of Fore-mast do		2
Rake of Mizen-mast do		10
Stive of Bowprit do	4	6
Fore-mast before Middle Length on Water-Line	.37	
Main-mast abaft	.633	
Mizen-mast	.347	

listed by Fincham in *Papers on Naval Architecture* are tabulated below in the same form in which he presented the material. As the rigging is taken to each mast at the hounds, the 'hounded length pole' of the topgallant mast refers to the upper part of the mast on which the royal yard would have been crossed.[31]

The model in the Science Museum, London, is equipped with curiously cut trysails on fore and main masts, and an oddly-shaped fore topmast staysail; the topgallant stays on each mast are placed so high that the royals require a huge roach to ride over the stays; and the heel of each topmast is extended sufficiently far below the trestletrees to sling the lower yards, thus permitting the yards to be braced up more sharply and performing the duty of a patent iron truss. The last arrangement is thought to be unique. A considerable degree of experimentation was being conducted in the 1820s with regard to improvements in masting, sails, rigging and ballasting, and numerous experimental cruises were undertaken by naval vessels to test the sailing qualities as the result of such alterations, and the *Falcon* may have contributed to such experiments. Alternatively, it may be that the topmast heel was lowered by the model's owner to rig her in a convenient way so that she could be sailed more easily.[32]

John Fincham had a few comments to make on the *Falcon*'s construction:

> It may be observed that the Falcon, the yacht of the Right Honourable Lord Yarborough, has cast-iron instead of wood chocks under the keelson, made so as to receive at the ends pigs of common ballast. The openings between the timbers of the frame, are filled in with oak and caulked to three inches from the outside, and then filled in with cast-iron fixed with Roman cement, which makes it a solid mass impervious to the water. The use of cement with oak fillings well caulked, in the openings between the timbers, has been sometime common in the royal dockyards, and was applied in the Right Honourable the Earl of Belmore's yacht, the *Osprey*, about ten years ago; but the application of iron with cement in the openings, was first used in the Falcon, and has since been introduced by Mr. Thorald, in his yacht, the *Coquette*. The advantages of filling the openings in this manner, are, preventing the openings being filled with dirt and builge water which produce an unpleasant and unhealthy vapour, giving stowage to the hold, giving security to the bottom, more generally diffusing the ballast, and, by lowering the centre of gravity of the ballast, increasing the stability.[33]

The *Falcon*'s later life in the world of commerce remained full of interest. Among Baring Brothers' letters to their Canton agents, Russell & Co, there are several references to the desirability of using fast ships for the carriage of silk or opium, which presumably led to her purchase from Lord Yarborough in 1836 at a cost of £5500.[34] In a letter written to Russell & Co by one of the partners, Joshua Bates, on the occasion of the commencement of the *Falcon*'s first voyage to China in October 1836, the ship is described as 'formerly Lord Yarborough's yacht' and later in the letter it states:

> 'The ship seems admirably calculated for an opium ship between your port and Bombay or Calcutta. We believe she will sail faster than any ship in that trade and it is possible some of your opium traders may take a fancy to the *Falcon*; if so, you hereby have our authority to sell her, provided you can obtain for her a sum of £10,500 net. She is perfectly sound as on the day she was built and entirely fastened with copper. You will see that her decks and topsides, also her spars, are quite new. She was originally built with great care at an expense of £18,000, so that she may be considered now as good or better than the best class of River-built ships. . . We rely much on your good judgement in making the most of this Fast ship. . '[35]

In the autumn of 1837 the *Falcon* loaded tea for the London market and arrived back in February 1838, thus gaining the distinction of being one of the earliest British tea clippers. Then followed an outward passage of 110 days to Canton from Cowes, 1 April to 20 July 1838, which included a stay of four days at Batavia from 2 to 6 July. This was under the command of Captain Middlemist with a crew of 21 and a cargo of 'woollens'. She loaded tea at Whampoa and sailed on 2 October the same year, passed through Gaspar Straits on 23 October and reached London on about 6 February 1839, after a passage of approximately 127 days. She then ferried 3150 chests and 794 half chests of tea round to Liverpool later the same month. Basil Lubbock's story about an auxiliary engine being fitted for the outward passage is thus proved incorrect.[36] As Fincham states, the engine was fitted about 1825 to Lord Yarborough's earlier yacht of the same name, the discarded brig *Falcon*.[37]

Again Baring Brothers vainly tried to sell the ship in 1839, but now their asking price had fallen to £6000.[38] To improve cargo capacity and her sailing capabilities the following work was carried out at Liverpool in that year:

Outline specification of alterations to the *Falcon*[39]

> 'Step bowsprit on deck to increase space below for crew accommodation; bring catheads up to top of bulwarks so that anchor flukes can be carried on deck, when at sea; channels impede her sailing and no fender will protect them in dock, so remove them and bring deadeyes to head of bulwarks; quarter galleries so large and low that when ship is loaded, they almost touch the water; remove the hammock nettings in the waist; small hatchway to be formed in deck abaft capstan; far too much iron ballast; state rooms too extensive and by reduction would give more cargo stowage.'

This covers all the visible work; the other concerned water tanks, pumps, chain lockers, after peak and orlop deck under fo'c'sle.

Baring Brothers could not have found a purchaser in Liverpool after these alterations were completed as a new master was appointed in September 1839 with orders to take charge of the ship on a new voyage.[40] But due to the Anglo-Chinese war the ship did not leave Liverpool until 1840 and Jardine Matheson & Co must have bought her sometime in that year, because in December 1840 she left Macao for Calcutta to load opium.

T G Dutton's lithograph entitled *Clippers in the China Trade* is dedicated to Alexander Matheson and, although undated, obviously portrays the ship after the proposed alterations were carried out in Liverpool. This is reproduced in figure 87 where it may be observed that, although the man-of-war appearance has not altogether been removed, yet she has a sleeker hull with a continuous sheer line.

In the opium trade, the *Falcon* was occupied

87: Thomas G Dutton's lithograph of the *Falcon* is entitled 'Clippers in the China Trade' so that this picture of the ship is really a detail of the whole. She is pictured under Jardine, Matheson ownership *MacGregor Collection.*

88: *Dash.* Lines plan: Built in 1828 by T & J Brocklebank at Whitehaven. Redrawn from builder's plan by courtesy of T & J Brocklebank, Liverpool. Dimensions: 66ft-3in × 17ft-3in × 10ft-2in; 86 tons. Reconstruction: sheer elevation and half-breadth plans, based on body plan, elevation of topsides and other Brocklebank plans.

regularly between Calcutta and China throughout the 1840s. A fast passage from Macao to Calcutta occupied 35 days between 4 December 1840 and 8 January 1841 under Captain Pike. She remained in this trade until her disappearance sometime in the mid 1850s.

T & J Brocklebank's brigantine *Dash* and barquentine *Bonanza*

A good example of a fine-lined brigantine is afforded by the *Dash* (figure 88) which T & J Brocklebank built for themselves in their own yard at Whitehaven in 1828. Both *Lloyd's Register* and Brocklebank's own history refer to her as a 'schooner'; but the latter's water-colour of her shows that she was a brigantine. This painting is in the unmistakable style of Jacob Petersen of Copenhagen,[41] and the rig is further confirmed by a sail plan in the Brocklebank archives. Before the middle of the century, most of the Brocklebank plans were not drawn to scales of fractions of an inch, such as ⅛in, ¼in, ⅜in or ½in to 1ft-0in, but to proportional scales such as 1:25, 1:30 and so forth.

It has been possible to reconstruct the lines of the *Dash* using a scale of 1:30 and to space out the stations in conformity with the plans of other Brocklebank ships. The basis of this reconstruction was a body plan and sheer elevation of the topsides. Her measurements, as given in Brocklebank's history, are 66ft-3in by 17ft-3in by 10ft-2in and 86 tons; the draught of water of nine feet is taken from the green *Lloyd's Register*. This Register also describes her as 'sharp', and her name suggests a fast vessel, but the reasons why Brocklebank's should have built her on

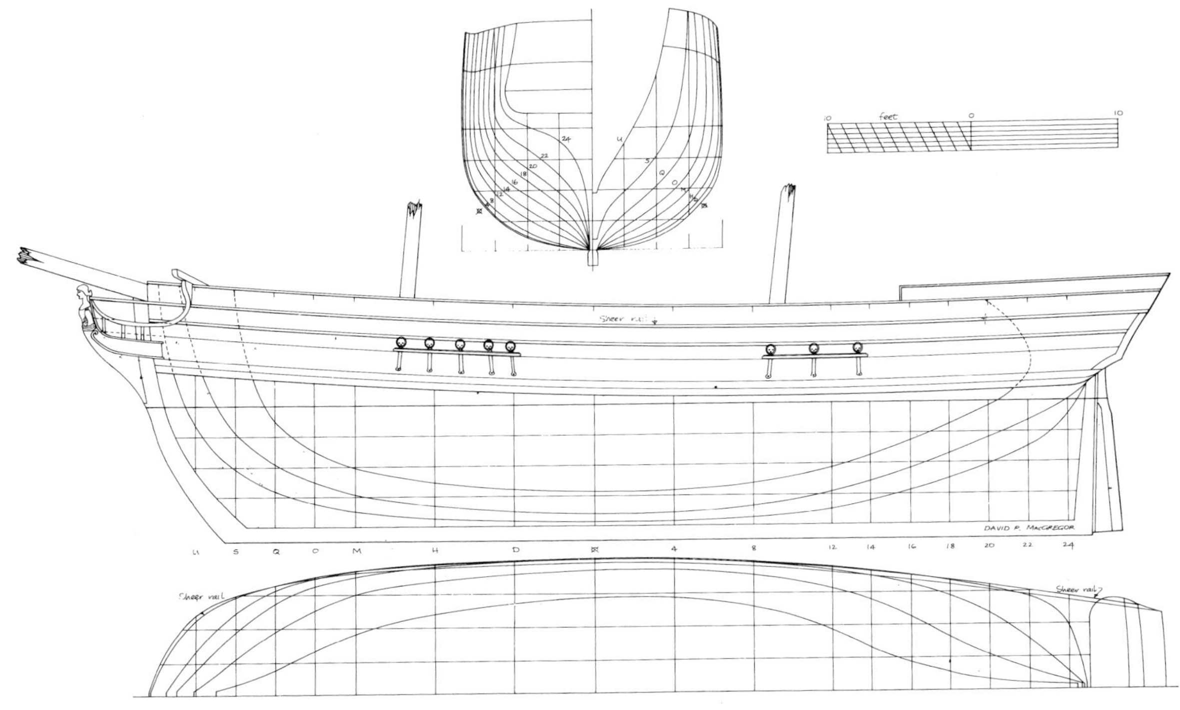

90: This painting of the *Dash* has formed the principal source for completing the builder's sail plan. She is shown passing Elsinore, which was a favourite background for Scandinavian artists. There are no braces to the fore royal yard. *Merseyside County Museums.*

moderately fine lines are unknown, particularly as she was merely placed in their usual trade routes, North and South Atlantic, Baltic and Mediterranean.

Compared with *Neilson*, she is somewhat finer-lined and the whole after body tapers away from the midship section; there is considerable deadrise and the floors curve all the way to the bilges. It looks as if the body plan was designed on arcs of circles which was becoming an old-fashioned practice by this date, although occasional examples persist for another 25 years. Where less resistance was wanted, it was becoming fashionable to give a straight rise of floor up to the bilge. Perhaps the shortage of grown oak bends for the floors and first futtocks forced designers to avoid the use of rounded bottoms. Unfortunately, no deck layout was found for the *Dash* but she probably had a raised quarter-deck as in the *Neilson*.

A few alterations were made to the sail plan so that it accorded generally with Jacob Petersen's painting, notably the addition of stunsails and running rigging. Neither the sail plan nor the painting shows a flying jib set, but doubtless such a sail could have been hoisted high up on the topgallant or royal stay like a jib topsail; and a storm staysail was probably available for the fore stay. The fore royal is set flying without braces or lifts, being intended as a light weather sail. When so many brigantines at this date had a fore trysail set from a standing gaff, such as in the *Hellas*, or even hoisting on a separate trysail mast, it is interesting to find instead this sail plan of a brigantine with two huge staysails set between the masts. In 1829, the *Dash* was valued at £1500 or £17.8s. per ton and had a crew of seven.

The *Oberon*, built the year before and of 150 tons, has practically the same rig, accord-

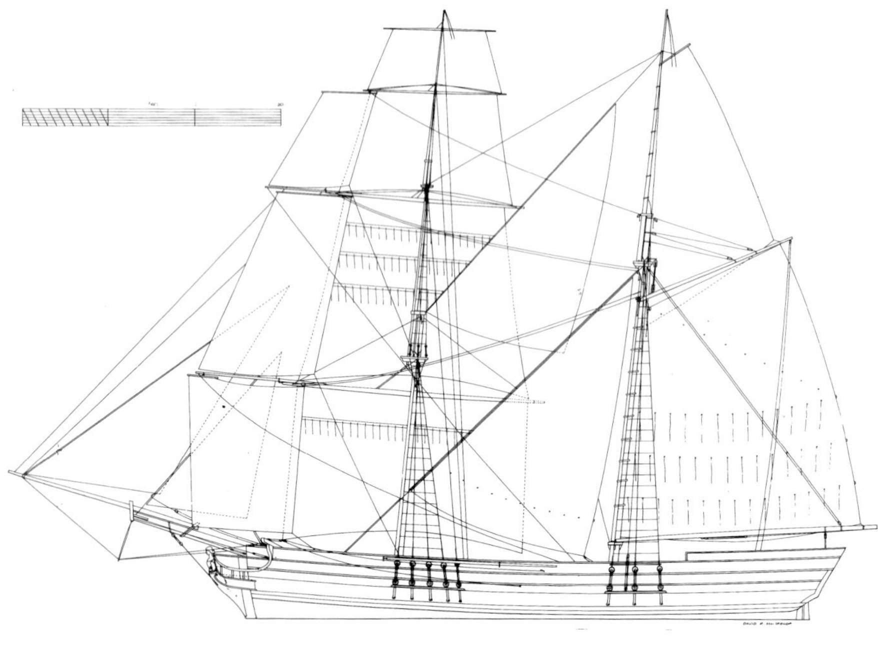

89: *Dash*. Sail plan: redrawn from tracing made of builder's plan in the offices of T & J Brocklebank. Reconstruction: running rigging and studding sails, based on painting by Jacob Petersen (see figure 90).

ing to the sail plan, although Brocklebank's history lists her as a brig. The *Courier* of 1826 was a topsail schooner, as proved by her sail plan, which is reproduced in *Merchant Sailing Ships 1815–1850* figure 78.[42] Offsets indicate that the shape of *Courier's* midship section was similar to that of *Maypo* and *Bonanza* as drawn in figure 91, with sharply rising floors that round up the whole way, and so she was obviously intended to make fast passages. Her midship section is placed about nine feet forward of amidships.

The discovery that *Bonanza* was a barquentine and not the 'three-masted schooner' so described in the yard book is remarkable and makes one wonder what other barquentines might have been afloat in these years, perhaps disguised under the pseudonym of 'three-masted schooner'. The so-called 'first' vessel of any rig is often proved to be a myth by later discoveries. Apart from the *Transits*, rigged as five-, four-, and three-masted barquentines in the years 1800, 1809 and 1819, it had been assumed that the first 'orthodox' three-masted barquentine was the *Fanny* of Bremen, built in 1850. Illustrations of the *Transit* appear here as figures 55 and 56. The lines plan and sail plan of *Bonanza* given here prove that she was an 'orthodox' barquentine, in spite of the shape of the mizen.

The lines plan in figure 91 has been drawn from offsets given in Thomas Brocklebank's notebook for the barque *Maypo*, ship No 93, laid down in May 1828 and launched on 17 June 1829.[43] The reason for using these is because the entry for *Bonanza* in the notebook begins: 'Dimensions New Ship No 94 same as No 93 except about 1½ins fuller upon O, P & 2 at the Main Deck Rail Harpin'. The *Bonanza*, ship No 94, was launched the following year. The dimensions of the two vessels are compared here:

	Maypo	*Bonanza*
Length aloft [= from foreside stem to taffrail measured along sheer line]	84ft-8in	85ft-6in
Length of keel [= tonnage length of keel and fore rake]	82ft-6in	82ft-7½in
Breadth extreme	21ft-9in	21ft-8in
Depth of hold	13ft-4in	13ft-2½in
Tonnage	174 70/94	173 79/94

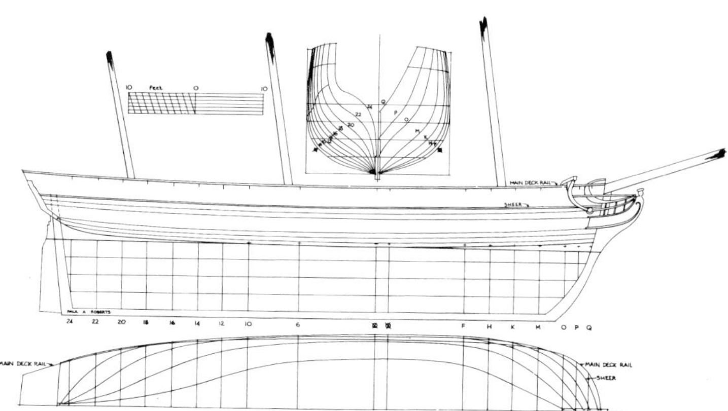

91: *Bonanza*. Lines plan reconstructed by the author from builder's offsets in yard book at Merseyside County Museums; ink tracing of this for reproduction made by Paul A Roberts. Built 1830 by T & J Brocklebank at Whitehaven; dimensions 85ft-6in × 21ft-8in × 13ft-2½in and 173 tons. Reconstructed: head rails &c from schooner. *Courier*.

The offsets principally consist of measurements for the hull within the rabbet line of keel, stem and sternpost, and up to the 'sheer'. First a list is given to enable the diagonals in the body plan to be drawn and then a table gives dimensions for constructing the cross sections in it. There are six diagonals in this case. Although other columns give the 'main breadth' and the 'sheer height' above the keel rabbet, there are no further dimensions to extend the body plan sections between the top diagonal and the sheer. However, by using the same Dixon Kemp curve which had faired in the body plan, the sections were extended upwards. Additional data had given the bulwark height as three feet, and the tumblehome at sheer and main deck rail, so that the midship section was certainly correct. The rake of the sternpost and the shape of the stem rabbet were given. The breadths at main deck rail from stations H to Q were also given, so that the flare at the bows was correct.

Fortunately, a copy had been made of a Brocklebank lines plan of an unnamed vessel of '175 tons' with the Whatman paper on which it was drawn bearing a watermark of 1821. The hull form turned out to be very similar. At first it was thought that it might be the *Maypo* herself as she is the only vessel around this period of 175 tons, and the figures '84 22 & 13-4' appear under the stem on this plan — figures which are surely the three principal dimensions and which closely approximate those of the *Maypo*. This plan provided useful data for the shape of the stern and rudder, keel and stem thickness, and run of topsides. No head was shown, and this has been taken from the sail plan of the schooner *Courier* and adjusted to suit the scale. The plan was drawn at ¼in scale as it enables the sail plan to fit conveniently on the sheet, whereas the Brocklebank plans at this date were in proportional scales such as 1:30 for *Oberon*, 1:25 for *Dash* and probably 1:35 or 36 for *Courier*, which would make the head of the masts disappear off the sheet.

The resultant plan is a fine-lined hull with considerable deadrise, floors that curve up into slack bilges and topsides which tumble home to give an elegant body plan. The conventional waterlines have been plotted and these produce a short, sharp convex entrance, a long middle body which really curves all the way although there are two deadflats; and finally a long fine run with some hollow near the sternpost. It is certainly a hull form designed for a fair turn of speed, and hulls of this kind indicate that Brocklebank ships were not intended to carry the maximum amount of cargo without regard to their sailing qualities. It is often said that shipbuilders who built for their own account did not require fast vessels but merely ones to carry the maximum amount of paying cargo, but it looks as if some reappraisal of the design of Brocklebank ships is now due.

The sail plan of *Bonanza* in figure 92 is full of interest, and the most notable feature is the great rake of the masts. Most entries in Brocklebank's notebook do not give either mast spacings or the rake, but both are given here, presumably because she departed from the customary sail plan. The foremast rakes 1½in to a foot, the mainmast 2in and the mizen 2½in. In the mast spacings, dimensions

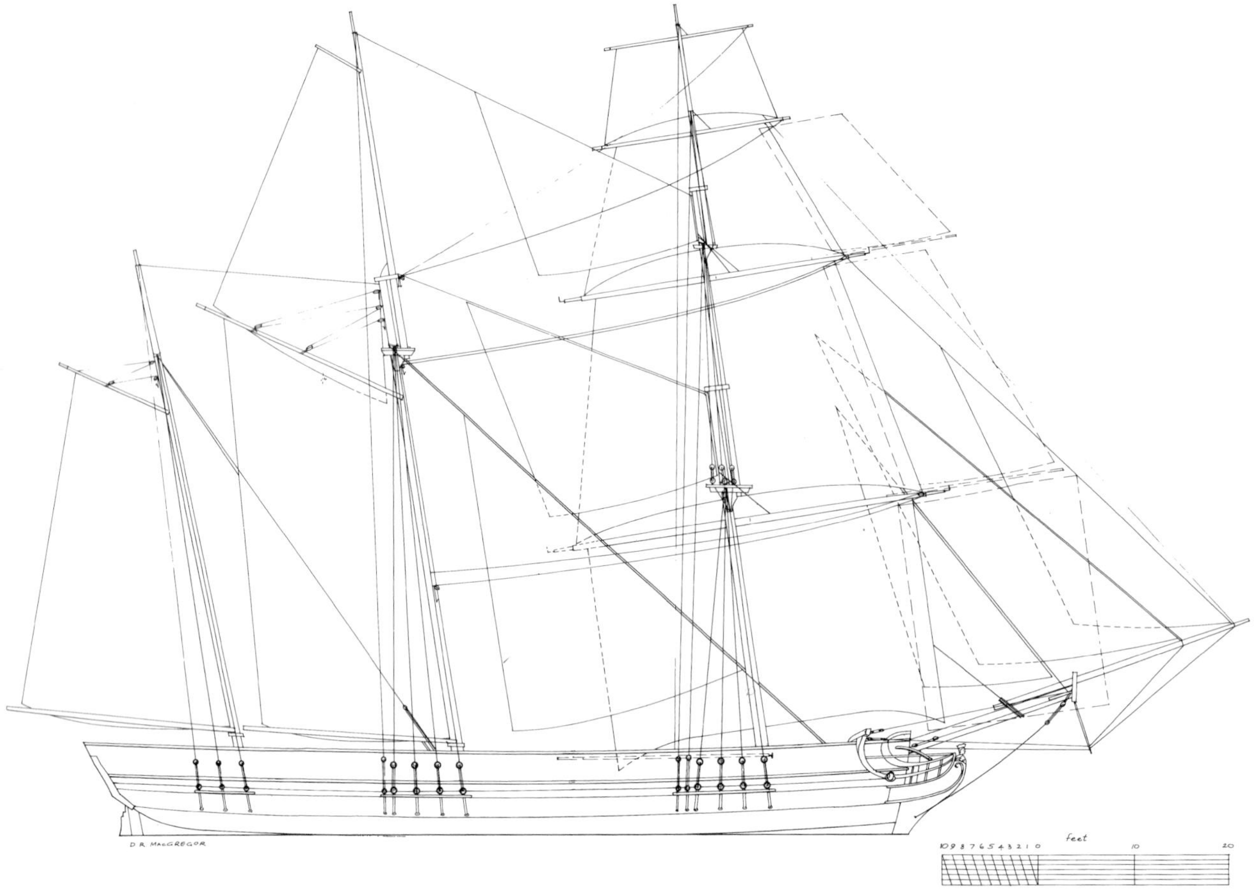

92: *Bonanza.* Sail plan: Reconstructed by the author from builder's spar dimensions. Reconstruction: bowsprit, jibboom, dolphin striker, yardarms, mizzen gaff, length of doubling on mainmast, all rigging, all stunsail booms and yards, all sail outlines.

93: With a broad white band on a black hull, the brig *Rimac*, and an unidentified Brocklebank brigantine, are in company. This picture is included to illustrate the sort of appearance which the *Bonanza* would have had. *Merseyside County Museum.*

are taken from the 'huddin' which is assumed to mean the 'hood ends' or where the planking fits into the stem rabbet. No dimensions are given for bowsprit or jibboom, for yardarms, mizzen gaff, doubling on mainmast, or dolphin striker. Nor are any stunsail booms listed; they hardly ever were by shipbuilders, but they always formed part of the inventory. The absence of a trysail gaff on the foremast makes the rig of an 'orthodox' pattern, but the stepping of the foremast so far forward results in having to provide a bumpkin to bowse down the fore tack, even though the leeches of the fore course are cut without a gore. It seems unlikely that the foot would have been shorter than the head. The staysails from the mainmast follow the pattern of those in the sail plan of the brigantine *Oberon*, as do the headsails. The head yard of the main topsail is drawn on the evidence of the words 'Gaff Top Gaff' under the list of mainmast spars, although no figure is entered in the column. She was later converted into a brig between the years 1841–43, but no dimensions of the new rig have been found.

The Brocklebank ships appear to have been expensively built at prices double those charged by Alexander Hall & Sons and must have had a very complete outfit. Because they built their own ships there was no need for Brocklebank's to obtain competitive tenders and there may have been different bookkeeping methods. The barque *Irt* of 215 tons, built by them in the same year as the *Dash*, cost £29 per ton.[45]

Some 50 years were to elapse before the barquentine rig was widely adopted but the brigantine rig became increasingly popular as the century advanced, and apart from distinct changes in hull form, it varied little with the passing years, while the deck arrangements and rigging details proved to be repetitions of those found on brigs and schooners. Numerous illustratons suggest the rig was much in use with slavers and opium clippers, both of which types needed fine-lined hulls.

Leith smacks

The cutters of the nineteenth century combined the sharp hull-forms and large sail plans of those seen before 1800, although the use of square canvas was lessening until only a single yard was carried.

One of the best known examples of the sloop or cutter rig was to be seen in the Leith smacks which carried passengers and cargo between Scottish ports and London, and which were at their perfection in the 50 years before the railway linked London and the north. Their design was a compromise between a fast passenger boat, a big cargo carrier and a weatherly vessel; and the result, according to Peter Hedderwick's plan and a model in the Science Museum, London, of the *Comet* (built 1809 at Bridport of 156 tons), was a fairly full-bodied hull incorporating a fine run and capable of high sustained speed. Living at Leith, Hedderwick was in a good position to observe and design numbers of these smacks and he wrote that 'the London and Leith smacks (about 200 tons register) are burdensome vessels; - and they steer and sail uncommonly well, and go but little by the stern'.[46] The surprisingly full-bodied hull given by Hedderwick to his smack of 173 tons makes her very little finer than his schooner *Glasgow* and therefore an interesting comparison with the Post Office packet *Sylph* which has much finer lines. There is a strong family likeness between Hedderwick's smack and the Berwick smack whose lines are given by David Steel in 1805,[47] and the shape of the midship section, hull-form, rake of bow and stern are almost identical. Steel's smack measured 140 tons and was already an established type, carrying passengers and fresh salmon from Berwick to London. When giving evidence before a Parliamentary Select Committee in 1819, Hedderwick thought that the design for a Post Office packet between Holyhead and Howth should be 'a little sharper' than the design for a Leith smack. Perhaps the Committee thought his designs for Leith smacks were too full-bodied because they thrice asked him if he could design faster and finer-lined vessels:

'If they were to be built merely for the purpose of carrying passengers and mails, would you construct them so as to sail faster than they now do?' — 'I think I could.'

'If you were to build a packet, you would build her with finer lines than that?' — 'Yes.'

'In constructing a packet to sail between Holyhead and Dublin, you would alter the lines, in as much as they would be calculated for sailing instead of stowage?' — 'Yes, taking off some of the bottom.'[48]

The proposed design submitted by Peter Hedderwick actually shows greater deadrise and easier bilges than his Leith smack.[49]

Peter Hedderwick stated that the shortest passage time he knew of between London and Leith, on a course of 460 miles, was 50 to 54 hours, which works out at the exceptionally fast average of 8½ to 9¼ knots, although a normal quick passage was of about five to six days, and with contrary winds and bad weather could run into several weeks. Captain Todd of the smack *Eagle* said in his evidence that his fastest speed by the log, when running free, had been 10½ knots. In going to windward, his smack was little inferior to the revenue cutters and once had the advantage over a Harwich Post Office packet. He explained that the *Eagle* had to take the ground and remain in a tolerably upright position, which is why the packets were built a little fuller than purely passenger craft. The *Eagle* was built in 1814 at 196 tons and Hedderwick considered her a perfect example of a smack.[50]

	Hedderwick's Smack	*Matchless (built 1810 at Bridport)*
Length for tonnage	73ft-2in	71ft-0in
Extreme breadth	23ft-6in	23ft-9in
Depth of hold	12ft 6in	12ft-0in
Tonnage	173 47/94	170 25/94

Whereas many of Peter Hedderwick's other plans have been identified as representing actual vessels, it has not been possible to repeat this with any certainty for his smack although the measurements of the *Matchless* agree very closely. This smack is one of six whose particulars he lists (see above).[51]

The lines of Hedderwick's smack have been redrawn as figure 94 becaue the plate in his

94: Hedderwick's Leith Smack Lines plan: Unidentified smack, but probably designed by Peter Hedderwick c 1820-25. Redrawn from Plate CVII in *Treatise on Marine Architecture* by Peter Hedderwick (1830); Dimensions on plan: 73ft-2in (keel and forerake) × 23ft-6in (breadth) × 12ft-6in (depth of hold); 173 47/94 tons. Reconstruction: diagonal lines and cant frames omitted; whole length of bowsprit drawn.

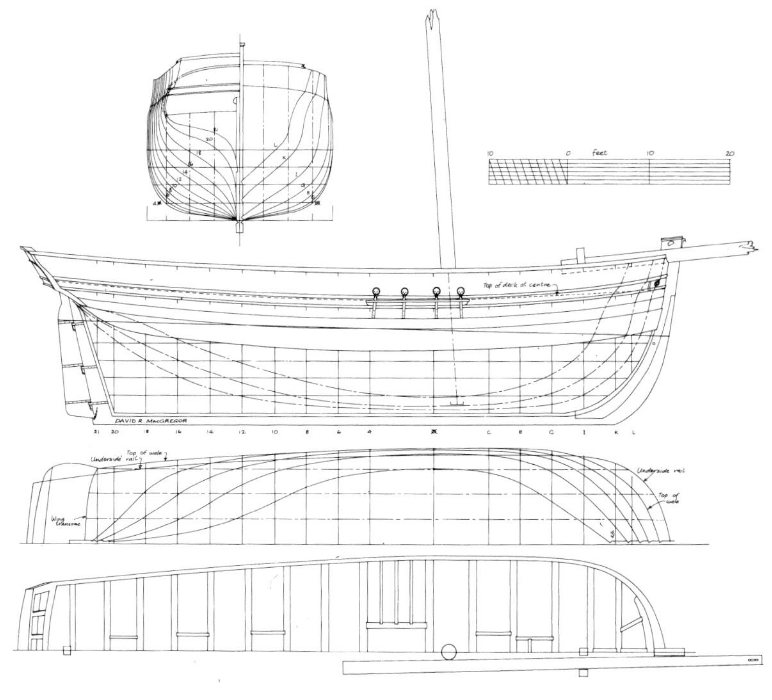

95: Leith Smack drawn by T W Ward. This is based on a model in the Science Museum, London, of the smack *Comet* built in 1809. This drawing is intended to show the deck fittings and the fullness of her hull.

book was confused with so many construction lines, and not all the waterlines and buttock lines were plotted. Compared with his schooner *Glasgow*, the deadrise and curve of the bilge are identical, but the smack has 14 inches more beam and 12 inches less depth of hold. The entrance is identical but the run is finer, which the additional rake to the sternpost assists. An interesting feature is the heavy shoulder worked into the bow sections with the flare above. On a load line length of 74ft-0in and an assumed maximum speed of ten knots, the speed-length ratio of this smack is the high figure of 1.16. On the deck plan, Hedderwick had only dotted on part of the bowsprit to show how it could be run in, but here the full length is drawn. Although there is no windlass on his plan, one is listed in his Table of Dimensions together with a winch.[52] A set of lines taken off the Science Museum's model of the smack *Comet* reveals that she and Hedderwick's smack spring from the same stock, although the *Comet* is of a somewhat fuller hull form.[53] From this model, the hull at least of which is contemporary, William Ward has made a drawing to depict the deck fittings and run of the planking (figure 95). The deck layout is basically similar to Hedderwick's smack, apart from minor differences which are centred on the number of deck openings abaft the main hatch: in Hedderwick's smack, the foremost of these three openings was probably a cargo hatch, and of the next two, one was a companionway and the other a skylight.

In the matter of costs, Alexander Hall built the *Rotterdam Packet* of 112 tons in 1816 for £12 12s per ton; in 1835 he built the *Cock of the North* of 59 tons — hardly in the same class — for £8. 12. 6. per ton.[54] At Ipswich, George Bayley contracted in 1822–23 for a Leith smack of 200 tons at £12 per ton.[55] Hall's costs included hull, spars and joiner's work.

The huge mainsail sported by the smacks was a great feature of the rig, together with the long bowsprit and lofty mast. Peter Hedderwick's smack has a main boom 66ft-0in long and a bowsprit projecting 38ft-0in outside the stem head. J C Schetky's painting of the Leith smack *Queen Charlotte* (1802) under a press of sail, figure 97, exhibits the triangular topmast stunsail that appears on Hedderwick's sail plan, and also the square topsail with its short head-yard that was probably bent to the sail before it left the deck. The short yard at the head of the square sail is similar to that on the schooner *Alexander*, as is the method of booming out the clew. The narrow foot of the lower stunsail is bent to a boom and set flying, rather like Steel's collier brig. These huge sails required large, skilful crews to manage them

96: Hedderwick's Leith Smack. Sail plan: Redrawn from Plate XXV in Hedderwick's book. Reconstruction: centres of gravity of each sail omitted; square canvas and triangular stunsail drawn dotted and latter corrected. No ratlines drawn by Hedderwick.

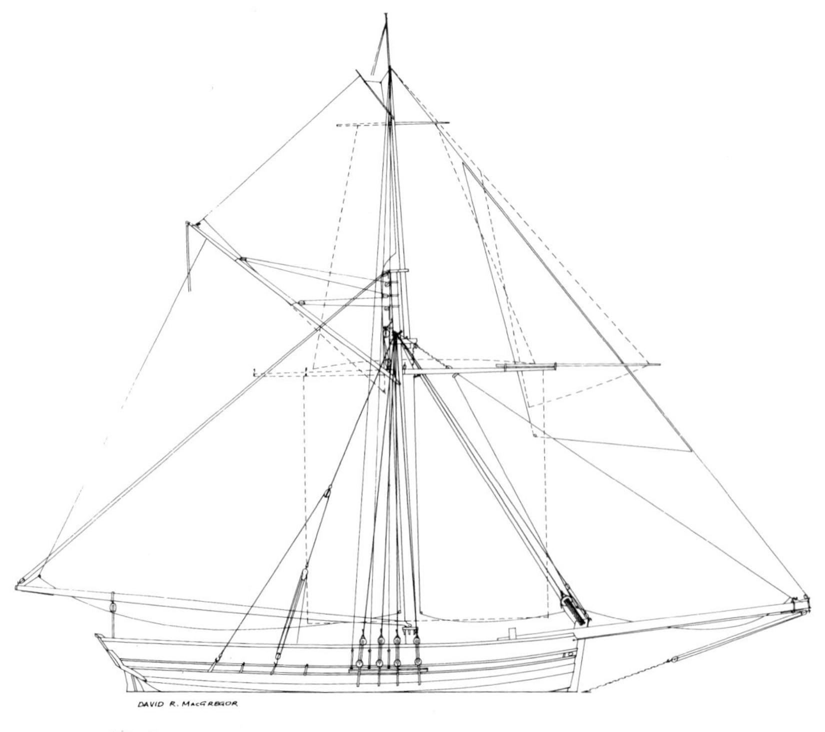

and it was by means of these excessive areas of canvas that the masters drove the straining hulls to obtain their fast passages. A typical crew comprised a master, mate, steward and eleven able seamen.

'Three taps on the forecastle hatch by the mate', records one who served his time in the smack *King William* in the 1830s, 'was the signal for all hands to turn out and reef down the mainsail. When this had to be done, they knew that there was no time to put off, for the sail was carried as long as the ship would stand up under it. It was no uncommon thing for the boom to be trailing in the water. To reef the big mainsail was no easy task, and when it had to be done in the middle of a dark and stormy night — perhaps during a blinding snowstorm — it was not completed without risk.'[56]

In 1819, a Holyhead packet of 102 tons could carry four carriages on deck and eight horses, and had berths for 22 passengers. The cabin passengers naturally fared best, the after of the two cabins being reserved for ladies. All the passengers dined in the main cabin around which were the beths — shuttered bunks or small staterooms — for the men. Steerage passengers had no cabin and slept anywhere they could.[57]

When beating up the congested River Thames, north country collier brigs with their bluff, sturdy hulls often forced other craft to give way, but they feared the Leith smacks. Captain Andrew Shewan relates why:

> 'When Geordie was a bit obstinate (requiring a lesson) the "Scot" would give way apparently; but with two or three hands standing by the heelrope of the jibboom he would carefully stick his "horn" through his rival's mainsail or trysail, which being rent, the offending boom was allowed to run inboard and the smack's stern allowed to graze Geordie's quarter and should his small boat be hanging in the stern davits, probably leave it dangling by one tackle. Poor Geordie had no remedy for this but language, which being received [with] laughter only, was entirely unsatisfactory.'[58]

These then were the smacks. But the question remains: why were so many built in the southwest of England, as a discussion in the *Mariner's Mirror* pointed out?[59] Out of 23 smacks sailing in and out of Leith in 1832–33, ten were built at Bridport, four at Topsham, two in 'Wales', one at Ipswich, one at Blythnook and five at Leith.[60] In his evidence to the Select Committee in 1819, Peter Hedderwick, who had had at least one smack built to his design at Topsham, gave his reason as to why smacks were built in southwest England: 'We think there is rather more choice of timber'. Such an answer is rather unsatisfactory in the present context. The 1824 edition of the *London and Leith Smack and Steam-Yacht Guide* describes Bridport as 'a maritime town of Dorsetshire noted for the skill with which its shipwrights build vessels of the class in question'.[61] Good was the principal builder of smacks there and had constructed the *Matchless*; Robert Davy was the principal builder at Topsham.

It is difficult to resolve problems concerning spheres of influence, but the ports of the English Channel had by 1810 achieved fame and notoriety for building fast naval cutters, smugglers and revenue cutters. One must

97: The Leith smack *Queen Charlotte* (1802), from a painting by J C Schetky. The triangular topmast stunsail and short head to the square topsail are similar to those on Hedderwick's plan (figure 96), but the head of the square foresail is different. *Mariners' Museum.*

98: *Harmony*. Outline sail plan: reconstructed from builder's cost account, as transcribed by James Henderson, and Hedderwick's proportions. Built in 1823 by A Hall & Sons, Aberdeen, of 75 tons. See David R MacGregor *Merchant Sailing Ships 1815–1850* (pages 72-3) for fuller details of this smack and her cost itemized.

suppose that a Leith firm of shipowners, requiring a smack for the booming Leith to London passenger service, decided to obtain one from an area known to build fast vessels and the smack so obtained, either second-hand or built on speculation, led the way to firm orders being placed for others. However, the lines of Hedderwick's smack, David Steel's Berwick smack, and the Science Museum's model of the *Comet* all show a flat-floored, powerful hull with undoubted ability to carry a press of sail in all weathers, features insisted upon and corroborated by the evidence given to the Select Committee by designers and skippers. Thus the finer lines and big deadrise of the English south coast cutters were not adopted in the Leith smacks. This suggests that Bridport and Topsham builders got the work because they were accustomed to build large cutters of up to 200 tons but that the design was based on the current northeast coast equivalent of the Berwick smacks, of which Peter Hedderwick was an important exponent.

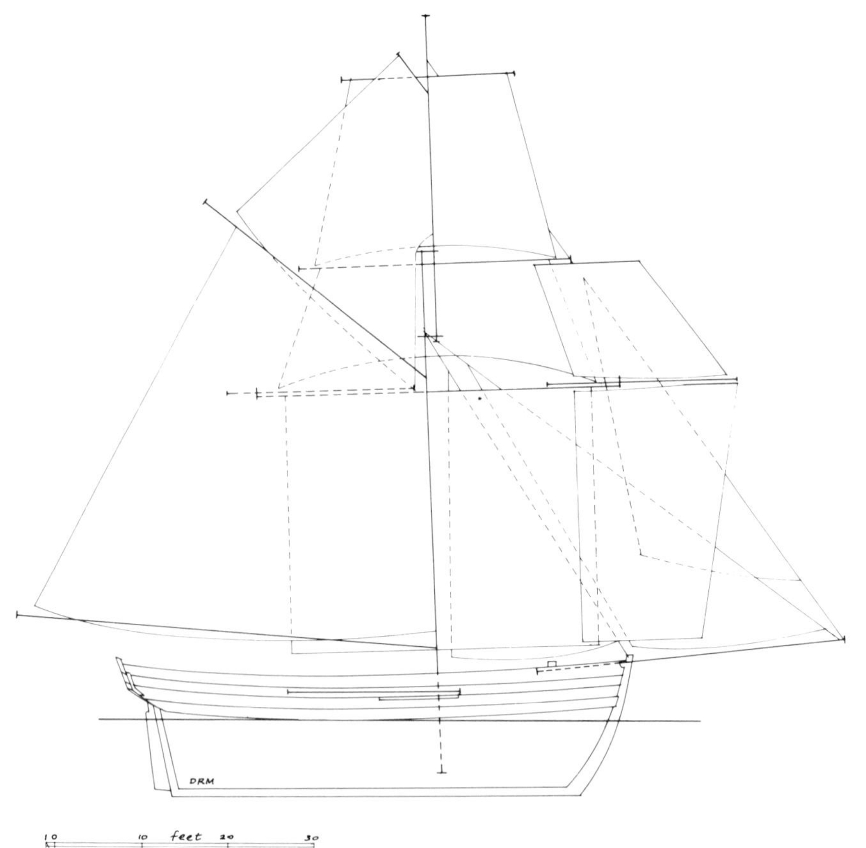

In the 1830s many of the smacks were lengthened and converted into schooners. In the following decade, several companies re-equipped themselves with fast Aberdeen schooners similar to the *Scottish Maid*. Captain Ritchie, manager of the Leith & London Shipping Co, reported most favourably on their three new Aberdeen schooners, *Nonsuch, Rapid* and *Swift*, both as regards speed of sailing and cargo-carrying abilities. 'I can say with truth, that any of these clippers will go twice as fast by the wind (that is, to windward) in blowing weather as the *Robert Bruce*, the best and only smack of the Company's old ships they have not sold . . .'[62] In the 1850s the packet companies began to replace all their sailing vessels with steamships.

Clipper schooners

Although cutters and sloops were employed in ocean trade until the middle of the century – in the fruit trade several were in constant use – the schooner rig was gradually gaining in popularity, particularly after the 1820s.

99: The Dartmouth-built schooner *King of Tyre*, pictured in 1837 when passing Gibraltar on passage from Messina to London, carries as much square canvas as a brigantine. The passaree boom to the clew of her square foresail is effective with a quartering wind. *F A L Fairweather.*

The use of square canvas on a schooner's foremast, sometimes so great in area as almost to convert the craft into a brigantine, enabled her to make ocean passages with greater reliability, while the large area of fore-and-aft canvas gave her good speed to windward. The Dartmouth-built schooner *King of Tyre*, pictured off Gibraltar in 1837, figure 99, is a good example of such a vessel; she even has a spar to boom out the foot of her square sail. The perishable nature of fresh fruit cargoes always required fast vessels, although speed was not quite so vital with dried fruit. Due to the delicate condition of fresh fruit, only small vessels of under 150 tons were employed, else the cargo would be crushed in too large a vessel and the speculative risks inherent in such a cargo would be too highly concentrated. Although no single book has yet been written on the fruit trade, it has been treated in some detail in works by Basil Greenhill, Michael Bouquet and others.[63]

A builder of several fruit schooners was James B Balley of Shoreham (1788–1863). About 1818 he was taken into partnership by the shipbuilder John Edwards so that the business went under the name of Edwards & Balley, but later it passed entirely under Balley's control. From the early 'thirties he was building clipper brigs and schooners for trade to the Mediterranean, Africa and South America. These included such names as the *Sancho Panza* (1828), *Saucy Jack* (1834), *Aimwell* (1835), *Minstrel Boy* (1839), *Parga* (1840), *Dusty Miller* (1841), *Freak* (1845) and *Spirit* (1845).[64] Another such vessel was the *Emma*, built in 1830, which measured 142 tons; she was framed with English oak and equipped with a longboat, a jolly boat, and a windlass, but no capstan. Against her entry in the 1831 edition of *Lloyd's Register* (red volume) is the abbreviation 'Shrp', standing for 'Sharp', an abbreviation which occurs occasionally in the registers; in this case it corroborates the type of hull form for which James Balley was celebrated. Had there been no windlass, the schooner *Emma* might have been considered a suitable candidate for the Science Museum's model of the *Emma* of Sidmouth. James Balley was probably also

100: The significance of two vessels together in a painting usually indicates some common ground, and the reason in this case is because both vessels were owned in Limerick, although *Lloyd's Register* gives assigns a different owner to each. The brig lowering her skysails, is the *Minstrel Boy* which Balley of Shoreham built in 1839 with a tonnage of 244; the schooner *Harriet* is assumed to be the one built at Southampton in 1834 with a tonnage of 186. The rock of Gibraltar is in the background and the artist is W J Huggins. *Parker Gallery.*

101: Here is another of Balley's schooners, although she looks more like a brigantine with four square sails set on the foremast and three stunsails on each side. The label at the bottom reads: 'The Schooner *Parga* of London/Samuel Tozer Sanders, Commander, 1852'. The *Parga* was built in 1840. *MacGregor Collection.*

102: Three schooners built at Shoreham in 1833 which were employed in the Waterford and Bristol packet trade. Their names, left to right, are *Alexander, Rapid* and *Martha,* and this engraving was made in the year they were built. The *Alexander*'s square sail is of a style to be found in large cutters, with its short head yard. *Parker Gallery.*

responsible for building in 1831 the fruit schooner *Pera* of 143 tons, which in 1834 sailed from London to the Greek island of Syra in 21 days.

Prior to the mid 'thirties, few packet companies employed schooners although the Waterford Line, which connected with Bristol, did so. An engraving from a painting by John Lynn, dated 1833 and reproduced in figure 102, shows the three sister ships *Alexander, Martha* and *Rapid* which were each of about 175 tons and were built in 1833 at Shoreham by James Balley. The *Alexander* and *Martha* were owned by Pope & Co, but the *Rapid* was owned by her master, W Millar, who probably chartered her to Pope & Co. In 1839 the *Rapid* passed into the hands of the London and Waterford Shipping Association, but not before she had made a fast passage out to Mauritius where she came under the notice of James Blyth, as will be reported later. Large schooners thought nothing of participating in ocean trade if their services were in demand. These three schooners would have been little different from the fruiters of their day and the engraving shows them under different points of sail. The head of the *Alexander*'s square sail is laced to a short yard at the centre and is reminiscent of the square sail set by cutters like the *Fly* (figure 17), and John C Schetky's water-colour of the Leith smack under sail (figure 97) shows a similar version of this sail. The *Alexander*, like the *King of Tyre*, has the weather clew of the square sail extended on a passaree boom which virtually does duty for a square lower stunsail.

Several of the fast fruit schooners, such as the *Hellas* (1832) and *Time*, were purchased at the end of the 1830s for the opium trade. The *Time* was built at Poplar in 1832 by Fletcher, Son & Fearnall, being designed by Thomas J Ditchburn who was Fletcher's manager; she measured 85ft-9in by 19ft-9in by 10ft-9in and 139 tons. This was undoubtedly the ship that Ditchburn referred to in 1860 during a discussion at the Institution of Naval Architects on raking midship sections, when he remarked:

'I built a vessel for the Smyrna trade upon the principle described by Mr Maudslay, with a diagonal midship section, and as far as sailing qualities are concerned, she answered exceedingly well, although she did not carry cargo enough to make her answer pecuniarily. After making a few voyages she was sold as a yacht. But there was good in this principle – that she had an increased amount of stability, which prevented oscillation in a transverse direction, and checked the longitudinal pitching, which it is so desirable to get rid of.'[65]

103: *Susanna.* Built in 1838 by T & J Brocklebank at Whitehaven. Redrawn from builder's plan by courtesy of T & J Brocklebank, Liverpool. Dimensions: 59ft-9in × 15ft-9in × 8ft-2in; 65 tons. Reconstruction: upper deadeyes, shrouds and backstays. Scale of original probably 1:36.

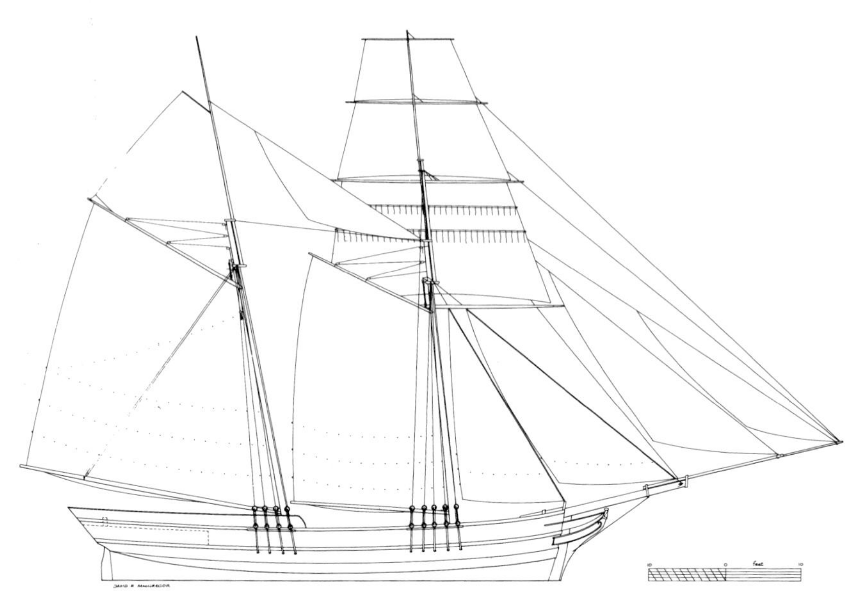

In vessels with a raking midship section, as proposed by Joseph Maudslay, the entrance became longer and finer but the fuller run was compensated by an increased fineness of the buttock lines.

When examined for possible use as an opium clipper, the *Time* is reported to have had so much deadrise that it was necessary to stand with one foot on the keelson and the other on the ceiling.[66] Presumably this must have meant anywhere in the hold, otherwise the statement is valueless. She had the reputation of being the smartest vessel in the Mediterranean fruit trade and was rigged as a ranterpike schooner, but was altered to an ordinary topsail schooner when entering the opium trade.

The ranterpike rig is rarely referred to but apparently necessitated that one of the upper masts on the foremast was stepped abaft the other. The ranterpike schooners built on the Clyde from the 1840s had their long fore topmasts fidded abaft the head of the lower masts.[67] Alternatively, the fore topgallant mast could be stepped abaft the fore topmast, as was reported by one who had sailed aboard a 'Glasgow Rantipike' in the 1870s.[68] This latter arrangement would be an apt description of that drawn in the sail plan of a schooner identified as the *Susanna* and built by T & J Brocklebank in 1838. The plan is reproduced in figure 103 and included here as representing a heavily-rigged schooner of the type that might have been engaged in the fruit trade. The topgallant mast is a light spar and could be sent down in heavy weather without endangering the effectiveness of the rig, because all the headsails lead from the topmast or the lower mast. In square-rigged vessels, a spar such as the *Susanna*'s topgallant mast would be described as a 'sliding gunter pole'. It is suggested that the *Time* was rigged in the same manner as the *Susanna*.

The *Susanna* was never owned by Brocklebank's but built by them for others, although her first owners have so far not been traced. She measured 59ft-9in by 15ft-9in by 8ft-2in and 65 tons. As she was registered at Dublin in 1861 it may be that she began life in Ireland, perhaps at Limerick or Waterford where quite a number of Mediterranean traders seem to have been owned.

By the mid 'forties the very lofty rig to be seen in schooners like the *Susanna* or the *King of Tyre* was being replaced by shorter masts,

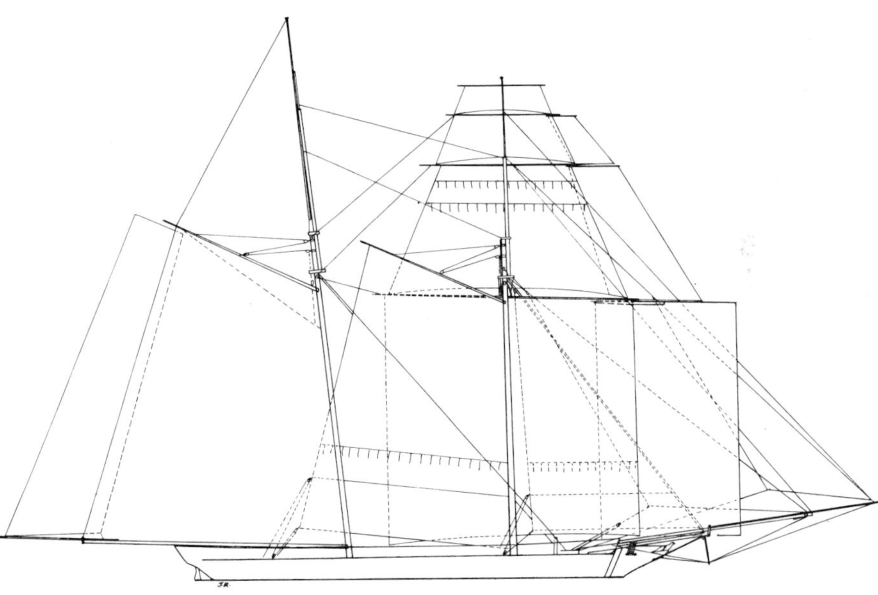

104: HMS *Jackdaw*. Built in 1829–30 at Chatham as a cutter. Reproduced from Admiralty plan in National Maritime Museum. Dimensions: 60ft-9in (length on deck) × 20ft-3in (breadth extreme) × 9ft-0in (depth in hold); 107 73/94 tons. Converted to schooner in 1832; this plan shows manner of lengthening spars at a later date. This plan was redrawn for greater clarity. Reconstruction: sails and rigging behind other sails are drawn dotted; reef points added.

but this slight reduction in canvas area was compensated by the sharper entrance given to the hull; simultaneously, to avoid the bow being buried in the sea, the foremast was stepped further aft. The hull was now increased in length and most schooners set three headsails from the fore crosstrees. In many cases the rabbet of the stem was given considerable rake, like an Aberdeen schooner, although the bow was not usually terminated in quite the Aberdeen manner. The freeboard was also reduced somewhat and the new style of clipper schooner is depicted in the painting of the Salcombe schooner *Queen of the West*, built in 1849. Some fine-lined schooners were built of iron during the 'forties and there are small sketches of midship sections on the Lloyd's Register survey reports, which indicate considerable deadrise. During the 'forties, clipper schooners were employed even more extensively in the fruit, fish-carrying, opium and packet trades.

An idea of the amount of canvas carried by a schooner is given on the sail plan of HMS *Jackdaw*, reproduced in figure 104.[69] The *Jackdaw* was one of six cutters of the *Lark* class, built in 1829–30 and converted to a schooner in 1832 for surveying purposes, but this plan is of a later date after the spars had been lengthened. In some merchant schooners the fore staysail would have been divided into two sails by the end of the 'thirties. Notes on the *Jackdaw*'s sail plan specify that the lowermast heads should be square without sheave holes; that for the 'foremast fore crosstree should be very much curved'; that the trestletrees and crosstrees were to be as light as possible without cheeks at the hounds; that the dolphin striker should be fixed to an eyebolt in the bowsprit and allowed to 'work free'. Like the *King of Tyre* and some other schooners, the fore royal yard is not fitted with braces.

The *Hellas* was the other fruiter mentioned as becoming an opium clipper. Like the *Time*, she was launched n 1832, being built at Waterford, and measured 91ft-4in by 23ft-0in by 14ft-10in and 209 tons. With a hull look-

105: The *Hellas* was in the fruit trade before she became the opium clipper pictured here. Like most brigantines of this date, she carries a standing fore gaff. Until the 1840s and even later, this sort of rig usually went by the name of 'schooner'. *Parker Gallery.*

ing more like a gun-brig, she was then described as a 'schooner' although to judge by Brierly's lithograph of her we should call her a 'brigantine' (figure 105). As this lithograph was dedicated to A Grant, it probably shows her during her days as an opium clipper. She is depicted with sliding gunter poles running abaft the heads of the masts, which shows more clearly on the mainmast.

Some fine-lined slavers were captured in these years and one, the *Theresa Secunda*, was taken in 1832 by HM brig *Pelorus* when flying Spanish colours. She had 460 slaves aboard, was condemned at Sierra Leone, and sold to the Hon R F Greville who converted her into a yacht with the name of *Xarifa*. Lines taken off after she became a yacht were published by Howard Chapelle in *Search for Speed under Sail* (figure 89), and these show that she had a long, shallow hull with big deadrise and sharp, convex waterlines. She measured 90ft-8in by 21ft-11in by 9ft-6in and 177 tons. Chapelle lists her spar dimensions but does not reconstruct her sail plan. These dimensions allow for lower, topsail and topgallant yards on the foremast to give her a conventional schooner rig of her date. She is recorded as having been constructed at Philadelphia in 1831. Greville sold her in 1839 and she eventually became an opium clipper on the China coast.[70]

During the 1820s and 1830s, shipbuilders on Chesapeake Bay turned out a number of fine-lined craft for the fruit trade to Florida and the Bahamas, the coffee trade to Brazil, the slave trade to Africa and the coastal packet trade for passengers and selected merchandise. Many of these vessels were given a schooner rig. A few even had three masts.

A demand for clippers

A demand for fast ships was gradually developing in the 'thirties as a result of competitive business, when it was found that speculative deals had outpaced the modes of transport available and that the supply of fast ships was limited. Two London merchant houses provide examples. 'In 1834 the Barings had to abandon a silk venture for lack of a fast ship, by which they hoped to get control of the European market for two months. (Barings to Bryant & Sturgis 22nd

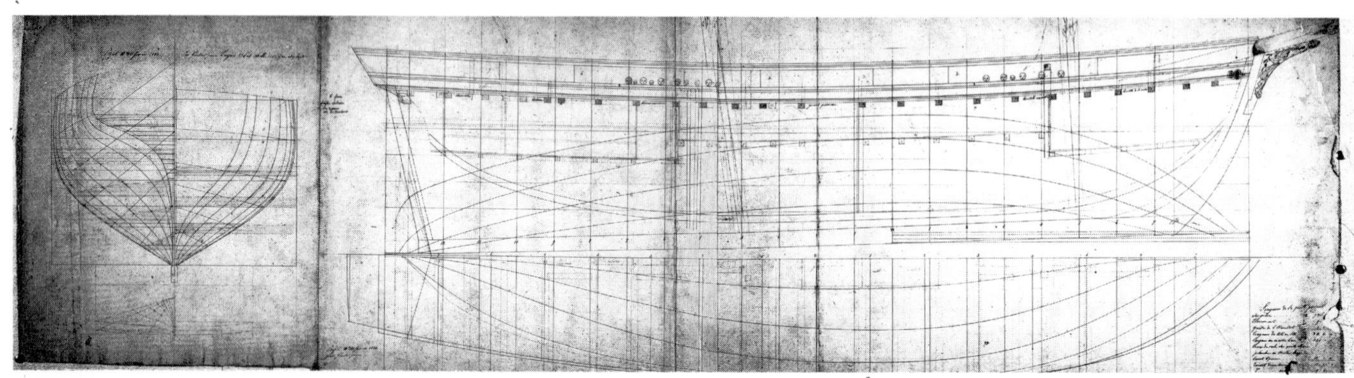

106: *Design for French schooner or brig.* Projected design dated February 1824 by Guibert Jnr. Reproduced from plan in Collection of Guibert drawings at Mariner's Museum, Newport News. Dimensions on plan in 'pieds': 84-2 (length from outer edge of stem to outer edge of sternpost) × 23-0 (breadth at midships) × 12-1 (depth of hold); 9-5 depth of water forward; 11-7 depth of water aft; 243 tons; [second figure superimposed on a '2']. No rig specified and no spar dimensions given.

July 1834.) They also wanted a fast ship for an undesignated purpose in 1835. . .'[71] This possibly resulted in their purchase of the ship-rigged yacht *Falcon* in 1836.

The other example comes from extracts of letters written from Mauritius by James Blyth to the London office of Blyth, Green, Jourdain & Co. In April 1834 he wrote that loaded merchant ships seldom took less than 100 to 110 days to make the passage out to Mauritius,[72] but in October he records that the *Manchester* arrived on the 5th, 82 days from Falmouth,[73] and 11 months later the *Courier de St Paul* arrived only 64 days out, the shortest passage ever known.[74] Earlier the same year, perhaps realising the potentialities available by employing a fast ship, he had written to London: '. . . [If] you can make *sure of a rise* in sugar to an *important extent* and of sufficient *duration* to operate, despatch

107: An early photograph taken near Swansea in about 1845 by Calvert Jones. The bilge keel indicates a hull with more than the normal amount of deadrise and an attempt to prevent it heeling so far over when dried out. The schooner also has a fine, hollow run. The topsail yard is slung from the cap which was a rig very common on both sides of the North Sea prior to 1850.

110: This lofty brig is the slaver *Black Joke* which was built at Baltimore about 1824 and originally bore the same *Henriquetta*. She was captured in 1827 by HMS *Sybille* after making 6 trips and carrying 3040 slaves to Brazil. She had a length of 90ft-10in on the gun deck and a beam of 26ft-7in. She was taken into the Royal Navy but never got her lines taken off; after serving for four years she became strained and was burned at Sierra Leone in May 1832. This drawing was made from a watercolour sketch done by J W Carmichael which is now in the Laing Art Gallery, Newcastle.

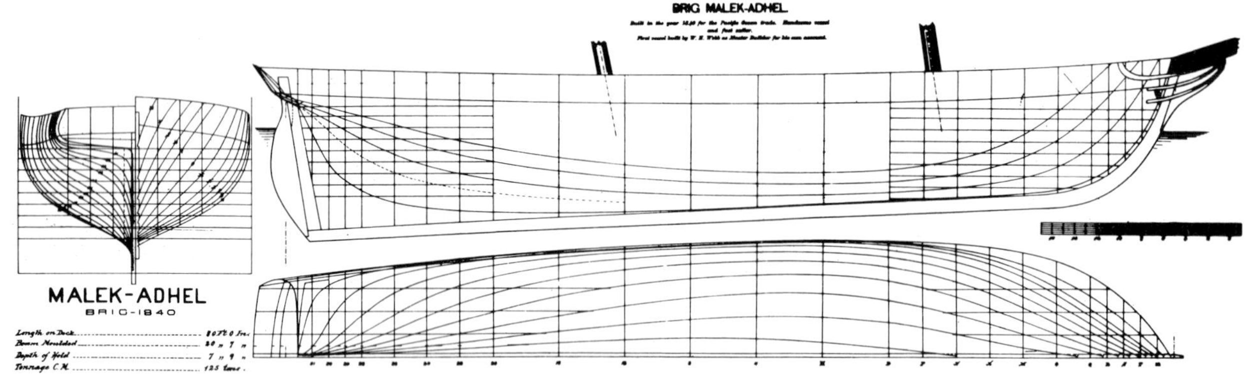

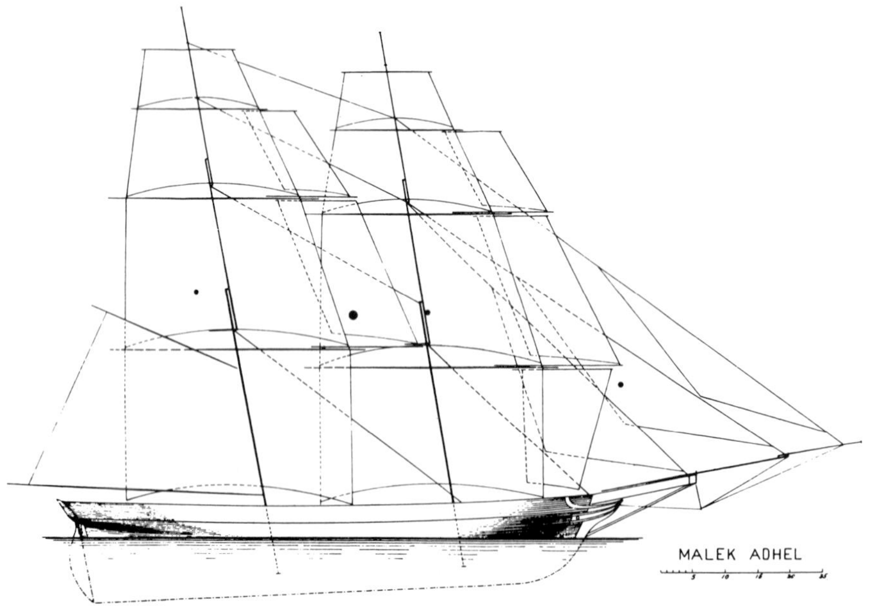

108: *Malek-Adhel.* Built in 1840 by William H Webb at New York. Reproduced from plan in his book, *Plans of Wooden Vessels.* Dimensions on plan: 80ft-0in (length on deck) × 20ft-7in (moulded breadth) × 7ft-9in (depth in hold); 125 tons. Built for Pacific Ocean trade. Webb called her a 'handsome vessel and fast sailer'. Rigged as a brig. A fairly typical example of a modified Baltimore clipper model, as built in New England, for use in trades where speed was of paramount importance.

109: *Malek-Adhel.* Outline sail plan: Reproduced from W H Webb's *Plans of Wooden Vessels.*

a *thorough* clipper to me . . . '[75] In October 1836 he wrote: 'I do not recommend the building of *clippers* carrying less than their tonnage, but of vessels rather sharper than the *Annabella* . . . The *Symmetos* (Riley), *Louisa* (McCatcheon) and *Annabella* (Anstruther) are the finest merchant ship models I have seen here.'[76] In the same letter he explained that the *Annabella* measured 199 tons and that her cost, together with 12 months' provisions, was £3,800 and that she carried 35% more deadweight than her register tonnage. This barque was built in 1834 at Port Glasgow, was owned there and classed 10 A1. *Lloyd's Register* for 1837 does not list any vessel named *Symmetos* but there is a ship called *Symmetry*, Captain W Riley, owned in London and built at Hull in 1833 of 293 tons. The same Register records that the *Louisa* was a brig of 181 tons, built at Yarmouth in 1834 and owned by her master.

Another letter from James Blyth at the end of 1836 stated that the brig *Lord Saumerez* had been sold for $6000 because she did not pay and that finer-lined craft were needed.[77] In 1837, he wrote that the *Rapid* was the only deep-laden clipper ever to have made a quick voyage.[78] This is undoubtedly the schooner of that name built at Shoreham in 1833 of 179 tons, which forms the centrepiece of figure 102.[79] Of interest is the fact that the vessels employed in the trade to Mauritius were frequently of less than 200 tons, which provides a useful reflection on the market and harbour conditions which only permitted the use of small ships.

James Blyth's remarks on the use of fast ships in commercial enterprises form a useful comment on the change of thinking that was overtaking the entrepreneur.

The Symondites

The building of large yachts which were intended to emulate and even surpass the naval brigs was another form in which the design of fast ships was stimulated. The arguments surrounding the supposedly inferior design of British men-of-war made headline news for a decade from the early 'twenties and resulted in a stream of books and pamphlets which increased to a torrent when Captain William Symonds was appointed Surveyor of the Navy in 1832 in succession to Sir Robert Seppings. Symonds' pamphlet, *Observations on Naval Architecture*, had appeared in 1824, but he was a naval officer with no training as a naval architect. His yacht designs, when he was stationed at Malta, had attracted the attention of the Hon George Vernon and eventually such highly placed influence and patronage induced the Navy Board in 1826 to have the 12-gun sloop *Columbine* built at Portsmouth to Symonds' own design.[80] Two smaller copies as ketch-rigged yachts were at once put in hand by George Vernon and the Duke of Portland, and the latter commissioned Symonds to build an improved version of a 10-gun brig as a yacht for himself. Named the *Pantaloon*, she was bought by the Navy in 1831. Three

111: HMS *Dolphin*. Lines plan: Built in 1836 at Sheerness; designed by Sir William Symonds. Redrawn from Admiralty plans in National Maritime Museum. Dimensions as built: 90ft-8in (between perpendiculars) × 29ft-3½in (extreme breadth) × 14ft-7¾in (depth in hold): 319 62/94 tons. Reconstruction: particulars from several plans combined on one sheet.

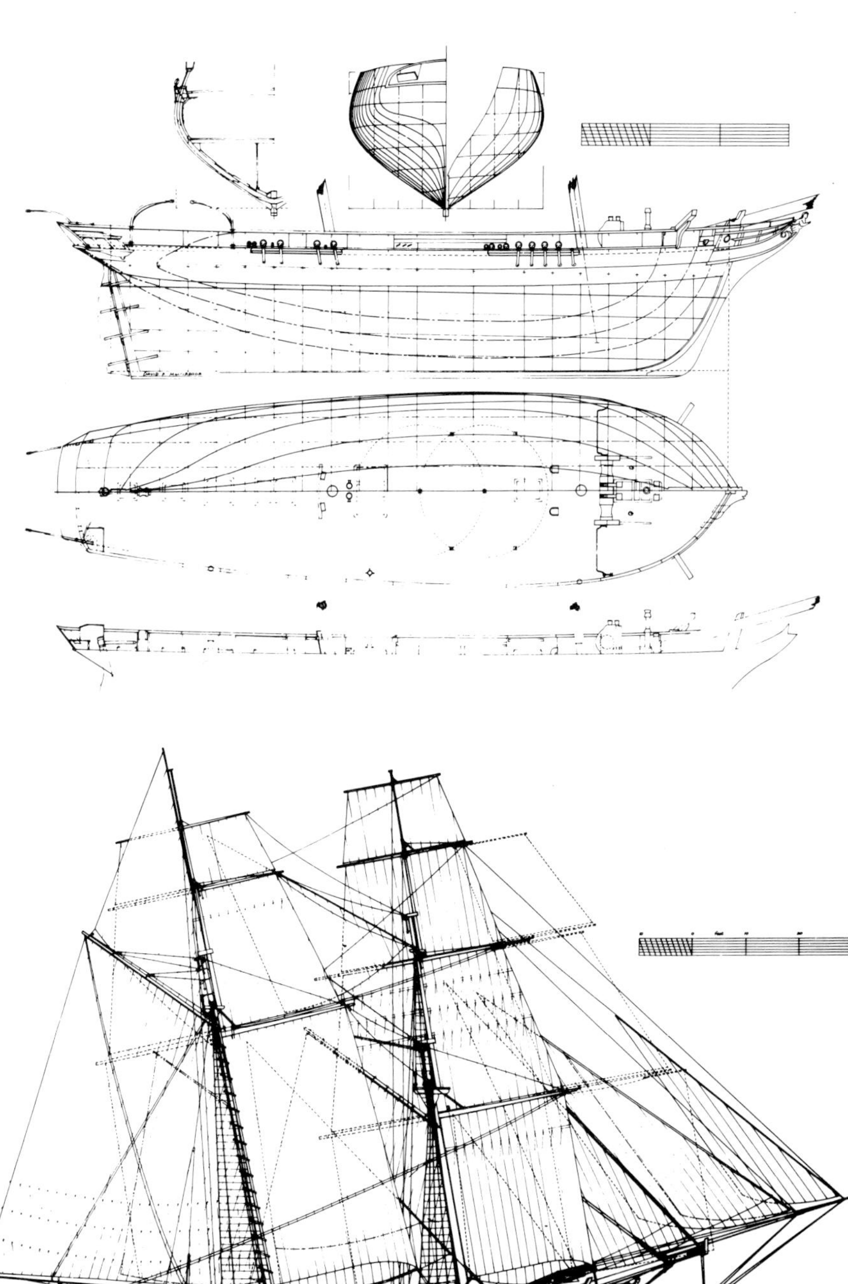

112: HMS *Dolphin*. Sail plan: Reconstructed from sheer elevation and outline sail plan showing sail cloths dated 'Jno Peek Oct 1836'. Reconstruction: thickness of masts and spars, standing and running rigging, stunsails. A lithograph by H J Vernon, dated 1836, shows no square sails on the main mast.

years later Lord Belfast commissioned Joseph White of Cowes to build a 10-gun brig that would be superior to Symonds' ships in all points and the resultant vessel, the *Waterwitch*, proved so fast and successful that the Admiralty in turn bought her.

An interesting sideline on the design of the *Waterwitch* is given by Thomas White Jnr, who recommended 'building all vessels designed for the same service from the same draft, by the mere application of different scales'. He continued: 'We find that the exact midship section of the *Harriet* cutter yacht, of 120 tons, built some twenty years since for the Marquis Donegal, then Lord Belfast, was extended and adopted in the *Waterwitch* brig, of 330 tons; and the same has been carried out in the *Daring*, of 450 tons, sufficiently so for the illustration of this point...'[81]

William Symonds was Surveyor to the Navy from 1832 to 1848, but all his ships had the same features: very steep deadrise with the turn of the bilge at about the load line or just above, and the maximum breadth at the height of the main deck. There was also great beam in proportion to length, the ratio being as low as 3¼ to 1in many cases. The ships he designed sailed fast and performed valuable work in chasing slavers, although their hard rolling made them unsteady gun platforms. The plan of HMS *Dolphin* (figure 111) has been redrawn from the original at the National Maritime Museum, Greenwich, and is included to show a typical example of Symonds' work. In the body plan, the steep deadrise, big tumblehome and maximum beam above the load line are all present. There is very little sheer but marked rake to the stem and sternpost. She was armed with one 32-pounder on a pivot and two 32-pounders on carriages. The method shown here of turning the windlass was employed in a number of warships of her size at this date. The detailed sail plan (figure 112) is redrawn from a small original plan showing the cloths, and from contemporary sources. Such a sail plan of a true brigantine was fitted in several opium clippers, slavers and other fast vessels. Tremendous overlap by a variety of sail combinations is a feature of this rig. Other points of interest show the head of the fore trysail hooped to the standing gaff; the absence of any roach in the foot of the square sails sheeting to a yard; the presence of a square sail below the main yard; and the tremendous hoist of the fore topmast staysail.

An account by the *Dolphin*'s mate, John Sibbald, tells of a race with White's *Waterwitch*, when looking for slavers off the African coast:

> 'We fell in with the *Waterwitch* off Cape Coast... and kept company until Wednesday 30th [November 1836], when we tried rate of sailing, with a fine breeze on the quarter, going 6 and 7 knots. At daylight the

113: HMS *Dolphin* chasing a slaver brig, from a lithograph by H J Vernon. It will be noticed that no square canvas is drawn here on the main topmast, although there is a vast amount on the sail plan. *Parker Gallery.*

114: This painting by W J Huggins represents the *Red Rover* which was built in 1829 by the Howrah Dock Company at Calcutta. She measured 97ft-7in × 24ft-0in × 11ft-10in and 254 tons. She was flush decked with raking stem and sternpost, and drew 2ft-6in more aft than forward. She is considered to have been one of the early opium clippers; unlike many of her contemporaries, she was not unduly lofty and so probably possessed fairly sharp lines. *Martyn Gregory Gallery.*

> *Waterwitch* was about half a mile on the weather-quarter, and at sunset she was astern 5 or 7 miles. The following day, and Friday, in sight; . . . The whole of the *Waterwitch*'s officers agree that we beat them at the rate of half a mile an hour, and are more surprised at being beaten than we are. Now we are the clipper of the Navy.'[82]

Opium clippers

Similar enthusiasm was felt amongst the opium clippers in Chinese waters as the following remarks in the *Canton Register* of 1835 suggest:

> 'We are happy to learn that the trials which are being made in England to ascertain the rate of sailing of many of the ships lately built by the surveyors of the navy on improved principles, are not disregarded in this distant quarter; but that they have given birth to a spirited emulation between the American and British ships at Lintin. It is well known that the merchant vessels of the United States are the fastest that sail the seas; their builders having paid more attention to this most essential quality of a ship than to construct them for the stowage of large cargoes; . . .'

The article continues with an account of two sailing trails between the American brig *John Gilpin* and the British brig *Fairy*. The latter was best on the starboard tack and the other on the port tack, but could not beat the British brig, being 'always abaft the *Fairy*'s beam; both trials were much alike and equally in favor of the *Fairy*, she having given the *Gilpin* her royals'.[83]

The maiden passage of the opium clipper *Red Rover*, whose design was based on that of the Baltimore clipper *Prince de Neuchâtel*, was made up the China Sea against the monsoon in February 1830, being only 22 days from Singapore Strait to Macao Roads, and her first three complete voyages between Calcutta and China were completed within 12 months.[84] This set in motion a new shipbuilding programme for the construction of fast ships of which the *Waterwitch* and the *Sylph* were among the first to be built. The former had no connection with the 10-gun brig built by Joseph White, but was a magnificent clipper barque built at Kidderpore, Calcutta, in 1831 by J Kyd & Co and designed by Captain Andrew Henderson, who comments on her in a paper he read to the British Association in 1854:

> 'The term "clipper ship" is applicable to all vessels in which speed is made the primary object. Acting on this principle, in 1831 Mr Henderson built the clipper *Waterwitch* (a model was placed on the table) so sharp and shallow, as to stow a cargo of only one-half the 380 tons registered; while carrying the sails of a 500 tons ship, having a numerous crew to man her efficiently, experience proved her very long masts and square yards were within the limits of safety. The ship being still employed in the China trade, though twice twelve years old, is evidence of her being safely built, rigged and well proportioned as a sailing clipper, her length being 3.75 times her breadth. In 1842 he built the *Kelpie*, of the same tonnage register, but increased the length to four breadths, with less rise of floor, as shown in model and diagram of midship section.'[85]

Basil Lubbock gives *Waterwitch*'s tonnage as 363 and dimensions as 104ft-11in by 27ft-10in by 17ft-6in. This is surely not the shallow depth to which Henderson referred in his paper; indeed, very few of the ships listed by Basil Lubbock in the 'Opium Fleet' had a depth in excess of 17ft-6in.[86] Support for Lubbock's figures, however, is to be found in another paper which Henderson read in which he listed the opium clipper *Kelpie*'s measurements, and in these the breadth and depth are very similar to those of the *Waterwitch*. The *Kelpie*'s measurements are given as 108ft-0in by 27ft-4in by 17ft-5in and 355 tons om, and the proportion of breadths to length is 3.94 to 1.[87] It is to be noted that Lubbock describes the *Kelpie* as an ex-slaver, captured in 1836 and 109 tons, which suggests that there was another vessel of the same name. The *Waterwitch* had 'tween decks with a headroom of 5ft-3in, a small poop and topgallant forecastle. An old lithograph depicts her under a vast spread of canvas, rigged as a barque with very deep topsails and courses but comparatively shallow topgallants; skysails are carried on fore and main, and on the mizen, a jackyard topgallant is set above the jackyard topsail; the fore and main trysails are enormous and numerous headsails are set. F G Hely's chalk drawing of the barque at the National Maritime Museum, gives a fairly similar view. Captain Henderson held 16 shares in the ship and remained her master until 1837. In the 'forties he designed the steamers *Assam, Naga* and *Nautilus* for the Assam Co to carry passengers and to tow barges on the Brahmaputra River in East Bengal.

The *Sylph* was built two months after the *Waterwitch* and also in the region of Calcutta. She was designed for the Calcutta merchant Rustomjee Cowasjee by no less a person than

115: An unnamed British barque from a watercolour drawing. Comparison of two illustrations of the *Waterwitch* in the Natiional Maritime Museum — a chalk drawing by F G Hely and the photograph of an old print — strongly suggest that this painting also depicts here. The barque shown here is very heavily rigged, and it seems remarkable that she should have her trysails set as well as so many stunsails. It is unusual to see a nineteenth-century barque setting a square sail from a yard on the mizen, and a staysail is rigged on the windward side of this yard to act as a stunsail. *Mariners Museum.*

Sir Robert Seppings, and was constructed on his diagonal principle with dimensions of 100ft-5in by 26ft-0in by 12ft-5in and a tonnage of 305, the height in the 'tween decks being only 4ft-6½in.[88] These measurements reveal a hull of much shallower draught than other opium clippers of similar length and breadth. Seppings later designed two further vessels for the same owner, the opium clipper barque *Cowasjee Family* of 431 tons built in 1835, and the ship *Rustomjee Cowasjee* of 764 tons built in 1839. A painting of the *Sylph* shows a heavily-rigged ship with trysails on each mast and a very tall, high-peaked spanker; the topsails and topgallants are shown drying with the yards lowered and the sails spread across stays and braces in a manner not seen after the introduction of double topsails. In the Royal Navy the sails would be described as 'hauled a-bowline'.

It is unfortunate that no copies of Seppings' designs for these opium ships appear to have survived, but one can conjecture as to the *Sylph*'s hull form by studying the lines of the

116: The opium clipper *Sylph* designed by Sir Robert Seppings. The topsail and topgallant yards have been lowered to dry the sails which are draped across stays and braces; the bow-lines are hauled taut to prevent the leeches from sagging. There is a trysail to each mast and the headsails have enormous overlap. With the fore mast stepped further aft than her contemporaries, she has more the appearance of a clipper of the forties. On the left is a true brigantine like the *Psyche*. *C A Bull.*

three-masted schooner *Seagull* which he designed in 1829, and whose plans in the National Maritime Museum, Greenwich, have been re-drawn and are reproduced here in figure 117. The *Seagull*'s dimensions of 97ft-3in by 11ft-2in and 280 tons closely resemble those of the *Sylph*, and her design follows the style adopted by Seppings during the previous ten years, which is basically a development of the fast cutter hull which proved so successful in numerous vessels. In the *Seagull* there are hollow garboards, steep deadrise and very slack bilges, with the maximum beam kept just above the load line; the half-breadth plan exhibits convex waterlines and a long, tapering run. The additional length, when compared with a cutter, produces a shallower type of hull with a drag of 2ft-9in aft. It is highly probable that the *Sylph* and the *Seagull* were of very similar hull form even down to the raking stem rabbet which is present in the painting of the *Sylph*, although the opium clipper has in addition an outreaching head knee and the usual trail boards.

In his design for the *Cowasjee Family*, Sir Robert Seppings increased the measurements to 106ft-10in by 30ft-3in by 13ft-6in and 431 tons. Basil Lubbock writes that 'she is described as having a very rising floor with great area at the line of flotation' which could have resulted from this four-feet increase in beam over the *Sylph*, especially if the deadrise was increased.[90] She might in fact have been approaching the style to be seen in the plan of the *Anonyma*, figure 119, which is a further modification of the original cutter hull. Here beam and depth are practically similar to *Cowasjee Family* but the length has increased by 11 feet making the measurements 118ft-3in (scaled off plan from foreside stem to after side sternpost) by 29ft-10in by extreme breadth by 13ft-9in, 459 tons om and 257 tons nm. In the absence of plans the much smaller tonnage figure by the new measurement tonnage rule would have suggested an extremely sharp hull, and in this case the lines plan confirms the correctness of such a diagnosis.

The *Anonyma* has straight, steeply rising floors with her maximum beam above the load line which produces a midship section almost identical to the gun brig, ex-yacht *Waterwitch* when the two body plans are superimposed, although *Waterwitch* has a little hollow in her floors. The *Anonyma*'s extra length of 25ft-0in gives her very fine lines with easier curves and practically no hollows anywhere, and makes her a good example of how a clipper hull need not be dependent on concave lines. With a load line length of 114ft-9in she would have had to sail at 13.4 knots to attain the high speed-length ratio of 1.25.

The *Anonyma* was built as a yacht by William Camper at Gosport in 1839 for the Hon R F Greville who sold her the following year, and after passing through several hands she entered the opium trade in 1842 under the Jardine Matheson house flag. The plan in the Admiralty collection at the National Maritime Museum was drawn by George Atkins from lines taken off the brig in December 1839.

A few comments are required on the *Anonyma*'s lofty sail plan as reproduced in figure 120, which is a reconstruction based on John Fincham's *Treatise on Mastingships* and in accordance with the lithograph of her made in 1846. The first edition of Fincham's work, published in 1829, contained tables for

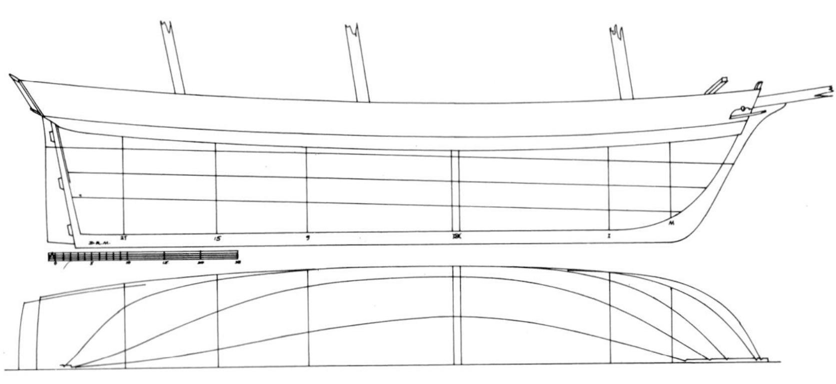

117: HMS *Seagull*. Lines plan: Redrawn from Admiralty draught at the National Maritime Museum. Dimensions on plan: 95ft-0in (length of deck), 77ft-9¾in (length of keel for tonnage), 26ft-3in (extreme breadth), 11ft-2in (depth of hold), and 279 74/94 tons. Reconstruction: number of stations much reduced; chain plates and deadeyes omitted, and also fittings to rudder.

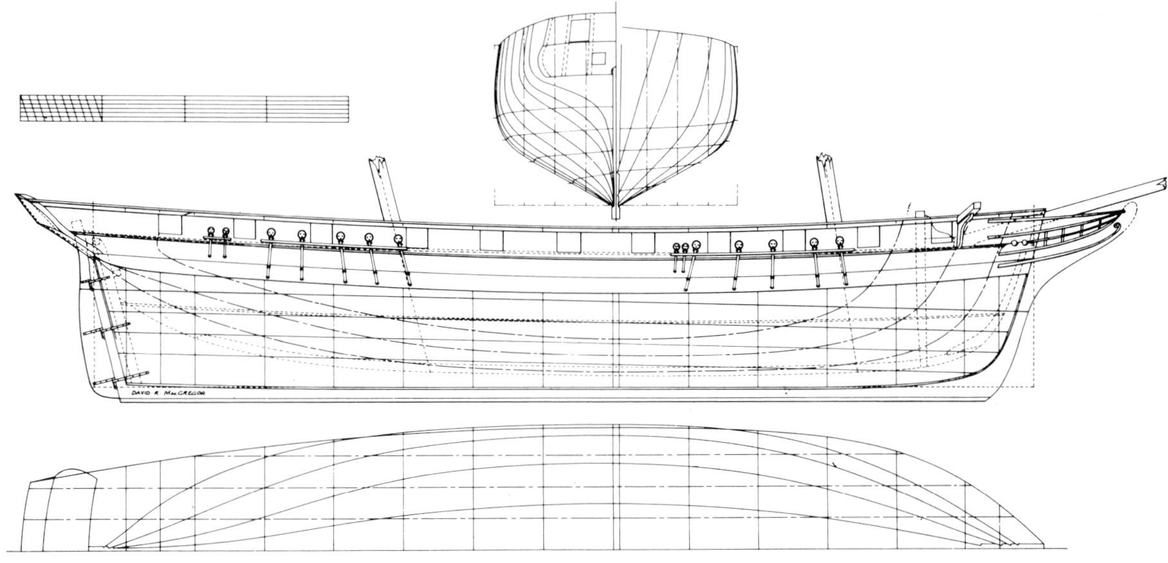

119: *Anonyma.* Lines plan: Built in 1839 by William Camper at Gosport. Redrawn from Admiralty plan in National Maritime Museum. Dimensions on plan: 115ft-4in (length on deck) × 29ft-10in (extreme breadth) × 13ft-9in (depth in hold); 458 85/94 tons. Reconstruction: buttock lines projected, and angles of chain plates re-aligned to suit sail plan.

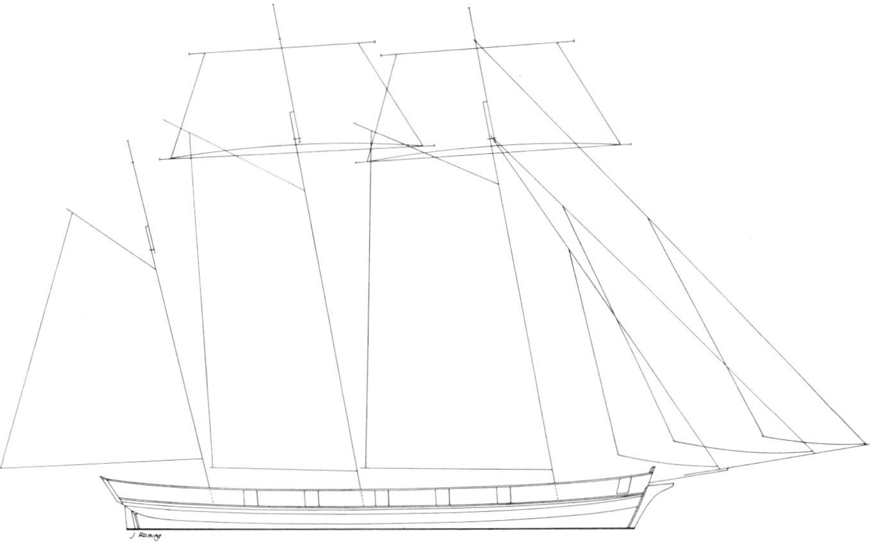

118: HMS *Seagull.* Sail plan: This plan has no connection with opium clippers, but as it was a rig given to her, it is included to illustrate the three-masted schooner rig in vogue at that date with some fast-sailing craft. Some American schooners also carried this rig. Redrawn by Janette Rosing from an Admiralty draught which had this rig and that of a brig combined on one sheet.

120: *Anonyma.* Sail plan: Reconstructed from sheer elevation, position and rake of masts and bowsprit, and position of lower deadeyes. Reconstruction: dimensions of spars and masts from *Treatise on Masting* by John Fincham (1st and 3rd editions) using a table of brigs rigged as yachts: sails and rigging from lithograph of brig as an opium clipper, and of other similar vessels; stunsails follow contemporary proportions.

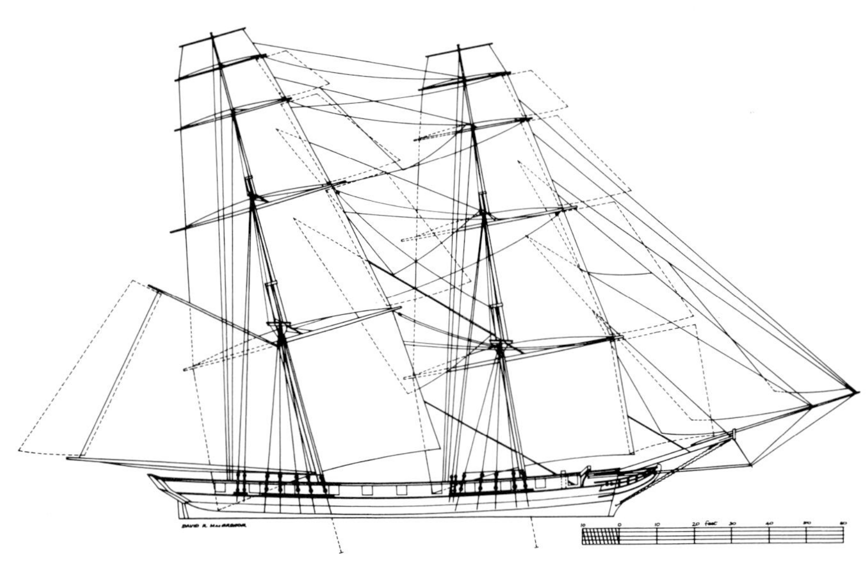

masting brigs (repeated in subsequent editions) and amongst these are sections for 'yachts as brigs'. Figures of spar lengths can be read off direct in the tables: those for masts and bowsprit are graded according to the maximum beam, and those for yards and booms according to the hull length. There is also a table covering all masts and spars which can be calculated by proportion, providing the maximum breadth is known. But although *Anonyma* and Lord Belfast's *Waterwitch* are virtually of similar beam, the former's spars work out according to Fincham's rules to be longer than those scaled off the latter's con-

121: According to the title, this lithograph by James Peck was taken from a sketch done by Norman Hill if 1846, and depicts the *Anonyma* in the Straits of Malacca while 'crossing the North Sands off the 2½ Fathom Bank'. Below this is the list of the firms to whom the print is dedicated. *Paul Mason Gallery.*

temporary sail plan.[91] This looks eminently satisfactory on the sail plan of *Anonyma* as she is some 25ft-0in longer than *Waterwitch*.

The length of the *Anonyma*'s spars, their great rake and the large sail area produce an extreme example of a clipper both in rig and hull form, the limits of which are rarely exceeded. The aquatint of the clipper brig *Governor MacLean* shows an equally extreme, rakish vessel[92] and similar pictures of this date corroborate in showing that there were a number of such craft afloat, engaged in various specialised and often illicit trades. Even by 1834 the *Canton Register* was referring to the 'clippers' that carried opium from India and mentioning the 'deeds of speed' when commenting on passage times, as if describing a steeplechase.

In a rare book on shipbuilding in India, John Phipps lists the *Red Rover, Sylph, Waterwitch, Cowasjee Family, Syren, Rob Roy, Ariel, Nymph, Syed Khan, Lady Grant* and *Ardaseer* as the opium clippers built in India before 1840.[93] The majority would have been built of teak with a generous amount of gilding and gingerbread work, so beloved of Country-built ships. Although the best materials were used in the construction it is probable that the final cost would have been lower than in the United Kingdom owing to the cheapness of labour in Bombay and Calcutta. The barque *Ariel*, listed above, was built in 1837 at Kidderpore with a round stern, which was unusual at that time.[94] It is worth noting here that other ships built in India with round sterns included the *Lady William Bentinck* built at Howrah, Calcutta, in 1833 as a Bengal pilot brig; and the *Mermaid* built at Bombay in 1825, also as a Bengal pilot brig.[95] The former probably became the *Bentinck* that was purchased at Canton in 1841 for a survey ship and renamed *Plover*.

122: A chalk drawing by F G Hely showing the true brigantine *Psyche*. She has a small square topsail and topgallant on the main mast, with space for a royal as well, rather like the sail plan of HMS *Dolphin*. It will be noticed that she also sets a large gaff sail on the fore mast. She had been the Spanish slaver *Indagador* when captured by a British sloop in 1834.

Although the smuggling of opium into China had continued throughout the eighteenth and early nineteenth centuries, it was only after 1830 that the days of the clippers began. In a 'Register of the Opium Fleet', Basil Lubbock lists 32 vessels of all rigs that entered the trade for the first time between 1830 and 1839, but between 1840 and 1843 (inclusive) there were no less than 48 new entrants, this large increase being probably due to the open-

123: A watercolour drawing of HM gun brig *Grecian* and an opium clipper schooner in company. The schooner is better drawn that the brig and it is possible that the picture was drawn by one of her crew. It is signed 'M E M 43'. Naval officers and ship masters were often competent artists in those days. The schooner is unidentified but is flying the Jardine Matheson house flag; her bowsprit is unusually long. *James Dickie Collection.*

ing of the China coast to general trade as a result of the first Anglo-Chinese war. After 1845, fewer ships entered the trade although some finely-modelled schooners were built especially for it.[96]

In a booming trade it was sometimes found desirable to purchase second-hand ships which is why yachts like the two *Falcons* and the *Anonyma*, the ex-fruiters *Time* and *Hellas*, and several former slavers and warships found their way out East. The *Hellas* made several voyages out to China before joining the opium fleet in 1838 and her last outward passage between Gravesend and Canton took 124 days in that year. As an opium clipper she had a crew of 50 and was heavily armed. The other fruiter *Time* was armed with a brass 12-pounder pivot gun amidships and six 4-pounders.

Fast ships in eastern trades

Although the abolition of the Honourable East India Company's monopoly at the beginning of 1834 encouraged the construction of several new ships built specifically for the China trade, it was not until the termination of the Anglo-Chinese war in 1842 that the design of fast ships to carry tea really commenced. Even then, the demand for new ships was closely interwoven with trade requirements, lowering of tea duties, foreign competition, and the awareness of the public of the distinction of drinking the new season's tea at enhanced prices. All this took time to accomplish.

By inference, a few of the new ships built in the 1830s were designed on finer lines than formerly although there are no plans to prove this. Henry Hall commented on the situation in his *Report on the Ship-Building Industry of the United States:*

> 'Americans earned a world-wide reputation for speed soon after 1814, and finally put the English so much on their mettle that the latter sent out a new and finer class of merchantmen than they had ever before owned to contest for the palm of superiority. The *Alexander Baring, John o'Gaunt, Euphrates, Monarch, Foam* and other ships of that class, were equal to any under the flag of the United States in capacity, spread of canvas and speed. This, in turn, stimulated the pride of the American houses, who responded between 1840 and 1850 with vessels of good and carefully studied form.'[97]

The names of these ships have been quoted before but always out of context. The *Alexander Baring* was built at the Blackwall Yard, London, in 1834, on dimensions of 132.4ft by 28.8ft by 13.8ft and measured 505 tons om and 612 tons nm. Owned by Baring Brothers she 'had been built to the specification of the managing partners. [She] was a fast sailer. . . '[98] In 1838 she went out to Hong Kong in 105 days from Deal, but took 149 days to return from Canton, leaving on 22 January 1839. In 1842 she took 127 days to sail from Canton to London, leaving in January. Barings sold her in 1845 for about £4500.[99] On her first voyage in 1834 they had anticipated that she would get a homeward freight of £7 per ton.

The *Euphrates* and the *John o'Gaunt* were built in 1834 and 1835 at Liverpool by John Wilson, a shipbuilder who between 1807 and 1845 constructed 56 vessels.[100] Of the two, it was the *John o'Gaunt* that was talked about for two decades and her fast passages became suitably embellished. Here are two examples of passages she made between China and England in the late 1830s, under the command of Captain John Robertson:

124: Paintings of merchant ships in the China trade are rare before 1848 or so. This painting depicts the *Arabia* which was built at Scarborough in 1844 with tonnages of 330 om and 362 nm. *Paul Mason Gallery.*

1838	Canton to Liverpool	6 January to 29 April	113 days
1838	Liverpool to Anjer	12 June to 8 September	88 days

She continued this last passage to Canton by way of Batavia. A year later she took 84 days to Batavia, remained there 10 days, and then sailed up to Canton in 9 days.

The identity of the *Monarch* is uncertain, but there are two possibilities: either the ship of 464 tons om and 551 tons nm built at Leith in 1840; or the barque of 338 tons built at Scilly in 1844 by Thomas Edward and launched fully-rigged with all yards crossed and sails bent. Reference has already been made to the significance of the *Falcon* as an early British tea clipper, but without plans of the Liverpool ships a valid comparison is impossible.

Another ship of the 1830s was the *James Matheson*, built in 1836 at Dartmouth of 408 tons om, and described in 1844 as 'a crack ship and one of the fastest sailers out of [Liverpool].'[101]

Prior to 1840 the fastest passage out to China was possibly that claimed for the *Mangles* which was said to have gone from London to Macao in 94 days in 1829. This ship was built in 1802 at Calcutta of 545 tons.[102] The fastest homeward passage up to the year 1845 might be the 91 days taken in 1844 by the brig *Bonanza* between Shanghai and Liverpool. This vessel was built in 1830 by T & J Brocklebank as a three-masted barquentine of 176 tons, as described earlier in the chapter.

One could continue with further samples of ships and passages that were considered fast in their day, although without the evidence of plans to support them such descriptions are valueless in a study of this kind. But prior to the year 1840 it would be instructive to learn whether any British ships approached the fineness of hull form to be found in the American ship *Ann McKim*. This

125: *Ann McKim*. Lines plan: Redrawn from part-plan of ship which was printed in *Report of the Ship-Building Industry of the United States* by Henry Hall (1884 p 84). The published plan consisted of the bow and stern ends in profile separated, with the body plan between and the half-breadth plan below. Reconstruction: sheer elevation; LWL and mast positions from lines plan of ship in *Search for Speed under Sail* by Howard I Chapelle (plate 83).

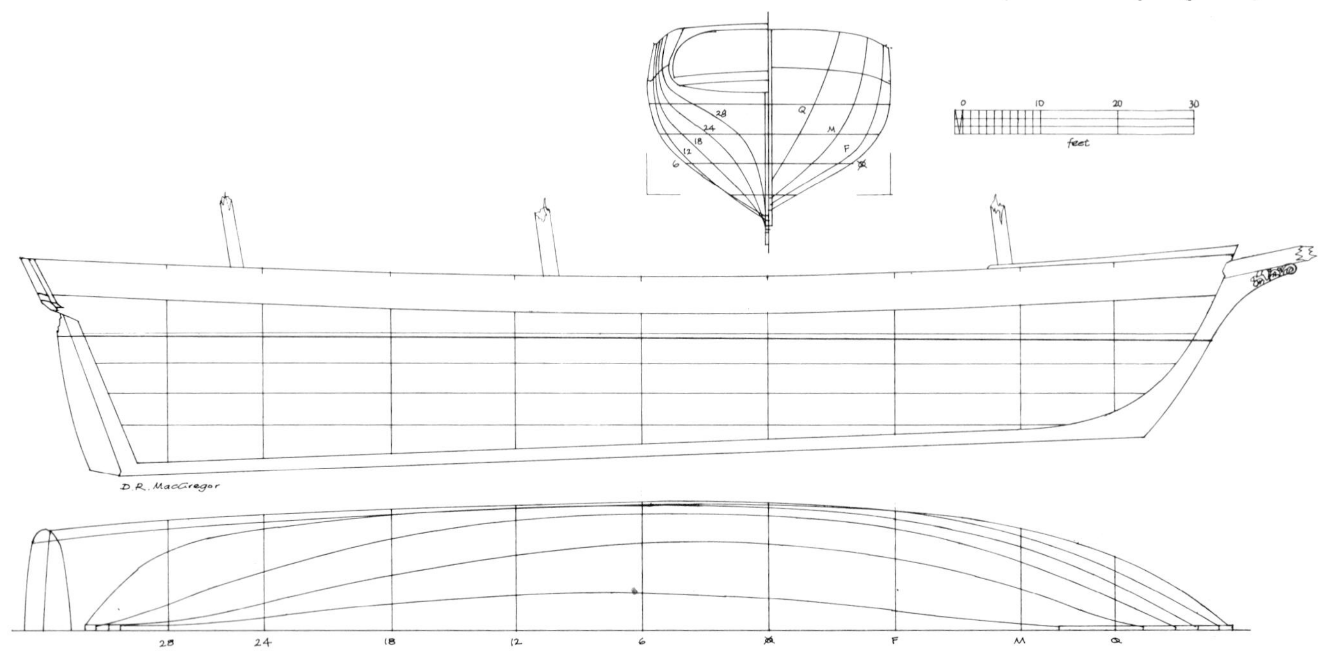

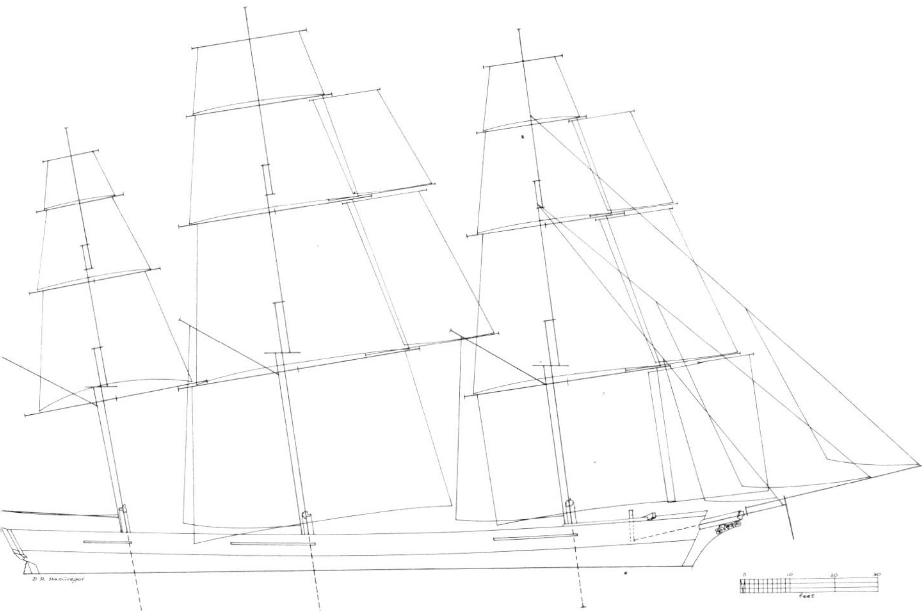

126: *Ann McKim*. Outline sail plan: Entirely reconstructed from sheer elevation in figure 125 and from spar dimensions listed on lines plan of ship drawn by Chapelle; see caption to figure 125. Rake of masts from Chapelle's plan, but his list of spar dimensions does not give length of mast heads or of yardarms. These were calculated from tables in *A Treatise on Masting Ships and Mast Making* by John Fincham (2nd ed 1843); sail outlines from contemporary text books. Stunsail booms and yards were those listed by Chapelle.

full-rigged ship of 494 tons was built by Kennard & Williamson at Baltimore in 1832 with dimensions of 143ft-0in (between perpendiculars) by 31ft-0in (moulded) by 15ft-10in (moulded) and when fully loaded, drew 5ft-2in more aft than forward. The first seven years of her life were spent in the South American trade, but in 1839 she was diverted to the China trade for the remainder of her career.[103]

Howard Chapelle published his draught of her lines plan and gave a 'European drawing, possibly copied from the builder's draught' as his source material.[104] Unfortunately, he does not acknowledge the source. The plan reproduced here in figure 125 has been redrawn from the lines plan which appeared in Henry Hall's *Report on the Ship-Building Industry of the United States.*[105] This shows a hull with very steep deadrise so that the maximum beam is placed above the load waterline; also extremely long and sharp ends which are generally convex, having only a trace of concavity in the lower portions of the run. Chapelle has drawn trailboards, bracket knees and a figurehead, whereas Hall has only a fiddlehead; Chapelle has also included a topgallant rail, but there is none in Hall's plan.

Spar dimensions are tabulated on Chapelle's lines plan, and these have been employed to produce a rudimentary sail plan in which the masts and yards are drawn according to their correct length but by a single line only. The lengths of the studding sail booms and yards are also listed. The position and spacing of the masts, as well as their rake and the angle of steeve of the bowsprit have been scaled off Chapelle's plan. Like the opium clippers, the *Ann McKim* was designed for speed, not for cargo capacity, and she could only earn a living with high freight rates. A model such as hers was certainly capable of high speed, and her fastest passage in the South American trade was one of 59 days from Coquimbo, Chile, around Cape Horn to Baltimore, made in 1837. In the China trade she ran from New York to Anjer in 79 days in 1842, and returned home in the spring of 1843 in only 96 days. However, like other extreme clippers, she also recorded some lengthy passages such as 150 days between Macao and New York from 26 June to 23 November 1840. She had been obliged to beat down the China Sea against the southwest monsoon which was a passage which had received little attention up to that time, although a bare ten years later it was judged to be a fine test of nerve and seamanship.[106]

The generation of fast sailing American ships in the China trade were not to be modelled on hulls of Baltimore clippers like the *Ann McKim*, but rather on sharper versions of the North Atlantic packet, as will be described in the next chapter.

New measurement tonnage

Following the inability of the 1821 Commission on Tonnage Measurement to arrive at a practical solution, a second commission was appointed in 1833, whose report, issued the following year, was accompanied by a long list of sample ships whose internal volumes had been computed by the naval architect, H Cradock. Several rules for measurement, submitted by members of the Commission, were based on the dimensions obtained by Cradock, but these rules applied primarily to the measured examples rather than being devised independently to suit any vessel that might be designed. The scheme suggested by Edward Riddle of Greenwich Hospital appears to have been the basis for the Commission's recommendation, and like the one submitted in 1821 it attempted to obtain the internal volume by means of three crude cross-sectional areas. 'The principle which guided the Committee in their selection was that a rule of such general application should depend on the smallest number of measurements necessary to give the figure of the hull, and that it should afford results sufficiently exact for the required purpose, by an easy arithmetical process.'[107] For the first time, dimensions were taken in feet and tenths of a foot. The recommended rule was passed by Parliament in 1835 and became law as from January 1836.[108]

Under the new law which became known as New Measurement, the deck was divided into six equal parts between the after part of the stem and the foreside of the sternpost, and at the first, the middle and the last of the five points so obtained, a primitive form of cross-sectional area was measured internally, although the measurements only consisted of two breadths and one depth at each point. The actual method of calculating the tonnage is irrelevant here but a full account may be found in George Moorsom's *Brief Review and Analyses of the Laws for the Admeasurement of Tonnage*.[109] The annexed diagram (figure 127) shows the location of the measurements, and those requiring to be multiplied two or three times are drawn as double or triple lines. This diagram was inspired by a drawing made by John Lyman

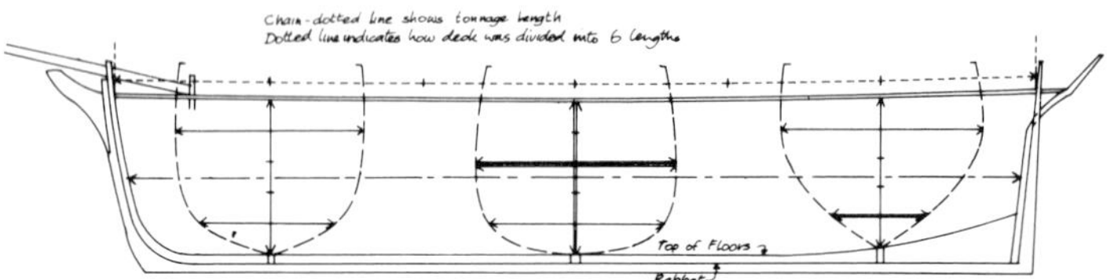

127: Tonnage by 1836 rule. Diagram to show points at which dimension were taken to calculate tonnage. Double or treble lines indicate that these measurements were doubled or trebled in calculations.

for his articles on tonnage measurement.[110]

The paucity of measurements resulted in numerous attempts at evasion and the publicly stated opportunities for this which Alexander Hall & Sons announced, drew the attention of all to the urgent need for yet another reform in the mode of assessing tonnage. In Hall's case, a new approach to fine-lined ships was the result which was copied by many other builders, as outlined in the next chapter. Thus the New Measurement can be thanked for stimulating inadvertently a reappraisal of naval architecture and a radical alteration of hull proportions. It was found that a redistribution of the ship's body into a shallower and longer hull permitted the same amount of cargo to be carried, yet reduced the actual register tonnage figure. Of course, this was an unintentional by-product of the new law.

The points between which the principal measurements were taken were now radically different from the old measurement rule, so that it is necessary to restate the definitions. Enclosed spaces above the level of the upper deck, such as the poop or raised quarter-deck, were also measured for tonnage for the first time. All new ships were measured in feet and tenths of a foot and appear thus in the Certificate of Registry, in *Lloyd's Register of Shipping*, and in the Lloyd's Register survey reports. Existing ships did not have to be re-measured unless radical alterations were made to the hull or if the owner desired it. Thus the figures of old and new tonnage are quoted simultaneously for most ships until 1854, when the Moorsom system was introduced, and in many cases the two figures lingered on for another ten years if a ship had not been re-measured according to the Moorsom rule. In *Lloyd's Register of Shipping*, the uppermost tonnage figure — as printed in the appropriate column — is usually that by the old measurement rule; the lower figure is according to the new measurement rule, and is often printed in a slightly smaller type face. If only one tonnage figure is given, it will be the old measurement for ships built prior to 1836, but the new measurement for ships built subsequently. The new divisor in the calculations was 3500 which resulted in awkward factions. (See Appendix I for definitions and measuring instructions.)

These instructions for measurement in the tonnage and Registry Acts are very sparse and liable to gross misinterpretation today, although contemporary surveyors doubtless received copious explanations. Technical language suffered from lack of precision and the writer in those days was virtually inarticulate when obliged to describe practical operations. The use of words, hitherto entirely adequate in literature, required redeployment by specialised writers who gradually asserted their mastery in this new medium and eventually created a new vocabulary.

Four

THE ABERDEEN BOW 1839-50

The *Scottish Maid*

Around the coasts of the British Isles the packet services for the swift conveyance of passengers and cargo had been growing in importance and in the volume of their business, but the introduction of steamers began seriously to threaten the prosperity of the sailing packet companies. The cutter-rigged smack was dominant, such as the Leith smacks which were described in chapter three, and to increase the speed of their services many companies invested in schooners or had their smacks converted to that rig. The London & Edinburgh Shipping Co of Leith owned seven smacks in 1830 but between 1835 and 1839 six of them were converted to schooner rig and the remaining smack sold.[1] Many of these schooners would have resembled those employed by the Waterford Line in the 1830s, as in figure 102.

The London & Edinburgh Shipping Co did not acquire their first steamer until 1853, but the Aberdeen & London Steam Navigation Co was in operation at the end of the 1830s, and it was partly to compete with the latter firm and partly to take advantage of the booming trade conditions that a group of Aberdonians ordered a schooner from Alexander Hall & Sons in 1839. This firm was well equipped to handle the new order as they had constructed no less than ten schooners since 1830. The new schooner was christened *Scottish Maid* and measured 92.4ft by 19.4ft by 1.7ft and 142 tons new measurement. Her plans are reproduced in figure 129.

This schooner has received so much publicity over the last 65 years that it is necessary to give careful consideration to her design and its results, but without isolating her from the general development of which she forms an integral part.

Her design must have been evolved partly with the idea of reducing the taxable figure of register tonnage and partly to improve her sailing qualities. The implications of the New Measurement tonnage law, introduced in 1836, and the manner of measuring the vessel and making the calculations are discussed in chapter three.

There are loopholes in most laws and Alexander Hall & Sons began early to examine ways of reducing this taxable register tonnage figure. James and William Hall took control of the firm from their father in about 1830, and commencing in 1837 they measured all their new vessels by the new measurement rules, even though they still estimated their costs by the old measurement figure. Thus, when they received the order for the *Scottish Maid* they were fully conversant with the new rules and the opportunities to be gained by changing the

128: A lithograph by the Hull artist, John Ward, of a clipper schooner with very raking masts and lengthy jibboom. The spar hinged outside the fore rigging indicates that she set a square lower stunsail. *MacGregor Collection.*

hull form. Indeed, the brothers James and William, then in their early thirties, may have frequently discussed such an opportunity.

As depth was now taxed, the paramount need was to make the ship of shallower form, and in order to retain the same capacity it became necessary to lengthen the hull. Fortunately, the length was only measured at half the depth and so it could be increased considerably above such level at each end to gain additional 'free' tonnage. The deck length was now much longer than the keel length, and the stem and sternpost were sharply raked to connect the two. The increased deck length stretched out the divisions for measuring the breadth and depth, as specified in the Registry Act, and in consequence the foremost and aftermost stations became positioned where the cross-sectional areas were less or where they could be made so. In addition, by working thicker timbers locally where the internal measurements were taken, further reductions could be made to the tonnage figure.[2] The diagram in figure 137, reproduced from a publicity drawing issued by Alexander Hall & Sons, will clarify these observations. A particularly desirable feature in a fast vessel on a short sea route, where port and dock charges would frequently occur, was to keep the register tonnage figure as low as possible, because it was on this figure that the charges were levied.

Nothing is known about the hull form of any craft built by Hall's shipyard before the *Scottish Maid*, so comparisons are really impossible. Nine years after the schooner was launched, the *Aberdeen Journal* contributed a description of her construction which is probably the most accurate available as it was made comparatively near to the time of her building. From this it appears that the model approved by the owners was for a fast schooner but with a 'common bow'. Bearing in mind that she was ordered to compete with a line of packet steamers it is reasonable to assume that she was designed with fine lines. But let the *Aberdeen Journal* continue the story:

> 'The Messrs Hall commenced framing the schooner from aft, and continued the frames until they reached the fore end of the keel. Thus far the work had proceeded, when the builders suggested a deviation from the models, which they believed would prove to be a decided improvement. They proposed to run the stem out so as to form the cutwater, the effect of which would be to draw the waterlines finer at the bow and, as a natural consequence, the vessel would divide the water easily, be more buoyant forward, and of less register tonnage than if she were built on the old plan. The idea did not at first meet the views of the owners. A skeleton bow was then erected, and not a few of the curious examined it and were skeptical of the uncommon design. After due consideration, the owners gave consent to proceed with the vessel according to the skeleton model, and in that style she was finished and launched. The look of the schooner in the water was encouraging. It was evident from the appearance of her waterlines that the idea of a perfect bow was realized, and some of those who were at first opposed to the project were now among its warmest commendators.'[3]

It was judged necessary to fit the *Scottish Maid* with a 'new style of masting and rigging . . . and give her spars a good rake aft'. The former critics were further encouraged when the new schooner frequently made the passage between Aberdeen and London in 49 hours.[4]

Some idea of the difficulties involved in departing radically from the normal design

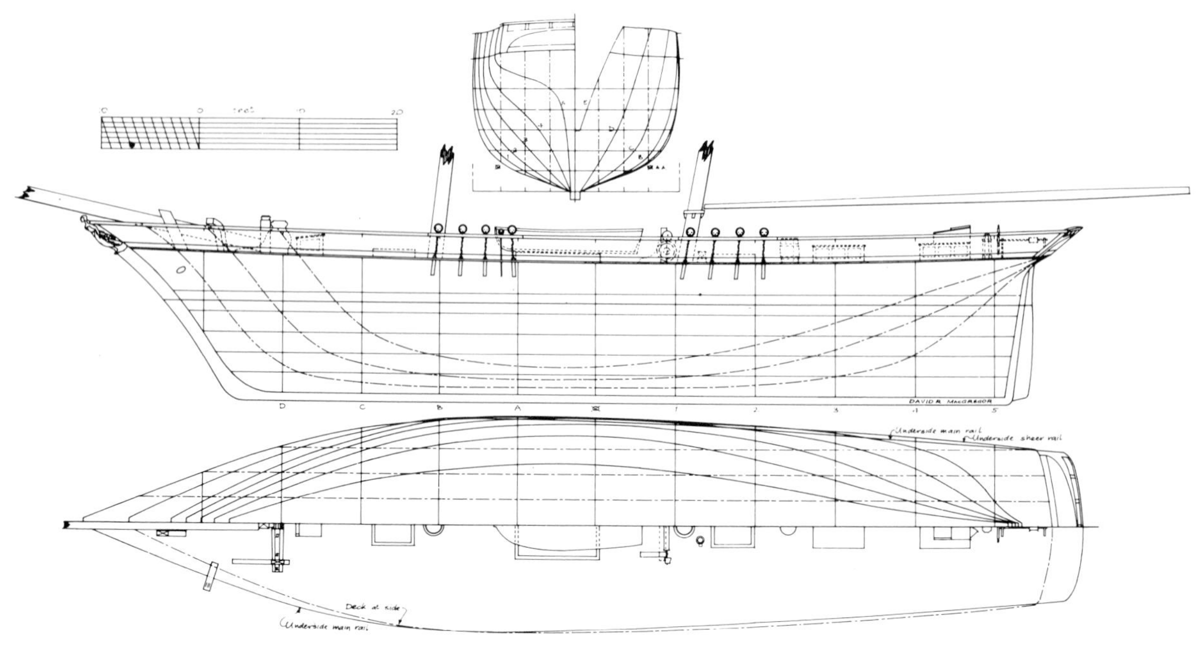

129: *Scottish Maid.* Built in 1839 by Alexander Hall & Sons at Aberdeen. Lines taken off builder's half-model in possession of Glasgow Museum and Art Gallery, Kelvingrove. Model labelled '*Scottish Maid* and *Non-Such*'. Dimensions: 92ft-4in × 19ft-4in × 11ft-4in; 142 tons n.m. Reconstruction: figurehead, mast positions, bowsprit, load waterline, all deck fittings. Principal source: painting of schooner *Non-Such*; also other contemporary plans and paintings.

130: This painting depicts the *Non-Such*, built three years after the *Scottish Maid*, but very similar to her in size, rig and general appearance. Here she is close-hauled under all plain sail. The artist's name on the buoy cannot be deciphered.

to be found in Aberdeen may be judged from the fact that 18 persons held shares in the schooner, many of whom might wish to air their views. Alexander Nicol and George Munro were the principal or managing owners with a joint holding of 12 shares. So successful was she that Nicol and Munro had two very similar schooners built the following year, the *Aberdonian* and the *London*. The successful reception of this new schooner hull was only the prelude to worldwide recognition by the end of the 1840s.

The building costs for *Scottish Maid* were as follows:[5]

Carpenters' wages		£ 333.14. 4½
Iron work for hull	£ 63. 2.10	
Iron work for rigging	£ 39. 1. 7	£ 102. 4. 5
Block making		£ 35.16. 8
Boat building		£ 23. 3. 6
Cooper work		£ 8. 8. 6
Sailmaking		£ 167. 5.11½
Compasses		£ 6. 2. 5
Chandlery		£ 7. 0. 0
Colours [ie flags, signal flags & c]		£ 6. 0. 5
Painting		£ 24.12. 3
Timber and plank used		£ 603.16.10
Cash paid: Crockery & c	£ 6. 2. 5	
Rigger	£ 11.11. 0	
Rope makers	£146. 0. 0	
G Watt & Co	£ 13.10. 0	
Twine	£ 20. 0. 0	
W Simpson & Co [for anchors, chains, & c.]	£178.13.0	
Sacking, & c.	£ 2.18. 9	
		£ 378.15. 2
Allowances		£ 2.19. 6
TOTAL		£1700. 0. 0

There is no reference to profit made. The contract price was £1700, to fit her 'completely ready for sea'.

The importance of the *Scottish Maid* lies in her being an early example of the streamlined type of hull that rapidly became popular in the 1840s. The absence of trail boards and head rails made a very light, graceful bow with 'the stem forming the knee of the head' as the Lloyd's Register surveyors put it. The waterlines in the entrance are all convex with no hollows and there is hardly any flare to the bow which makes the shape of the forebody conform to the cutter style of British fast sailing theory. She has a finely modelled run, considerable deadrise and easy bilges; the outline of the midsection might be said to have been modelled on Sainty's packet sloop *Sylph* (figure 68). Of course, the raking stem rabbet was not entirely new, but Aberdeen clippers carried it to excess. Previously, it was seen in Baltimore clippers, but without any concavity in the stem profile; and also in the three barquentines named *Transit* (see chapter three), and other vessels.

According to the Lloyd's Register survey report, some of the *Scottish Maid*'s scantlings were as follows:[6]

Floors, sided 10in and moulded 12in; top timbers, sided 7in and moulded 6in; keel, sided 11in and moulded 15in; keelson sided 12in and moulded 17in; 18 deck beams sided and moulded 9in; timber and space 24in; outer planking, keel to bilge and bilge to wales 3in; bilges 4½in; wales 4in; topsides 2½in; upper deck 2½in.

She received a low classification of 5 A1 because she was largely built of fir with the exception of the stem, sternpost and some of the outer planking above the bottom, which were in oak. Some beech was used in the floor timbers. The surveyor reported that the workmanship throughout was good and likewise the quality of the timber and fastenings. A midship section of Hall's schooner *Swift*, built 1843, is included to illustrate the type of construction embodied in these clippers.

The deck layout is entirely reconstructed from a painting of the *Non-Such* (figure 130), and of other Aberdeen ships of the 1840s. According to the Lloyd's Register survey report, the *Scottish Maid* carried a clinker-built longboat and jolly boat which, from the sizes of boats carried by Hall's schooner *Water Witch* (1843), are here drawn as 15 feet and 14 feet long respectively. No mention is made of a patent windlass in the survey report, so a normal handspike variety was presumably fitted, but she did have a patent winch. These clipper schooners did not show any knighthead timbers above the rail; what looks like them further aft are the raking bowsprit bitts.

The spar dimensions from the builder's cost account have been employed to reconstruct a sail and rigging plan, with the assistance of James Henderson's research and contemporary illustrations. The painting of the Aberdeen schooner *Pera* shows several fancy sails: a square sail sheeted to a boom; a rectangular lower stunsail on a swinging boom; and and a small topgallant stunsail. As such sails were only set in fair weather, they are shown by dotted lines on the plan. The painting of the *Scottish Maid*, reproduced by Boyd Cable, shows double topsails and is therefore evidently of a date about 30 years later than the building of the schooner; consequently, the earlier painting of the *Non-Such* has been the one most used. Two brails are shown on the forerail as it was then customary for schooners to brail it into the mast rather than lower the gaff.

Many of the points referred to above may be observed in William Ward's drawing of the *Scottish Maid* which he has depicted lying alongisde a wharf at low water. Here can be seen the framing of the stern, and the relationship of spars and hull form.

An article by Boyd Cable which appeared in the *Mariner's Mirror* in 1943 unwisely described the *Scottish Maid* in forthright terms as 'the world's first clipper'.[7] Even a title such as 'Aberdeen's first clipper' would have been open to question. Three excellent articles in reply completely demolished his claims,[8] yet there are a number of important issues that require comment and in particular the source of the plans used by Boyd Cable.

His article contains some useful factual data on Aberdeen ships and shipbuilders but is based on the pedantic and untenable hypothesis that no vessel can be classed as a clipper unless she has hollow entrance lines, and Boyd Cable accordingly dismisses all Baltimore clippers from the clipper category because their entrance lines were sometimes convex. Similarly he states that 'it is beyond doubt that the *Scottish Maid* was the first vessel of clipper design to be built in Great Britain'.[9] The plans presented in this book completely refute the second statement. In the reply made by Howard I Chapelle is to be found a very lucid comment on the designation of 'clipper' to any fine-lined, fast sailing vessel irrespective of rig or hull form.[10] The hollow in the entrance can be found either in the waterlines or in the flaring sections of the body plan, and an observer can easily be misled into believing a ship has a hollow entrance when the only hollows are in the flaring topsides. Considering Boyd Cable's insistence on this hollow entrance as the very core of his argument, it is incredible to discover that in the plan he submitted of the *Scottish Maid*'s lines there is practically no hollow visible in the entrance waterlines. Although no scale is given on his plan, the beam dimension shows it to be very close to ⅛in to 1ft-0in and at this scale the maximum hollow in the lowest waterline measures only about 2in at a height of 1ft-9in above the rabbet. The hollow in the waterline next above is barely discernible and above this the waterlines are convex. A straight edge on the body plan or bow lines reveals practically no hollows. Thus Boyd Cable demolishes the argument with his own evidence.

The lines presented here are not those used by Boyd Cable, which he had received from Alexander Hall & Sons, but were taken off the half-model which was at that time in the Glasgow Museum and Art Gallery, through the courtesy of Mr Browning, the Curator of Technology. Builders' half-models of the

131: *Scottish Maid.* Sail plan: Entirely reconstructed with assistance of James Henderson. Sources: lines plan; spar dimensions from builder's cost account; spar diameters and mast positions from contemporary practice; paintings of ships built by same builder, especially *Non-Such* and *Perá*.

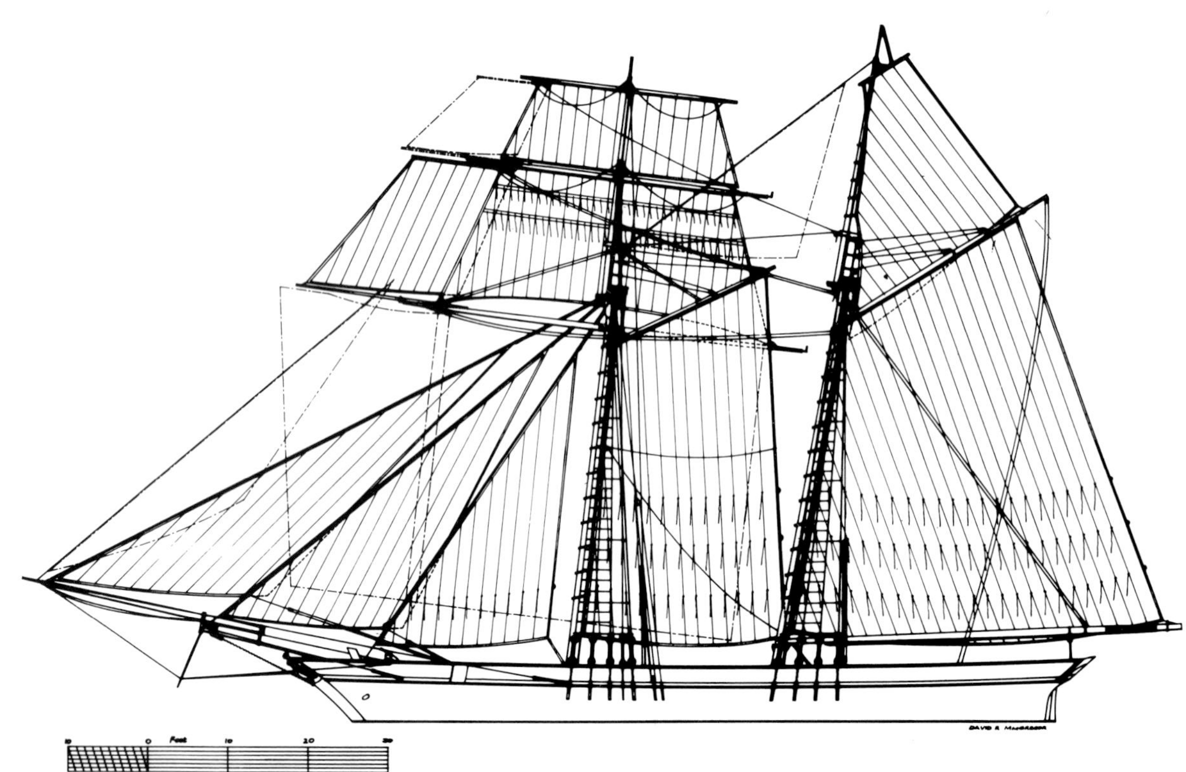

132: A reconstructed drawing of the *Scottish Maid* unloading at a London wharf. This is based entirely on the plans, but additional detail has been added to portray the schooner as she might have looked. Drawn by T W Ward.

clippers *Scottish Maid, Reindeer, Stornoway, Chrysolite, Cairngorm, Vision* and *Schomberg* were loaned by Alexander Hall & Sons to the Glasgow Museum for an exhibition in about 1880 and were never returned. This model is entitled '*Scottish Maid* and *Non-Such*', the latter having been built in 1842 for the London & Edinburgh Shipping Co. The dimensions given by the builder are for the 1836 new Registry Act and are measured internally. The length is from the inner part of the main stem to the fore part of the sternpost aloft; the beam is the maximum inside at half the length and all measurements are in feet and tenths of a foot. A small calculation is required to determine how closely the model fits the dimensions of the schooners, as it is almost certainly carved to the inside of the plank, as was normal practice. The model gives the moulded beam, that is to say the beam inside the plank, as 21ft-0in. The Lloyd's Register survey report shows that the top timbers were moulded 6in and that the ceiling plank was 2½in thick. Thus 8½in must be deducted each side from the moulded beam, resulting in an inside beam of 19ft-7in or 19.58ft. This is almost identical to the inside beam of *Scottish Maid* which Hall lists as 19.4ft. As to the length, the model measures, as near as can be estimated, 89.25ft as opposed to 92.4ft for the *Scottish Maid*. The depth is difficult to check without having a midship section, but is approximately correct on the model.

The conclusion is therefore that the model is correct for breadth and depth but 3ft-0in too short for the *Scottish Maid* and 9ft-0in too short for the *Non-Such*. The relevant dimensions are tabulated below:

Comparison of *Scottish Maid*'s dimensions

	length	*breadth*	*depth of hold*
Scaled off Boyd Cable's plan	88.0ft nm	19.85ft moulded	9.75ft (approx)
Builder's certificate of *Scottish Maid*	92.4ft nm	19.4ft inside ceiling	11.4ft
Short notice in *Aberdeen Herald* 20 July 1839 on *Scottish Maid*	100.0ft extreme on deck 80.0ft keel	22.0ft extreme on deck	12.0ft
Half-model at Glasgow Museum, drawn as figure 129	89.25ft nm 78.0ft keel	19.6ft inside ceiling 21.0ft moulded	11.4ft (approx)
Dimensions of schooner *Non-Such*, from builder's certificate	98.6ft nm	19.4ft inside ceiling	12.8ft

(all dimensions in feet and decimals of a foot)

133: The four surviving half-models in the possession of Alexander Hall & Sons. Top left, an unidentified clipper, similar to *Reindeer* but of size; bottom left, claimed to be *Scottish Maid* and source for the plans of this schooner used by Boyd Cable; top right, barque *Alexander Hall*; bottom right, full-rigged ship *Thomas Arbuthnot* (1841).

It will readily be seen that the lines drawing made from the half-model and the plan submitted by Boyd Cable are of two different vessels. Boyd Cable's plan shows a fuller vessel with less deadrise, a fuller run, a more raking sternpost and a different rake to the stem. In addition, the sheer elevation is not continued above deck level which gives a false impression of a long, low hull. As the deck to rabbet measurement is only 11.25ft the depth of hold would measure about 9.75ft. The last dimension is very critical and the fact that two of the three measurements are incorrect throws grave doubts on the authenticity of the plan. Had this plan been traced or redrawn from the original, Boyd Cable would surely have emphasized the fact in his article in no uncertain terms, but he merely refers to 'the lines of [the *Scottish Maid*] supplied to me by Alexander Hall & Co Ltd and... the model they still possess'.[11]

During the Second World War, a fire in Alexander Hall's offices destroyed what was left of the old plans and models with the exception of four half-models that are mounted on a display board and are still in the possession of the firm. None of these models is named but adjacent initials such as A H or S M and confirmatory measurements suggest the following names: the barque *Alexander Hall*, bluff-bowed; the ship *Thomas Arbuthnot*, also bluff-bowed; a clipper similar to the *Reindeer*, but larger in tonnage; and another clipper which Mr Smith, the late managing director, used to call *Scottish Maid*. These four models are shown in figure 133, as mounted on a communal backboard. The dimensions and form of the model called '*Scottish Maid*' agree exactly with the plan reproduced by Boyd Cable in his article.

I have seen these four models myself but my old friend, James Henderson, a native of Aberdeen, has carried out considerable research there over the last 20 years and has been unable to find any other source for Boyd Cable's plan than the model mentioned above. It is Henderson's suggestion that this was a prototype model or an unfinished design. It does not suggest that of a hull built for speed as much as does the Glasgow half-model. On the information at present available, the plan of the *Scottish Maid* as taken from the *named* builder's half-model at the Glasgow Museum is accordingly submitted as the most reliable plan of the schooner so far produced.

Returning to the hull design, James Sellar, who had spent a lifetime in shipyards and had been a friend of William Hall, wrote a letter to *Sea Breezes* in 1924 in which he said that William Hall very much disliked having a hollow waterline forward. He also referred to tank tests conducted by James and William and said that they were carried out in about 1837.[12] Corroborative evidence is, however, lacking and several possibilities present themselves. The brothers could have

134: An explanatory diagram issued by Alexander Hall & Sons in 1846 to draw attention to the benefits of the Aberdeen bow. The glass tank measured 10ft long, 16in wide. Two inches of red turpentine (CB) floated on the water. The hulls were of actul vessels, 24in long. Figure 3 is the shape at the load waterline and figure 4 is the midship section. The conclusion was that the buttock lines in the fore and after bodies should rake as much as possible.

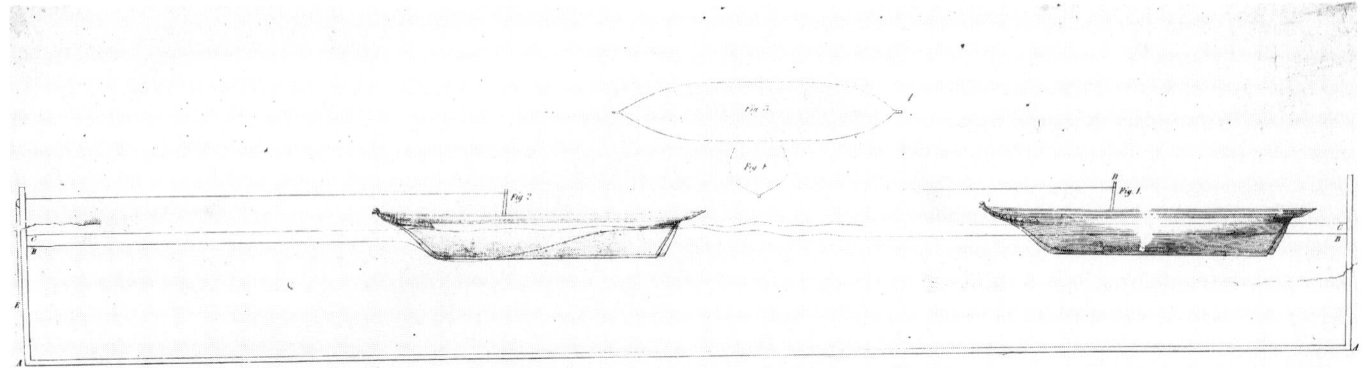

The above Drawing represents an experiment made in order to observe the motion created in Water by a Vessel passing through it, and to ascertain the best form of Bow for dividing the water. A.A. is a Canal 10 feet long, by 16 inches deep, and 12 inches broad; the sides composed of Glass, so as to enable the motion of the Fluids to be observed when disturbed by a Vessel passing through them. The Canal was filled with clear water to the line B.B., say 10 inches deep, Spirits of Turpentine (of a red transparent colour) were then poured on the water to the line C., being 1¼ inches deep. Various models were provided, made from the Plans of Vessels which had been built—these were tried separately, and at various depths. The results, from the various models, all showed the decided tendency of the upper Fluid to pass downwards; but the model drawn above gave the clearest demonstration thereof. Fig. 1 shows the Vessel in a state of rest—a line was attached at D., and carried over the end of the Canal—an observer, by looking through the Glass sides, could see the motion made in the Fluids when the Vessel was set in motion, by a small weight being made fast to the line E.—the result was, as shown in Fig. 2.—the velocity at the time being two feet per second, or 2¼ miles an hour. It is, therefore seen, that the red Fluid, although lighter than the water, runs down, when pressed on by a body in motion; and to the best of the observer's judgment, at least one third of the red Fluid displaced by the Vessel, escaped by passing downwards along the bottom and bilges; and the cause of its rising upwards, before it reaches the quarters, must be attributed to its difference in density. The thinness of the red Fluid at the Rudder is deserving of notice, as the remainder of it passed off from the quarters of the Ship, forming what is called the Wake or Track, which must be considered as being the water rushing up at the quarters from under the Bottom. The confinement of the water, by the sides of the Canal was not the cause which produced this effect, as the Fluid did not rise in the least degree on the sides of the Glass, which it would have done had that been the cause, and there was a clear space, of 4 inches, at each side between the vessel and the side—the size of the model being 24 inches by 4; neither can it be owing to any peculiarity in the horizontal or transverse shape of the Ship, as may be seen—Fig. 3. being the Load water line, and Fig. 4. the midship section. Although the above is at variance with the Hypothesis formed by most Writers on the subject, yet, judging from the above fact, it must appear evident that the perpendicular Longitudinal lines of the Fore Body ought to be as acute as the horizontal lines—thereby giving as fair course for the water downwards, as for dividing it horizontally. This is most fully attained by raking the whole Bow forward, which enables the Longitudinal lines to be made more acute, and the shape approaches nearer to the appearance of a fast swimming Fish than any form that has hitherto been tried; and, as all Vessels are designed for moving on the surface of the water, the great Fore-rake above is designed to keep up the sharp lower Bow, which it does most effectually, as in Vessels built on this plan, the fore-parts have always been found to be driest, however acute the horizontal lines may have been. Concerning the after body, although the above experiment does not make the case out so clearly, in consequence of the low density of the red Fluid, yet, from the fact of the water having to rush up the after run, it follows that the after perpendicular lines, (usually termed Buttock lines,) ought to be formed as acute as the horizontal—this is accomplished best by raking the whole after body along with the Stern Post—it is not proposed to shorten the Keel to obtain these uncommon rakes, but to make the Vessel longer above; which has also a very important effect in reducing the Tonnage, as taken by the new Registry Act, without curtailing the capacity. The improvement of the Marine of this Country being of the utmost importance, we consider it the duty of all connected therewith to make known to the profession everything which may tend to elucidate Truth, and we, therefore, submit the above to their inspection.

Aberdeen, April, 1846

James & William Hall

135: This painting of the *Pera*, which Hall built in 1843 of 191 tons nm, shows the sort of kites carried by Aberdeen clipper schooners in a fair wind. The foot of the square foresail is set on a boom, and there are stunsails to each of the three square sails. It is interesting to note how far aft the fore mast is stepped. The figurehead is now supported by a trailboard sweeping up to the feet, whereas the *Non-Such* had a much plainer bow. The artist is Skillott, who has signed his name on the buoy. *Science Museum.*

experimented before the *Scottish Maid* order was received, yet built a model for approval with a common bow, fearing to lose the order if an unconventional design was submitted. For them, it might have been the thin end of the wedge to commence construction and then make this vitally explosive suggestion which they had probably always intended to make. Or they could have been conducting their tank tests while the hull of the *Scottish Maid* was being framed.

Knowledge of these tests is obtained from a printed report that is dated April 1846 and which was issued by Alexander Hall & Sons to inform the shipping community of the benefits to be obtained by employing ships of the new design. A copy of this report which describes the tests in detail is reproduced here and it is worth noting that it is signed by James and William Hall. No date is assigned for the experiments, but the general inference is that they must have been conducted several years after the building of the *Scottish Maid* since it is reported that 'various models were provided, made from the plans of vessels which had been built'.[13] Of course, this does not invalidate the claim that the original tests were made back in 1837. However, at this late date it is not clear whether the tank experiments of James and William Hall resulted in the *Scottish Maid* or were conducted afterwards to establish and improve their empirical designs.

Recent research has shown that model tests were made in England as early as 1670 and further examples are recorded as taking place in the middle of the eighteenth century under the auspices of the Society of Arts. The Society for the Improvement of Naval Architecture was founded in 1790 and conducted numerous experiments on which reports were published. On the Continent, tank testing was employed in a theoretical manner although Chapman utilised the results in his designs.[14] In the nineteenth century, model testing was adopted as a means to achieve better designs. In America the engineer and yachtsman, Robert Stevens, conducted experiments in 1838–39 with schooner hulls, employing actual models and thereby anticipating modern practice.[15] In Dumbarton, the firm of William Denny & Brothers was making tank tests at about the same time.

One important trade-mark of Hall's clippers was the manner of fitting the bowsprit. By referring to the plan of *Scottish Maid*, it will be seen that it did not protrude from the hull like the brig *Anonyma* but entered the hull on top of the sheer and clear of the figurehead. It was a low-steeved spar, the heel tenoned into the pawl post, the raking bitts giving additional support, and the bobstay and bowsprit shrouds securing it firmly to the hull. This method of fitting the bowsprit was the crowning glory of the Aberdeen bow.

Development of the Aberdeen bow

The Aberdeen clippers that Alexander Hall & Sons set afloat in the 1840s were in every trade throughout the world. The schooners were often in the East Coast packet trade and were based largely on the *Scottish Maid* in general appearance, to judge by various paintings. The midship section of the *Swift* shows that the deadrise was increasing in some instances. Many of the schooners were rigged with royal yards and short poles above this, as the firm appear to have disliked terminating the masthead close above the rigging. Many of the clippers were painted with the now-famous Aberdeen green above the load line and even the half-model of the *Scottish Maid* in the Glasgow Museum has a dull version of this. The *Torrington*, built in 1845, was their first opium clipper. Although their first iron hull was not constructed until the late 1860s, they sometimes supplied all the woodwork for one, as in the packet schooner *Prince of Wales* for which they made all the timber spars and deck fittings. They not only gave her a royal mast and yard but a skysail pole two feet long! Some of the schooners set three headsails from the crosstrees, others only two, and the sails often ran the entire length of the stay so that the halyard blocks were close up to the lower yard. The pictures reproduced here show that the Aberdeen schooners set no precedent in this respect but continued the existing practice.

Captain Ritchie, manager of the Leith & London Shipping Co, wrote of the three schooners owned by the company, in a letter dated 16 October 1847:

> 'The *Nonsuch* was launched on the 12th, the *Rapid* on the 19th January 1842 and the *Swift* 12th October [1843]. The *Nonsuch* and *Rapid* have made ninety-six voyages each, and the *Swift* sixty-four. I have made several passages in each of them, and always found that they were much dryer in bad weather, and sailed much faster, than any other sort of vessels, besides carrying a large cargo for their tonnage. I can say with truth, that any of these clippers will go twice as fast by the wind (that is, to windward) in blowing weather as the *Robert Bruce*, the best and only smack of the Company's old ships they have not sold . . . I have never seen any sort of vessels to equal the clippers for sailing, cargo carrying, and making good weather in a gale.'[16]

There is a useful contemporary sketch of the *Torrington* reproduced in *The Opium Clippers.*[17] An eye-witness described her arrival on the China coast:

'The *Torrington* caused a great deal of interest by her appearance, among the merchants and shipowners in Canton and Hong Kong, and now that she is returned from the voyage, after performing such an extraordinary passage, there is quite a sensation among them.' And 18 months later the same correspondent wrote: 'The *Torrington* is still in all her glory – beating every clipper on the coast.' He added that she was cheap to run and, unlike the other clippers, had not been dismasted, although she had once sprung and lost her bowsprit.[18]

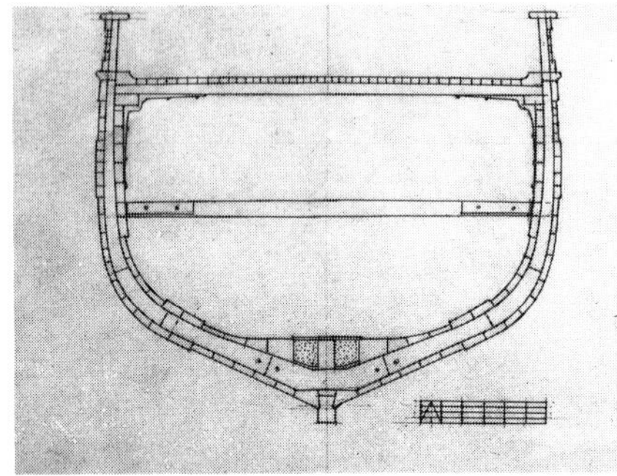

136: *Swift.* Midship section. Built in 1843 by Alexander Hall & Sons at Aberdeen. Traced, with some reconstruction, from drawing in *Lloyd's Register* survey report, so show sort of construction built into the small Aberdeen clippers in these years. Frames of oak; outer planking in elm and oak; beams of oak; deck of yellow pine. Measurements: 105ft-0½in × 22ft-9in × 13ft-4in; 253 tons om and 184 tons nm. Research by James Henderson.

The master of the schooner *Curlew*, launched in 1847 for the Cape of Good Hope trade, claimed a speed of not less than 13 knots during a period of six hours.[19]

A variation on the schooner model was required for vessels that were to carry a paying cargo and Hall's first attempt at this was to place a full midship section between extreme raking ends. The interesting and in some ways unique result may be seen in the lines of the *Acasta* in figure 139, which has been developed from the diagram issued by Alexander Hall & Sons in 1845 to sell the idea of their new design. Reproduced as figure 137, this diagram contrasts the barque *Acasta* with a ship of 'ordinary proportions' in which both have the same length of keel and midship section. Printed at the foot of the diagram, the builders comment on their design as follows:

> 'It is evident from the above that the register tonnage is reduced actually by enlarging the capacity, as not only is the measurement reduced 30 tons, but all the additional length is added to the contents, being almost the entire forecastle forward and a considerable space aftward; and at the same time the symmetry, sailing qualities and the dryness on deck are greatly increased, as has now been fully proved by the experience had from 20 to 30 vessels during the last six years.'[20]

The comparable dimensions for new measurement tonnage as printed on the diagram are set out below:

'Vessel of ordinary proportions'	102.8ft × 23.4ft × 16.7ft	356¾ tons nm
Acasta	111.4ft × 23.4ft × 16.7ft	327 2/5 tons nm
		385 15/94 tons om

137: The diagram issued by Alexander Hall & Sons of Aberdeen boosting their bow to reduce tonnage under the New Tonnage regulations of 1836. The ship with the Aberdeen bow in the diagram is the *Acasta.*

In the register dimensions listed on page 107, only the length is different, because it is measured on deck; breadth is still measured internally:

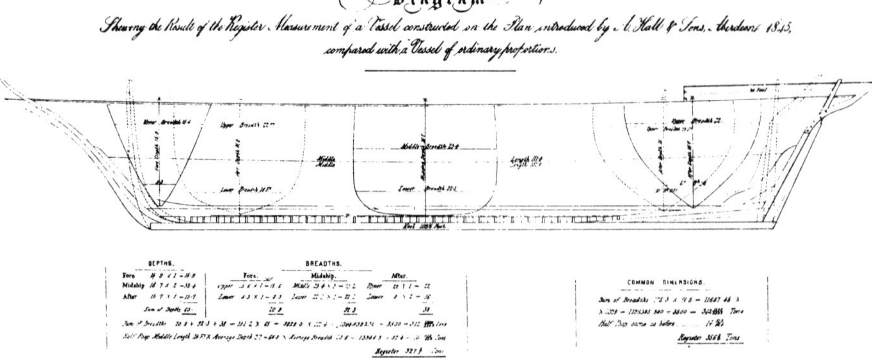

'Vessel of ordinary proportions'	104.0ft × 23.4ft × 16.7ft (length scaled off plan)
Acasta	128.3ft × 23.4ft × 16.7ft (length from builder's cost account)

These figures show the ridiculous position reached when an increase in overall length results in the figure of register tonnage being decreased. The steamer *Bonnie Dundee* was lengthened in about 1847 by 22 feet, when an Aberdeen Bow was given her; the result was that her register tonnage was *reduced* by seven tons.[21]

A useful point of comparison arises from these figures which helps in determining a vessel's fine-lined characteristics. The proportionate difference between the old measurement and new measurement tonnages provides an approximate guide to the degree of fineness, because fine-lined vessels usually possessed a lower tonnage figure by the new measurement than by the old. Thus *Scottish Maid* measured 142 tons nm and 195 tons om; *Acasta* measured 327 tons nm and 385 tons om; *Vision* (figure 236) measured 563 tons nm and 723 tons om. Conversely, full-bodied ships had a bigger new measurement tonnage and so *Thomas Arbuthnot* measured 621 tons nm and 523 tons om; *Alexander Hall* measured 403 tons nm and 358 tons om. This yardstick applies to all classes of vessels within the years 1836–54 when the new measurement tonnage rule was in force, and numerous opportunities will show its use.

It should not be imagined that after 1839 every vessel launched by Alexander Hall & Sons had a clipper bow. Far from it. Fortunately, in 1848 the *Aberdeen Journal* gave a definitive list of vessels built since 1839 'with the improved bow'. This list provides valuable evidence as to the progress made with the experimental bow in these years. The yard numbers in the composite list printed below show that in the first four years only 11 ships received the Aberdeen bow out of a total of 34 built, but that from 1843 the position was reversed and only occasional ships were built without it.

The list that appeared in the *Aberdeen Journal* gave name, rig, port of registry, register tonnage and intended trade, in addition to the date of build. These particulars have been rearranged in the following list, and the yard number and om tonnage added. It should be noted that for the year 1845 the *Aberdeen Journal* lists a brig called '*Wm. Renton*' registered in Newfoundland. No such brig was built by Hall, and the name has obviously been transposed from that of *William Punton* which is incorrectly inserted in the list under the year 1848. The list given below has corrected this error.

This list numbers thirty-six sailing craft and must obviously be the one referred

List of clippers with Aberdeen bow built by A Hall & Sons 1839–48[22]

Yard no	*Date built*	*Name*	*Rig*	*New tons*	*Old tons*	*Port of registry*	*Intended trade*
101	1839	*Scottish Maid*	sch	142	195	Aberdeen	Aberdeen & London
109	1840	*Aberdonian*	sch	146	?	Aberdeen	Aberdeen & London
110	1840	*Elizabeth*	sch	136	190	Aberdeen	Aberdeen & Newcastle
111	1840	*London*	sch	142	?	Aberdeen	Aberdeen & London
112	1840	*Port Fleetwood*	sch	162	180	Fleetwood	Cape of Good Hope
127	1841	*Lightning*	sch	177	?	Glasgow	Grangemouth & London
116	1842	ps *Iris*	sch	187	310	Copenhagen	Baltic
128	1842	*Rapid*	sch	149	217	Leith	Leith & London
129	1842	*Non-Such*	sch	151	?	Leith	Aberdeen & Leith
130	1842	*Fairy*	sch	150	?	Aberdeen	Cape of Good Hope
132	1842	*Mountain Maid*	bg	192	226	Aberdeen	Cape of Good Hope
135	1843	*Border Maid*	sch	90	135	Berwick	Berwick & London
136	1843	*Water Witch*	sch	92	146	Berwick	Berwick & London
137	1843	*Pera*	sch	191	235	Peterhead	Mediterranean
138	1843	*Ebenezer*	sch	67	100	Wick	Wick & Leith
139	1843	*Swift*	sch	183	252	Leith	Leith & London
142	1843	*Hero*	sch	52	85	St Andrews	St Andrews & Leith
143	1844	*Colloony*	bk	287	335	Glasgow	Montreal
		['rake of stem 21ft-0in from fore end of keel' LR report]					
144	1844	*Heroine*	sch	75	109	Wick	Wick & Leith
145	1844	ss or ps *Queen* 3	sch	384	?	Aberdeen	Leith & Inverness
146	1844	*Dart*	sch	88	132	Arbroath	Arbroath & London
147	1845	*Acasta*	bk	327	385	Aberdeen	General
		['clipper bow, the stem forming the head knee' LR report]					
148	1845	*William Punton*	bg	170	?	Newfoundland	Newfoundland
149	1845	*Prince of Wales*	sch	178	?	Leith	Leith & London
150	1845	*Torrington*	sch	144	237	London	Coast of China
152	1845	*White Mouse*	sch	72	?	Dartmouth	Fruit trade
153	1846	*Bon Accord*	S	380	432	London	East Indies
155	1846	*Sir William Wallace*	sch	115	165	Fraserburgh	Coaster
156	1846	*Matchless*	sch	107	170	Lerwick	Lerwick & Leith
157	1946	*Gitana*	sch	92	?	Aberdeen	General
158	1846	*Electra*	bk	306	364	London	West Indies
159	1847	*North Star*	S	385	459	London	East Indies
160	1847	*Amelia*	sch	150	240	Glasgow	Coast of China
161	1847	*Victoria*	sch	66	111	Leith	Leith & Rotterdam
162	1847	*Curlew*	sch	116	166	Aberdeen	Cape of Good Hope
163	1848	*Pilot Fish*	S	303	400	Liverpool	Brazils
164	1848	*Ben Muick Dhui*	bk	244	306	Aberdeen	Brazils
		['square stern and bow termed clipper with considerable outreach' LR report]					
165	1848	*Bonita*	S	299	398	Liverpool	Brazils
						['is formed with usual so called clipper bow carried rather to excess' LR report]	

138: Here an unmistakable Aberdeen clipper-bowed barque like *Acasta*, seen through the rigging of the ship in the foreground, is contrasted with ships of conventional design. This photograph was in possession of an Aberdeen captain, which confirms an Aberdeen origin to that raking stem. It is not known where the photograph was taken, but the date must be about 1865. No names are visible.

to in contemporary commentaries, especially when the magic number of 36 vessels is specifically mentioned.[23]

The following names are submitted as an addenda to the above list, in order to advance it to the close of 1849. The port of registry and intended trade are taken from *Lloyd's Register* and the vessels selected are those which, by contemporary description had an 'Aberdeen Bow'.

The first three-masted square-rigged vessel built with the Aberdeen bow is shown by the above list to have been the barque *Colloony* of 1844 and the first full-rigged ship to have been the *Bon Accord* of 1846. But Boyd Cable would have us believe that the *Glentanner* of 1842 was the first full-rigged ship to be built on clipper lines.[24] If it was on the question of date alone, why did he not select the *Thomas Arbuthnot* which was built the year before and was the first full-rigged ship to be constructed by Hall since the launch of the *Scottish Maid*? Boyd Cable assumed that once the Aberdeen bow had proved successful it would be built unquestioningly into every vessel produced by the yard. But many ship-owners did not require fine lines or disliked such a raking bow. In any case, it has already been shown by the surviving half-model that the *Thomas Arbuthnot* had a bluff bow and vertical stem, and the remarkable similarity of *Glentanner*'s measurements strongly suggests that she was a sister-ship. Compare these figures:

Thomas Arbuthnot .... built 1841	131.0ft × 26.4ft × 19.1ft 621 nm and 523 om tons
Glentanner .... built 1842	130.1ft × 26.2ft × 19.5ft 610 nm and 524 om tons

The beam to length ratio is approximately 5 to 1 which inevitably assisted their sailing speeds; this ratio is higher than the average for ships at this date.

The following table lists all the full-rigged ships and barques built by Alexander Hall & Sons from the launch of the *Scottish Maid* until 1849, but excluding those given in the previous table. It will be noticed that in every case, the new measurement tonnage is larger than the old measurement figure, a sign that the Aberdeen bow was absent and that the vessel was built on fuller, more conventional lines. It is submitted that none of these ships and barques can be classified as clippers. The missing yard numbers not included in either list refer to steamers, brigs, and fore-and-aft vessels which were not built with the Aberdeen bow.

Yard no	*Date*	*Name*	*Rig*	*New tons*	*Old tons*	*Intended trade*
168	1848	*Reindeer*	S	328	427	Liverpool/East Indies [see figure 113]
169	1849	*Princeza*	bg	149	?	Liverpool/Mexico ['Usual flared out clipper bow' LR report]
170	1849	*Benjamin Elkin*	S	367	425	Liverpool/Australia ['has a flared out clipper bow' LR report; half-model has lines similar to *Reindeer*]
172	1849	*Emperor*	bk	368	418	Liverpool/Brazil ['flared out bow termed clipper carried to an extreme' LR report]

(no 172 was the last vessel launched by Hall in 1849)

List of non-clipper ships and barques built by A Hall & Sons 1839–1849

Yard no	*Built*	*Name*	*Rig*	*New tons*	*Old tons*	*Remarks*
103	1839	*Ann Smith*	bk	292	?	very lofty
105	1840	*Lord Western*	bk	530	445	
106	1840	*Crusader*	bk	224	210	
115	1841	*Thomas Arbuthnot*	S	621	523	full and lofty; photograph of half-model in figure 102.
117	1841	*Trio*	bk	388	355	
122	1842	*Queen of the Isles*	bk	278	261	
123	1842	*Glentanner*	S	610	524	possible sister to no 115
126	1842	*Humayoon*	S	530	446	in China tea trade
134	1842	*Cynthia*	bk	251	242	
151	1845	*Alexander Hall*	bk	403	358	full and lofty; photograph of half-model in figure 102
167	1848	*Peruvian*	bk	413	387	'This is a full-built burdensome vessel with the common bow, nearly upright stem with cutwater and bust figure-head. . .' (LR report)

It is interesting to note that many of the fuller-built ships had lofty, narrow sail plans after the style of Hedderwick's 500-ton ship.

Some of Hall's clippers compared

The evolution of the Aberdeen bow into this splendid and raking stem is unique in British naval architecture. It recalls the long over-hang to the bows of the North American Grand Banks schooners or, nearer home, the forward raking stems of the Emsworth smacks such as the *Echo*. On the plans of *Acasta*, *Reindeer*, and *Benjamin Elkin* the forward rake measures no less than 28ft-0in from the forward end of the keel and it seems highly possible that all the ships and barques fitted with the Aberdeen bow, from the launch of the *Colloony* in 1844 until the advent of the *Stornoway* in 1850, possessed this extreme rake to a greater or lesser degree.

The lines of *Acasta* (figure 139) have been drawn from the sections and profile given on Hall's tonnage diagram and although only three sections were given, the lines plotted in very easily. A brief comment on the method employed to obtain the lines may be of interest.

The waterlines were faired in with a spline and the relation of the foremost section at station E to the positions where the waterlines intersected the stem forced the spline to produce these convex shapes at the bow. A little more care was required at the stern; here, some hollow was introduced and ship curves had to be used as the bend was too steep for the spline. The quarter-beam buttock was plotted to check the waterlines and after a little fairing, the missing sections were drawn on the body plan. Using one of Dixon Kemp's pear shaped body plan curves ensured that the sections bore the correct related shapes. Additional buttocks were drawn but very little fairing was required. It was essential, of course, to know the general hull form of Aberdeen-style ships in the 1840s and the lines of *Scottish Maid* and a Sussex copy, the *Watkins* (figure 160), were studied. Although the *Watkins* had about 28 feet of dead flats amidships, none has been given to *Acasta*. The ends of these two ships are very similar as regards the contours of the waterlines, the flatness of the floors and the full-bodied midship section. A midship section of the *Colloony* is drawn in the Lloyd's Register survey report and shows a similar shape to the *Acasta*. These square-rigged ships of the mid 'forties probably mark the extreme limit of rake to both the stem and the sternpost, although the rake to the stem did continue in this excessive form until the end of the 'forties or early 'fifties. One feature in the

139: *Acasta*. Lines: built in 1845 by Alexander Hall & Sons at Aberdeen. Redrawn and reconstructed from a diagram issued by her builders to show advantages of their new design methods. Dimensions for register: 128.3ft × 23.4ft × 16.7ft; $327\frac{2}{5}$ tons nm and $385\frac{15}{94}$ tons om. Reconstruction: figurehead; bulwarks; cathead; mast positions; lines developed from three cross-sections in above diagram.

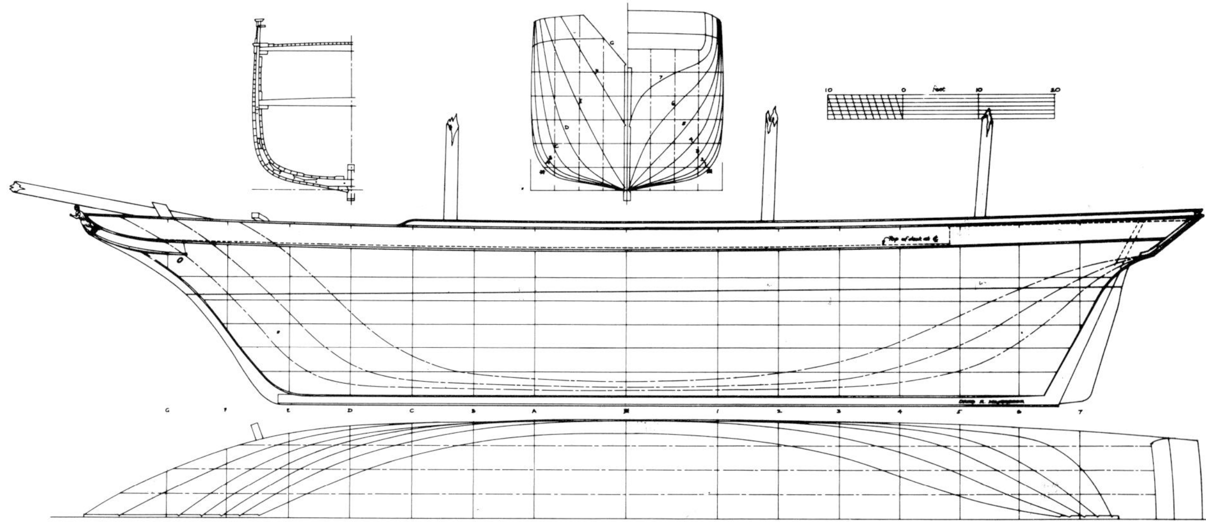

forebody of these ships is that the waterlines in the half-breadth plan run almost parallel to each other, due to the extreme rake of the stem. Similar effects can be observed in Baltimore clippers and other craft with boldly raking stems. By making the sections convex at the forefoot of the *Acasta*, the builders provided initial resistance to correct the probability of the head pitching into the sea, rather than relying entirely on the rapidly increasing latent resistance as the flaring bows cleaved into the sea, sometimes with a frightful impact. Nevertheless, some of the Aberdeen clippers did earn a reputation for pitching badly, although the master of the *Bon Accord* praised Hall for the easy motion in a head sea, as his letter, given below shows.

Arthur Smith's painting, reproduced in figure 140, of an unnamed clipper barque nearing Aberdeen harbour, probably portrays one of Hall's clippers of this period and may possibly represent the *Acasta* or the *Ben Muick Dhui*, as they were the only two such barques owned in Aberdeen between 1844 and 1852. Smith has shown her under close-reefed canvas, with topgallant masts and jibboom partly housed. The rigging of *Acasta*'s sail plan has been based on this painting. The *Acasta* had a longboat 20 feet long and a jolly boat 18 feet long; the former would have been on the main deck and the latter could well have hung in the davits which Smith's painting shows to be on the port side only. The fitting of a topgallant rail that stopped just forward of the foremast was peculiar to these Aberdeen clippers and to some other small ships of the period. It is shown in the above picture, in the painting of the clipper brig *William Punton* (figure 141) and in the engraving of Walter Hood's clipper barque *Phoenician* (figure 142), built 1847. If there was no

140: This painting by Arthur Smith pictures a barque nearing the mouth of Aberdeen harbour in heavy weather, with her top-gallant masts partially housed, her jibboom run in, and her sails furled or close-reefed. She possibly represents the *Ben Muick Dhui* (1848) or *Acasta* (1846).

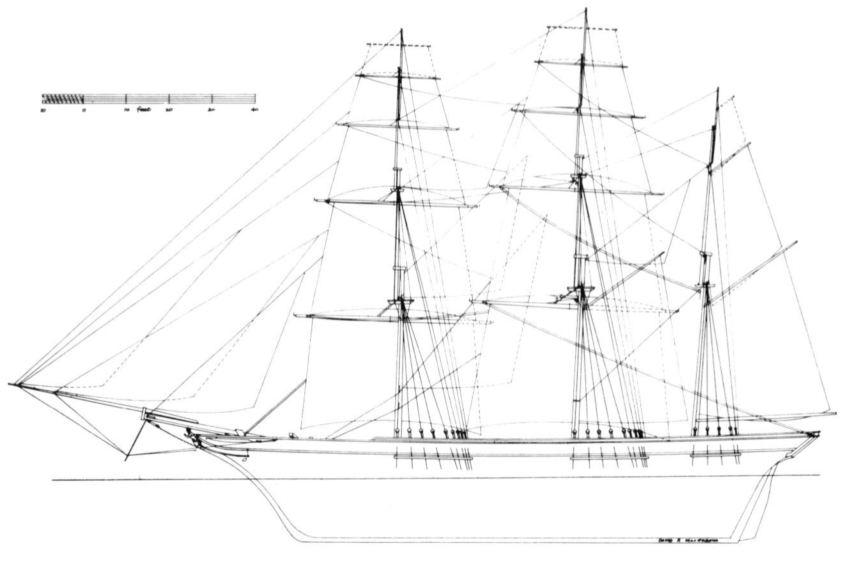

141: *Acasta*. Sail plan: Entirely reconstructed and based on a plan drawn by James Henderson. Sources: lines plan; spar dimensions from builder's cost account; spar diameters and mast positions from contemporary practice; painting of Aberdeen ship. Skysail yards not listed by builder are dotted.

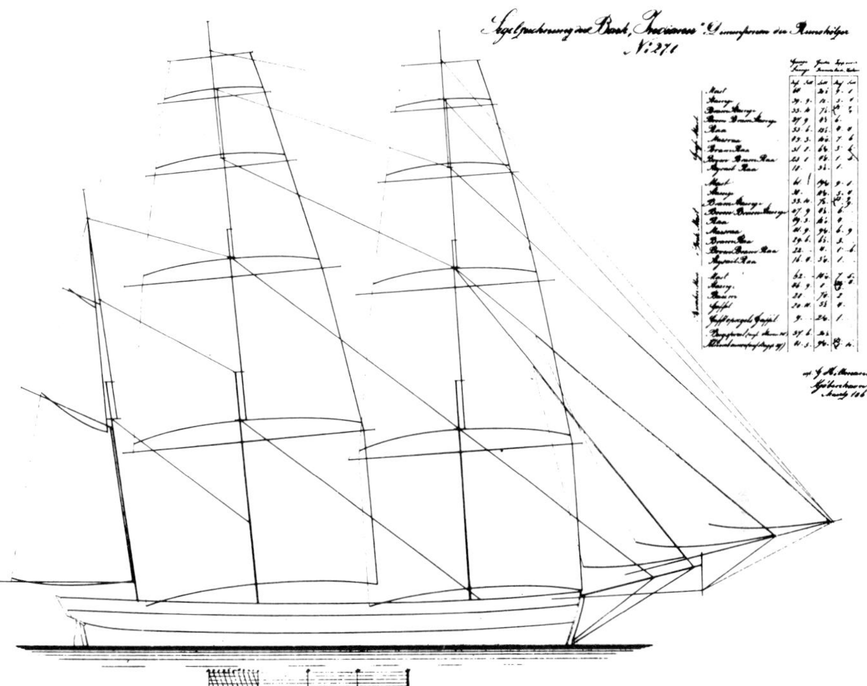

142: *Indianer*. Sail plan signed and dated: 'G. Hillmann, Copenhagen, 186[1]'. Reproduced from plan in Mariner's Museum, Newcastle News, Virginia. 150 Com. Lasten. This plan has been selected to show the lofty sail plans given to full-bodied vessels, as confirmed by her lines plan. It also indicates the use of sliding gunter poles on fore and main masts, and an alternative method of rigging the mizen mast.

anchor deck forward, the topgallant rail would have had to unship to permit work on the anchors, and so this arrangement was used in some vessels.

The *Acasta*'s sail plan shows the fitting of sliding gunter masts which are listed in the spar dimensions, the extension above the cranse iron being specified. On the fore and main, skysail yards were obviously carried in light winds although on the mizen the gunter mast was of questionable use.

As some of the Arthur Smith's paintings are reproduced here, some remarks about the artist might be of interest. Writing at the beginning of the century, William Skene recalls a scene in Aberdeen of 50 or 60 years earlier:

> 'A few doors down the Quay from Marischal Street was a shop at the windows of which the East End boys — especially those with nautical proclivities — were wont to stand for hours criticising a picture shown therein — a representation of the latest clipper ship fitted out from Aberdeen. The painting was minutely correct in every particular — ropes and spars and all.
>
> 'The artist was Arthur Smith, marine painter; and I do not think a new vessel left the port for very many years without Arthur transferring her to canvas. The only adverse criticism I ever heard on Mr Smith's painting was that he invariably had his ships sailing with a fair wind, and always sailing off Girdleness.'[25]

The two paintings by Arthur Smith included here depict an unknown barque and the *Bonita* in anything but fair winds, as both the vessels are snugged down under reduced canvas.

Some interesting comments on deck arrangements and fittings are given by the Lloyd's Register survey reports which the surveyors had to complete and send to the head office in London together with their recommendations for classification. Now preserved at the National Maritime Museum, Greenwich, they form a valuable comment on ships for whom no other technical description or appraisal has survived. When R Robinson was the surveyor at Aberdeen in the 1840s, he gave beam spacings along the side of his report which greatly assists the reconstruction of a deck plan or the positioning of the masts. Sometimes the surveyor made sketches of iron knees, keel and garboard construction, and occasionally drew a midship section, a few of which have been mentioned.

The deck layout of the *Pilot Fish*, launched in 1848, is described thus by the Lloyd's surveyor:

> 'Has a flush main deck throughout with raised house on deck for cabin extending in breadth to within 2½ feet of rail each side and in length to 3 or 4 feet of sternpost. The passage on each side and the portion abaft the house covered in and decked with 2½in yellow pine to level of lower part of main rail and made watertight. The whole forming a raised quarter deck on each side and abaft the house... Is formed with a clipper prow and round stern.'[26]

This arrangement aft was sometimes termed an 'Aberdeen house' (see plan of *Vision* figure 236).

The form of patent windlass commonly used by Hall in the 'forties was Tyzack & Dobson's although the latter name was sometimes written 'Dobinson'.

It is interesting to note that the *Bon Accord* was equipped with a longboat made of iron, in addition to three other boats. Her master, Captain Buckle, reported on his ship's performance in a letter to Alexander Hall & Sons, dated 5 February 1846 from Dover, which was reprinted in the *Aberdeen Journal*:

> '"In coming from Newcastle with 25 keels of coal we passed all we saw, both on and off the wind, with the exception of a clipper schooner, one of your own build, which was too much for us, close-hauled." The only inconvenience we felt with the long bow was in handling the anchor, a defect which has since been remedied; but, adds Captain Buckle, "the easiness it gives in riding, and in a head sea, more than compensates for this."'[27]

The sail plan of the *William Punton* is given in figure 143 to illustrate the type of clipper brig being constructed by Alexander Hall & Sons. It is reconstructed by James Henderson from the builder's spar dimensions and a painting of the vessel. The excessively long jibboom and rake to the masts form an interesting comparison with the opium clipper *Anonyma*. The *William Punton*, of course, would have set stunsails on each mast to augment the narrow sail plan, and in addition main topgallant and royal staysails would almost certainly have been carried. The trail

144: A painting of the Aberdeen brig *William Punton* in a gale. She has an extreme version of the raking stem with lengthy jibboom and flying jibboom beyond. There is a blackpainted trysail mast for the main trysail to hoist on.

143: *William Punton*. Built in 1845 by Alexander Hall & Sons at Aberdeen. Entirely reconstructed by James Henderson. Dimensions: 104.0ft × 19.6ft × 12.7ft; 170 tons nm. Square stern. Sources of reconstruction: builder's spar dimensions; painting of brig in National Maritime Museum. Owned in Harbour Grace, Newfoundland. Some accounts spell the name *Panton*.

145: *Reindeer*. Lines: Built in 1848 by Alexander Hall & Sons at Aberdeen. Drawn from lines taken off builder's half-model in Glasgow Museum and Art Gallery, Kelvingrove. Dimensions: 141.5ft × 22.7ft × 15.5ft; 328 tons nm and 427 tons om. Reconstruction: the figurehead, mast positions, cathead.

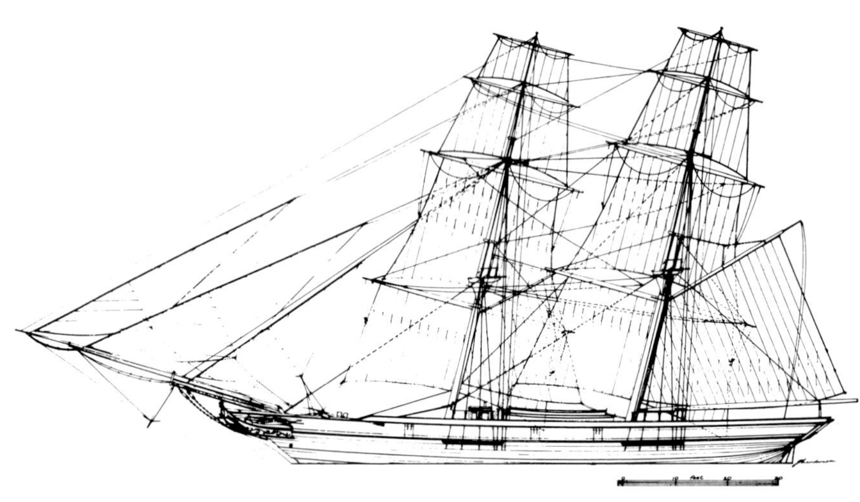

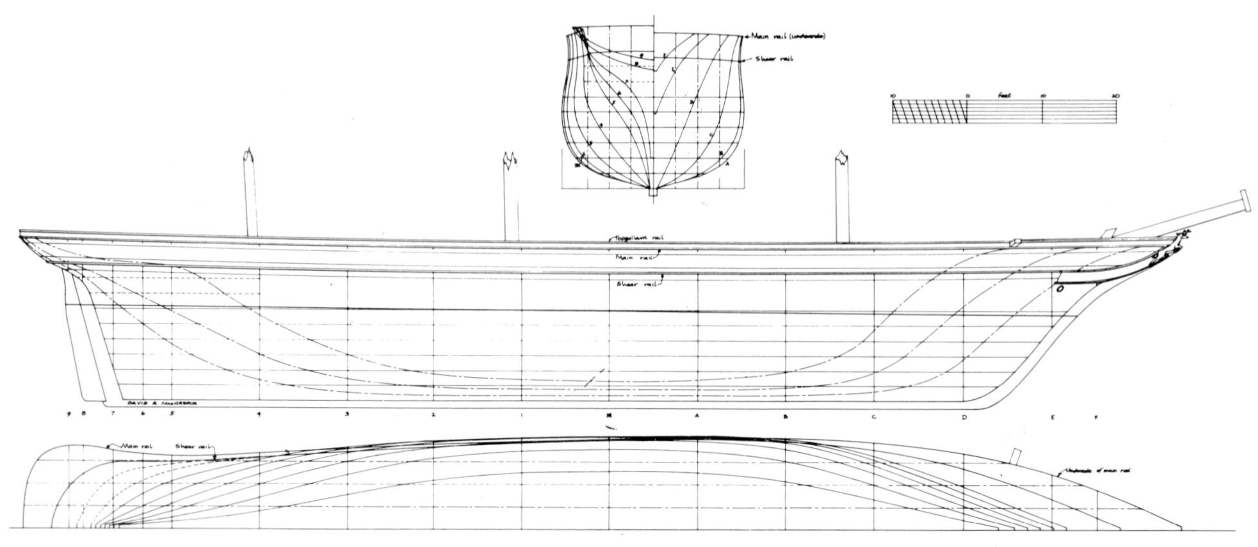

board, bow decoration and name badge correspond with those shown on paintings of Hall's clippers. No lines of the *William Punton* are known. She has a square stern. The first of Alexander Hall's sailing ships to be fitted with a round stern was the ship *North Star*, launched in 1847, but after 1849 almost all his ships had round sterns. However, this was not quite the first time he had built a round stern on a vessel as he had given one to the paddle tug *Paul Jones* in 1827.

The design of the *Reindeer* is a radical change from that of *Acasta* although the extreme rake of the stem is repeated. The lines plan in figure 145 shows that the *Reindeer* is much sharper in the entrance and run, has greater deadrise, and is longer in proportion to breadth and depth; the ratio of beams to length is almost 6¼ to 1. The body plan is now bell-shaped with slack bilges and tumblehome, above which the topsides flare outwards. The load line at the entrance is straight but there are hollows lower down. An indication of high potential speed is the fact that the quarter-beam buttock crosses the load line aft in a straight line. The *Reindeer* was indeed one of the sharpest clippers yet built up to this time in Great Britain, but two experimental features are to be seen in her plan, namely, the shape of her stern and the flaring topsides.

146: This painting by Arthur Smith depicts the *Bonita* under reduced canvas. Built the same year as *Reindeer*, she was thirty tons smaller, but probably very similar in appearance. What a different form of hull this was to nearly every other ship afloat.

The stern is most unusual but cannot be a pure flight of fancy for her alone because the half-model of the *Benjamin Elkin*[28] incorporates such a stern, and so does an unidentified half-model in Alexander Hall & Sons' office, as illustrated in figure 133. In addition, there is a significant entry about a brig (c. 1845) in the National Maritime Museum's *Catalogue of Ship-Models* which reads: 'The shape of the hull forward is an extreme example of the "Aberdeen Bow" . . . In the present case this may be exaggerated, while the pinched effect towards the stern is also somewhat doubtful'.[29] Unfortunately, a search at the Museum in 1965 failed to dis-

147: *Reindeer.* Sail plan: Entirely reconstructed and based on a plan drawn by James Henderson. Sources: lines plan; spar dimensions from builder's cost account; spar diameters and mast positions from contemporary practice; painting of *Bonita* and other Aberdeen clippers.

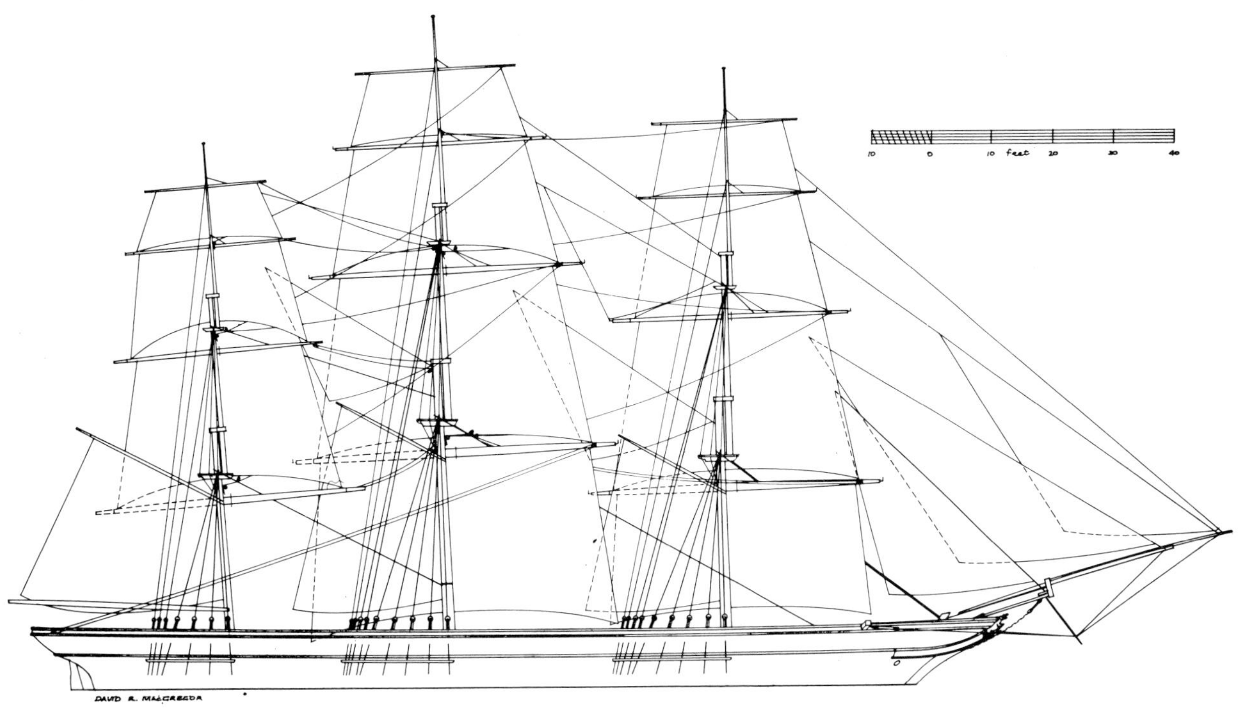

148: This watercolour was painted by the Dutch artist D A Teupken and is dated 1850. The name *Emperor* was identified by Marryat's signal flags. Lloyd's Register survey report assigns her 'flared out bow termed clipper carried to an extreme'. See further comments in text. *Private Collection.*

cover the whereabouts of this model, but Dr R C Anderson who compiled the catalogue was surely describing a hull similar to the *Reindeer*. The dimensions for this model are given as 96ft-0in (length) by 21ft-0in (beam), but no depth is stated, and the figures are undoubtedly external dimensions. They fail to agree with the dimensions of any brig built by Hall during the 'forties, the nearest being the *Mountain Maid* (1842) which had internal measurements of 99.5ft by 19.2ft by 13.1ft. Under external measurement, the breadth might increase to approximately 20.7ft. This 'pinched effect toward the stern' may have been intended to decrease the measurements for the calculation of tonnage, as the aftermost set of breadths were taken just where the hull becomes narrowest. Or perhaps it was intended to afford additional buoyancy aft when running before a following sea. It is claimed that the painting of the ship *Bonita* (figure 146) illustrates such a stern, but it is hard to determine if this is so.

In the same way, the introduction of tumblehome may have reduced the measurements for tonnage breadths and the flaring topsides were possibly introduced to retain a good beam for spreading the lower shrouds, which was important on such a narrow hull.

The *Reindeer*'s lines were taken from the builder's half model in the Glasgow Museum and Art Gallery, and the sail plan is drawn from the builder's spar dimensions and a reconstructed spar plan prepared by James Henderson. The builder's figures do not give the rake or position of the masts and these have been reconstructed with the assistance of the beam spacings and mast centres for the *Benjamin Elkin*, which the Lloyd's Register surveyor noted on the edge of his report. *Reindeer* could not have been classed with Lloyd's as her name does not appear in the register book and this explains the absence of a survey report. The painting of the *Bonita* has been exceedingly useful in determining the run of the rigging and the deck layout. The *Reindeer* has a raised quarter-deck, a round stern, no quarter galleries, and the figurehead of a reindeer. As Thomas McTear and Robert Vining of Liverpool owned shares in both the ships listed below and negotiated their building and cost with Hall's, it is reasonable to assume that the deck layout and rigging would have been similar. Their respective measurements are:

Bonita	built 1848	299 tons nm, 398 om, 134.7ft × 22.5ft × 15.2ft
Reindeer	built 1848	328 tons nm, 427 om, 141.5ft × 22.7ft × 15.5ft

The contract with McTear and Vining had read, 'say 375 tons at £10 per ton' for building and fitting out, which works out at £3750; extras had amounted to £137.11.1, which produces a total of £3887.11.1.

Like many of the clippers at this time, *Reindeer* was sent out to China but after three such voyages — the first under the renowned Anthony Enright, later master of *Chrysolite* and *Lightning* — she was placed in the South America trade, as had been the *Bonita*. On her maiden voyage she sailed out to Hong Kong in 108 days from Liverpool and returned in 106 days. She was lost in 1856.

The *Benjamin Elkin* cost £15 per ton and the extra money went into the cost of timber which was mostly of mahogany, the deck fittings being of polished mahogany.[31] Making allowance for nine inches more depth of hold than *Reindeer*, her midship section is virtually of the same shape, as also are her lines and general hull form.

It also seems probable that the barque *Emperor* of 1849 was of similar hull form to these two, especially as her new measurement tonnage was only one ton more than the *Benjamin Elkin*. The *Emperor* is of particular interest, due to the discovery of a watercolour drawing of her done by the Dutch artist Teupken and dated 1850, and reproduced here as figure 148. The hull possesses the long raking stem to a marked degree and the care with which the rigging has been lined in, suggests that a sail and rigging plan of the barque was provided for the artist's use. A single reef has been taken in the topsails, but both the courses are set in addition to all sails set below the crossstrees. The royal yards, and main skysail yard, are not crossed. There are five shrouds to the foremast and mainmast, and four to the mizen.

The Aberdeen bow had been evolved as a result of the 1836 tonnage law and the arguments in favour of the bow remained valid for as long as the tonnage was measured in this way; but the 1854 Merchant Shipping Act introduced a new system of tonnage measurement which abruptly terminated the basis for the bow. In practice, the extreme raking stem of such ships as the *Reindeer* was not repeated after 1850, although the use of more

Building costs of the *Reindeer*[30]

Carpenters' wages	£1007. 8.4
Ironwork, to hull and rigging	£ 457.15.8½
Boat building	£ 58. 7.5
Block making	£ 78. 8.1
Painting	£ 64. 6.4
Cooper's work	£ 15.13.6
Pitch, tar and oakum	£ 52. 7.8
Wm Simpson & Co for chains, anchors, ropes and sails	£ 402.10.0
Peter McMillan	£ 8. 2.9
Cash paid; shore dues	£ 3. 2.0
Timber and plank	£1739. 9.3½
	£3887.11.1

moderate raking stem rabbets did remain in several designs such as those of *Vision* and *Schomberg*. By 1856, the builder's half-model of the *Robin Hood* shows the stem in transition from the raking Aberdeen bow to the more conventional clipper bow; by the mid 'sixties, the change was complete.

149: The Aberdeen raking stem of the early composite ship *Bristow*, built at Liverpool in 1854. This is a detail from the photograph reproduced in figure 190. The sheer rail terminates rather clumsily against the trailboard. *MacGregor Collection.*

Influence of the Aberdeen bow

It is now time to consider the influence of Hall's new design and the impact on other shipbuilders.

In Aberdeen itself it was a few years before other shipbuilders launched a vessel with Hall's raking stem, presumably because they were not immediately convinced of its utility or did not receive any orders from shipowners that would have changed their opinion. It was in 1844 that a Lloyd's Register surveyor first described as 'clipper' a schooner from a yard at Aberdeen other than Alexander Hall's. This was the 'clipper schooner *Queen of the Tyne*' which Walter Hood built, appropriately, for an Aberdeen shipowner and which measured 192 tons nm and 289 tons om on dimensions of 106.0ft by 24.25ft by 13.3ft. The surveyor wrote that 'she has a raking stem forming the knee of the head'.[32] Later the same year, another Aberdeen yard, that of Alexander Duthie, built the 'clipper schooner *Favourite*' for a Burghead owner with tonnages of 80nm and 130om. According to the Lloyd's Register survey reports extant and the relationship of the new and old measurement tonnages, Walter Hood's yard produced about a dozen vessels with the Aberdeen bow between 1844 and 1849 and Alexander Duthie's yard eight such vessels in the same period.

Although the Aberdeen bow became generally accepted as producing a graceful apperance with improved sailing qualities, the principles behind its introduction became greatly modified in the process. Many ships copied the hull only above the waterline,

150: The Aberdeen clipper brig *Granite* under close-reefed topsails, courses, fore topmast staysail and spanker, as depicted by the artist E J Gregory. This brig was built at Aberdeen in 1846 by Walter Hood and she had a tonnage of 186 nm. *Private Collection.*

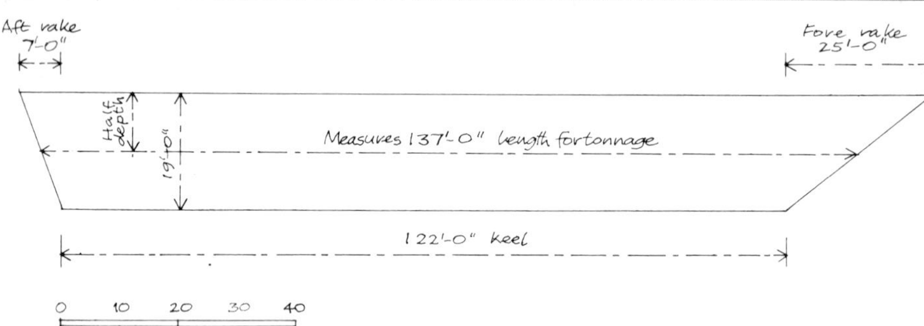

151: *Phoenician.* Diagram to show how the *Phoenician*'s tonnage length could be 10ft-0in shorter than the register length.

retaining the traditional shape below. Such examples include the iron schooners *Proto* (1841) and *Caledonia* (1850). But early interest was undoubtedly expressed and one mark of this was the copying of the schooner *Rapid*, as claimed by the *Aberdeen Journal* in 1848: 'The *Iris* was the first steamer built [by Hall] with the "Aberdeen bow", but now it is generally followed in the Clyde; the model having been taken, in the first intance, from the *Rapid* of Leith . . .'[33] Her lines may have been taken off although it does not specifically state this; however, a visual copy is liable to misinterpretation before the impression is transferred to paper. A copy of the *Acasta*'s type can be found in the plan of the barque *Watkins*, built in 1847 at Newhaven. Speculative interest has been shown by recent authors in the order placed for a fruit schooner by a Dartmouth owner which resulted in the *White Mouse* being delivered in 1845.[34] More than mere curiosity must have prompted such an order and one wonders what shipping centres James and William Hall visited, displaying models of their new design and seeking orders for new ships. Alexander Stephen's diary of the 'fifties and 'sixties reveals the large amount of travelling he undertook to the principal ports and tells of the other shipbuilders he met there, amongst whom the name of William Hall features prominently.[35] After 1845 many orders were received in Aberdeen from owners in London and Liverpool which must have been based on real satisfaction and competitive prices. Even the naval architect John Fincham was influenced and the plate of a 'Clipper Schooner' of 240 tons om, in his book *Outline of Ship-Building*, although of an unnamed and so far unidentified vessel, clearly indicates the Aberdeen bow.[36] Examples can be cited from foreign countries where plans show that the Aberdeen bow was copied: a 'clipper schooner-brig' from Holland in the late 'forties, with vertical stem below the load waterline and raking stem rabbet above;[37] in the brigantine *Harmonie* built at Troense, Denmark, in the 'fifties with a stem raked like *Acasta*'s;[38] and vessels built and designed by Ebenezer Moseley at La Have, Nova Scotia, in the 'fifties.[39]

It is worth looking at some of these examples in greater detail, commencing with ships built at Aberdeen in yards other than that of Hall's.

Of Walter Hood's ships not a single plan or model appears to exist except for the *Thermopylae* and possibly for the *Salamis*, so one is left to speculate on the hull form from descriptions, which the evidence of plans show to be notoriously unreliable, and pictures. Two of Hood's clippers in this early period were schooners, seven were brigs and the others barques and ships. The *Illustrated London News* gives the dimension of the *Phoenician*'s rake of stem as 25ft-0in and that of the sternpost as 7ft-0in.[40] This places her in the same category as *Acasta* and *Reindeer*. George Thompson of Aberdeen who ran the 'Aberdeen White Star Line', owned her and also the *Oliver Cromwell* and *John Bunyan*. It seems probable that all three were of similar hull form, in spite of a discrepancy in *John Bunyan*'s dimensions which will be discussed below. Here are the measurements by the 1854 Register Act:

Three clipper ships built by Walter Hood & Co.

Name	*Date*	*Rig*	*Tons nm*	*Tons om*	*Register dimensions by 1854 Act*
Phoenician	1847	bk	478	521	147.0ft × 27.4ft (external) × 19.0ft (122.0ft keel)
Oliver Cromwell	1847	S	478	527	148.5ft × 27.3ft (external) × 18.7ft
John Bunyan	1848	S	466	526	150.3ft × 27.7ft (external) × 18.3ft

To indicate the difficulties involved in tonnage and registry measurements, it may be mentioned that the Lloyd's Register survey report assigns the *John Bunyan* dimensions of 137.3ft by 25.0ft by 18.3ft. With almost identical tonnages, these smaller dimensions are obviously incompatible and are undoubtedly those used for tonnage measurement. Clarification is obtained in several ways: first, by the *Illustrated London News* which gave an extreme breadth of 27ft-5in to *Phoenician*, thus showing that the breadth listed in the above table is not internal; second, by drawing a trapezium with *Phoenician*'s measurements of keel, fore and aft rakes, and depth of hold, wherein the tonnage length at half the depth measures approximately 137ft-0in; third, by discovering that *John Bunyan* was never lengthened.

Of *Phoenician*, the *Illustrated London News* remarked with some pride that 'sailing and carrying powers were never more happily combined than in this vessel; which has discharged 780 tons of deadweight, and invariably made such passages as have not been surpassed either by British or American-going ships'.[41] These passages had resulted in her making a round trip from Sydney to London and back in eight months during 1851, but what the papers particularly liked at the time was that she could carry a cargo that measured 50 per cent more than her register tonnage. A clear engraving of her was given, as reproduced in figure 152, which resembles in several respects Arthur Smith's painting of the unknown Aberdeen barque: the termination of the topgallant bulwarks forward; the gallows top to the winch; the position of the davits; the shape of the stern; and the iron railing around the raised quarter-deck. The *Phoenician* carried a 23-foot long-boat, which is not shown in the engraving, and two other boats. The line of the main and mizen topmast stays suggests she had trysail gaffs on the foremast and the mainmast which was a regular Aberdeen feature until well into the 'fifties. It is assumed that the *Oliver Cromwell* and the *John Bunyan* were ship-rigged versions of her, and an oil painting of the latter by a Chinese artist largely confirms this.[42] The *John Bunyan* has been chiefly remembered for a passage from Shanghai of 98 or 99 days which turned out to be of the same duration as one made by the American clipper *Oriental* of over twice her tonnage.

152: The *Phoenician* built by Walter Hood & Co in 1847 had a bow which imitated Hall's designs. This engraving appeared in February 1852, five years after her launch. The topgallant rail only commences some distance abaft the cathead.

153: The clipper barque *Ocean Queen* which John Duthie built in 1846. This painting is by J Heard. The topgallant rail starts much further aft than usual. *Parker Gallery*.

The facts were twisted by British journalists to boost our clippers; but it is impossible adequately to compare passages made at different seasons and from departure ports 860 miles apart. A fuller comment can be found in *The Tea Clippers*.[43]

John Duthie's clipper ship *Countess of Seafield* was launched on the same tide as the *John Bunyan* and like her was placed in the China tea trade. Her measurements were 140.2ft by 25.0ft by 18.2ft with tonnages of 450 nm and 520 om. The Lloyd's Register surveyor reported that she had the 'clipper bow as termed carried rather to an extreme in outreach and a full length figurehead'. Of two of Duthie's other clipper ships the surveyors wrote: the barque *Ocean Queen* (1846) 'has no knightheads or hawse timbers.

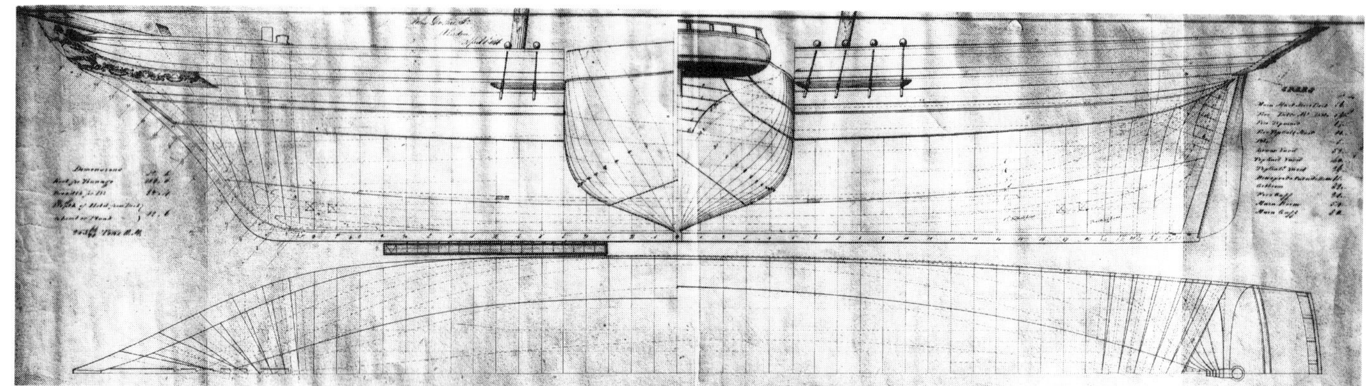

154: Aberdeen schooner. Unidentified. Signed and dated: 'John Duthie Jnr, Aberdeen, April 1, 1846'. Reproduced from original plan in Nederlandsch Historisch Scheepvaart Museum, Amsterdam. Dimensions on plan: 106ft-0in (keel for tonnage) × 12ft-6in (depth of hold from deck to limber plank); 253 64/94 tons.

155: The *Proto*, built in 1841, was an early copy in iron of an Aberdeen clipper schooner. *Parker Gallery*.

The bowsprit is secured by stout bitts bolted to the upper deck and hold beams, and shackled to the inside of stem'; the barque *Shepherdess* (1850) is 'formed with the flared clipper bow carried to a considerable extent'. The clipper schooner *Thames* was built in 1847 of 126 tons for the Berwick Shipping Co, which was already running two steamers between the River Tweed and London. The local Berwick shipbuilding firm of AB Gowan & Son built a further two schooners for the company, based on the design of the *Thames*, and a picture of one of them, the *Teviot* (1848), shows a bow with a rake like the *Reindeer*'s.[44]

There is a lines plan of a clipper schooner with an Aberdeen bow in the Nederlandsch Historisch Scheepvaart Museum at Amsterdam, which is dated 1 April 1846 and is signed by John Duthie jnr. Measurements in English are inscribed on the plan: 106ft-0in keel for tonnage, 22ft-4in breadth for tonnage, 12ft-6in depth of hold and 253 64/94 tons om. As this is old measurement tonnage, 3/5 of the beam should be added to find the length 'aloft' which would result in a length of 119ft-4½in from the forepart of the stem to the after side of the sternpost. However, no vessel in the Lloyd's Register survey reports fits these dimensions and as the drawing has been endorsed 'English schooner' in Dutch it may have been a projected design for use in Holland, where the Aberdeen bow was occasionally copied. The figurehead represents a winged angel. The total depth of the keel is 1ft-8in, the floors 11in, and the keelson 1ft-3in, as scaled off the plan. The cant timbers run forward at a very acute angle to the centre line. Spar dimensions are listed on the original and are virtually identical with those of the *Scottish Maid*, apart from the topsail yard and main boom which are 3ft-0in and 5th-6in longer respectively. The lines are also much alike but with firmer bilges, a slightly concave entrance, and greater rake to both stem and sternpost.

It is now time to mention in more detail vessels built in yards outside Aberdeen, but designed with an Aberdeen bow.

Among these is an early example of an iron schooner named *Proto* which was built by John Laird at Birkenhead in 1841 for the London & Liverpool Shipping Co. Whereas a lithograph portrays her as similar to *Scottish Maid* above the load line, a lines plan indicates considerable differences below with hollows in the lower waterlines, more balanced ends and flatter floors.[46] Perhaps her master or owners saw the *Scottish Maid* in the Thames, admired her clean entrance and ordered a schooner from Laird of similar appearance without knowing the principles behind the Aberdeen schooner's design. The inscription to the lithograph assigns the *Proto* with dimensions of 87ft-0in length on deck by 20ft-2½in by 12ft-4½in and tonnages of 128 nm and 155 om. All John Laird's ships were built of iron, his first being launched in 1829. *Proto* was the forty-first. The late Brian Savin-Taylor traced this plan when he was an apprentice draughtsman at Cammell Laird's yard and gave me a blue print of it. It is reproduced here as figure 156.

Another iron schooner is the *Caledonia*,

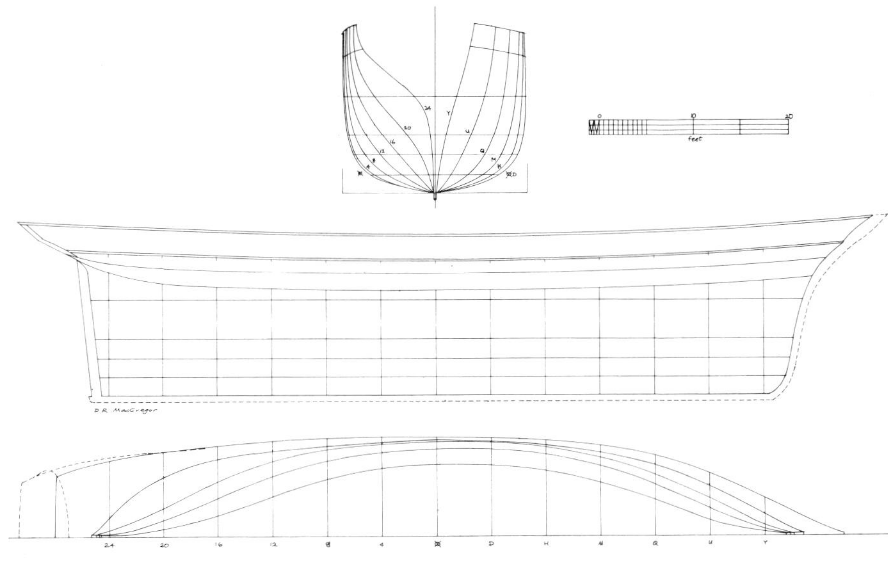

156: *Proto*. Lines plan. Built of iron at Birkenhead in 1841 by John Laird. Redrawn from tracing made c1938 by Brian Savin-Taylor of builder's plan; his blueprint donated to me in 1949. See text for dimensions. Reconstructions: stern overhung on half-breadth plan; stations in bodyplan from sheer line to rail cap; two lower waterlines omitted in half-breadth plan, but waterline no 4 was omitted on blueprint.

built by William Denny & Brothers at Dumbarton in 1850, with measurements of 99-3ft by 21-2ft by 12-5ft and 187 tons nm; she was owned in Stockton by the Stockton & London Shipping Co. The Lloyd's Register surveyor describes her as a 'clipper schooner' in his report. Her plans are in the National Maritime Museum, Greenwich, and are reproduced here in figure 158 to illustrate

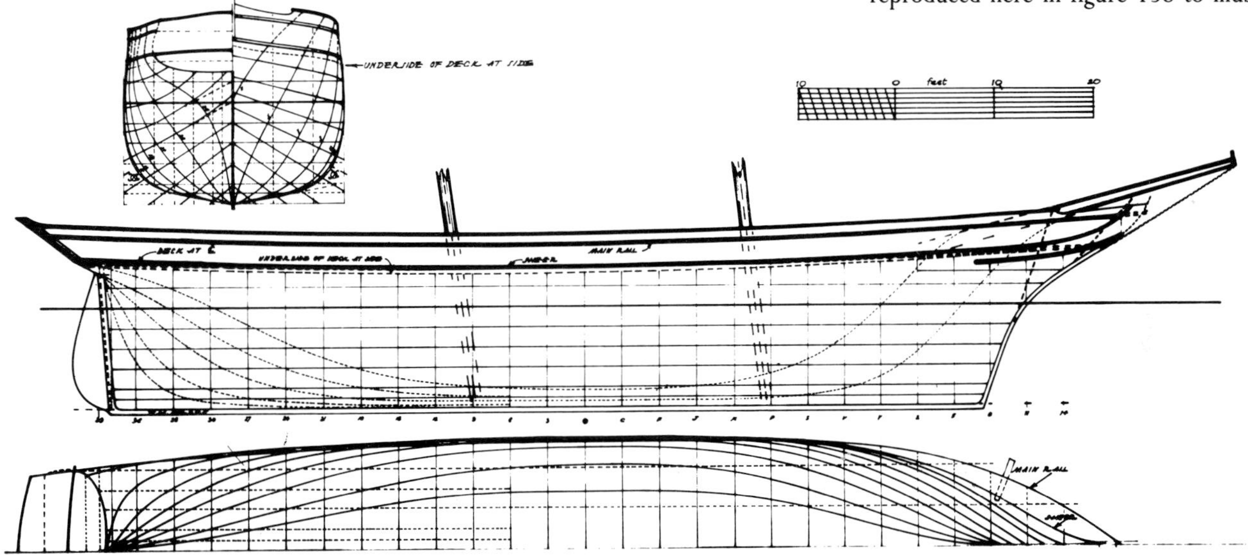

158: *Caledonia*. Lines: Built of iron in 1850 by Denny Bros at Dumbarton. Redrawn from original plan in National Maritime Museum. Dimensions: 99.3ft × 21.2ft × 12.5ft and 187 tons nm. Dimensions of hatchways written on sheer elevation in pencil.

157: A painting by John o'Brien of the Nova Scotian barque *Stag* indicates an extreme form of Aberdeen bow adopted by some copyists. She was built in 1854 at La Have, Nova Scotia, and measured 103.8ft × 22.6ft × 12.6ft and 209 tons. Her fastest speed was 12.6 knots and her best day's run was 225 miles. *Maritime Museum of Canada.*

the style of draughtsmanship at Denny's yard. Like *Scottish Maid*, there are few hollows in the waterlines, but she has flatter floors and in this respect bears greater similarity to the barque *Acasta*. Unfortunately, there is no deck plan, but some of the hull plating is drawn on the body plan. There is a fair amount of detail on the sail plan which like all of Denny's plans clearly indicates the stunsails

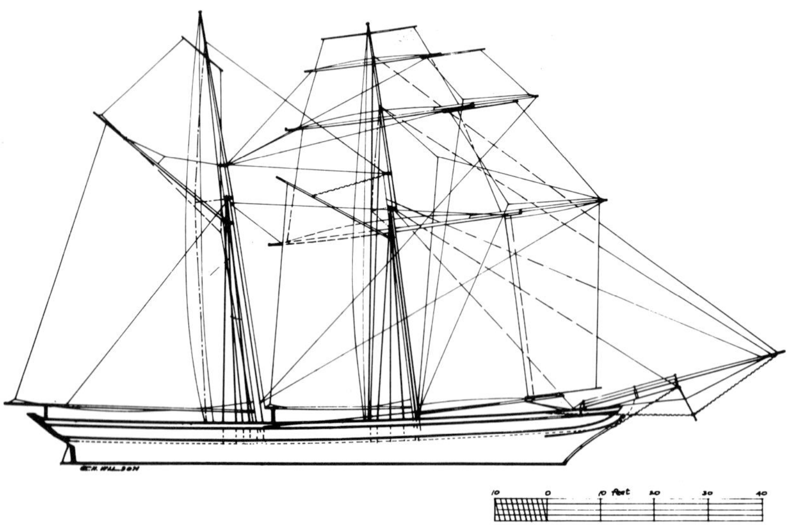

159: *Caledonia.* Sail plan: Redrawn from original plan in National Maritime Museum. Waterline made to agree with lines plan.

160: *Watkins.* Built in 1848 by John Gray at Newhaven. Redrawn from original plan in National Maritime Museum, signed and dated 'John Gray, Newhaven July 1847'. Dimensions on plan: 122ft-0in (extreme length for old tonnage) × 24ft-0in (extreme breadth for old tonnage) × 15ft-6in (depth of hold); $329^{62}/_{94}$ tons om and $288^{1307}/_{3500}$ tons nm. Reconstruction: height of masts from angle of chain plates; length of bowsprit; separation of sheer elevation and longitudinal section. Body plan did not exist and is reconstructed from half-breadth plan and midship section.

and their gear. Presumably, the square sail boom hooked on to the foremast like a passaree boom and was only employed to boom out the weather clew, but the lower stunsail boom was also secured to the boom's outer end which is an arrangement shown in several of Denny's sail plans. Short-dotted lines indicate chain rigging. The inner fore topmast stay has been crossed out in pencil and a third stay drawn in pencil from the fore crosstrees to the jibboom end.

The circumstances which resulted in the Stockton & London Shipping Co adding the iron schooner *Caledonia* to their fleet are now forgotten, and one can only surmise on the circumstances which led them to order from a Clyde-side yard rather than from a builder on the Wear or the Tyne. The contract price of £2900 was accepted on 22 April 1850 by C Martin on behalf of the owners, on a visit he made to Denny's yard. The breakdown of costs is as follows: iron hull £1288; woodwork £816 (presumably including spars); furnishing £478. Allowing for some extra disbursements, this gave a net profit on the contract of £267.[47]

This was the Company's only iron vessel and on her first appearance in Stockton the local paper commented on the 'beautiful new iron schooner arrived Thursday last named *Caledonia* from Dumbarton where she was built. . . model and rig greatly admired, the like of her having never been seen on the river'.[48] She was sold in 1857 for £1800. During the 'fifties she is reported, by a later writer, as having capsised two or three times in the Tees. Her first owners employed her to carry cargo and a few passengers between Stockton and London.

Other iron clipper schooners built by William Denny & Brothers in these years were the shallow draught *Annsbro'* (1846) built with a centreboard working on a pivot, which could project eight feet below the keel when lowered; the *Shamrock* (1849); and the *El Zeide* (1851). Most of the steamers produced by the yard until the mid-fifties also had the Aberdeen bow.

At the National Maritime Museum, Greenwich, there is an untitled drawing, signed by John Gray and dated 'Newhaven July 1847', which Michael Bouquet identified as the *Watkins.* This barque was built in 1848 by Gray at his Newhaven shipyard and the plan shows her to be a copy of an Aberdeen clipper such as *Acasta.* She has the raking stem rabbet, absence of sheer, full midship section, convex entrance, raised quarter-deck, square stern, and bowsprit entering the hull on top of the sheer. Tonnages of 288 nm and 330 om, written on the plan, are confirmed in the Lloyd's Register survey report of the *Watkins.* The plan also gives dimensions of 122ft-0in length for old tonnage, 24ft-0in extreme breadth for old tonnage, and 15ft-6in depth of hold. The half-breadth plan, longitudinal and midship sections are redrawn in figure 160 from the original. Strangely enough,

161: The *Swordfish*, which Thomas J Ditchburn designed, was built by Joseph Cunard at Miramichi in 1845. Her figurehead of a swordfish can just be discerned. The standing trysail gaffs were regular equipment for many ships at this date. She makes an interesting comparison with the Aberdeen clippers of the forties.

there was no body plan, but this has been easily reconstructed with the help of a cross-section which shows her construction. Nor are any of the deck fittings drawn in plan. The Lloyd's Register survey report allots her three boats: a longboat of 23 feet, a gig of 22 feet, and a jolly boat of 18 feet. Her windlass was Tyzack & Dobinson's patent; she had a double winch; she was rigged with trysails on all three masts and carried a full suit of stunsails. In appearance, she must have closely resembled the barque *Lewes* which John Gray built seven years later.[49]

On 21 April 1852 John Gray launched the barque *Electric Telegraph* which George Moorsom refers to in his book on tonnage measurement as 'very long, very shallow, full in midships and very sharp at extremities' and further that she was a 'remarkable vessel - of most unusual form and proportions'.[50] This sums up the general hull form of the *Watkins* or possibly a finer lined version of it, and suggests that many of Gray's ships at this date were influenced by the Aberdeen bow. The *Electric Telegraph* measured 215 tons nm and 285 tons om with a length on deck of 113ft-0in. She was sold to Liverpool owners in 1852–3 and renamed *Novidade*.

The widespread demand in the early 1850s for sailing ships of maximum potential speed brought the Aberdeen model into greater prominence and the national press acclaimed it, particularly when comparing passages in the China tea trade made between British and American ships. This fame undoubtedly brought orders to the Aberdeen yards, but although shipbuilders throughout the kingdom were besieged with demand for better and faster ships and some firms were influenced by the Aberdeen model, there were others who considered they could improve on it or produce superior designs. Naval architecture then, as now, was a question of personal opinions, tastes and whims, and each shipbuilder fiercely contended that his own products were the best.

Other clippers of the 1840s

Not every naval architect was regularly employed in a shipyard and many acted purely as consultant designers, a practice that was to increase as ship design became more specialised, as new materials were introduced and as competition increased together with the combination of higher speeds and maximum capacity. Traditional methods of construction remained but the length of the contract was frequently shortened. Owners would learn of a profitable trade and would sanguinely expect to place a ship in it overnight and this they would sometimes accomplish if suitable ships were on the market. The new designers had to think equally in terms of wood and iron, of sail and steam.

One such naval architect was William Rennie who designed many fast-sailing ships in the quarter century from 1845. The first record of a clipper ship designed by him is contained in the inscription on a lithograph, representing the barques *Beraza* and *Raphael* under sail, which reads: 'These two barks of most extraordinary speed were designed by Mr William Rennie, and built by Joseph Cunard Esq, expressly for the trade between Liverpool and Vera Cruz'.[51] The *Beraza* was built in 1846 and measured 339 tons nm and 375 tons om. Joseph Cunard's shipyard was at Miramichi and both vessels were owned in London by McCalmont. At that time Rennie had a shipyard near Miramichi, but moved to Liverpool in 1848; he will be referred to in more detail in chapter six.

The year before, Cunard had built another vessel for McCalmont which was the full-rigged ship *Swordfish* of 345 tons. She was designed by Thomas Joseph Ditchburn

(1801–1870) as stated in the inscription to a lithograph of this ship: 'Celebrated for the rapidity of her voyages between Liverpool and Brazil and especially for having performed a remarkable passage from Pernambuco to Liverpool in 22 days. Was built by Joseph Cunard & Co of Miramichi from a drawing by T J Ditchburn Esq of Blackwall'. This lithograph is reproduced in figure 161; the ship's hull is green and the figurehead represents a swordfish. A contemporary newspaper confirmed this fast passage which terminated at Liverpool in the first week of January 1846, and added:

> 'Her average speed for the voyage (with the exception of one day calm and last five days) was 220 miles per day of 24 hours; and, until the last few days, she experienced very mild weather, and had her studding sails set the entire passage. This vessel performed the outward passage, leaving here in October last, in 27 days, and on a former occasion went out in 25 days.'[52]

T J Ditchburn was manager of Fletcher, Son & Fearnall's works at Poplar for 15 years from about 1824, following his seven years' apprenticeship in Chatham Dockyard. During his time at Fletcher's, he superintended the alteration of the bow and reshaping the entrance in numerous steamers which greatly improved their performance. As Fletcher's built the fruit schooner *Time* in 1832, it follows that Ditchburn must have designed her. He favoured a long, fine entrance and the total abandonment of the 'cod's head' form of bow. He gained considerable praise for the beauty of form and speed of the steam yacht *Fairy*, built of iron in 1845 as a tender to the Royal yacht. From about 1838 and in association with Charles Mare, he built over 400 steamers at Blackwall in the space of ten years.[53] In 1846, he designed and built in his own yard the iron brig *Recruit*, one of the early iron warships. She had a very fine entrance and run with exceedingly hollow floors and big deadrise which emphasised great depth of keel; maximum breadth was at the load line and there was a fair tumblehome above.[54] It is obvious, therefore, that the *Swordfish* would have received very fine lines and possibly considerable deadrise when built in 1845 to his design. It is probable that Thomas Ditchburn played an important role in the development of fine-lined sailing ships in the 'thirties and 'forties which has since been forgotten and overshadowed by the success of his paddlewheel steamers. Two of his iron yachts, the *Mystery* of 1841 and the *Mosquito* of 1848, were well-known in their day; the latter 'possessed many of the qualities for which the *America* was so much admired three years afterwards'.[55]

Another example of a fine-lined merchant ship of the 'forties may be found in the iron barque *Richard Cobden*, which was designed by Thomas R Guppy of Bristol, who also prepared the specification. Thomas Guppy had been associated with the building of the steamers *Great Western* and *Great Britain*. The *Richard Cobden* was built in 1844 at Liverpool by James Hodgson and measured 137ft-7in by 27ft-6in by 19ft-2in, 461 tons nm and 522 tons om. A paper read in 1871 before the Institution of Naval Architects by John Grantham gave brief particulars of her construction, but the most remarkable thing about her is the shape of her midship section which is shown in figure 162. This drawing was submitted by Grantham and it is a pity that the lines plan did not accompany it. Such extreme deadrise was unusual in a merchant ship of this tonnage and greatly reduced her stowage capacity compared with vessels of the same dimensions and not of such an extreme form. She was well spoken of as regards speed and delivering her cargo in good condition, and as she was engaged in the China trade it was presumably hoped to recover the receipts lost by the small capacity in the higher freights available to fast vessels. The swell shown in the midship section just below the loadline, together with the tumblehome and flare, are reminiscent of the SS *Great Britain*, completed in 1844. Like her the *Richard Cobden* was built of Coalbrookdale iron, the plates being immensely thick. There

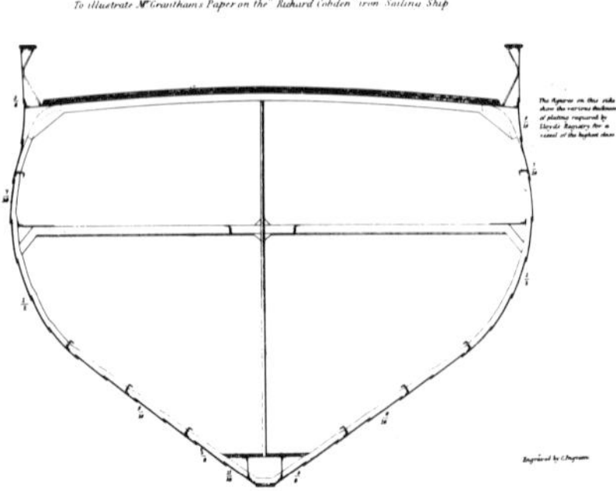

162: Richard Cobden. Midship section. Built at Liverpool in 1844. There is no external keel and the iron plates are arranged as a clinker-built wooden hull. This degree of deadrise is very steep. The U-shaped longitudinal riders, formed of two angles, can be seen attached to the plates. The waterways are of iron and there are two skins of deck planking.

163: This painting by D A Teupken is typical of his work and depicts the *Farewell* of St Ives which was built at Harrington in 1847 with tonnages of 111 nm and 142 om; she was in the Mediterranean trade for ten years. Her fore lower mast is short enough to make her a brigantine, although she sets a large trysail. *MacGregor Collection.*

164: This pencil sketch of the *Virginia* is entitled: 'The new fast sailing clipper-built ship *Virginia* on her day's run of 279 miles, from land to land 11 days.' The passage has not yet been traced but was presumably made in 1845, the year she was built. As she was built at St John and owned in Liverpool, it might have been her maiden passage between these ports. Her builder was A Titus and her tonnage was 733, but *Lloyd's Register* only classed her at 4 A1. *MacGregor Collection.*

is no external keel and the frame spacing is double what was required, but there are a number of longitudinal riders to give extra stiffness; the stem and sternpost are of solid iron with overall measurements of 6in by 3in and 6in by 2¼ respectively. She lasted 26 years before being broken up.[56]

It is of interest to note that T R Guppy built in Bristol the iron screw steamer *Tintern* and the iron schooner *John Bright* for Darby & Sim, owners of the *Richard Cobden*. The former was built in 1845 as a coaster of 90 tons; the *John Bright* was launched in 1846 as a topsail schooner of 298 tons and it was intended to fit a screw propellor and engines after a voyage to New York, although when surveyed at the start of a passage to Valparaiso in 1848 this had not been done.[57]

Early American clipper ship development

The North Atlantic packet trade was largely dominated by American ships which were designed with flat floors and full ends, but their big sail plans and hard-driving masters ensured that reasonably quick passages were achieved on a regular basis. It was to this sort of hull form that American designers turned when commissioned by shipowners to produce fast vessels with good carrying capacity for the newly-opened China trade in the early 1840s. However, these powerful hulls were given more deadrise with a somewhat finer entrance and run, as can be seen in the lines of the *Helena* which William H Webb built in 1841 (figure 168).[58] This ship measured 135.0ft by 30.5ft by 20.0ft and 856 tons. Three years later, Webb constructed two other China packets, the *Panama* and the *Montauk*. The former was of approximately similar dimensions to the *Helena*, but the *Montauk* was about 12 feet shorter, and she was also of slightly finer lines. A lines plan of the latter is published by Howard I. Chapelle in *Search for Speed under Sail*[59] and a painting of her is reproduced here in figure 166 which indicates that she was very lofty, and capable of crossing skysail yards on each mast. By later standards, these China packets were rather full-bodied and yet they made some fast passages.

A word should be said here about Isaac Webb and his influence on the clipper ship. He had been apprentice, foreman and finally successor to Henry Eckford at his New York yard. He had the ability to impart his knowledge and three of his apprentices became leading ship designers: his eldest son, William; John W Griffiths; and Donald McKay. Each of these three left their mark on the clipper ship era.[60]

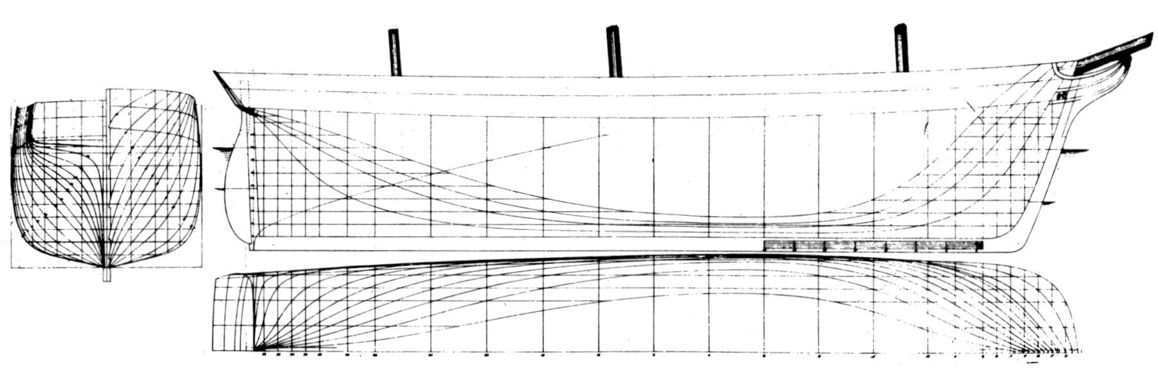

165: *Helena*. Built in 1841 by William H. Webb at New York. Reproduced from plan in his book, *Plans of Wooden Vessels*. Dimensions on plan: 135ft-0in (length on deck) × 30ft-6in (moulded breadth) × 20ft-0in (depth of hold); 856 tons. Built for the China trade where she made some fast passages home to America.

166: A painting by the Chinese artist Sunqua showing the *Montauk* hove-to. She was built by William H Webb at New York in 1844 and was in the China trade. *Peabody Museum, Salem.*

167: *Sea Witch.* Lines plan. Built in 1846 by Smith & Dimon of New York with register dimensions of 170ft-3in × 33ft-11in × 19ft-0in and 907 35/95 tons. She was designed by John W Griffiths. Redrawn from plan in the Smithsonian Institution by Paul Roberts.

From 1843, Griffiths lectured on his theories of improved naval architecture for fast-sailing ships, of which the principal points were to rake the stem forward above the load line, although the success of the Aberdeen bow in this respect was not mentioned; to introduce hollows in the waterlines at the ends; and to raise the level of the quarters by reducing the overhang of the stern. He designed the clipper ship *Rainbow* which Smith & Dimon built in New York in 1845 for Howland & Aspinall. She was really an elongated version of a China packet with more hollows in the ends and a much longer run. On her sail plan, moonsails are drawn on each mast. Her measurements were 159ft-0in by 31ft-10in by 18ft-4in and 752 tons. *Rainbow* was hardly afloat before one of the firm's other ships, the *Natchez*, under Captain Robert Waterman, reached New York only 78 days out from Macao, a remarkable performance for a 14-year-old trans-Atlantic packet. Howland & Aspinall determined to build for Waterman the fastest clipper they could and commissioned Griffiths accordingly.[61]

John Griffiths was apparently given *carte blanche* to design the fastest ship he could, and Smith & Dimon built her. The result was the *Sea Witch* built in 1846 with dimensions of 178ft-2in (on deck) by 33ft-0in (moulded) by 21ft-6in (moulded), and 907 tons. In design she had departed from many of the packet ship features and now exhibited more of the clipper ship hull form to be seen from 1850 onwards. Her raking stem rabbet was akin to the clippers being built in Aberdeen, although her bowsprit did not spring from the hull in the same manner. She had a very hollow entrance and as the midship section was kept well forward of the centre of her hull, there was a long convex run. There was

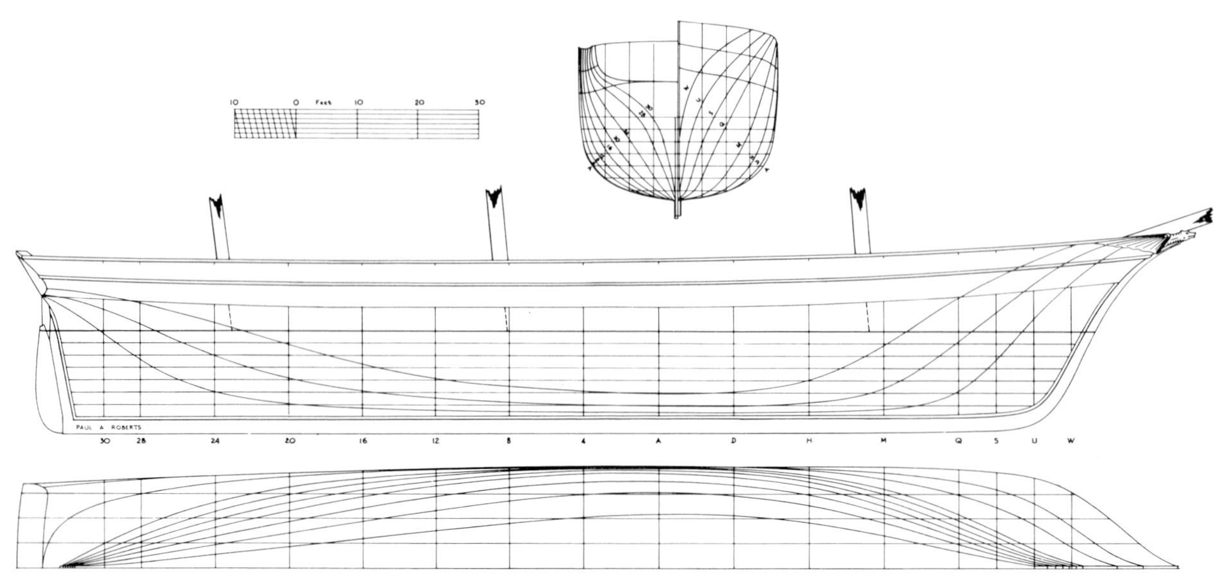

good deadrise with very slack bilges and hardly any tumblehome. In her sail plan, skysails are not drawn above the royals.[62]

Under the command of Captain Waterman, the *Sea Witch* performed some of the fastest passages ever made in the trade between America and China. In 1849, she sailed from Canton on 9 January, reached Anjer only seven days later and arrived at New York 74 days 14 hours out on 25 March 1848. Thirteen months earlier she had sailed from Canton on 29 December 1847 and had taken the remarkably short time of 77 days to New York which she reached on 15 March 1848.[63]

Her two passages from China of 74½ and 77 days have never been beaten, but it is important to note that they were both made with the favourable north-east monsoon. On the other hand, her run of 83 days on her maiden voyage was made against the monsoon, which made this passage exceptionally fast. Ships bound to England were estimated by Matthew F Maury to take an extra 12 days on the passage after crossing the Line in the North Atlantic, so supporters of British clipper records can take comfort in this. The clippers being currently produced in Aberdeen were less than half the size of ships like *Sea Witch* so that their speed potential was that much less.

169: Close hauled on the port tack and under all plain sail, the *Sea Witch* approaches the anchorage at Whampoa. An unidentified Chinese artist has given her too many rows of reef points. *Peabody Museum, Salem.*

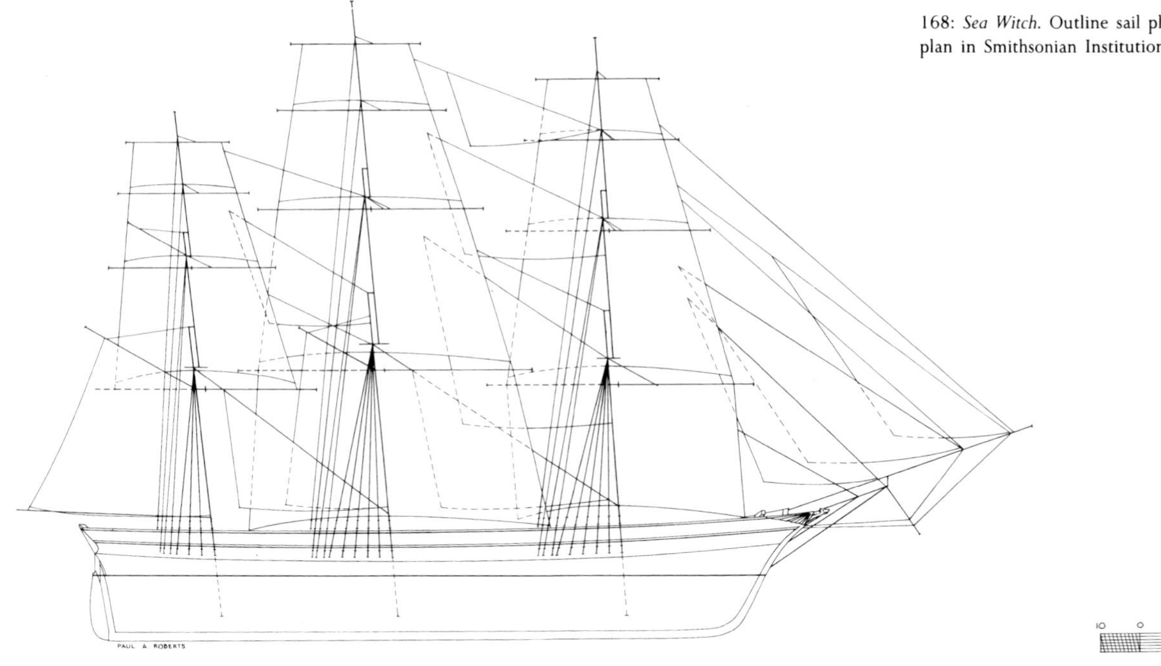

168: *Sea Witch.* Outline sail plan. Redrawn from plan in Smithsonian Institution by Paul Roberts.

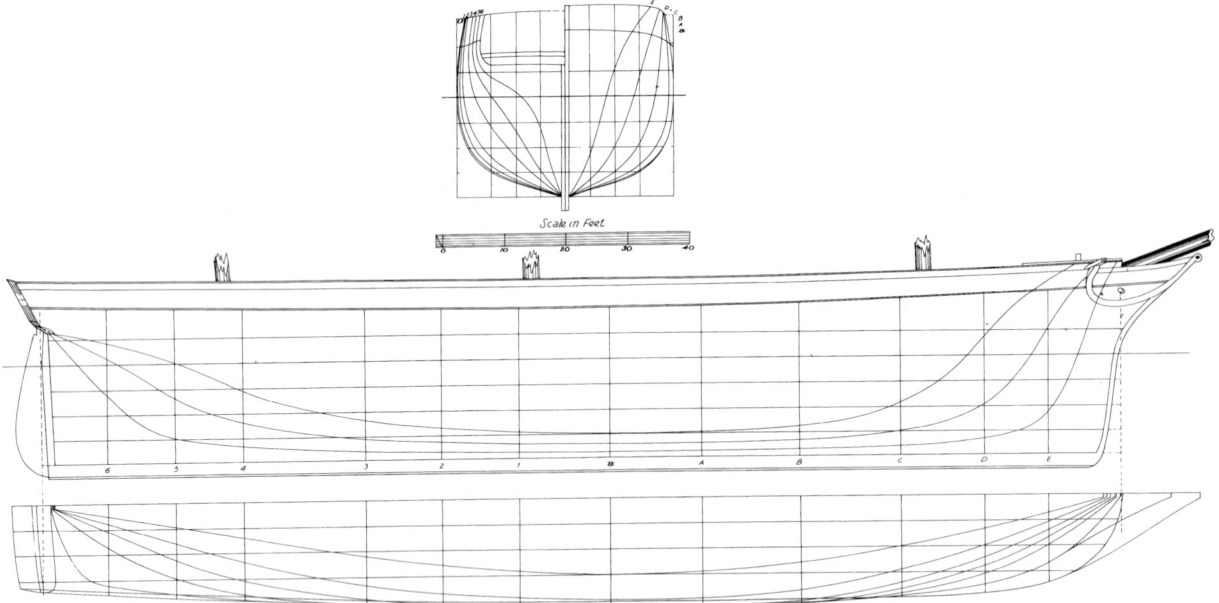

170: *Oriental.* Lines plan. Built in 1849 by Jacob Bell at New York. Dimensions: 185ft-0in × 36ft-0in × 21ft-0in and 1003 tons. Redrawn by E N Wilson from plan in National Maritime Museum which records the lines taken off the ship at Blackwall in January 1851. Reconstruction: scroll head; cathead and moulding; rudder; masts and bowsprit.

In 1847, Brown & Bell of New York built the *Samuel Russell* of 957 tons for the China trade, with big deadrise and sharp lines; her fastest passage was one of 81 days from Canton to New York in 1848. A year later, Jacob Bell, who had succeeded Brown & Bell, built the *Oriental* on fairly similar lines but with less deadrise. She ran in the tea trade to London for several years and was reported to have sailed at 16 knots. After her arrival in London in December 1850, her lines were taken off in Green's Blackwall Yard in the following January.

The only plans so far found of a British ship with hull form equivalent to these China packets are of the *Camertonian* which was built at Workington in 1848, as described in the next section.

The *Camertonian*

Considering the proximity of the Cumberland shipyards to the coal fields and iron deposits that lie close to the shore, it is surprising that iron did not supplant wood in ship construction. At the port of Workington, seven miles north of Whitehaven, the firm of Peile, Scott & Co produced some ships of excellent workmanship during the years 1834–57, and when the Visitation Committee of Lloyd's Register inspected the yard in 1851 they remarked that 'it seemed scarcely possible to produce a finer standard of naval architecture'.[65] At this date the manager was Jonathen Fell and he was therefore responsible for the design and construction of the *Camertonian*, which the firm built in 1848 as a fine-lined ship for Eastern trades.

A local newspaper described the launch in the typical, highflown jargon of the day:

> 'On Friday [18th August], there was launched from the building yard of Messrs. Wm. Peile, Scott & Co., at Workington, a splendid new ship, 550 tons register measurement, called the *Camertonian*, built for Isaac Scott Esq. The symmetry of this vessel, in the opinion of judges, has not been equalled, and the character of the builders sufficiently guarantees that the materials and workmanship cannot be surpassed. This is the third new ship launched by the above firm within twelve months, making together 1700 tons; probably the most tonnage ever turned out of any yard in the country in so short a time.'[66]

Local newspapers are always very loyal to the local industries and very parochial in their views, and it is rare to obtain a launching account which has penetrated the bland aloofness to offer an observed appraisal. The accounts of American ships in the 1850s, written by Duncan MacLean for the *Boston Atlas*, some of which were reprinted in 1952, were unique in the detail they gave; but then the author was a seaman.[67] British ships arriving at Australian ports received better write-ups than they ever got in the Mother country. The reader can judge for himself the quality of reporting by the quotations em-

171: Starboard quarter of the *Camertonian* drawn by T W Ward.

bodied in this book but the hackneyed phrase, 'symmetry of this vessel', is absolutely meaningless.

Fortunately, there is a superb contemporary model of the *Camertonian* to ¼in-scale in the possession of William Salisbury and from it the plans in figure 171 have been drawn. At present the model is not rigged, but all the masts and spars are extant and so is much of the rigging and blocks. The ship measured 128ft-0in aloft by 28ft-9in by 20ft-3in, 485 tons om and 543 wagons nm. The Lloyd's Register survey report gives the dimensions of the keel as 14in sided and 15in moulded; floors 13½in sided and moulded; keelson 14in sided and 21in moulded; external planking 4in thick, with bilge planking 5 in and wales 5½in. The framing was composed of oak, the beams of teak, and the decks of yellow pine. A class of 12 years A1 was obtained. It must have been a splendid sight when the ship was completely framed awaiting the planking, with the bottom of the ship almost solid across the floors and the top-timbers somewhat thinner as they stood out against the sky. Using long pliable battens, the shipwrights would have checked the outer faces of the frames for fairness and taken off any unwanted material with adzes. Experienced shipwrights knew through long practice how best to convert their timber, a factor which permitted a business to be run profitably when English oak was such a scarce and valuable commodity.

The hull design shows considerable rise of floor with very slack bilges. The entrance is long and convex, and the body tapers appreciably towards the run, although great fullness is retained at the quarters above the light-waterline level, which results in marked hollows as the hull sweeps into the sternpost. On the model the keel is sided 18in at the rabbet and moulded 30in which greatly exceeds the survey report dimensions. It also gives the hull a false appearance of great depth in proportion to length. From the register dimensions these are 4.4 breadths to length and 6.33 depths to length, proving that the hull is fully contemporary in proportions; but the heavy head and cumbersome, square stern, with imitation quarter galleries, dignified though they may, look incongruous with the sharp bottom.

There are points of similarity with the lines of the clipper said to *Scawfell* (figure 269) as regards the deep keel, rise of floor and convex

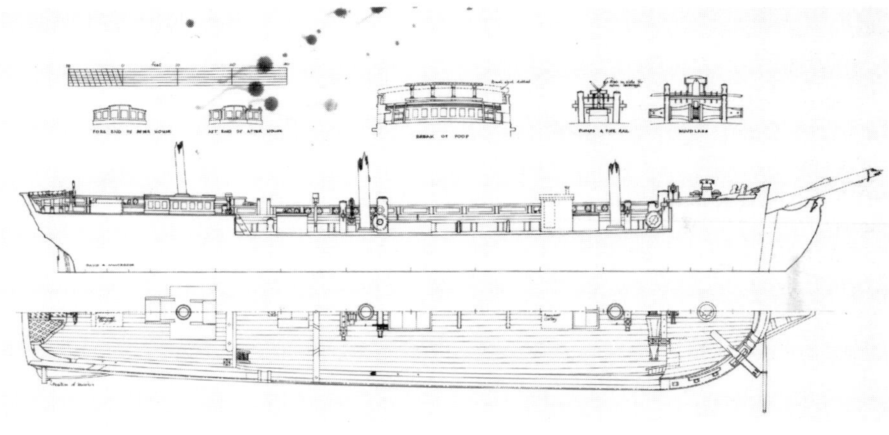

173: *Camertonian.* General arrangement plan: Drawn from same model as lines plan. Reconstruction: bulwarks made thinner; galley; boat chocks on main deck; skylight on raised quarterdeck; and main brace bumkin (all dotted); figurehead.

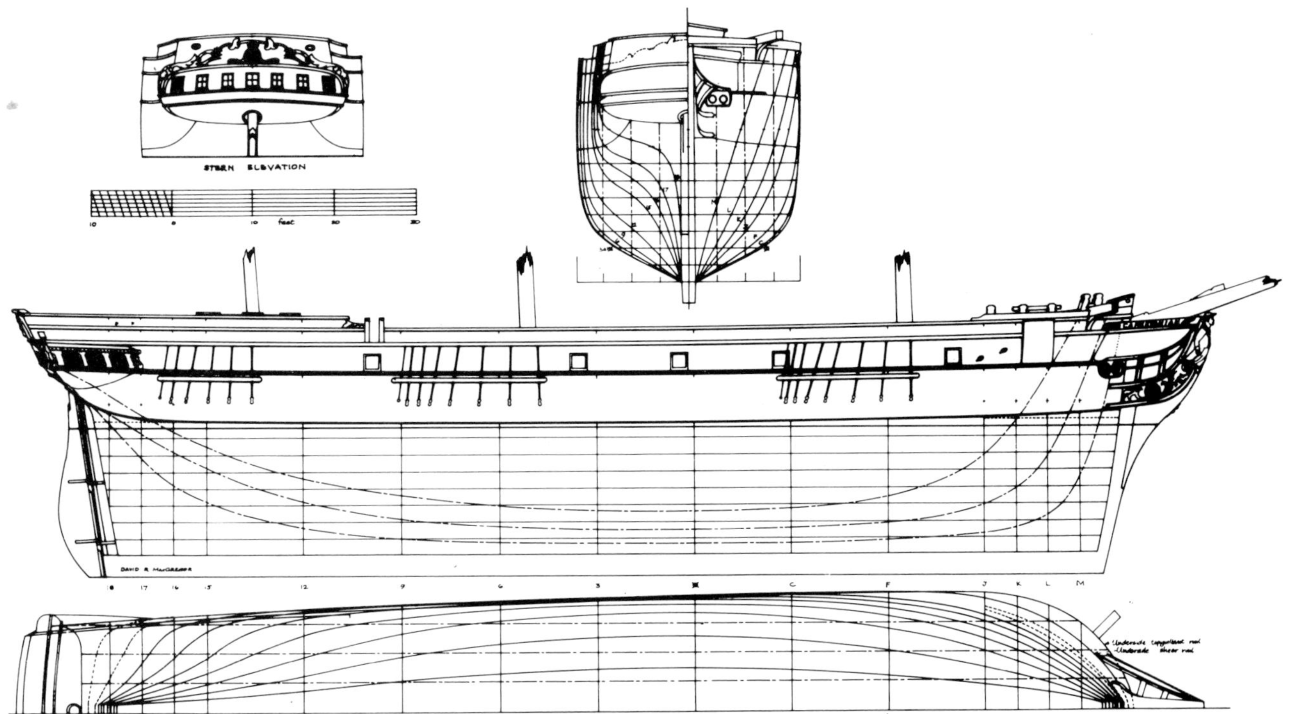

172: *Camertonian.* Lines: Built in 1848 by Peile, Scott & Co. at Workington. Drawn from lines taken off contempoararary ¼in model in possession of William Salisbury. Dimension: 128ft-0in × 28ft-9in × 20ft-3in; 485 tons om and 543 tons nm. Reconstruction: figurehead.

waterlines, which would be reasonable as Jonathan Fell may have been involved in both designs.

The opportunity has been taken to present several sketches of the *Camertonian*, because the model is unusually well detailed. In figure 174 the windlass has been manned and the starboard anchor is being heaved up; this is a scene that has rarely been captured with a camera. Other sketches show the foretop and truss to the lower yard; and a starboard quarter view with stern carving, quarter galleries and a boat hanging in fixed iron davits.

Some of the bulwarks of the model of the *Camertonian* are rather too massive and a few of the fittings are obviously missing, such as the galley, one of the longboat chocks, and the cabin skylight, but the difference of colour on the deck shows the extent of such omissions. The reconstructions have been dotted on the plan. The Lloyd's Register survey report assigns to the *Camertonian* one longboat, a quarter boat and a yawl. No davits are fitted on the model, but by this date they would have undoubtedly been carried, at least on one side of the ship, if not on both.

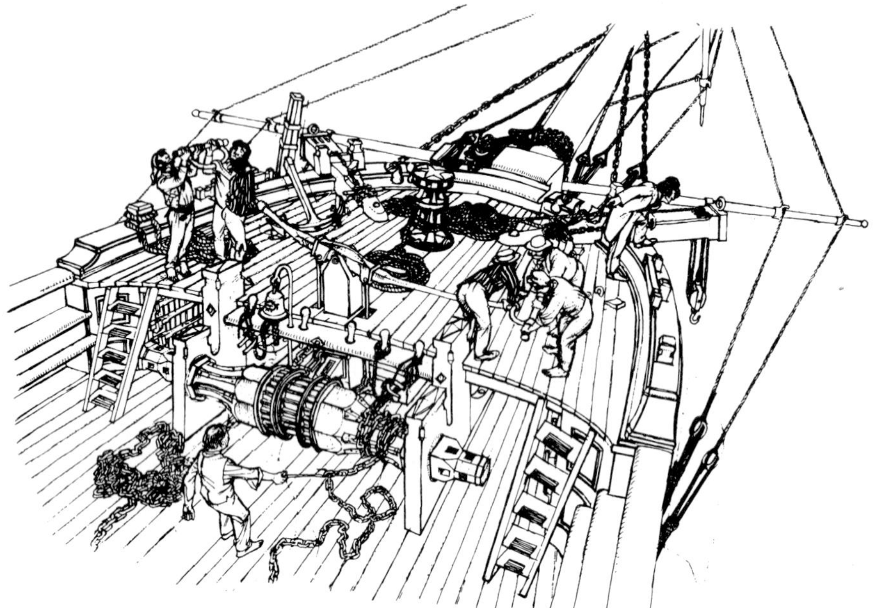

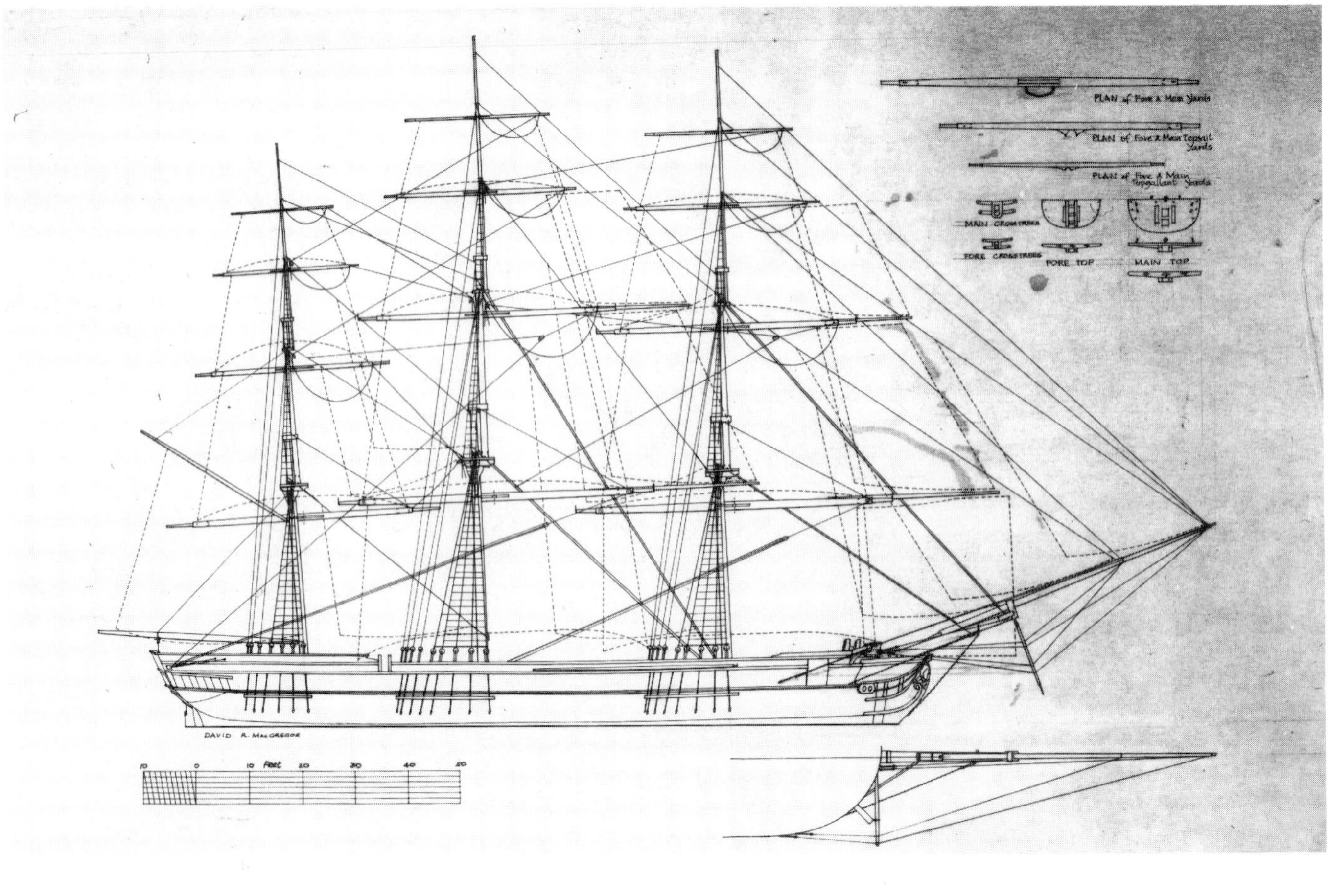

174: Heaving up the starboard anchor aboard the *Camertonian* by means of the windlass. Such a scene is rarely found in a photograph. The first mate is looking over the side to see when the anchor breaks water. There are three men manning each of the rocker arms of the windlass; another man, with an iron claw, hauls the chain clear of the barrel. The norman, which is used when letting go the anchor, is held up clear of the barrel. The massive whisker booms for the bowsprit rigging pass through an iron fitting on the catheads.

175: *Camertonian.* Sail plan: Although model was not rigged, all spars are lengths of those lying on the mode, and the rigging agrees with what remains attached to model and spars. No skysail yards found in model. Reconstruction: sail outlines, which are dotted.

Although the boat skid has a pair of slanting grooves for boats to rest on, no complimentary marks appear on the balustrade rail at the break of the raised quarter-deck, where the after end of each boat would be secured. The *Camertonian* was supplied with three bower anchors (25, 25 and 24 cwt), one 10 cwt stream anchor and one 3 cwt kedge anchor. The asymmetrical structure on the quarter-deck with two companionway tops is a curious feature.

No sails existed on the *Camertonian*'s model, but their possible outlines have been dotted on the reconstructed spar and rigging plan (figure 175). The amount of rigging shown agrees with what has survived on the model's spars. The dolphin striker is made of timber and is exceptionally long, and the high amount of steeve to the bowsprit follows the tradition of earlier years. A tall sail plan emerges, but the amount of overlap between the square sails reveals that yards were becoming longer with the result that a 'squarer' sail plan was evolving. The stunsails on the mainmast are larger than those on the fore. No skysail yards have survived on the model, but the run of the stays and height of the poles permit quite large skysails to be set.

Unfortunately, there is no information about living accommodation, but the crew probably entered their airless fo'c'sle, situated in the 'tween decks, through a scuttle located beneath the anchor deck, which they would approach bent double. Access to the officer's quarters was through the aftermost companionway on the quarter deck; the other sliding scuttle top probably led to sail locker and store rooms.

The *Camertonian* spent her short life in the India trade. In 1854, she was wrecked at the Sand Heads, bound for Calcutta, after a passage of 114 days from Liverpool.

Few British clippers were larger than 500 tons in 1849 but the whole concept of fast sailing was on the threshold of a great boom, stimulated by international competition as the result of the repealing of the Navigation Laws and by the discovery of gold in California and Australia, which produced unprecedented demands for the transport of gold-hungry persons and the goods they required, all at maximum speed. The size of British clippers doubled, then trebled, but it was the even larger American and Canadian ships that really satisfied the demand and which in turn provided the biggest challenge to the native British shipbuilders.

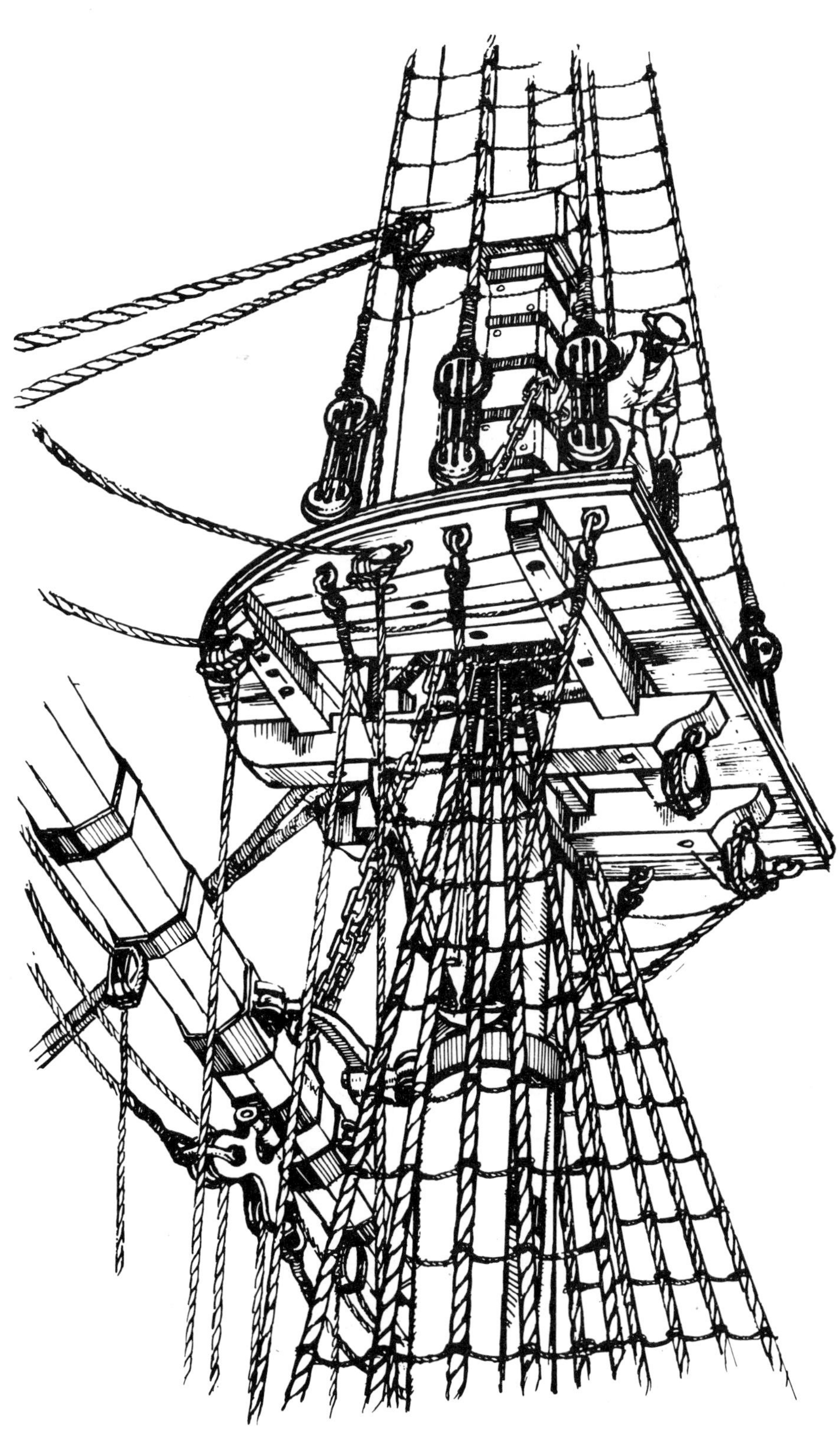

176: Fore top of the *Camertonian*. For the sake of clarity, some rigging is omitted.

Five

PROGRESS OF SHIPBUILDING 1850-75

Iron as a shipbuilding material

The official catalogue of the 1851 Great Exhibition reveals the great inventiveness being released in the shipbuilding industry and this catalogue forms a valuable compendium of some of the new techniques then in process of development. In many cases there were no precedents on which shipowners or surveyors could base their opinions, so that it became literally a matter of trial and error before a product or process was judged to be completely satisfactory and foolproof.

On the development of iron shipbuilding, that lucid expounder of naval architecture, J Scott Russell (1808–1882), wrote in 1864:

> 'The kind of skill, required for the proper design of an iron ship, was new as well as rare, because of the total want of precedent for iron structure and seagoing ships. At first we naturally looked up to the wood shipbuilders, and to wooden ships, for the proper proportion of the iron parts of iron ships. Unluckily, the wood shipbuilders hated iron ships, and therefore little help came from them. Besides, they knew little or nothing either of the properties of iron, of its right strength and proportions, or of the right ways to fashion it. The men who did know something of the qualities and properties of iron were quite another race, occupied in thinking of quite other things. The smith and carpenter had little knowledge in common between them, and the smiths alone understood how to handle iron, and what they could make it do. There was also a race of iron boiler-makers, who were known to understand how sheets of iron were to be cut and bent, and shaped and joined to one another. Therefore there was some help to come from them in the way of workmanship; but as to general design, large mechanical principles and skill, enlightend by science, there was no race except the civil and mechanical engineer, who had already acquired great skill in using iron, by the extent to which he employed it in forming all parts of his machinery, where it had a very great deal of hard work to do, and had to be most skilfully proportioned to that work, in order to do it. Here was found a considerable amount of skill of the right sort, to be drawn upon whenever the necessities of iron shipbuilding required it; and as soon as they did very extensively require it, and iron ships became urgently needed, it was from the mechanical engineers mainly, and not from the wood shipbuilders, that help ultimately came; and the new art and science of iron shipbuilding had to be worked out mainly by mechanical engineers.'[1]

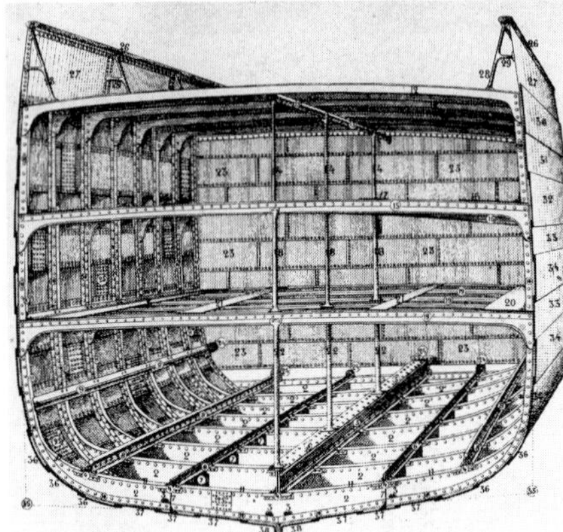

177: Perspective view of an iron hull, from Captain H Paasch's *Illustrated Marine Encyclopedia.* 1 Keel. 2 Floors. 3 Water-courses; Limber-holes. 4 Lug-pieces. 5 Keelson; Middle-line-keelson. 6 Side-keelson. 7 Intercostal-keelson; Side-intercostal-keelson. 8 Bilge-keelson. 9 Bilge-stringer. 10 Frames. 11 Reversed-frames. 12 Upper-deck-beams. 13 Central-stringer. 14 Upper-deck-pillars; Upper-deck-stanchions. 15 Main-deck-beams. 16 Main-deck-beam-stringer-plate. 17 Main-deck-beam-tie-plate. 18 Main-deck-pillars; Main-deck-stanchions. 19 Lower-deck-beams. 20 Lower-deck-beam-tie-plate. 22 Hold-pillars; Hold stanchions. 23 Bulkhead. 24 Collars. 25 Butt-straps. 26 Main-rail; Roughtree-rail. 27 Bulwark-plating. 28 Bulwark-stays. 29 Spurs (of Bulwark-stays). 30 Upper-sheerstrake; Upper-deck-sheerstrake. 31 Topside-strake. 32 Main-sheerstrake; Main-deck-sheerstrake. 33 Side-plating (inside-strakes). 34 Side-plating (outside-strakes). 35 Bilge. 36 Bilge-strakes. 37 Bottom-strakes; Strakes in flat of bottom. 38 Garboard-strakes.

Wrecks and disasters attending early iron ships focussed widespread attention on the strength and durability of the material with which they were constructed and undoubtedly encouraged others to invest in ships of this kind. A particularly well-known case is that of the steamer *Great Britain* which lay ashore on the Irish Coast from September 1846 to August 1847, completely exposed to the winter gales, and although 'every part of the bottom had been battered and damaged by the rocks upon which it was beaten, yet . . . it was difficult to perceive the slightest strain in the upper sides, or to detect any alternation in her form'.[2] The fact that she also floated when finally towed off, together with her huge size and the widespread publicity of the feat of survival, gave great impetus to iron shipbuilding.

It would be as well to list the qualities which commended themselves most strongly to iron shipbuilders of the day.

John Grantham gave the following 'objects most desired by the merchant in the choice of a ship . . .: strength combined with lightness; great capacity for stowage; safety; speed; durability; economy in repairs; cost; draught of water'. And he added that iron vessels were eminently superior to wooden vessels in each of these items.[3]

In a letter to a London shipowner, dated November 1858, Alexander Stephen Jnr listed what he considered were the advantages of an iron ship:

1 First cost at present less than wooden ship of equal class.
2 In many trades iron ships command a preference for carrying in greater safety.
3 Capacity is much greater on the same tonnage.
4 Durability is immensely in their favour.
5 Economy in upkeep; no longer carpenters' bills for internal decay.[4]

Letters embodying similar arguments were sent to possible clients in London, Hull, Liverpool, Glasgow, Dundee and Peterhead.

In 1858, the price differential in favour of an iron ship was approximately 10s to 30s for a 13 A1 ship with a complete East India outfit. Prices for iron ships were falling towards the end of the 1850s to as low as £14.10s per ton at 12 A1 with a full East India outfit, some £4 lower than had been seen earlier in the decade at the height of the boom. During the 'sixties, iron sailing ships cost between £14 and £16.10s per ton on the Clyde.

In the matter of capacity, John Grantham estimated that whereas a given wooden ship could carry 500 tons, an iron ship of identical shape and size could carry 600 tons, because the shell of the wooden ship was so much thicker, particularly in the ends.[5] This difference became especially marked in sharp vessels where more timber was required in the construction of the frames, and in the case of extremely long wooden ships the proportion was strongly in favour of an iron vessel.[6] The midship section of the extreme clipper *Annandale* reveals the vast amount of timber required to stiffen her, while the iron clipper *Hurricane* had comparatively thin sides. It should be noted in passing that ships built of oak required their frames and planking to be thinner than softwood ships, with a resultant increase in capacity. The table (right), which was compiled by George Moorsom in 1852, compares ships of iron and wood.

Some interesting figures could undoubtedly be calculated for individual ships which could explain the relatively high profits in some cases. Little work has yet been undertaken on the calculation of earnings after every factor has been taken into account.

Needless to say, there were many difficulties to overcome in iron construction: plates corroded in the hold through the action of bilge water lying on them, which was overcome by covering the plates with a layer of Portland cement or asphalt; the mass of iron in the hull caused considerable deviation of the compass, which scientists strove to recompense; cargoes were said to be seriously damaged until ventilation was improved; lack of experience and difficulty in assimilating new techniques of construction was slowly improved in time. In addition, the competence of shipwrights in far distant ports to work satisfactorily in iron was becoming less of a hazard as dock and harbour facilities improved throughout the world.

But fouling of the bottom by the adhesion of barnacles and marine growth was still proving a serious problem in 1870. Many authors lamented the lack of success achieved; John Grantham referred to it as 'the old enemy to iron'.[8] It was shown that excessive marine growth could reduce the

Additional capacities according to materials (expressed as percentages)[7]

Tonnage of ship	*Excess of oak over fir*	*Excess of iron over oak*	*Excess of iron over fir*
1000	7.54%	14.0%	21.46%
500	6.8%	16.0%	22.8%
200	10.0%	18.6%	28.6%

178: An iron hull from the outside, showing the run of the plating. This view shows the bows of the iron ship *Rodney* of 1447 tons, built in 1874 by William Pile & Co. at Sunderland. *Cyril Hume.*

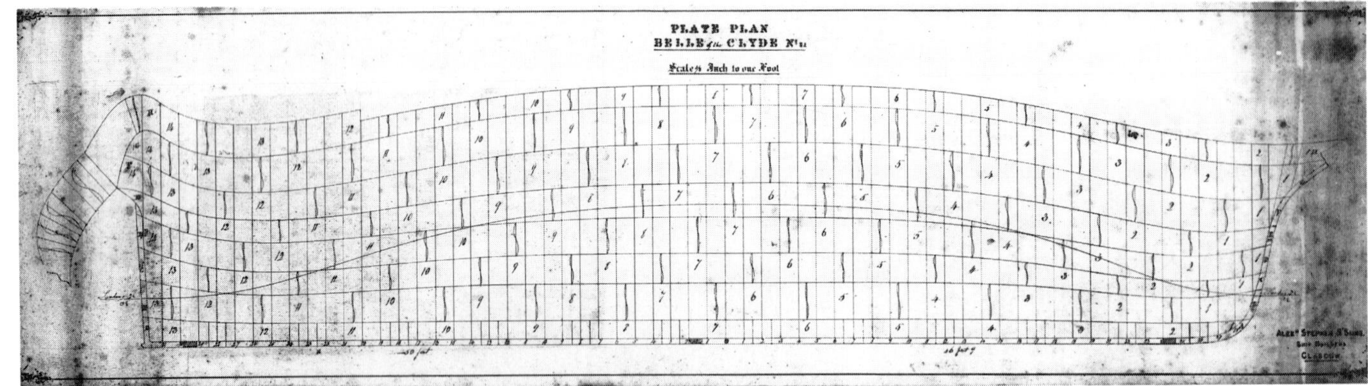

179: *Belle of the Clyde.* Shell expansion drawing photographed from original when in possession of the builder's, A Stephens & Sons. Here the iron plates of the hull are drawn out as though each was flat which results in this shape for the profile.

speed of a steamship by three to four knots and that of a sailing ship by the same proportion. After going into dock, iron ships often had tons of barnacles scraped off the bottom, particularly after passing through tropical waters, although by lying in freshwater rivers further accretion was checked and sometimes a partial cure was effected. It was recommended that iron ships be docked once or twice a year to have the plating scraped and an anti-fouling paint applied.[9] Alexander Stephen Jnr gave in 1858 his view of the comparative costs involved: to scrape and paint in dock one of George Smith & Sons' 900-ton sailing ships after a voyage to India cost £70, which he observed was 'obviously cheaper than stripping, caulking and recoppering' a wooden ship, but he gave no comparative cost for the latter.[10]

A wide variety of anti-fouling paints and compounds was used, many with little success, and a list of strange conglomerations was given by Charles Young.[11] Meanwhile, a firm founded in 1848, Peacock & Buchan, enjoyed better results than most.[12]

The lack of success with anti-fouling paints led to ships of the Royal Navy having one or two layers of wood planking bolted to their bottoms so that copper sheathing could be applied. The galvanic action occurring in water when copper and iron were in contact produced rapid and serious corrosion of the iron, which is why wood planking had to be inserted between the two metals. However zinc sheathing, which over wood was far less successful than copper, had no deleterious effect on iron; indeed the iron stimulated the zinc to exfoliate more rapidly and so deter barnacles and weeds from adhesion. By the close of the 1860s, zinc sheathing was being applied to naval vessels, but only very occasionally to merchant sailing ships.[13] The lack of success with anti-fouling preparations was an important reason in favour of composite construction, in which the hull benefitted from the strength of the iron frame as well as the ease with which copper sheathing could be applied to the timber planking. This method of construction will be discussed later.

Rules for iron ships

Iron construction was in a relatively experimental stage until 1840, but the building of three larger ships that year — the *Iron Duke* of 392 tons nm, *Vulcan* of 318 tons nm and *John Garrow* of 711 tons nm — was convincing evidence that such a form of construction was satisfactory. In 1836, Lloyd's Register surveyed their first iron vessel, the ketch *Goliath*, and in 1846–7 they issued an amended survey form for reporting on iron ships. This form was the result of Augustin FB Creuze's visits in 1846 to several shipyards to study in detail the constructional methods employed. A year later, Lloyd's Register sent him to Liverpool to report on the condition of the steamer *Great Britain* after she had been refloated, following her long stranding on the Irish coast. Thereafter, they endeavoured to improve their surveying methods for iron ships and establish suitable rules that would suit all parties.

Beginning in the summer of 1851, Lloyd's Register annually despatched a committee to visit shipyards in different parts of the country to foster a closer spirit of co-operation between shipbuilders and the Society. In 1853, when this 'Visitation Committee' toured the north of England and Scotland, they were struck with the number of iron ships under construction, particularly on the Clyde, and reported in these words:

> 'These visits could not fail to produce a deep impression of the rapidity with which the substitution of iron for wood in shipbuilding is progressing and of its great importance. There appeared to be no want of hands, although it was said more could be employed, but nevertheless the great activity which generally prevailed in every branch was truly astonishing.'[14]

The Committee concluded its 1853 Report with a chronicle of the events attending iron shipbuilding from their point of view, and stressed the great importance of introducing some rules 'by which, at least, the surveyors and the Committee might be enabled to judge the fitness of the iron, from its size and quality, for the ribs, plates, beams &c. of iron ships'.[15] Reading between the lines one gets the impression that some of the local surveyors were rather in the hands of the shipbuilder and required the full support of the Society. Even in the case of timber construction, the surveyors had to be very knowledgeable and capable men, otherwise some builders were apt to take advantage of them; so now in the matter of iron the position was accentuated.

In September 1850 the Visitation Committee had sent Augustin FB Creuze to visit yards specialising in iron shipbuilding in order to obtain data on constructional methods from which rules could be drawn up. He reported that the establishment of any rules would prejudice the improvements which shipbuilders were making in iron construction. Here the matter rested until August 1852 when enquiry forms were circulated to a number of shipyards in connection with the matter of framing a set of rules. The ques-

180: The iron structure is shown well in this photograph of the *Ranee* undergoing repair in New Zealand. The bow has been raised out of the water to removes the plates safely. The trailboards have disappeared although when built in 1864 it is inconceivable that she was fitted without them. She was built by Hart at Liverpool of 1264 tons and was originally named *Cowasjee Jehangeer. Alexander Turnbull Library, Wellington.*

tionnaire consisted of the normal Survey Report for iron ships with the request that the builder insert the scantlings he would specify for ships of the following tonnages: 100, 200, 400, 600, 800, 1000, 1300 and 1800.

To the Committee's chagrin not a single form was completed.

Robert Napier replied that he was very anxious that iron ships be built as soundly as possible, but added:

> 'I cannot see my way to filling up the forms satisfactorily as I consider the subject so involved with practical difficulties that it would be impossible to make rules to meet the different cases honestly and so as not to do much injury to this new and growing branch of shipbuilding and trade.'[16]

Similar answers were received from Smith & Rodger and A Stephen & Sons of Glasgow, Denny & Rankin of Dumbarton and Coutts & Parkinson of the Tyne.

By this time the Committee, while appreciating the reasons behind Napier's reply, were feeling a growing concern that the entire matter was getting out of proportion. The result was that the Society's principal surveyors, Messrs Martin and Ritchie, carried out a tour of inspection of the chief iron shipbuilding establishments and, based on their findings, a set of rules was drafted in February 1854 at a conference of senior surveyors at Glasgow. These rules were read to the Liverpool sub-committee in August 1854 and generally approved.[17] The rules appeared in the 1855 Register Book for the first time, and the opening paragraph begins:

> 'Considering that Iron Ship-building is yet in its infancy, and that there are no well-understood general rules for building Iron Ships, the Committee have not deemed it desirable to frame a scheme compelling the adoption of a particular form or mode of construction, but that certain general requirements should be put forward, having for their basis thickness of plate and substance of frame, showing a *minimum in each particular* to entitle Ships to the Character A for a period of years . . .'[18]

These rules, with slight modifications, remained in force for about ten years and their mild tenor was calculated to achieve the fullest degree of co-operation between the builders and Lloyd's Register. During their annual tour of inspection in August 1855, the Visitation Committee observed that there were but few objections raised to the new rules for iron ships.[19] However, the various shipbuilding centres held widely diverging views on the practice of iron shipbuilding and Lloyd's Register was obliged to act with extreme tact and wisdom to avoid a head-on clash with the builders. Many owners indeed refused to submit their vessels to Lloyd's for classification, a situation which resulted in the formation of the Liverpool Underwriters' Association in May 1858 for the survey and classification of iron and, later, composite ships. They issued their own register and set of rules in 1862: the register books are oblong in shape and are valuable for the comparison of purely iron vessels.

In the article on shipbuilding contributed by Andrew Murray (1813–72) to the *Encyclopaedia Britannica* and re-printed separately in 1861, he made a strong attack against what he called the 'dead and spiritless mediocrity' of merchant ships built under Lloyd's rules.[20] (Murray was chief engineer at Portsmouth Dockyard, 1846–69.) J Scott Russell, on the other hand, while acknowledging the criticisms held by many builders, stressed the 'even-handed justice and impartiality' with which the rules were administered; and as an example of the willingness of Lloyd's Register to consider new methods of hull construction, he cited the case of the auxiliary iron steamer *Annette*, which was built in 1861 according to his own 'longitudinal system', and with full co-operation of Lloyd's surveyors. She received the highest class for iron ships of 12 A1.[21] The register book also assigns the notation 'Experimental B.S.' [subject to biennial survey] to her which some builders considered objectionable for a strong, well-built ship.

Spread of iron shipbuilding

The end of the 1840s and beginning of the 1850s saw many shipyards building in both iron and wood, while others concentrated almost entirely in iron but with an occasional wooden vessel. Yards on the Thames, Mersey, Tyne and Clyde were working hard on iron ships, particularly on iron paddle steamers. For instance, in January 1846 37 vessels were under construction on the Clyde, of which 26 were iron steamers of a total tonnage of 14,137 and the remaining were wooden vessels of a total tonnage of 8890.[22]

The Dundee shipbuilder, Alexander Stephen Snr, opened a new yard on the Clyde at Kelvinhaugh in 1850. The following year, when reviewing the work accomplished, he remarked that 'shipbuilding has been at a very low rate and latterly still worse'; yet he concluded his summary with the statement: 'Settled to commence Iron Ship Building'.[23] During the late 'fifties, Alexander Stephen Jnr reported a conversation held with James and William Hall at Aberdeen who stated that if they were not both old men they would already have adopted iron shipbuilding; and he added that they were 'men of great experience and shrewdness'.[25] These were the brothers who built the *Scottish Maid*.

Reliable figures of tonnage produced at individual ports are lacking for the 'fifties, but a report in the *Glasgow Herald* of 25 March 1853 listed the following classes of vessels as under construction on the Clyde: 13 iron sailing ships; 26 iron paddle steamers; 52 iron screw steamers; six wooden sailing ships; one wooden screw steamer. Fourteen of the iron ships were intended for the Australian trade.

Whereas most of the iron sailing vessels built prior to 1850 were schooners, brigs or barques of small tonnage, an abrupt reversal to this trend materialised in 1852 with the construction of iron full-rigged ships of large size, and this new development became the established pattern. In future, iron schooners, brigantines or brigs were none too common, nor too were any iron sailing ships of under 100 tons. In the majority of cases it was the larger shipyards which built in iron because of the bigger capital outlay required for the necessary machinery and stock, and this precluded the participation of many small yards which specialised in building schooners. Large yards tended to receive orders for big ships although an occasional schooner appears in the building lists of most shipyards.

The list below names the majority of iron sailing ships of over 900 tons which were

Iron sailing ships above 900 tons built in UK 1850–59

Year	*Name*	*Tons nm*	*Builder*
1850	nil		
1851	nil		
1852	*W S Lindsay*	900	Coutts & Parkinson, Newcastle
1853	*Ellen Bates*	1098	Neath Abbey Iron Co, Neath
1853	*Evangeline*	954	Jordan & Getty, Liverpool
1853	**Hurricane*	979	A. Stephen & Sons, Glasgow
1853	*Swarthmore*	1381	Coutts & Parkinson, Newcastle
1853	**Tayleur*	1979 om	Bank Quay Foundry Co, Warrington
1853	*Tornado*	1229	William Simons, Glasgow
1854	*Conflict*	1326	Cato, Miller & Co, Liverpool
1854	**Cairnsmore*	1086	J. Reid & Co. Port Glasgow
1854	*Ellen Stuart*	1373	Getty, Jones & Co, Liverpool
1854	*Flying Venus*	1393	Mare & Co, London
1854	*Henry Moore*	1117	J. Scott & Sons, Greenock
1854	*Glen Roy*	1220	Denny & Rankin, Dumbarton
1854	*James Pilkington*	1350	John Getty & Co, Liverpool
1854	**John Bell*	1208	A. Stephen & Sons, Glasgow
1854	*Lady Octavia*	1319	Bank Quay Foundry Co, Warrington
1854	*Mary Stenhouse*	1289	R. Hickson & Co, Belfast
1854	**Storm Cloud*	908	A. Stephen & Sons, Glasgow
1854	*Talavera*	1160	Cato, Miller & Co, Liverpool
1854	*Winefred*	1468	H. Cram, Chester
1855	*City of Madras*	914	R. Steele & Co, Greenock
1855	*Howden*	1322	C. & W. Earle, Hull
1855	*Pride of Canada*	1013	Laurence, Hill & Co, Port Glasgow
1855	**Sarah Palmer*	1325	Bank Quay Foundry Co, Warrington
1855	*Sir Charles Napier*	1161	Coutts & Parkinson, Newcastle
1855	*Startled Fawn*	1164	Bank Quay Foundry Co, Warrington
1855	**White Eagle*	993	A. Stephen & Sons, Glasgow
1856	*Kirkham*	1061	J. Laird, Birkenhead
1856	*Khimjee Oodowjee*	909	Josiah Jones Jnr, Liverpool
1856	*William Fairbairn*	1293	J. Laird, Birkenhead
1857	**Charlemagne*	1014	A. Stephen & Sons, Glasgow
1957	*City of Canton*	909	R. Steele & Co, Greenock
1857	*Defiance*	955	W.C. Miller, Liverpool
1857	*James Livesey*	1072	T. Vernon & Son, Liverpool
1857	*Philosopher*	1059	T. Vernon & Son, Liverpool
1858	**Aphrodita*	1601	Josiah Jones Jnr, Liverpool
1858	*Edith Moore*	1429	W.C. Miller, Liverpool
1858	*Knight Errant*	1312	? Hull
1858	*Norah Greame*	1001	R. Hickson & Co, Belfast
1858	*Simla*	1444	Canada Works, Birkenhead
1859	*Bates Family*	2154	Samuelson & Co, Hull
1859	**City of Madras*	999	A. Stephen & Sons, Glasgow
1859	**City of Nankin*	986	Barclay, Curle & Co, Glasgow
1859	*Slieve Donard*	1498	T. Vernon & Son, Liverpool

*plans or half models known to exist

built in the United Kingdom in the 1850s. As previously mentioned, Lloyds Register did not classify every iron ship and this list is accordingly not claimed to be absolutely complete, although various other sources besides Lloyd's Register have been consulted.[25]

It is interesting to note the preponderance of yards in the Liverpool area and on the Clyde and that London contributed only a single vessel. The peak year was 1854 when the boom was at its height. Auxiliary ships have been omitted from the list and also cases when it is doubtful if the ship had engines fitted or not, such as the barque *Tynemouth* (1854 of 1228 tons) which Lloyd's Register class as a sailing ship. One account credits the *Thomas Hamlin* (1851 at Newcastle) with 1300 tons but Lloyd's Register allots her only 832 tons om.

These ships represent a wide variety of types from the extreme clipper *Storm Cloud* to the full-bodied carrier *Aphrodita*. It is also probable that the ships built in 1853, 1854 and 1855 were generally finer in form than those launched at the end of the 'fifties when the boom for fast ships had collapsed and freights had fallen. The *Tayleur* and the *Bates Family* are by far the largest ships as regards register tonnage, but in some vessels considerable length was achieved in proportion to breadth, a feature which was becoming increasingly common in iron ships. In contrast, the two largest ships built of wood in the 'fifties were the *Schomberg* of 2284 tons nm and the *Eastern Monarch* of 1631 tons. Immense wooden ships were of course being constructed in North America during the 'fifties, which greatly stimulated British builders and owners.

During the 'sixties, shipbuilding in iron became more commonplace and many ships of over 1400 tons were regularly built, together with a few of over 1500 tons. As regards total output, 1864, 1869 and 1875 were the boom years for sailing ships built of iron and in the early 'seventies many ships of between 1500 and 2000 tons were under construction.

It has already been observed that published particulars on sailing ships are scarce, although this lack is remedied slightly in the case of iron ships for the simple reason that they were built of iron and therefore were objects of interest. John Grantham published specifications of the iron ships *Josephine, Deerslayer, Lady Octavia, Sarah Palmer* and *Philosopher*;[26] Professor W J M Rankine printed a full set of plans of the steel sailing ship *Formby*, which was built by the successors to Josiah Jones Jnr;[27] and there are other scattered examples.

Steel shipbuilding

The first vessel built of steel may have been the *Ma Roberts* which John Laird built in 1858 for Dr Livingstone's use in Africa, whence it was shipped out in pieces for re-assembly.[28] She was followed by some steamers built on the Tees: *Little Lucy* of 20 tons, built 1859 by Richardson, Duck & Co at Stockton; *Cuirassier* of 73 tons, built in 1860 by the same firm; and *Talpore*, built in 1860 at Stockton by M Pearse as a troopship on the River Indus.[29] The Liverpool shipbuilders Jones, Quiggin & Co, successors to Josiah Jones Jnr, built a number of early steel vessels according to a list of the ships built in their yard. The first was either a cutter yacht for J Jones, laid down about 1860, or the paddle steamer *Light of the River*, 289 tons, for use on the River Nile. Three small steamers were built in 1861, numbers 94, 102 and 105. A schooner was also built in 1861 for Horsfall & Co of Liverpool, probably named *Donietta*, of 134 tons at a cost of £2050. In December 1862 the paddle steamer *Banshee* was built, as a Confederate blockade runner of 432 tons, yard number 146. In 1863, the schooner *Domitila*, number 151, was constructed; also the full-rigged ship *Formby*, number 152, of 1271 tons, costing £24,003. Two more steel full-rigged ships were launched in 1864, the *Clytemnestra* (number 154) and *Altcar* (number 156).[30]

On the Clyde in September 1862, Alexander Stephen Jnr quoted John Campbell of Glasgow a price of £20 per ton BM 'complete' to build a ship entirely of steel of approximately 950 tons.[31] This was the sort of price being asked for a composite ship to class 14 or 15 A1.

All the above named ships were built of Bessemer steel but high costs generally restricted its use to small vessels and special contracts. Masts and yards were occasionally made of steel but it appears that no more large sailing ships were constructed with it until the launch of the full-rigged ship *Bay of Cadiz* in 1878. She was built by J & G Thomson, of Glasgow, of 1700 tons gross, and the steel was manufactured by the Siemens-Martin process. Thereafter, the use of steel for sailing ships became more popular.[32]

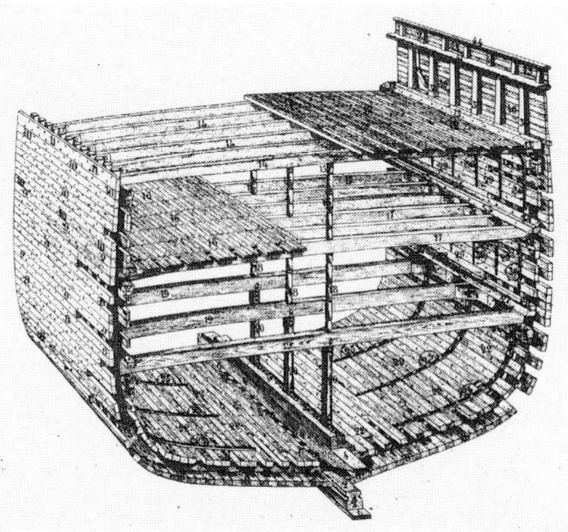

182: A cross-sectional drawing of a wooden ship to illustrate the construction. The iron hanging knees can be clearly seen. This is a three-deck ship, and the lower deck beams were rarely planked over. 1 False-keel. 2 Keel. 3 Frame. 4 Keelson. 5 Rider-keelson. 6 Limbers; Water-course. 7 Garboard-strakes. 8 Bottom-planing. 9 Wales; Bends. 10 Topside-planking. 11 Sheerstrake. 12 Upper-deck. 13 Upper-deck-waterway. 14 Upper-deck-beams. 15 Upper-deck-stanchions. 16 Main-deck. 17 Main-deck-beams. 18 Main-deck-stanchions. 19 Hold-beams; Orlop-beams. 20 Hold-stanchions. 21 Limber-strakes. 22 Hold-ceiling. 23 Hold-beam-knee-riders. 24 Hold-beam-lodging-knees. 25 Hold-beam-clamps. 26 Hold-beam-shelves. 27 Hold-beam-waterway. 28 Hold-beam-spirketting. 29 Twixt deck-ceiling; Tween-deck-ceiling. 30 Main-deck-beam-hanging-knees. 31 Main-deck-beam-clamps. 32 Main-deck-shelves. 33 Main-deck-waterway. 34 Main-deck-spirketting. 35 Main-deck-lodging-knees. 36 Upper-deck-beam-hanging-knees. 37 Upper-deck-beam-clamps. 38 Upper-deck-beam-shelves. 39 Bulwark-stanchions. 40 Bulwark-planking. 41 Main-rail; Roughtree-rail. 42 Topgallant-bulwark-stanchions. 43 Topgallant-bulwark-planking. 44 Topgallant-rail.

Review of wood shipbuilding

Just as the writers a century ago tended to disregard timber construction in favour of new materials, so the author finds himself attracted in like manner. Nevertheless, in the description of individual vessels there have been references to the types of timber employed in the building and also to the manner of the construction, and it is hoped that this will provide an adequate commentary. By the middle of the century the chief concern for wooden shipbuilders was the acute shortage of native hardwood, which resulted in large imports of oak and teak. Timber merchants

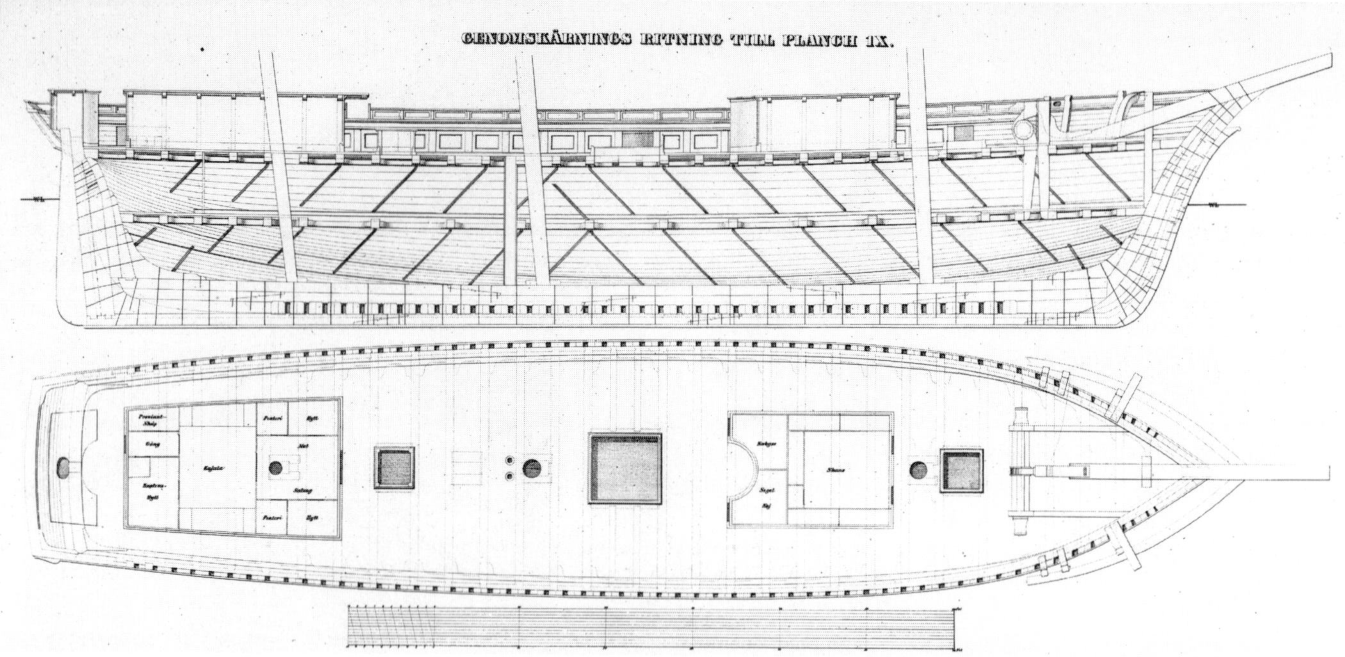

181: Wooden construction. Longitudinal section drawn by N C Kierkegaard and dated Gothenburg 22 September 1862, and published portfolio of plans entitled *Plancher till Praktisk Skeppsbyggnadskonst*. This section accompanies Plan IX of a barque of about 180 Lasts with dimensions of 125 (length on load line between rabbets) × 29 × 18. (All measured in Swedish feet; 1 fod .974ft.) *Peabody Museum, Salem.*

were scouring the forests of the world for suitable wood and by degrees a variety of new timbers made their appearance, which obliged Lloyd's Register to recast somewhat their grading classifications. The situation was considerably aggravated by the vast amount of new tonnage required in the early 1850s and many softwood or part-softwood ships of lower class were built to take advantage of the high freights. This meant that in the early 'sixties these ships of 5 to 7 A1 were due to be reclassed and to avoid this expense many were sold or broken up and new ships were ordered to replace them, a fact which gave useful orders to shipyards and helped to stimulate a new trade boom that was just beginning.

The acute shortage of good timber and the great demand for ships naturally had the effect of artificially raising prices for ships of high class, but simultaneously benefitting iron shipbuilding. In 1855, wooden ships classed at 14 A1 cost between £17 and £20 per ton with an East India outfit, if ordered from Alexander Stephen & Sons. Sometimes a ship built on speculation could fetch a high price if market conditions were right, but often a builder was left with an unsaleable ship on his hands. As many of the smaller wooden ships were built on speculation, the master shipwright was obliged to study the market very closely and to gauge astutely the requirements of potential customers.

The additional strength afforded by the use of iron for knees, beams, hold pillars and diagonal trussing permitted large wooden ships to be constructed without the cumbersome timber members which would otherwise be indispensable. With the building of very long ships which only possessed a comparatively narrow beam, the need for longitudinal stiffness became essential, and the use of iron allowed built-up girders to provide sufficient longitudinal strength while at the same time occupying little valuable cargo space.

An American ship and a British vessel are here contrasted to illustrate two differing approaches to wooden construction. In all-timber ships, massive scantlings were required to obtain the necessary strength, and cargo stowage became a problem in such a forest of hold pillars, sister keelsons and hanging knees. The American method was to employ wood almost exclusively throughout the hull and a coloured drawing in the Peabody Museum, Salem, reproduced here as figure 183, shows the structural timbers of the American packet ships *Star of Empire* and *Chariot of Fame*. These two ships had a length on deck of 220ft-0in, a beam of 43ft-0in, a depth of hold of 27ft-6in, and a tonnage of 2050. The keelson was composed of eight logs, each probably measuring 15 inches square: there were two rows of three each, placed one above the other, and the other two logs were above each other on the centre line. There were three pillars to each beam in the lower and middle holds; the hanging knees were huge and heavily bolted to the frames;

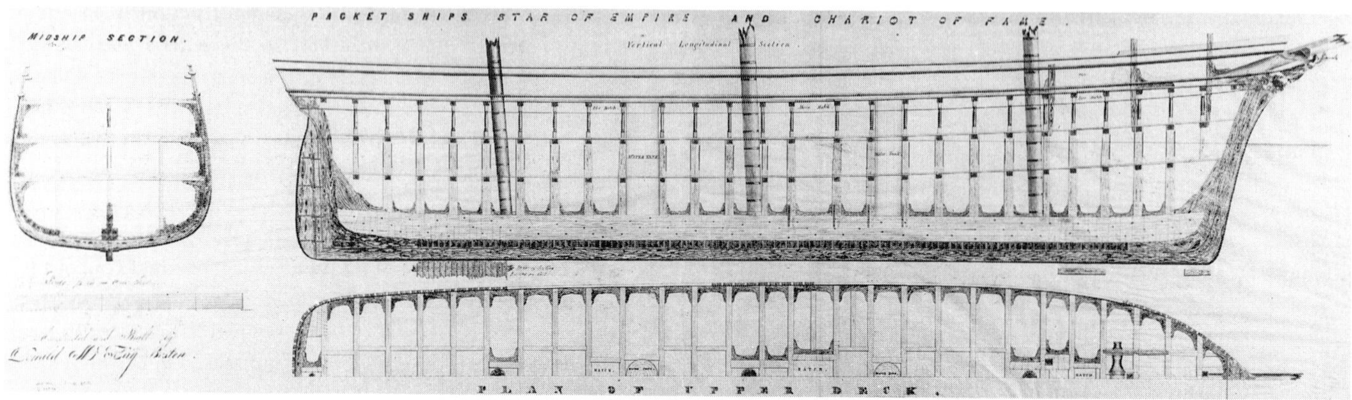

183: A tinted drawing of Donald McKay's ships *Start of Empire* and *Chariot of Fame* shows the massive timber construction required in these huge wooden ships. The cross-section indicates the enormous timbers that were laid longitudinally to give the ship support. The *Chariot of Fame* measured 220ft × 43ft × 27.6ft and 2050 tons.

184: The 'tween decks fo the *Jhelum*, looking forward when photographed at the Falkland Islands in 1966. This gives a good impression of the massive construction in a timber hull. All the upper deck beams have a moulding formed on the two lower arrises; there is a similar moulding on many of the ceiling planks. The long iron hanging knees are visible and also the T-shaped iron brackets instead of timber lodging knees. On the left are iron hold pillars. In the hold is the huge barrel of the windlass, and reaching as far down as the lower deck is the pawl post. *Karl Kortum.*

there were heavy bilge stringers and the ceiling at the bilge looks at least 12 inches thick. All these massive timbers occupied much space and one can readily appreciate the great gain in capacity given by an iron ship of identical form and dimensions.

By contrast, the Scottish-built clipper *Annandale*, launched in 1854 with measurements of 226.8ft by 28.5ft (inside ceiling) by 18.5ft and a tonnage of 759 nm, employed iron hold pillars, iron hanging knees, iron breasthooks, and 14ft-0in by 4¼in by ⅞in iron plates across the scarphs of the lower deck clamps. Nevertheless, her great length and narrow beam obliged a rider keelson to be added with two heavy limber strakes each side; the ceiling at the bilge was 9½in thick; externally the planking at the bilge was 6½in thick and at the wales 7½in. The midship section of this ship appears on her lines plan in figure 228. Such heavy timbering was the price for a clipper of extreme proportions. The insertion of diagonal iron trussing, let in flush with the outer face of the frames, gave great longitudinal strength and permitted planking of smaller scantling to be used. The West Indiaman *Renown*, built in 1824 by J M Hilhouse, has diagonal trussing shown on her plan, and this probably represents a fairly early use of it.

In spite of the big demands for tonnage in the first half of the 1850s, comparatively few wooden ships of over 1000 tons were built in the United Kingdom. Although no exhaustive check has been made through every available list, the samples taken bring up only an occasional ship that fulfils the above requirements. Furthermore, with a single exception, there is no tradition of large wooden ships having been built. The exception refers to the building of the so-called 'Blackwall Frigates' which formed the elite of the passenger fleet to India, Australia and the East. Some large ships of this type were built in the' forties such as the *Monarch* (1444 tons), *Marlborough* (1402 tons) and *Blenheim* (1314 tons); in the 1850s, Basil Lubbock lists 51 of these passenger frigates of which 22 measured 1000 tons or more.[33] By far the largest of the latter were the *Agamemnon* of 1431 tons built by Richard Green at Blackwall in 1855, measuring 252.3ft by 36.2ft by 23.2ft; and the *Eastern Monarch* of 1631 tons built by Alexander Stephen at Dundee in 1856, measuring 239.0ft by 40.3ft by 24.9ft (1849 tons om). The former was very long, having a proportion of almost seven beams to length.

With a tonnage of 2600 om and 2284 nm, the Aberdeen clipper *Schomberg* was by far the largest wooden merchant sailing ship built in the United Kingdom in the 1850s or probably at any other period, and also larger than any iron sailing ship built in the 'fifties. Launched in 1855 for James Baines as the British answer to the huge American clippers, this ship had a length of 247.7ft (after part of main stem to fore part of sternpost), a beam of 42.2ft (inside), and a depth of hold of 28.9ft. She will be described fully in the next chapter.

185: Aboard the hulk of the *Actaeon* in the Falkland Islands in 1966. The lower deck wooden beams are badly decayed, but the massive iron knees are still there. On top of the beams and going up the side are staple knees, the tops of which have been cut off. It is interesting to note the contours which the knees must adopt to pass over all the structural wooden members. The *Actaeon* was built at Miramichi in 1835 of 561 tons. *Karl Kortum.*

186: Beside the River Wear at Sunderland, the shipyards were laid out on the narrow foreshore beneath the high banks. In this old photograph, taken prior to 1858 on the north bank and looking downstream, Wearmouth Bridge frames the background. Brigs lie at moorings in the river. On the left, in a tiny dry-dock, a brigantine is being fitted out with sails and rigging. The angle of the shrouds suggests this rig instead of brig. In the foreground, a ship is in frame with ribbands in place but no deck beams yet laid. Nearer still, a stem piece has been erected in the left foreground but no frames can as yet be seen. *Copied from old print in Sunderland Museum.*

With old and new measurement tonnage figures to choose from before 1855, a ship can be listed as above 1000 tons with one figure and below with the other. As American ships were measured until 1864 by a formula roughly equivalent to the British old measurement tonnage, it is obvious that no rigid line can be drawn. The following table lists approximate numbers of wooden ships which registered over 1000 tons and it can be seen that Sunderland was the source of many wooden ships of the 'fifties.

If tonnages by old measurement were allowed, this would increase the number of ships registering more than 1200 tons and include *Omar Pasha* (1279 om), *Matilda Wattenbach* (1300 om), *Sarah Neumann* (1220 om), and probably others. It would also advance *Rajmahal* to 1467 tons om.

In the matter of steamships, some large wooden vessels of over 2000 tons were constructed, such as the *Arabia* of 2402 tons, which shows that shipbuilders were fully capable of building big wooden vessels.

Wooden ships of over 1000 tons built in UK 1850–59

This is an exploratory table and the figures are only approximate. Of ships built after 1854, the tonnage is either nm or according to the new 1854 rule.

Year	*Total*	*Named ships above 1200 tons*
1850	1	—
1851	1	—
1852	4	—
1853	9	*Dunbar* (1321 by J Laing, Sunderland)
1854	9	*Earl of Eglinton* (1270 at Troon); *George Marshall* (1361 by G Marshall, S Shields); *Orwell* (1220 at Harwich)
1855	6	*Agamemnon* (1431 by R Green, Blackwall); *La Hogue* (1331 by J Laing, Sunderland); *Schomberg* (2284 by A Hall, Aberdeen)
1856	5	*Eastern Monarch* (1631 by A Stephen, Dundee)
1857	3	*Duncan Dunbar* (1374 by J Laing, Sunderland)
1858	5	*Holmsdale* (1257 by J Reed, Sunderland); *Rajmabal* (1302 by Brocklebank, Whitehaven)
1859	3	—

By comparison, Canada produced vast numbers of ships which registered over 1000 tons and such vessels, which were built of softwood and received a low A1 classification, could be bought cheaply in Bristol and Liverpool and thereby enabled their owners to obtain a quick profit when freight rates rose in the early 1850s. Frederick W Wallace, writing about the shipbuilding boom in the Canadian maritime provinces, says that so many big vessels were launched 'that it became a common place happening, and a corporal's guard would not muster to see a 1500-ton ship take the water'.[34] For the decade of the 1850s, it is almost a foregone conclusion that any ship of over 1000 tons which is listed in *Lloyd's Register* was constructed in Canada. A cursory perusal of published works has indicated that over 30 ships were built in Canada which measured

187: An interesting photograph of Donal McKay's shipyard at East Boston with the midship section of a ship framed up on the stocks and a full rigged ship fitting out close beside her. The ground is covered with piles of timber sorted out for planking or grown bends. *Peabody Museum, Salem.*

more than 1500 tons and of these four were above 2000 tons – the *Guiding Star* (2012 tons), *White Star* (2467 tons), *Morning Light* (2377 tons), and *Acadia* (2030 tons).[35]

The same remarks on size apply to America, except that here the production was on an even bigger scale and the maximum sizes proportionately increased. A few British shipowners ordered clippers from well known American shipbuilders to satisfy passenger requirements at the height of the Australian gold rush, but otherwise the entire range of tonnage was absorbed initially by American interests to cater for the California gold rush and allied trade expansion. Towards the end of the 'fifties, many American ships were sold to British owners at probably very low prices. Running one's eye down the list of clippers in Carl Cutler's *Greyhounds of the Sea*, one is struck by the immense size of these well-known ships that were double or treble the size of their British counterparts, and one wonders how many acres of forest were razed to the ground to provide timber for these gigantic vessels.[36]

The number of ships listed by Cutler which measured over 1500 tons is considerable, as the following figures prove:

Clipper ships built in America of over 1500 tons, 1850–59[37]

Year	*Total*	*Named ships above 2000 tons*
1850	1	—
1851	11	*Challenge* (2006, *Trade Wind* (2045)
1852	6	*Sovereign of the Seas* (2420)
1853	29	*Chariot of Fame* (2050), *Empress of the Seas* (2197), *Great Republic* (4555 originally; 3357 as rebuilt after fire), *Queen of Clippers* (2361), *Red Jacket* (2035), *Star of Empire* (2050)
1854	15	*Champion of the Seas* (2447) *James Baines* (2515), *Lightning* (2084)
1855	7	*Donald McKay* (2595)
1856	2	—
1857	—a	—
1858	1	—
1859	—b	—

a: largest was 1482 tons b: none above 1000 tons

188: An example of decoration and carving at the stern to be seen aboard the *Stratford* ex *Arctic* which was built in 1850 at Williamsburg, New York. She had a tonnage of 1157 and was an Atlantic passenger packet. She was an old ship when this photograph was taken.

Because the tonnage of American ships was roughly equivalent to that of British old measurement tonnage, it is evident that the *Schomberg* of 2600 tons om was equal to the largest American ship. Head and shoulders above them all stands the leviathan *Great Republic*, even in her reduced form after the fire.

The merit of the British shipping policy lies in the fact that it took advantage of the big ships available in American and Canadian yards when a temporary boom period existed, but when depression followed, its own productions in the 500-1000-ton range were still in demand. The smaller ships were more adaptable and better suited to the small undeveloped harbours and narrow rivers into which they traded.

Diagonal and experimental construction in wood

The application of diagonal framing and planking as practised in the first half of the nineteenth century by Annesley, Seppings, Fletcher & Fearnall, and others, was described in chapter one. During the 1850s it came into vogue again and the two yards which built ships with diagonal planking and the minimum of frames were J & R White at Cowes and Alexander Hall & Sons at Aberdeen. On the Thames, Bilbe & Perry employed diagonal framing with conventional planking in the years 1851–56.

Beginning in 1850, John and Robert White conducted experiments for three years into the merits of diagonal construction and patented their process in March 1852, at which time they also issued a prospectus describing their methods.[38] There was a keel, floor timbers, keelson, and external longitudinal planking in the normal way, but there were no frame timbers above the head of the first futtocks. The floor timbers were spaced at about 3ft-4in-centres. Then skeleton frames were erected with longitudinal ribbands outside them, over which two skins of thin diagonal planking were laid in opposite directions, and finally the third layer which was the longitudinal one. By degrees, the skeleton frames were struck as beams and planking were added, but the longitudinal ribbands were retained as part of the structure. There were long hanging iron knees to alternate beams, and in the hold these knees reached sufficiently far down to allow a single bolt to be driven into the heads of the floor timbers. Originally, screw threads were cut in the treenails but later this was dispensed with. John White estimated that the diagonal system added a charge of about £1.15s per ton to the normal costs. Most of the sailing ships he built were classed by Lloyd's Register, some receiving 13 A1. In the ship *Empress*, the diagonal skins were each 2¼in thick, and the outer planking was 4in to 5in; there was also a complete ceiling of 2½in to 4in planking.

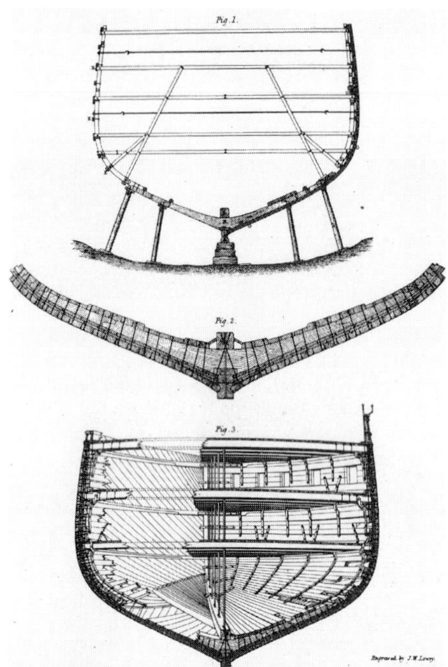

189: A drawing to illustrate J & R White's method of diagonal construction. On the left of the drawing, the ceiling and beams are omitted to show one of the diagonal skins; on the right, the hull is shown in a complete state.

The principal differences between the systems employed by J & R White and Alexander Hall & Sons were that Hall used widely-spaced frames both to form the shape of the hull and as permanent parts of the structure; Hall also led the diagonal planking between the keel and floors for half the ship's length. The three skins of outer planking were secured with screw-threaded treenails which produced a very solid hull. Hall's method of construction is described fully in the section on the clipper *Vision* in chapter six.

In his article on 'Shipbuilding' in the *Encyclopaedia Britannica*, Andrew Murray spoke well of Hall's diagonal system and described the construction of *Schomberg* and *Vision* with the aid of a midship section and diagrams.[40]

The *Vision* cost £16.15s per ton on 563 tons nm but only classed 7 A1; *Cairngorm* cost £14 per ton on 1094 contract tons and also classed 7 A1. The latter was built in the conventional manner which illustrates the additional expense involved in the specialised diagonal system.

Ships built by J & R White on diagonal system[39]

Date	Name	Rig	Tons	Owner
1853	PS *Vectis*	sch	983 om	P & O, London (first of this system)
1853	PS *Solent*	sch	1804	Royal West Indian Mail Co
1853	*Patricia*	bk	267 nm	James Shepherd, London
1853	PS *Tartar*	sch	471 om	P & O, London
1854	*Royal Blue Jacket*	sch	105 nm	Ivens & Chessel, Bristol
1855	*Heroes of Alma*	S	651 nm	James Shepherd, London
1855	*Cecile* (yacht)	sch	200 om	Marquis of Conyngham
1857	*Solent*	S	732 nm	James Shepherd, London
1857	*Medina*	S	410 om	James Shepherd, London
1858	*Empress*	S	480 nm	E I Wheeler & Co, London

Ships built by Alexander Hall & Sons on diagonal system

Year	Name	Rig	Tons	Port of registry
1854	*Vision*	S	563 nm	Liverpool (first of this system)
1855	*Schomberg*	S	2284 nm	Liverpool
1856	*Kitta Wake*	sch	150 gross	Ayr (yacht)
1856	*Salamander*	sch	115 gross	Kirkcudbright (yacht)
1860	*Chaa-sze*	S	556	London

190: The small barque *Prince Alfred* on the stocks at the yard of Duthie Jnr at the Inches, Aberdeen. She measured 258 tons and was launched in 1862; the copper sheathing shows clearly and the black hull above gleams brightly from its fresh coats of paint. *Nautical Photo Agency.*

Earlier in the 1850s, Hall had built the ship *John Taylor* and the barque *Marion* with a diagonally-laid ceiling in the lower hold and succeeding vessels are described as being trussed or stropped with 4½in × ⅝in iron bars, all of which suggest that the firm was experimenting with new constructional methods. The *Schomberg* was fitted with iron beams and so was the *Charles Horsfall*.

In 1855, another Aberdeen builder, Thomas Wright (also described as F Wright), employed diagonal planking in the *Admiral Collingwood*. This flush-decked barque was given three skins of larch and fir, and received a class of 7 A1; she was sheathed with zinc.[41] Diagonal planking in various forms was employed by a number of shipbuilders at this period, although the additional expense incurred prevented its more general adoption.

Some interesting experimental construction was carried out by Charles Harratt of Barking, London, who launched the three-masted schooner *Isis* in 1853, the ship *Sphynx* in 1856 and the schooner *Louisa* in 1858. The construction was a combination of diagonal planking over longitudinal timbers, although each three were different. H J Boolds signed the drawing of *Sphynx* and a similar style of lettering suggests that he drew all three plans.[42] His name appears as a member of the Scottish Shipbuilders Association in the proceedings of 1863–64 and his address is given as Greenock.

The enterprising shipbuilders, Bilbe & Perry of Nelson Dock, Rotherhithe, were also experimenting with diagonal and composite structures. At the Great Exhibition of 1851 they exhibited the model of a merchant ship in which the timber frames were diagonally arranged; this, they claimed, gave additional strength and would prove economical in the use of timber owing to the elongation of the curves.[43] The surveyor to Lloyd's Register describes the system of radiating frames in the construction of the *Orient*:

> 'Built on Mr Bilbe's diagonal plan, that is to say, the midship frames are placed perpendicular to the keel while those in the fore and after body gradually radiate until the foremost frame is inclined *aft* at the gunwale to an angle of fifty degrees with the keel, while the frames of the after body incline to the same extent forward at the sheer strake... All her workmanship is of the best description. She is beautifully formed and neatly and carefully finished.'[44]

A half-model in the Science Museum catalogue of a ship with radiating frames is probably the very model that was exhibited by Bilbe at the Great Exhibition in 1851. This model was returned prior to 1939 to Lloyd's Register of Shipping, but it cannot now be found.

The following table lists such ships built by Bilbe which were surveyed by Lloyd's Register. It is not known when he adopted this system nor which was the first ship so built.

Bilbe & Perry may also have built the *Koh-i-noor* and *Victoria* between the launching of the last two vessels. When the firm began composite building in 1856, it is possible that no more ships with radiating timber frames were built.

Composite construction

Although it is commonly believed that the first composite vessel was the schooner *Excelsior*, built in 1850 in accordance with John Jordan's patent, there are earlier patents and actual vessels which preceded Jordan's work by some years. John Walters took out a patent in 1814 for various methods of combining iron and wood in hull construction; William Watson in 1839 specified iron angle or T-bars with wooden planking; Thomas J Ditchburn in 1841 patented the combination of wooden inner and outer planking with iron angles or T-bars as frames.[46] Names of actual vessels are difficult to collect because the experimental nature of their construction discouraged the owners from classing them with Lloyd's Register who would probably have

Some ships built by Bilbe & Perry with radiating frames[45]

Year	*Name*	*Rig*	*Tons*	*Remarks*
1851	*Celestial*	S	438 nm	room and space on keel 30in; at gunwale 24in; 13 A1
1852	*Ignis Fatuus*	bk	173 nm	probably built on speculation as Bilbe was owner; 10 A1
1853	*Orient*	S	1032 nm	Only received 7 A1 which owner rejected; not classed
1854	*Gazehound*	bk	350 nm	
1856	*Alhambra*	S	335	

made them subject to annual survey. The steamer *Assam* built in 1839, perhaps in India, by Captain Andrew Henderson, is an early example of a composite ship. T J Ditchburn built small steamers for use on the Thames, according to his patent, 'but [they] did not last two summers'.[47] The *Archduke, Maximillian* and *Little Western* were built at Bristol about 1842 with a part frame of light iron T-bars, wooden beams and floors, and two skins of diagonal planking.[48] A study of journals such as the *Mechanics' Magazine* or the *Artizan* would probably reveal other names.

So John Jordan's patent of November 1849 was not without precedent, although he later contended that his was the first to specify a complete iron frame — ribs, keel, beams, stem and sternpost. In conjunction with John Getty, the firm of Jordan & Getty built the following vessels at Liverpool on this composite principle: the schooner *Excelsior* (1850 of 33 tons); the barque *Marion Macintyre* (1851 of 283 tons); the ship *Tubal Caine* (1851 of 787 tons); and the flat-bottomed schooner *George Jordan* (1853 of 91 tons). The *Marion Macintyre* and *Tubal Caine* were both built for L H Macintyre & Co of Liverpool, and cost £10 per ton for hull, masts and rigging which was very cheap; but they were iron-bolted which caused chemical action between the copper sheathing and the iron bolts, resulting in corrosion of the latter.[49] By October 1853 the business was being referred to as 'John Getty (later Jordan and Getty)',[50] so that the composite barque *Bristow* (1854 of 374 tons) must have been built by Getty under agreement with Jordan. Jordan & Getty got into difficulties and so parted, but Jordan seems to have continued as a ship surveyor and during the 1860s, as we shall see, he was very busy furthering the cause of composite ships and protecting his patent.

191: An engraving from the *Illustrated London News* during 1851 bearing the caption: 'Launch of the *Marion Macintyre* and part of the ship *Iron Frame* at Messrs Jordan and Getty's Building-Yard, Liverpool'. *MacGregor Collection.*

In 1854, the SS *Union* was built on the Thames for a Southampton company and it is possible that she may have been constructed to Jordan's system, as he knew a great deal about her.

Thomas Bilbe of Rotherhithe had built many experimental ships with diagonal frames during the early 1850s, and in 1856 he took out a patent for a form of composite construction in which he employed two angles facing each other to make a U-section, with timber laid between to form a compound

Ships built by Bilbe & Perry 1857–60 on composite principles[51]

Year	*Name*	*Rig*	*Tons*	*Description of build from Lloyd's Register*
1857	*Red Riding Hood*	S	709	'frame iron, pitch pine and hackmatack; plank pitch pine; experimental; biennial survey'
1857	*Gondola*	bk	407	'iron and teak frame, mahogany planking'
1858	*Lauderdale*	S	851	'iron frame, diagonal build'
1859	*Demerara*	K	81	'iron frame, diagonal build'
1859	*Gleam*	bk	292	'iron frame, diagonal build'
1860	*Woodpecker*	sch	175	'iron frame planked Pugit Sound pine (biennial survey)'

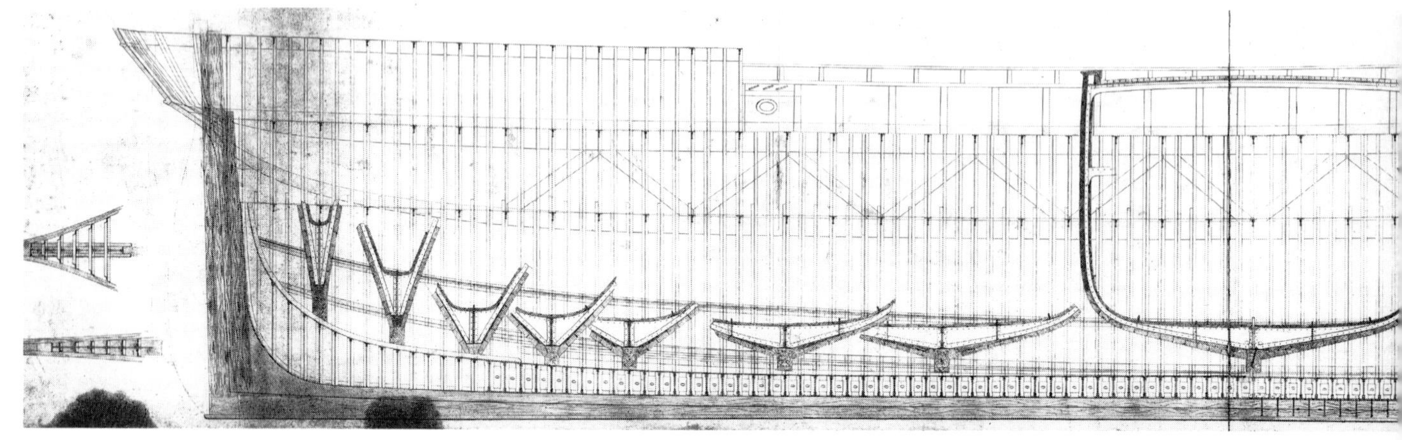

member. This served either as a frame or a beam, and bolts or other fixing could be passed through the angles or the timber filling piece. Bilbe's first ship by this method is generally considered to be the *Red Riding Hood*. The comments on her and other composite ships he built are listed below.

Bilbe & Perry built further composite ships during the 1860s.

Across the Channel, in France, composite ships were being built at Nantes and Bordeaux during the fifties on composite principles.

But composite shipbuilding did not become really popular until after 1863, and on the occasion of John Jordan's paper on the subject to the Scottish Shipbuilder's Association on 7 December 1863, the President, Peter Denny, remarked that 'everyone must be indebted to Mr Stephen for the attention he has bestowed upon it. I think, if it had not been for Mr Stephen, this part of the art of shipbuilding would not have progressed as it has done; . . . Meantime, I daresay all will admit that Mr Stephen has the field: . . .'[52]

The part played by Alexander Stephen Jnr in broadening the appeal of composite construction and obtaining a proper class for it at Lloyd's Register has never been described before, but it is interesting to see how the initiative of one man can effect so large a change.

The earliest reference to composite ships found in Alexander Stephen's diary is dated 31 March 1856 and concerns a conversation about them which he had with his brother William. Ten days later he made a full size model of part of the iron framing of a 1000-ton composite ship. The model was 3ft-4in long and 18in broad and the iron angles were 5in by 3in by ½in at 16in centres. The copper screw bolts which fastened the planking were prevented from coming into contact with the iron frames by a piece of rubber placed inside the bolt hole and under the washer. This attempt at isolating the copper bolts from the iron frame was essential to prevent the corrosion of the iron by the galvanic action which occurred when the copper got wet. Later, Stephen dealt more effectively with this problem by covering the angle-iron frames and copper bolts with cement which effectively prevented water getting to them and so avoided any ill-effects. He took out a patent for this idea in February 1862.[53] Some builders later employed galvanised iron bolts.

Meanwhile, Stephen took every opportunity of enquiring into other methods of composite construction, got to know John Jordan, examined a 260-ton ship building at Sunderland in 1861 and frequently discussed the matter with his brother, William. He considered that the great obstacle to progress of this system would be to get orders for such vessels and only lack of capital prevented him from building a small vessel on speculation to demonstrate the feasibility of the scheme.[54] Correspondence followed with John Jordan and L H Macintyre & Co, the builder and owner respectively of *Marion Macintyre* and *Tubal Caine*, on the merits of the system and its success. At Stephen's request, the Visitation Committee of Lloyd's Register visited his yard on 30 July 1861 and discussed with him the construction of ships with an iron frame and wood planking to be built under a roof. They tended to treat the subject on an experimental basis just as they had done with other similar applications for classification in the past, and although their initial reaction was favourable, they later reversed their opinion. Simultaneously, Alexander Stephen discovered that composite construction would cost more than he had originally anticipated: a ship of 1000 tons similar to his number 27 (*City of Calcutta*), built under a shed to class 15 A1 would cost £12.8.3 per ton; to this an East India outfit would add £2 and copper sheathing another 16s making £15.4.3 in all. Profit and overheads would further increase the cost.[55]

Undismayed by the lack of interest at Lloyd's Register, Alexander Stephen visited them in London, but found they would not commit themselves until he had submitted a written statement. Meanwhile, he was visiting shipowners and expounding on the advantages of combining an iron frame with wood planking. The matter was now right out in the open, and on 23 September he learned that John Willis was getting a quotation for a composite ship from a Sunderland builder. (This vessel was probably the *Amur*, built in 1862.) On 25 September he sent Lloyd's Register his specification and drawings for composite ships, and followed this up with another visit to London when he discussed this system of building with Frederick Somes, Lidgett & Co, John Willis, Lloyd's surveyor J H Ritchie, and George Marshall. The latter promised to use his influence at Lloyd's.

Another visit to London followed soon after and on 10 October Stephen obtained Lloyd's verbal consent. 'I can now build as high class as 15 years A1. This is a great matter and I feel thankful to God for his kindness in guiding me in this.'[56] His diary entry for 11 October reads:

> 'Called at Lloyd's and received letter from Mr Seyfang with Committee's decision which is all I could wish. It is dated yesterday. I have got the plans also and the models, with the bolts we had intended to use in the construction of these ships and which I had laid before the Committee. This is the first time Lloyd's have decided to assign a number of years for ships built with an *entire* iron frame and wood planking.'[57]

192: Composite construction. Longitudinal section drawn by Alexander Stephen & Sons and dated 15th October 1861. This must have embodied the proposals for composite construction which he made to Lloyd's Register earlier that month. The original cartridge plan was mounted on linen and was drawn to a scale of ½in to 1ft which made it very long. Photographed from original in builder's possession. *Norman Brouwer.*

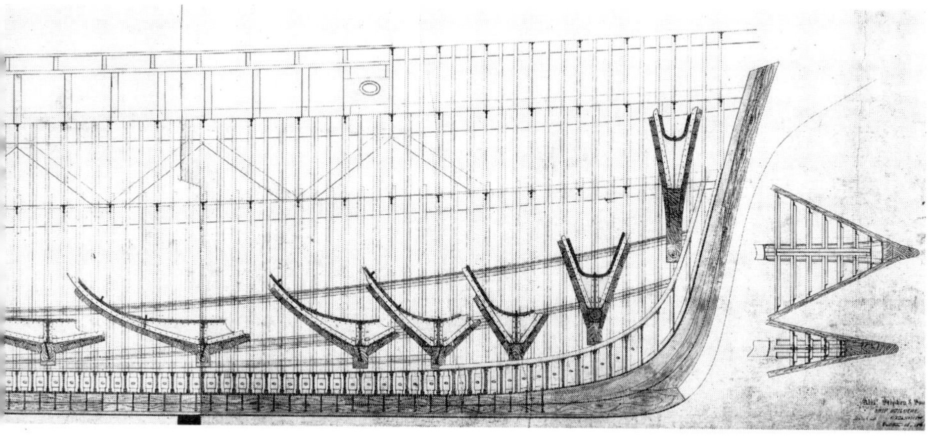

The following day he contracted with John Lidgett & Co to build for them his first composite ship of 750 tons BM, at a cost of £18.18s per ton BM, to class 15 A1 with an East India outfit. He estimated the actual cost to himself as follows:

All prices are calculated per ton BM

Cost with E.I. outfit	£15 5. 4
less for galvanized iron bolts	£ 1. 0.10
	£14. 4. 6
add greenheart ceiling	£ 3. 1
doubling of elm	£ 1. 3. 0
shed	£ 6. 6
	£15.17. 1
Contract price	£18.18. 0[58]

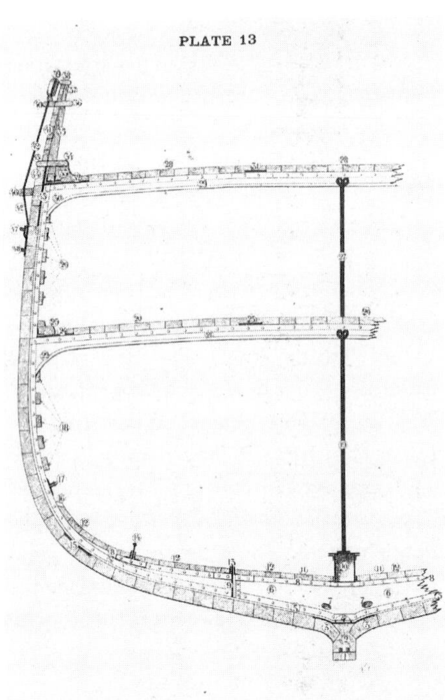

193: Part section of a composite ship, with names of the different members, from Captain H Paasch's *Illustrated Marine Encyclopedia.* 1 False-keel. 2 Keel. 3 Garboard-strake. 4 Keel-plate. 5 Frame. 6 Floor. 7 Limbers; Water-course. 8 Reversed-frame. 9 Side-intercostal-keelson. 10 Middle-line (box) keelson. 11 Limber-boards. 12 Ceiling. 13 Side-keelson. 14 Bilge-keelson. 15 Bilge-plate; Iron-bilge-strake; Bilge-strake-plate. 16 Covering-board. 17 Bilge-stringer. 18 Cargo-battens (in hold). 19 Hold-pillar; Hold-stanchion. 20 Lower-deck. 21 Lower-deck-beam. 22 Bracket-end (of lower-deck beam). 23 Lower-deck-beam-tie-plate. 24 Lower-deck-stringer; Lower-deck-beam-stringer-plate. 25 Lower-deck-waterway. 26 Cargo-battens (betwixt-deck). 27 Upper-deck-pillar; Upper-deck-stanchion. 28 Upper-deck. 29 Upper-deck-beam. 30 Bracket-end (of upper-deck-beam). 31 Upper-deck-beam-tie-plate. 32 Upper-deck-stringer; Upper-deck-beam-stringer-plate. 33 Upper-deck-waterway. 34 Covering-board. 35 Bulwark-stanchion. 36 Main-rail; Roughtree-rail. 37 Topgallant-bulwark-stanchion. 38 Topgallant-rail. 39 Dead-eye. 40 Upper-channel. 41 Bulwark-planing. 42 Chain-plate. 43 Planksheet. 44 Sheerstrake. 45 Iron-sheerstrake. 46 Lower-channel. 47 Chain-bolt. 48 Preventer-bolt. *Norman Brouwer.*

The keel of this ship, number 34, was laid on 4 March 1862. She was christened *John Lidgett* at her launch.

Lloyd's Register insisted on describing the ship in the Register Book as subject to biennial survey, and to placate Lidgett, Stephen agreed to pay any expenses in repair of the frames at the first biennial survey, up to a limit of £500. But Lidgett need not have worried as the first biennial survey in March 1866 proved entirely satisfactory to all concerned.

Now that Lloyd's Register had permitted a high class in years to be awarded, enquiries flowed in to Alexander Stephen & Sons and many quotations were made, the second contract for a composite ship being obtained on 21 January 1862. This ship, number 35, was the *Arima*, built for Gregor, Turnbull & Co. Needless to say, other shipbuilders were quick to take advantage of the approval given by Lloyd's Register to Alexander Stephen & Sons, and by April 1862 five more builders had submitted their own proposals to Lloyd's. Alexander Stephen must have realised the inevitability of this, although he was chagrined to learn that James Hall of Alexander Hall & Sons had written to William Robertson, his chief draughtsman, telling him that they were building a composite ship and hoped to launch her in June 1862. This could have meant that Hall's would get their ship into the water first, because Stephen could not lay the keel of the *John Lidgett* until George Smith's *City of Bombay* was launched.[59] As it happened, Hall's ship, the *Reindeer*, was only half framed by August and was not completed until February 1863, so Stephen had the satisfaction of being the first builder to finish a composite ship under the new conception of this old principle. Stephen's yard must have got a move on as they launched the *John Lidgett* on 29 August 1862, only five months and 24 days after laying the keel.

What originally was considered to be an individual and novel attempt at yet another composite ship, rapidly changed into a well-supported movement by numerous shipbuilders and backed by firm orders secured after much deliberation and discussion with shipowners, who required convincing arguments about the new system. In addition to the often quoted ease of applying copper sheathing to a wood hull, shipbuilders might have remarked on the high cost of docking and scraping an iron-hulled ship in China; or perhaps of the big saving in stowage capacity that a composite ship had over a wooden one, where the shell was greatly reduced in thickness, thanks to the iron frame. Lloyd's Register viewed this rush to composite construction with suspicion, as the following report of January 1863 indicates:

> 'The Sub-Committee gave a very anxious attention to "the principle recently come into practice of building ships with iron frames and wood planking", referred them per the General Committee's minute of 18th September 1862. In approaching this important subject the Sub-Committee was fully impressed with the desirability of not repressing the efforts of individuals who are desirous of making experimental improvements in the construction of ships. At the same time it may be necessary to lay down some general principles for the construction of ships for iron frames planked with wood, a mode of building which has recently come much into practice, nearly every vessel however, differing in some respect from any other.'

Then followed three pages of suggested building specifications. The report concludes:

> 'Further it is recommended that all such ships be noted as "Experimental" and be classed subject to a biennial survey, and that it be made a condition that "to entitle such experimental ships to classification, the plans on which they are to be built shall be submitted to the Committee for their approval".'[60]

As it transpired, these 'experimental' ships achieved extremely long lives.

It was not until 1867 that Lloyd's Register issued rules for building composite ships, which by then were well-established items in a shipbuilders' list. The word 'experimental' was then dropped.

An interesting but forgotten feature of the era of composite ships was the part played by John Jordan after 1862. His patent of 1849 specified a complete iron frame and Alexander Stephen offered him a royalty of £40, one week after the order to build the *John Lid-*

194: The stem and lower part of the figurehead of the tea clipper *Ambassador*, as she lay at Punta Arenas, Straits of Magellan, in 1970.

gett had been obtained. This was refused. The patent was due to expire in 1863 but by March of that year George and Henry Jordan had acquired John Jordan's rights in it. Alexander Stephen failed to convince George Jordan that he should charge no royalty, in spite of the fact that 'our firm - were means of reintroducing [composite construction] after it was abandoned years ago'. It was finally agreed that the royalty should not exceed 3d per ton register on any future vessels.[61]

This was only the beginning of numerous protracted negotiations and it appears that George and Henry Jordan, who in July 1863 succeeded in renewing the patent rights for another seven years, attempted to extort the maximum royalties from every shipbuilder on each occasion that a composite ship was built. There are repeated comments in Alexander Stephen's diary to fresh agreements with George Jordan over other composite ships. In October 1863 it was agreed between them that the royalty charged Alexander Stephen & Sons should be 75 percent less than that charged to other firms. As Jordan was proposing to charge 2s per ton, Stephen's would pay only 6d per ton. The royalty attributable to building the auxiliary steamer *Sea King* and the clipper *Eliza Shaw* amounted to £37.3s.[62] Alexander Hall & Sons, however, paid Jordan a royalty of £48.5s for building their first composite ship *Reindeer*. To enquiring shipbuilders, Stephen pointed out that the disproportionate royalty rates were because his firm had re-introduced the system.

In 1865 some shipbuilders formed a league to dispute Jordan's rights and the case of 'Jordan *v* Moore' was heard in December. G S Moore was the Sunderland builder who produced the small composite barque *Amur* in 1862 with a frame partly of iron and with iron beams. George Jordan won the case and was awarded £2 damages.[63] Moore appealed on the grounds that the patent was far too

195: Inside the hold of the tea clipper *Ambassador* at Punta Arenas in 1970 showing the iron frames, pillars, keelson and lower deck beams. The wooden planking of the composite construction has been virtually stripped off. This ship was built in 1869 at Rotherhithe by William Walker, and measured 692 tons.

wide in its claim and that previous patents, such as Ditchburn's, had specified a framework of iron. The appeal was heard in April 1866 and the previous verdict was quashed. 'In the opinion of the Court the invention was not novel and not the subject of a patent.'[64]

However, George Jordan continued to claim his royalties even demanding 6s per ton from Alexander Stephen in November 1867, whereas Robert Steele was only paying 1s per ton. In February 1868, Stephen paid him 3d per ton on a new ship. Meanwhile, litigation against other shipbuilders continued. It is likely that George and Henry Jordan obtained considerable financial recompense for all the bother they caused, but by 1870 when their patent rights finally expired composite construction had practically ceased as well.

Although the majority of composite ships were in the 500- to 1000-tons range, there were several smaller ones and a few very much bigger in tonnage. Of the latter, the largest was the *Sobraon* which Alexander Hall & Sons built in 1866 of 2131 tons; following her came the *Andromeda* of 1876 tons, built in 1864 by Jones, Quiggin & Co, Liverpool. Hall paid Jordan a royalty of £173 in building the *Sobraon*.

Variants on Jordan's system were naturally introduced, such as Charles Lungley's in 1864, and by this method were built the *Dilpussund, Dilawur* and *Dilbhur*. In 1869, Alexander Stephen & Sons built the clipper *City of Hankow* and the steamer *Tsz'ru* in which the iron frame was planked with wood to a foot or so above the load line, above which the topsides were covered with iron plates. The last year that composite merchant vessels were built in Great Britain was probably 1876 when Stephen built the barque *India* and Robert Thompson Jnr constructed the barque *Helena Mena*. The system was much liked in Holland where it persisted into the 1880s.[65]

Improvements to deck fittings and rigging

Experiments and improvements above deck and aloft were much in evidence in the 'fifties and 'sixties and many patents were registered for fittings of all kinds.

Considerable attention was given to the improvement of windlasses, and in particular the more economic and efficient use of manpower and the application of steam power. The drawing in figure 196 of *Camertonian*'s windlass shows a standard fixture which remained in constant use in modified form throughout the remnant of the sailing ship era. It is generally referred to as 'Armstrong's Patent' but as no Mr Armstrong appears to have registered a patent windlass, it is usually assumed that a pun is intended, the patent gearing being in the form of the crew's strong arms. Various patentees invented methods of transferring the lateral action of the windlass arms to the revolving of the barrel and names such as Tyzack & Dobinson, Bowman & Vernon, Pow & Fawcus are to be read in surveys and specifications, but the two firms which gained predominance were Brown & Harfield and Emerson & Walker.

Brown & Harfield continued to improve the 'Armstrong patent' variety and moved the handles to the after side of the windlass barrel

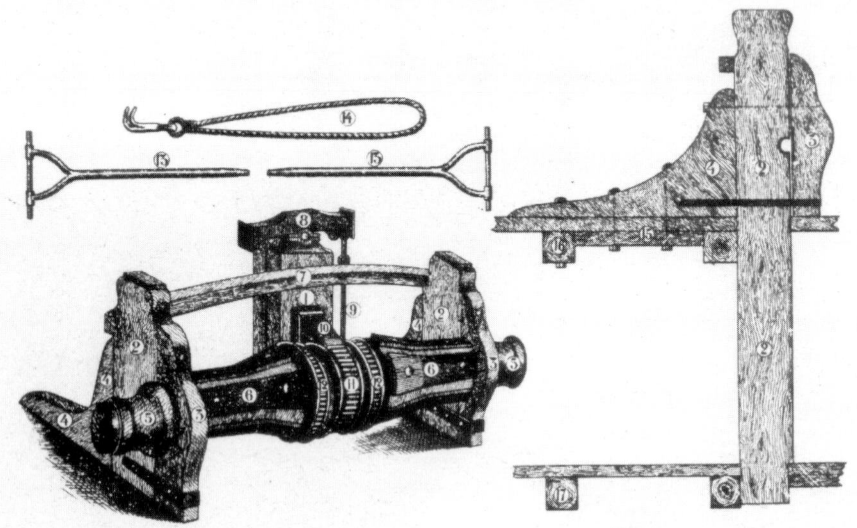

196: Perspective view and side elevation of an 'Armstrong Patent' windlass, with which the majority of ships heaved in their anchor cables. It might take four hours to heave in forty fathoms of chain at the approximate rate of one link per minute. 1 Pawl-bitt; Pall-bitt. 2 Carrick-bitts. 3 Cheeks (of Carrick-bitts). 4 Standard-knees (of Carrick-bitts). 5 Windlass-ends. 6 Whelps (on main-piece of Windlass). 7 Strong-back. 8 Crosshead. 9 Purchase-rod. 10 Pawl; Pall. 11 Pawl-rim. 12 Purchase-rims. 13 Hand-levers. 14 Chain-stopper. 15 Beam-carling. 16 Upper-deck-beam. 17 Lower-deck-beam.

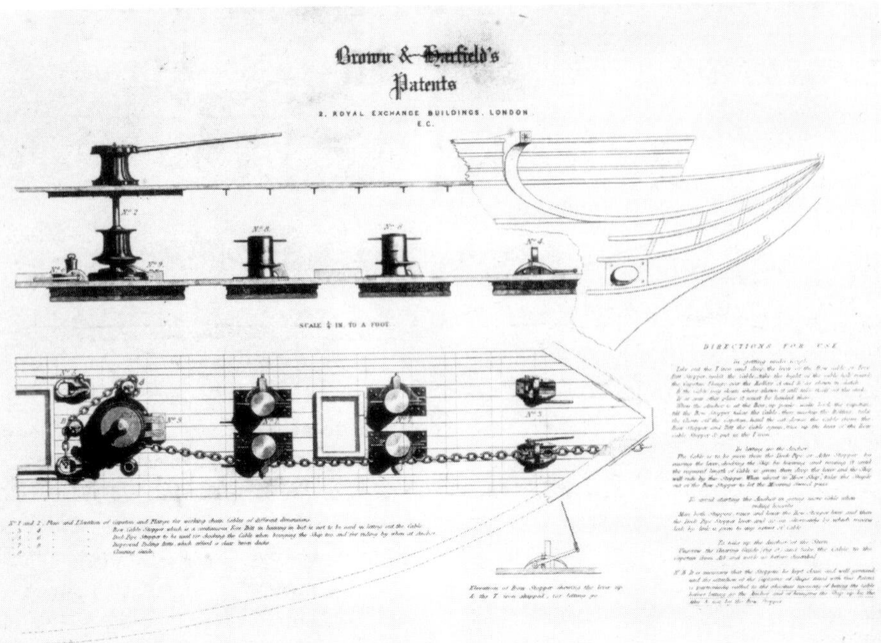

197: Brown & Harfield's patent windlass. This type was mostly fitted in large vessels and can be seen in the plan of the iron clipper *Hurricane*.

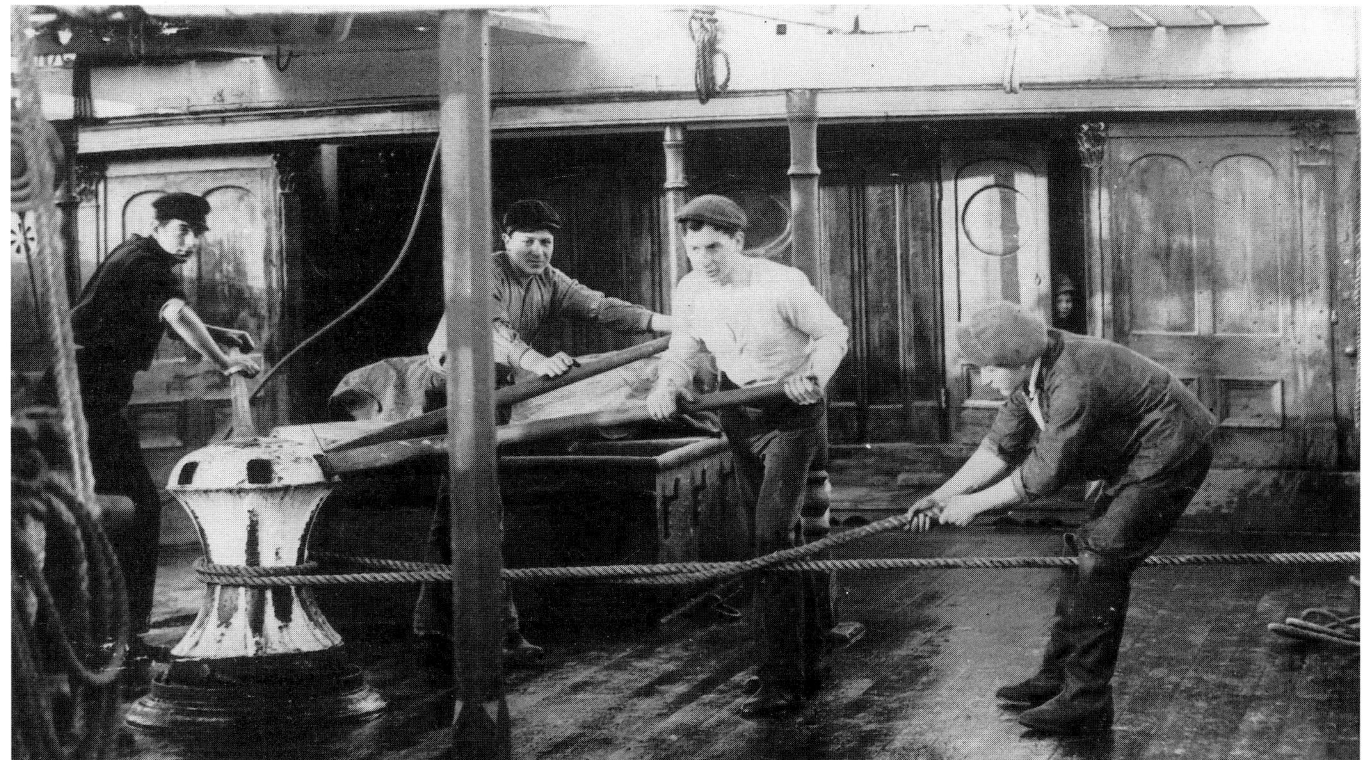

199: Manning the after capstan aboard the full-rigged ship *Agdo* ex *Waitangi* (1874). Supports to the boat skids are in the foreground and beyond are the high coamings to the after hatch. In the background is the break of the poop with corinthian capitals adorning the pilasters and round-headed panelling in-between. *Nautical Photo Agency.*

198: Drawings of the Emerson & Walker windlass of the pattern possibly fitted to the *Formby* (built of steel in 1863) from the catalogue issued by the Emerson Ship's Windlass Co of Boston, Mass. I am grateful to Karl Kortum, Director of the San Francisco Maritime Museum for these particulars. The following description and key to the letters is best described in the words of the original catalogue. Incidentally, the letter on the deck beams below the capstan looks like a 'C' but perhaps is really a 'G'. Description of the windlass: Figure 1, represents the windlass, as standing under the topgallant forecastle and a common capstan above. Figure 2, is a sectional side view of windlass and stopper. The same letters have reference to the same parts as in the other views. This view shows plainly how the windlass should stand when in place. A, is a common capstan working on the shaft J, of the windlass, but having no connections otherwise. B, is the lever head keyed to the shaft J. Turn the head round with the sun and the upper pawls O, catch into the pinion C, which turns the large gear on the starboard end of the windlass and gives great power. Turn the head against the sun the lower pawls O, catch into pinion D, which works small gear F, on the port end of the windlass and gives speed. The lower end of the shaft J, steps into a hole in the top of the centre piece V, the forward part of which extends sufficiently to reach the pawl bitt when the windlass is in place. The wheels which hold the chains we call wild cats; these are connected to the gears when heaving in chain by the keys N N. When paying out chain they are controlled by the friction bands H H. E, is the base of the capstan. W, is the cam which works the friction bands being connected by the rods M. P, is pawl plate firmly secured to the pawl bitt. T, is a hook which is hooked into the friction band at the top and fast to the deck at the bottom. S, is the clearing guard which prevents the chain from fouling. K, K, are the following pieces made as shown by the line on the side of the bitt; they open abaft the box, up to the top of the box; above that they open at the centre of the box.

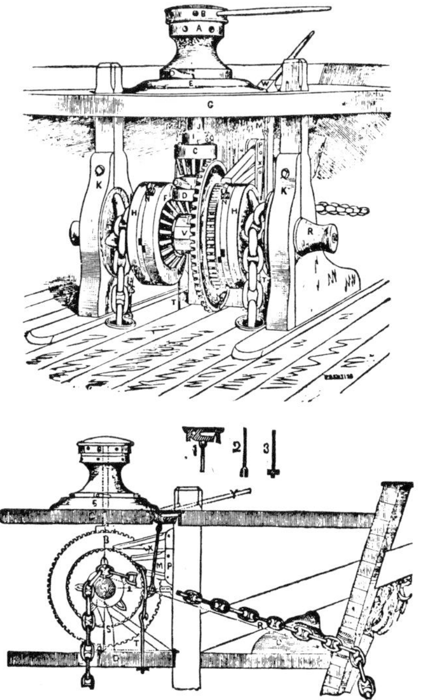

as can be seen on the deck plan of the clipper *Ariel* (figure 320). They also patented in 1847 a modernised version of the old naval practice in which the motive power was supplied by a capstan. In its new form the chain cable led directly to the capstan and was not shackled to a messenger. A circular, slotted flange below the capstan barrel accepted the chain cable, which passed around rollers and through a cable stopper down into the chain locker. Everything was of iron to minimise wear. The capstan bars could be manned on the topgallant forecastle while the cable came in on the main deck, a long spindle passing from one level to another. T & W Smith's passenger frigate *Hotspur* was fitted with one of their capstans in 1851.

Emerson & Walker also employed a capstan, but their spindle transferred the drive by a worm gear to a windlass barrel. There were two slotted flanges on this barrel to accept a cable each, in the same manner as with Brown & Harfield's pattern, but the cable only made a half revolution before continuing towards the chain locker. In ships with no topgallant forecastle, the capstan was dispensed with and the bars were fitted into a slotted head at the upper end of the spindle. The *Chaa-Sze*, built in 1860, was Alexander Hall's second ship to be equipped with Emerson & Walker's windlass; in her case the cost to supply it was £100.[66]

Other labour saving devices were beginning to make their appearance such as anchor davits, small winches on the rail for braces or sheets, more efficient cargo winches and pumps, and more reliable boat lowering gear. The long boat remained encumbered with sheep, hen and pig pens and a variety of means was employed to accommodate it conveniently on deck. Aloft, iron and steel masts and yards, wire and chain rigging, and roller-reefing sails increased safety and reliability.

Iron masts were referred to in a patent taken out in 1809 by the engineers Richard Trevithick and Robert Dickinson. In 1825, following a suggestion to the Admiralty by Robert Bill who had experimented with iron T-bars in hull construction, the 46-gun frigate *Phaeton* was fitted with an iron mainmast and bowsprit. Unfortunately, the bowsprit was carried overboard and the mast exhibited signs of weakness which necessitated its being shifted. Prior to these setbacks, valuable experiments were conducted into the deviation of the compass caused by the presence of the iron spars; but the conclusion was that 'the guns &c had greater effect on the needle than the mast and bowsprit . . .'[67] The iron mast measured 92ft-6in with an average diameter of 2ft-0in; the iron bowsprit was 54ft-6in with an average diameter of 19½in. Each spar was composed of hollow wrought iron cylinders, ¼in thick and 3ft-6in long, which were rivetted together at their ends and stiffened there and at their middle with iron hoops; in the bowsprit the cylinders overlapped each other by half their length.[68] There does not appear to have been any vertical stiffening inside or out, so that the spars must have buckled under their own weight. This seems surprising as Robert Bill's first patent in 1820 for iron masts refers to the use of T-bars with iron plates wrapped round them.[69] Experience gained in civil engineering contracts proved of value in iron shipbuilding, and masts were later composed of several iron plates, rivetted together and stiffened internally with angle irons.

The auxiliary barque *Q.E.D.*, built in 1844 at Newcastle by Coutts & Co, must have had an iron mizen mast because she used it as a funnel; perhaps the other lower masts were also of iron. The standing rigging was of iron wire, set up with rigging screws. An early example in the 1850s was the Dutch East Indiaman, *Olivier van Noord*, which was already fitted with iron lower masts when she visited Salthouse Dock, Liverpool, in January 1851.[70] The spread of iron as a building material naturally led to the wider adoption of this metal for masts, particularly lower masts and yards, although a barque often retained a timber mizen lower mast. During the 1850s, steel became increasingly popular for hollow spars, possibly because its greater strength allowed thinner plates and therefore made the spars lighter in weight, which was a great saving aloft, especially when lengthy lower and topsail yards had to be supported. Wire standing rigging was experimented with in the early decades of the century, but was not a commercial success until the 1830s, and rigging screws were also tried out. Patents by Andrew Smith in 1841 and Robert S Newall in 1848 improved the techniques of rigging, with wire, the iron ships of the 1850s.

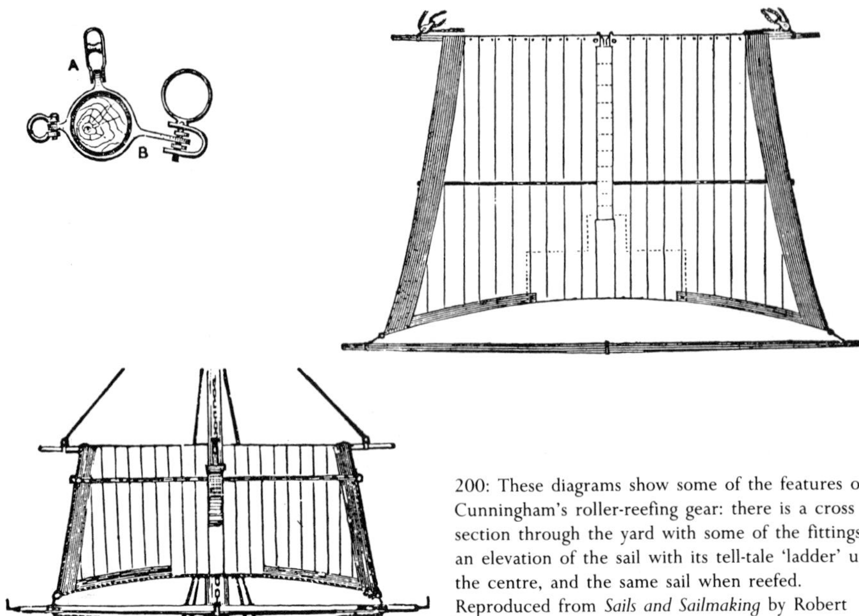

200: These diagrams show some of the features of Cunningham's roller-reefing gear: there is a cross section through the yard with some of the fittings, an elevation of the sail with its tell-tale 'ladder' up the centre, and the same sail when reefed. Reproduced from *Sails and Sailmaking* by Robert Kipping (12th ed 1887 pp 168-69).

The control of square sails by various reefing processes was a prolific field for inventors, but the stern test of practicality under duress of weather apparently terminated any hope of success for the majority of patentees, because only a few names are encountered. Of these, Henry D P Cunningham and Colling & Pinkney were the best known, but Robert Kippling also illustrates Captain Samuel Dyer's patent, which was first granted in April 1856.[71] Henry Cunningham first registered his patent in November 1850 and so gained a long start on the others.'[72]

Under Cunningham's system the yard revolved as it was lowered due to the chain tye engaging in a whelped sleeve fitted around the yard at the slings. The name of the first vessel so rigged is not known, but the P & O steamer *Iberia* carried one in February 1851, and brigs, barques and ships were soon being fitted with them. Robert B Forbes wrote to the *Nautical Magazine* in April 1853 drawing the attention of readers to his own system for furling topsails. The following month there was a letter from H D P Cunningham recommending his own method for preference and giving a list of 12 vessels so fitted, including the PS *Iberia*.[73] Masters wanted time to experiment with such novelties, as in the ship *Madge Wildfire* which had Cunningham's roller-reefing system first fitted to the mizen topsail on a voyage to India and back; on her return to Liverpool in May 1855 she had one fitted to her fore topsail.[74] Other ships played for safety. The *Fairlight* (1858) was equipped with three Cunningham topsails and also three rows of conventional reefs point to each.[75]

Cunningham's gear was fitted in a lesser number of cases to topgallants: in the early 'sixties, the ships *Nelson* and *Victory* had them on each mast; the *Elizabeth Nicholson* had one on the mainmast only; in 1864 the tea clipper *Fiery Cross* was reported to have been fitted with them on each mast in addition to roller-reefing topsails; the iron ship *Shandon* (1855) also had them, in addition to roller-reefing topsails and courses.

Henry Cunningham continued to issue modifications to his patent throughout the 'fifties and 'sixties so that by 1865 some 4000 ships were using his topsails, yet in that year the switch to double topsails was accelerating. An indication of the cost of fitting Cunningham's topsails is given in a quotation by Alexander Stephen & Sons, dated April 1858, in which these topsails on fore and main only were to be charged at £32, excluding the cost of canvas, patent cloth or bonnets.[76]

John Colling brought out a patent for a roller-reefing topsail in April 1862 and 18 months later he and David G Pinkney registered a joint patent. Their gear was less

201: This photograph of the *Wild Duck* (1859) in dry dock at Auckland contrasts double topsail yards on the foremast with single roller-reefing yards on the other two masts. Photographs only rarely record the mixtures that used to occur in ships' rigging. *Alexander Turnbull Library, Wellington.*

complicated than Cunningham's; the yard did not rotate but only a light spar on which the sail was bent. Several ships in the 'sixties were fitted with it, such as the white-hulled Aberdeen ship *Kagosima* and the iron brig *Belle of the Clyde*; the *Christiana Thompson, Leander, Thermopylae* and others had a main topgallant sail on this principle, above double topsails. Walter Hood's *Ethiopian* (1864) set all her topsails and topgallants by this method.

In 1841, R B Forbes had introduced double topsails for American ships, and his system was very similar to that fitted prior to about 1835 in many sloops, schooners, and brigs on both sides of the North Sea including Scotland and north-east England, in which the lower topsail hoisted on the head of the lower mast between the cap and the trestletrees. In Forbe's rig, the topmast was fidded abaft the lower mast, and both upper and lower topsail yards hoisted. The system did not become so popular as that initiated in America in 1853 by Captain Frederick Howes, who rigged his ship with an additional yard permanently secured to the lower mast cap, thus effectively splitting the big single topsail in two. His arrangement did not require any change in standard masting techniques and there remained only one yard to hoist or lower. It is not known how many British ships were rigged according to either of the above methods, but Captain Howes' system early gained support and Robert Kippling advocated it in his 1858 edition of *Sails and Sailmaking*, adding three explanatory diagrams.[77]

The auxiliary steamer *Royal Charter*, which was built of iron at Chester in 1855 and measured 2719 tons, was fitted with Howes' topsails, as the following account from the *Illustrated London News* infers:

> 'The *Royal Charter*, independently of her steam power, is a full-rigged ship, and is the first English vessel which has adopted the American plan of double topsails on each mast. This rig gives the ship a most formidable appearance, by having on each mast five yards. The difference between this and the ordinary rig consists in the lower topsail-yard being secured to the cap of the topmast by a truss; and, in the absence of slings,

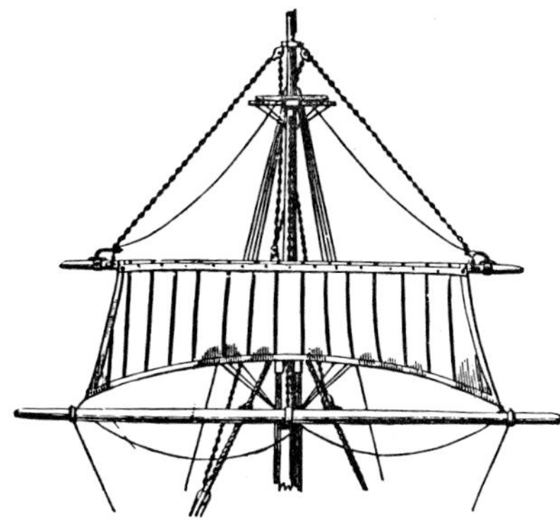

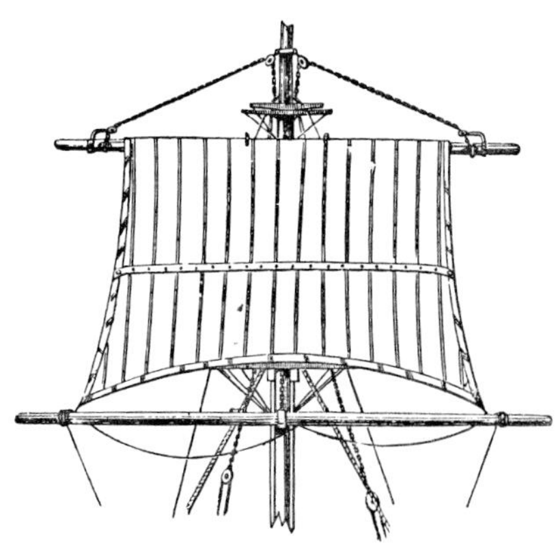

202: These two diagrams show some features of Colling & Pinkney's roller-reefing gear: the front of the sail set and the same when close reefed. Reproduced from same source as figure 200 (pp 176-77).

203: The iron passenger ship *Cornwallis* combined double topsails with Cunningham's reefing gear. From an engraving published in 1862 in the *Illustrated London News*.

> the yard is supported in the centre from below by a crane, stepped upon the heel of the foremast. [As the heel of the foremast actually stepped on the keel, perhaps 'topmast' should be read instead of 'foremast'.] Thus the lower topsail is the size of a close-reefed topsail of the old rig, and sets entirely by the sheets...the ship can be reduced to close reefed topsails at any time by lowering the upper topsails.'[78]

An accompanying engraving depicts a single row of reef points on both upper and lower topsails.

The American-built ship *Donald McKay*, built to the order of James Baines, reached Liverpool in March 1855 with Howes' topsails and as a result probably influenced other ships, like the *Royal Charter*.

In 1858, Josiah Jones Jnr built the iron ship *Aphrodita* at Liverpool. She was a large ship for her day, measuring 1601 tons, and designed to carry a large cargo irrespective of speed. Her sail plan at the National Maritime Museum, Greenwich, may be presumed to show the ship when new. She was square-rigged on all three masts, with double topsails on fore and main and a single mizen topsail. The lower topsail yards were held by a truss to the lower mast cap, and the foot of both lower and upper topsails was slightly roached. The *Aphrodita* may be regarded as another early example of a British ship with double topsails.

Three years later, a few owners were cautiously making enquiries about double topsails and by 1862 several ships had them fitted. The iron passenger ship *Cornwallis* (1862) had the best of both worlds: double topsails on all three masts with Cunningham's roller-reefing gear fitted to the fore and main upper topsails.[79] A sail plan of the *John Lidgett* (1862 by A. Stephen & Sons) has double topsails drawn; they are depicted on fore and main masts in a lithograph of the *Kosciusko* (1862 by Walter Hood & Co), which was published the year she was built; a plan of the *Montrose* (1863 by Barclay, Curle & Co) has them. They are listed in the spar dimensions of Alexander Hall's composite ship *Reindeer* (1863); and one is constantly coming across other examples. By 1865 they were fairly commonplace and rapidly growing in popularity.

Double topgallant sails did not apparently make their appearance until the mid 'sixties, and Basil Lubbock claims that the first British vessels so fitted were the iron ships *Antiope* and *Marpesia* which John Reid built at Port Glasgow in 1866.[80] Some of George Thompson's clippers, such as *Thermopylae*, were given double topgallants in the early 'seventies and by the middle of this decade they were being generally adopted in the larger iron ships. F W Wallace records that, prior to a passage to South Africa in 1869, the *Sea Gull* of Toronto was re-rigged as a brigantine and was fitted with double topsails and double topgallants.[81] The full-rigged ship *Mermerus*, built in 1872, was one of Barclay Curle & Co's earliest ships to be fitted with double topgallants.

Many other improvements were of course being made in deck fittings, rigging, ironwork aloft and the control of sails, which are too numerous to describe here, although one other of Henry Cunningham's inventions can be mentioned. This was his device to control

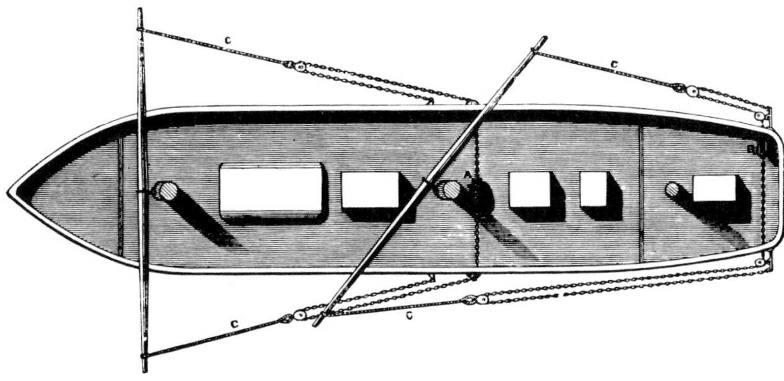

204: Plan of a three masted ship with Cunningham's braces fitted to the foreyard and the mainyard.

the braces on the fore and main lower yards which he did by means of making the running part of chain, continuing it across the deck from side to side, but passing it around the barrel of a winch. This winch supplied the motive power and by heaving in on one side, the yard was let go on the other. Cunningham patented this system in September 1864. Three years later he referred to the following full-rigged ships as being fitted with it: *Dragon* (1864), *Colonial Empire* (1861), *Rosneath* (1857), *Indian Chief* (1864), *Christiana Thompson* (1866), *Saint Vincent* (1865) and *Maitland* (1865).[82] Some ships had it on the mainyard as well as the foreyard. Later ships to be fitted were *Ben Voirlich* (1873), *Thermopylae* (1868) and *Salamis* (1875). The *Mary Moore* (1868 by A. Stephen & Sons) was designed with one on the foreyard but it is uncertain if it was fitted. Further research will add additional names.

205: The winch mounted on deck to operate Cunningham's braces. When bracing sharp up, the lever at 'a' locked the chain brace in position; the slack in the weather brace could then be heaved in and the weather lever locked.

Tonnage measurement by 1854 rule

The subject of a more correct method of measuring for tonnage had resulted in considerable discussion, and in 1849 a third Commission was appointed by the Government to inquire into the matter and submit a more satisfactory rule. The Commission was made up entirely of practical men — shipowners, shipbuilders and naval architects — who believed that only by a careful measurement of the hull and the computation of the cubic contents, could an exact tonnage figure be estimated. But their proposals, based on a scheme by the naval architects William Parsons and George Moorsom, required external measurement in which offsets were taken at a number of stations and from them a curve of areas drawn to calculate the gross cubic content of the hull.[83] This required considerable expertise that was incompatible with the nature of the work. It discriminated unfairly against ships with thick wooden frames and planking as against thin iron plating, because an iron ship would have a greater internal volume than a wooden ship of the same tonnage and could accordingly load a larger cargo.[84] The proposals were received unfavourably by the shipping industry and the Government declined to adopt the Commission's report.

But animated discussion continued, and the Board of Trade and other societies were bombarded with suggestions and proposals. Meanwhile, a system of internal measurement was proposed by George Moorsom, who acknowledged in his writings that external measurement was not the correct answer. It was conceded by all that a thoroughly reliable and accurate mode of measurement must be adopted and one that acted indiscriminately on all classes of vessels, and Moorsom's proposals did just this. His scheme proposed the measurement of a series of transverse sections in the hold and, from the areas so obtained, the internal volume was calculated by Simpson's rule. The number of transverse sections varied from between 4 and 12, depending on the length of the hull, and the areas were to be measured below the *tonnage deck*, which was defined as the upper deck, or the middle deck in three-decked ships. To the figure so obtained was added the volume of poop, forecastle, and deckhouses to produce a gross figure, and when divided by 100 the quotient was the tonnage.[85] This divisor was deduced by dividing the aggregate tonnage of the United Kingdom in 1833 into the estimated cubic capacity of this tonnage. The answer was 98.22 or 100 for convenience.[86] The choice of this divisor facilitated the calculations and meant that 100 cubic feet equalled one ton.

George Moorsom's proposals were embodied in the Merchant Shipping Act of 1854[87] and have remained ever since 'the foundation of the tonnage registry laws and measurement rules of the maritime nations of the world'.[88]

There were three tonnage figures: under deck, gross, and net register. Crew accommodation *above* the tonnage deck was exempted from inclusion provided it did not exceed one-twentieth of the gross tonnage; if it did, only the excess was to be included. This provision induced crew accommodation to be placed above the tonnage deck in a topgallant forecastle or large deckhouse, so that there was no taxable space below the upper deck that could not carry cargo. For many years the gross and net tonnages of sailing ships were identical and in many cases that

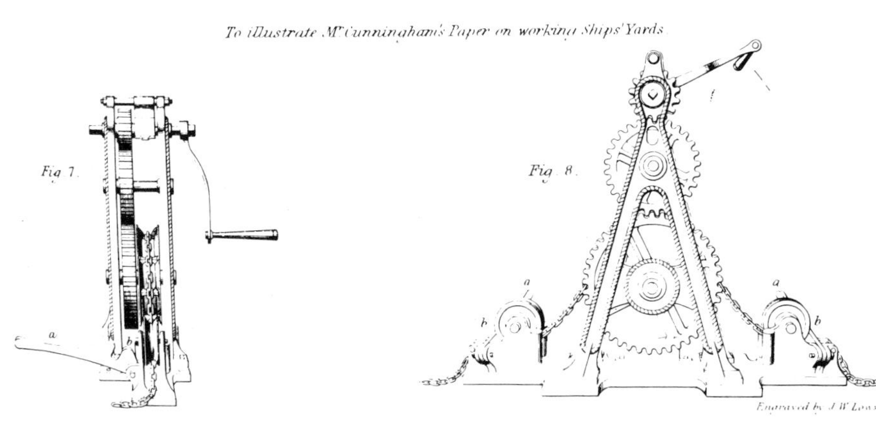

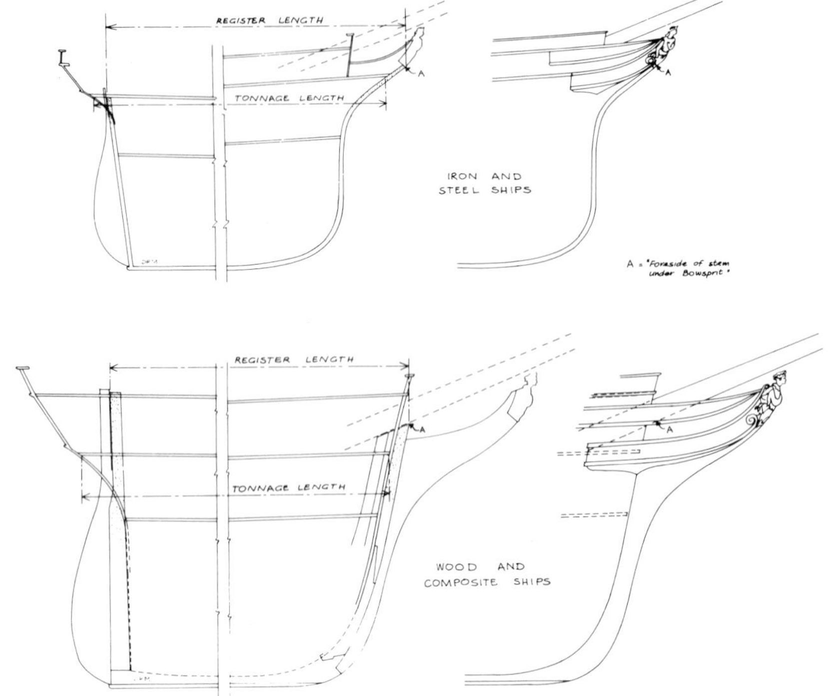

206: Tonnage by 1854 rule. Diagrams to show differences between 'tonnage length' and 'register length'. Register length was from foreside of stem to afterside of sternpost along the deck. Tonnage length was from inside of inner plank by stem to inside of stern timber. Although this was ideally measured on the underside of the tonnage deck, in practice it was measured on top of it and deductions were made for rake of stem and stern, and thickness of planking.

of the under deck tonnage as well. In 1854, the only permissible deduction from the gross tonnage total was the engine room in steamships. In 1867, a new law allowed crew accommodation, wherever situated in the hull, to be deducted from the gross tonnage figure, and from this year the net register tonnage of sailing ships could be less than the gross tonnage. Other deductions have since been allowed, such as master's accommodation and various store lockers.

W S Lindsay gives an interesting sideline on Moorsom's efforts to solve the tonnage conundrum.

> 'It would not be easy to concoct a more just and wise mode of ascertaining the register tonnage of merchant vessels than that which Mr. Moorsom, a man of remarkable genius, after years of labour, submitted for the consideration of Government, and which, through the instrumentality of Mr. Farrer,[89] was in a great measure, adopted and embodied into the Merchant Shipping Act of 1854. I look back, as one of the pleasing reminiscences of my public life, to the hours I spent with Mr. Moorsom in going through the details of his scheme before it was submitted to the public; but, though I may have ventured to offer an amendment here and there, as others may have done, the merit of the scheme belongs to him alone. It is now adopted by nearly all the maritime nations. Mr Moorsom was the most modest of men; and I have the greatest pleasure in adding my humble testimony to the public labours of this most excellent and unassuming man.'[90]

It is once again necessary to define the points between which dimensions were taken both for tonnage measurement and for registry, and to illustrate these with diagrams for absolute clarity (figure 206). The definitions themselves will be found in the Appendix.

Six

THE CLIPPER SHIP BOOM 1850-59

Introduction

Considerable space has already been devoted here to considering various aspects of the clipper ship and sufficient examples have been given to demonstrate how a strong tradition of fast sailing ships was established by the middle of the century and that the long-held myth of a 'first clipper' is no longer acceptable. The force behind the desire for faster ships may be traced to the changing outlook on international trade that was overtaking the entrepreneur, whose orders for new, fast ships were closely interwoven with trade requirements. Growing international trade received an important filip in 1849 with the repeal of the Navigation Laws although many pessimists predicted dire results. The effect on the shipbuilders was that output fell slightly between 1849 and 1851 as some owners waited to see the outcome of the termination to protection. But neither builders nor owners were ruined because the repeal coincided with gold discoveries in California and Australia which, coupled with free trade, brought a vast demand for ships of all kinds and kept British yards busy for some years at full stretch. In the China tea trade, competition with America produced orders for faster and larger clippers and proved a great incentive to British shipyards. All forms of trade were stimulated to require speedier deliveries, and

207: The American ship *Archer* is probably in dry-dock at Foochow after going ashore in the River Min in 1865. She was of 905 tons nm and was built in 1852 at Somerset, Mass, near Boston. This is a clear photograph of the beautiful hull-form possessed by a fine-lined wooden ship. *A J Nesdall.*

208: A model of the *Stornoway* made by James Henderson. No painting has ever been found of this ship and so the details are entirely reconstructed from a half-model, spar dimensions and survey report. (Model in *Aberdeen Museum.)*

higher freights were offered to faster ships. Orders from interested owners were late in reaching the builders so that it was not until 1853 that the first really extreme clippers were launched.

The boom for building clippers was at its peak in the years 1853-55 during which a greater number of extreme clippers were built and for a wider range of trades than was ever the case again. The heavy demands of the Crimean War for additional tonnage to serve as transports resulted in a combined record total of 323,200 tons of sail and steam shipping being built in 1855, but in April of the following year the War ended, with the inevitable result that freight rates dropped and shipbuilding orders were cut back. This slump was superseded by steadier conditions towards the end of the 'fifties and shipbuilding orders revived, but orders for clippers dwindled, except in the tea trade, for which fine-lined ships were occasionally built.

In America, the building boom for clippers lasted from 1851 to 1854, thus virtually coinciding with that in Britain. On both sides of the Atlantic many of the ships can be looked upon as experimental, but in its way this provides greater interest in tracing how various builders evolved their designs.

By contrast, only a handful of extreme clippers were built in the period 1865–69, but owing to the singular fact that plans have survived for the majority, they have achieved greater prominence and fame than the clippers of the 'fifties which posterity has treated unfairly by ignoring or belittling. It is hoped that the plans presented here will at long last rectify this state of affairs.

An early lesson to British shipowners of the value of possessing a clipper of proved renown was the arrival at London in December 1850 of the American clipper *Oriental*, 97 days out from Hong Kong and with 1600 tons of tea aboard. She had loaded at a freight rate of £6 per ton whereas the best British ships could only obtain £3 to £4 per ton. She was the first American ship to take advantage of the lifted restrictions in the British tea trade, and the money-making potential of a clipper must have been quickly realised.

Had there been earlier opportunities of obtaining high freights in return for fast passages there is little doubt that British ships would have been built on finer lines, as occurred in America, where the clipper ship era took place while the tonnage laws closely approximated the British 'Old Measurement' rule. Their tonnage law lasted in this form from 1789 to 1864 with very similar measurements to the British old rule for length and breadth including an assumed depth, although single-decked vessels did have their depth of hold measured. After 1864, they adopted the Moorsom system that was embodied in the British Merchant Shipping Act of 1854. This point about the long continuation of the old law or its equivalent in America has been stressed, because many writers state that the clipper was designed in America due to favourable tonnage measurement, whereas it was designed in spite of unfavourable measurement. This false premise has led to false conclusions that the poor British were penalised by unfair legislation, and numerous excuses are trotted out to account for the sad state of the shipping industry. The truth of the matter is that after 1835 the British employed a form of tonnage measurement that encouraged better ship design, and the Navigation Acts gave considerable protection from foreign competition. Protection, however, like monopoly, can result in stagnation.

There were a handful of small, newly-built clippers operating in the tea trade in 1850, such as the *Reindeer*, whose plans are given in figure 145, but there was obviously scope for more and larger ships. The *Reindeer* had been built in 1848 by Alexander Hall & Sons and this firm provided the greatest inspiration to other builders at this date, besides designing some of the fastest ships. Existing half-models show that they built eight important clippers between 1848 and 1856, most of which exerted considerable influence on current fast sailing theories. These ships were *Reindeer, Benjamin Elkin, Stornoway, Chrysolite, Cairngorm, Vision, Schomberg* and *Robin Hood*. It became common practice at this date to associate British clippers almost exclusively with Aberdeen so that a journalist at Launceston, commenting on the arrival of the extreme clipper *Storm Cloud* after a run of 71 days from the Clyde, described the ship as 'a noble specimen of naval architecture, and Aberdeen iron built clipper', whereas she was built at Glasgow by Alexander Stephen & Sons.[1] Here is another example: on the occasion of a race with the *Joseph Fletcher* from Shanghai, the Liverpool-built ship *Wild Flower*, launched in 1852, was referred to as the 'clipper ship (Aberdeen model) *Wild Flower*'.[2]

These and other similar references make one suspicious of newspaper attributions in general, particularly when the vessel's clipper build and hull form are discussed. It is intended to attribute the clipper distinction to ships whose plans or models have been inspected, and to subject to critical analysis other claims for clipper build. In addition, there are ships which, though possessing no plans, deserve to be rated as clippers on account of technically reliable descriptions and calculations. Beyond these are many vessels to which the word 'clipper' has been attached on the strength of one short passage, the appearance above the waterline or just

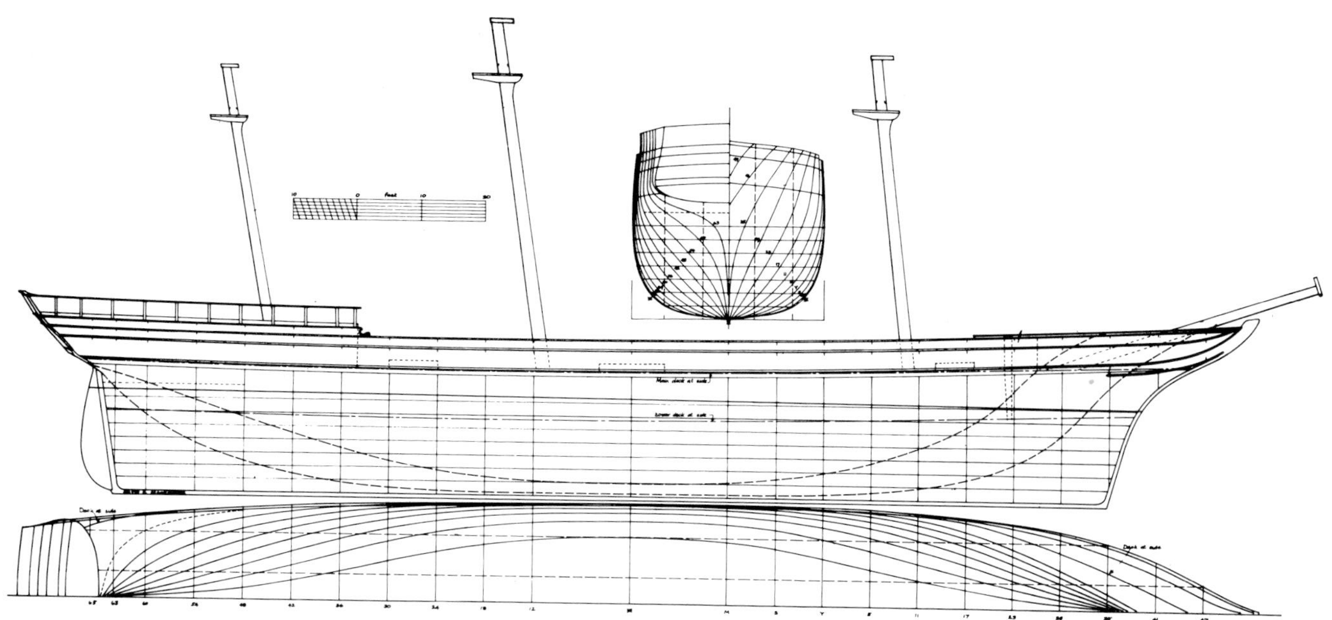

209: *Three Bells*. Lines plan: Built of iron in 1850 by William Denny at Dumbarton. Lines redrawn from builder's plan at National Maritime Museum. Dimensions: 171.0ft × 29.0ft × 16.7ft; tonnages 649 nm and 730 om. No reconstruction, other than addition of lower masts from builder's sail plan.

plain advertising. By the 'fifties an advertisement demanded that a ship be called a clipper to attract business, and if that word seemed a bit hackneyed, then possibly 'frigate-built yacht' or some other lurid title might sound more original.

Some of the methods for judging fineness of hull form were outlined in 'Criteria for Hull Analysis' in chapter one, and these consisted of the speed-length ratio, prismatic coefficient, and coefficient of under deck tonnage. The comparison of old and new measurement tonnages as an approximate guide is referred to in chapter four. A high ratio of beams to length is not necessarily a sign of a clipper.

It will be noticed that the appellation 'extreme' is sometimes added to 'clipper' to define a ship which is unusually sharp in the entrance or the run or at both ends, or that perhaps has maximum deadrise. *Three Bells* would be a clipper, but *Annandale* an extreme clipper. 'Medium clippers' are often little more than sharpened versions of general cargo ships, and as such are, with one or two exceptions, not considered here.

The question of additional capacity which iron ships, with their thinner outer shell gained over wooden ships, was discussed in the last chapter, and this must have proved an important point in boosting the earnings of the narrow, sharp-ended iron clippers which began to make their appearance early in the 1850s.

The *Three Bells*

William Denny (1815–54) had served for a few years as designer with the shipbuilders Coats & Young of Belfast, and in 1842 he joined his distant cousin Robert Napier in the same capacity at the Govan Shipyard on the Clyde, but left to go to America. He returned in 1844 and with his brothers Peter and Alexander formed a partnership at Dumbarton, but when Alexander retired in 1849 to begin business on his own it was dissolved, and the new-styled firm of William Denny & Brothers was founded, the partners being William, Peter and James. The firm built entirely in iron and apart from a few schooners and the clipper *Three Bells*, which was launched in 1850, only steamers were constructed. The plans from this yard have been deposited at the National Maritime Museum, Greenwich, and an inspection reveals that all Denny's ships of this date were similar in hull form and appearance. The occasional schooner launched by Denny at this time, such as the *Caledonia* (figure 158), was a reduced version of *Three Bells*.

The plans of *Three Bells* were redrawn from the original and show an iron clipper with a long raking Aberdeen bow above an angular forefoot, in comparison with which the heavy square stern looks incongruous. Imitation galleries were applied to the stern, and the bow finished in a billet figurehead. The entrance and run are concave below the light load line but convex above, and the midship section is positioned approximately amidships giving evenly balanced ends. The entrance is much sharper than *Camertonian* or *Ballarat* and the line of the buttocks indicates easy, curving lines. Although not drawn here, the quarter-beam buttock is straight where it crosses the load line, indicating a fast vessel. The floors sweep into the bilges which round up into a slight tumblehome.

Unfortunately, no deck details are known other than the position of the three hatches and the extent of the forecastle and poop, but she would undoubtedly have had a deckhouse abaft the foremast to contain the galley, if nothing else. The forecastle is 5ft-6in high at the break and probably accommodated the seamen in the same manner as did *Black Prince*, forcing the men to bend double as they passed through the door on to the main deck. There were four watertight bulkheads with brass force-pumps in the three middle com-

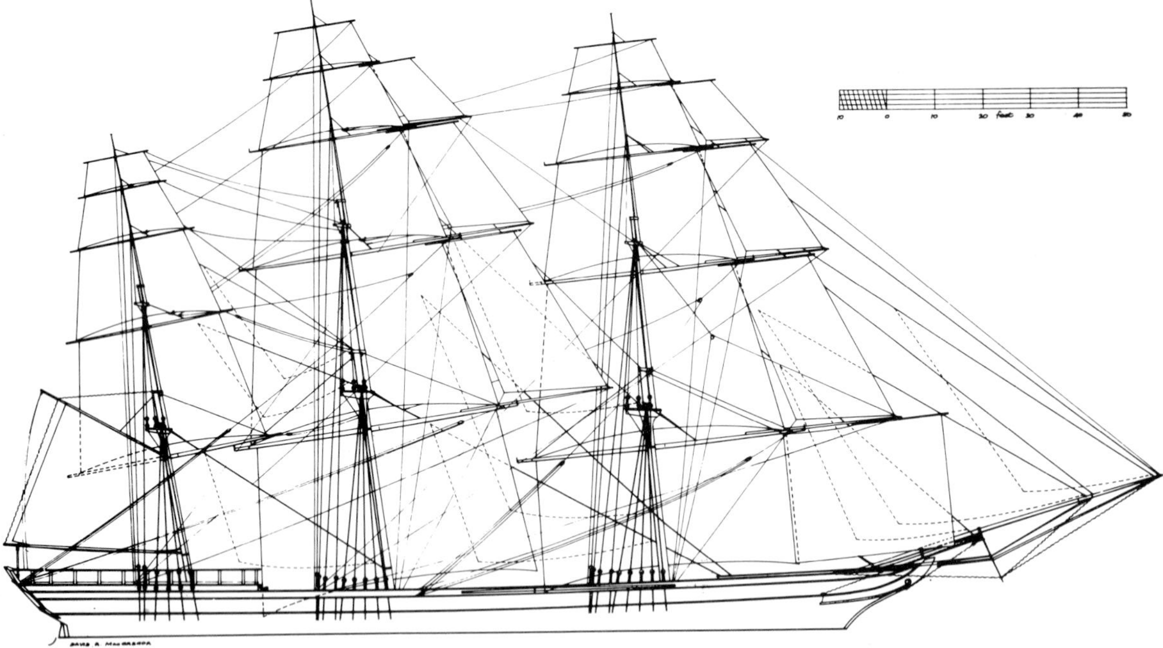

210: *Three Bells*. Sail plan: Redrawn from builder's sail plan at National Maritime Museum. Reconstruction: Staysails; lower stunsail boom; foot of courses and lower stunsail; chain plates and deadeyes; almost all the braces. An unusual feature of this plan was that the builder had drawn the stunsails with their booms, yards, sheets and tacks in such detail.

211: In this typical example of a watercolour by the Dutch artist J Spin, the *Ternate* (1855) is portrayed as a very lofty ship. The skysail masts are fidded abaft the royal masts, and the skysail poles are long enough to carry moonsails. *Scheepvaart Museum, Amsterdam.*

partments; the foremost and aftermost compartments drained into the adjacent ones with adjustable cocks. Three boats were carried and the upper deck was of wood. The measurements were 171.0ft by 29.0ft by 16.7ft with tonnages of 649 nm and 730 om.

On her first voyage to Australia, an Adelaide paper said that she was 'the first iron vessel to visit this colony' and commented on her 'steamer-like' bow and 'beautifully clean run'. In the 'tween decks there was space for 250 passengers; further aft her 'cabins were fitted up with oak'. Maximum speed was given as 12½ knots and the best day's run was 273 nautical miles.[3] On a load line length of 163ft-6in, the speed-length ratio works out at .98 for 12½ knots, but to attain a high ratio of 1.25 a speed of 15.98 knots would have been required.

The first owners were Glasgow fleshers (butchers to Sassenachs): John Bell held 32 shares, and William and Findlay Bell 16 shares apiece, so that the name of *Three Bells* is entirely appropriate. They also owned shares in the wooden barque *Alceste* (1839) in the same proportions. John Bell later held 32 shares in the extreme clipper named after him.

In the early 1850s iron ships were inevitably making history, so that besides the *Three Bell*'s claim being the first iron ship to visit Adelaide, there is also a similar one in respect of Montreal, where she went on her maiden passage, returning to Glasgow in 16 days. In November 1850, she sailed for Adelaide and claimed a fast passage of 86 days from Cape Clear, Ireland, to the Adelaide light ship. She returned to Glasgow via Melbourne and Calcutta and on 24 March 1852 sailed from Glasgow for Melbourne, which she reached 96 days later. On a later Atlantic passage she stood by the sinking steamer *San Francisco* for a week and rescued over 200 passengers, a feat which was immortalised by Walt Whitman.[4] The Bell brothers retained ownership until she disappeared from Lloyd's Register after 1871.

The sail plan, reproduced in figure 210, shows a lofty rig with three skysails. The narrowness of the rig prevents overlap of the yards, except in a single case, but this is fully compensated by a full suit of stunsails, the fore lower stunsail being unusually square. Reconstruction has been restricted to the following: outline of the staysails, which have been accordingly drawn dotted; foot of the fore and main courses (the leeches were already drawn); braces; chain plates and deadeyes; and lower stunsail boom. It is unusual to find a builder's plan on which the stunsails and their gear have been so clearly drawn.

Another clipper launched in 1850 was the *Stornoway*, whose design is referred to later in this chapter. With a similar beam to the *Three Bells*, the *Stornoway* was 14 feet shorter in length but one foot deeper, and not quite so sharp in the ends. The *Three Bells*' iron construction permitted a longer, narrower hull and this greater length in turn made a higher speed possible. Most of the iron clippers had a proportion of six beams to length and upwards.

The Australian gold rush

At the beginning of the 1850s, the advance in shipbuilding techniques had barely begun and the British shipping industry was ill-equipped to meet the excessive demands made on it for tonnage to transport persons and goods to the gold fields of Australia. Gold was first discovered in Australia in 1841, but the subject did not reach the editorial columns of the *Sydney Morning Herald* until 15 May 1851, when it burst upon the pastoral society of New South Wales. All were agreed that 'the curse of gold-digging mania' was irresistible and four days later there were 600 men at the Bathurst diggings. In London, the first news of the discovery appeared in an editorial in *The Times* on 2 September 1851. Research does not reveal how the news was obtained, but an Australian 'Gold Circular' of 1852 stated:

> 'By the *Vimeira*, we hear that intelligence of our gold discovery had reached England on the 28 August by the Overland Mail via Southampton . . . Two other parties were in possession of the news — in all probability from the same source: and one of them proposed to sell it to *The Times* for £200.'[5]

The first gold from Australia reached England aboard the *Thomas Arbuthnot* in September 1851, a matter usually overlooked, but because she had put into Pernambuco, her letters and papers were transferred to the mail steamer *Teviot* and reached Southampton on 10 September. A letter from the *Thomas Arbuthnot*'s master, G H Heaton, was printed in *The Times* three days later and describes the state of affairs in Sydney — a situation which changed little while the gold rush was at its height in the early 'fifties.

The letter is addressed to the owners, Phillips, Shaw & Lowther, later tea clipper owners, and was dated Pernambuco, 20 August 1851:

> 'Gentlemen — I suppose you have had rumours of the extensive gold fields discovered in New South Wales, causing as sudden a revolution as I believe ever could have visited any country. The colony is completely paralysed. Every man and boy who is able to lift a shovel is off, or going off, to the diggings. Stations are in many parts completely deserted; consequently sheep and cattle are left to go and do as they like. Nearly every article of food has gone up, in some cases 200%; and seeing that a great reduction in the grain crops next season must ensue for the want of labour, it will necessarily follow that maintenance for man and beast will be both scarce and high. No doubt there will be extensive emigration from all parts of Europe, when once the news gets wind.
>
> 'We have on board about £800 worth of Australian gold, the first shipped from the Colony. It was purchased on the spot (in fact dug up before their eyes) by four gentlemen, managing partners of different mercantile firms in Sydney. It is all in lumps, nearly pure, the largest weight 4 lb less 2 oz. When this was brought down there was a large amount at Bathurst waiting for a military escort, which the people were in hopes the Government would allow to them. What we have on board was brought down by four gentlemen, they being armed to the teeth.
>
> 'I had great difficulty in getting away from Sydney. Although I promised my crew double wages, some six or seven left me as soon as the affair became known. Forseeing what would most likely be the case, I got a steamer and towed the ship down towards the Heads. I placed two armed policemen, night and day, one at each end of the ship. Still, those that could swim got off somehow. All this caused much expense. I left the *Lady Clarke* ready for sea without a soul on board but the Captain. I believe he was about starting, with his articles in his pocket, on the road towards Bathurst, thinking he might induce some sailors to return and ship. They were coolly (I mean what sailors were left in Sydney) asking £80 for the run home, and a guarantee of procuring them a ship to return direct to Sydney. I paid £5 and £6 per month for what I wanted.
>
> Yours very faithfully,
>
> (signed) G.M. Heaton'.[6]

212: Ships clustered along both sides of the Railway Pier at Sandridge, near Melbourne. The ship on the left has double topsail yards with a stunsail boom above the lower yard; the ship on the right has single topsail yards with the stunsail boom under the lower yard. *J Rosing Collection.*

Gold was found in Victoria in July and August 1851 and soon the yield became very high. Melbourne eventually attracted more shipping from abroad than Sydney. The first gold to be shipped from Victoria consisted of only 18oz which the *Honduras* took when she left Melbourne on 29 August 1851. The *Phoenician*, which has sometimes been claimed as being the first ship to take gold from Sydney, did not sail until 12 November 1851 after 20 other ships had already loaded some gold in their cargoes.[7]

Alexander Duthie and Walter Hood

The plan of the Aberdeen-built ship *Ballarat* represents a fast cargo carrier and approximates the type of medium clipper that was beginning to appear in the early 'fifties — a type of ship that with good seamanship and hard driving could and did produce short passages. The incentive which drove her out to Australia in gold rush days was a vitally important factor in making short passages, and it was responsible for many comparatively full-bodied ships achieving faster runs than some of the extreme clippers.

The *Ballarat*'s lines, reproduced in figure 213, have been taken by James Henderson from the builder's half-model, and are redrawn from his rough draft. Her lines show a powerful vessel with a short, moderately sharp entrance but a longer run; also a wall-sided hull with noticeable deadrise and slack bilges; the hull tapers very little towards the stern, which is broad, and there is a poop of full height. Her measurements are 141.9ft by 27.4ft by 20.0ft (1836 Registry Act) with tonnages of 637 om and 713 nm. Based on these register dimensions, she has a ratio of 7.1 depths to length.

213: *Ballarat*. Built in 1852 by Alexander Duthie & Co. at Aberdeen. Lines taken off builder's half-model by James Henderson and drawn from his draft. Dimensions: 141.9ft × 27.4ft × 20.0ft: 637 tons om and 713 tons nm. No reconstruction.

214: This engraving of the *James Booth* suggests the probable appearance of the *Ballarat*, whose lines are given here.

The *Ballarat* was built in 1852 at Aberdeen by Alexander Duthie & Co, who had succeeded William Duthie Bros in the 1840s, and was owned by the London shipowner Duncan Dunbar who had amassed a vast fleet. On her maiden passage in 1852 she took 78 days to Melbourne from the Lizard and on the succeeding voyage was 79 days between identical points. Later voyages took her also to China and New Zealand. The engraving of the *James Booth* (1851), also built by Duthie, suggests the probable appearance of *Ballarat*. Thanks to James Henderson, the half-models of these two ships have survived, but the *James Booth* had a fuller hull form in spite of the fact that the *Illustrated London News* described her as 'a remarkably fine specimen of the clipper built vessels'. Of her builders the paper wrote that they were 'distinguished for their models of beautiful symmetry'.[8] The Lloyd's Register surveyor at Aberdeen described each ship in more prosaic terms as having a 'common bow', or in other words, not having an Aberdeen clipper bow.[9]

The following comments, bearing clipper connotations, were given by the Lloyd's Register surveyor in the early fifties: *Brilliant*

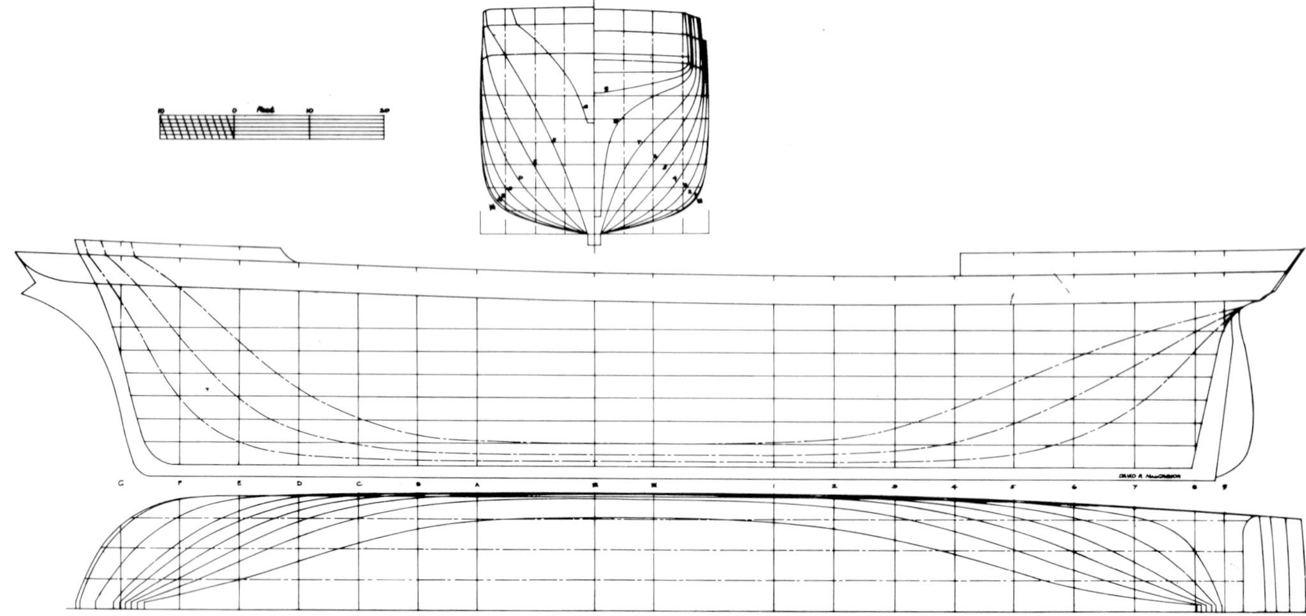

215: The *Star of Peace* photographed at Circular Quay, Sydney, c1865, when she was still fitted with single topsail yards, each of which was equipped with Cunningham's roller-reefing gear. This picture gives a good idea of what one of Walter Hood's clippers was like in the 1850s, as this ship was built in 1855 by him with a tonnage of 1113 and a length of 208ft. The stern was somewhat heavy. *C L Hume.*

(1850) 'formed with clipper bow carried to a moderate extent'; *Rubens* (1853) 'This vessel is formed with fine ends'; *Raphael* (1854) 'moderately fine in ends'.[10] All are Duthie-built ships.

The *Aberdeen Journal* of 17 May 1854 described the launch of two vessels from these yards in these words:

> 'Launches.—On Saturday last, there was launched from the building-yard of Messrs W Hood & Co, a magnificent clipper ship of the following dimensions:—extreme length, 230 feet, breadth of beam, 36 feet, tonnage, 1224 N.M., 1271 O.M. The vessel was named the "Omer Pasha"—a highly popular name at present; and is registered A 1 at Lloyds for ten years. The "Omer Pasha" is the property, chiefly, of our enterprising city member, Mr Thompson, and will probably be employed in the Australian or China trade. She is to be commanded by Capt. Thomson, formerly of the "John Bunyan", whose services in the latter vessel have been very efficient. The "Omer Pasha" is the largest vessel ever launched at Aberdeen, and is really a magnificent specimen of naval architecture.—Same day, Messrs A. Duthie & Co. turned out an excellent ship—clipper-built of course—named the "Ben-Avon," of 684 tons, N.M., the property of Mr G. Leslie, for probably the India or China trade, to be commanded by Capt. Budge, formerly of the "Balmoral." The "Ben-Avon" is a very beautiful model, will sail fast, and carry a large cargo. The launches passed off very successfully, and to the gratification of a great concourse of spectators.'

Little can be deduced of Walter Hood's ships as, apart from *Thermopylae*, no plans or models appear to have survived, but a photograph of his *Star of Peace* suggests that she was not unlike the *Ballarat* above the load line and possibly may have been fairly similar in hull form below. Walter Hood built approximately one ship per year for George Thompson & Co's 'Aberdeen White Star Line', whose green-hulled ships such as the *Phoenician, John Bunyan, Walter Hood, Maid of Judah, Omar Pasha, Star of Peace*, and so on, were well known in the Australian and China trades. The latter two were ships of 1100 tons and so somewhat bigger than the average size of British-built wooden merchantmen. From 1853, many of his ships were built under a roof.

Many of Hood's ships were described by the Lloyd's Register surveyor as having a 'clipper stem' or a 'clipper bow', but the barque *John Knox* merited a more specific comment: 'This is a vessel of long, low, sharp construction, little outreach forward'.[11] This definitely suggests a fine-lined hull. She was built in 1852 for the China trade with measurements of 128.2ft by 21.7ft by 14.0ft, 296 tons nm and 358 tons om, and she drew 1ft-3in more water aft than forward. A painting of the barque was reproduced in *Mariner's Mirror*.[12]

The *Hurricane* and other iron clippers

By the autumn of 1852 the rush to Australia was in full flood and shipowners, finally convinced that this was no nine-days wonder, began placing orders for the sharpest and finest-lined ships ever built in the British Isles. The Australian clippers required fine lines to take them down the Atlantic but also power to carry sail in the roaring forties. Many had exceedingly sharp ends but with a full midsection, or alternatively a midsection with sharp deadrise and hard bilges. A new feature was the appearance of so many iron clippers of greatly increased size and dimensions, the majority of which came from yards on the Clyde. The lines of one such ship, the *Lord of the Isles*, were published in 1861 by Andrew Murray, and again in this century by Basil Lubbock and due to this she has attracted most publicity.[13] Another similar ship was the *Hurricane* for which more detailed plans are available.

In 1843, Alexander Stephen (1795–1875) moved his shipyard from Arbroath to Dundee where he built for the next 50 years, but in 1850 he was ambitious enough to open a second shipyard on the Clyde at Kelvinhaugh and decided to adopt iron shipbuilding from the start, although two wooden ships were built in the 1850s. The first ship laid down at Kelvinhaugh was the wooden *Cyclone*, and the iron *Typhoon* was the second; but as the latter was launched on 20 August 1852, only four months and ten days after the keel was laid, she became the first ship launched from the new yard. The external iron plating, consisting of 994 plates, had been rivetted to the frames in only six weeks.[14] This was very quick work and presumably the owners

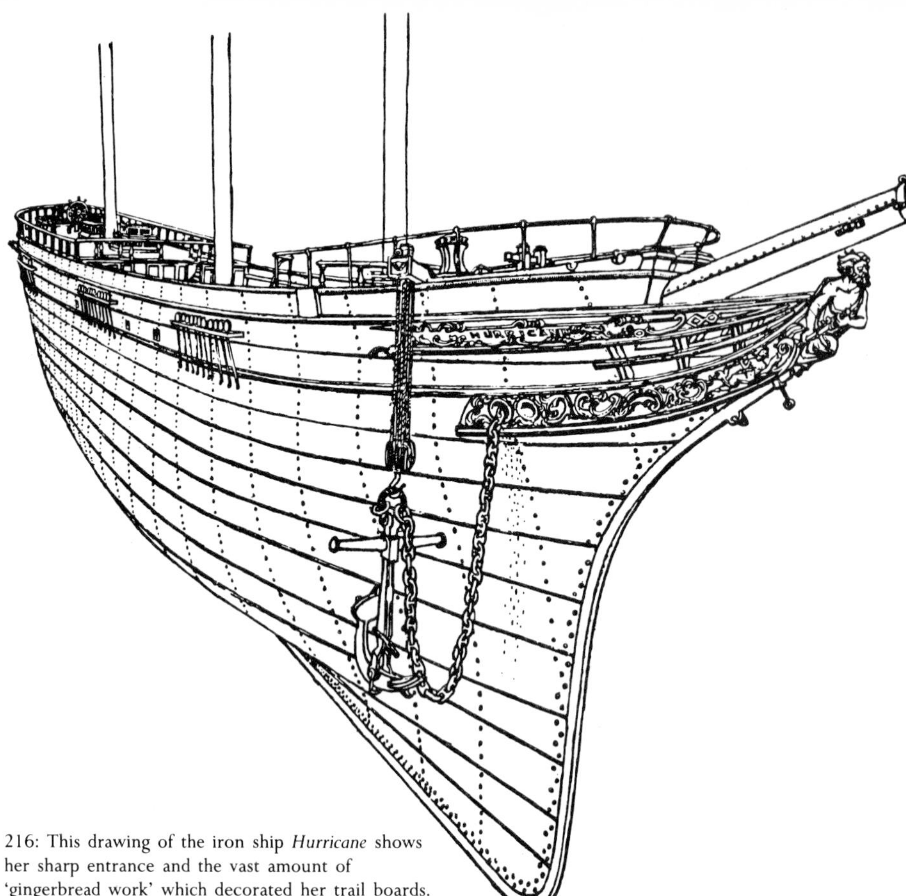

216: This drawing of the iron ship *Hurricane* shows her sharp entrance and the vast amount of 'gingerbread work' which decorated her trail boards.

 wanted the ship in a hurry for the booming Australia trade. A quotation made to Potter, Wilson & Co in February 1852, presumably for *Typhoon*, totals £12,270 or £12.14s.2d per ton on 965 tons om. This must be for hull and spars only as Stephen's were asking £14.13s.6d per ton complete for sea for another ship of similar size.[15] The *Typhoon* had dimensions of 196.1ft by 31.1ft by 20.0ft and 965 tons, and was built for Potter, Wilson & Co's Clyde & Australian Shipping Co. She was a long, narrow ship with a fair amount of deadrise, slack bilges and slight tumblehome; the stem raked forward and there was a heavy round stern. This profile was repeated in the *Hurricane*, but the hull form was made somewhat sharper. When commenting on the *Typhoon*'s heavy construction, the *Glasgow Herald* remarked that 'the three lower masts are of iron; the topmasts and jib-boom of wood; the latter sliding out and in the tubular bowsprit like a telescope or pencil case'.[16] Many of Stephen's ships were so fitted, as shown on the *Hurricane*'s sail plan, and many were given four headsails from the fore topmast. The *Typhoon* was dismasted at the outset of her maiden passage and put into Lisbon where she was given new all-timber masts; from there to Melbourne her passage lasted 100 days.

William Stephen remained at the Dundee yard but his younger brother, Alexander, who was 20 years old in 1852, went to Glasgow and presumably Alexander senior travelled between the two yards. In 1852 he was 57 years old with a lifetime's experience of building, although quite fresh to the subject of all-iron construction. Presumably, he also designed the ships, probably by first carving a half-model and later drawing a plan. However it is not known how large a hand Alexander junior had in the design. Beginning with the *Hurricane*, the plans are drawn in a similar style and some of them are signed 'W. Robertson'. William Robertson was appointed chief draughtsman in 1852 and was perhaps responsible for applying the finishing touches to the designs. He remained with the firm ten years, finally leaving on 31 December 1862 to become assistant surveyor for Scotland to the Liverpool Association of Underwriters. It is more than likely that Alexander junior was given increasing opportunities to make use of his talents as a designer; in any case the Kelvinhaugh business was transferred in 1858 to him and his brother James.

Like the *Typhoon*, the *Hurricane* was ordered by the Clyde & Australian Shipping Co for whom the Glasgow firm of Potter, Wilson & Co appear to have been the managers. Certainly, Lewis Potter (born 1807) was the first-named trustee of the company and a co-partner with Alexander Potter in Potter, Wilson & Co. In addition to *Typhoon* and *Hurricane*, the firm owned the *Melbourne, Geelong, Admiral* and other ships in the Australian trade. The *Hurricane*'s measurements were 214.9ft by 30.7ft by 20.0ft with tonnages of 979 nm and 1110 om. She was launched on 26 April 1853, handed over to her owners on 11 May and started on her maiden voyage towards Melbourne on 15 June. The above measurements give her a similar depth to *Typhoon*, a fractionally narrower breadth, but an increased length of no less than 19 ft.

The cost of *Hurricane* is not known, but supposing it to be £12.15s per ton old measurement for hull and spars only, which is fractionally above what the same owners paid for the *Typhoon*, the contract price would have been £14,152.10s. The owners could have spent another £2 to £3 per ton to equip her for sea with an East India outfit, thus making the first cost to them in the region of £16,500 to £17,500.

When the *Hurricane* was nearing completion in April 1853, the *Glasgow Herald* reported as follows:

> 'The largest iron sailing ship perhaps ever built is the one at present near completion under the shed at Kelvinhaugh. Messrs. Stephen and Sons were the first in Scotland, we believe, to build their ships under cover, which apart from the increased comfort to the shipwrights is considered favourable . . . as to rank one year extra at Lloyd's.'

After remarking that 'an iron ship of upwards of 1300 tons is really worth seeing on the stocks or afloat', the account continues:

> 'The model of the *Hurricane* is far sharper than is usual in mercantile ships. Her rise of floor is greater than in most men-of-war; whilst her greater length in proportion to beam gives her a much sharper entrance and finer run than are to be seen in any frigate afloat . . .
>
> 'The stem . . . terminates in one of the finest figureheads we have seen. We presume the good-looking he-deity is intended to represent the Spirit of the Storm with his locks blown back and his "eye in a fine frenzy rolling" . . . We were struck with the elaborate and careful carving of the whole figure, which would have done credit to the atelier of a sculptor; and very different indeed from the ordinary run of figureheads. It was sculptured by one of Messrs. Stephen and Sons' workmen, and deserves more than a mere passing encomium.'[17]

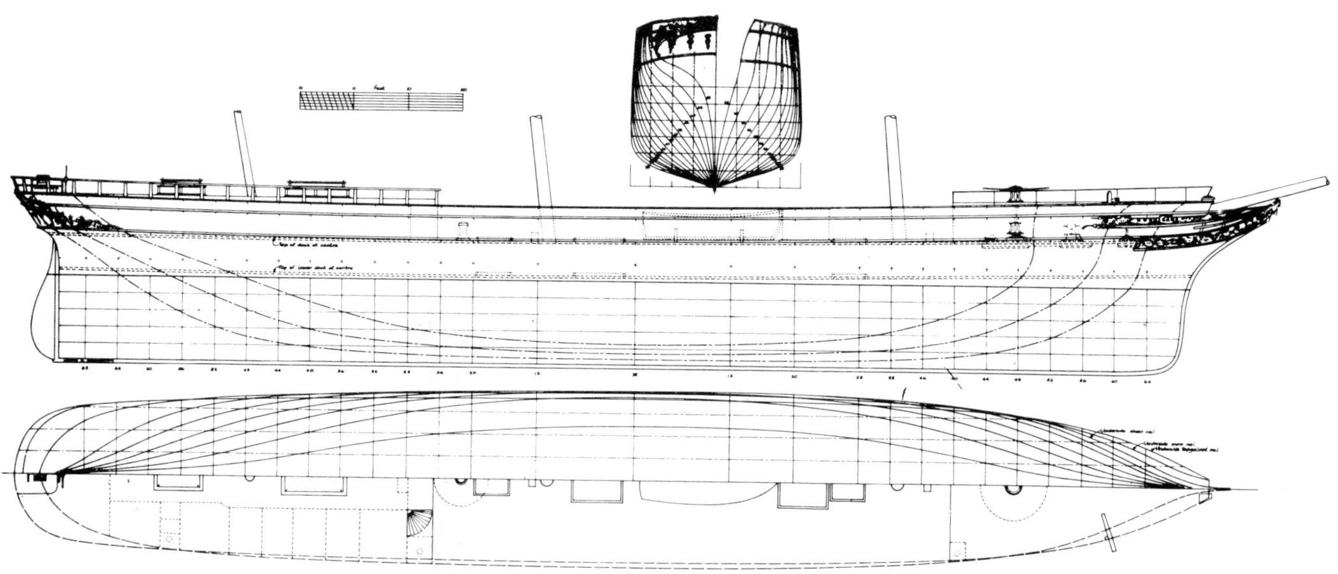

217: *Hurricane.* Lines plan: Built of iron in 1853 by Alexander Stephen & Sons Glasgow. Plan redrawn from a tracing made of the builder's lines plan and separate deck layout. Dimensions: 214.9ft × 30.7ft × 20.0ft; tonnages of 979 nm and 1110 om. No reconstruction.

This description agrees so well with the plans that it must have been composed by an expert. Many ships of this date bore names relating to the winds, such as *Typhoon, Hurricane, Storm Cloud, Whirlwind, Monsoon, Tornado* and *Tempest*, suggestive, perhaps, of their contempt for the elements.

The design of the *Hurricane* embodies all the concepts of an extreme iron clipper: great length in proportion to breadth; very sharp lines and minimum sheer. There are no deadflats shown on the plan although a lack of beam sometimes resulted in this; instead there is still a small curvature where the entrance and run meet. As in many iron clippers, the load line has considerable hollow both in the entrance and run as it approaches the stem or sternpost, and this hollow extends all the way down. A shoulder is worked into the forebody, just above the load line, as can be seen in the body plan and the buttocks; this was intended to give bearing forward and reduce the tendency to pitch. It also has the result of making the entrance somewhat fuller on the load line compared with *Lord of the Isles*, where the forebody is filled out lower down. The *Hurricane* has straight floors with marked deadrise but the turn of the bilge is kept low and so is maximum beam; there is also some tumblehome. The *Lord of the Isles* had greater deadrise and very slack bilges. The *Hurricane*'s quarter-beam buttock is straight where it crosses the load line, a sure indication of a fast vessel.

The lines plan and deck arrangement in figure 217 have been redrawn from a tracing made of the original when still in the possession of Alexander Stephen & Sons.

218: *Hurricane.* Sail plan: Redrawn from a tracing made of the builder's plan, with following reconstruction: Load waterline found to be 1ft-6in longer than lines plan, and here shortened to agree with lines plan; probable outline of three courses dotted on; channels, chainplates and deadeyes added; fore and main lower stays drawn double; top added to trestletrees. The pole iron masts and bowsprit are as drawn on the original.

Now their plans are on permanent loan to the National Maritime Museum, Greenwich. The deck layout was obviously varied slightly in the finished ship because a deckhouse for passengers was sited between the foremast and mainmast. If the fore hatch was positioned in front of the foremast, a house 27ft-0in long could have been accommodated. The Lloyd's Register survey report lists the following boats: 28ft longboat; two 24ft cutters; 26ft gig; 25ft lifeboat. The height of the bulwarks was considerable being 7ft-3in above the deck, which gave a flush appearance fore and aft, and easily accommodated a full height poop and topgallant forecastle. There was a pump in each of the four watertight compartments. She was fitted with three of Porter's patent bower anchors, weighing between 31 and 33 cwt, together with Brown & Harfield's capstan for operating the anchor cable, as described in the last chapter. The upper capstan was manned on the forecastle deck and the chain cable led to the lower capstan inside the foreastle; in here were also placed a pair of cable stoppers close to the hawse holes, a pair of riding bitts, and abaft the capstan another pair of cable stoppers above the spurling pipe leading to the chain locker. Thus the forecastle was well occupied, quite apart from the seamen's berths and the heel of the bowsprit. A number of similar deck fittings are shown in more detail on the plan of *Storm Cloud*.

In the 'tween decks, about 250 passengers could be carried and there were also 12 to 15 staterooms in the long poop. Access to the poop deck was obtained by means of two quarter segments of circular stairs at the break; between these staircases the break of the poop was set back but the deck was carried overhead. It is probable that the door to the wc beside the stairs faced on to the main deck. Wire netting was provided between the timber stanchions on the poop; some of Stephen's ships also had similar protection on the forecastle.

William Ward's drawing shows the splendid figurehead and the carved trail boards which extend no less than 36ft from the shoulder of the storm god. This decoration is matched by equally elaborate carving at the stern.

The load line is drawn at a mean draught of 15ft-9in which permitted about 1600 tons of cargo to be carried, according to a displacement scale. At a draught of 18ft-9in, equivalent to the upper waterline on the plan, cargo capacity would be 2007 tons.

The sail plan shows two interesting features: pole masts, and telescopic bowsprit and jibboom. It is generally accepted that the first ship with pole masts was the iron ship *Patriarch*, built in 1869 by Walter Hood & Co, and in the absence of her sail plan the claim is substantiated by photographs. In the case of *Hurricane*, the original plan was drawn in ink on semi-opaque white linen and was entitled: 'Rigging Plan of Ship *HURRICANE* Launched 26th April 1853 Kelvinhaugh', and along one edge 'Copy Rigging Plan'. This plan was found to be 1ft-6in longer on the load line than the lines plan; this difference was corrected when making the drawing, but otherwise the sail plan in figure 218 is a true copy. The only reconstruction has been the outline of the three courses, and the addition of channels, chainplates and deadeyes. Other plans of Stephen's ships indicate that channels were generally fitted. Ambitious builders undoubtedly visualised their ships constructed of iron from keel to truck, and this sail plan would have been accepted as sure evidence that pole masts were fitted but for a comment in the excellent description by the *Glasgow Herald*, already quoted, which stated that the masts were of pine, dowelled together with the usual bolts and hoops.[18] The evidence of the pole masts is thus open to doubt; a Chinese painting of the ship, at the National Maritime Museum, Greenwich, has the lower masts and bowsprit hooped, and the topmasts and topgallants fidded in the usual manner. However, the fact is undeniable that pole masts were proposed for the ship. Perhaps the dismasting of the *Typhoon* in October 1852 caused the iron masts to be abandoned. The fitting of the telescopic bowsprit and jibboom was referred to in describing the *Typhoon*.

It should be noted that shipbuilders often drew the yards parallel to the waterline, as in this case, and not at right angles to the mast. In the latter manner, the actual shape of the sails is correct, but in the *Hurricane*'s plan the leeches are merely drawn to connect the yardarms which results in incorrect shapes. The lead of running rigging and fitting of stunsails would be similar to the *Storm Cloud*'s plan (figure 227).

A good idea of the appearance of an iron clipper of this date can be obtained from the engraving of the *Gauntlet* built in 1853 by Denny & Rankin. The long hull, lack of sheer and apparently short masts are a repetition of *Hurricane*'s appearance. The bands on the built-up masts can also be seen.

The *Illustrated London News* published the portrait of the *Gauntlet* in August 1852 and accompanied it with this description:

'The "Gauntlet," clipper ship.

> This beautiful specimen of naval architecture, has just been built in the Clyde, to compete with the screw steamers and clipper ships in the Australian and Indian trades; and, from her fine model and rig, bids fair to be a formidable competitor to the swiftest of them.
>
> The *Gauntlet* is considered the most perfect clipper ship ever launched on the Clyde, and appears more like a yacht of large tonnage than a private merchant ship. Her saloons on deck are very elegantly fitted up, and the sleeping accommodations are entirely below, the lighting and ventilation of which are upon the principles adopted in the Cunard line of steamers, and the completeness of which will be apparent on inspection. The after saloon is fifteen feet in width; the sides are paneled and divided by narrow pilasters. The roof is covered at the sides, and is painted white and gilded; the coving being filled with pierced brasswork, which adds much to the beauty of the saloon, and assists its ventilation. The panels of this saloon are of painted glass, having circular compartments in them, surrounded by very handsome arabesque ornaments; and within these circles are medallion views of Bamborough Castle in England; Castle Howard, in Scotland; Phoul a Huca, in Ireland; and Llanberis, in Wales; besides subjects illustrative of chivalry, such as a knight arming for battle, going to battle, the return, &c.: the ground-colour of the panels being deep blue, with a damasked pattern in a lighter tint of blue. The pilasters are maple and gold, with panels of glass, on which are painted groups of weapons and shields of arms of the ancient nobility of Great Britain. The seats are covered with crimson velvet, and a rich carpet adds to the luxurious appearance of the whole; a fine-toned pianoforte completing the elegancies for the use and comfort of the passengers. The fore-saloon is much plainer

219: In the accompanying text to this engraving of the iron ship *Gauntlet*, the *Illustrated London News* in 1853 called her the 'most perfect clipper ship ever launched on the Clyde'. Drawn by E Weedon.

in its decoration, but is very nicely and appropriately furnished. Indeed, in every respect, no expense has been spared in making provision for the comfort of the passengers; shower and plunging-baths and also an ice-house being fitted.

The *Gauntlet* is built of iron, double riveted; and her plates and framing are of much greater thickness and strength than any other iron vessel yet built of the same dimensions; and yet her appearance is remarkably light and symmetrical. She is divided into five water-tight compartments, by strong iron bulkheads reaching from the lower hold to the upper deck. A powerful fire-engine is provided. The riveting was the object of the most especial care of the owners, who employed an experienced superintendent to inspect and test every rivet put into the ship. The measurements of this vessel are:—Length of keel and forerake, 182 feet; length over all, 194 feet; breadth of beam, 30 feet 6 inches; depth of hold, 19 feet; rise of floor at the quarter-deck, 3 feet 9 inches. Her tonnage is 784 tons of old measurement, 693 tons new measurement, or about 1200 tons burthen. Her stern, which is elliptic, with quarter galleries looks remarkably light and elegant; and her bow terminates in a pointed scroll figure-head.'

On her maiden passage under Captain R Tait, the *Hurricane* took 85 days to Port Philip Heads from Glasgow and reached Melbourne two days later on 10 September 1853. She landed 256 passengers. Her return passage to London, with 54,000oz of gold in the cargo, occupied 83 days from the Heads to the Isle of Wight and lasted from 3 November to 25 January 1854. Loading again in Glasgow, she sailed on her second voyage from Greenock on 12 May 1854, was towed 40 miles out to sea and passed the Tuskar Light two days later. She crossed the Line on 7 June and after a period of adverse winds, she made up lost time by running from the meridian of the Cape of Good Hope to Port Philip Heads in 24 days. The *Argus* reported her run as 74 days from the Tuskar Light to Cape Otway, which would have meant that she sighted the latter on 27 July, but it apparently took another three days to reach Port Philip Heads, which lie only 75 miles away in a direct line.[19] She returned to London via Bombay and in about July 1855 her owners sold her for £14,000 to Swayne & Bovill, a London engineering firm.

The *Hurricane*'s earnings are not recorded, but it is probable that by carrying 1600 tons of cargo at a minimum of £3 per ton and 200 steerage passengers at £15 each with a few first class, the freight list would amount to at least £8,300 in June 1853 and might reach £10,000. Alexander Stephen calculated that their *Storm Cloud* earned £8,700 net profits on her first two Australian voyages, as will be related later. *Hurricane*'s owners possibly made a clear profit of £6,000 when they sold the ship, if all profits and expenses are considered.

Her new owners arranged for Stephen's to form an aperture in the stern to take a screw propellor at a cost of £761, and to place the engines in position together with coal bunkers and other necessary work at a further cost of £25 per ton weight of metal used. This was executed on their slipway and finished by the end of 1855. Fifty-five tons of metal were used and the total was finally agreed at £2,807. Unfortunately, Swayne & Bovill were found to be overdrawn at the bank by £15,000, and no payment could be obtained. She cost £5.0s.3¼d each day she remained on the slip and was not finally launched until 2 August 1856, thus denying Stephen's much valuable business.[20] She was still afloat in 1867 when she made a 96-day passage to Melbourne.

With a load line length of 210 feet, the *Hurricane* was potentially capable of a speed of 18 knots, at which rate her speed-length ratio would be approximately 1.25. The clipper *Lord of the Isles* claimed such a speed on her maiden passage to Sydney, which on a load line length of 187 feet gives a speed-length ratio of 1.31. This is a very high rate, and anything above 1.25 rarely occurs. The ratio for the American clipper *Lightning* at a speed of 19 knots is 1.26.[21]

The maiden passage of *Lord of the Isles* between Greenock and Sydney occupied 74 days between passing the Tuskar Light on 19

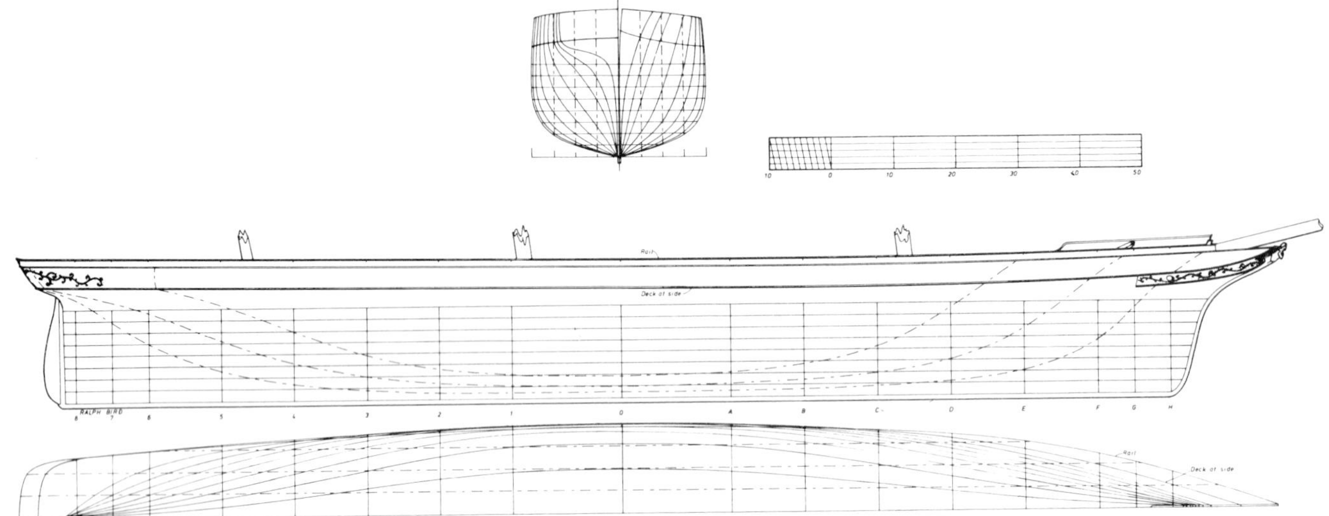

220: *Lord of the Isles*. Lines plan. Drawn by Ralph Bird from plan published as Plate IV in *Theory and Practice of Ship-Building* by Andrew Murray (1861). Built in 1853 by Charles Scott & Co, Greenock, with dimensions: 185ft keel, 210ft overall, 27.8ft beam, 18.5ft depth of hold, 691 tons nm, 770 tons om. Reconstruction: re-plotting waterlines to ensure they conformed to sections in body plan; omitting some stations for greater clarity in reproduction.

November 1853 and entering Sydney harbour on 1 February 1854; the meridian of Melbourne was passed when only 66 days out from the Tuskar Light, a fast run indeed. A passenger's letter, presumably based on data from the log book, contains the following remarks:

> 'When it appeared to myself and the rest of the passengers that there was scarcely any wind, the ship was going 8 or 9 knots. In a strong breeze the rate attained has been as high as 18 knots per hour. Several days' runs reached from 360 to 400 miles, and in one day the distance sailed, with only a few hours of maximum speed, was 428 miles.
>
> 'The distances given above, as having been run in one day, were ascertained by observation, substantiated by Massey's patent log.'[22]

Although not official log book extracts, these figures sound as if they were taken from a statement issued by the master, Captain Peter Maxton. If correct, they would be some of the fastest runs ever accomplished by a British-built sailing ship.

As the length and narrowness of these extreme iron clippers were such a feature of their design, the following list has been prepared of beam to length proportions, based on the dimensions in the Lloyd's Register survey reports.

Some sailing ships with a ratio of more than 6½ beams to length 1853–56[23]

This list is confined to ships surveyed by Lloyd's Register and of over about 800 tons. The ratios are computed on the register dimensions, but slightly different values will be obtained by using the dimensions of the 1854 Act, as against the new measurement rule of 1836.

Date	Ship	Ratio of beams to length	Material
1853	Hurricane	7.0:1	iron
1853	Swarthmore	6.6:1	iron
1853	Lord of the Isles	6.8:1	iron
1853	Tornado	6.6:1	iron
1854	Annandale	7.1:1	wood
1854	John Bell	7.3:1	iron
1854	Storm Cloud	6.5:1	iron
1854	Greenock	6.7:1	iron
1854	Glen Roy	7.0:1	iron
1855	Tempest	7.5:1	iron
1855	Cairnsmore	6.8:1	iron
1855	Agamemnon	6.9:1	wood
1856	Queensberry	7.2:1	wood
1858	Fairlight	7.1:1	wood

Further research would enable more examples to be added to the above, but at least it proves that neither does the oft-quoted *Lord of the Isles* have the highest ratio, nor even the *Annandale* and *Queensberry* which Dr R C Anderson was never tired of championing.

The *Greenock* was built by Smith & Rodger of Govan, Glasgow, who were also launching numerous steamers in the early 1850s; their yard operated from 1842–64. The *Tempest* was built by Sandeman & McLaurin of Whiteinch, Glasgow, with measurements of 845 tons and 214.2ft by 28.7ft by 19.1ft to the order of Handyside & Co, managers of the Anchor Line. Her maiden voyage took 105 days to Bombay from where she returned in 111 days to Liverpool. In 1856 she was converted into an auxiliary screw steamer and placed in the north Atlantic trade, but went missing the following year. A painting of her as an auxiliary shows the foremast situated a great distance abaft the bows and suggests a very long, sharp entrance.[24] Her appearance was very similar to the *Hurricane* or *John Bell*.

The plan of another Clyde-built iron clipper, the *Cairnsmore*, confirms the features seen in *Hurricane* and *Lord of the Isles*. She has steep deadrise with very rounded bilges

221: This painting by Samuel Walters, dated 1856, of the iron ship *Tornado* illustrates a vessel with 6.6 beams to length, although the artist has not really conveyed this impression. She was built in 1853 at Glasgow by William Simons with a tonnage of 1229. *Colin Denny Gallery.*

and considerable tumblehome, but her waterlines in the entrance and run are no sharper than *Hurricane*. Basil Lubbock published her lines and remarked that 'she was a long way ahead of her time', a statement now shown to be incorrect by the numerous other plans of contemporary ships, which have been assembled.[25] She was laid down in December 1853 but not launched until January 1855, which was a long time for capital to be tied up in boom conditions. The builder was John Reid of Port Glasgow, and she measured 222.5ft by 32.6ft by 20.7ft with tonnages of 1086 nm and 1211 om. Lubbock never published her sail plan.

In the Glasgow Museum there is a half-model of another of Reid's ships, the iron *Vanguard* of 687 tons, built in 1852 for the China trade. The model shows a vessel with a fair amount of deadrise, slack bilges and tumblehome, which was intended to produce a fast cargo carrier, but not nearly so extreme as *Cairnsmore*.

The 'splendid' *Glen Roy*, as a newspaper advertisement acclaimed her, was built by Denny & Rankin of Dumbarton, who began business in 1839 and took over Charles Wood's yard in 1843; Peter Denny (1788–1856) and Daniel Rankin (1787–1862) were the partners, and the firm continued in business until about 1867. The iron clipper *Gauntlet* which they built in 1853 was designed by William Rennie. Although the *Glen Roy*'s maiden passage to Melbourne was rather protracted at 99 days, she claimed to have run 1099 miles in three days, making a daily average of 366⅓ miles and an average speed of 15⅔ knots. Her measurements were 1219 knots nm and 229.0 ft by 32.6ft by 21.0ft. The *Gauntlet* had a coefficient of underdeck tonnage of .58, similar to *Titania* and *Thermopylae*, so it seems safe to class her as a clipper.

Although not included in the above list because her ratio of beams to length was only 6.45, the iron ship *Pride of Canada* had some interesting mechanical equipment: a steam winch, two iron double winches, Brown's patent capstan, a common capstan, and four pumps. This ship was built in 1855 by Laurence Hil & Co at Port Glasgow and registered 1013 tons.

In 1855, Barclay Curle & Co launched the iron ship *Shandon* of 729 tons net with dimensions of 183.7ft by 32.5ft by 19.0ft, being yard number 44. The builder's plan shows a short entrance with little concavity to be seen and there is about 18 feet of deadflats amidships, but she has a longer run. The fairly flat floors soon round up into slack bilges with considerable tumblehome. She was equipped with roller-reefing gear on all her topgallants, topsails and courses, which was a fairly unusual arrangement.

William Rennie

Perhaps no other naval architect is better known for his clipper ship designs than is William Rennie, and yet the references to him are always so fleetingly brief that it has taken some years to piece together this summary of his shipbuilding activities and the names of some ships he designed.

The earliest reference yet found refers to the schooner *Florence* which he built at Aberdeen in 1831; perhaps he was in his mid-'twenties by then after serving his apprenticeship in a local yard. One might observe, in passing, that Aberdeen always claims to beget the best clipper ship designers! By the end of the 1830s he had moved to Canada where he set up a shipyard at Bathurst, New Brunswick; there are records of ships built there from 1839, and in 1846 he designed the clipper barques *Beraza* and *Raphael* which another local builder, Joseph Cunard of Miramichi, built for London ownership. These barques are described in more detail in chapter four. On the survey report of the 5 A1 barque *Caroline* (1839) the surveyor wrote of Rennie: 'This is a good builder.'[26]

William Rennie returned to Britain in the

late 'forties and settled at Liverpool; the first reference to him in the directory is dated 1848 and he is described as a 'marine architect'. By 1851 he had joined with John Johnson to become Rennie, Johnson & Co, shipbuilders at Brunswick Dock. Soon after, William Rankine joined them and the title was changed to Rennie, Johnson & Rankine. No attempt has yet been made to record names of ships designed or built by him in Liverpool prior to 1853, although a perusal of Liverpool papers in these years would undoubtedly reveal some.

In 1853, the iron ship *Gauntlet* was completed at Dumbarton by Denny & Rankin and William Rennie is said to have designed her. It is unknown whether Daniel Rankin was any relation to Rennie's partner, William Rankine. Most sources assign an 'e' to the Rankine in Liverpool, but none to the builder at Dumbarton. The *Gauntlet* was described as 'more like a yacht of large tonnage than a private merchant ship'.[27]

In the same year Rennie designed and built in Liverpool the wooden ship *Margaret Deane* and although no plan or model has been located, the following description from the *Albion* provides a tantalising account of the hull form:

> 'Mr. Rennie who drafted this ship, and whose vessels have had no superiors, has adopted his principle of hollow lines, which are carried out through the entire ship. The lines form an infinite variety of curves, all of which blend into each other with flowing ease. The ship has good bearings, but the keel is made to fall gently from the vessel, so that the curved line is really carried out through the entire frame of the ship, the eye being able to trace the line of beauty from any point on which it may rest to any other point within the range of vision. Mr. Rennie has applied this principle before, but never so admirably as in the vessel now being built. Mr. Rennie has in his possession a beautiful model of an iron ship of 1000 tons, drafted by himself, which will probably be built in this town.'[28]

This 1000-ton iron ship has not yet been traced; perhaps she was never constructed or else built outside Liverpool.

The *Margaret Deane* was launched on 30 November 1853 by Mrs Green, wife of the future master who had previously commanded the *Swordfish* (referred to in chapter four) on some of her fast passages to and from Brazil. Measurements of the new ship were given as 144ft keel and fore rake, 28ft extreme beam, 16ft depth of hold, 460 tons nm and 530 tons om. The larger tonnage by the old measurement rule infers a sharp hull form.

In 1854, the firm began building iron ships with the launch of the barque *Sappho* of 359 tons nm. The surveyor reported that 'workmanship and model are both good' but that she was 'not a vessel of large capacity', which infers a sharp hull form.[29] There are also records of one, perhaps two, ships designed by Rennie which were launched in 1854.

The first of these was the 'frigate' *Earl of Eglinton* described in an advertisement as 'Designed by the celebreted draughtsman, W Rennie Esq of Liverpool, on model to secure great sailing powers'.[30] This ship which was built of oak and teak by the Portland Shipbuilding Co of Troon, was launched on 13 June 1854, and measured 208.4ft by 31.4ft by 21.9ft, 1274 tons nm and 1270 tons om.

There is some uncertainty over the other ship, the iron 'clipper' *Vision* of 422 tons, built in 1854 by Sandeman & McLaurin of Whiteinch, Glasgow. A contemporary report stated that she 'is built from the designs of G Rennie Esq of Liverpool'.[31] Although a George Rennie was an engineer and shipbuilder at London in 1860, William is the only shipbuilding Rennie found at Liverpool, and it is probable that the wrong initial was used.

During 1855 two steamers were completed by him at Liverpool and also four sailing ships. Simultaneously, the firm went bankrupt in January, and in June their yard was taken over by Thomas Vernon.[32] Life must have been very complicated that year, but all the above ships are ascribed to Rennie, Johnson & Rankine or to Rennie & Co in spite of this failure.

The most notable of the sailing ships built in 1855 was the 'beautiful wooden clipper' *Fiery Cross* and a report of her launch states that she was purchased by John Campbell of Glasgow, which suggests that she was built on speculation.[33] The launch took place at the Brunswick Dock on 31 July 1855, and although Rennie, Johnson & Rankine are described as the builders, the ship may have been completed by other parties. Perhaps this is the reason why Basil Lubbock states that the ship was built by Chaloner.[34] The *Albion* clarifies the matter somewhat by referring to 'the late firm of Rennie, Johnson & Rankine' and adding: 'The lines of this magnificent vessel are by Mr. Rennie, of Liverpool, celebrated as the finest marine draughtsman in England.'[35]

The lines plan of this ship, reproduced by Basil Lubbock, is the earliest known drawing of one of William Rennie's designs.[36] The ship is spoiled by a heavy, square stern in addition to a full poop, although in Melbourne she was called 'a smart and race-horsey looking ship'.[37] The entrance and run are hollow in the lower waterlines but sharp and convex at the load line. The main rail at the forecastle flares out beyond the line of the rail further aft to form a similar outline to that seen in the *Reindeer*'s hull, only in reverse. There is appreciable deadrise with hollow garboards, but the bilges are kept low and there is slight tumblehome. It is interesting to speculate

List of ships built by Rennie, Johnson & Rankine[38]

Date	Name	Rig	Tons nm	om		Dimensions
1853	*Margaret Deane*	S	468	530	wood	144.0ft × 28.0ft × 16.0ft
1854	*Sappho*	bk	359		iron	138.5ft × 22.9ft × 14.8ft
1854	buoy tender		90		wood	
1854	*Esther*	bk	264	280	wood	
1855	*Elizabeth Barter*	bk	210		iron	
1855	*Fusilier*	S	503	552	iron	152.7ft × 25.6ft × 16.9ft
1855	ss *Empress Eugenie*		441	686	iron	(not in *LR*)
1855	*John Campbell*	S	?	?		(not in *LR*)
1855	*Fiery Cross*	S	672	688	wood	174ft (keel & fore rake) × 30ft × 19ft
1855	ss *Carbon*		440	587		(not in *LR*; built under supervision of Jas Hodgson)

222: The starboard quarter of the iron ship *Storm Cloud* drawn to show her unusually shaped rudder and counter. The long, concave entrance stretches away into the distance. Her channels were formed of angle iron brackets and were left open for the sea to pass through.

how nearly this design could follow that described for the *Margaret Deane. Fiery Cross* made some fast passages, such as 81 days from Liverpool to Melbourne in 1855; 94 days Foochow to Dartmouth in 1857 with tea (she sailed on 9 August); and 96 days London to Hong Kong in the first months of 1858.

The following is a list of ships built by Rennie, Johnson & Rankine at Liverpool, so far as present researches are concerned:

William Rennie is reputed to have designed the barque *Strathmore* which was launched at Dundee in 1856 for the China trade. The following year he is listed in the Liverpool directory as a shipbuilder, and in that year built the wood barque *Sharston* of 353 tons register. By this date he had become consulting engineer to the Royal Mail Steam Packet Co, and was responsible for the design of their iron paddle steamer *Paramatta* of 3092 tons, launched in November 1858 by the Thames Iron & Shipbuilding Co at Blackwall. In 1860, he moved to London where he designed ships and acted as a consultant under the style of Rennie & Marshall at King and Queen Dock, Rotherhithe. By 1864, they described themselves, in addition to naval architects, as 'shipbuilders and repairers', but 1868 is the date of their last entry in the London directory. From 1860 until 1871 William Rennie lived at Railstone Villas, Campbell Road, E, but after that he cannot be traced with any certainty among others of the same name. By that time he would certainly have spent 40 years designing and building ships and would be in his middle to late 'sixties.

During the 1860s, William Rennie designed the tea clippers *Fiery Cross, Black Prince, John R Worcester and Norman Court*, the auxiliary steamer *Sea King*, later to become the Confederate cruiser *Shenandoah*, and the whaler *Chaa-sze* which became a China trader. He may have obtained the commission for the *Black Prince* through Captain William Inglis who was both her master and part owner, and who had commanded the *Gauntlet* which Rennie designed in 1853. His work in connection with these ships is treated more fully in the next chapter.

Alexander Stephen Jnr and the *Storm Cloud*

The *Glasgow Herald* of Monday 17 July 1854 carried the following report:

> 'On Thursday afternoon at four o'clock a magnificent new iron clipper ship, named the *Storm Cloud*, was launched from the building yard of Messrs Alexander Stephen & Sons, at Kelvinhaugh. This truly noble ship has been constructed expressly with the view of attaining a higher rate of speed than any vessel ever built in this or any other country; and, if we may judge from the exquisite beauty of her mould, she promises to fulfill all that is expected of her. It is difficult to explain her remarkable and novel build. We may state, however, that her lines are an approximation to those of the celebrated yacht *America*, the sharpness of her bows being carried aft to near the stern. Her keel is not level, but curves up fore and aft, which it is calculated will make her more readily answer her helm.'

The *North British Daily Mail* of 15 July 1854 allotted a column of 13in to describe the ship, and the *Artizan* gave a full technical account on design and performance a year after her launch. Three such lengthy reports were a big press coverage in those days for a merchant sailing ship.

The lines of the *Storm Cloud* are certainly unique, particularly for a ship of her size, and it may be that the reporter on the *Glasgow Herald* was groping for some similar hull with which to compare the lines, when he referred to the *America*. The lines of this schooner yacht had been taken off by Admiralty surveyors in 1851 or 1852 and the technical press was full of diagrams and detailed descriptions of the hull form. The lines were also reproduced in the third edition of John W Griffiths' *Treatise on Marine and Naval Architecture*, which appeared in 1853.[39] The title of this book is listed on the last page of a notebook covering the years 1851–53 which

Alexander Stephen Jnr kept. Also listed was John Scott Russell's *Theory of the Wave System of Naval Architecture* and Lardner's *Hydrostatics*. Stephen was therefore conversant with the contemporary theories on hollow lines as advocated by the chief proponents in Britain and America.

J W Griffiths approved of the design of the *America* and maintained that a long, sharp, concave entrance was necessary for maximum speed, and that the midsection be placed abaft the mid-point on the load line, thus giving a rather short run. He also denied that the concave lines in American clippers were the result of Scott Russell's theories, but were due to progressive development.

After considerable practical experiment, J Scott Russell propounded his theory on wave form to the British Association in 1842–43 and developed it over the years. He stated that the hull of a well-formed ship could be driven through the water up to a certain maximum speed, dependent on the length of the load line, above which wave-making resistance would build up to such a degree that it was uneconomical to obtain a higher speed. His theory showed the relation of maximum economic speed to be approximately the square root of the length of the load line, whereas later research has proved it to be 1.25 × the square root. He also contended that the length of the run should be two-thirds that of the entrance, thus placing the midsection abaft the mid-point of the load line. He claimed that 'the form of least resistance for the water-line of the bow is horizontally the curve of versed sines and that the form of least resistance for the stern of the vessel is the cycloid'.[40] These forms produce a long concave entrance and a shorter but concave run.

In the *Storm Cloud* the proportion of the entrance to the run at the load line is not 3 to 2 as in the wave-form theory, but 2.8 to 2.0. However, the difference is too slight to effect the conclusion that this ship was designed in conformity with the general principles of J Scott Russell's wave-form theories. The length of the load line scales 195ft-3in at a draught of 15ft-9in, and by his theory the designed economic speed would be the square root of this length, which can be calculated as 13.97 knots — say 14. But a technical appraisal of her design and her maiden passage, published in the *Artizan*, records a speed of 12 knots when close-hauled 5½ points into the wind, speeds of 15 and 16 knots when running with a quartering wind, and a day's run of 345 nautical miles which gives an average of 14.37 knots.[41] A Tasmanian paper claimed that on her second voyage she made 17 knots and a day's run of 370 nautical miles.[42] A speed of 16 knots gives a speed-length ratio of 1.14 and 17 knots gives 1.22.

223: This engraving from the *Illustrated London News* depicts HMS *Brisk*, in August 1860, receiving the surrender of the slaver *Manuela*, which has been hove-to with all sail set. The *Manuela* was originally the extreme clipper ship *Sunny South* and was built and designed in 1854 by George Steers at Williamsburg, New York. She measured 702 tons and became a store ship for the Royal Navy on the African coast, named *Enchantress*.

Further confirmation that Alexander Stephen Jnr was activated by an interest in Russell's theories may be judged from written notes he made in March 1853.

> 'Got the idea of a particle of water when it first comes in contact with the fore part of a ship in motion in not giving it its final velocity at once, but to increase its velocity gradually by means of the hollow water-line; and in this way also of preserving the water from accumulating at the entrance, but throwing it nearer the centre of gravity.' And a week later he was considering making a scale model of a proposed draught, hollowing it out, and then floating it. 'In experimenting with this, turn the model end for end. Try the Wave Line with this.'[43]

Accompanying sketches showed a long, sharp, concave bow, and the use of the words 'Wave Line' clinches the argument that Stephen Jnr was strongly influenced just then by Russell.

It must be presumed that Stephen Snr allowed his son Alexander a free hand in the design of the *Storm Cloud*, as the hull form was so radically different from anything yet produced by the yard that the hand of a new designer is immediately apparent. Another important fact effecting the design is that Stephen's built her for themselves and so did not have to sell their ideas to another party; this gave them complete freedom to back their own inspiration, which is remarkably rare in the shipbuilding industry. *The North British Daily Mail* also commented on the 'indifference to precedent' occasioned by having the builders as the owners and added that 'it is so rarely that a vessel is fashioned entirely according to the scientific judgement of the builder, and independent of the wishes of the owner, that we often wondered... who the owners were that had been so bold as to set at defiance in such important particulars, the ordinary rules of shipcraft...'[44] From diary entries, Alexander Stephen Jnr makes it clear that his firm were builders, not owners, and consequently it is not surprising to learn of their efforts to sell her.

A month before *Storm Cloud* was launched, the firm completed the clipper *John Bell* which might be said to mark an approach towards the wave form theory of design because the midsection was moved further aft. In the *Hurricane*, the midsection was positioned at the mid-point of the lood line, but in the *John Bell* it is four feet abaft the centre. Because of this the entrance was longer and slightly sharper than that of *Hurricane* and the run was shorter and slightly fuller; the amount of deadrise remained the same and also the profile.

In February 1855, Stephen's launched the *White Eagle* as a virtual repeat of *Storm Cloud*, and in June of the year came the fully square-rigged auxiliary steamer *Euphrates*, as a sightly fuller version. Both these two were also owned initially by the builders.

Tracings of the builder's plans of *Storm Cloud* and *White Eagle* have been laid over each other and these show an identical length from stem to sternpost. Other similarities are the bow profile, figurehead, amount of deadrise, shape of the run, rockered keel at forward end, and tiny counter stern. But in *White Eagle* the rockered keel aft is abandoned in favour of a straight keel. Another difference is the position of the midship section: in *White Eagle* this is six feet forward of that on *Storm Cloud*, resulting in a shorter entrance which is slightly fuller, although still sharp and concave.

In the *Euphrates* there is a basically fuller version of *White Eagle* although the dimensions have increased all round and the addition of 18 feet in length, as noted on the plan, seems to have introduced about 12 feet of almost deadflats. The bow profile is not so cut away, the figurehead is supported by light trail boards, and there are alternate positions aft for a rockered keel or a horizontal one.

The measurements of these four unusual ships are tabulated for easy comparison:

Date	Name	Tonnage UD	Net	1836 nm	Dimensions by 1854 Registry Act[45]	Coefficient by UD tons
1854	*John Bell*	940	1057	1207	231.5ft × 33.2ft × 20.6ft	.61
1854	*Storm Cloud*	688	798	907	201.6ft × 33.0ft × 20.33ft	.51
1855	*White Eagle*	756	879	997	203.3ft × 32.8ft × 20.9ft	.54
1855	SS *Euphrates*	1144 gross	658	—	257;6ft × 29.1ft × 20.0ft	—

In America, George Steers, designer of the yacht *America*, also designed the extreme clipper *Sunny South* which was built in New York in 1854, and was very similar to the *America* in principle. Her midsection was positioned at the mainmast and she had a long, concave entrance and a shorter but sharp and concave run; her keel was rockered for its entire length. This design is the only American one that resembles Stephen's ships, but her dimensions of 135ft-4in by 30ft-4in (moulded) by 17ft-3in makes her much broader than *Storm Cloud* in proportion to length; in addition, her entrance is not so long, sharp or concave as Stephen's clipper, although the run is very similar and she has greater deadrise.[46]

Although there is a builder's plan of *Storm Cloud*, the lines reproduced in figure 224 were drawn from an offset table found among papers in Alexander Stephen & Sons' archives, but the profile was taken from the lines plan. In the plans of both *Storm Cloud* and *White Eagle* the body plan is arranged as drawn here, with the fore body and after body stations arranged according to normal practice. The builder's lines plans for these two ships, in addition to the *John Bell*, were drawn to a scale of ⅜in to 1ft-0in rather than ¼in to 1ft-0in. This produces very large drawings which in the case of *John Bell* results in a lines plan eight feet long. In her case no body plan was drawn, but merely the outline of the midsection superimposed on the sheer elevation beside the appropriate station.

It is immediately evident that the *Storm Cloud*'s entrance is one of the longest and sharpest ever put on a clipper, either in Britain or America, when the overall length of the ship is considered. In this case the entrance measures 114ft-0in along the load line between the stem and the midsection, which

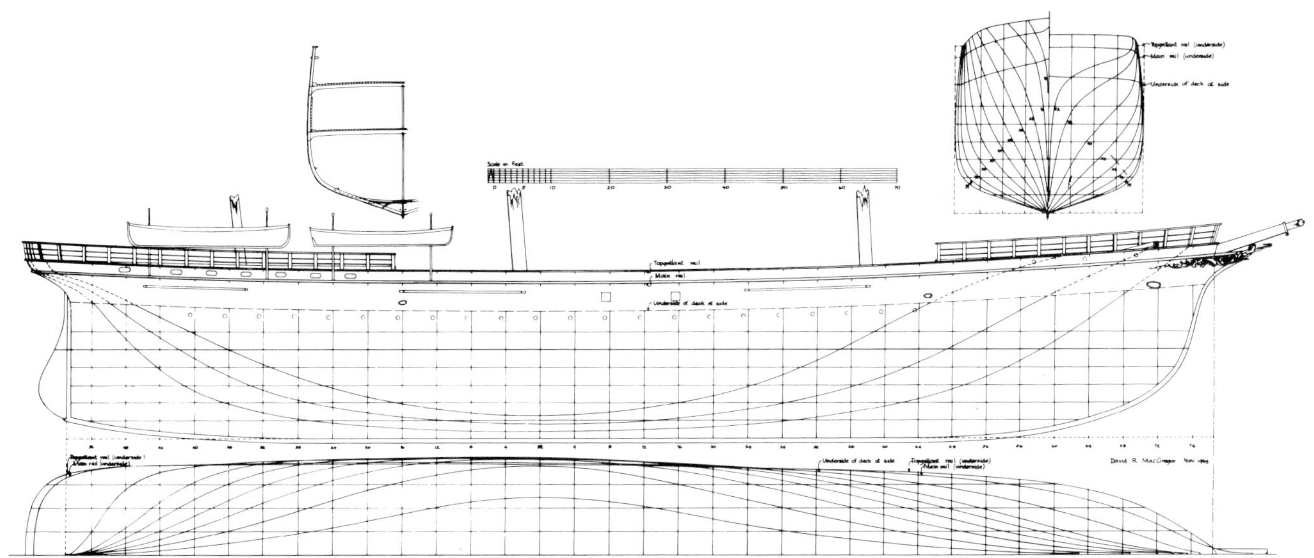

224: *Storm Cloud.* Lines plan: Built of iron in 1854 by Alexander Stephen & Sons at Glasgow. Drawn from builder's offset table and undated lines plan. Dimensions by 1854 Act: 201.6ft × 33.0ft × 20.33ft; tonnages 688.20 under deck, 797.85 gross and register. Reconstruction: Midship section from plan of Stephen's auxiliary steamer *Euphrates* and from scantlings in the Lloyd's Register survey report.

225: The *White Eagle* was an extreme iron clipper launched by Alexander Stephen & Sons in 1855. The long sharp entrance can be judged from the fact that the hull retains some flare at the position of the third painted port. A bowsprit similar to *Storm Cloud*'s is fitted. In this photograph taken in New Zealand, her name had been changed to *Pareora* after her sale to the New Zealand Shipping Co. *Alexander Turnbull Library, Wellington.*

is ten feet more than in that remarkably sharp clipper the *Annandale*, but then the latter has much more balanced ends as her plan indicates. Although the *Storm Cloud*'s run is much shorter than the entrance, it is sharp and concave, and the minimum amount of solid body is given. The quarter-beam buttock is curved, not straight, where it crosses the load line but the general run of the buttocks show no hard shoulders. A fair amount of deadrise occurs at the midsection with straight floors, firm bilges and some tumblehome. The rounded sterm is exceedingly broad on plan and there is little tapering of the deck as it moves towards the stern. Abaft the midsection for some 60 feet, the topgallant rail runs almost dead straight and parallel to the centre line.

Unusual differences can also be seen in the sheer profile: the keel is rockered both fore and aft to the amount of 52ft-0in forward and 40ft-0in abaft, measured in from each perpendicular; the stem terminates in a figurehead but there is none of the usual hair rails and brackets of the sort seen in other ships; the stern is also very light and employs shapes only possible in iron vessels. The profile at the ends is quite the opposite of the *Hurricane*, and an idea of the simple bow can be seen in the photograph of her near-sister *White Eagle* (figure 225). A large number of portholes are placed in the 'tween decks and good ventilation was provided. The channels are framed with angle iron, not solid timber, and are supported by diagonal struts, thus offering little resistance to the sea.

As shown by the survey report, heavy scantlings were used in the *Storm Cloud*'s construction: the keel was a solid bar measuring 10in by 2½in, which was also the size of the stem; the sternpost measured 8in by 3½in; the keelson was an iron plate 22in by ½in with 4 in by 3 in by ½in angles top and bottom; the frames, at 18in centres, were 5in by 3in by ½in angles with 3in by 3in by ⅜in angles to alternate frames; and the floor plates were 20in deep on the centre line. The garboard strakes measured ¾in thick, diminishing to 9/16in at the wales and ½in at the topsides. Although there was an iron gunwale plate of 24in by ½in, bulwark construction was not specified, but the waterway was of teak, 12in by 6in, and the decks were 3½in yellow pine. Manufacturers of the iron employed are not named but it was 'said to be the best'! The only test certificates required were for the chain cables.[47] The builder estimated that the *White Eagle* contained 388 tons of iron and 144 tons of timber, and the figures for *Storm Cloud* must have been somewhat similar.

There is a builder's plan for *Storm Cloud* showing main deck beams, hatchways, after accommodation, and length of poop and forecastle. Although some of the detail is reconstructed, there is considerable information to be found on plans of contemporary ships built by Stephen, particularly *White Eagle*, SS *Euphrates, Hurricane* and *Charlemagne*. The ladders from the lower deck to the main deck are shown in a plan of the latter ship, which was commenced in 1856. The survey report lists seven boats, although only five are drawn

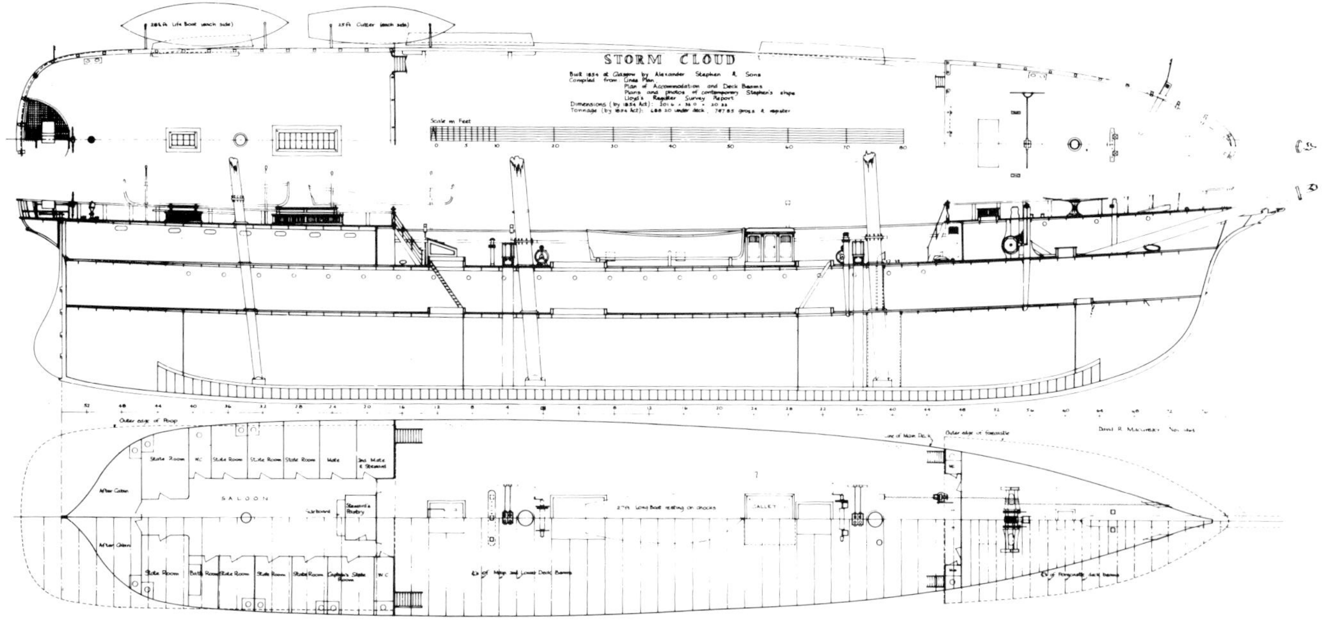

226: *Storm Cloud.* General Arrangement Plan: Mostly reconstructed. Sources for reconstruction: Lines plan; plan of accommodation and deck beams; plans and photographs of contemporary ships built by Stephen's; Lloyd's Register survey report.

227: *Storm Cloud.* Sail plan: Traced from plan in builder's possession signed and dated 'W. Robertson 18th June 1855'. Fore trysail and jackyard topsail were drawn in pencil on this plan and are here shown dotted. Reconstruction: Stunsails; iron plating (from builder's lines plan); channels, chainplates and deadeyes; braces to mizen yards and main skysail.

here, as it is uncertain where they were all stowed. The sizes given for them are: one 27ft longboat, two 28½ft lifeboats, two 25ft cutters, one 28ft gig, and a 14ft dinghy. The *White Eagle*'s plan shows a pawl post indicative of a windlass barrel which is reconstructed here. There is no indication of the curved stairways to the poop fitted in *Hurricane*, although the poop skylights with surrounding seats are similar. The general arrangement is typical of the Stephens' ships of the period 1852–58.

The *Storm Cloud*'s sail and rigging plan is traced from a builder's plan signed 'W Robertson 18th June 1855'; this date is ten months after the launch. This is important in showing that the sail plan is not a fanciful one which was never carried out, but shows the ship as she was just prior to her second voyage. There is also a separate list of spar dimensions which agrees fairly well with this plan. The 1855 sail plan shows the curved flying jibboom, the two dolphin strikers, the six headsails, and all the braces to the fore-and mainmasts. The reconstruction has been confined to the stunsails with their booms and yards; the braces on the mizen; the rows of reef points; the deadeyes, channels and chainplates. The latter appear in sail plans of SS *Euphrates* and *Charlemagne*, but there is no surviving sail plan of *White Eagle*. The fore trysail and mizen gaff topsail are in pencil on the builder's plan and so are dotted here. The standing rigging and stays are of wire. It is interesting that the old method is retained of leading the fore brace to the main top, and of taking the tackle of the topsail braces to the topmast stay instead of the standing part. The latter arrangement had been generally superseded by the early 'fifties but it occurs on the Stephens' plans of SS *Euphrates, Charlemagne* and *Sea Queen*. The run of the plating drawn here was marked by the builder on his large ⅜in-scale body plan.

The height of the load line shown for *Storm Cloud* is that used on the builder's sail plan and represents the ship on her earlier passages when the 'tween decks carried only passengers and the hold did not contain too much heavy deadweight cargo. There is so little body to the ship that when examining the builder's half-model it was difficult to realise that here was a vessel designed to earn a living by carrying freight and fare-paying passengers, and that she was not just a pleasure yacht. Some indication that prospective owners did not view her earning capacities at all favourably may be had from the fact that Stephen's did not manage to sell the ship until 1862, in spite of continuous efforts on their part and the granting of four certificates of sale to her master which empowered him to sell the ship anywhere outside the United Kingdom.[48]

Alexander Stephen Jnr estimated the first cost and interest on *Storm Cloud* from August 1854 to February 1856 to amount to £16,741; her old measurement tonnage, on which prices were usually quoted, was 1012 tons which means that she cost approximately £16 per ton, including a full East India outfit. On her first two voyages which lasted 21 months, the Stephens made a net profit of £8,700 after the payment of all expenses. In February 1856, they wrote: 'We feel reluctant to sell our ships *Storm Cloud* and *White Eagle* [which are] at present yielding us very sound returns and have made very successful passages.'[49] On these two voyages, freight rates were still high and she probably loaded at between £4 and £5 per ton to Melbourne on her first voyage. On her second voyage bound home from Calcutta to London, she carried 1000 tons of deadweight and measurement goods for a freight of £4,700; disbursements at Calcutta had been £700. Of course, 1000 tons of cargo in a ship of just under 800 tons register is a poor haul and heavy disbursements could whittle away all the earnings. A ship of 800 tons would normally expect to load 1300 to 1600 tons. Extreme clippers certainly required high freights to earn a living, but a fast passage could save them money when passengers were carried, because surplus provisions could be sold. Thus *Storm Cloud* saved £1,200 in this way on her fast run of 71 days to Launceston in 1855, when she carried 364 emigrants.

In February 1856, Alexander Stephen & Sons offered *Storm Cloud* for sale at £14,978 including her very full outfit, and *White Eagle* at £15,986.[50] In April, it was thought the sales would not occur owing to a fall in the price of iron, but *White Eagle* was sold in September 1856 to J G Macfarlane of Glasgow for £11,500. However, *Storm Cloud* remained unsold. In October 1859, they offered her to Handyside & Henderson for £7,000 plus £5,700 for lengthening her by 60 feet and altering her to a screw steamer, but the price proved too high.[51] Instead, she was chartered to Patrick Henderson for £5,412 to carry emigrants to New Zealand and sailed in January 1860.[52] She was finally sold in July 1862 to Captain James Adams of Helensburgh for £7,250 and was wrecked the following year off Akyab. There was a good demand for ships in the early 'sixties, particularly iron ones, hence the good price obtained for her.

Although she was claimed to have been built for the conveyance of coolies from India to the West Indies, her first two passages were made out to Australia. Her maiden passage occupied 88 days between Glasgow and Melbourne in 1854, from 6 September to 3 December, and she returned to London in 97 days. After sailing round to Glasgow to load and probably to have her bottom scraped and painted, she sailed from the Clyde on 17 June 1855 and was off Launceston Heads 71 days later on 27 August. A Tasmanian paper commented on her passage as follows:

> 'On the present voyage she reached Madeira in six days; made the run from Sicily to Cape Otway in 66; and sighted the shore of Tasmania on the 69th day. In twenty-four hours she logged 370 nautical miles — a feat which equals if it does not surpass, the performances of the celebrated *Marco Polo*.'[53]

From Tasmania she sailed to India and brought back to London a cargo from Calcutta, making the passage in 94 days.

On her maiden passage in 1855, the *White Eagle* had been forced into Cape Town to repair heavy weather damage, the total elapsed time from Glasgow to Melbourne being lengthened to 119 days. She came home via Calcutta, being 114 days from that port to Deal, and then was chartered for the Crimea to help in the evacuation during the summer of 1856. She had a long life under various owners and was bought in 1877 at Dunedin by the New Zealand Shipping Co for a sum in excess of £7,000. They renamed her *Pareora* and she was not broken up until 1885.

The *John Bell* was a another of Stephens' clippers to be converted into a steamer. This work was carried out in 1857 and from then until 1863 she sailed for the Anchor Line, during which time John Bell remained the principal shareholder, apart from two periods when he held no shares at all. Her changes of name and ownership were frequent, but from the mid 'seventies she sailed once more as a sailing ship and was not broken up until 1905 at Genoa.

Surprisingly, Stephen never built another clipper at the Glasgow yard that was as sharp as *Typhoon, Hurricane, John Bell, Storm Cloud* or *White Eagle*. Perhaps they were never given a suitable order even during the clipper ship boom of the late 'sixties or possibly their prices were always too high, and the China clipper *Eliza Shaw* (1863) appears to have been the next finest-lined ship, to judge by surviving plans. For many years their ships were fuller or sharper versions of the medium clipper *Tyburnia*, which was launched in 1857.

Benjamin Nicholson and the *Annandale*

The extreme clippers being built during 1854 had been conceived twelve months before, and the *Annandale* which was launched on 10 August 1854 had been commenced in January 1853. It was only a comparatively small yard which carried out the building, but 18 months is a long time for a radically extreme clipper to be maturing on the stocks, and any intervening trade depression would have ruined the whole enterprise and turned this noble venture into an economic catastrophe. As it was, she was probably completed just in time to secure some good freights before the depression of the late 'fifties although, like the *Storm Cloud*, she required highly priced freights to earn a living owing to her small carrying capacity. Another thing in common with *Storm Cloud* is that her builder and owner were partners in a family firm — in her case John Nicholson & Co, and so had a freer hand to adopt this extreme build.

Annan lies in Dumfries on the River Annan, a bare mile from the north shore of the Solway Firth, and sloops, schooners, brigs and barques were built there by the Nicholson family. John Nicholson was in charge from 1825 until his death in 1853 and prior to that date the largest vessel was the ship *Annandale* of 338 tons, launched in 1827 fully rigged and masted. In 1853, came the ship *Burns* of 375 tons, a full-bodied carrier, and

Square rigged ships built by B E Nicholson 1853–65[54]

Year	Name	Rig	Tons nm	Tons om	Dimensions
1853	*Burns*	S	363	375	124.0ft × 25.5ft × 16.8ft (R)
1854	*Annandale*	S	759	1131	226.9ft × 28.5ft × 18.5ft (1836 Rule) (extreme breadth 31.8ft) (R)
1856	*Queensberry*	S	635	767	206.9ft × 28.6ft × 19.2ft (R)
1857	*Shakspere*	S	486	565	164.8ft × 27.2ft × 18.0ft (R)
1859	*John Nicholson*	S	685	—	177.6ft × 29.4ft × 20.0ft (R)
1861	*Mansfield*	bk	357	—	133.1ft × 25.6ft × 16.9ft (R)
1862	*Burnswark*	bk	323	—	121.5ft × 24.5ft × 14.8ft
1863	*Elizabeth Nicholson*	S	904	—	192.5ft × 32.5ft × 22.2ft
1865	*Sarah Nicholson*	S	934	—	194.7ft × 32.7ft × 22.6ft

(R) signifies built under a roof; the last three ships were probably built under a roof, but the Lloyd's Register surveys have not been checked.

thereafter some much bigger ships were built beginning the following year with a new *Annandale*. John Nicholson's son, Benjamin (1833–1913), who was 20 years old on his father's death, took control of the yard and immediately embarked on an ambitious project of building much larger wooden ships, all of which were owned by the builders. Their cousins in Liverpool who had the firm of Nicholson & McGill, provided additional expertise in running the ships profitably.

During the years 1853–65, two smaller vessels were also constructed by Nicholson: the schooner *Syren* (1856) which was built astern of the *Shakspere* on the same slip, with wood left over from the construction of the *Queensberry,* and the brig *Solway Queen* (1864).

When the *Annandale* was measured in 1858 according to the 1854 Registry Act, the breadth became the maximum outside rather than the internal between the ceiling, and so the figure increased to 31.8ft. This was undoubtedly the reason for people assuming that she had been altered or rebuilt. The hull length scales 224.0ft on the plan, which suggests that an additional frame was added during building, and as the room and space measured 30½in, this would have had the effect of lengthening the hull to 226.5ft, which is almost the register length. The great narrowness of the hull, comparing beam to length, was emphasised in a special table of other such ships, earlier in this chapter.

Commander Francis Tweedie, who did the spadework on much of Annan's shipbuilding history, suggested that young Benjamin Nicholson got the inspiration to design and build an extreme clipper whilst working in the Liverpool office of Nicholson & McGill. A local newspaper partly confirms this when describing the launch of the *Annandale* and its remarks are of interest as coming from a largely agricultural district:

> 'We need not inform our readers, that the sharp narrow class of ships called clippers have come into repute of late, on account of their sailing qualities, and that they are for this reason in particular request for the China trade. M'Kay and other Americans took the lead in this manufacture, and for a while, indeed, monopolised the market; but of late, the Piles of Sunderland, and several firms in Aberdeen, have successfully rivalled and occasionally surpassed, the Yankee builders. The Messrs Nicholson of Annan, who have produced not a few fine vessels, resolved on building a very large one in the clipper style, and that not according to any of the existing models, but after an original design, which they considered would secure unequalled speed, without any serious sacrifice of carrying power. The required design was furnished by a young member of the firm — Mr Benjamin Nicholson, who has since his boyhood shewn a great aptitude for naval architecture. Its chief peculiarity consists in extreme length as compared with breadth, the latter being only a seventh of the former.'[55]

228: *Annandale.* Built of wood in 1854 by Benjamin Nicholson at Annan. Lines taken off builder's half-model in possession of Mr B E Nicholson. Lines drawn to inside of plank. Dimensions by 1836 Act: 226.9ft × 28.5ft (inside) × 18.5ft; maximum outside breadth 31.8ft; tonnages 759 nm and 1131 om. Reconstruction: Head, trail boards, cutwater, mast positions and quarter galleries from painting of the *Queensberry*; midship section from drawing in Lloyd's Register survey report.

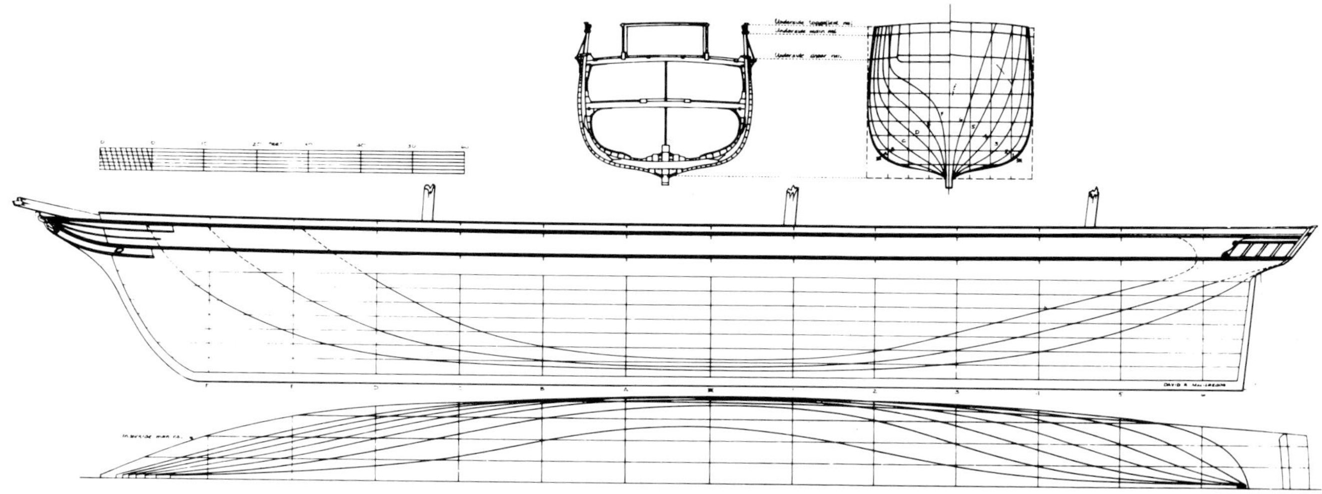

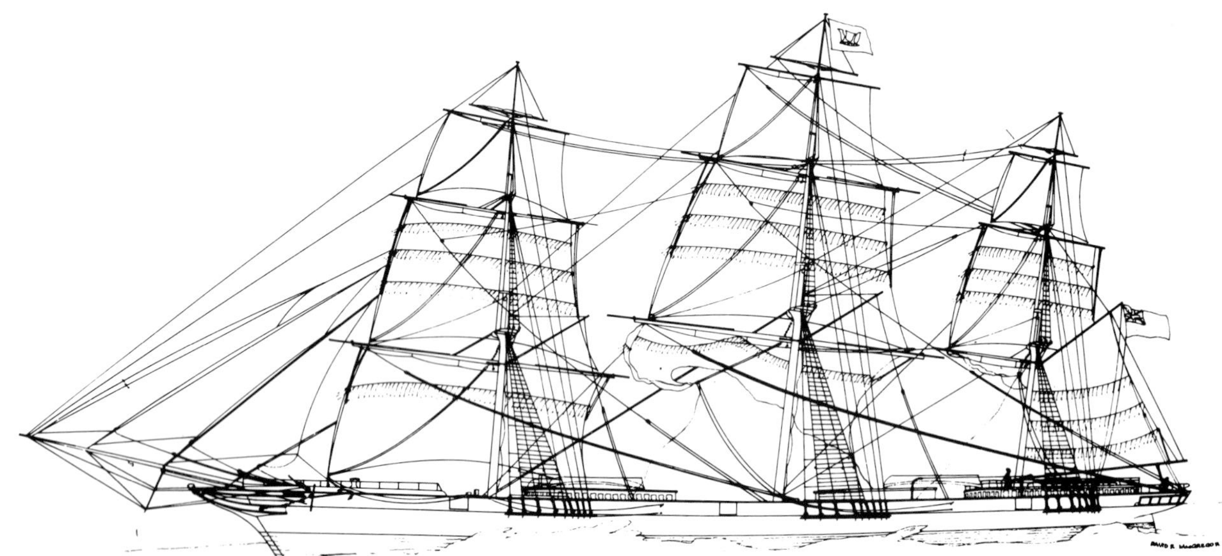

229: *Queensberry*. Built in 1856 by Benjamin Nicholson at Annan. She was of the same extreme proportions as their *Annandale* and in the absence of any illustration of the latter, probably yields a fairly accurate picture of her. *Queensberry* was slightly smaller with a tonnage of 635 nm. This drawing was made directly from Samuel Walter's oil painting of the ship by laying tracing paper over the glass to ensure accuracy. Painting in possession of Mr B E Nicholson.

The keel was laid in January 1853 and the ship was built under a shed; she was sheathed with yellow metal before launching, but no masts were stepped. There was only 11 feet depth of water for the launch at Welldale and the heel caught the ground slightly. The same newspaper compared *Annandale*'s size and measurements with the Sunderland-built passenger ship *Dunbar*, which was launched in December 1853. The paper was intrigued that *Annandale*'s keel was 20 feet longer than the *Dunbar*'s but that her tonnage was considerably less.

The *Annandale* was masted, rigged and fitted out at Annan, but owing to damage to her copper sheathing, presumably occurring through taking the ground at low water, succeeding ships were towed to Liverpool and fitted out there. The two partial dismastings at the start of her maiden passage and the breaking of her main truss which caused the mainyard to fall on deck, may also have influenced the desire to have the ship masted and rigged by men accustomed to bigger ships. Her sails were made at Annan, and the rigging by the Gourock Rope Co. Her accommodation consisted of berths for 24 seamen in a forward deckhouse and another deckhouse further aft contained the master, three mates, boatswain, carpenter, steward and three apprentices. This would be similar to the accommodation shown in a painting of *Queensberry*.

A few years ago Benjamin Nicholson had collected under one roof all the half-models of vessels designed by his grandfather, with the exception of the *Queensberry*, which could not be located. Of these, the *Annandale* was by far the finest-lined, and following her in order of sharpness come *Mansfield, Shakspere, Elizabeth Nicholson*, with the others all full-bodied carriers. Most of the models were made to ⅜in-scale which makes them large and unwieldy. *Annandale*'s model was 7 feet 6 inches long and in the enclosed cellar where I took off their lines, it felt like attending a group of sleeping alligators. The model of *Burns* was mounted on a rectangular backboard, but all the others had backboards shaped to the profile of the hull and projecting about one quarter of an inch beyond it, on all sides. This was common practice in many shipyards.

The *Annandale* forms one of the principal examples of the extreme clipper model in the British Isles and represents an ideal which was for the most part unattainable for practical purposes. Her entrance is very long, sharp and concave and so is the run. If one assumes that the sixth waterline represents the load line to give a draught of 17ft-9in, then the midsection is placed some 3ft abaft the midpoint. The buttock lines have very easy curves and the quarter-beam buttock is straight where it crosses the assumed load line. There is absolutely no sheer. There are hollow garboards with little deadrise and the floors curve into slack bilges, above which there is some tumblehome. A speed of 18 knots is claimed for her by her master, William Crockett, which results in a speed–length ratio of 1.21 on a load line length of 220ft-4in. During the 24 hours when this high speed was made the ship ran 381 miles by observation which gives an average of 15.87 knots.

The juxtaposing of the constructional midsection and the body plan provides a useful comparison, because the hull lines are drawn to the inside of the planking which forms a steady line against the frame, whereas the outer line of the planking swells and diminishes up the side. At the garboard the half-model is formed in an imaginary continuation of the frame down to the bearding line; above the main rail, the sides of the half-model ignore the angle of the topgallant rail and the fact that it is set forward, but sweep up grandly in a continuation of the topsides. Mouldings are generally ignored on such a model, although they are sometimes applied as if the model were planked.

The *Annandale*'s construction was referred to in the last chapter when wood shipbuilding was under discussion. It should be added that the floor timbers were sided 14½in and moulded 14in, diminishing to 10 in by 10in at the top timbers, and that because of her great length considerable trouble had been taken to provide unusually heavy longitudinal timbers, as shown in the midsection. The frame was of English oak, but foreign oak and larch were used for the beams and knees, and Baltic fir, red pine and American elm and oak for the outer planking. The Lloyd's class was 8 A1. Thomas W Wawn, the surveyor, reported:

> 'This vessel is so sharp aft that it is impossible to fit an ordinary crutch; her deadwood 20ft from aft being 12ft in depth. Pointers have therefore been fitted and through bolted from side to side. Her frame is generally sided much more than is required by the Rules and the workmanship is of a very good description.'[56]

Unfortunately, no deck plan is known, but the surveyor reported the presence of a longboat and three others, a patent windlass, two winches, an iron capstan and two metal pumps. Other descriptions indicate she carried a main skysail. Samuel Walter's painting of the *Queensberry*, for which he is said to have been paid £21, is in the possession of Benjamin Nicholson, and the drawing in figure 229 was made directly from it at the same size, the lengths of the various parts being carefully measured from the original. For lack of other evidence it gives the best picture we have of what the *Annandale* may have resembled, especially if a main skysail was added. Owing to the great length of the hull the masts look foreshortened, but such a sharp body did not require a towering sail plan to drive her along. It is more than likely that Walters was furnished with a sail plan and that the painting could be scaled up satisfactorily to yield a reconstructed sail plan. Using *Annandale*'s length of 226.9ft, the painting is almost exactly at a scale of $^{3}/_{32}$in to 1ft-0in. This gives a mainyard of 70ft-0in and a height on the mainmast from rail to truck of 114ft-0in, both of which are equivalent to the sizes in other clippers, although the upper yards are rather on the short side.

The fact that she was obliged to put back twice at the commencement of her maiden passage, with loss of topmasts on each occasion, suggests either that she was originally over-masted or that the local Annan riggers were not equal to their task. She had originally sailed from Liverpool on 7 December 1854, but after putting into Liverpool and Queenstown for repairs, she finally did not sail from the latter until 23 March 1855, and made a passage of 83 days out to Bombay, returning in 98 days to Liverpool.

The entire second voyage lasted from 30 January 1856 to 12 October 1858 during which time she tramped the world for freights, and visited in turn Melbourne, Hong Kong, Singapore, Hong Kong, Melbourne, Callao, Barbadoes, Bahia, Bombay and Liverpool. The first leg of this long voyage had taken her out to Melbourne in 78 days from Liverpool and this was followed by a very short passage of 31 days to Hong Kong, from 11 May to 11 June. Later that year she took the incredibly short time of seven days to sail from Singapore to Hong Kong, from 6 to 13 September 1856, during which time she had steady south-westerly winds and had two royal stunsails and the main skysail set for several days. Her first master, Captain W Crockett, left at the end of the second voyage. Writing some years later after he had retired to Australia, Captain Crockett penned these lines to the *Sydney Daily Telegraph*:

> 'I notice in your issue of the 17th instant, you gave some glowing accounts of some famous clippers. I have not seen any of the ships you mention. Being an old sailor myself, I do not consider the doings of the clippers you describe as marvellous. Yet I take exception to the statement that the *Thermopylae* has made the greatest 24-hours' run that has ever been made by any craft dependent on the wind as motive power. In the ship *Annandale*, under my command on the passage from Bombay to Liverpool in 1855, we made a distance in one day, from noon to noon, of 381 miles by observation. During the 24 hours, we passed the Island of Roderiques at midnight very close. I am satisfied that during part of this day's run the ship travelled at 18 knots an hour. We tried the log three times, and each time ran off upwards of 18 knots, and each time lost the log chip.
>
> 'I left the ship *Annandale* in Liverpool in 1858, and I have never hard anything of her, only that she was altered. She was too long for her beam. The *Annandale* was built at Annan, in the Solway Firth, in 1854, and was the longest sailing ship afloat for her beam at the time. I notice the *Thermopylae* sailed best with the wind abeam. The *Annandale* sailed well with the wind abeam, but she ran before the wind best. On her passage from Liverpool to Melbourne in 1855, the best day's run was 375 miles. At midnight the main skysail was taken in, and with this exception all sail was set the 24-hours. Close-hauled she was nowhere past the usual; and there was no reliance on her staying. She was built of larch, and she used to run the copper off her bottom. I should mention that I took charge of the *Annandale* when she was launched, and sailed her for four years. Messrs John Nicholson & Co of Annan, were the builders and owners.'[57]

In 1860, John Nicholson & Co sold the ship to Stuart & Douglas of Liverpool for £5,287. Five years later she went ashore at Key West, in December, was condemned, and the hull was sold the following March.

Although the half-model of *Queensberry* was missing in 1955, there is evidence to suggest that she was a smaller version of *Annandale*: the midship section is similar; the surveyor called her 'exceedingly fine forward'; the painting shows a clipper-like vessel, with the foremast a long way aft; her dimensions of 206.9ft by 28.6ft by 19.2ft make her equally narrow. Tonnage was 635. Her keel was laid in October 1854 and she was launched on 8 February 1856, having been built under cover. On her maiden passage she sailed out to Hong Kong in 97 days from Liverpool, from 14 April to 20 July. Another fast passage occurred in 1861 when she was off the Scillies on 7 April, 99 days from Canton; the gross earnings on this voyage, which began in November 1859 and included being chartered as a transport, totalled £6,092, before deductions. She was sold in 1863 for £4,327.[58]

The *Shakspere*, built in 1857, had the same shaped bow as *Annandale* but a fuller body which made her a fast medium clipper; her entrance was fine and convex but there was a full body amidships; the run was concave and sharper. The midsection was the same shape as the *Annandale*. Such a hull form resulted in a fine, powerful ship for her many passages around Cape Horn to the West Coast of South America, and in 1857 she took only 71 days between Caldora and Swansea, from 29 September to 9 December, which is a very quick passage.[59] From 1860 until her wreck in 1870 off the French coast, *Shakspere*'s gross earnings before deduction of expenses mounted to £21,447.[60]

Alexander Hall's tea clippers

Sufficient has already been written about

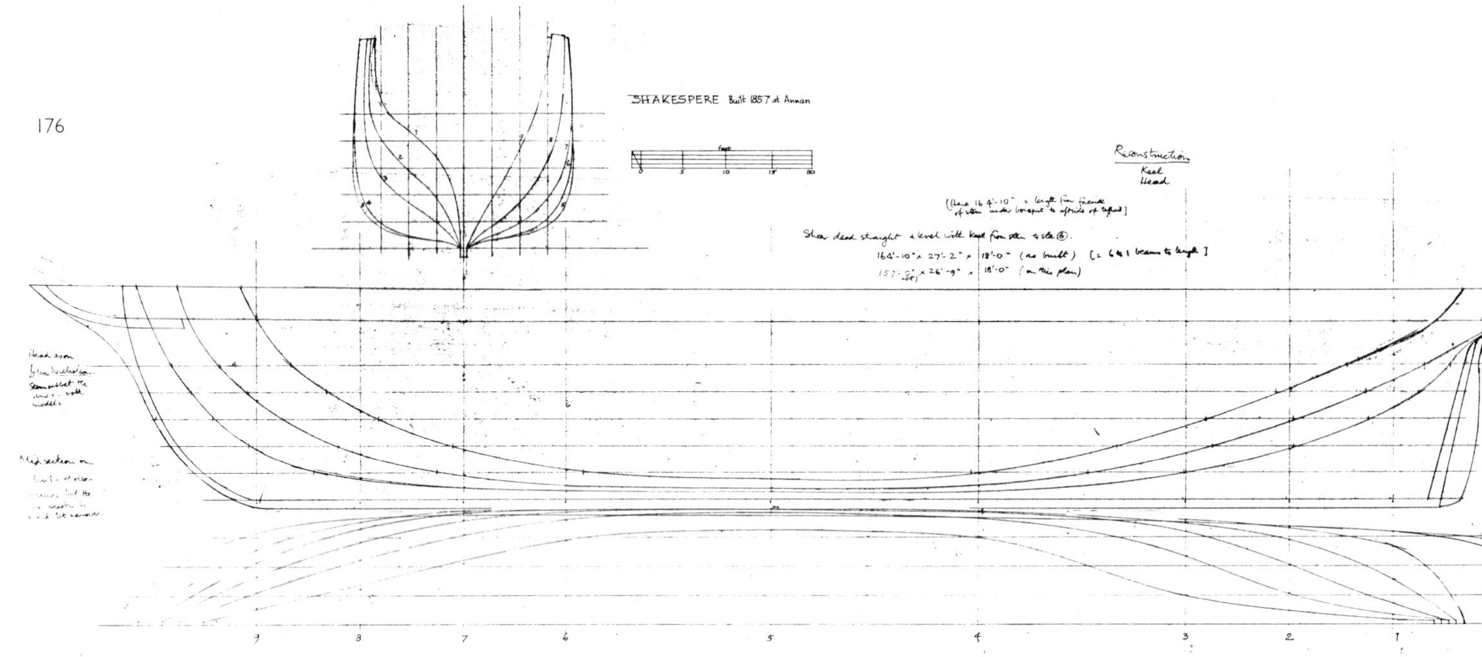

230: *Shakspere.* Lines plan. Drawn from lines taken off builder's half-model when in possession of B E Nicholson. Built in 1857 at Annan by Benjamin Nicholson. Dimensions scaled off this plan: 159ft-0in × 26ft-9in × 18ft-0in (approx). Dimensions of vessel as built: 164ft-10in × 27ft-2in × 18ft-0in; tonnages were 496 nm and 565 om. Reconstruction: head, from half-model of *John Nicholson*, and keel depth.

Alexander Hall & Sons to make unnecessary any introductory remarks about this firm, who were the builders of many extreme clippers. Contemporary papers were never tired of reporting the successes of the Aberdeen ships against the 'boasted American clippers' but it is only by reference to the surviving plans that really accurate comparisons can be made. Although half-models exist of many of the Aberdeen clippers, they do not agree too accurately with the register dimensions, which complicates the assessment, and the table below lists the conflicting measurements. Half-models of the *Scottish Maid, Reindeer, Stornoway, Chrysolite, Cairngorm, Vision* and *Schomberg* were loaned to Glasgow's museum in 1881 for an exhibition and were never returned, so that they survived the fire in Alexander Hall's offices which destroyed the majority of the other models and all the plans. Lines plans of *Stornoway, Chrysolite* and *Cairngorm* were reproduced in *The Tea Clippers* from the above source[61] and plans of *Scottish Maid, Reindeer, Vision* and *Schomberg* are now presented here, as well as a new set of lines of the *Cairngorm*.

A difference of two or three feet in the length may signify nothing more than the addition of a frame or two during the course of construction, but one foot in breadth or depth can make a considerable difference in hull form. In the above list, some discrepancies occur in each ship and perhaps it is only a table of offsets that produces the most reliable evidence of hull form, but these seem very rare and none has been discovered for any of the above ships.

From the *Stornoway*'s published lines, it will be seen that she possesses a good deadrise, rounded bilges, and sides which tumble home to some distance above the load line where they flare out much as in *Reindeer* (figure 145). This feature also appears in the half-models of *Chrysolite* and *Schomberg*. *Stornoway*'s entrance and run are shorter than in *Reindeer*. James Henderon's fine model of *Stornoway* in the Aberdeen Maritime Museum, shows the bow profile, the poop with its rounded sides, the short, sharp entrance, the two deckhouses and probable layout of the rigging. The latter is fairly typical of the day, although some ships would take

Comparison of dimensions for surviving half-models of ships built by Alexander Hall & Sons 1850–56

		Tonnage New	Tonnage Old	Register dimensions of ship (nm Rule)	Dimensions scaled off model
1850	*Stornoway*	527	595	157.8ft × 25.8ft(I) × 17.8ft 28.8ft(X)	157.8ft × 27.6ft(M) × 17.8ft
1851	*Chryoslite*	440	570	149.3ft × 26.1ft(I) × 17.0ft 29.0ft(X)	147.0ft × 27.5ft(M) × 15.5ft
1853	*Cairngorm*	939	1246	193.3ft × 33.6ft(I) × 20.2ft 36.6ft(X)	190.0ft × 35.6ft(M) × 20.2ft
1854	*Vision*	563	720	170.0ft × 27.6ft(I) × 18.2ft 29.3ft(X)	170.0ft × 27.6ft(M) × 19.0ft 156.5ft × 29.5ft(X) × 17.5ft model at Liverpool Museum
1855	*Schomberg*	2284	2600	247.7ft × 42.2ft(I) × 28.9ft 45.5ft(X)	257.7ft × 42.9ft(M) × 25.5ft
1856	*Robin Hood*	853 (reg)	1185	204.0ft × 35.3ft(I) × 21.0ft (by 1854 Rule)	223.0ft × 40.0ft(M) × 22.0ft model in Aberdeen Public Library

(I) internal breadth by NM rule
(M) moulded breadth
(X) maximum external breadth

All the models are at Glasgow Museum, except where stated.
Vision and *Schomberg* were diagonally built without ceiling and so their internal breadth and moulded breadth are almost identical.

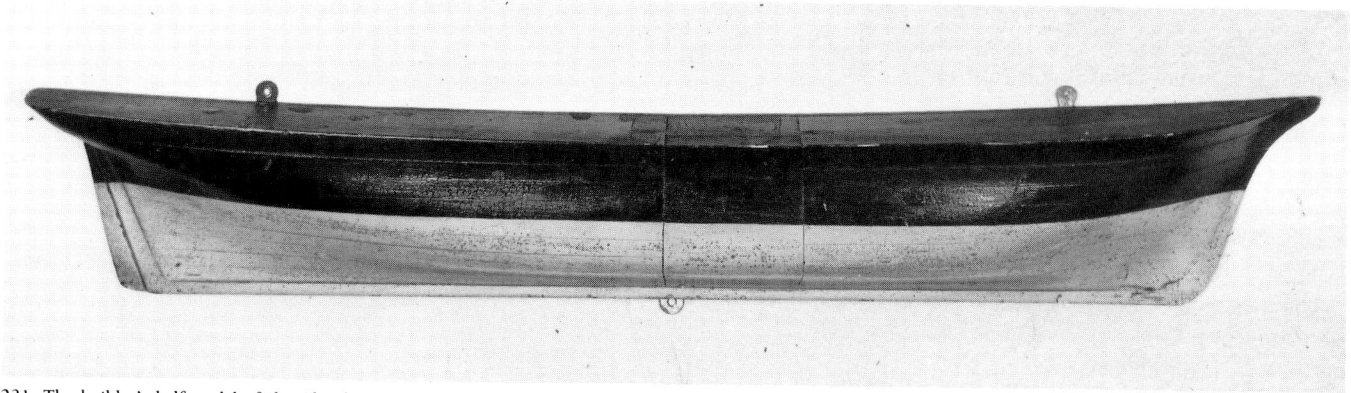

231: The builder's half-model of the Aberdeen clipper *Chrysolite* in the Glasgow Museum. The two saw cuts indicate that a new piece was added to the model during the design process.

232: The builder's half-model of the extreme clipper *Cairngorm*, built by A Hall & Sons in 1853. She had great rise of floor and long, sharp ends. Model in Glasgow Museum.

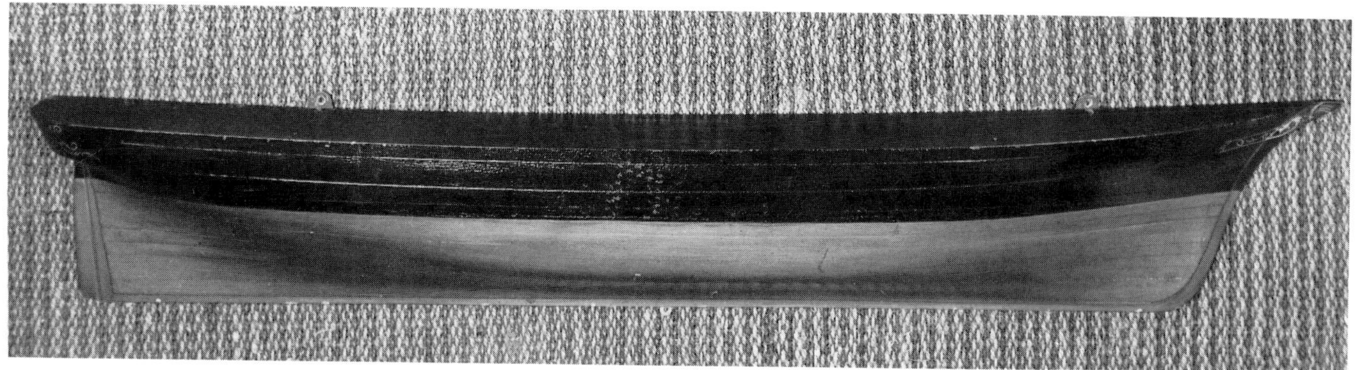

the main stay and main topmast stay across the foremast at a higher point.

The *Chrysolite*, launched in March 1851, seven months after the *Stornoway*, is, according to the half-model, of a different style with a short, sharp, concave entrance, but with a longer concave run; there is considerable deadrise and the floors are hollow; the curve of the bilges is very pronounced and the maximum beam occurs here; the topsides flare out as in *Reindeer*, but in spite of this the breadth at rail height is 18in less than at the bilges. The length and breadth scaled off the model agree moderately well with the register dimensions, but the model's depth of hold is obviously 18in too shallow. In the revised edition of *The Tea Clippers*, I explained how James Henderson had reconstructed her lines plan to overcome this discrepancy by proportionately increasing the spaces between the waterlines.[62] There is no harm in emphasising again the great difference prior to 1855 between internal beam for tonnage measurement and maximum external beam: in *Chrysolite* the former was 26.1ft and the latter 29.0ft. The photograph of her half-model indicates two vertical saw cuts in the centre of the hull, suggesting that the design was modified at some stage and a longer piece inserted.

The *Chrysolite* has a sharper entrance than *Ballarat* and a longer, finer run. She is of roughly the same type as William Webb's clipper *Swordfish*, but with less beam and more deadrise.[63] The *Swordfish* was built at New York in 1851 of 1130 tons and made some fast passages out to San Francisco and home with tea from China.

A short article and lines plan of *Chrysolite* was published in the *Monthly Nautical Magazine*, which John W Griffiths edited at New York, but the lines bear no resemblance to the half-model not to any of Hall's ships for which models exist. In this plan, the rising floors are drawn almost straight with very slack bilges; there is some tumblehome, no flaring topsides, but excessive sheer forward; the stem is definitely not from Aberdeen. The entrance and run are sharp and evenly balanced. The dimensions on which Griffiths based his calculations bear no resemblance to the register dimensions for the actual vessel, nor with the half-model. He was also under the impression that Aberdeen was on the Clyde! The possibility of contemporary corroborative evidence is thus lost.[64]

During the early passages, these Aberdeen clippers beat down the China Sea against the south-west monsoon and averaged 104 to 108 days from Whampoa to England. On her maiden passage, *Chrysolite*'s biggest 24-hour run is given as 320 miles and her highest speed as 14 knots.[65] The load line length on the half-model scales 143ft-3in, which gives a speed-length ratio of 1.17, indicating a fast hull form. The Lloyd's Register surveyor reported that she was 'formed with fine ends and great rise of floor; clipper bow with moderate outreach'.[66]

In the early 1850s, newspapers never tired of repeating the names of *Stornoway* and *Chrysolite*, and later adding *Cairngorm*, when commenting on other clippers or fast passages. Andrew Shewan remembers them as 'sharp-bowed, taunt-rigged, narrow ships, with the peculiar entrance, their planking carried right forward to the stem (with a great rake) and no head knee or cutwater, which did not add to their beauty in my impression'.[67]

For the *Cairngorm*, the Lloyd's surveyor

reported: 'This is a vessel of sharp construction having great rise in floor and finely tapered ends. Stem raked to form cutwater with little overhang. Stern round with full poop, beams of which round down at ends and are united to poop timbers in a circular form along the sides.'[68] This has since been described as a 'half-round' and it became very common in later iron and steel ships.

Detailed particulars were very sparse in the pages of newspapers and the *Aberdeen Journal* published the following account:

> 'LAUNCH OF A MAGNIFICENT CLIPPER.—Last week there was launched, from the building yard of Messrs A Hall and Sons, a splendid clipper-ship, named the "Cairngorm". The vessel, owing to the extreme sharpness of her bottom, was launched on a cradle yesterday week, when there was not sufficient water to float her off; it was then deemed necessary to remove the cradle, and on Saturday the launch was accomplished, to the entire satisfaction of all concerned, and she was floated into the Victoria Dock to receive her equipments. The dimensions of the "Cairngorm" are—length, 200 feet between perpendiculars; extreme breadth, 36½ feet; depth of hold, 20½ feet. Her tonnage is 1250 om, or 980 nm. Messrs Jardine, Mathison, and Co, China merchants, are the owners; and the vessel is built expressly for the China trade. She will be commanded by Captain John Robertson, whose services, first in the "John O'Gaunt", and more recently in the "Stornoway", are well known. In the latter vessel he has, for the last two years, successfully run the race of competition in carrying the first of the new teas from China to this country. The "Cairngorm" is, we believe, the largest sailing vessel ever before built in Scotland; and is certainly about the finest. Her sailing qualities, we are confident, will prove of the very first order, and in carrying power there is every reason to believe she will be equally capable. The "Cairngorm" lies at Waterloo Quay, and is well worth seeing, as an admirable model of a vessel combining immense size with great elegance of appearance.'[69]

233: This engraving of the *Cairngorm* is the only illustration ever found of this famous ship, but fortunately there are spar dimensions and a half-model. It is surprising that Hall continued to give his ships channels right through into the 1860s. *MacGregor Collection.*

It is not absolutely clear from the above account just how much of the launch took place on the first attempt, but the mention of a cradle to support the hull indicates what concern was expressed by the builders to present her yacht-like hull from heeling over as it went down the ways.

The *Illustrated London News*, when publishing her portrait, inferred that owners' wishes had restricted Alexander Hall & Sons' clipper designs, and that the builders decided to design and construct their embodiment of the ideal clipper, which is precisely what Alexander Stephen did with *Storm Cloud* and Benjamin Nicholson with *Annandale*.

After extolling the Aberdeen build, the periodical explained how her design was conceived, in these words:

> 'But while the passage to China has thus been greatly shortened, . . . it was still felt that the Americans had a great advantage in the large size of their clippers, some of them being double the registered tonnage of the largest British ships. To meet this objection,

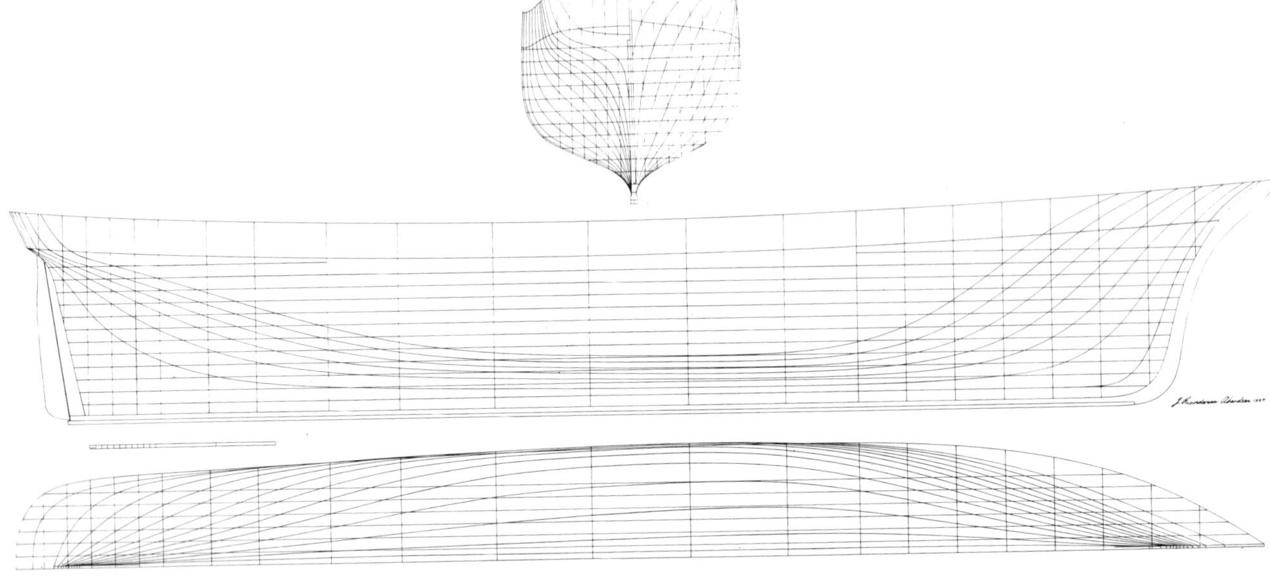

234: *Cairngorm*. Lines plan. Built in 1853 by Alexander Hall & Sons at Aberdeen with register dimensions of 193.3ft × 33.6ft (internal) × 20.2ft, and tonnages of 939 nm and 1246 om. Lines drawn by James Henderson from lines taken off builder's half-model in Glasgow Transport Museum.

235: *Cairngorm* sail plan. Entirely reconstructed by James Henderson. Sources: lines plan; spar dimensions from builder's cost account; engraving of ship in *Illustrated London News*. Although both the latter and the painting of *Mimosa* show no stay from main topmast to head of fore lower mast, I have added one to Henderson's plan. Stunsails would have been set up to the royals.

> the Messrs Hall resolved to lay down a clipper of larger size and finer lines than had been previously built in Scotland; and to construct her so that any purchaser might challenge in good faith the fastest of the American fleet. This vessel was brought under the notice of the house of Jardine, Matheson & Co, through the enterprising commander of their *Stornoway* clipper, Mr Robertson, and purchased for them to bring home the new teas.'[70]

The *Cairngorm* was thus built on speculation. For a vessel of her size, she had enormous deadrise which amounted to 22 degrees along her floors between the hollow garboards and turn of the bilge. Of the American clipper ship plans reproduced by Howard Chapelle in *Search for Speed under Sail*, only *Samuel Russell* (1847) has this amount of deadrise, but without the hollow garboards and with fuller ends. *Nightingale* (1851) also has great deadrise but the midsection profile curves all the way from rabbet to tumblehome.[71]

The *Cairngorm*'s lines have already been published in my work, *The Tea Clippers*.[72] I took lines off her half-model in about 1950 when it was in the Glasgow Museum at Kelvingrove, but this plan was amongst my earliest attempts at drawing a lines plan and certainly needed to be re-drawn to provide such a unique hull form with first-class draughtmanship. When discussing this with my friend, James Henderson, he asked if he might supply a new lines plan of the ship which could accompany his reconstructed sail plan. He accordingly took lines off the builder's half-model in the spring of 1987 in order to prepare a brand-new set of lines, and now the full glory of the *Cairngorm*'s extreme clipper design can be studied.

After being dismasted at the start of her maiden passage, *Cairngorm* sailed from Lisbon to Hong Kong in only 72 days, from 1 May to 12 July 1853. Although only one of her tea-laden passages occupied less than 100 days, she obviously commanded a high rate of freight such as £7 per ton in 1855 and £4 per ton in 1857. Her fastest homeward run was in 1859 when she reached Deal on 5 February, only 91 days from Macao. Although William Pile's *Lammermuir* gave her a close race on this fast passage, Andrew Shewan wrote that *Cairngorm* was the 'acknowledged "Cock of the Walk" ' and was 'considered the crack tea clipper with the exception perhaps of *Robin Hood* (built 1856). There was nothing to equal her in speed, though her day was nearly over.'[73] It hardly mattered that she only classed 7 A1, because Jardine, Matheson & Co owned her and could secure all the best tea they wanted. The smaller quantity of hardwood used in the construction reduced the initial cost from £18.18s. per ton in the case of *Stornoway* down to £14 per ton for her, and the high freights she obtained secured larger profits. When her original class terminated in 1860, she was sold to avoid the cost of repairs necessary for reclassification.

The *Vision* may be considered a smaller version of *Cairngorm* because her lines are so similar. From the plan in figure 236 it will be seen that *Vision*'s midsection is placed about 4ft forward of the mid-point on the load line which makes the entrance slightly shorter than the run. The entrance is, nevertheless, very sharp, long and concave, and the load line even shows concavity; the run is of the same calibre, being beautifully drawn out, with very fine quarters. The quarter-beam buttock is straight where it crosses the load line aft. The hull is given great rise of floor and the hollows at the garboard are continued to the bilge, which is slack with slight tumblehome above. She was launched on 31 December 1853 but as she was not completed until 1854 the latter year becomes the date of build generally assigned to her. Her owner was James Beazley of Liverpool. Her measurements were 170.0ft by 27.6ft (inside) by 18.2ft, 563 tons nm and 720 tons om, which makes her a smaller vessel than *Cairngorm*. The absence of ceiling takes the inside breadth measurement almost to the outer face of the frames thus virtually equating it with the moulded breadth.

There is also a half-model of *Vision* in the Liverpool Museum and the lines of this were taken off by William Salisbury and published in the *Mariner's Mirror*.[74] The dimensions already tabulated show this model to be 13ft-6in shorter than the register dimensions, about correct for breadth after some 10in of

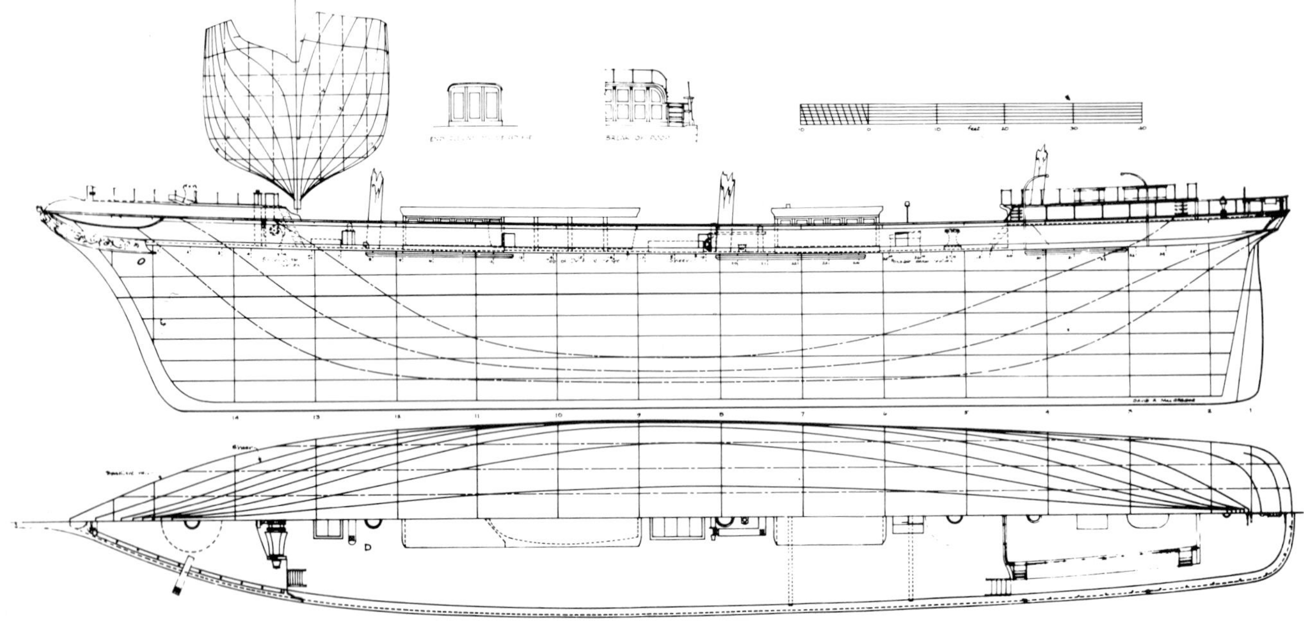

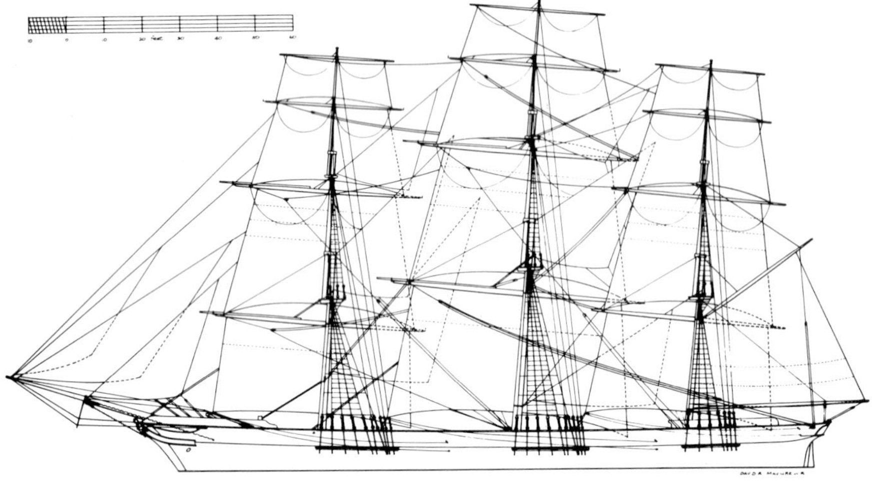

236: *Vision*. Lines plane: Built of wood on diagonal system in 1854 by Alexander Hall & Sons at Aberdeen. Lines taken off half model in Glasgow Museum and drawn to inside of plank. Dimensions by 1836 Act: 170.0ft × 27.6ft (inside) × 18.2ft; tonnages 563 nm and 720 om. Reconstruction: All deck fittings, based on painting of ship by S Walters, owned by Gracie, Beazley & Co., Liverpool, and half-model of ship in Liverpool Museum; Lloyd's Register survey report: and contemporary paintings of other ships built by Hall.

237: *Vision*. Sail plan: Reconstructed from builder's spar dimensions, painting of ship by S Walters, and contemporary illustrations of ships built by Hall; also from research by James Henderson. The spike bowsprit accords with the spar dimensions but is not shown in Walters' painting. No stunsails are listed in the spar dimensions, but a full suit would have been carried.

planking layers are added each side, and 9in too shallow. Compared with the Glasgow half-model, the lines are much fuller and there is considerably less deadrise. The big deadrise on the Glasgow model is confirmed by a drawing with the Register survey which assists establishing the Glasgow half-model's authenticity.

The back-board of the Glasgow model was cut to the same shape as the hull, and allowance had to be made for the total thickness of the keel. The deck details shown here are largely based on the Liverpool model, another model in the possession of James Henderson, the survey report, and a painting of the ship by Samuel Walter which is in the possession of Gracie, Beazley & Co. A curious method of stowing the longboat was adopted, with the deckhouse roof continued over it, and some of the stanchions must have been demountable else the boat would have been a permanent fixture. The American clipper *Witch of the Wave* (1851) had a similar arrangement, in which the boat was placed on rollers for easier handling. The *Vision* was fitted with an Aberdeen house on her quarter-deck. The shape of the topgallant forecastle is most odd.

'This is a very sharp vessel in ends and bottom', remarked the Lloyd's surveyor, 'built upon the diagonal principle; flared stem and bow; round stern, no transomes; main deck runs fore and aft from stem to stern having a round house abaft for cabin, well-raised quarter deck on each side of it and across the after part of it.'[72]

The surveyor then proceeded to give a detailed description of Hall's diagonal construction. The frames were spaced at an average of 4ft-6in centre to centre with a short intermediate floor timber between. One 1¾in skin ran vertically between the frames. Outside the frames, two 1¾in skins of larch and red pine were laid, the one crossing the other diagonally, and for a length of 85ft-0in amidships these diagonal skins ran from gunwale to gunwale without a break, being taken right across the top of the keel. An inner keel separated them from the floors. To do this, the frames must have been shored up outside and temporary blocks between the keel and the floors inserted and removed as the diagonal planking progressed. Forward and abaft this centre section of 85ft-0in the diagonal skins terminated at the keel and

238: The *Bristow* loading grain in bags at King's Lynn at the end of the last century. Her Aberdeen clipper bow is prominent. She was built at Liverpool in 1854.

were rabetted into it. An outer skin of 3½in to 5in thickness was laid longitudinally and rabetted into the keel with garboard strakes in the normal way. The layers of plank were united by treenails cut with a screw thread and formed with a square head; greenheart or African oak was used for these treenails, and they produced an exceedingly solid and highly durable hull. (William Hall had taken out a patent in June 1853 for screw treenails.[76]) The main deck was 3in thick, laid over two diagonal skins, each of which was 1¼in thick. There were beams to alternate frames with long iron hanging knees to each beam.

The *Vision* was the first of five diagonally-built vessels and *Schomberg* was similar in construction. There were also two schooner yachts — the *Kitta Wake* and the *Salamander* — and the ship *Chaa-sze*. A midship section of the *Vision* was published by Alexander Hall & Sons to illustrate their method and this was in turn printed by Andrew Murray in his article on 'Shipbuilding' in the *Encyclopaedia Britannica*.'' However, the shape of the midship section is fuller and with less deadrise than that in the Lloyd's Register survey report or in the Glasgow half-model.

The sail plan has been reconstructed from Walters' painting and the builder's spar dimensions; included in the latter are positions for the mast centres. There are four particular points of interest. First, the greater length given to the yards on the mainmast compared with those on the foremast, and the great length of the main royal yard; the mainyard is one-fifth longer than the fore yard, the difference being 11ft-6in. Second, the foremast is only two feet taller than the mizen, measured from the rail, whereas in most vessels the mizen is appreciably shorter; the yards on the fore are slightly longer than on the mizen, although the fore course has one foot less drop than the crossjack. Third, the yard arms of the fore yard are amazingly short, being only two feet each; perhaps because no reef band was fitted. Fourth, only a spike bowsprit is carried as the spar dimensions do not list a jibboom; many Aberdeen clippers have a bowsprit which is so short that the cap is only a few feet outside the figurehead, hence a single spar would be equally suitable.

The main stay and the main topmast stay are led to the deck at the foot of the pawl post, although to do so they have to pass only a few feet above the fore hatch, and they are also double at this point. But this appears to be normal practice as may be seen in various illustrations such as the photograph of the barque *Emigrant* stranded in the River Avon at Bristol. Many of the features seen in the model of *Stornoway*, both as regards deck fittings and rigging, would be applicable to *Vision*.

On her maiden voyage the *Vision* went out to Hong Kong in only 95 days from Liverpool, from 18 March to 21 June 1854. Then, laden with 720,000 pounds of tea she left Whampoa on 16 July and reached Liverpool 103 days later, on 27 October. The following year this fast passage secured a freight of £6 per ton although her passage on this occasion occupied no less than 139 days. She was wrecked in China in 1857.

Of other ships built by Hall in the early 'fifties, those reported by the Lloyd's Register surveyor as having a 'clipper bow' consisted of *Conqueror, John Taylor, Francis Henty, Hannibal, Marion, Velocidade* and *Woodlark* (brig); *Leichardt* had a 'flared-out stem and bow'. The only ship whose hull form was

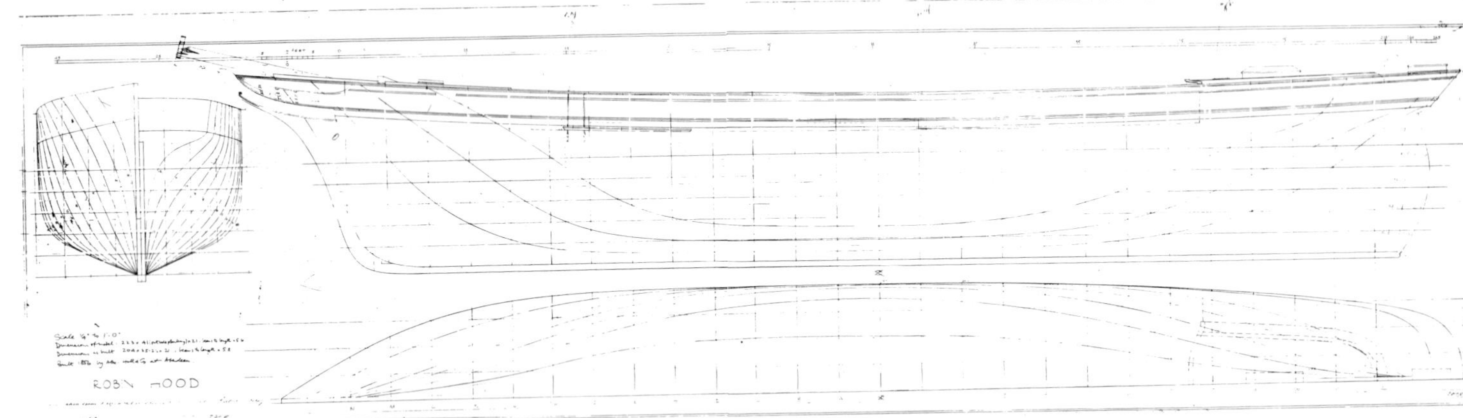

239: *Robin Hood.* Lines plan. Drawn by James Henderson from lines taken off builder's half-model which is now in the Aberdeen Maritime Museum. Built by Alexander Hall & Sons, Aberdeen, in 1856. Dimensions scaled off this plan: 223ft register length, 220ft keel and fore rake, 41ft extreme breadth, 21ft depth of hold (approx). Dimensions of vessel as built: 204ft-0in × 35ft-2½in × 21ft-0in, and tonnages of 853 register and 1185 om. This plan is reproduced from a pencil draught made by James Henderson in 1949 and is not in his present immaculate style.

referred to was the ship *Julia*, built 1852 of 510 new and 624 old tons: 'This is a sharp low vessel with considerable rise in floor formed with the clipper bow and round stern.' It seems reasonable to class her as a clipper, perhaps similar to *Chrysolite*; both had the same breadth, but *Julia* was nine feet longer.[78] Many of the Aberdeen ships were painted green, regardless of who the builder was, although *Cairngorm* is thought to have been black.

Numerous ships built outside Aberdeen had Hall's version of a clipper bow and some examples are seen in paintings, such as that at the Liverpool Museum of the barque *Rapido* which was built at Harrington in 1855 of 328 tons and with a green-painted hull. Another example is the barque *Bristow* built in 1854 at Liverpool on the composite principle; for her an actual photograph exists, as seen in figure 238. This view of the bow shows the application of the trail board and fiddlehead, and due to the wedge shape of the forecastle deck no hair rails can be fitted. She appears to have a reasonably fine entrance, but no plan or model of her is known.

It is a tragedy that the beautiful half-model of the *Robin Hood* obviously does not represent the ship as built and we therefore have no exact knowledge of this ship's hull form. One reads that Alexander Hall & Sons received a *carte blanche* order from James Beazley, who already owned the *Vision*, 'to build a ship that either for speed, strength or finish should not be excelled by any vessel afloat' and that the result was perfect.[79] The *Aberdeen Journal* of 6 November 1856 described her in these words:

> 'LAUNCH.—On Thursday last, there was launched from the spacious new building shed of Messrs Alexander Hall and Sons, a beautiful ship named the "Robin Hood," 1184 tons measurement. This fine vessel has been built to the order of James Beazley, Esq, shipowner, Liverpool, expressly for competing in the yearly race for the first cargo of teas from China in this century. For this particular trade no expense has been spared that experience could devise to eclipse all competitors on that field. The "Robin Hood' is classed 13 years A1 on Lloyd's register of shipping, whose rules would have granted her an additional year, had her owner allowed her to remain two months longer under cover. The "Robin Hood' being an extremely sharp ship was launched on her keel, supported to the extreme ends with midship bilge ways, to steady her upright. She made a beautiful launch, and was lustily cheered by a large concourse of spectators. She was immediately taken under the large harbour shears, where her masts are being put in and her other equipments completed, when she will sail for Liverpool to lay on the berth for China, and will be commanded by an experienced captain in the trade, whose exertions will not be wanting to recover the palm from our Yankee cousins, as it has this year been lost by the "Chrysolite" taking the Sooloo passage home.'

On her maiden voyage a speed of 15 knots has been claimed and a 24-hour run of 364 miles. This in itself required an average of 15⅙ knots so that speeds of at least 17 knots would have been attained at times. Hall's projected design for *Robin Hood*, as illustrated by the half-model now in the Aberdeen Maritime Museum, is for an extreme clipper with greater breadth in proportion to length than his previous ships and of a design broadly similar to the lines of the American extreme clipper *Sweepstakes*, both as regards the long sharp entrance and run, and also in the steep deadrise and straight floors, although *Robin Hood*'s model has no tumblehome.[80] Her half-model, made to ¼in-scale, is built of mahogany and is a superb example of craftsmanship. In 1960, this model was at the Aberdeen Public Library which could find no better place to hang it than the men's wash room, which is where I saw it. It was subsequently damaged but has now been restored.

John and William Pile

These two brothers have many clipper ships attributed to them, but no plans or models of this type appear to have survived of ships of the 1850s, which renders an effective appraisal of their designs impossible and the correct attribution of the term 'clipper' a matter of guesswork. Although there is a half-model of the *Chowringhee* and a lines plan of the *Roxburgh Castle*, both of which William built in the 'fifties, neither are of the clipper model. The *Crest of the Wave* which William built in 1853 has a coefficient of under deck tonnage of .55 which is the same figure as *Cutty Sark*, thus inferring a very fine-lined hull. As to performance, her maiden passage was one of 73 days from Liverpool to Melbourne in 1854, which was considered very fast.

John Pile built *Spirit of the North* (1853), *Flying Dragon* (1853) and *Spirit of the Age* (1854), all of which were said to be clipper build. An engraving of the *Flying Dragon* was

240: The barque *Flying Dragon* was typical of ships built by John Pile of Sunderland.

printed in the *Illustrated London News* and her measurements were given as 190ft-0in (overall) by 31ft-6in by 18ft-1in, with 675 new and 780 old tons.[81] On her maiden passage she sailed from the River Wear to the Thames in 28 hours, and then made the passage to Melbourne in 77 days from Deal. All these three were barque-rigged.

Other ships built by these two brothers which claim to be clippers are the *Norna* (1851), brig *Lizzie Webber* (1852), *Mirage* (1855) by John Pile; also the *Aurora* (1852), *Spray of the Ocean* (1854), *Kelso* (1855), and *Lammermuir* (1856) by William Pile. A whole-hull model of the *Mirage* is in the West Hartlepool Museum but she has been rigged as a brigantine and set in a sea, thus making it impossible to measure the hull. A brig named *Annie Dixon* was described in a contemporary report as having an Aberdeen clipper bow and a Baltimore clipper bottom, and that her model was exhibited at the Paris Exhibition of 1855.

William Pile continued to build on the Wear all his life. The earliest set of lines for one of his clippers comes from a half-model of the iron ship *Ganges* (1861); the only half-model of one of his tea clippers is the second *Maitland* (1856), lines of which appear in figure 312.

The last ship built on the Wear by John Pile was the *Port Jackson*, launched in March 1854, but she was taken round and coppered in his new yard at West Hartlepool; and the first ship to be built in his new yard was the China clipper *Mirage*, launched in December 1854 but completed in 1855. During the 1850s he built nine sailing ships there as well as 18 steamers. His activities continued during the 'sixties in many other fields, such as running a line of steamers to the Continent and owning his own blast furnaces, rolling mills and foundry. Unfortunately, when the bankers Overend, Gurney & Co failed in 1866, he was forced into liquidation, and Denton, Gray & Co took over his yard. The firm had become Pile, Spence & Co in about 1860, when Joseph Spence was admitted to partnership. Paintings exist of many of John Pile's ships, but no plans or models are known.[82]

American and Canadian clippers

No direct evidence has come to light that British builders actually copied American clipper ship design even though American maritime writers have claimed as much. After the lifting of the Navigation Laws, American clippers made many passages to British ports with tea from China, and the *Oriental* had her lines taken off at the end of 1850 or early the following year in Green's Blackwall Yard. But for the reasons given in my book *The China Bird*, the *Challenger*, which Richard Green completed in January 1852 for the tea trade, bore no evidence of American influence.[83] Later, the huge American clipper

241: A rigged model of the American clipper ship *Light Brigade*, the hull of which is composed of contrasting laminations of wood, suggesting it is an old model or one built in a shipyard. This clipper was built in 1854 by J O Curtis at Medford, Mass, and originally bore the name *Ocean Telegraph*. Tonnage was 1495. *MacGregor Collection*.

Challenge had her lines taken off in London, but this did not happen until the end of 1852 and no plans of any British clippers have been discovered which could be called copies of her.

British shipbuilders undoubtedly took note of American vessels as they would have been curious to see ships which had been written up in the papers. The Glasgow shipbuilder, William Simons, listed the spar dimensions of the *Star of Empire* and *Sovereign of the Seas*, both by Donald McKay, and the *Red Jacket* designed by Samuel Pook. (He also listed the spars of Stephen's iron clipper *Typhoon* and of numerous other Scottish vessels, possibly because he sometimes built spars in timber or iron for other yards.[84]) In his notebooks, Alexander Stephen Jnr listed spar dimensions of the American ships *Enoch Train* and the *Queen of Clippers*, the latter being acknowledged to the *New York Tribune*; on 18 July 1854, he sketched the bows of *Champion of the Seas* at Liverpool.[85] Occasionally, Stephen's took an American vessel on their slipway for repairs, such as the three-masted schooner *Eckford Webb*, which explains why a copy of her sail plan was found amongst their plans, but they did not copy the design. Alexander Stephen Jnr also knew of John W Griffith's book on naval architecture and may even have possessed a copy. Sometimes the British newspapers devoted half a column to a detailed description of an American clipper – a description possibly copied verbatim from the Boston *Atlas* where spar dimensions and scantlings were listed in detail.

William Webb designed and built a large number of clippers at his yard in New York, but none was more extreme than the *Challenge* which was constructed for NL & G Griswold of New York in 1851 and was intended to be the finest and fastest clipper afloat. She measured 230ft-6in by 43ft-2in by 26ft-0in and 2006½ tons register. Webb's

242: This painting by the well-known marine artist John Stobart portrays the American clipper ship *Comet* which William H Webb built in 1851 of 1836 tons. The artist has shown her with double topsails which were presumably Howes' patient. In 1854 she took only eighty-three days twenty-one hours, pilot to pilot, on a passage from Liverpool to Hong Kong.

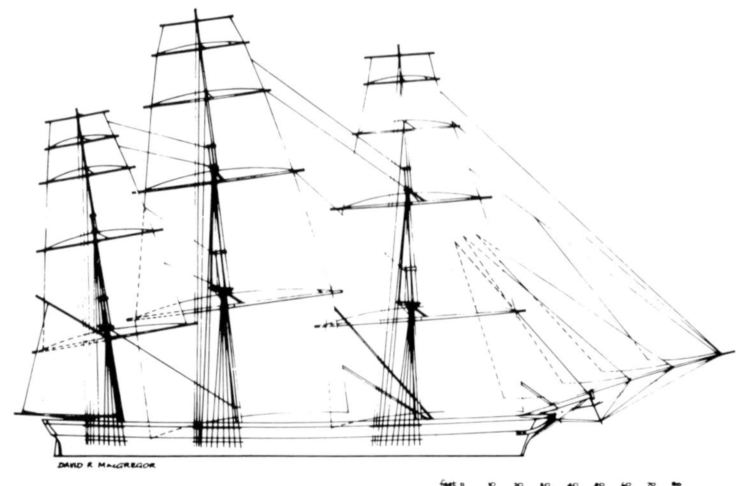

243: *Nightingale.* Sail plan: Entirely reconstructed from hull profile, mast positions and rake of masts on lines plane. Sources for reconstruction: spar dimensions from *American Clipper Ships* by O T Howe and F C Matthews 1927, vol II, p. 427, with exception of bowsprit, jibboom, flying jibboom, spanker boom and gaff; rigging from oil painting of ship in *American Sail* by Alexander Laing, 1961, p. 264.

244: *Nightingale.* Lines plane: Built in 1851 by Samuel Hanscom Jnr, at Portsmouth, New Hampshire. Redrawn from plan drawn by G Hillmann (probably in Liverpool c. 1860) in the Mariner's Museum, Newport News. Dimensions (customs measurement): 185.0ft × 36.0ft × 20.0ft; 1060 tons. Dimensions on plan: 171ft-3in (length on load waterline) × 35ft-0in (moulded breadth) × 20ft-0in (depth of hold); 1100 tons burthen. Reconstruction: figurehead and trailboards.

ships usually had a short sharp entrance, so his design for the *Challenge* formed a radical departure from his normal practice. Her entrance was very sharp and concave, even at the load line; there was considerable deadrise with rounded bilges which flowed into the tumblehome; the maximum beam was placed midway between the foremast and mainmast, and then the extremely long run flowed aft with much hollowness in the lower body. She had a long, open deck with only a small deckhouse abaft the foremast, a very short poop, and only a monkey forecastle. The owners secured Robert Waterman from the *Sea Witch* as master and, in superintending her construction and outfit, he obliged Webb to increase the lengths of the masts and spars considerably beyond what had been designed for her. The distance across from the outer leech of one of her square lower stunsails to the outer leech of the other was 160ft. The sail plan reproduced here shows that her upper yards were short although she was very lofty. She was undoubtedly 'overhatted' and this probably contributed to her poor performance on the maiden voyage.[86]

She was launched on 24 May 1851 and her maiden passage to San Francisco took 108 days, but Waterman had to relinquish his command after a near-mutiny and other problems. She crossed over to Hong Kong and on the return trip was only 18 days from opposite Japan to San Francisco, which remains the record.[87] Recrossing the Pacific she loaded tea at Whampoa for London and leaving in August 1852 took 105 days to the Downs. Attempts were made to compare her passage with that of the British clipper *Challenger*, presumably because of a similarity of names, but the latter had taken her departure a week earlier from Shanghai which was 850 miles dead to leeward in the south-west monsoon and the equivalent of one or two weeks' sailing.

The appearance of these huge wooden clippers in British waters created intense interest throughout the kingdom, but only a single British ship was built to respond to this competition. This clipper was the *Schomberg* and she will be discussed in the next section. For the most part, British owners could obtain large wooden ships for the asking from Canadian shipyards and again there is no evidence that British builders copied them or even wished to do so. In one instance the

245: *Challenge*, built in 1851 by William Webb at New York. Lines plan redrawn and reconstructed by E N Wilson from take-off (dated 1852) in National Maritime Museum. Dimensions: 230ft-6in × 43ft-2in × 26ft-0in and 2006 tons.

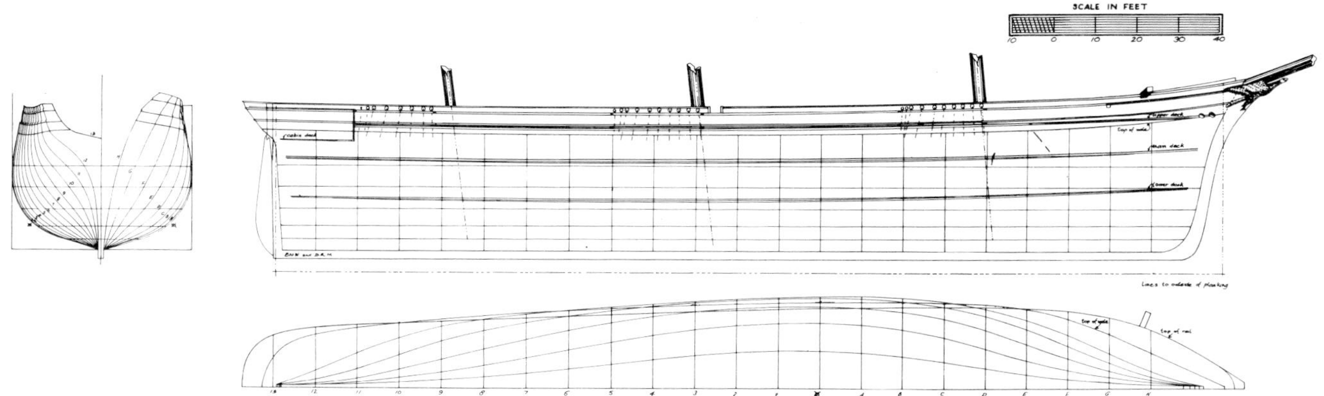

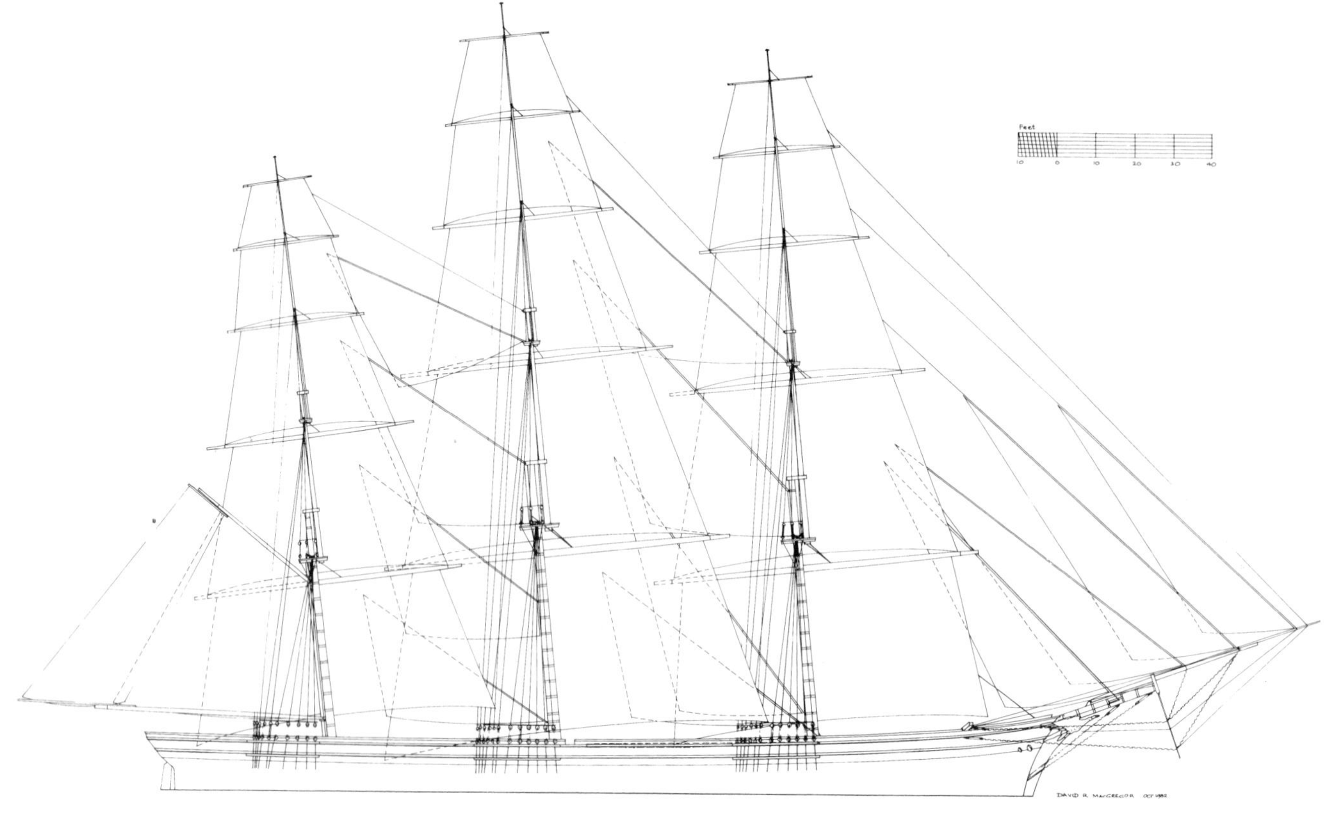

246: *Challenge*. Sail plan. Entirely reconstructed to show ships as first built. Sources: lines plan; spar dimensions listed on plan of lines taken off in London, December 1852, by Admiralty Surveyors and from spars in Howe & Matthews' *American Clipper Ships* (1926); headsails based on Lebreton's lithograph.

reverse proved to be the case when the St John shipbuilder, Walter Brown, commissioned a design from the British naval architect, Oliver Lang, and the resulting ship was christened *Oliver Lang*. The popular *Marco Polo* was frequently credited with fast and satisfactory passages, yet no copies of her extraordinarily deep hull were perpetrated over here. If British naval architects and builders had sincerely wanted to copy American clippers they would not have attempted to fill in the *Lightning*'s hollow bows. As Howard Chapelle once remarked: 'The English development was independent of American evolution of the clipper. Both were the product of trade requirements, but the requirements were not the same for each, and thus the design characteristics of English and American clippers were quite different.'[88]

Of the many Canadian ships achieving distinction with fast passages in the Australian trade, none was better known than *Marco Polo* whose maiden passage to Australia took only 68 days to sighting Cape Otway. A half-model of the ship has survived and is located at the Mariner's Museum, Newport News. John R Stevens measured it there and drew out a set of lines which is reproduced here through his courtesy (figure 247).

The *Marco Polo* was built to carry a large cargo and was fitted with bow ports for the loading of timber.[89] Her great depth of hold must have made her an ideal ship for the cotton trade where bulk rather than weight had to be catered for. Her measurements by the 1836 Registry Act were 184.1ft by 36.3ft by 29.4ft, with tonnages of 1625 nm and 1400 om.[90] The half-model measures approximately three feet longer than this given length, and the moulded breadth is 38 feet which is almost correct. Lloyd's Register assigns her a class of 6 A1. Although her design was conceived 12 months before the discovery of Australian gold she was, according to Frederick W Wallace, of 'sharper model under water than the usual craft built at St John'.[91] Her builder and first owner was James Smith. Her excessive depth is the most prominent feature of

247: *Marco Polo*. Built of wood in 1851 by James Smith at St John, New Brunswick. Lines taken off builder's half-model in Mariner's Museum, Newport News and drawn by John R Stevens. Dimensions in 1852 in England: 184.1ft × 36.3ft × 29.4ft; tonnages of 1625 nm and 1400 om. Reconstruction: position of masts; head rails and figurehead; cathead; painted ports.

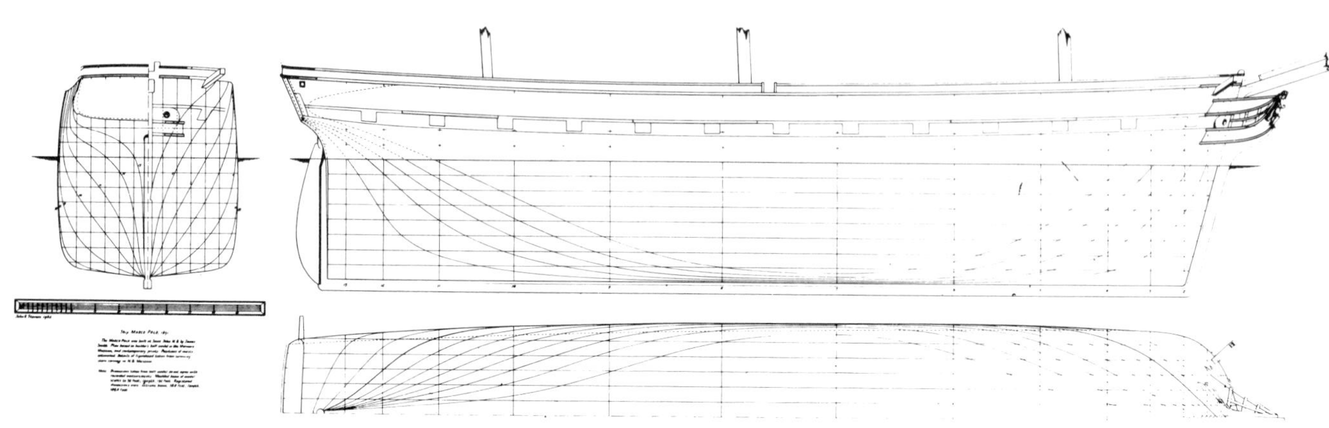

her design, and her flat floors, hard bilges and wall sides give her an almost rectangular midship section. The entrance is short and sharp with some hollow in the lowest waterlines. Her run is longer, slighly concave at the load line and considerably so below that. There are heavy quarters and she has a broad, square stern decorated with an elephant's head and a figure of Marco Polo reclining gracefully at each side; the bow is cumbersome with a full-length figurehead of Marco Polo himself.[92] The unusual form of the ship was noticed by the reporter of the *Illustrated London News* who referred to 'the peculiarity of her hull' as her 'distinguishing feature'.[93] Taken altogether, the hull form represents a very powerful ship possessing good stability from which a daring and capable could extract a high turn of speed; and it was her good fortune to be commanded successively by two such men on her first three voyages to Australia.

Her maiden voyage was across the Atlantic to Liverpool which she reached on 19 June 1851 19 days out from St John. Then she sailed to Mobile and brought back a cargo of cotton in 35 days. Lloyd's Register shows that Smith remained the owner during this period. On her return from Mobile in 1852, James Baines bought her in Liverpool, possibly from an intermediary called Paddy McGee. He realised her potential as a large passenger ship and immediately set about fitting her out as one of his Black Ball Line of packets to Australia. It is reported that she cost £9,000 delivered in Liverpool, but that on her first voyage to Australia she 'netted the handsome sum of £13,000'.[94]

The Parliamentary report on 'Mortality in Emigrant Ships' gives some useful information of the deck arrangements in the *Marco Polo*. She had a topgallant forecastle extending to within three feet of the foremast; abaft the foremast was the forehatch. This indicates that the mast was placed well forward. Aft of the hatch came a large deckhouse measuring 30ft-0in long and 22ft-8in wide and with a gangway of only seven feet on each side. The main hatch was placed abaft this deckhouse followed by the mainmast in the usual way. The poop extended to within seven feet of the mizen, leaving a gangway on each side of only 4ft-8in. This suggests that the centre portion of the poop projected more than at the sides, a fairly common arrangement. The deckhouse between the fore and main hatchways was due to be removed before her second voyage, as the charter party did not permit it. The clear height on the main deck was 7ft-9in and on the lower deck 7ft-4in, although the Passenger Acts only called for six feet in the clear. From the lines plan and the depth of hold, it can be calculated that the bulwarks were about six to seven feet high.[95]

248: This painting of the *Marco Polo* was executed by Captain Tom Robertson. The late David M Little who sent me a photograph of the painting considered it a good likeness of the ship.

Her fittings were considered better than those usually found in Liverpool ships, but the galleys were too small, the plumber's work was bad, and the skylights and ventilators were carelessly made. On the other hand the wcs were in good condition, although it was observed that many emigrants had probably never seen one before. (The *Ticonderoga* which carried 795 passengers was provided with 20 WCs.) An area of 15 square feet was allowed for each person below deck. In the *Marco Polo*, the provisions and water were reported to be good, and the regulations were enforced. The ship carried a surgeon, an assistant surgeon, a matron and a 'religious instructor'. On the passage out in 1852 she carried 930 emigrants: there were 52 deaths — nearly all infants — and nine births, but the ship was considered clean and orderly on arrival, which was very different from the scene of confusion and disorder at the time of departure, when drunkenness and fighting amongst emigrants and sailors was common. On such occasions the ship's band was a

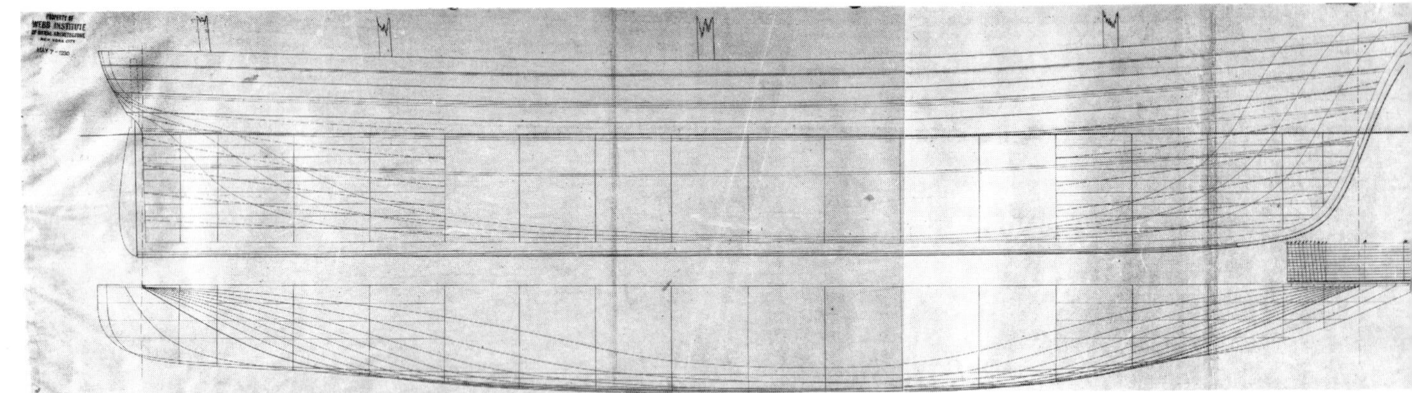

249: *Great Republic*. Lines plan. Drawn by G Hillmann and photographed from a plan in the Mariners Museum, Newport News. Built in 1853 by Donald McKay at East Boston. Dimensions of ship as first built: 335ft × 53ft × 38ft and 4555 tons.

250: Right-hand half of a stereo photograph showing the *Great Republic* at San Francisco when rigged as a four-masted barque. Her first voyage there was in 1856-7 and her last in 1864. *National Maritime Museum, San Francisco.*

decided asset, to cheer up everyone's spirits. The charter party in 1852 allowed a crew of 70 but this was considered excessive and was reduced to 59.[96]

Before 1852, the duration of an outward passage to Australia was rarely less than 100 to 120 days, and the 76 days taken in 1850 between Plymouth and Port Adelaide by the barque *Constance*, was considered sensational. Thus the time of only 68 days, land to land, occupied by the *Marco Polo* in 1852, placed her in the forefront of the passenger trade.

This passage by the *Marco Polo* lasted from 4 July 1852, when she left Liverpool, until she reached Melbourne on 20 September, which gives an elapsed time of 78 days. She sighted Cape Otway on 10 September, 68 days out from England; she passed through Port Phillip Heads on 16 September and then touched a sandbank. She returned to Liverpool in 77 days, from 10 October to 26 December. On the next voyage, still under Captain Forbes, she was 76 days from Bardsey Island to Port Phillip Heads, and returned to Liverpool in 97 days, having spent five days among ice in 60 degrees south latitude. On her third voyage she was commanded by Charles MacDonnell and was towed to Cork by two steam tugs. Leaving that port on 12 November 1853, she was off the Tuskar Light in southern Ireland on 16 November from where she was only 69 days to Port Phillip Heads, which were reached on 24 January 1854. Running ashore the following day, she was hove off undamaged six days later and proceeded to Melbourne. On a subsequent passage to Melbourne in 1855–56, the *Marco Polo* carried one milch cow, 30 sheep, 30 pigs, 360 fowl, and a large supply of rabbits, hares and game. A band, a printing press for a newspaper, and photographic equipment were also available to the 520 passengers, but as her

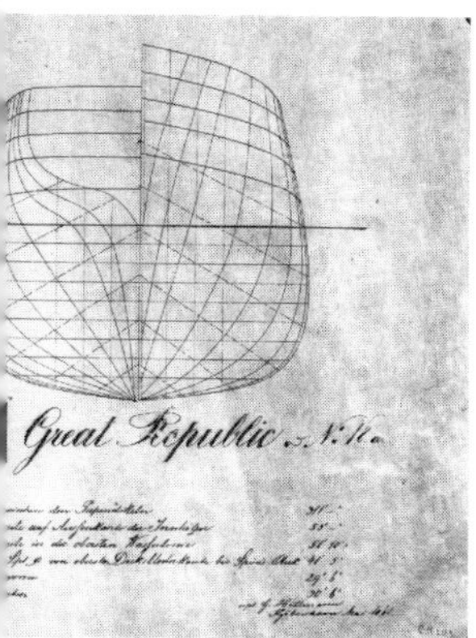

owners contracted to deliver the mails in 65 days, one wonders if the passengers had much peace.[97]

The following incident was one of many which coloured the career of the *Marco Polo*, and relates to the end of her first passage to Australia in 1852:

> 'On arrival of the *Marco Polo* at Melbourne, such was the excitement on account of her rapid passage, that the people threw small nuggets of gold on board amongst the crew. The crew having become unruly, Captain Forbes had the whole of them imprisoned till his departure, and thus was able to get off again without loss of time. Many ships are laid up in Melbourne from want of hands, which cannot be obtained at any price. One ship had advertised for men at the rate of £30 per month, but no application was made.'[98]

On his visit to Liverpool in the summer of 1853, Donald McKay secured an order from James Baines to build four large clippers for the Australian run, the first of which was the *Lightning*, delivered in March 1854. She was followed by the *Champion of the Seas* and *James Baines*, both delivered in 1854, and the *Donald McKay*, completed in 1855. McKay's 'inconsistency in design', as Howard Chapelle calls it, is apparent in these four ships: *James Baines* was an extreme clipper but not quite so sharp as *Lightning; Champion of the Seas* was slightly fuller in the ends than the former, whereas *Donald McKay* was only a medium clipper with a deep, flat-floored hull and fullish ends; *Lightning* on the other hand was an extreme clipper with a very fine, hollow entrance and run.[99] James Baines was presumably astute enough to realise the coming depression in the Australia trade and to instruct McKay to build the last of the quartette on fuller lines.

The lines of the *Lightning* are here reproduced in figure 251 to show one version of an extreme American clipper. This plan was redrawn from the ⅛in-scale plan in the Clark Collection.[100] By British standards the midsection is unusual for its fullness, with the almost flat floors rounding into bilges that are kept low, and with considerable tumblehome above. The run is long and concave and the entrance even exceeds this with considerable hollow along the load line. The midsection is placed abaft the middle point of the load line, thus agreeing broadly with JW Griffith's theories for a fast ship. The draught line is low due to the preponderance of passengers on two decks and the minimum of cargo, which made the large passenger ships dry vessels in big seas. Although she was not deep, the *Lightning* has more beam in proportion to length than most British clippers, her measurements being 237.5ft on deck, 44.0ft extreme breadth, 23.0ft depth of hold and 2084 tons. On the dimensions, the ratio is 5.4 beams to length. The deck of the topgallant forecastle joins the top of the big deckhouse abaft the foremast and from thence a gangway each side connects with the forward end of the long poop. Later in life the poop and forecastle were completely joined, making a continuous fourth deck with an open bulwark railing on all sides. Needless to say, the sail area was immense with a mainyard 95ft-0in long. The spar dimensions given in America when the ship was new make provision for a skysail on the mainmast only, but because all contemporary illustrations show skysails on all three masts and a moonsail above the main skysail, it is probable that new and longer topgallant masts were made and fidded in England. Alternatively, sliding gunter masts or separate royal masts could have been fidded, but there is no evidence to this effect.

The maximum speed in knots claimed for *Lightning* is 19, but 21 knots were achieved

251: *Lightning*. Built of wood in 1854 by Donald McKay at Boston, Mass. Drawn from lines plan in Clark Collection at Francis Russell Hart Nautical Museum, Massachusetts Institute of Technology. Dimensions: 237.5ft (length on deck) × 44.0ft (extreme breadth) × 23.0ft (depth of hold); 2084 tons. Reconstruction: Figurehead; lower masts and bowsprit, but lengths are from contemporary records.

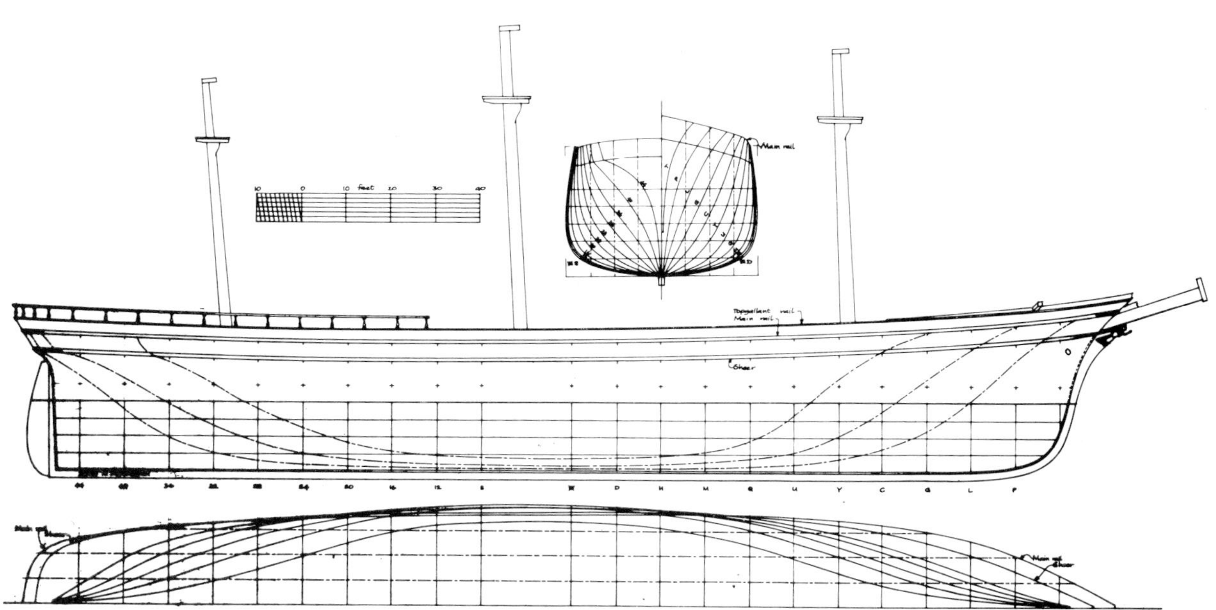

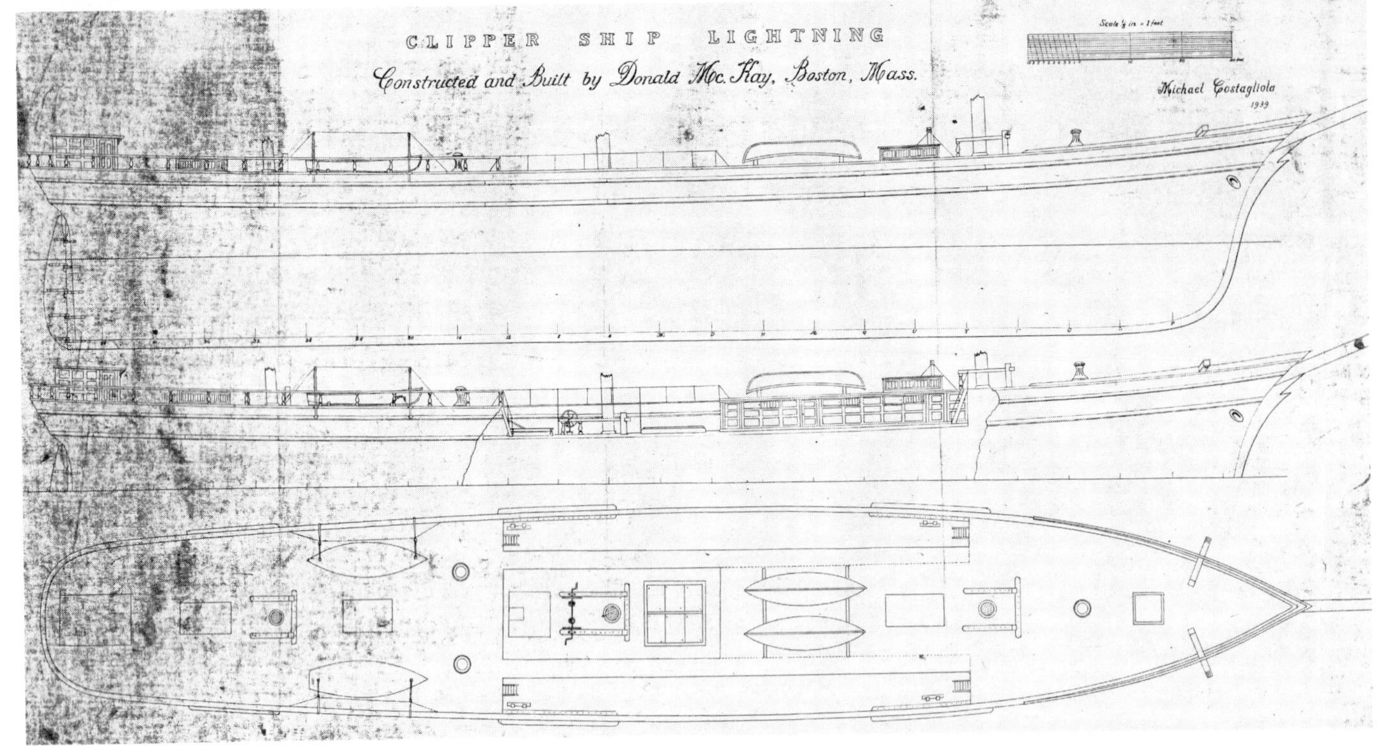

252: *Lightning* General arrangement plans. Drawn by Michael Costagliola and reconstructed from contemporary descriptions, especially Duncan McLean's account in the *Atlas* of Boston, dated 8 February 1854.

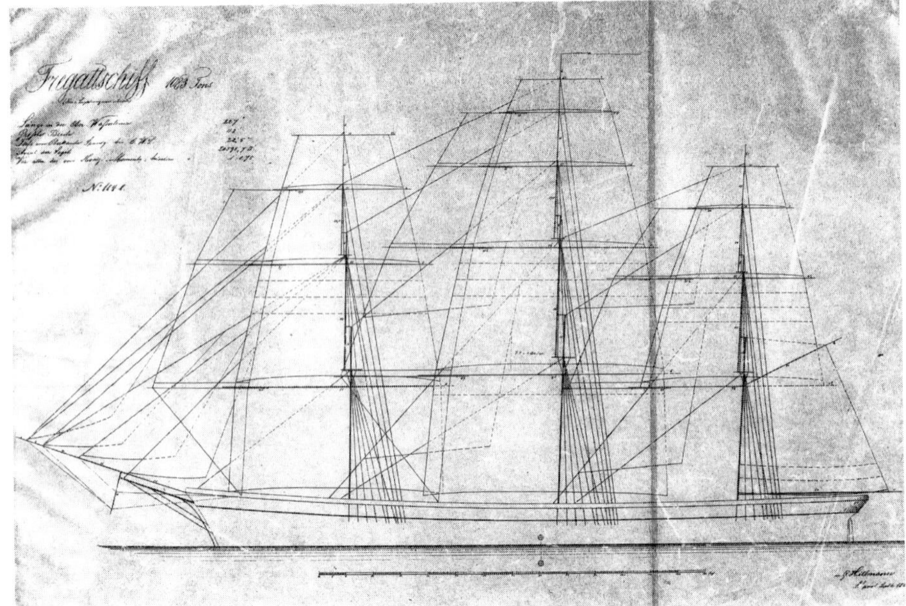

253: Fregattschiff. Sail plan of unnamed ship, signed and dated: 'G Hillmann L'pool Sept 8 1862'. Reproduced from plan in Mariner's Museum, Newport News. Dimensions (given on plan): 227ft-0in (length on waterline); 45ft-0in (maximum breadth); 22ft-5in (depth below LWL); 1083 tons. Sail area 20,595.7 sq ft. This in all probability represents the *Lightning*, because the measurements are almost identical with the exception of the tonnage. The great beam of this ship could not result in a tonnage as small as 1083, and the explanation may be that Hillmann inadvertently wrote this figure instead of 2083, which is the *Lightning*'s tonnage. A feature of this plan is the great area of square canvas which has been achieved by breadth rather than height. By contrast, the area of fore-and-aft canvas is small. The presence of stunsails on the mizen is unusual. Many of the spar dimensions agree with those of *Lightning* as first built, including the mainyard of 95ft-0in.

by *James Baines*, and 20 by *Champion of the Seas; Sovereign of the Seas* claimed 22 knots, and several of the big American passenger clippers reported similar speeds. In the matter of noon to noon runs, Carl Cutler has collected 14 which are more than 400 miles. The greatest is for *Champion of the Seas* which reported 465 miles between 11 and 12 December 1854; next comes a doubtful one for *Flying Scud* of 449 miles; then 438 for *Marco Polo*; 436, 430 and 421 for *Lightning*; 423, 407 and 404 for *James Baines*; 421 for *Donald McKay*, and so on.[101] This subject has always provoked discussion but in the *Mariner's Mirror* in 1957 and 1958 sufficient arguments were advanced to show that many of these fast runs were not mythical but fully capable of attainment. Many of the ships obtaining these speeds were British-owned at the time with British masters; they were large ships, designed for speed, and carrying cargoes considerably less in tonnage than their register. Many of the large iron and steel ships of later years attained high speeds in knots and big 24-hour runs in the 380-mile range, but they were primarily designed to carry huge bulk cargoes. So what could not a large ship, designed for speed, achieve?[102]

The sailing ships which received the biggest amount of publicity in the British or Australian press were undoubtedly the American-built ships for the Liverpool Black Ball and White Star lines. These ships made news wherever they went, and the Melbourne *Argus* quoted verbatim the fulsome reports which first appeared in the Boston *Atlas*. Perhaps the owners studied public relations by ensuring that their masters were furnished with full press comments to hand over to other reporters and so secure free advertising matter. Probably the only British-built sailing ships to receive such lengthy press reports, but lacking the technicalities of the Boston reporter, were the *Schomberg* and the *Storm Cloud*; most other British ships received a paragraph or two, but without much technical detail.

In those days, newspaper readers quite obviously gained their news because a certain clipper had outdistanced its rivals and so brought 'advices' of a week or so later. For instance, the fall of Sebastopol and the arrival of the iron clipper *John Bell* were reported in the same headline of the *Tasmanian Daily News*.

255: *Red Jacket:* Lines plan: Built in 1853 by George Thomas at Rockland, Maine, from a design by Samuel H. Pook of Boston. Redrawn from plan and spar dimensions in *The United States Nautical Magazine and Naval Journal*, 1856, vol. IV, between pp. 198-9. Dimensions: 251.2.ft × 44.0ft × 31.0ft; 2305 tons. Reconstruction: forefoot and forward end of keel; mast positions from spar dimensions in above Journal (these do not agree with mast positions on published plan); rigging from contemporary illustrations of ship; sail outlines; spar diameters based on contemporary American clippers; figurehead; mizen trysail mast; hoops to lower masts and bowsprit; rudder. No stunsails are listed in the dimensions, but they would have been carried. In spite of the very long lower yards there is practically no overlap to the sails.

254: A spirited engraving of Donald McKay's huge clipper *James Baines* under full sail, taking troops out to the Indian Mutiny in 1857. She is carrying sky stunsails, and a moonsail on the mainmast.

Contemporary newspapers enjoyed reporting the achievements of the clippers in terms usually reserved for a steeplechase, but perhaps the account in the Melbourne *Argus* of the 'Great Ocean Regatta' between *Red Jacket* and *Lightning* was the most original:

'The race is, as our readers know, from the mouth of the Mersey to Hobson's Bay, round the white buoy off Gellibrand's Point, and back — an open course.' And so on. The 'first heat' for the whole course was won by *Lightning* with 162 days to the 164 of *Red Jacket*.[103]

The average day's run for a passage of less than 70 days to Melbourne worked out at about 200 miles per day, which made sail a very sound commercial proposition. The gross earnings of the *Red Jacket* on her passage from Melbourne to Liverpool in 1855 amounted to £12,500: the 2305-ton ship was full with cargo, passengers, mail and 138,643 ounces of gold. During 1855 the White Star Line and the Black Ball Line each contracted with the Post Office to dispatch one ship per month to Australia with the mails, the regular steamers having been chartered for the Crimean War; the Black Ball Line rashly agreed to land its mail within 65 days and accepted a penalty clause.

It is difficult to assess the clipper attributes of Canadian ships because plans are so scarce, although authentic descriptions can sometimes be found. In an effort to surpass his

256: The Canadian clipper ship *Star of the East* hove-to. She was built for the Australian gold rush in 1852 by W & R Wright at St John, New Brunswick, of 1219•tons. The skysail masts are gunter poles, rigged abaft the royal masts.

fellow shipbuilders, Walter Brown of St John commissioned the British naval architect Oliver Laing to design a ship for him, and the product, christened *Oliver Laing*, was launched in 1853. She measured 1236 tons nm.

Her lines plan in the New Brunswick Museum shows a vessel that is reminiscent of one of Laing's warship designs, particularly in the run and profile. She has a long, fine entrance and the top of the topgallant forecastle was very wedge-shaped on plan. She was also owned by James Baines.

A ship built the previous year for which I have found no plans but which was probably of clipper status was the *Star of the East*. A contemporary description paints a fine picture of the new ship on her arrival in Liverpool, and I have quoted it in full, with the exception of the reference at the beginning to the engraving which appeared above it because the painting of the ship in figure 256 is so much clearer.

> 'The beautiful Clipper, "Star of the East," [was] launched in the early part of this year at St John's, New Brunswick. She was built by the celebrated firm of William and R Wright, who constructed the famous Clippers "Constance," "Miles Barton," and other vessels well known in the Australian trade. She made her first voyage across the Atlantic, against strong north-east winds, under twenty days, beating by several days two of the crack St John ships. Her arrival at Liverpool caused the greatest sensation in nautical circles; and as she lay in the river for two days after her arrival, she was the centre of attraction to every eye, and the general conclusion on all hands was that her equal had never before been seen on the Mersey. The symmetry of her appearance made her true size very doubtful, and it was only on close inspection that any one could believe she was a ship of 1,219 tons instead of 700. Most people took her for a yacht, from the exquisite proportions of her hull and spars, and much surprise was manifested by many when they were informed that she was a veritable merchantman, with a cargo of deals on board. She was almost immediately purchased by Mr James Beazley, of Liverpool, and as promptly secured by Messrs Millers and Thompson for their Golden Line of Australian Packets. She was purchased for £16,000, the largest sum ever paid for a colonial ship.
>
> 'A brief description of her hull and fittings will be interesting. Although extremely sharp fore and aft, she has great beam, which makes her a most comfortable vessel in a seaway. The principal dimensions of her hull are as follows:—Length of keel, 206 feet; over all, 237 feet; beam, 40 feet 10 inches; depth of hold, 22 feet; register, 1,219 tons; depth of keel and kelson, through and through, 8 feet 8 inches (17 inches sided). The trusswork forward is most substantial from the keel up, for the support of the sharp bow, which is ornamented with a full-length female figure-head, richly gilt. She is copper-fastened throughout. Her stern is elliptical, and, with the quarters, ornamented by a neat design in gilt scroll-work, the "Star" being conspicuous, and in which two circular windows are ingeniously and prettily introduced as part of the pattern. Her deck arrangements are very compact, and the houses include galleys, hospital, two forecastles for the seamen, &c, the ship's "people" being well cared for. She has a long poop-house aft, with passages on either side, and containing two saloons. The fore one is 44 feet long, and is chastely ornamented in white and gilt pannelling. There are ten state-rooms here, fitted with every convenience. The after-cabin is 30 feet long, and contains four state-rooms. This apartment is superbly finished with panellings and pilasters of mahogany, satinwood, and rosewood. A rich carpet, handsome mirrors, and chairs, tables, and lounging sofas, give the chief saloon an air of ease and comfort equal to a drawing-room on shore. Her 'tween decks are particularly deserving of notice, and must merit approval whenever looked at. Her external appearance is very graceful,

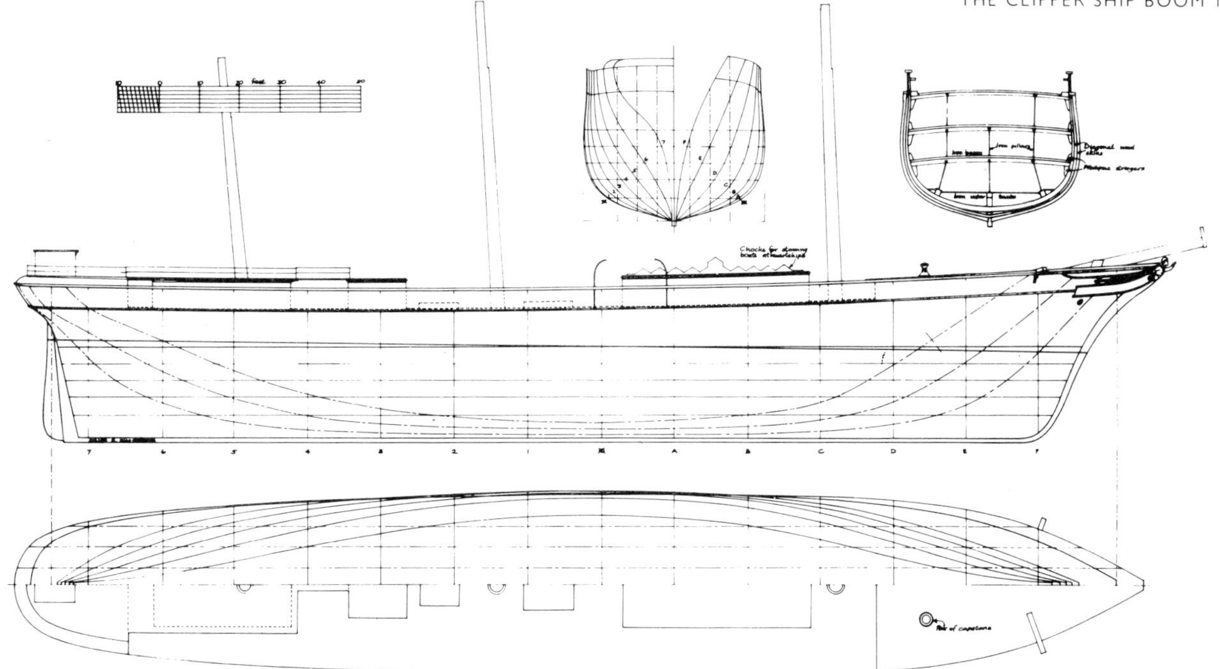

257: *Schomberg.* Lines plan: Built of wood on diagonal system in 1855 by Alexander Hall & Sons at Aberdeen. Redrawn from shipyard blueprint, loaned by F C Poyser, and bearing the builder's rubber stamp. Dimensions according to 1836 Act: 247.7ft × 42.2ft (inside breadth) × 28.9ft; external breadth 45.5ft; 2284 tons nm. Reconstruction: Deck layout; midship section; spars. Sources for reconstruction: Photograph of ship at Aberdeen; plans in *Encyclopaedia Britannica* (1861); builder's spart dimensions; contemporary descriptions. The curious shape of the boat chocks, which permit eight boats to be stowed athwarthship on the deckhouse, is taken from the photograph of the ship.

and her model is curious, and well worthy of mention, being very sharp at both ends, and yet so flat on the floor as not to require any ballast in launching. Go where she will, she must command the attention of all beholders.'[104]

The *Schomberg*

The incidents attendant on placing the order for this large ship have been forgotten, but it is a strong probability that the enterprising builders, Alexander Hall & Sons, would have been the party who first made the proposals and convinced James Baines & Co that they could build a clipper similar in size and performance to those being delivered by Donald McKay. Of course, James Baines would know their name and work intimately, and James and William Hall must have visited him on many occasions when calling on clients in Liverpool, probably submitting their current shipbuilding prices to him on each occasion. But when Baines decided to contract with them in March or April 1854, he wanted the ship in a hurry, so that construction of the huge vessel occupied only 12 months. The ship was launched on 5 April 1855 and the builder's certificate was dated 14 June. The cost was calculated as follows:

'By Jas Baines & Co for building, finishing and equipping vessel according to specification, said vessel measures 2600 tons BM, but deducting one foot of breadth as agreement—

then 2492 8/94 tons at £14	£34,889. 3. 9
extras as per journal, July 1855	£ 4,623. 0. 0
tanks	£ 3,463. 0.10
extras as per end of day book	£ 128.15. 1
discount rec'd on chain stoppers	£ 1.14. 1
	£43,105.13. 8[105]

The final price on 2492 tons can be calculated as £17.6s per ton.

The dimensions of the ship were 247.7ft length from after part of main stem to fore part of sternpost, 42.2ft inside breadth, 28.9ft depth of hold; tonnage by new measurement was 2284. Her moulded breadth was 42ft-6in but the very thick diagonal skins of which she was composed, raised the maximum external breadth to 45ft-6in. A table in chapter five shows that she was the equal in size to the largest American clipper, excepting the *Great Republic*.

The lines reproduced here in figure 257 have been redrawn from a blueprint bearing the rubber stamp of Alexander Hall & Sons, and which was loaned to me by the late Frederick C Poyser of the Nautical Photo Agency. The lines of *Schomberg* which appeared in Murray's article on 'Shipbuilding' in the *Encyclopaedia Britannica* are undoubtedly from the same master plan, although the engraver has made some curious errors.[106] The similarity of the engraving helped to establish the authenticity of the blueprint, but as the latter contained no midship section, a reconstruction has been made, based on Murray's engraving and published

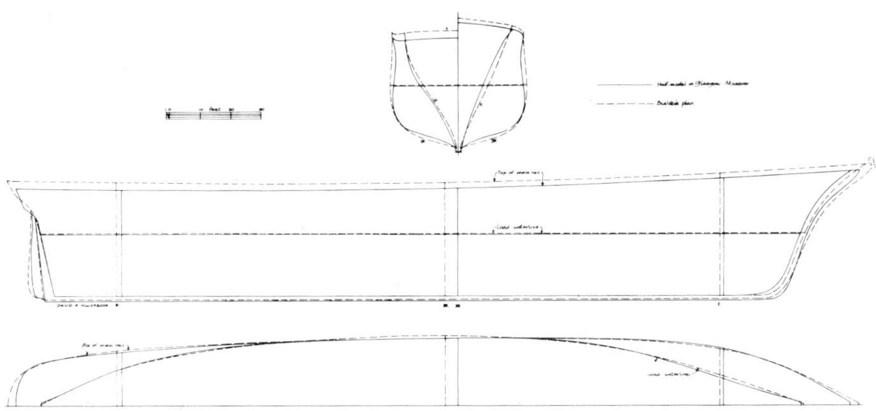

258: *Schomberg;* Superimposed plans: This plan compares Alexander Hall & Sons' original concept for their mammoth clipper, according to a half-model in Glasgow Museum, with the plan of the ship given here in figure 208. Three bodyplan stations have also been selected from each ship for comparison. The solid lines show the half-model in Glasgow Museum, the broken the builder's plan.

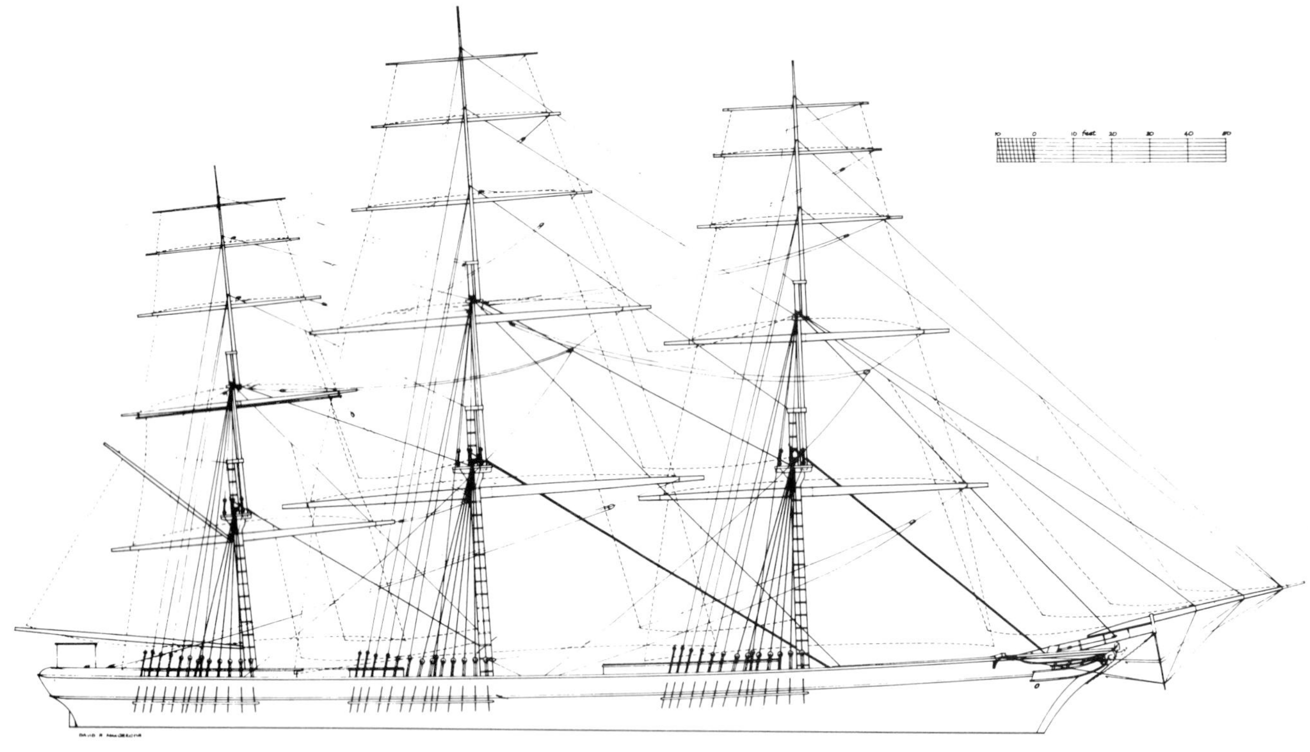

259: *Schomberg*. Sail plan: Reconstructed from builder's spar dimensions, hull lines, and contemporary photographs and illustrations. The mizen topsail is fitted with Cunningham's roller-reefing gear. The builder's spar dimensions include no stunsails, but these sails would undoubtedly have been carried. Two iron yards, each 90ft long, made in Liverpool and presumably fitted prior to maiden voyage.

descriptions. The research already carried out by James Henderson has proved particularly useful. Deck details are entirely reconstructed with his help and that of newspaper reports, and for the sail plan a full set of spar dimensions was fortunately available in the builder's cost account; a photograph of the ship at Aberdeen has also provided data unattainable elsewhere.

The half-model of the ship at the Glasgow Museum and Art Gallery does not agree with the plan used here; this is proved conclusively by the lines taken off the Glasgow model by James Henderson. In figure 258 the sheer profile, three sections and load line of the two plans are superimposed, the firm line representing the half-model and the dotted line the plan in figure 257. It can be seen that the half-model has hollow garboards and greater flare to the topsides, a hollow load line in the entrance, and a slightly shallower hull. There is no indication at what stage the design was amended, but perhaps James and William Hall took the actual half-model to Liverpool when they first broached the subject of a large clipper to Baines. Their proposition meant considerably more if they had a half-model and outline specification with them, and they may easily have visited the managers of the White Star Line and other owners before contracting with Baines. Perhaps Donald McKay had prejudiced Baines in favour of American ships and the lines on which *Schomberg* was built were possibly a compromise. However the Aberdeen bow has been retained. At the time of the launch, her builders are reported as expressing satisfction with the design, but thought the length could have been increased by 50ft.[107]

The lines on which the *Schomberg* was built make her an extreme clipper with a long entrance that has some hollow in the lower body, but the load line is slightly convex; the midsection is positioned seven feet forward of the middle point of the load line, thus making the run longer than the entrance. The buttock lines run in easy curves and the quarter beam buttock is straight where it intersects the load line. There is no hollow at the garboard, but the floors are straight with big deadrise and the bilges are slack as they turn gently into the sides; there is some tumblehome and a small amount of flare occurs to the topsides. The keel is only 12in deep below the rabbet which is small compared with many of the clippers being built: *Annandale* and *Lightning* have 18in below the rabbet and the American *Sweepstakes* has about 30in.

On her one and only passage to Australia her highest recorded speed was 15½ knots and her longest 24-hour run was 368 miles. On a load line of 246ft-0in, the speed-length ratio is .97 which is low for a ship of her length and hull form. On the other hand a run of 368 miles produces an average of 15⅓ knots, so that speeds of 16 to 17 knots must inevitably have occurred that day, although the log was not perhaps heaved. With 17 knots the ratio rises to 1.06. The square root of the load line is exactly 16, and to achieve a speed–length ratio of 1.25, *Schomberg* would have had to sail at 20 knots.

The diagonal construction of her build was similar to the *Vision* but the skins of planking were naturally thicker: the layer between the frames, the two diagonal layers, and an outer transverse layer, were each 2½in thick of Aberdeenshire larch; the longitudinal layer averaged 6in thick of Baltic oak and pitch

260: In this early photograph, the huge clipper ship *Schonberg* can be seen almost ready for sea in the summer of 1855. Unfortunately, the figurehead is covered over, presumably because it was incomplete. The curiously shaped life boat chocks on the deckhouse, just below the church tower, are visible. The port is Aberdeen. *Nautical Photo Agency.*

pine; between each layer there was felt and tar, and the whole mass was fastened by screw treenails of African oak, 1⅜in diameter. Thus outside the frames, the sides were at least 13½in thick and probably more in places. The frames were of English oak. Andrew Murray states that she had three tiers of iron beams, but the two accounts in the *Aberdeen Journal* speak of iron for main and upper deck beams, and pitch pine for the lower deck beams.[108] There was one beam for each frame; the beams rested on pitch pine stringers and were secured with iron staple knees. Iron hold pillars were employed as shown in the cross-section. A fourth deck was laid in the lower hold across the keelson and between the bilge stringers, and below this iron water tanks were fitted to contain about 300 tons of fresh water. Considerable thought was given to the problem of ventilation.

'For ventilation, the spaces three feet wide between the frames were boarded up, and formed excellent ventilators from the various decks and hold, leading up to a space immediately under the main rail, which was fitted all round with venetians. She was also fitted with large funnels, and with a fanner for forcing the air down to the keel, besides scuttles on every six feet on the middle deck. The saloon was on the upper deck, and was fitted with a double roof for causing a current of air, with orifices all round under the cornice outside.'[109]

On the main deck, 60 staterooms were provided at the after end for the first-class passengers and the remainder of the deck was occupied by second-class passengers. Square glazed ports gave light to this deck. The lower deck was for third-class passengers.

The actual poop was quite short in length, being probably reserved for the master, officers, stewards, doctors and apprentices, but forward of it was a separate house which could have contained the library, smoking room, and ladies cabin; the dining saloon was 30ft long and was also situated on the upper deck. A moveable house fitted over the main hatch when at sea, and the decks were well encumbered with sheep and hen coops, cow stall, and so forth. The boats were stowed on top of the big deckhouse and placed athwartships, a pair of davits amidships being used to hoist them overboard. The crew and officers numbered 130 and it was said she could carry 1000 passengers.

One point of special interest in the sail plan, given in figure 259, is the lack of hoist to the topsails, which is emphasised on the mainmast by the great length of the lower and topsail yards. The mainyard measures 111ft-6in, the main topsail yard 90ft-6in, and the main course and topsail overlap the sails on the mizen considerably. The long skysail poles are tall enough to set moonsails on each mast. The mizen topsail was fitted with Cunningham's patent roller-reefing device, hence the second smaller yard. Stunsails would have been carried on each side of the foremast and mainmast up to royal or even sky stunsails, but as the lengths are not listed by Hall's, the sails are not drawn here. In contrast to the long yards, the bowsprit and jibboom look very short. The lengths of the staysails on the stays can be gauged from the photograph of the ship, because the majority of the staysails are seized to their hanks and then hoisted up the stay. The yard book uses a curious description for the spar lengths: the overall length of the lower yards is termed from

261: This engraving from the *Illustrated Times* depicts the *Schonberg* going about in the Mersey at the start of her maiden voyage. In spite of the fact that the artist has managed to get her hull twisted, her general proportions can be observed clearly.

'shoulder of socket to shoulder of socket', and the yardarms from socket to pin; for the other yards the over length is described as such, and the yardarms as 'arms to pin'. The pin is presumably the sheave pin to take the sheets from the sail above.

A few other British ships were fitted with mainyards measuring 100ft or more in length, such as the *British Ambassador* (1873) with 108ft-0in and *Stuart Hahnemann* (1874) with 100ft-0in. Of the McKay quartette, *James Baines* had a mainyard of 100ft-0in and *Donald McKay* of 115ft-0in, the latter's foreyard measuring 105ft-0in.

On her maiden voyage to Melbourne, *Schomberg* experienced light winds for much of the way and was becalmed on the Line for about ten days. Leaving Liverpool on 6 October 1855, she took 28 days to the Line and 55 to the Greenwich meridian, but thereafter met steady and favourable winds. She made the land near Cape Bridgewater on 25 December, 81 days from Liverpool. The following day, when about 35 miles from Cape Otway, the wind dropped and the westerly current took her ashore. She soon became a total wreck. But other ships had been making slow passages that autumn: between Liverpool and Melbourne *Lightning* took 81 days or 77 land to land, and *James Baines* took 84 days or 79 land to land, so that *Schomberg*'s was no disgrace. Although exonerated at the Court of Enquiry, Forbes never got another command with James Baines & Co, nor for that matter did the firm ask Alexander Hall & Sons for another ship to replace the *Schomberg*.

Although other large sailing ships were built in the British Isles, it was 11 years before a clipper of comparable size was launched, namely the *Sobraon* of 2130 tons, and she was another product from Alexander Hall's yard.

Sarah Neumann and the clippers of southern England

Although yards on the Thames produced ships of clipper build, there are no surviving plans to show any of the extreme clipper range. Indeed the only known plans of a London-built clipper apply to the *Challenger* which R & H Green completed in 1852 for the China trade with measurements of 174.0ft by 32.0ft by 20.0ft and 699 tons nm. Her lines have been published in my two books *The Tea Clippers* and *The China Bird* and show a hull form with a sharp entrance and run, a small amount of deadrise, firm bilges and little tumblehome.[110] This places her in the clipper category, and although not producing extreme speed, she maintained a very consistent series of passages from China which averaged only 115 days between Shanghai and London during James Killick's tenure of command, 1852–60. It may be that *Challenger* could be considered typical of some of the faster Blackwall passenger ships built on the Thames.

Elsewhere in the shipyards of southern England there was a great deal of activity for fast vessels of up to 500 tons, but there is

262: Oil painting of *Challenger* by S D Skillett (fl 1845-56). Here there are many flying kites set, such as ringtail, royal stunsails, and a jib topsail. There are trysails on fore and main as well as skysails on all three masts, although the latter could have been set on gunter poles. *Courtesy of John Perret.*

264: This painting of the *Shuttle* by Joseph Heard indicates the type of vessel being produced by George Cox of Bideford in the fifties. The hull was painted green, and she has an Aberdeen style bow. *Gomshall Gallery.*

little positive evidence to go on and almost nothing in the way of plans or models. John Gray's *Electric Telegraph*, built at Newhaven in 1852, has been described as probably like the *Watkins* (figure 160). The *Illustrated London News* carried engravings of ships such as the *Speedy*, which Cox & Son built at Bridport in 1853 'on lines said to be unsurpassed by any vessel afloat'![112] She was built for the Liverpool house of J Prowse & Co and was expected to make the passage to Sydney in 70 days. Actually, she took 88 days land to land in 1854 which the *Sydney Morning Herald* described as 'an excellent passage'.[113] Her second outward passage to Sydney occupied 96 days from Portsmouth in 1855. The *Speedy* was classed at 8 A1 and measurements were given of 192ft-0in 'stem to sternpost', 33ft-0in beam and 21ft-0in depth of hold; tonnage was 1031 nm and 1002 om.

In the 1950s there was a half-model of a large ship in the possession of Vernon Boyle of Westward Ho! and when the lines were taken off, the dimensions from the resultant plan, assuming the normal scale of ¼in to 1ft, gave 203ft-0in (foreside of stem under bow-

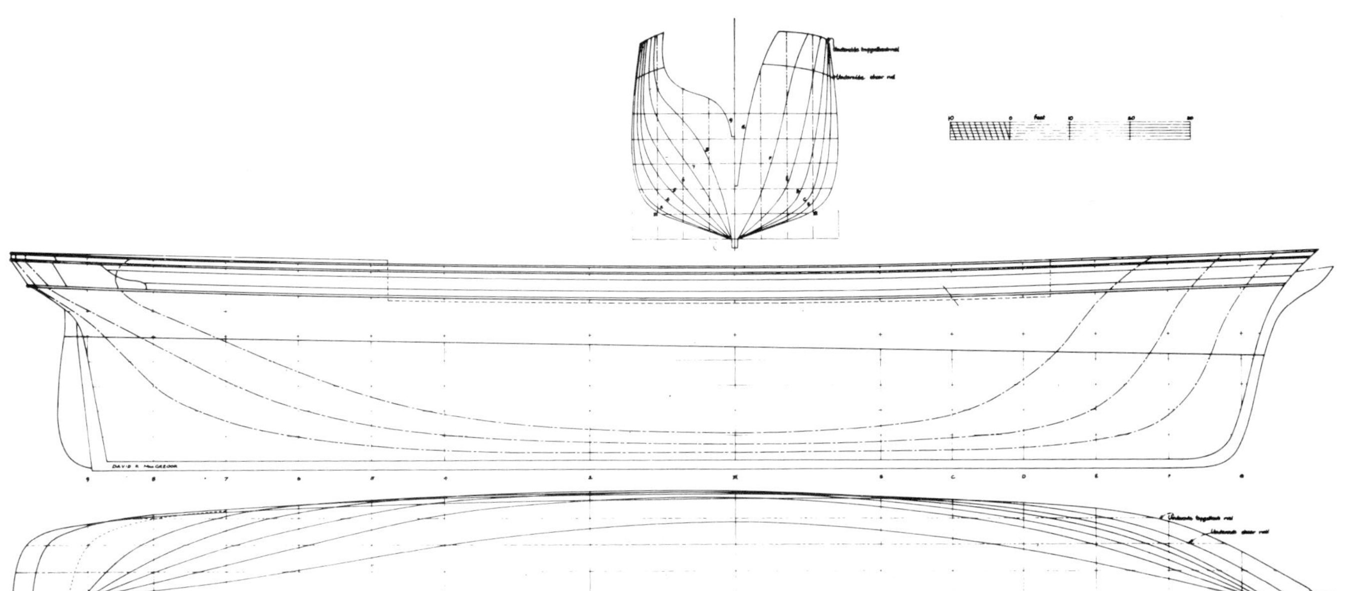

263: *Sarah Neumann.* Built in 1855 by George Cox at Bideford. Lines taken off un-named half-model in possession of Vernon Boyle, Westward Ho! Dimensions: 201ft-8in (between perpendiculars) × 35ft-9¾in × 21ft-4in; tonnages 1004 nm and 1220 om. Reconstruction: attribution of name.

sprit to after side sternpost), 34ft-0in (moulded breadth) and 22ft-0in (approx depth of hold). George Cox of Bideford was the only local builder to construct ships of this size and his biggest, the *Sarah Neumann*, measured 201ft-8in (between perpendiculars) by 35ft-9¾in by 21ft-4in, with tonnages of 1004 nm and 1220 om. Given Vernon Boyle's intense interest in local shipbuilding history it seems safe to state that the model came from a local yard and, from the similarity of the two sets of dimensions, that it represents the ship *Sarah Neumann*.[114]

The lines show a vessel that is definitely of the clipper mould with a long, convex entrance and a longer, convex run, although a little hollow is worked into the lowest waterline. The midsection is placed 10ft-3in forward of the middle point of the load line; the latter was marked on the half-model to show a draught of 21ft-6in aft and 17ft-9in forward, which gives a larger drag aft than usual. The floors are straight with appreciable deadrise and the bilges round gently into the curved sides, with a fair amount of tumblehome above. The forward sections are formed very full at their lower ends to give good initial stability, and the convexity of the entrance and run is the most prominent feature of the lines. The quarter-beam buttock is straight where it crosses the load line, which indicates a fast hull form. If the ship's beam of 35ft-9¾in was measured externally, then 5in or 6in could be deducted each side for planking to give a moulded breadth of 34ft-9in to 35ft-0in which is not very different from the model.

The Lloyd's Register surveyor described the *Sarah Neumann* 'as a clipper style and handsome model; materials, workmanship of the best description'.[115] She was classed 13 A1 and was equipped with a longboat and three other boats; the poop measured 62ft-0in long and 6ft-6in high, the forecastle 44ft-0in long and 6ft-0in high. The floor timbers were sided 15in and moulded 16in. She was launched on 15 May 1855 and reached Liverpool on 2 August to load for Australia. Her owner, John Leech, already owned the *Jane Leech* and *Shuttle*, both built by George Cox in 1854.

At Barnstaple in 1853, John Westacott was building the 425-ton *Sea Snake* 'of a clipper style', and the 'long, sharp ship' *Spring Bok* of 198 tons nm and 230 om. The latter was barque-rigged with dimensions of 120.0ft by 20.0ft by 12.0ft and the differences between the two tonnage figures suggest a fine-lined vessel. No models of these or similar ships have been located but some were probably of the clipper model.

Experiments in hull form were being conducted by various builders. At Bristol Museum, for instance, there is a half-model of a ship bearing the name *Idea*, which about sums up the design. The model has very hollow garboards, steep floors, a hollow run, and the attempt at an Aberdeen bow, but the form is much fuller above the load line. It is doubtful if any ship was built from this model, which probably dates from about 1850.

Charles Tayleur & Co, Warrington

The first record of iron shipbuilding at Warrington dates from 1840 when the Bridge Foundry Co built four small iron paddle steamers for use on the Mersey and also the iron schooner *Warrington*. They continued to build occasional iron vessels during the 1840s.

Another business was founded in 1844 when Charles Tayleur and George S Sanderson obtained a 99-year lease on 18,000 square yards of land owned by J Wilson Patten MP, of Bank Hall, and the resulting firm of Tayleur, Sanderson & Co named its works Bank Quay Foundry. The previous engineering experience of the two partners has not been traced. In 1847, George Sanderson retired and Charles Tayleur's son Edward became a partner. Originally, the firm cast cannons for the Navy but gained prominence with their work for the Britannia Tubular Bridge, and heavy castings and forgings were a speciality. In 1846, they launched two 75-ton iron schooners on the same tide, the *Enterprize* and *Neptune*. No more names of ships launched have been traced until 1852 when the shipyard was extended by leasing more land and an ambitious but short-lived building project ensued. The shipyard was situated close to the London & North Western Railway station, and due to a bend in the River Mersey there was a clear space of 200 to 300 yards for launching ships.[116]

No ships appear to have been built after 1855. Charles and Edward Tayleur were also partners in the Vulcan Foundry of Newton-le-Willows, probably dating from 1847, but further research into the interlocking partnerships is required. Work at the Bank Quay Foundry declined after 1855 and finally ceased.

A builder's half-model of the *Tayleur* was in the possession of the Vulcan Foundry Ltd when I measured it in October 1958 at their offices at Newton-le-Willows. It was labelled 'Original Model', and scaled by the 1836 Registry act 204ft by 36ft by 23ft. As built, the *Tayleur* was enlarged somewhat in all directions at the owner's request so that the dimensions became 225.0ft by 39.4ft by 27.6ft. With tonnages of 1750 tons nm and 1979 om, she was the largest iron sailing ship until the launch of the *Bates Family* in 1859. Lines taken off the 'original model' show that she is a clipper, but not an extreme one; she

Iron ships built by C Tayleur & Co 1852–55[117]

Year	*Name*	*Rig*	*Tons nm*	*Tons om*	*Dimensions*	*Owners*
1852	PS *Invincible*		111			used in R. Mersey
1853	PS *La Perlita*		140			PSN Co
1853	*Tayleur*	S	1750	1979	225.0ft × 39.4ft × 27.6ft	C Moore
1854	*Lady Octavia*	S	1319	1272	200.3ft × 34.7ft × 22.3ft	
1854-5	*Deerslayer*	bk	390		142.0ft × 26.1ft × 15.7ft	Blyth
1854-5	*Liverpooliana*	S	390		149.0ft × 26.0ft × 15.0ft	C Moore
	name changed to *Medora* in 1855 when sold to Shallcross & Co					
1855	*Retriever*	bk	410		164.4ft × 26.2ft × 15.7ft	
	name changed to *Mystery* by July 1855					
1855	*Startled Fawn*	S	1165	1329	200.3ft × 36.9ft × 22.3ft	Fletcher
1855	*Sarah Palmer*	S	1325		225.5ft × 36.6ft × 22.3ft (builder's measurement)	Palmer
1855	*Conference*	S	531		164.8ft × 26.4ft × 16.0ft	H Moore

265: The iron ship *Tayleur* from an engraving dated 16 November 1853, as the artist imagined she would look when at sea, but only two days were to elapse between her sailing and the day she was wrecked.

has a long, convex entrance with some hollow lower down and a run of similar form; the midsection is placed at the middle point of the assumed load line; there are 12½ degrees of deadrise with slack bilges and not much tumblehome. She is after the style of *Sarah Neumann* but broader and deeper, and with that heavy rounded stern which many iron ships possessed.

The enlarged version that was built must have had some similarities with the half-model. 'She is perceptibly hollow in her entrance and clean in her tail, her bow as well as her stern lines commencing near to amidships, whilst her large extent of floor will ensure her carrying canvass and making rapid way through her destined element.'[118] So spoke the *Liverpool Standard*, as reported in Australia. Another report gives the rise of floor as 10 degrees. There were three decks but passengers were to be carried on the main deck only, the lower deck and hold being reserved for cargo, and it was estimated that she would load 4200 tons on a draught of 21ft-0in. The garboard strake was 1in thick diminishing to ½in; the keelson was a box girder 2ft-6in by 2ft-0in composed of ½in plates and there were two sister keelsons; frames were spaced at 18in centres but at only 15in centres amidships. The ironwork weighed 780 tons. The lower masts were of iron, braced inside with transverse plates; the fore and main yards were 84ft-0in long but no other spar lengths are reported. Contemporary engravings and illustrations of her at sea, executed before she ever set sail, show skysails on all three masts, single topsails with point reefing, trysails on fore and main, and channels for the rigging. There was a full-length figurehead of Charles Tayleur, and on the stern his family crest and other emblems. From the signing of the contract to the launch on 4 October 1853, only six months elapsed, which was very fast work. Mr Heathcote, manager of the Bank Quay Foundry, supervised her construction. Tugs were in attendance at the launch and she was immediately towed to Liverpool to be fitted out. The total cost was reported as £34,000 which works out at £17.3s per ton om.[119]

While she was under construction, Captain Noble, her future master, fell into the hold, and the Carpenters Society foretold disaster; unfortunately, they were proved correct, because the ship was totally wrecked on Lambay Island in Dublin Bay on 21 January 1854, two days after starting her maiden voyage. About 300 people were drowned. The Court of Enquiry found that her crew of 55 was largely composed of Chinese and Lascars who were no good in cold weather; that her owners were at fault in not adjusting the compasses, which were wrong, and for not giving her a trial trip; and that Captain Noble was wrong in not taking soundings.[120] Trial trips for sailing ships were unheard of then. Adjustment of compasses in iron ships was little understood and the Liverpool Compass Committee submitted three reports to the Board of Trade between 1855–60. Such a disaster made owners reluctant to order an iron ship so that when the *Startled Fawn* was about to sail for Melbourne in May 1855 it was reported that 'the prejudice against iron vessels created by the *Tayleur* catastrophe is fast yielding to good sense and increasing intelligence, and as it cannot be denied that iron as a material for shipbuilding is lighter than wood, so most certainly is it cheaper'.[121] On this occasion the *Startled Fawn* was chartered by James Baines & Co.

Charles Moore & Co of Liverpool who had ordered the *Tayleur* and *Liverpooliana* from Charles Tayleur & Co, now ordered another large iron clipper of about 1300 tons om, but sold her to Jones, Palmer & Co before she was launched, so that the latter were able to give the ship the name of their choice which was *Sarah Palmer*. Miss Sarah duly arrived at the shipyard on the launch day, 31 July 1855, but through some accident the new ship slid gently down the ways sooner than intended, without the daggers being loosed, and so Sarah Palmer was never able to christen her namesake properly.[122] There is no record as to whether the local sages prophesied doom for the new ship, although after a life of five years she foundered in 1860 when bound to Queenstown with guano from Callao.

A lines plan and sail plan of the *Sarah*

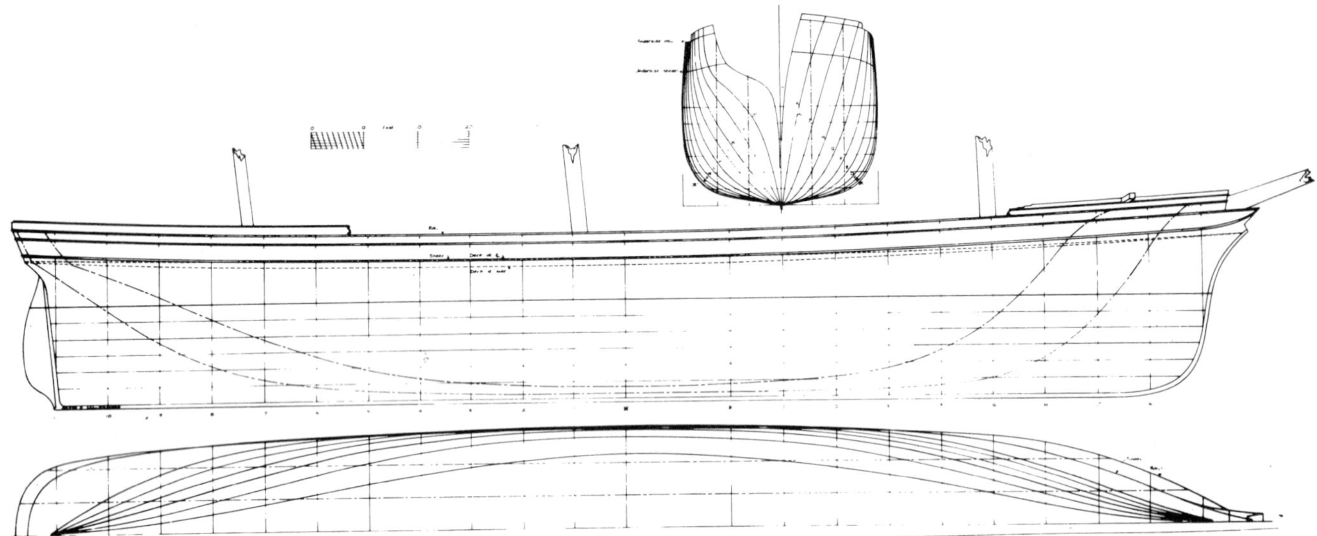

266: *Sarah Palmer*. Lines plan: Built of iron in 1855 by C Tayleur & Co at Warrington. Redrawn from old, possibly contemporary, plan on opaque linen cloth in National Maritime Museum. Dimensions: 225.5ft × 22.3ft; 1325 tons. Reconstruction: position of masts adjusted to agree with sail plan.

267: *Sarah Palmer*. Sail plan: Redrawn from old, possibly contemporary, plan on opaque linen cloth in National Maritime Museum. Reconstruction: deadeyes and lanyards added to fore and main rigging; outline of staysails dotted.

Palmer from the National Maritime Museum, Greenwich, are reproduced here to prove that she is an extreme clipper. There is a long, concave entrance with marked hollow in the load line, and due to the good breadth of beam the entrance is taken to the midsection which is situated at the middle point of the load line; the run commences here and is equally long with hollows in the lower waterlines, but the upper ones are more convex. Two buttock lines are drawn at one-third and two-thirds of the half beam, and they show very clean ends without any hard shoulders. Deadrise is the same as the *Tayleur*'s, and the midsection profile is closely similar to the latter's original half-model with slack bilges and little tumblehome. As might be expected, several design points resemble the *Tayleur*'s 'original model' such as the midship section, the heavy round stern and the deck profile; but the forefoot is no longer angular and the projection of the head is much reduced.

These Warrington-built clippers have not the narrow hulls of the Clyde-built iron clippers like *Hurricane*, but they have additional beam of the proportion to be seen in *Schomberg*. It also looks as if there were two basic sizes built by the yard: the smaller kind, such as *Deerslayer, Liverpooliana, Retriever* and *Conference*, with almost identical beam and depth measurements, but with hull length added or subtracted according to the owner's wishes; and the larger kind consisting of *Tayleur, Lady Octavia, Startled Fawn* and *Sarah Palmer*, with beam and depth again virtually identical but with length of either 200ft or 225ft. The naval architect, John Grantham (1809–74), supervised the construction of the *Sarah Palmer* and listed the specification of her ironwork. The latter is reprinted here in Appendix IV. He also gave specifications for the *Lady Octavia* and *Deerslayer*, so perhaps he also supervised their construction or at least acted in an advisory capacity.[123] The *Sarah Palmer*'s constuction was not in accordance with the rules of Lloyd's Register but the surveyor spoke highly of the method adopted, the workmanship, materials and outfit. The gunwale was formed by a box girder, but the waterways were of teak; there were four watertight bulkheads, and six boats were provided.

The sail plan of *Sarah Palmer*, redrawn from the original as figure 267, depicts a rather unattractive ship, with cumbersome bow and stern details, and the shortish masts, in relation to the length of hull, do nothing to assist her appearance. The main lower mast is 3ft-6in longer than the fore lower mast, otherwise all the other parts of the fore-and mainmasts are of similar length, as also are the respective yards. The lower yards scale 76ft-6in which is rather on the short side for a ship of her proportions, even allowing for her very fine lines, and produces a big gap between the sails. Stunsails would of course help to fill the gap and she would definitely have carried these on the foremast and mainmast. The absence of a crossjack is unusual by this date and the running topmast backstay is an uncommon feature in a square-rigged ship of this size. The lower masts are of iron and according to a newspaper report were 'filled with what is technically called "feathers"'.[124] Was this a local engineering term? I have been unable to trace the meaning of this expression but it has been suggested that in bending the iron plates, slivers of the metal flaked off inside.

The *Lady Octavia* and *Startled Fawn* both took their maiden passages to Australia, but the *Sarah Palmer* went to India.

268: A painting by a Chinese artist of the *Scawfell* at anchor off Hong Kong. *Merseyside County Museum.*

Clippers of north-west England

At Whitehaven, Thomas and John Brocklebank operated a shipyard which built almost exclusively for their own requirements, but few of their ships were of the clipper category. In 1852 they launched the flush-decked wooden ship *Martaban* of 852 tons nm and 827 tons om which was a much longer and somewhat finer-lined ship than previously, the ratio of beams to length being almost 5½ to 1. A plan in the Brocklebank archives[125] has some waterlines of this ship superimposed on a lines plan of the *Aracan*, launched two years later, which indicates that the latter was a longer and sharper vessel, measuring 186.6ft by 32.0ft by 21.6ft, 864 tons nm and 911 tons om. She had a crew of 35. Her plan shows a fair amount of deadrise which quickly rounds up into very slack bilges, but there is about 30ft of dead flats amidships although the ends are fairly sharp and convex at the load waterline. On her maiden voyage she sailed out to India and returned to Liverpool in 85 days from Bombay.

We now come to a hull form of very different proportions and of a much more experimental nature. The lines in question were taken from a beautifully-made half-model, composed of the normal laminated sections, in the shipping collection of Liverpool Museum. The scale of the model is assumed to be ⅛in to 1ft-0in, and is said to represent the tea clipper *Scawfell*, which Charles Lamport built at Workington in 1858. Lamport had already produced many fine ships in this decade such as *Cambalu, Sebastian Cabot* and *Lodore*, but possibly his only vessel of real clipper build so far was the *Aerolite*. This is assumed from the big difference between the new and old tonnage figures, which in her case are 911 nm and 1160 om, and there are many other cases on record to substantiate this particular point.

The *Aerolite* was built in 1853 of wood, with a diagonal ceiling, and fore and main lower masts of iron. Her dimensions were 183ft by 36ft-6in by 20ft-0in. Her maiden passage took her out to Melbourne in 93 days in 1853 and in the early 1860s she was sailing home from China with times such as 98 days from Shanghai to Liverpool in 1864–65.

Many fine ships were built at Workington towards the end of the 'fifties for the China trade and of very similar size, and their measurements and builders are tabulated below for comparison.

Jonathan Fell ran the Workington & Harrington Shipbuilding Co and the *Jubilee* was their first ship. Previously he had been manager for Peile, Scott & Co, so that every ship listed above, except *Scawfell*, would have fallen under his influence.

The table below throws up several possibilities for identification of the model of which the strongest, purely on the evidence of the dimensions, is the *Dunmail*. Strangely enough, the *Scawfell*'s dimensions yield the largest discrepancy. Arguing in favour of the *Scawfell*, one could add four inches each side

Ships built at Workington with dimensions similar to prototype half-model of *Scawfell*

Year	*Name*	*tons reg*	*UD coeff*	*Dimensions*	*Builders*
—	Half-model (figure 259)	—	—	184.0ft × 31.5ft × 18.0ft (approx)	—
1856	*Banian*	760	—	186.0ft × 30.5ft × 20.8ft	Peile, Scott & Co
1857	*Jubilee*	764	.57	192.4ft × 31.0ft × 21.3ft	Workington & Harrington SB Co
1858	*Scawfell*	826	.57	198.0ft × 32.6ft × 21.8ft	Charles Lamport
1859	*Dunmail*	768	—	184.7ft × 31.5ft × 21.4ft	Workington & Harrington SB Co
1863	*Belted Will*	812	.59	186.5ft × 32.4ft × 20.9ft	Jonathan Fell

for plank thickness, thus advancing the moulded beam of the model to 32.0ft. An extra two feet in depth could be added by raising the deck level during construction. The extra length is more of a problem and could only be accommodated if the model were to represent a preliminary design, as in the case of the *Tayleur* or the *Robin Hood*. Whether in this case 14ft was merely added to the design or an entirely new design produced would be hard to say, but her record passage of 85 days from Macao to Liverpool betokens a sharp hull, as does her low coefficient of underdeck tonnage, .57, which is less than *Titania*'s .58.

The lines of this half-model show a hull designed with a raking midsection, the broadest point of each waterline being further aft than the one below. This has the effect of making the run longer and finer than the entrance in the lowest waterlines, but conversely of making the entrance longer and finer than the run at the load line. This helps to increase stability and decrease pitching, and assists in producing a hull that will sail fast. In this case the entrance and run are entirely convex and there are no hollows in the waterline lines. The broadest part of the lowest waterline is at the middle point of the load line, but the broadest place on the load line is about 25ft abaft the middle point. The buttock lines are very easy forward, and fuller, but still easy, aft. There is very steep deadrise, and the floors are slightly convex, rounding into very slack bilges and flaring sides, so that the maximum beam is at rail height. Joseph Maudslay, the London shipbuilder, read a paper on the subject of raking midsections to the Institution of Naval Architects in 1860 and submitted a lines plan of such a ship, but the present half-model is no copy of Maudslay's plan. Charles Lamport was a member of the Institution, but Jonathan Fell was not.

On this model the keel is four feet deep aft, below the rabbet, but only 2ft-3in forward and the waterlines have been drawn parallel to the base of the keel. A ship built to this model would probably draw about three or four feet more water aft than forward. The slaver brig *Diligente*, captured by the Navy in 1837, had a similar type of keel.[126]

Two interesting facts point to *Scawfell* having a really sharp hull. First, when abandoned in 1883, she was carrying 50 tons of permanent iron ballast, whereas the clippers like *Sir Lancelot* had had theirs removed in the early 1870s to improve their stowage. Second, apart from the ballast, she was carrying 1059 tons of coal and coke when she was lost. This represents only 28¼% more than her net register tonnage, whereas most ships expected to carry at least 50 per cent more than their register tonnage and many twice as much. She must have had a very sharp hull to carry so little.

Her fast passage of 85 days from Macao was made in 1861 with the fair monsoon; she sailed on 16 January and arrived off Point Lynas, near Liverpool, on 11 April. In 1866–7 she took 97 days between Foochow and Deal, leaving in October.

There is a splendid painting reproduced in figure 270 of *Dunmail* off Hong Kong with several flying kites set: jamie green, ring tail and moonsail. According to the booms provided, royal stunsails could be set on both foremast and mainmast. She had no specially fast passages to her credit, nor had the *Jubilee*, but a good average. The latter was only broken up in 1944. *Belted Will* was a faster ship than either of these two and her first four passages from Hong Kong or Whampoa to London, all made against the monsoon, averaged 109½ days.

Clippers of the late 1850s

Following the termination of the Crimean War in 1856, there was a surplus of unwanted tonnage and freight rates fell, with the result that orders for new ships were severely restricted for a few years, although a limited number of clippers were built for the India and China trades, such as those listed in the last section. Further north, at Greenock, Robert Steele & Co built the *Ellen Rodger* (1858) and *Falcon* (1859) and a plan of the latter appeared in *The Tea Clippers*.[127] This plan shows her to have been a clipper, but not an extreme one, with a fair amount of deadrise and slack bilges; she has long,

269: *Scawfell*. Built of wood in 1858 by Charles Lamport at Workington. Lines taken from half-model in Liverpool Museum. Dimensions of *Scawfell:* 198.0ft × 21.8ft; 826 tons. Dimensions scaled off this model: 184.0ft × 31.5ft × 18.0ft (approx.). No reconstruction.

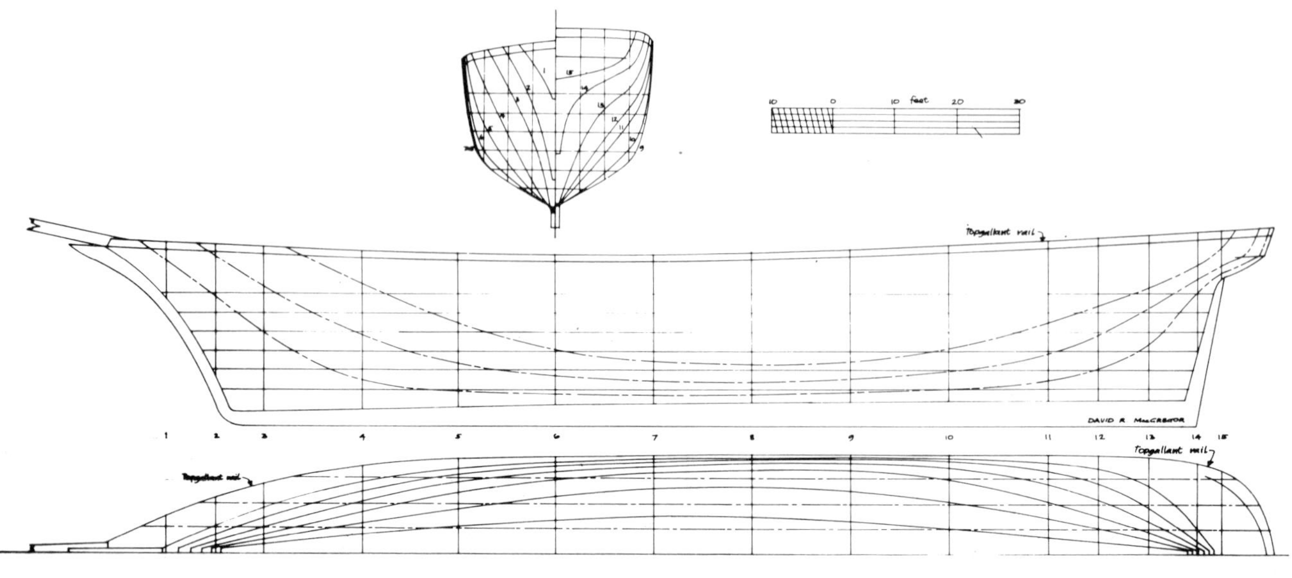

270: The Workington-built ship *Dunmail* under all plain sail, as seen by a Chinese artist. The flying kites set comprise a main moonsail, ringtail, jamie green and main sky staysail. *Parker Gallery.*

271: This is an oil painting attributed to the Chinese school depicting the *Summer Cloud* reefed down in a moderate gale. She was built in 1859 by John Pile at West Hartlepool and constructed of iron; here he built many fine ships like her. The hull was painted a bluey-grey colour in the painting. *Martyn Gregory Gallery.*

272: The *Matchless* looks built for speed in this little-known lithograph by the artist T G Dutton. This attractive rig usually goes by the name of 'jackass barque', but in Guernsey where she was built the rig was called 'barquetta'. She was built in 1859 by Marquand & de la Mare and measured 241 tons. *Lavinia* was another.

sharp ends, with slight concavity near stem and sternpost.

At Port Glasgow, John Reid & Co built the iron ship *Weymouth* in 1858 for the China trade, and a whole-hull model which I measured in 1949 showed a moderately fine-lined ship with a fair amount of deadrise and very slack bilges. In 1866–67 she sailed from Foochow to London in 104 days.

Up the Clyde, nearer to Glasgow, Barclay, Curle & Co built several clippers for George Smith & Sons' 'City Line' which traded to India, and plans of the ships can now be inspected at the National Maritime Museum, Greenwich. Earlier in the 1850s, these builders had mostly produced moderately full-lined cargo ships for Smith's, but a lines plan of the *City of Perth*, launched in 1857, shows a fine-lined vessel with a long, sharp entrance and run, little deadrise, firm bilges, but with about 13ft of dead flats amidships. She was yard number 53 and measured 459 tons, being built of wood with iron beams.

A lines plan dated October 1859 shows the sister ships *City of Nankin* (1859) and *City of Shanghai* (1860) to have been sharp-ended ships with a long fine run but a shorter, more convex entrance. Like the *City of Perth*, they had little deadrise which must have improved their stowage capacity. They were long iron ships with square sterns, and had dimensions of 212.1ft by 32.2ft by 21.4ft and 986 tons in the case of *City of Nankin; City of Shanghai* was almost identical. Unlike Smith's flush-decked ships of the earlier 'fifties, these ships had full height poops and forecastles.

Alexander Stephen & Sons also received contracts from George Smith & Sons at this date.

273: 'Clipper Frigate Ship'. Lines plan of unidentified three-masted ship drawn by G Hillmann, and photographed from his plan at the Mariner's Museum, Newport News. Dimensions on plan have been interpreted as follows: length on W L 200ft, breadth on W L 39ft, depth in hold [?] 16ft. Body plan indicates a wooden keel although thinness of stem might have indicated an iron hull.

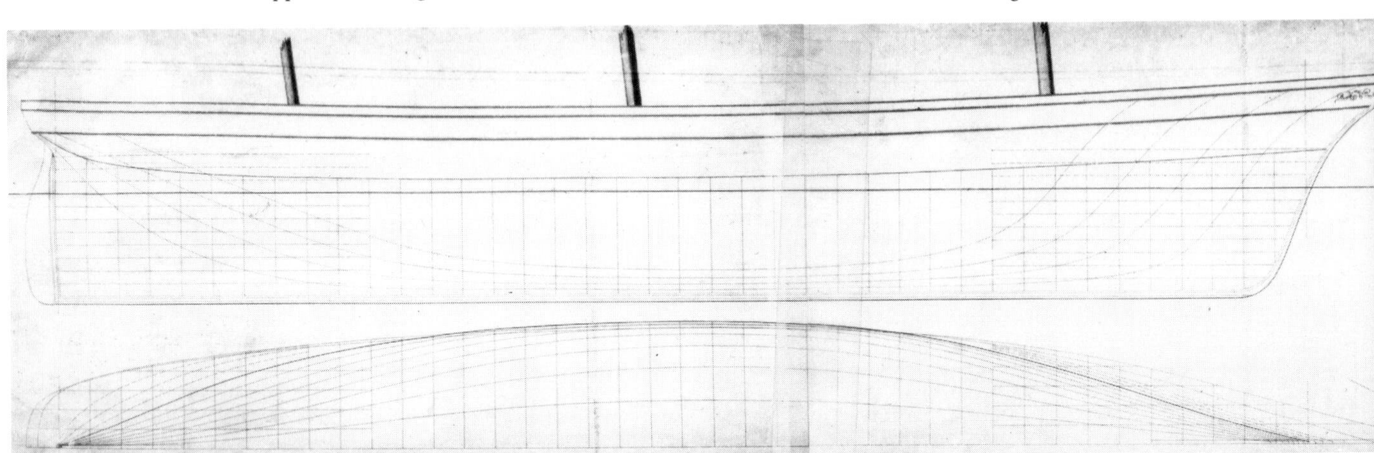

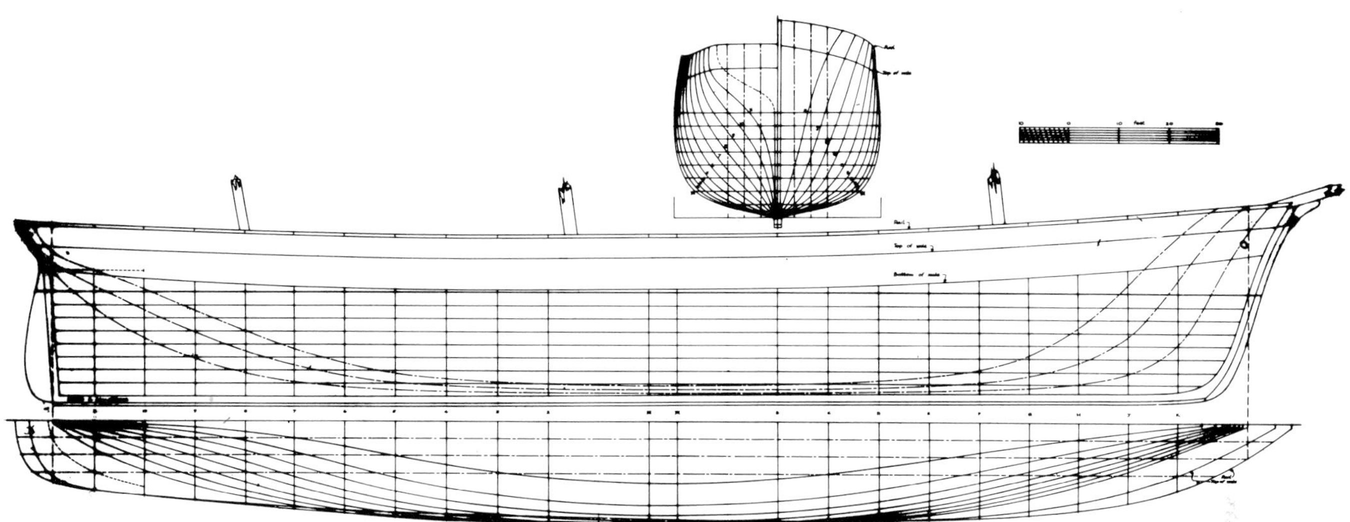

At Aberdeen, Alexander Hall & Sons built the jackass barque *Ziba* in 1858 for the China tea trade, with a net tonnage of 465. I have reconstructed a sail plan for her from the builder's spar dimensions, as reproduced in *The Tea Clippers*,[128] but no lines plan or half-model have been found, which means that her clipper status cannot be verified; however, it is probable that she was a fine-lined ship because she has a coefficient of under-deck tonnage of .57. Several jackass barques were built in the Channel Islands and at Salcombe in the late 'fifties; some of them were unattractive but others like the *Matchless* were very graceful.

Several examples are presented here of clippers built in other European countries and the research suggests that although they were not isolated examples, there was hardly the great boom in the designing and construction of clippers to be seen in Great Britain and America. A number of vessels from Holland and Germany were chartered by British owners at the time of the Australian gold rush in the first half of the 1850s. However, the plans submitted here come from the second half of the decade and are of extremely fine-lined vessels. At Copenhagen, the naval architect, G Hillmann, was producing copies of plans of many different craft around 1860–61, and amongst these were the plans of the large Danish clipper *Cimber*. The lines are reproduced here in figure 274 to show a long hull with an extremely sharp entrance and run, a fair amount of deadrise and rounded bilges. The outline sail plan indicates a conservatively sparred ship without any large sail area. A description in the *Illustrated London News* describes her in these words:

'There is now lying in the East India Docks a remarkably fine clipper ship, the *Cimber*, a vessel of immense strength and durability; and matching, if not excelling, in dimensions and sym-

274: *Cimber*. Lines plan: Built 1856 by Jörgen Bruhn at Apenrade, Denmark. Redrawn from plan drawn by G Hillmann dated Copenhagen 1861 in the Mariner's Museum, Newport News. Dimensions scaled off plan: 237ft-9in (length on load waterline between perpendiculars) × 41ft-0in (moulded breadth) × 22ft-0in (depth of hold approx.); approx. 2000 tons om. Reconstruction: rudder, stem, fiddlehead.

275: *Cimber*. Sail plan: Redrawn from plan drawn by G Hillmann dated Copenhagen 1861, in the Mariner's Museum, Newport News.

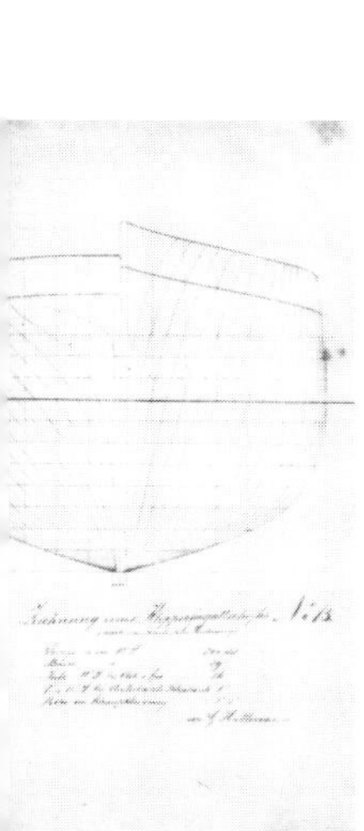

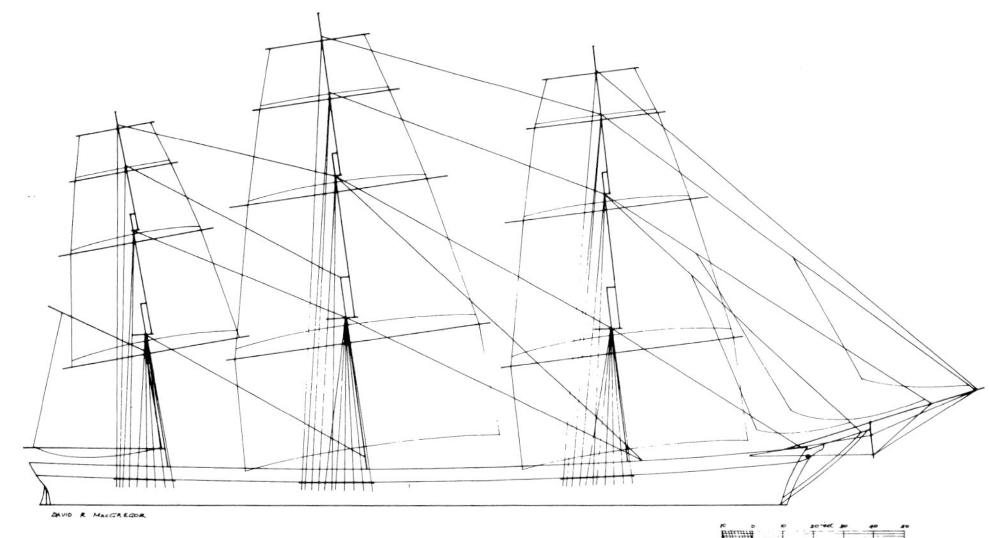

276: An engraving dated 17 April 1858 of the Danish clipper ship *Cimber,* built at Apenrade 1856, which reached San Francisco on 3 March 1857, 106 days out from Liverpool.

metry the most exquisite American clippers, being ten feet longer than the once celebrated *Sovereign of the Seas*. Her length is 250 feet, her beam 42 feet, and her burden about 2800 tons. We take the greater pleasure in engraving this fine specimen of naval architecture as she comes from a country that has not hitherto put forth ships of her size and class. The *Cimber* was built by the late Mr Jörgen Bruhn, of Apenrade, in Denmark, on his extensive establishment near that port, and is constructed throughout of picked Danish-grown oak—equal to the best descriptions of British. She is one of the fastest vessels afloat, having made her run from Liverpool to San Francisco in one hundred and four days, being twelve days less than any other passage on record; and her commander, Captain Bruhn, is sanguine of beating all competition on his intended passage to Australia.'[129]

The record claimed was presumably between Liverpool and San Francisco. As to the anticipated fast run to Australia, there seems to be no knowledge as to the result.

Clipper Schooners and Brigs

The difference in size between the majority of clipper ships and clipper schooners had grown so large after 1850 that direct comparison is unsatisfactory, and it is more suitable to analyse schooners as a class by themselves.

Fast schooners and brigs were in demand for a number of trades including the carriage of fresh fruit, vegetables, fish, livestock, and opium, and many shipyards produced beautiful examples of these vessels according to the evidence of paintings and contemporary descriptions. But needless to say, plans and models are fairly scarce, and it is probably safe to state that, with the exception of yachts and naval craft, the only proof of clipper form comes from a handful of yards, as given below.

In Scotland, William Denny & Brothers of Dumbarton built two iron clipper schooners at the beginning of the 1850s, as shown by surviving plans at the National Maritime Museum, Greenwich: these were the *Caledonia* (1850) reproduced in figure 158 and the *El Zeide* (1851). Alexander Stephen & Sons produced no clipper schooners at Glasgow in the 'fifties, and none of the

277: *Hebe.* Built in 1856 at Bergen. Reproduced from plan in *Transactions of the Institution of Naval Architects,* 1866, vol. VII, plate XV. Dimensions on plan, probably in English feet: 143ft-7in (length between perpendiculars on waterline) × 31ft-8in (moulded breadth) × 19ft-6in (depth from keel to planksheer); 664 ½ tons om; 232 Norwegian laster. Described in 1866 by the Bergen naval architect, A Dekke, as 'very sharp'. Employed in Transatlantic trade. Caption fig 217 FSS but now a sail plan is also included, either at end of plan or it could be placed above or below.

To illustrate M

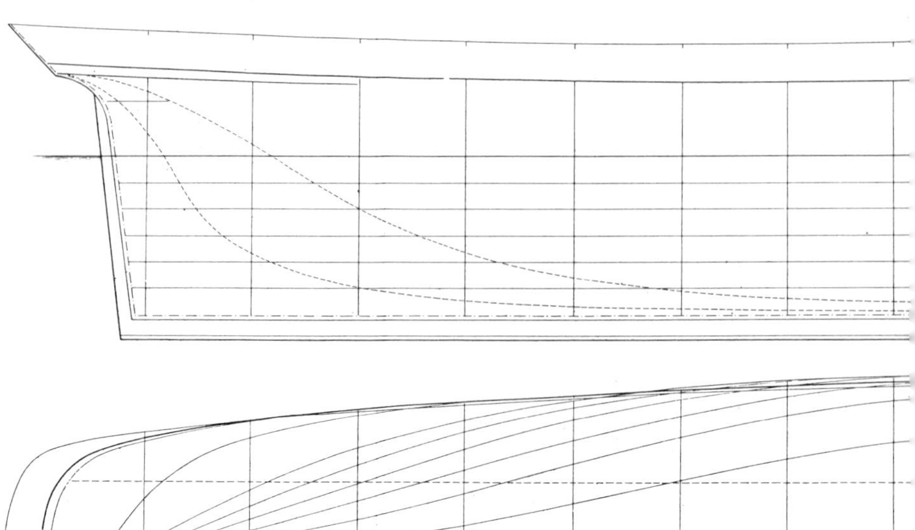

278: This splendid photograph was taken at Havana, Cuba, in 1860 and is part of a stereo plate. It shows an unidentified schooner entering the harbour, with Morro Castle on the port bow. Whether she is of clipper build cannot be determined but she looks like a survivor from the past. It is worth noting that the colour of her bowsprit and of her main boom changes from dark to light where it projects beyond the limits of her hull. *Peabody Museum, Salem.*

Geddie schooner plans from Garmouth have fine enough lines for this category.

At Aberdeen, Alexander Hall & Sons built schooners, some of which must be assumed to be of clipper type because they were built as yachts or for the opium trade, and although no models have survived to confirm this, there are spar dimensions and one photograph. For example, the *Vindex* was built for the opium trade in 1855 at a cost of £18.10s per ton om on 264 tons, and the builder's spar dimensions give her a lofty rig of four yards on the foremast, the fore topsail being fitted with roller-reefing gear.

The following year came the *Salamander*, built as a yacht for the Earl of Selkirk, with measurements of 109.5ft by 21.8ft by 11.1ft, 115.86 tons UD and 214 tons om. She was diagonally built and cost £5,000 to 'build and finish', which works out at about £23 per ton om. No lines plan or half-model are known of this schooner, but there are the builder's spar dimensions and a unique photograph taken in Aberdeen harbour when she was new. As a yacht she must have been a very fine-lined craft. She has a round stern and the figure-head of a salamander. The most prominent feature of her rig is the close spacing of the masts and the long distance from the stemhead to the foremast, which equals approximately the distance from the mainmast to the counter. The main boom measures 54ft-0in with a maximum diameter of 13½in. The poles to the topmasts look much loftier on the photograph than in the sail plan, in which they are drawn as five feet long.[130]

In a photograph of *Salamander*, the longboat is stowed keel uppermost between the masts, which gives the appearance of a steamer's boiler. Forward, the two WCs in white boxes form a distinctive feature.

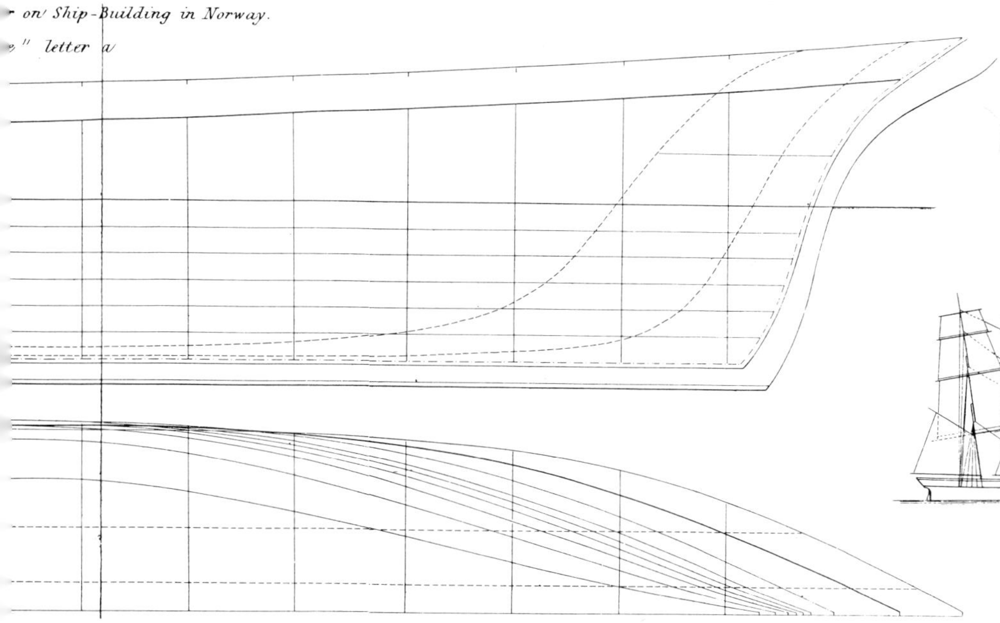

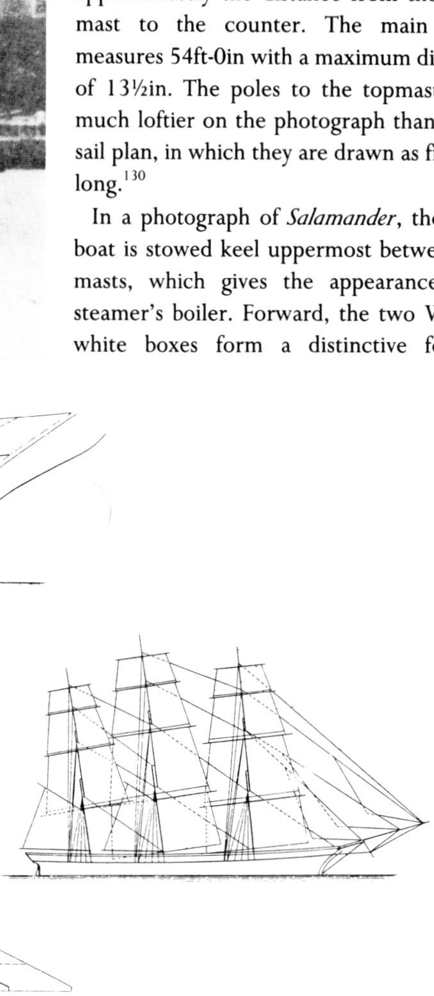

279: The brig *Teazer*, seen here off Sandy Hook, is a splendid survival with her Cunningham pattern roller-reefing topsails, bowlines to the courses, trysail mast and flying jibboom. According to the volumes of *Lloyd's Register*, she was only rigged as a brig between the years 1868-71 inclusive, but they may have got it wrong in previous years. She was built in 1858 by W Kelly at Dartmouth for the South American trade. She registered 293 tons with dimensions of 131.0ft × 25.1ft × 14.8ft; an under deck tonnage of 285 gives her a coefficient of under deck tonnage of .58 which indicates a sharp hull. *Peabody Museum, Salem.*

Although the fore gaff is fitted with halyards it remains aloft and the sail is brailed into the mast, which was then the usual practice, particularly when the sail had no boom, as in this case. The fore gaff is also fitted with vangs. The fore topsail was a roller-reefing sail for which a sum of £14.15s was allocated to its gear in the builder's account. On the mainmast, the topping lift is led to the hounds, which was still normal practice, and a running backstay can also be seen. The fore staysail is an immense sail and there must have been considerable overlap to the headsails, because the stays are so close together. The schooner was probably also equipped with a square sail set from the foreyard; then there would have been lower, topmast and topgallant stunsails, with a flying jib, main topmast staysail and, perhaps, even a ringtail. In 1859, she must have been sold as she sailed out to Hong Kong that year in 110 days, and thereafter was employed on the China coast as an opium clipper.

Descriptions in Lloyd's Register survey reports suggest that various other builders in Scotland were employing some degree of clipper hull form, and the brig *Lady Saltoun* built in 1854 at Fraserburgh by J Webster merited the description of 'flared clipper stem and bow of moderate overhang'.[131] Her tonnage was 132 nm and 190 om, an indication of a sharp hull.

Many small clippers for the fruit trade were built by yards along the south coast of

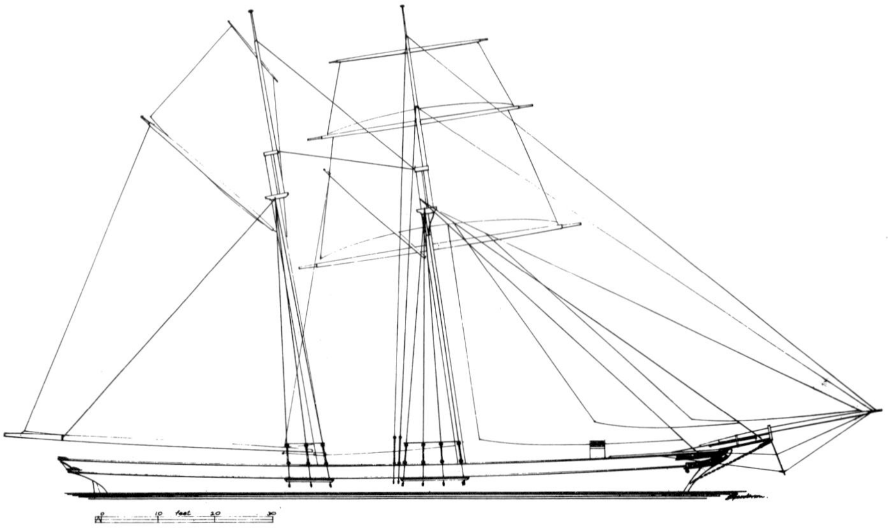

280: *Salamander.* Built in 1856 by Alexander Hall & Sons at Aberdeen. Drawing entirely reconstructed by James Henderson. Dimensions: 109.5ft × 21.8ft × 11.1ft; 115.86 tons under deck and 214 tons om. Reconstruction: hull from photograph of schooner in Aberdeen harbour; spars from measurements in builder's cost account; sails and rigging from photograph (right) and illustration of contemporary schooners. *James Henderson.*

England but the names of the builders are too numerous to mention. The construction of these schooners was at its height in the years 1850–70. Soon after the repeal of the Corn Laws in 1846, the duties on fruit imported from the Mediterranean were likewise repealed, and this greatly stimulated the trade and 'encouraged the production of vessels so superior to those previously in use, as, in speed, to outrival the once celebrated Baltimore clippers'. W S Lindsay, who wrote these words, remarked on how the successful employment of these fast schooners had retarded the introduction of steamer services to the Mediterranean, and he recollected 'the fleets of beautiful small Mediterranean

281: This early photograph was taken in 1856 in Aberdeen harbour and showed the Earl of Selkirk's new yacht, the *Salamander,* just built for him by Alexander Hall & Sons. Her fore mast is stepped a long way aft which suggests a sharp entrance, and the masts are very close together.

284: The Kiel ship portrait painter, H Reimer, painted this view of the *Courant* which was built at Kiel in 1856. She has a sort of Aberdeen bow. *F Holm-Petersen.*

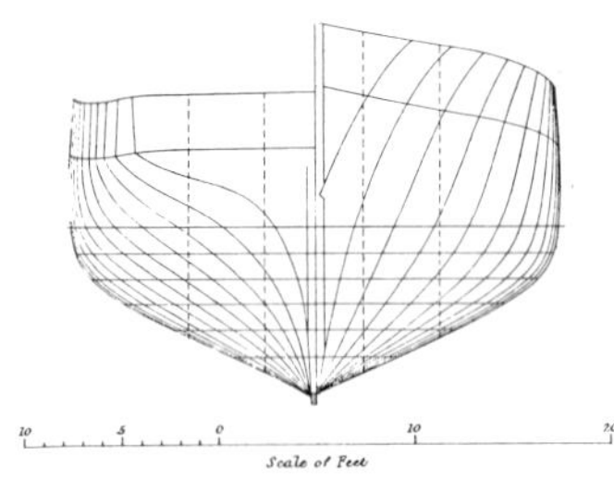

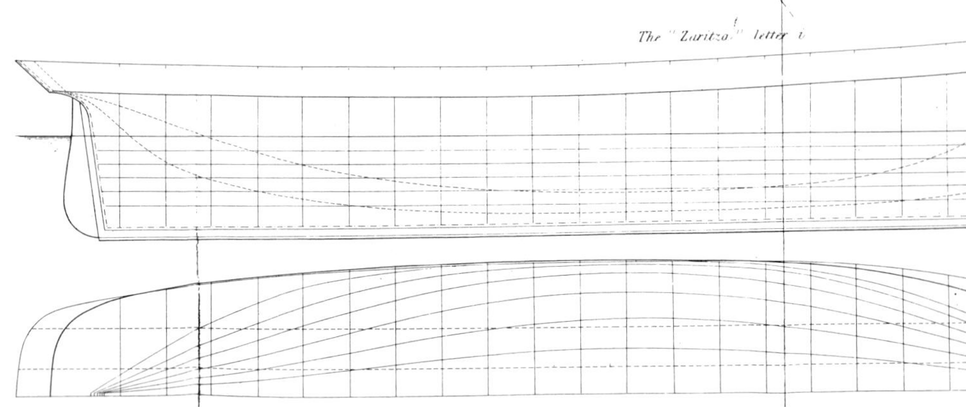

285: *Zaritza*. Built in 1857 at Bergen. Reproduced from plan in *Transactions of the Institution of Naval Architects*, 1866, vol VII, plate XV. Dimensions on plan, probably in English feet; 97ft-9in (length between perpendiculars on waterline) × 24ft-9in (moulded breadth) × 12ft-0 ¾in (depth from keel to planksheer); 270.12 tons om; 67 Norwegian laster. Employed in fruit trade between Sicily and Russia via the Baltic, making most voyages in January and February; thus she had to be a good sea-boat as well as fast.

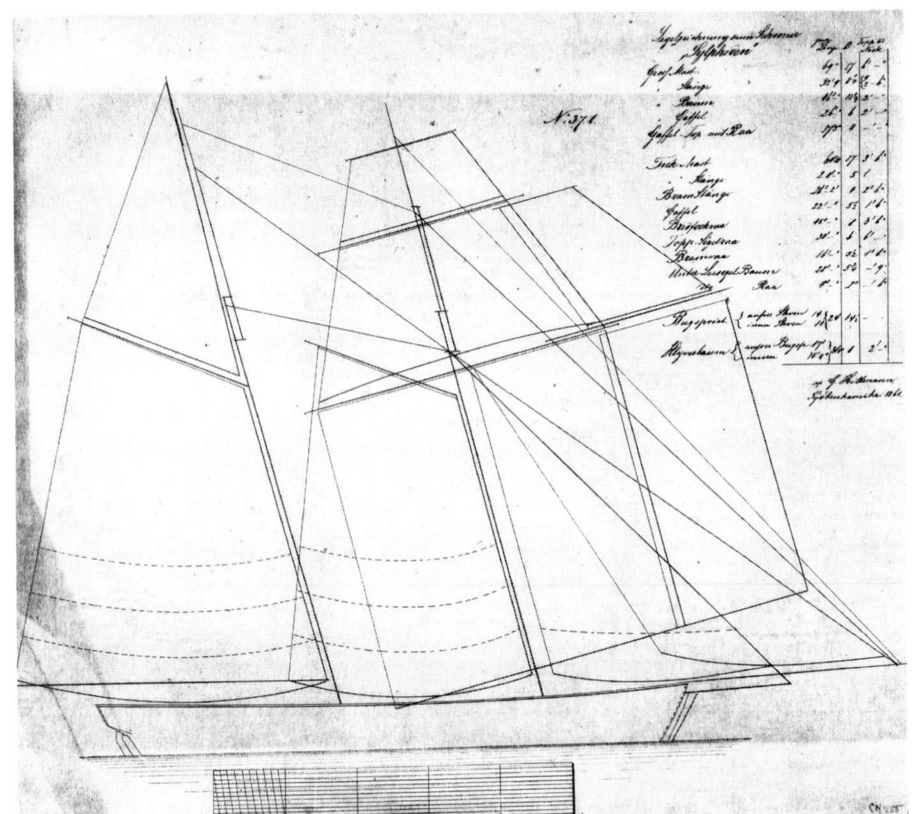

283: *Sylphiden*. Outline sail plan: Drawn by G Hillmann from same source as figure 282. Dated Copenhagen 1861. The shrouds and backstays are missing, but it would be correct for the sailmaker's use.

282: *Sylphiden*. Lines plan: Drawn by G Hillmann. This schooner was probably built in 1854 at the Danish port of Nakskow. I have not translated the measurements. She has steep deadrise, large beam above the LWL, and convex waterlines. Photographed from Hillmann's plan at Mariner's Museum, Newport News.

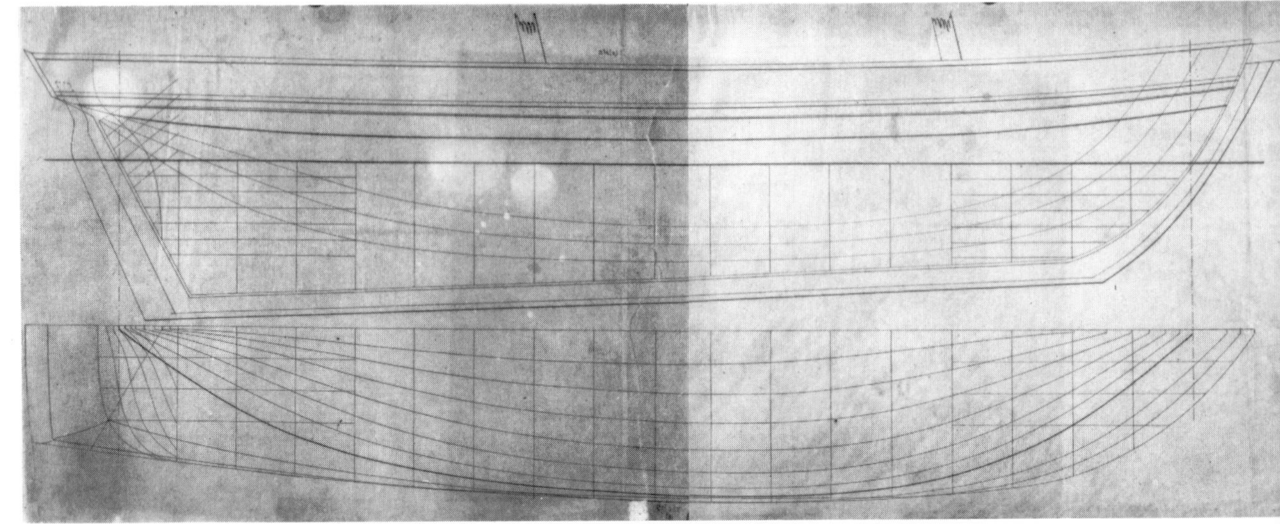

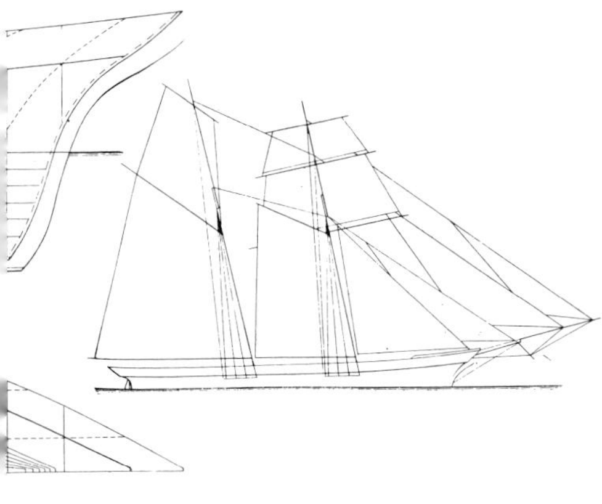

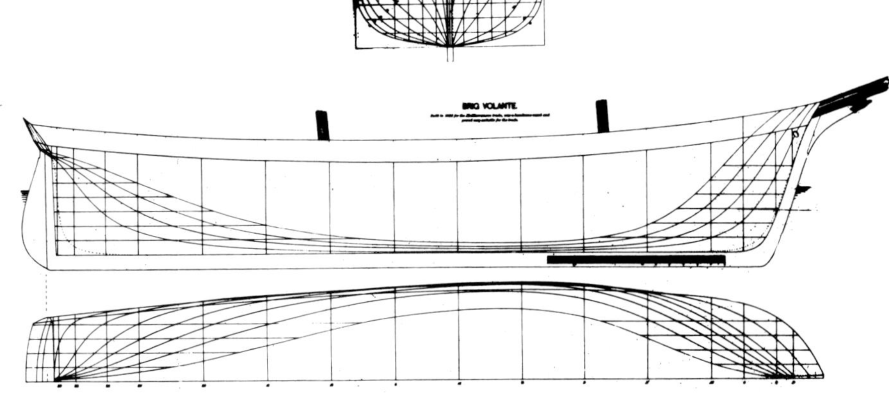

287: *Volante*. Lines plan: Reproduced from *Plans of Wooden Vessels* by William H Webb. Built by Webb at New York in 1853. Dimensions written on plan: length on deck 112ft-0in, beam moulded 26ft-6in, depth of hold 11ft-3in, tonnage C M 300 tons. The wording beneath the main title reads: 'Built in 1853 for the Mediterranean trade, was a handsome vessel and proved very suitable for the trade'.

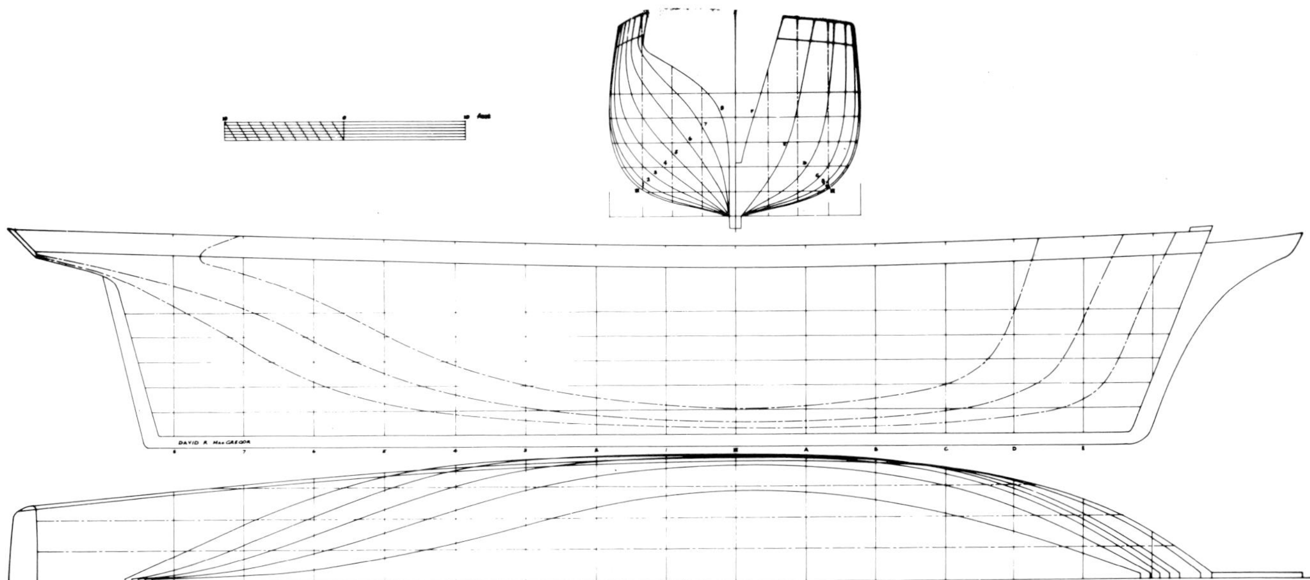

286: *Fling*. Built of wood in 1858 by J W & A Uphsam at Brixham. Lines taken off half-model in builder's possession. Dimensions: 92.5ft × 21.0ft × 12.5ft; 139 tons. No reconstruction. Rigged as two masted topgallant-yard schooner.

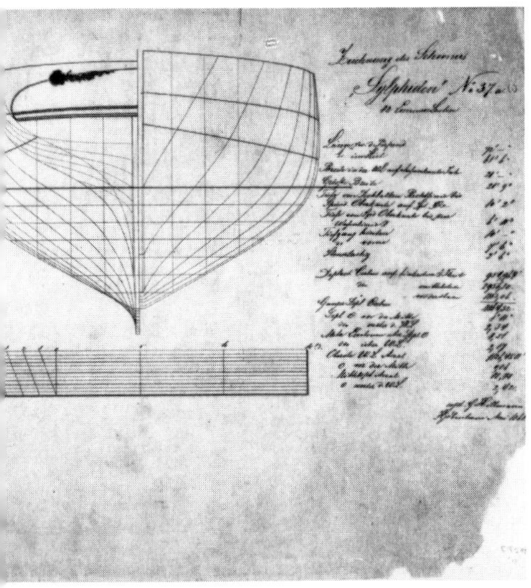

clippers which were wont to crowd our docks' and the 'extraordinary rapidity and regularity' of their voyages.[132] It was estimated that in 1854 some 240 craft were engaged in the Azores fruit trade, mostly carrying oranges.[133]

Many such splendid schooners were built in south Devon, and J A & W Upham of Brixham produced some fine examples, such as the *Fling* whose lines are reproduced in figure 286. Her convex entrance, long concave run, good deadrise and slack bilges were typical of many other schooners from south-west England; a few small square-riggers also received such a hull form.

The half-model of the *Fling* was made to ½in-scale and is of the bracket or 'bird's nest' type (figure 7). It agrees closely with the register dimensions which consist of 92.5ft by 21.0ft by 12.5ft and 139 tons. Her keel was laid on 26 December 1857, and she was launched on 7 October 1858 at a cost of £10.10s per ton builder's measurement. Only good quality timber went into her construction to achieve a class of 12 A1, and her Dartmouth owners, Browning, Drew & Co, undoubtedly received an excellent vessel. When the lines were taken off some years ago, the model

288: The Salcombe-built schooner *Queen of the West* was built in 1849 of 120 tons nm and 155 tons om. Her closely-spaced masts and lofty rig were typical of clipper schooners in the fifties and sixties. A square foresail was doubtless set when running before the wind. *F A L Fairweather.*

reposed in her builder's office, but now it is deposited at the National Maritime Museum, Greenwich.

No load waterline is given on the model, but there would have been a freeboard of about three or four feet amidships, and there was probably a drag of two or three feet aft. No spar dimensions are known, but she must undoubtedly have been rigged as a two masted schooner with a square topsail and topgallant on the fore; she may have even carried a royal as well, and she would certainly have been fully equipped with all the necessary staysails and stunsails for a clipper of her class, and her appearance could well have resembled the Salcombe-built schooner *Queen of the West*, a painting of which appears in figure 288.

Other clippers for the fruit trade were built in East Anglia, such as the schooner *Peri* which was launched in 1858 by Thomas Harvey & Son of Wivenhoe. Hervey Benham writes that she was 'famed for her phenomenally fine run'[134] and a set of lines drawn out by Charles G Davis confirms this. Figure 289 shows these lines which have been redrawn from an article in the American magazine *Yachting*.[135]

The *Peri* measured 98 tons nm and 170 tons register, was classed 14 A1, and was owned in London by T Nelson & Co, who already owned the schooner *Lightning*, which Harvey had built in 1852. The *Peri* must have ben lost in 1861 because she is not in *Lloyd's Register* for 1862. Dimensions scaled off the plan give register dimensions of approximately 86ft-3in by 19ft-3in by 9ft-0in. She has a raking midsection which Davis attributed to all Harvey's boats and this gives her very easy buttock lines. The entrance is long and convex, and the run very concave, and there is a fair amount of deadrise with firm bilges. The shape of the sections in the body plan are unusually regular in the fore and after bodies. According to the plan, she drew 8ft-3in of water forward and 10ft-6in aft.

Charles Davis calls the *Peri* a 'butterman', because he says she raced milk, cheese and butter up the Channel from Guernsey, and he has drawn her with five headsails and four yards on the foremast, but with a rig so lofty that the height of the foremast from rail to truck is equal to the hull length from taffrail to figurehead. This is exceptionally tall by any standard, especially for a fine-lined hull such as hers.

Thomas Harvey & Son produced many clippers and yachts, in addition to a schooner-rigged pilot cutter for Liverpool.

For a schooner, speed was all-important, and the sort of voyage time hoped for was the 17 days which the schooner *Elinor* took in 1869 from London Bridge to St Michaels in the Azores and back home again.

In his celebrated handbook entitled *On The Stowage of Ships and Their Cargoes*, R W Stevens wrote in the 1869 edition under the section on 'Fruit':

> 'Several schooners belonging to Brixham are built purposely for the Mediterranean trade, and are engaged almost entirely in it; they are long flat vessels with sharp ends, but much sharper aft than forward, so much so that little or no dunnage is required beyond the ballast, which is all placed in the narrow part of the hold. One of these schooners, the *Ocean Bride*, registers 144 ton, is 120ft overall; keel 92ft; extreme beam 20ft; and depth of hold 11ft 6in. She took in at Patras, in 1860, 180 ton (net) currants. The ballast, 20 ton, was all stowed abaft the main hatchway. She will stow 50 ton of St Michael's oranges — 20 boxes to the ton — with 55 ton ballast.'

The *Ocean Bride* cited here was built at Brixham by Richardson in 1859 and was owned in the same port by Sheers & Co.

Some three-masted schooners made their appearance in the 1850s: Gourlay Brothers of Dundee built the narrow iron-hulled *Alma*

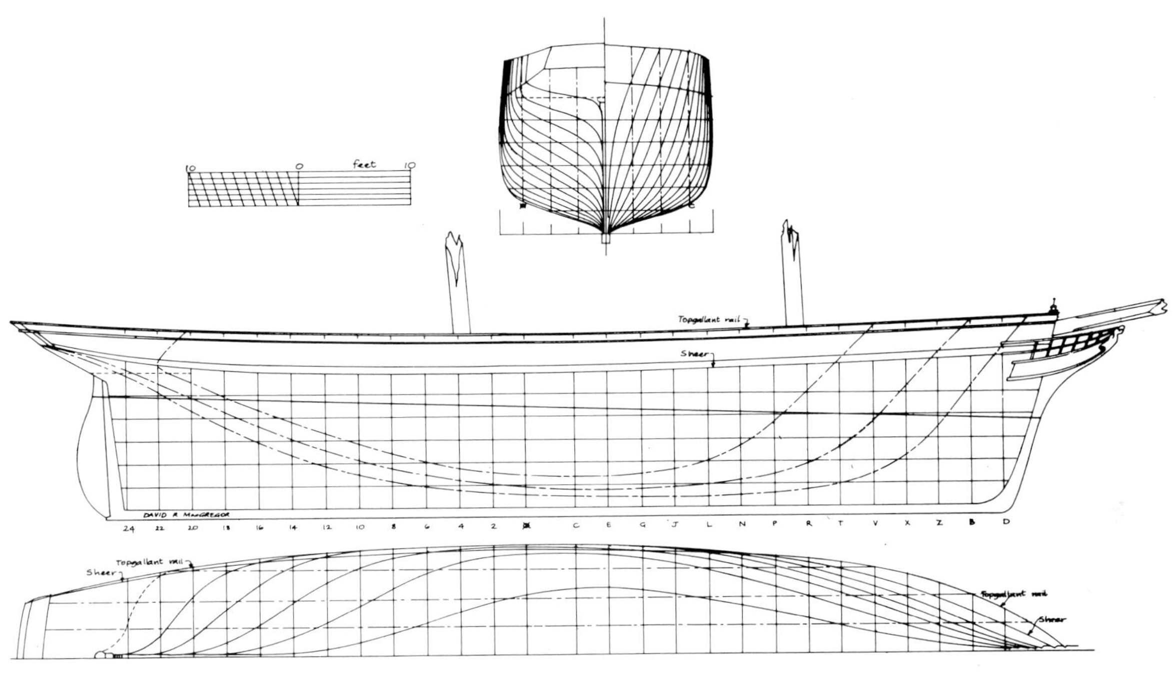

289: *Peri.* Built in 1858 by Thomas Harvey & Son at Wivenhoe. Redrawn from small reproductions of plans drawn by C G Davis in American Magazine *Yachting,* January 1925, p51. Dimensions scaled off plan (as for register): 86ft-3in × 19ft-3in × 9ft-0in (approx.); 98 tons nm and 170 tons register. Reconstruction: spacing of stations which had almost been obliterated in magazine article; positions of masts from sketch of sail plan by Davis in same article.

290: This freehand sketch of *Peri* under sail was done by D G Davis and published to accompany his plans of the schooner. She looks exceedingly lofty.

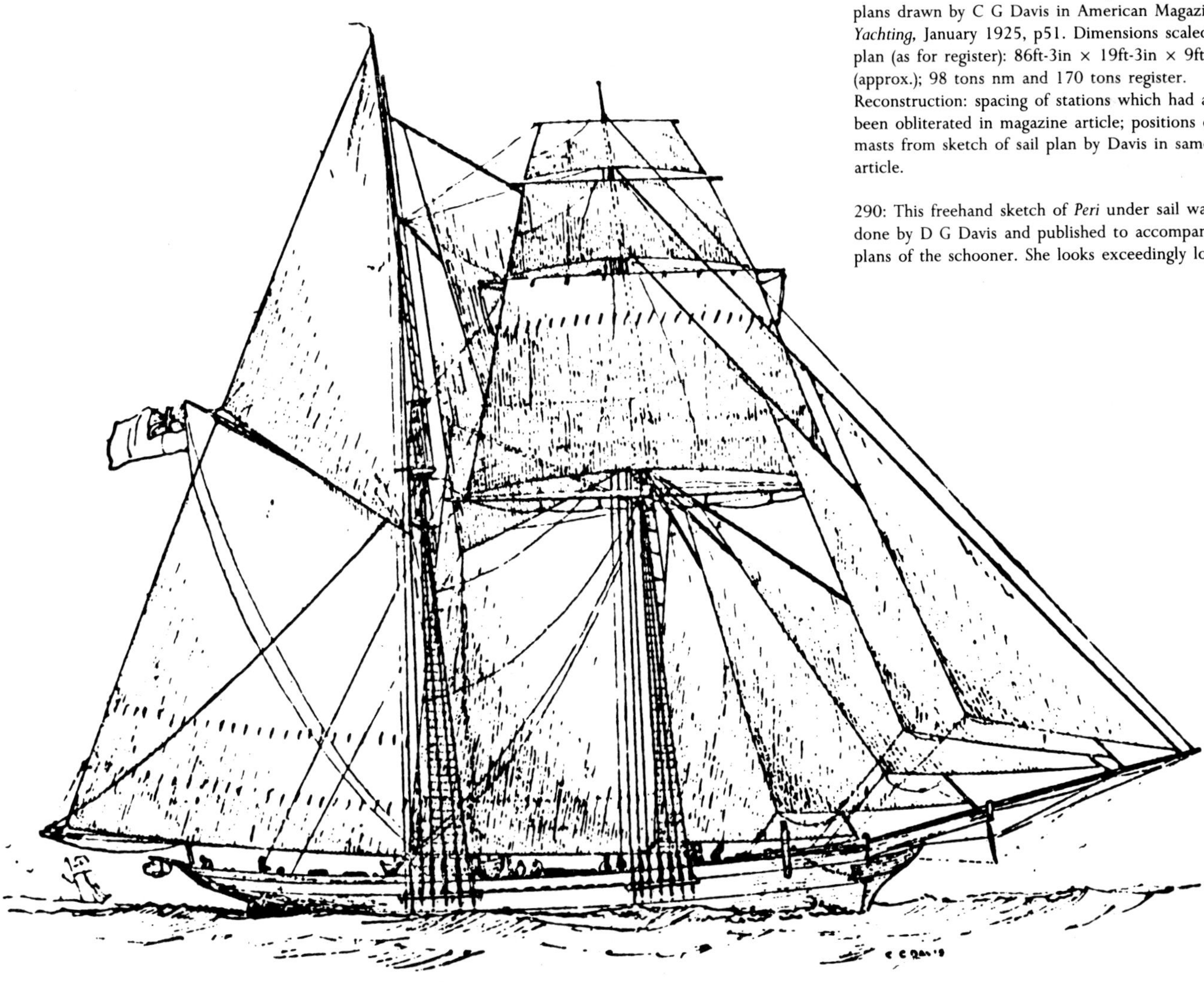

in 1854 to sail to the Australian gold fields. At Shoreham, James Balley launched the *Wild Dayrell* in 1856 of 310 tons, designed with hollow lines, but without any square sails and with a 'Yankee three mast schooner rig' of which great things were expected; in the same year, Balley built the *Osprey* at a cost of £3,164 with four yards of her foremast in the conventional style.[137] *Wild Dayrell* was possibly an attempt at copying an American 'tern' schooner which was a new style. Due to the fact that so many harbours dried out at low water, British sharp-lined schooners could not afford to have deadrise or else they were in danger of falling over on their sides as the tide ebbed. The design and construction of fine-lined schooners continued throughout the nineteenth century as there were always reasons why an owner wanted a fast vessel.

One fast deep-sea schooner was the *Susan Vitery* which was built at Dartmouth in 1859 by W Kelly, and after trading to the Azores and then carrying cod from Newfoundland she had the distinction of being the last schooner in the home trade to sail without an engine. Given a third mast in 1903 and renamed *Brooklands* she survived the Second World War and was finally lost near the Tuskar in 1953 when sailing under her original name.

291: This somewhat crude representation of the schooner-brigantine *Persian* was done by an unknown pierhead artist *who did not sign his work*. She was built in 1852 at Plymouth with measurements of 81.9ft × 19.2ft × 13.0ft and 142 tons, being in the Mediterranean trade. *MacGregor Collection.*

Conclusions

From the examples submitted for study there can no longer be any doubt that the extreme British clipper was as sharp as the American model and endowed with similar potential for speed. Furthermore, the so-called influence of American clipper ship builders has no foundation in fact because the British designers had their own traditions and the requirements for speed were not the same for the two countries. British iron clippers have received little recognition in the past but their builders made the most of the metal's qualities in their lengthy and beautiful hulls.

It has often been considered that hollowness of line was the trade mark of the clipper, but the plans given here show that a hull can be convex in one plane and concave in another over the same area. An observer is almost certain to say a bow is hollow when the topsides flare out, although the load line may in fact be convex.

Some of the most extreme clippers were built purely to satisfy their builder's whims on speed and design, and the results were not always productive of continually high average speeds, although fully capable of maximum speed for short periods. But the world would be sadder if they had not been built.

The large wooden-hulled American-built passenger ships received too large a proportion of praise and press comment which thereby prevented numerous other worthy clippers from receiving any mention at all. Many of these extreme clippers made slow passages which can often be attributed to the experience or ineptitude of the master, but another factor is the lack of knowledge about what courses to sail to find the best winds. The analysis of ships' logs by M F Maury and others led to the publication of recommended routes according to the season of the year, and in later years permitted comparatively full-bodied ships to achieve remarkably fast passages between ports where some of the extreme clippers in the 1850s had wasted days becalmed or beating against head winds. It may be said that the science of oceanography has contributed almost as much to a ship's speed as has the study of hydrodynamics.

292: This well-known photograph shows the schooner *Brooklands* under full sail in about 1930. She was originally built as a two-masted schooner under the name of *Susan Vittery,* having been constructed in 1859 by Kelly at Dartmouth, and she had a tonnage of 140. Her first years were spent in the soft fruit trade, bringing back oranges from the Azores. *Nautical Photo Agency.*

Seven

THE LATER CLIPPERS 1860-75

Introduction

One result of the first clipper ship boom of 1853–55 was that many classes of vessels were now built on sightly finer lines than previously so that the medium clipper began to replace the full-ended ship as the bulk carrier, the small loss of capacity in the finer ends being more than compensated by the longer hull. The slump of the late 1850s was followed by a shipbuilding boom for both steam and sail tonnage in the first half of the following decade and a number of fine-lined clippers for different trades were constructed. There was also a boom in building full-rigged auxiliary steamers, but these proved financially unsuccessful and several such ships later had their screws removed.

As pointed out before, this study of clippers is based entirely on the evidence of plans and models, and in their absence any description is treated with reserve. But it is thought that all the principal clippers to have been built on extreme lines are referred to, although later research may bring to light additional ships now forgotten or omitted through ignorance of their particulars. Clippers not

293: An amateur artist's impression of a clipper barque running before the wind under full sail. Obviously the hull interested him not at all as it is painted black all over without any detail; but the masts have a pale yellow wash. *MacGregor Collection.*

connected with the China trade appear to be less numerous although every effort has been made to present as representative a selection as possible. Only naval architects or shipbuilders with recognized skills in designing were entrusted by shipowners to create these clippers on which they decided to risk their capital.

A study of freight rates shows that fine-lined clipper hulls were employed only where rates were high enough to yield an above average return and so justify the small cargo capacity, permanent iron ballast, large crews, extensive area of canvas, racing spars and expensive maintenance. All these factors severely restricted the number of ships. Occasionally, a shortage of ships in even the humblest trade could force up the rate and so gain the full-ended carrier an additional five to ten shillings per ton, but this was not a predictable certainty; whereas at the annual opening of the tea season in China the 'full bloods' — as the clippers were sometimes styled — could regularly expect to load for London at about £4 per ton and upwards in most years of the sixties, although £6 was about the limit. The freight of £8 per ton which the *Falcon*

295: A magnificent photograph of tea clippers in their prime at Pagoda Anchorage, Foochow. The photograph is dated 1868 and the ships named as *Sir Lancelot* (nearest) and *Spindrift* on the right. But the ships did not look like this. The most likely candidates are *Ariel* (left) - as the ship is flush-decked and *Thermopylae* (right), and the year 1869. The flags are at half mast. I have reconstructed the rigging above the top of the hills where it had been printed out. *Peabody Museum, Salem.*

 obtained at Hankow in 1864 was exceptionally high and the result of unusual circumstances, such as an acknowledgement of the heavy risks attending ships on the River Yangtze, the expense of towing the ship, a possible glut of tea and shortage of ships to load it.

Although it seems unlikely that any extreme clippers were built exclusively for the Australian trade after 1860, numerous clippers and a host of medium-clippers were constructed for it, because large numbers of passengers and emigrants were still carried and so speed remained important. Many of the clippers returned home direct from Australia, but others carried coal or other products to China and then brought home tea or cotton, thus making a triangular return route. A few clippers were built for the coffee trade to South America, and other smaller clippers rigged as schooners and brigantines continued to be built for the soft fruit trade, although steam was gradually replacing sail. It was competition in all branches of trade that encouraged the design and construction of fast sailing ships.

Although the demand for new sailing ships fell away in the second half of the 1860s, a limited boom for extreme tea clippers in the period 1865–69 goes against the general trend, and can probably be attributed to the fall in tea duties. In 1863, the duty was lowered from 1s 5d to 1s per pound and two years later it was cut to 6d per pound. This resulted in orders for new clippers as well as the appearance of more steamers which were soon loading the new season's tea on equal or preferred terms. It is an unfortunate fact that the ships launched for the China trade in the last five years of the 1860s are the ones which so frequently collect the title 'tea clipper'. Thus it was the drop in tea duties which stimulated orders for new China clippers, not the introduction of composite construction.

In the 1850s, the mania for speed spread into all categories of shipping and designs varied considerably, not merely from yard to yard but also in the designs of a single builder. Experiment was all the rage as long as orders for fast ships continued to be received, but when bulk carriers were needed designers tended to concentrate on a single type which, lengthened or shortened, would economically meet the client's needs. This eventually en-

294: Some of the ships lying here in the upper anchorage of the Woosung River at Shanghai are undoubtedly clippers. It has been suggested that the full-rigged ship in the centre could be the *Blackadder* which loaded tea at Shanghai in 1872. On the right background are some of the large white paddle steamers which plied on the river; that on the extreme right is the *Mirage*. Reproduced from a photograph in *Far East* (April 1877) in the collection of Ken and Jenny Jacobson.

couraged each yard to produce a particular brand of ship, easily recognisable by the experienced eye and although designs were kept as secret as possible there was great rivalry between each yard. Like other builders, Alexander Stephen was very reluctant to part with half-models or lines plans to prospective clients for fear of them being copied, and he was always insistent in having a client return his proposed half-model at the earliest opportunity.

The builders were in constant touch with each other on their visits to the shipowing centres when looking for orders; here they would meet, discuss current trends and prices, and go aboard ships in dry dock. For instance, Alexander Stephen Jnr was at Liverpool in October 1863 and went aboard the clippers *Serica* and *Young Lochinvar*, built by Steele for the China trade; a few days later, when in London, he accompanied Captain Killick aboard Alexander Hall & Sons' new ship *Yang-tsze*, of which Killick was part owner, and noted in his diary that 'she is much inferior to the *Eliza Shaw*', which he had just built for Killick's firm, Killick, Martin & Co.[1] All this dissemination of knowledge resulted in the tea clippers being built of a more or less recognisable type, particularly as owners usually ordered from a small circle of builders. Robert Steele of Greenock, Alexander Stephen of Kelvinhaugh, and Charles Connell of Scotstoun were the principal tea clipper builders on the Clyde; Alexander Hall and Walter Hood built at Aberdeen; William Pile built at Sunderland. Other yards building on the Clyde, Wear or Thames tended to model the outward appearance of their ships on well known vessels.

In the newspapers of the 1860s, there are enough articles on clipper ship performance to satisfy the most voracious appetite, but it is probable that twentieth-century writers such as Basil Lubbock obtained much of their information on China clippers from an anonymous article in the July 1873 issue of *Naval Science*, which concentrated purely on the ships of the 1860s and listed the principal names. Although the conclusions on tonnage laws are entirely incorrect, the remainder of the long article is well-reasoned, albeit the clippers of the 'fifties are virtually ignored. The widespread interest aroused throughout the country is also touched upon. The following extracts are especially pertinent:

> 'The relative merits of our clippers, especially those known as the China clippers, engaged in carrying home the early teas from China to the London markets, used to excite as much discussion and speculation at one time as horse-racing . . .
>
> 'The *Falcon* was a vessel considered by many to be the first of the now really handsome clippers, and the model from which sprang the designs of the now famous vessels which followed her in rapid succession.
>
> 'With this increased demand for clipper ships came increased emulation and excitement, and this again reacting upon the designers and builders led to increased excellence, and all helped to lead up to the great ocean races of 1865, 1866, and later years . . .'[2]

This passage about *Falcon* was given prominence by Basil Lubbock in his great pioneering book entitled *The China Clippers*, which first appeared in 1914, but with the superior information available today, based as it is on numerous plans and wider research, it can be shown that there are other contenders for the *Falcon*'s claim to fame.

The *Fiery Cross* and *Black Prince*

Although about ten years were to elapse before any clippers were built to equal the fineness of those ships of 1853–55, yet William Rennie's design for the second *Fiery Cross* provides an example of a fast ship which was the most successful China clipper in the years 1861–65. Built in 1860 at Liverpool and constructed by Chaloner, this ship set the pattern for the first half of the 1860s and thereby influenced later vessels. In November 1861, Alexander Stephen went aboard her in London on one of his numerous visits to obtain orders; ten months later he wrote in his diary: '*Fiery Cross* is the fastest ship in the China trade at present.'[3] This statement was certainly borne out by her performance as she won the coveted premium of first ship home with new tea in the years 1861, 1862, 1863 and 1865, whilst her outward passages in the same period include three between London and Hong Kong or Shanghai, at the time of the north-east monsoon, which average 90 days. No wonder she was so much admired.

In 1862 John Campbell of Liverpool, the owner of *Fiery Cross*, asked Alexander Stephen to quote a price for a composite ship of 750 tons based on the model of this fast clipper, and Stephen had a useful talk with him about ships for the China trade.[4]

The lines of the *Fiery Cross*, which I took

296: A painting of the *Fiery Cross* (1860) which James Dickie found at an antique fair and traced to a photographic studio in Edinburgh. It was probably made from a copy negative taken by this studio from a customer's painting, but the owner of the painting has not been traced. The painting accords well with her sail plan which I published in *The Tea Clippers* (p 122), even to the absence of a crossjack and the height of masts sufficient to set skysails.

297: The *Black Prince* was just leaving the builder's yard when this photograph was taken in 1863. She was designed by William Rennie. *James Henderson.*

off from a whole model in the Science Museum, London, were reproduced in *The Tea Clippers* and show a long, sharp entrance with slight concavity near the stem and an equally long run; there are hollow garboards, moderate deadrise, slack bilges and little tumblehome in the body plan; the quarter-beam buttock is not really straight where it intersects the load line aft. The absence of a topgallant rail is noteworthy and gives a light appearance, unlike Steele's *Falcon* and *Taeping*. Her deck layout indicates a raised quarter-deck and forecastle level with the rail, and the fittings would have been typical of other ships. The sail plan, reproduced in the same work, allowed for skysails on each mast, although curiously the leeches of the square sails are all drawn curved; however, the original plan is incomplete as no courses are shown nor any fore-and-aft sails, although I have reconstructed these on the sail plan.[5]

Her appearance in a photograph dated 1866, wherein she is shown with double topsail yards on the main but single topsails on fore and mizen, is confirmed by a painting done in the years 1866-68.[6] She had dimensions of 185.0ft by 31.7ft by 19.2ft and registered 695 tons, Alexander Stephen recorded the following additional figures on her: capacity 1050 tons tea; area of midsection to load line 424.12 sq ft; displacement at load line 1615.24 tons; displacement per inch 10.46 tons; length on load line 181.6ft[7] [lines plan scales 184:01.]

The influence of the *Fiery Cross* was strongly apparent in the *Black Prince*, a clipper designed by William Rennie and constructed by Alexander Hall & Sons, a combination which should have produced an outright winner in the China trade. But we are led to believe, through the writings of Captain Andrew Shewan, that much of this skill was undone by the lack of drive of her master, William Inglis, and his 'inconstancy of purpose'. Doubtless there were many other clipper captains of similar disposition who lacked nerve or energy on occasions, as there were only a few dauntless spirits who drove their ships with that untiring and restless energy that alone could achieve a record passage. But there has been no Shewan to record the other dilatory masters. Unfortunately, for William Inglis' reputation, Andrew Shewan sailed as an apprentice with him in 1866–67 and also knew him well by repute, with the result that his characteristic subterfuges have been remorselessly dissected to the detriment of the splendid ship he commanded. However, in calling *Black Prince* 'this much maligned and unfortunate tea clipper',[8] Shewan has unwittingly provided most of the fuel to kindle the flames.

William Rennie's career was outlined in chapter six and will not be repeated here, other than to state that the ships at present known to have been designed by him in the 'sixties consisted of *Fiery Cross, Chaa-zse*,[9] *Black Prince*, SS *Sea King, John R Worcester* and *Norman Court*. In spite of the fact that no plan or model of *Black Prince* has been traced it is almost certain that her hull form differed little from *Fiery Cross*, and Shewan remarks that she was supposed to be an improvement on the design of the latter. The register dimensions of the two ships are almost identical:

Name	*Dimensions*	*Tons UD*	*Coefficient of UD tons*
Fiery Cross	185.0ft × 31.7ft × 19.2ft	695	.61
Black Prince	185.0ft × 32.0ft × 19.0ft	707	.62

Other points of similarity are the mast and spar dimensions. The lengths from Hall's cost account of *Black Prince* agree almost exactly in every case with the published sail plan of *Fiery Cross*, with the exception that *Black Prince*'s bowsprit and jibboom were each about five feet shorter and that the mainmast was stepped two feet further aft. Both ships were equipped with Cunningham's roller-reefing topsails. The *Black Prince* crossed three skysail yards, stunsails on fore and main up to royals, and even topmast stunsails on the mizen. The latter are most unusual, but the builder lists the length of these booms as 31ft-0in and 6½in in diameter; unlike naval ships, they would hardly have been rigged merely to exercise the apprentices. Figure 315 shows mizen stunsails set in HMS *Active*. The photograph of *Black Prince* as a brand new ship is the best portrait of her and indicates the slight differences in rig between her and *Fiery Cross*, such as having three head-sails instead of four, a hoisting spanker hooped to the mizen, and a spencer gaff. As an indication of the size of *Black Prince*'s spars, the main yard measures 72ft-0in long, the main skysail yard 25ft-0in, and the length of the mainmast from deck to truck is 137ft-6in. The lower masts and bowsprit are of iron, and the topmasts, lower yards and topsail yards of steel.

Alexander Hall & Sons were certainly giving flying kites to their ships in 1863 because the *Reindeer*, of similar size to *Black Prince*, was equipped with a sliding gunter moonsail mast which extended 10ft-0in above the main skysail mast. Altogether the from produced four first-class ships for the China trade in 1863: *Black Prince, Fy-chow, Reindeer* and *Yang-tsze*.

The contract price for *Black Prince* was £18 per ton BM on an agreed tonnage figure of 911 8/94 which together with an extra of £400 for planking the bottom in teak worked out to a total of £16,799.10s.7d. When ready for sea the first cost had risen to £17,540.16s.1d or £23.10s per ton register.[10]

When Captain Shewan visited the *Black Prince* in the West India Dock after she had newly arrived from Aberdeen in the autumn of 1863, he was accompanied by a man who had 'modelled and built fast ships, and for a season was with White of Cowes, the great yacht builders'. His friend thought highly of her looks and 'reckoned she would prove very fast – the finest clipper that Aberdeen had yet produced'.[11] Unfortunately Shewan could not bring himself to be so complementary and he wrote:

> 'It was an undoubted fact that puzzled me, but the Aberdeen shipbuilders did not seem able to give their ships the smart *finish* peculiar to the Clyde-built ships.
>
> 'Yet the *Black Prince*, though no perhaps endowed with the peculiar *grace* of Steele's creations, who excelled in the beauty of the figureheads (usually a graceful female), was a very handsome looking clipper, much like the *Fiery Cross* but with a more powerful appearance.'[12]

The above remarks sound strange, coming from a man brought up in Aberdeen ships.

During the 1860s many of the clippers were built with much lower bulwarks than formerly and as many builders felt that a topgallant forecastle or full poop spoiled the run of the sheer, if it projected above the rail, greater ingenuity was required to provide suitable accommodation. This conflict between design and practicality is well exemplified in Captain Andrew Shewan's comments on *Black Prince*:

> 'I am inclined to think [Rennie] had to modify the design to give her a topgallant forecastle. Her bulwarks were only four feet high and the after end of the said forecastle was lowered to match the bulwarks (at least there was only a slight break). Thus the iron beams of the [forecastle] were, at the entrance from the deck, not more than five feet high, so that every man had to bend nearly double. However, the height increased as one moved forward.'[13]

Shewan recalled that severe accidents occurred as men rushed out on deck.

This unfortunate arrangement may well have been adopted in other ships, and an examination of plans reproduced here will show how the problem was solved by other builders.

No plans have been found for *Black Prince* but it is evident that her deck layout was typical of other ships. She had a topgallant forecastle; a deckhouse abaft the foremast; a longboat on deck and serving as an animal pen with spare spars each side; a raised quarter-deck with the usual fittings; an arrangement, in fact, very similar to that aboard the *Maitland*, as may be seen in figure 312. The *Black Prince* began life with a second small deckhouse abaft the mainmast, which was presumably used by the apprentices, but Captain Inglis later had it removed. The stanchions around the quarter-deck were of wood and supported an ornamented and carved wooden rail, with stout rope netting below.

The passage times of *Black Prince* stand comparison with other ships. Leaving Hong Kong in March 1864, she took only 93 days home to Liverpool with 1150 tons of cotton at a freight of £4.10s per ton. In 1866, she took 109 days from Foochow to London with new tea, beating *Ziba, Chinaman, Flying Spur, Ada, Falcon* and *Min*, which sailed at about the same time. On this occasion she loaded 1148 tons of tea at £5 per ton. Her net earnings on the first four voyages total £10,060.19s.4d.[14] So even if the *Black Prince* was not winning tea races, the owners' account book shows that she was earning good profits.

The auxiliary steamer *Sea King*

This is the only steam-propelled vessel whose plans are included in this book, and it is done to indicate the similarities between an auxiliary steamer and a pure sailing ship, together with a description of how the contract was secured; in addition, some of the remarks made by her designer and her builder are worth recording. The ship herself had an interesting history, becoming the Confederate cruiser *Shenandoah*, and later the Sultan of Zanzibar's yacht.

The story is told through the diary of Alexander Stephen, and begins on 4 September 1862 when he called at Robertson & Co's office in London and was told that they wanted 'the fastest ship that can be got and to have auxiliary power for the China trade to bring the first of the season's teas to London'. He also learned that they had been in touch with the shipbuilders Robert Napier, Scott & Co, Robert Steele & Son, and Alexander Hall & Sons, for ships built of iron or wood. Stephen promptly offered to build the ship for £22 per ton complete but without engines.[15]

Two days later Stephen was at Robertson & Co's office again and made a formal offer in the presence of Messrs Robertson, McMinnis and Wade – possibly three of the

298: This model of the auxiliary steamer *Sea King* was probably that made by William Rennie which Alexander Stephen claimed was too ornate. The hull-form differs little from a pure sailing ship.*Science Museum*.

partners — to build a composite ship inclusive of engines at a price of £22 per ton BM, and to dimensions of 216.0ft by 32.0ft by 21.0ft making $1071^{87}/_{94}$ tons BM. Stephen was to return to Glasgow to prepare the specification, model and drawings, and to keep the matter confidential. 'Thanks be to God for all His mercies', he wrote.[16]

But the contract was not yet settled by any means, and Alexander Stephen was back in London ten days later to find out why he had been instructed to stop work on the model. He was told that Mr Chapman of Gladstone & Co, the China merchants, objected to such a large sum of perhaps £29,000 being concentrated in a single hull, and also that James Hall of Alexander Hall & Sons had called quoting lower prices for ships in general, although without special reference to his one. The upshot was that Robertson & Co said they would write to James Hall asking for a specific price and then give Stephen the opportunity to requote. On 20 September, Stephen heard from Robertson's that James Hall would be naming a price in their London office on 22 September, so down he travelled again, to find that Hall had made a written offer of £25,550 to build the ship including engines.[17]

'After a long conversation', noted Alexander Stephen in his diary, 'I was asked to write out my offer and seeing that I was promised a preference and I would only be put on the same footing as Hall's, I wrote out my offer at £25,540 for 216ft-0in by 32ft-6in by 20ft-6in = 1104 tons and 120 hp, all according to specification. 12 A1; teak planking outside, also bottom teak; iron fastened and built under our shed, and pure [?] copper on bottom.'[18] This sum was only £10 less than Hall's price.

Next day, 24 September, he received Robertson's written acceptance after Mr Chapman had signified agreement.

Alexander Stephen was now able to recommence work on the model, and on 1 October worked through the night until 2 am on it. On 21 October he was down in London again, and left his model and lines plan with Robertson & Co for their approval. Next day, however, he met Messrs Chapman and Rennie at Robertson's and was handed a model for the ship made by Rennie. How the conversation went is unknown but his diary entry reads: 'Our model is sharper than Rennie's; I think they will take Rennie's!'[19] This was, of course, William Rennie, the noted naval architect, and Stephen must have been disappointed at having his design superseded. (In view of Stephen's comments about his design being for a hull of sharper form than Rennie's, it is worth noting that no lines plan exist in the firm's archives that might be construed as Stephen's original design.)

This was confirmed when Mr McMinnis visited Alexander Stephen & Sons' yard on 6 November, which prompted the following entry: 'As to Mr Rennie's lines, we are to adhere to them as near as practicable and as breadth and depth of ship we are to adhere to the specification and the length only varying same to be measured by the Custom House people.' The engines were to be made by A & J Inglis of 150 horsepower.[20]

Further diary entries by Alexander Stephen illuminate the story. When in London on 12 November he wrote: 'With Robertson & Co. Saw Mr Rennie's model, but it is made with a lot of small fittings which renders it of no use to us. Expressed my opinion that the ship is not sharp enough for the trade intended.'

William Rennie's model may have been the whole hull model now at the Science Museum, London, which is illustrated in figure 298. In style it is very similar to the Museum's model of *Fiery Cross* (1860) which Rennie also designed. As Stephen's firm had built those most extreme clippers *Hurricane, Storm Cloud, White Eagle* and *John Bell*, Alexander Stephen was well fitted to express an opinion on the sharpness of William Rennie's lines, although neither Rennie nor Robertson & Co may necessarily have been aware of this, and it is the only known occasion prior to 1875 that he was obliged to build a ship to someone else's design.

As the engines' power was raised by 30 hp, the extra price was £1,510, making the total for ship and engines £27,050, of which the engines amounted to £6,600.

On 21 November Stephen's began laying down lines in the mould loft. On 26 November he wrote: 'Mr Rennie in yard and measured the lines in the mould loft. Says it is a matter of form and could not find anything wrong. He calls tomorrow to let us know.' Presumably there had been a discussion on the hull form.

29 November: 'Mr Rennie of London in yard again but merely glanced at the lines of after body of Robertson & Co's ship in the moulding loft. He said he thought they were

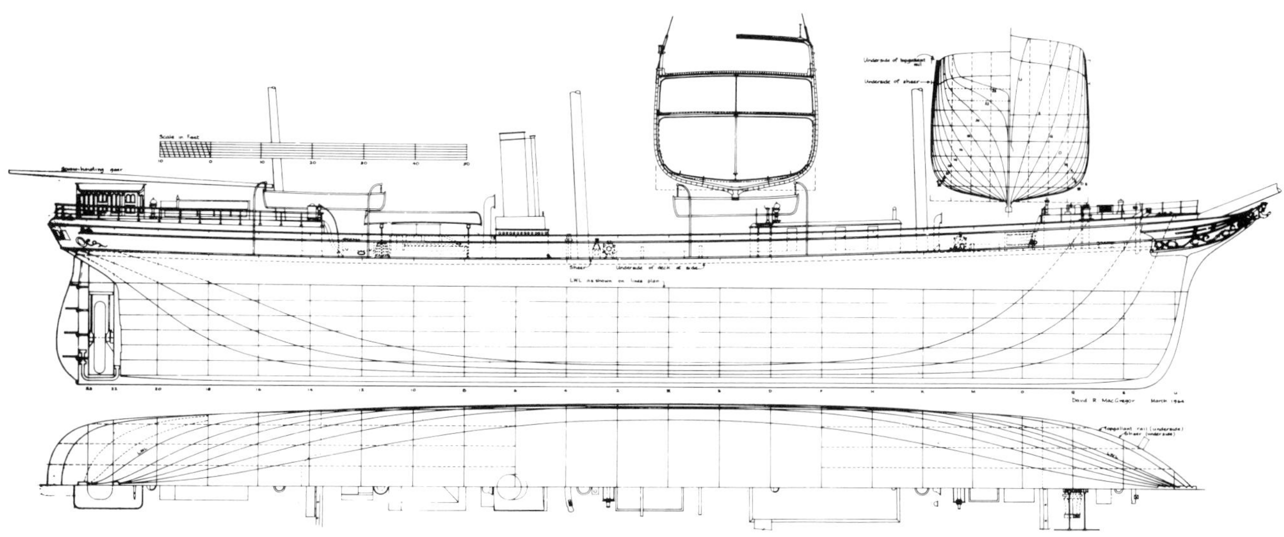

299: SS *Sea King*. Lines: Built of composite construction in 1863 by Alexander Stephen & Sons from a design by William Rennie of London. Redrawn from plan found in builder's archives bearing the stamp of 'Rennie & Marshall' and dated 1862. Dimensions for registry: 220.0ft × 32-5ft × 20.5ft; 790.28 tons net and 1017.82 gross tons. Reconstruction: deck level lowered, and stem and stern amended to conform to builder's longitudinal section. This longitudinal section and deck plan used for deck layout. Ship later became Confederate cruiser *Shenandoah*.

all correct. He goes to London tonight.'

This is the last reference to the subject of Rennie's lines, although William Rennie later visited the yard several times to inspect progress on the ship.

25 December: 'Received a tracing from Rennie & Marshall, London as requested by Robertson & Co for the latter ship's masts and yards.' Marshall was evidently Rennie's junior partner.

The lines reproduced here in figure 299 are redrawn from a lines plan discovered in Alexander Stephen & Sons' yard, being issued by Rennie & Marshall of London and bearing their embossed stamp. It is dated 'Oct 12th 1862' and again '6th November 1862 WR'. These initials could either stand for William Rennie or for William Robertson who was Stephen's chief draughtsman, and who could have dated and initialled the drawing when received. The plan does not bear William Rennie's signature. The figurehead is of a female and the only buttock line projected is the quarter beam buttock which is drawn dotted. The measurements on Rennie's lines plan are as follows, the words being in stencilled letters:

Length between perpendiculars	220ft-0in
Length at load line	216ft-3in
Breadth	32ft-6in
Depth in hold	20ft-6in
Depth in midships from top of keel	22ft-6in
Tonnage OM	$1126^{45}/_{94}$
Tonnage:	
under main deck	930.36
poop	95.41
gross	1025.77
Area of midship section to load line (moulded)	482.19 sq ft
Area of load line (moulded)	5499.65 sq ft
Displacement at do. (external)	2190 tons
Displacement per inch at do.	15.52 tons

The above table of dimensions is similar in the headings to that used on Rennie's original lines plan of *Norman Court*, and suggests that a special stencil had been cut for use in his office.

The first thing to notice in the hull form is the absence of deadrise, making the midsection quite unlike the second *Fiery Cross*. There is more similarity in the stem and lift of the head, and the shape of the entrance and run are broadly similar. The two ends are very long and sharp, but there is not much hollow to be found in the waterlines, although, like *Fiery Cross*, the buttocks are concave above the load line in the run. In this case, the maximum beam is kept low and there is a small tumblehome above, because deadrise in steamers was restricted by the necessity of fitting the machinery low down. There was some discrepancy in the hull profile between Rennie's lines plan and a longitudinal section prepared by Stephen, and the plan here is drawn according to the shipyard profile. This meant reducing the height from rabbet to underside of topgallant rail by nine inches, increasing the length on the loadline by one foot, and making the sheer slightly more pronounced. As the shipyard longitudinal section was headed '*Shenandoah*', it was probably of later date than Rennie's plan and therefore a more correct representation of the ship as built.

The *Sea King* was of composite construction and her keel must have been laid early in 1863, because the first frame was erected on 7 February, and the framing completed by the end of the month. The planking, of six inch stuff, took six weeks to lay on and was finished to the gunwale on 18 April. The *Lloyd's Register* survey report gave the keel as 15in by 18½in, floors 21in by 11/16in, frames 5in by 3¾in by $^{9}/_{16}$in, plate keelson 16in by $^{14}/_{16}$in with angles top and bottom; the room and space was 18in and the beams were secured to every third frame, there being 36 hold beams and 42 deck beams; four transverse bulkheads were fitted of ⅜in iron plate.

While the building work was progressing Alexander Stephen contracted with Confederate agents for building a paddle steamer to run at 20 knots, and he also became suspicious of a Captain Pearson 'whom I take to be a Federal spy'.

The *Sea King* was successfully launched on 17 August being, according to Stephen, the first screw steamer to be built of composite construction. Coinciding with the date of her launch was the arrival at Falmouth with the new season's teas of the steamer *Bahama*, 81 days out from Foochow, which Robertson &

Co had bought from the Confederate Government. The *Sea King* went down the Clyde on 7 October and ran her trial trip the following day between the Cloch and Cumbrae Lights. She took one hour, seven minutes to go down at an average speed of 12.25 knots and returned against a strong gale at 9.89 knots, making an average of 11.07 knots which pleased all on board. As the ship was underpowered, the speed was considered very satisfactory. The gross register tonnage after measurement was given as 1017.82 and the net register as 790. The class was 13 A1. The ship was sent round to London and was chartered to carry troops out to New Zealand. Alexander Stephen visited her there and reported that the whole transaction was very satisfactory to both parties, his net profit being £3,267 besides £500 for general charges, which was much better than he had anticipated when the contract was signed.[21]

The total cost of *Sea King* was estimated as follows:

Contract price	£27,050. 0s.0d
Extra tonnage 48 14/94 BM at £18 per ton	866.13s.7d
Three steel yards and topmasts	192. 0s.0d
Half Lloyd's special survey	25. 9s.0d
Launch money	5. 0s.0d
Extras	336.11s.6d
	£28,475.14s.1d = £24.12s.7d per ton BM
Paid in cash	20,287.10s.0d
Six months bill from 17 Aug	8,188. 4s.1d
Another calculation gave:	
Gross price	£28,470
less engines	6,600
Hull	21,870 = £19 per ton BM on 1152 tons BM[22]

Due to the low power of the engines, the ship had to be fully square-rigged, and presumably the engines were only used sparingly, or all fuel would have been rapidly consumed. This was the great disadvantage of auxiliary ships in that the money expended on fitting the machinery could rarely if ever be recouped, no matter how high the freights were. In this case the engines cost £6,600, and installation and other charges possibly accounted for another £500, added to which was the cost of carrying the special firemen, engineers and sufficient fuel. In turn, the latter serously reduced cargo capacity. Captain Killick told Alexander Stephen that the auxiliary steamer *Far East* was specially built in February 1864 to compete with *Sea King*. By the mid 1860s the rage for auxiliaries was dying out and some were having their screws unshipped. The *Sobraon* was designed as an auxiliary, to which reason she owed her flat floors, but the screw was never fitted and the aperture was filled in during construction.

Appropriately, the *Sea King* has a splendid figurehead of that nautical monarch and the deck layout in figure 299 is fairly typical for a ship of her type. The rocker arms to the windlass purchase are doubled to allow more men to man the handles; the pumps appear to be of the old up-and-down pattern; there are iron winches to the fore and main hatchways; on the poop there is mechanical gear in the large wheelhouse to hoist the screw clear out of the water when under sail alone. It is surprising that steam power was not harnessed to raise the anchor, heave out cargo or pump the ship. Many builders were slow to use steam power to ease some of the labour intensive jobs aboard. Some firms, however such as Barclay, Curle & Co and Jones, Quiggin & Co were beginning to use steam power even in pure sailing ships. The *Sea King*'s funnel is telescopic and can be lowered to lessen windage when under canvas alone.

Although not drawn on the plan in figure 299, there were 16 berths for seamen in the forecastle, where sufficient headroom was better contrived by William Rennie than in *Black Prince*. The forecastle also contained the windlass barrel, which was common enough although a messy affair for the men, but one to which they were accustomed. The big deckhouse contained the galley and a further 20 berths for the crew. There was accommodation in the poop for the master and two mates; also seven cabins for passengers, a pantry, a bath, and three WCs.

The sail plan is traced from one found in the builder's archives, which shows masts, yards, plain sails and standing rigging. The running rigging and stunsails were added according to a painting by W Napier dated 1865 which shows the ship as the Confederate cruiser *Shenandoah*, the lengths of the stunsail booms and yards being in accordance with contemporary practice. The builder's inventory does not list fore royal stunsails, any mizen staysails, nor a main trysail. The topsails are fitted with Cunningham's patent roller-reefing gear, and a newspaper report of 1865 infers that the royals were also fitted with this roller-reefing gear: 'She carries all the improved methods of reefing, furling and setting sails from the deck; has roller reefing topsails, royals, and a fly at each masthead'.[23] The lower masts, lower yards and bowsprit were of iron; the topmasts and their yards of steel. The absence of external chain plates to the mizen rigging was fairly common. She was a very handsome vessel, and undoubtedly was as well designed and equipped to make fast and safe passages as any ship of her type.

Her maiden passage took her out to Auckland in 74 days from London; thence to Sydney and from there to Shanghai in 23 days. Here tea was loaded and then she took 79 days home to Deal, which was reached on 7 September 1864. The time of 79 days included five days spent coaling at the Cape of Good Hope and the Cape Verde Islands, which suggests that she steamed a fair amount in calms. Robertson & Co were well pleased with their ship but thought some additional longitudinal strength would have been advantageous. Alexander Stephen visited her in Wigram's dry dock at Blackwall on 15 September and heard a report that she had been sold to a Liverpool firm for £35,500. If this is correct, the owners must have made a clear profit of £7,000 together with £2,000 or so net earnings on the voyage.

After transfer of ownership, the *Sea King* left London apparently for a voyage to Bombay, but off Madeira she was handed over to the Confederate Government and renamed *Shenandoah*, receiving at the same time arms and stores from a supply ship. Thereafter, she cruised in pursuit of Federal ships.

News that the Civil War had terminated was six months old when it reached her in the North Pacific ocean. Lieutenant Waddell, her master, thereupon decided to make for a European port, and 123 days later she entered the River Mersey on 6 November 1865. She made this passage without putting into any port for supplies. At Liverpool she

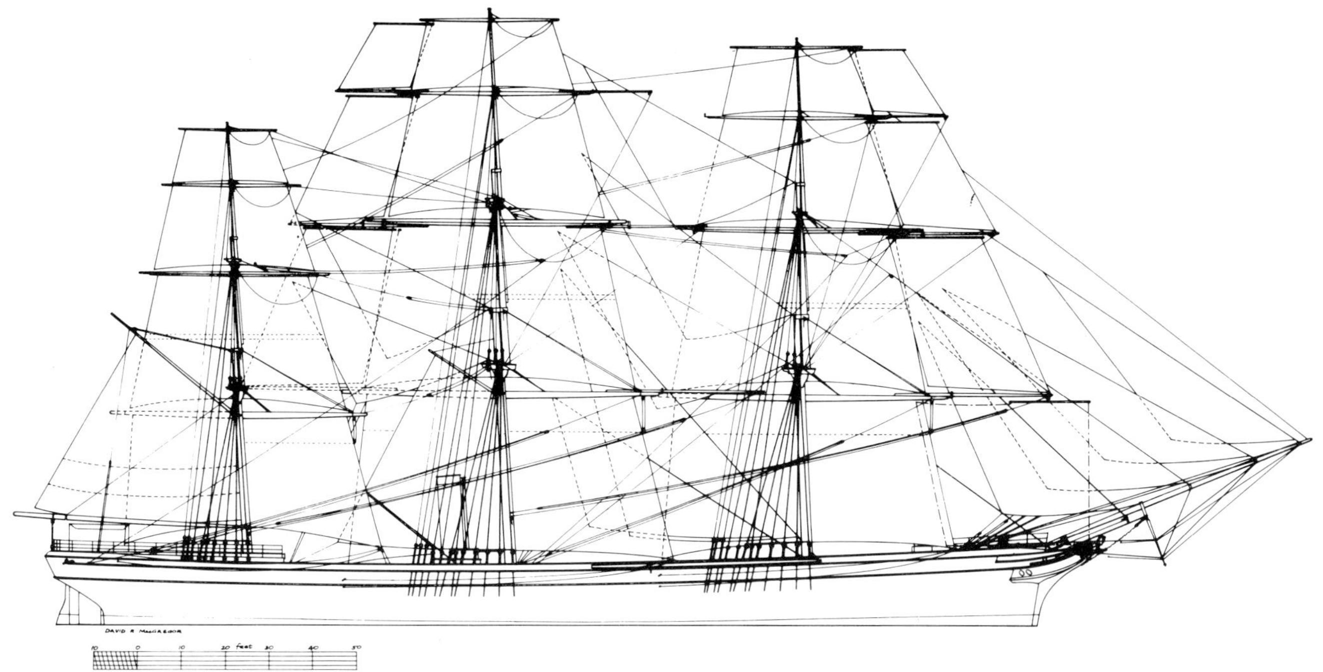

300: SS *Sea King*. Sail Plan: Redrawn from plan in builder's possession. Reconstruction: running rigging and stunsails from painting by W Napier dated 1865. Lengths of stunsail booms and yards in accordance with contemporary masting rules.

was handed over to the American consul, and later was despatched to New York but was driven back and disabled by severe gales. Kellock & Co were accordingly instructed to auction her, and in March 1866 she was knocked down to M R Wilson for £15,750.[24] She seems to have remained idle at Liverpool until October of the same year when Smith & Fleming bought her through Stoddart Brothers for use as a yacht by the Sultan of Zanzibar. She was renamed *Sea King* and she sailed for Bombay. In 1872, she was reported as having been sunk in a hurricane at Zanzibar in April but that the crew of HMS *Wolverine* succeeded in refloating her. She was finally wrecked in 1879.

Other clippers of 1860–68

From plans and models examined, ships that merit the classification 'clipper' or 'medium clipper' and which are not analysed elsewhere in this chapter are included in this section. A selection of some built in the boom of the early 1860s is tabulated below:

Further particulars of these and other clippers built after 1863 are given in this section.

Alexander Hall's first composite ship was the *Reindeer* built in 1863 — not to be confused with the clipper of the same name which he built 15 years earlier — and the *Aberdeen Journal* described her launch in its issue of 11 February 1863 in these words:

> 'LAUNCH.—On Wednesday last, there was launched from the lower building yard of Messrs Alexander Hall & Co, Footdee, a fine vessel of 904 tons register, and 903 tons builder's measurement, specially designed and built for the China trade, on the new principle of iron frame, planked with East India teak, fastened with screwed brass bolts galvanised, iron masts, steel yards and topmasts, wire rigging and all her equipments of the most modern style and finish. Her dimensions are—extreme length, 200 feet; breadth 32 feet; depth 21 feet. She is the property of Jervis Robert Wardley, Esq, of Liverpool, whose lady stepped forward and christened the vessel "Reindeer", as it gilded into its future element. Captain McClellan, late of the China tea clipper "Chrysolite," (turned out by the same builders) takes command. This vessel will take the highest class at Lloyd's, viz, 15 years A1, and will sail from this port direct for China in 8 or 10 days, to bring home the first teas of the season.

Some clipper ships built 1860–63

Date	*Name*	*Material*	*Rig*	*Dimensions*	*Tons*	*Builder*
1860	*Orange Grove*	iron	bk	146.6ft × 25.6ft × 15.9ft	398	Barclay, Curle
1861	*Ganges*	iron	S	192.0ft × 33.2ft × 20.6ft	839	W Pile
1861	*Highflyer*	wood	S	193.7ft × 35.5ft × 20.0ft	1012	R & H Green
1861	*Mansfield*	wood	bk	133.0ft × 25.6ft × 16.9ft	357	B E Nicholson
1862	*Helen Nicholson*	iron	S	180.0ft × 30.0ft × 19.7ft	717	J Reid
1863	*Childers*	wood	S	194.3ft × 35.4ft × 21.9ft	1016	R & H Green
1863	*Eliza Shaw*	comp	S	184.5ft × 30.6ft × 18.3ft	696	A Stephen
1863	*Everest*	wood	S	171.8ft × 30.0ft × 19.2ft	571	T & J Brocklebank

None of the above ships can be considered of extreme clipper form. The *Mansfield*, whose lines were taken from a half-model owned by Benjamin Nicholson of Carlisle, has a schooner-type hull formed after the style of the *John Williams III* but with a more hollow run.

Like some of John Reid & Co's other ships, the *Helen Nicholson* was of a good length with a fair amount of deadrise and slack bilges. Her half-model is in the Glasgow Museum. Her first few years were spent in the South American trade and then she was switched to the China trade.

Another iron ship, the *Ganges*, has an obvious kettle bottom hull, for whereas *Taeping*'s maximum moulded beam is 11ft above the rabbet, that of *Ganges* is only eight feet. The latter's deadrise is negligible, but the floors round up to the maximum beam which is placed close above firm bilges, and then the sides tumblehome 20in. However, the entrance and run are long and sharp and her dimensions give her approximately six beams to length. She was William Pile's first iron ship and was launched in July 1861 for James

Nourse's coolie trade; Basil Lubbock terms her 'the clipper of Nourse's fleet'.[25] Her half-model in the Sunderland Museum is made to the unusually large scale of ⅜in to one foot.

Everest was a square-sterned ship with big deadrise and fine ends, and undoubtedly the sharpest of all the ships built by T & J Brocklebank for the China trade.

Eliza Shaw was a finer version of the numerous clippers turned out by Alexander Stephen & Sons in the 1860s, but like some of his other ships she looks under-canvassed.

Highflyer, designed as an auxiliary steamer but built without a screw aperture, and also *Childers*, were fairly similar ships to come from Green's yard at Blackwall; their midship sections resemble that of *Eliza Shaw* but each had a finer entrance.

Another square-sterned vessel is the iron barque *Orange Grove* of 385 tons, built for the West Indies trade, and designed with little deadrise; some hollow is worked into the hull near stem and sternpost. She has a flush deck with a big deckhouse right aft while the petty officers and boys have a small house abaft the foremast, and the crew were quartered in a small forecastle entered through a scuttle on the fore side of the windlass.

Eliza Shaw, Highflyer and the Aberdeen ship *Ethiopian* (1864) had an interesting arrangement for their after accommodation, which was placed in a large deckhouse extending from side to side. The ship's main rail was approximately 4ft-6in above the deck and the sides of the house were rounded down on to the rail, just as in a poop extending right to the stern. However, there was a gap between the after end of the house and the taffrail — in *Eliza Shaw* it was 15ft — where there was a low deck occupied by binnacle, wheel and wheel box. To get forward from the wheel meant going up over the house by means of the ladders provided or else down steps, through the house and out on to the main deck. This arrangement was only found in a few sailing ships in the early 'sixties, although it can be seen in some steamers.

A rather lean year was experienced in 1864 and the only possible candidate for inclusion so far discovered is the *Mofussilite*, built by Alexander Stephen & Sons. She is a borderline case between a clipper and a medium clipper, with a short, sharp entrance but a

301: The iron ship *Mirzapore* of 1186 tons loading at Maryville, North Vancouver towards the end of the last century. With the *Cassipore* and *Dinapore* of roughly similar size, she was built by Pile, Spence & Co at West Hartlepool in 1863 for Mackinnon of Liverpool. As their names suggest, they were in the India trade. The quarter-deck arrangement is somewhat similar to *Cutty Sark*, with a house on deck and a raised quarter-deck surrounding it. *Provincial Archives, Victoria.*

302: *Everest*. Lines plan: Traced from shipyard plan in offices of T & J Brocklebank. Built in 1863 at Whitehaven by T & J Brocklebank with dimensions of 171.8ft × 30.0ft × 19.2ft and 571 tons. No reconstruction.

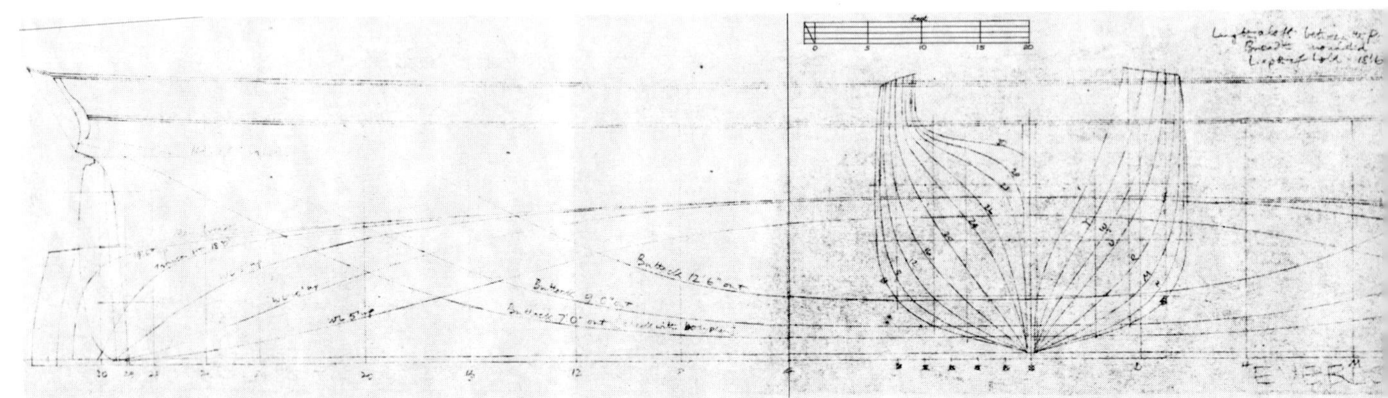

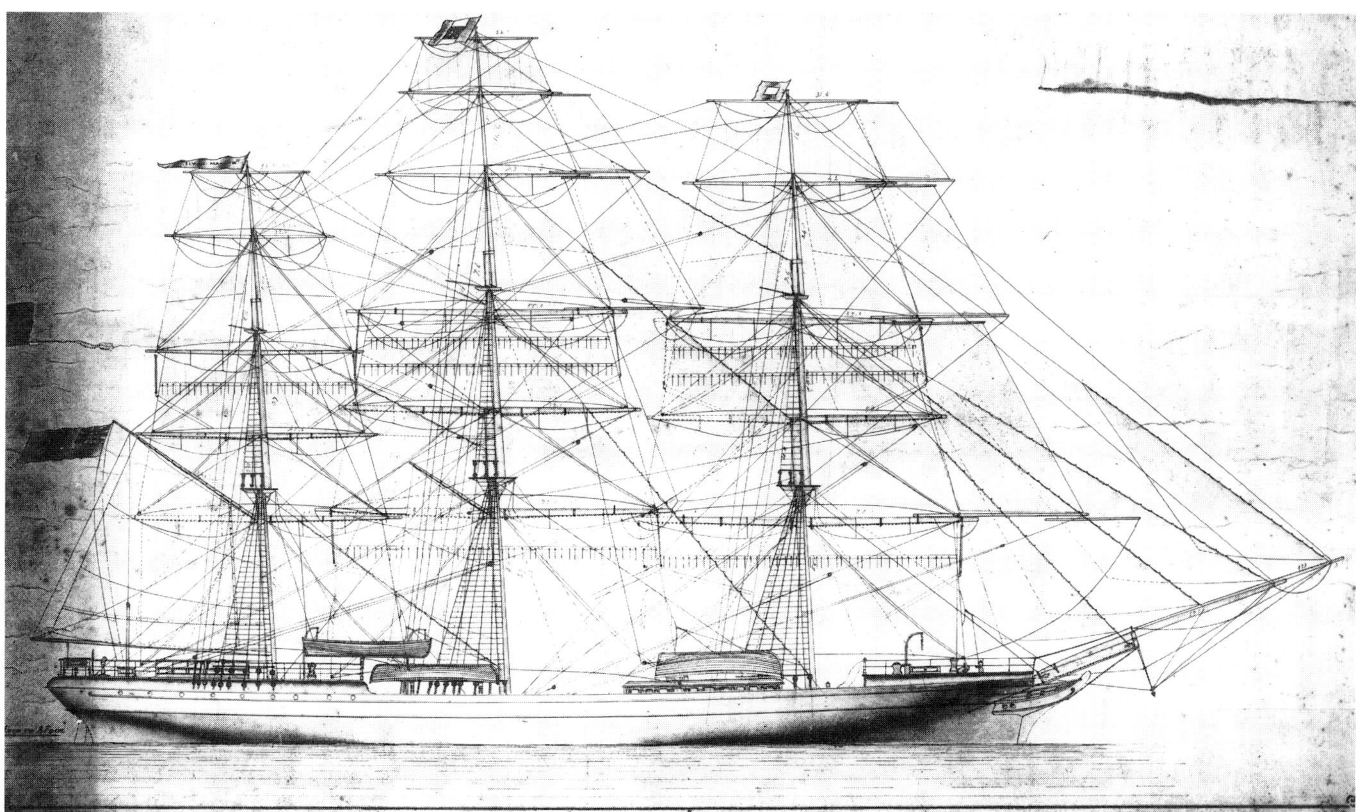

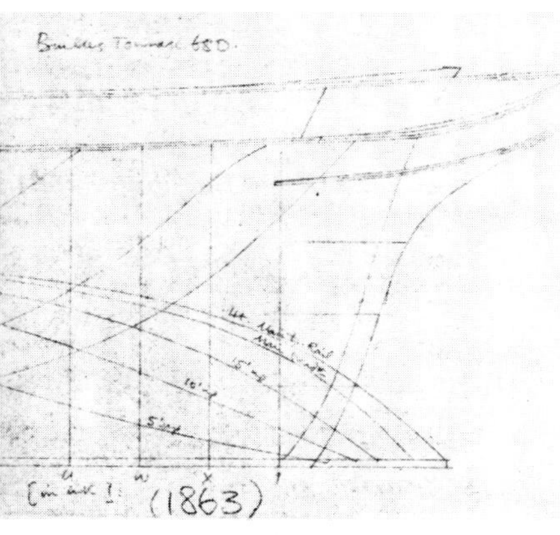

303: This watercolour of the medium clipper *Hoang Ho* shows the appearance of ships which Alexander Stephen & Sons of Glasgow were building for the China trade in the 1860's. She was constructed in 1864. In the painting the hull is given a bluey-geen colour; there is a Liverpool pilot schooner away on the left. *James Dickie Collection.*

306: *William Davey.* Sail plan: This is an unusually well-detailed plan for a builder to make of the sails, spars and rigging, particularly by including the stunsails and so much running rigging. Built 1866 by Alexander Stephen & Sons, Glasgow; plan photographed when in possession of the builder.

longer run; there was little deadrise but considerable tumblehome. The influence of *Tyburnia* (1857) is still apparent in her design. She was an expensively-built composite ship costing £20.10s per ton on $1043^{76}/_{94}$ tons BM and classed 15 A1. Plans of the clipper barque *Fusi Yama* are typical of the Stephen's ships of the 1860s as regards hull form and deck layout.

In Guernsey, the *William Le Lacheur* was built in 1864 by James Sebire and a photograph taken in the 1860s shows quite a fine-

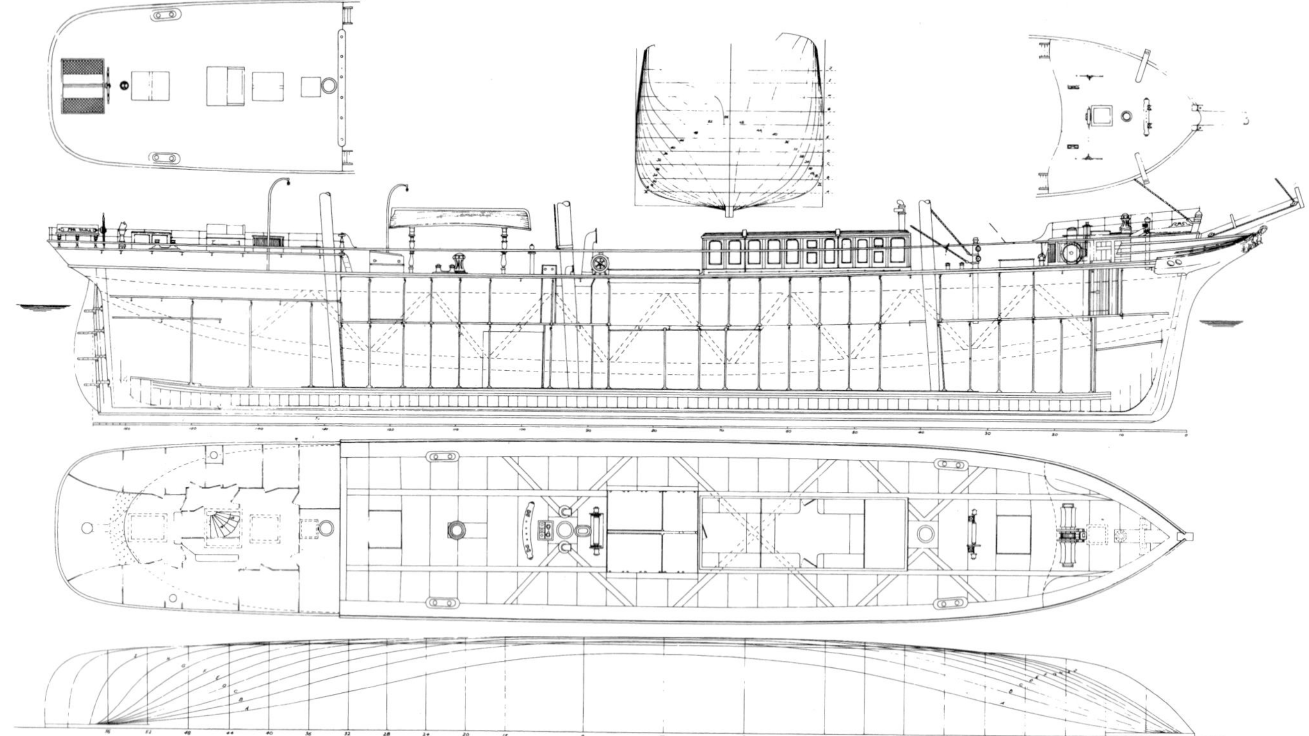

304: *Fusi Yama.* Lines, longitudinal section and deck layouts. Redrawn by E N Wilson from tracing made of builder's plan. Built in 1865 by Alexander Stephen & Sons, Glasgow, with dimensions of 165.5ft × 28.1ft × 17.0ft and 556 tons net and gross. Reconstruction: deck layouts for fo'c'sle and raised quarterdeck; some stations omitted amidships for sake of clarity. Diagonal iron trussing outside iron frames shown on dotted section.

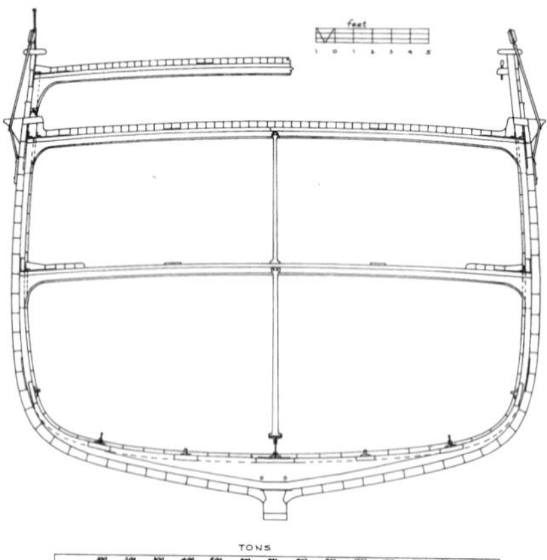

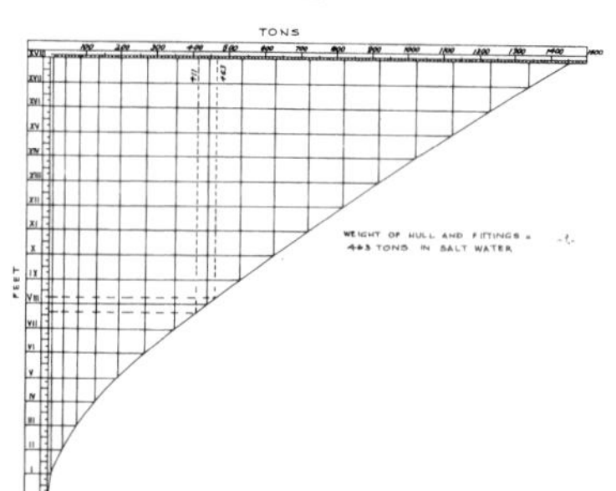

lined hull with some deadrise. This photograph, figure 307, is unusual in showing a ship of this date completely out of the water. She is still in her prime, crossing three skysail yards above roller-reefing single topsails. The proportion of hull depth to total mast height is rather similar to the *Maitland*. Her measurements were 165.8ft by 30.5ft by 17.7ft, 539 tons under deck and 573 tons net, and she classed 14 A1. These measurements give a

305: *Fusi Yama.* Sail plan: Redrawn by E N Wilson from tracing made of builder's plan. Reconstruction: chain plates and channels (from midship section). Running rigging and studding sails would be as on other vessels: the builder did not draw these.

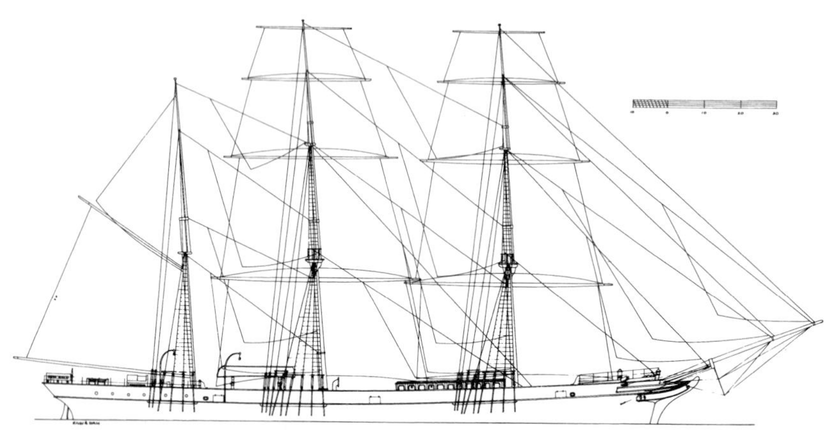

coefficient of under deck tonnage of .60 which is identical to the *Sir Lancelot, Ariel* and *Maitland*, and indicates that *William Le Lacheur* was a fine-lined vessel. She was built of wood for the Costa Rica coffee trade, which involved sailing round Cape Horn, and her maiden passage home from Punta Arenas on the Pacific Coast, north of Panama, was made in 97 days. The *Nicoya* was built three years later by Alexander Hall & Sons of very similar dimensions for the same trade and owner, followed in 1868 by the *Herradura*, also built by Hall.

Another of William Rennie's designs, the *John R Worcester*, was constructed by the Marine Investment Co at Port Glasgow and was launched in January 1866. Although no plans of her have been discovered, a contemporary report states: 'Her model is an improvement on the lines of the *Fiery Cross*.'[26] She measured 191.5ft by 32.4ft by 19.9ft and 844 tons net and gross. The London merchant, John R Worcester, who ordered the ship and gave her his name, failed a year after she was built and Thomas Patton Jnr bought the ship in 1867. She was employed in the tea trade, and a painting shows her to have been a flush-decked ship with two large deckhouses for accommodation, the wheel being mounted right aft on the main deck. On a passage from London to Sydney in July 1875, she ran 347 miles in 24 hours in the Roaring Forties.[27] In 1877, with a tea cargo from Shanghai she was in company with the *Cutty Sark* all the way down the China Sea during the north-east monsoon, but as soon as they picked up the south-east trades

308: I have attributed the name *John R Worcester* to this previously unidentified painting, firstly because she is wearing the flag of John Patten Jnr who became the owner after her first voyage, and secondly because her two large deckhouses so closely resemble those of the ship in the following illustration. Patton did own other ships but the sky stunsails indicate a clipper of the front rank, which is just what the *John R Worcester* was. *Parker Gallery.*

307: The *William Le Lacheur* dried out at St Peter Port, Guernsey, probably soon after she was built in 1864. This photograph does not do justice to the subject, but was the clearest found.

in the Indian Ocean the *Cutty Sark* left her astern.

In 1866, the wooden full-rigged ship *Stonehouse*, the construction of which had begun in 1864, was completed at Sunderland by John Smurthwaite. She measured 1014 tons under deck, 1153 gross, and possessed dimensions of 209.0ft by 36.25ft by 21.9ft. She was designed in 1863–64 by Gilbert Row of Topsham who called himself a 'naval draughtsman', and his plan of her lines together with a rigged model are in the Science Musem, London. She has very flat floors, hard bilges and vertical sides with slight tumblehome, but she has a long, fine, convex entrance and a fine run, although a little full on the load line aft. Intended for the Australian trade, she was given a poop 66ft-0in in length to carry about 40 first-class passengers with some more in the deckhouse, and a topgallant forecastle 43ft-0in long for the crew. No other work by Gilbert Row is known, but perhaps he was responsible for some West Country ships. His design for *Stonehouse* was obviously intended to produce a fast, powerful ship with large cargo capacity.

Another large wooden ship was the *Ann Duthie*, built in 1868 at Aberdeen by John Duthie Sons & Co with measurements of 200ft-0in by 35ft-2in by 20ft-10in and 993 tons net. James Henderson took her lines off

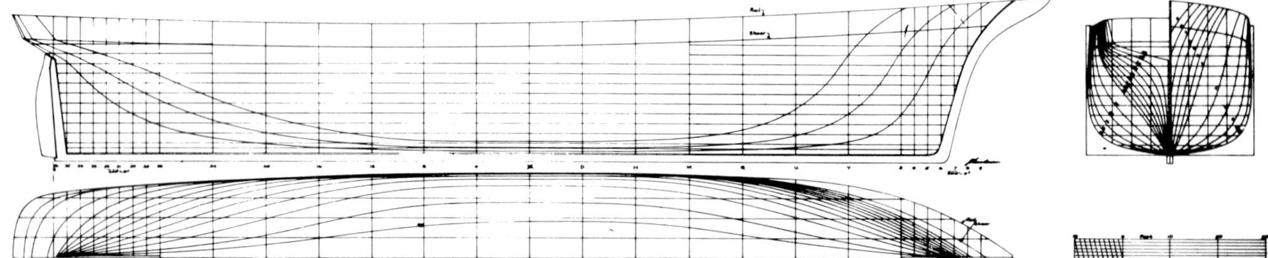

309: *Ann Duthie*. Lines plan: Built of wood in 1868 by Duthie, Sons & Co. at Aberdeen. Drawn by James Henderson from lines taken off builder's half-model in possession of Aberdeen Museum and Art Gallery. Dimensions (for Register): 200ft-0in × 35ft-2in × 20ft-10in; 883 tons under-deck, 993 tons gross. No reconstruction.

310: *Ann Duthie*. The sail plan, drawn by James Henderson, is entirely reconstructed, the principal sources being the half-model; the lengths of lower masts in the *Agnes Rose* of 991 tons net, built the year before by Duthie; a photograph of *Ann Duthie* at Aberdeen as a new ship; contemporary text books on masting and rigging; photographs of other Duthie-built ships.

a half-model in the Aberdeen Maritime Museum, which shows her to have moderately fine ends with floors that round up into very slack bilges. A half-model of the *Agnes Rose*, built the year before by the same yard, indicates that she had slightly finer lines. The reconstructed sail plan of *Ann Duthie* makes her very lofty with skysails on all masts, and stunsails would undoubtedly have been carried. All the masts were of wood.

The iron ships under construction by Barclay, Curle & Co were not very dissimilar to the *Stonehouse* but had more deadrise and slacker bilges. The iron barque *Derwent*, built by them in 1867 for trade to India and the East, was one of their finest-lined designs and has evenly balanced ends with a long, fine entrance and run, some concavity being worked into the lower waterlines near the stem and sternpost. A curious fact is that when a tracing of her plan to ¼in-scale and that of the larger *Mermerus* to 3/16in-scale are superimposed the body plans are almost identical in size and shape, and so also is the general configuration of curves formed by waterlines and buttocks. The *Mermerus* is a slightly fuller version but demonstrates clearly how Barclay, Curle & Co stuck to a well-tried design over the years. The *Derwent* measured 186.0ft by 28.8ft by 17.1ft and 599.37 tons under deck and net. Her bulwarks are 4ft-6in high and she is fitted with a short forecastle, a large deckhouse filling the space between foremast and main hatchway, and a raised quarterdeck. In her sail plan she has skysails on fore and main above double topsails, but there is no overlap to the courses, and indeed she looks a little under-canvassed without stunsails set. At a draught of 14ft-9in, as shown on the builder's plan, she displaces 1225 tons.

Unfortunately, no plans or models have been found of any ships built by Walter Hood

311: The *Ann Duthie* fitting out as a new ship at Aberdeen in 1868. *James Henderson*.

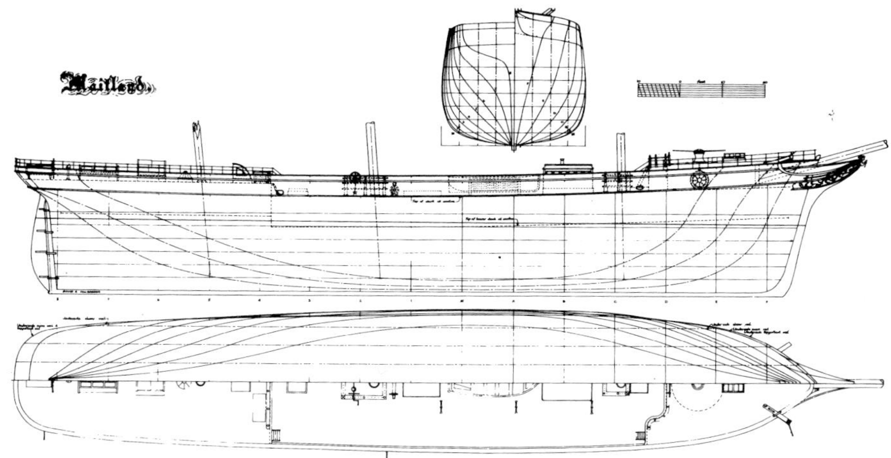

312: *Maitland.* Lines: Built of composite construction in 1865 by William Pile at Sunderland. Lines taken off builder's half-model in possession of Joseph L Thompson & Sons Ltd, Sunderland; deck details from plan in Science Museum, London. Dimensions for registry: 183.0ft × 35.0ft × 19.6ft; 798.72 tons gross and net. Reconstruction: plan view of deck fittings on raised quarter-deck; binnacle; wheel and wheel box; whisker booms on catheads.

313: The lofty sail plan of the tea clipper *Maitland* is ably captured in this lithograph by T G Dutton.

& Co, apart from *Thermopylae*, a half-model which may be *Salamis* (1875), and midship sections in the Lloyd's Register survey reports, so it is impossible to know just how fine-lined some of his ships were. His *Harlaw* (1866) has a coefficient of under deck tonnage of .58 which is equivalent to *Titania* or *Thermopylae*, and suggests that she was of sharp hull form. Her best passage was of 87 days between Shanghai and New York in the autumn of 1870.

William Pile and the *Maitland*

One ship for which the plans have been tantalizingly inadequate in the past is the *Maitland*, launched on 2 December 1865 and constructed by William Pile of Sunderland for John R Kelso of the same town. No plans of Pile's other tea clippers have been discovered and the only ones available until now for the *Maitland* were the general arrangement and sail plan, obtainable from the Science Museum, London. These two drawings were reproduced in the first edition of *The Tea Clippers* when an attempt was made to remove the aspersions cast on this ship by giving examples of her fine passage times such as 87 days on her maiden outward passage to Hong Kong from Sunderland, followed by 104 days home from Foochow against the monsoon, both being made in 1866.[28] Now with the discovery of the builder's half-model in the offices of Joseph L Thompson & Sons Ltd, the picture of this ship is utterly different because a complete set of plans can at last be presented. Joseph L Thompson & Sons Ltd were successors to William Pile and it was through their courtesy and by arrangement with M F Boyd, their commercial manager, that the lines were taken off.

The plan reproduced in figure 312 shows the lines from the builder's half-model combined with the deck layout and part of the longitudinal section from the Science Museum. As the latter drawing is clean, tinted and well-lettered, and bears the names of ship, builder and owner, it suggests an authoritative plan. However, the depth of hold is approximately one foot greater than either the midship section attached to the Lloyd's Register survey report or the half-model. The height from rabbet to sheer strake on the lines plan is that of the half-model, but the stem and square forefoot are made to agree with the Science Museum plans. The topgallant rail has been drawn with an unbroken sheer in conformity with the sail plan and T G Dutton's lithograph, and the amount of sheer agrees with the longitudinal section and the sail plan. The builder's longitudinal section goes through the centre line of the topgallant forecastle where the deck camber is highest and so the sheer of the topgallant rail is obscured, a fact which has caused confusion in the past. This emphasises the point that shipbuilders' plans require careful interpretation to obtain the best results. The problem of insufficient headroom at the break of *Black Prince*'s forecastle has already been described; in *Maitland*'s case a headroom of six feet is just obtained.

Compared with *Ariel*, which was also built in 1865, *Maitland* is a shorter but broader vessel: on the load line she is 15ft shorter, but 18in broader and shallower. By superimposing lines of the two hulls, it can be seen that *Maitland* has a long, sharp entrance with slight concavity on the load line close to the stem, but the additional breadth makes the entrance shorter than in *Ariel*, and the flatter floors accept the shape of the lower waterlines. The *Maitland*'s somewhat fuller entrance is more noticeable in the buttocks, particularly the shoulder at the load line and the

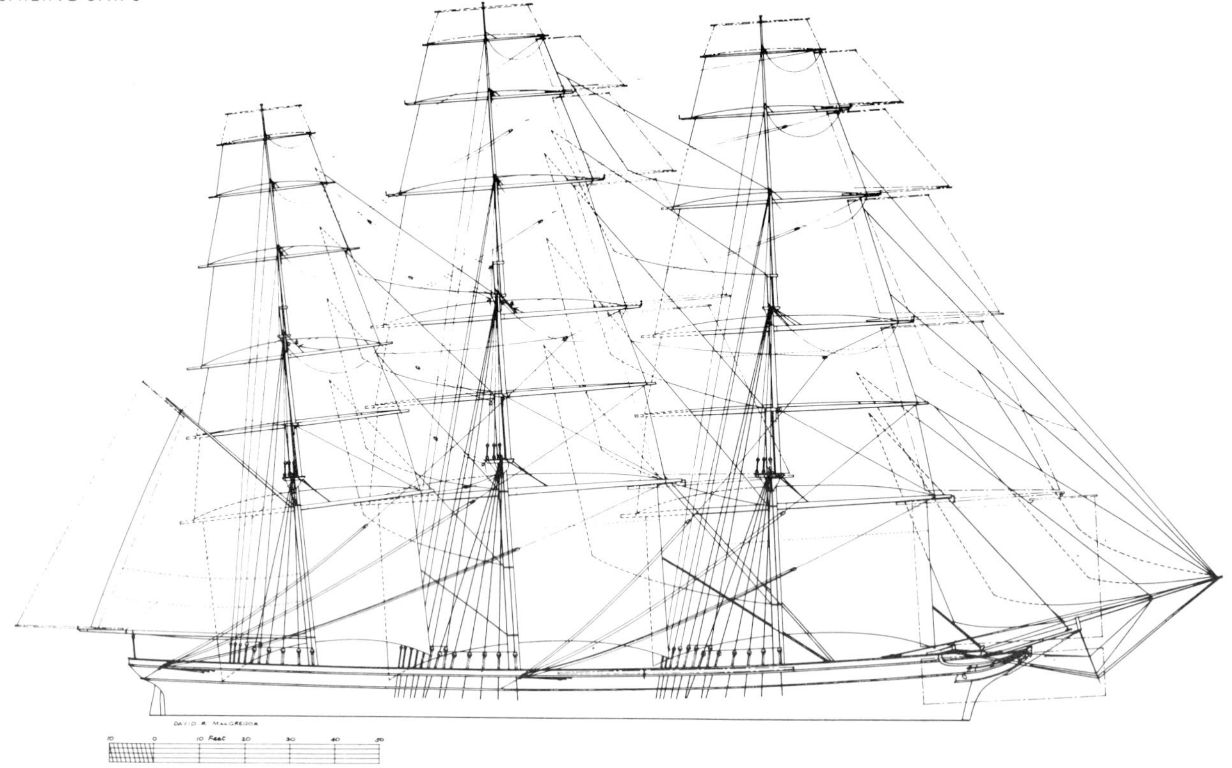

flair above. In the run, the buttocks are identical with *Ariel*'s above the lowest waterline, which is affected by the flatter floors, but the greater breadth produces a more concave run than in *Ariel*. The midsection is a less extreme version of the kettle-bottom seen in *Ganges*, but the floors have much less deadrise than in most tea clippers; the bilges are very slack and the sides round up easily with appreciable tumblehome. William Pile's reported liking for a 'good beam and a clean run' is well illustrated by this plan. In 1869 *Maitland* was credited with a speed of 15 knots. With a load line length of 179ft this gives her a speed–length ratio of 1.12. Two years earlier Basil Lubbock writes of the master claiming 17 knots on her outward passage which gives a ratio of 1.27, indicating a very fast vessel.[29]

The great similarity of the *Undine*'s measurements suggests that she was meant to be a sister to *Maitland*. She was built two years later, and the dimensions are compared below.

These similar measurements suggest that William Pile and the owner, John R Kelso, were so satisfied with *Maitland* that in their opinion her design could not be improved. The *Maitland* was wrecked in 1874 but the *Undine* survived until 1893.

The *Maitland*'s deck layout bears a close affinity to that described for *Black Prince*: there is the topgallant forecastle accommodated behind the topgallant rail; the large capstan driving Emerson & Walker's windlass; the small deckhouse; the longboat incorporating sheep and pig pens; and the long raised quarter-deck. *Maitland* is equipped with three other boats and a cargo winch, but there is no second capstan on the main deck. The height in her 'tween decks is 6ft-6in to the underside of the upper deck. In addition to the master's cabin and the pantry, the Science Museum plan shows nine cabins aft, of which one or two would have been allocated to the mates. The companionway stairs are offset to starboard, but a seat on the port side has been added to make the unit symmetrical about the centre line to conform with normal practice. The circular skylight gives light to a second saloon through which the mizen mast passes. Perhaps the apprentices berthed here as the small deckhouse only contains the galley and paint locker. There are berths in the forecastle for 22 seamen, with a separate compartment possibly for the petty officers. Inboard, the bulwarks are faced with carved or painted panels.

Any lack of sharpness in *Maitland*'s hull form was more than compensated by her large sail plan, which in addition to being very lofty was also square, as may be seen by the large overlap of the sails on the mainmast.

Ship	*Register dimensions*	*UD tons*	*Gross & net*	*Coefficient UD tons*
Maitland	183.0ft × 35.0ft × 19.6ft	754.58	798.72	.60
Undine	182.6ft × 35.1ft × 19.5ft	754	796	.60

314: *Maitland*. Sail plan: Redrawn from sail plan in Science Museum. Reconstruction: running rigging; stunsail booms, yards and their sails; moonsails; ringtail; watersail; jib topsail; crossjack. Ship was equipped with Cunningham's braces on fore and main lower yards, but this was not discovered until sail plan had been drawn with conventional braces. Principal source was T C Dutton's lithograph of ship; flying kites from eye-witness accounts. Unfortunately, position of masts on sail plan in Science Museum do not agree with position of longitudinal section, also in museum. This error has been repeated in drawings here. Neither plan in Science Museum is dated and so it is impossible to tell which is correct.

The respective yards on the foremast and mainmast are of equal length, whereas many clippers had shorter yards on the foremast. The table in the section on *Thermopylae*, comparing the length of lower and royal yards on six ships, indicates that *Maitland*'s lower yards are long in proportion to hull length and that her tall sail plan has less taper than most of the other six ships.

The *Spindrift*, with a load line 37ft-6in longer than in *Maitland*, has a mainmast only two feet taller from deck to truck. *Thermopylae*'s main topgallant sail is always commented on for its large size, yet *Maitland*'s main topgallant yard is only two feet shorter, with a drop at the bunt of 27ft-0in compared to 32ft-0in. *Maitland* is equipped with double topsails on each mast which were becoming increasingly popular in big ships, but as her topmasts are on the short side, the upper topsails have less hoist than the lower ones, which is the reverse of normal practice.

The *Maitland* was equipped with Henry Cunningham's brace winches on both fore

315: This photograph of HMS *Active* is intended to show what the flying kites, such as stunsails, watersails and spritsails, actually looked like when recorded by a factual camera, as opposed to the romantic shapes usually given them by artists with every spar and boom exactly parallel and every sail full of wind. here the main and mizen royals have been lowered to bring more wind on the fore royal. Although there is a fore lower stunsail boom, the clew of the lower stunsail has been hauled up. Sails not normally seen by a camera are the two spritsails, set from extended whisker booms; the watersail set below the lower stunsail; a lower stunsail on the main; the crossjack in a warship; the mizen stunsail. HMS *Active*, of 3980 tons, was built of iron at Blackwall in 1869 and sold out of the Navy in 1906.

and main lower yards, if the words 'fitted fore and aft' have been correctly interpreted from a lecture given by Cunningham. Captain Coulson, her master, makes this enthusiastic comment after his first voyage to China:

> 'They have many advantages over the old plan: you can spare so many men to the tacks and sheets: the *braces are always clear*, and the men amidships instead of in the lee scuppers. I hope never to be without them. The braces will last for years, there being so little wear and tear.'[30]

The *Maitland*'s sail plan is reconstructed from the following sources: the Science Museum's sail plan for masts, spars, plain square canvas, spanker and standing rigging; Dutton's lithograph for staysails, running rigging, and evidence of some stunsail booms, including those below the yards; and descriptions by Basil Lubbock and Andrew Shewan about the flying kites carried. It has never been stated clearly whether the moonsails carried yards or were really raffees, but the skysail mast poles are quite tall enough for the moonsails drawn here. Other flying kites to be shown are the jib topsail, skysail stunsails, watersail and ringtail. The high-sided HMS *Active* could set a watersail easily below the lower swinging boom (figure 315), but a hard-driven and tea-laden clipper could well have had it washed away in anything more than a light breeze, particularly in the conditions depicted in the *Illustrated London News*' engraving of *Taeping* (figure 323). Recent photographs of the barquentine *Regina Maris* taken about 1970 show such flying kites actually set and drawing.

Unfortunately, it was discovered too late when drawing up the sail plan that the mast positions do not agree with those on the longitudinal section, and there is no clue on the builder's plans as to which is the later drawing.

It is curious that the leeches of the mainsail should be cut vertically although not unusual for the foresail; the crossjack is reconstructed. It is probable that storm staysails were carried on each of the three lower stays. It should be noted that there were no external chain plates on the mizen.

The fore and main lower masts and bowsprit of *Maitland* are composed of iron plates 7/16in thick; the three lower yards, and the lower and upper topsail yards are made of steel plates 5/16in thick at the bunt and thinning down to 1/8in thick at the arms. The *Undine* had similar yards in iron and steel, and also an iron mizen lower mast and steel topmasts. Hers were fabricated by the Sunderland firm of Thomas W Puntun & Son.[31]

John R Kelso, who owned both *Maitland* and *Undine*, patronised William Pile who built a number of other ships for him such as *Maitland* (1851), *Kelso* (1855), *Vanguard* (1857), *Standard* (1858), *Kelso* (1861), *Herald* (1863), and *Deerhound* (1869). The first *Maitland* initially traded to the Mediterranean and later further afield, but the other ships traded regularly with China. The second *Kelso*'s coefficient of under deck tonnage, .60, was similar to that of the second *Maitland*.

William Pile also built for the China trade the barques *Miako* and *Osaka*, both launched in 1869 for Killick, Martin & Co; and the *Coral Nymph* built in 1864 for John Hay. No plans are known of these three, although there is a photograph of *Osaka*.

316: This photograph is rather pale, presumably having faded, so that the picture of the *Taeping* is rather indistinct. She is depicted under all plain sail including her crossjack, yet the skysail yard is not crossed. She was built in 1863 by Robert Steele & Co. *John Perret.*

Robert Steele & Co's tea clippers

The clippers built by Robert Steele & Co for the China trade are mentioned with such recurrence that it is worthwhile listing their names:

Date	*Name*	*Under deck tons*	*Coeff. of UD tons*	*Managing owners*	*Material*	*Register dimensions*
1855	*Kate Carnie*	573.69	.78	A Rodger	wood	148.4ft × 26.0ft × 19.0ft
1858	*Ellen Rodger*	554.93	.62	A Rodger	wood	155.8ft × 29.4ft × 19.5ft
1859	*Falcon*	729.41	.59	Phillips, Shaw & Lowther	wood	191.4ft × 32.2ft × 20.0ft
1861	*Min*	594.99	.59	A Rodger	wood	174.5ft × 29.8ft × 19.3ft
1862	*Guinevere*	603.33	.58	J MacCunn	wood	174.5ft × 30.1ft × 19.8ft
1862	*King Arthur*	654.47	.60	J MacCunn	iron	175.0ft × 31.7ft × 20.0ft
1863	*Serica*	652.44	.57	J Findlay	wood	185.9ft × 31.1ft × 19.6ft
1863*	*Taeping*	723.85	.63	A Rodger	comp	183.7ft × 31.1ft × 19.9ft
1863	*Young Lochinvar*	680.41	.61	McDiarmid & Greenshields	wood	181.7ft × 31.1ft × 19.8ft
1865	*Chinaman*	628.93	.62	Park Bros	comp	171.0ft × 31.1ft × 19.1ft
1865*	*Ariel*	852.87	.60	Shaw, Lowther & Maxton	comp	197.4ft × 33.9ft × 21.0ft
1865*	*Sir Launcelot*	847.04	.60	J MacCunn	comp	197.6ft × 33.7ft × 21.0ft
1866*	*Titania*	879.45	.58	Shaw, Lowther & Maxton	comp	200.0ft × 36.0ft × 21.0ft
1867*	*Lahloo*	756.54	.60	A Rodger	comp	191.6ft × 32.9ft × 19.9ft
1868	*Kaisow*	767.19	.61	A Rodger	comp	193.2ft × 32.0ft × 20.3ft
1869*	*Wylo*	766.67	.61	Killick, Martin	comp	192.9ft × 32.1ft × 20.2ft

*plans or models known to exist.

The comparison by the approximate block coefficient of under deck tonnage shows *Serica* as having the finest-lined hull and it is a pity that there is no lines plan of her to substantiate this, but as *Taeping*, built the same year, has fine waterlines, it is probable that *Serica* had great rise of floor of the kind to be seen in *Titania*. A half-model of *Taeping* at the McLean Museum, Greenock, shows that her maximum beam was kept lower than in *Falcon* or *Ariel*, but the entrance and run are long and sharp. Her larger coefficient could be explained by her flatter floors when compared with *Ariel*. The lines of *Falcon, Ariel* and *Sir Lancelot* were published in my book *The Tea Clippers*,[32] and the lines of *Titania* are given here.

'*Min* and *Guinevere* were of the same model', wrote James MacCunn to Basil Lubbock, 'So were *Ariel* and *Sir Lancelot* — the two latter 250 tons bigger than the former and finer lines altogether.'[33] James MacCunn had originally wanted *Sir Lancelot* to be ten feet longer. According to dimensions in the above list it looks as if *Kaisow* and *Wylo* were sisters.

After remarking that *Min* and *Guinevere* were fine sailers in quartering winds, MacCunn added that *Guinevere* 'was not clean enough about the buttocks, whereby when sailing at high speed, the water rather heaped up under the lee buttock.

'It was a "toss up" to *Sir Lancelot, Ariel* and *Titania* in regard to sailing speed. The extra beam of *Titania* gave her more stability.'[34]

Captain Andrew Shewan, master of the *Norman Court* at the age of 23 and well-versed in all the lore and ships of the China trade, considered *Ariel* to be the fastest China clipper followed by *Titania, Thermopylae, Cutty Sark, Spindrift* and *Leander*.[35]

'I regard [Robert Steele & Co]', wrote James MacCunn, 'as the premier designers and creators of the finest and most perfect models of sailing clippers.'[36]

The brothers Robert (1821–90) and William (1823–1917), grandsons of the first Robert Steele who founded the business, were the men who built the clippers. James Steele, grandson of Robert (died 1890), made a valuable point about the importance of good management in a shipyard when he wrote in a letter to me:

> 'With regard to the firm's success, especially with the China Clippers, I think the credit for all this should be attributed as much to my father, Robert Steele, and his father who managed and conducted the business, as to my uncle, William Steel, who was responsible for the designing. It was the superlative quality of the workmanship and materials which helped the designer to obtain his results.'[37]

An examination of the various plans of clippers built by Robert Steele & Co shows that *Falcon, Taeping, Ariel* and *Sir Lancelot* did not really possess the extreme clipper build to be seen in the design of *Titania*. Both *Ariel* and *Sir Lancelot* have more deadrise than *Falcon* although the waterlines and buttocks are very similar; the additional six feet in length would also increase their speed potential slightly and the builders had probably improved the position of the masts, and the balance of the sail area in relation to the hull. *Taeping* on the other hand had a fuller midsection. The block coefficients of under deck tonnage are not so accurate as would be the case if displacement tonnage was used, but at least they give an approximation of hull form. *Ariel*'s tenderness in following seas has frequently been mentioned by other writers although her lines are not so sharp aft as some extreme clippers, but it is likely that the low bulwarks — only three feet high — flush decks and general balance of the ship contributed to these dangers. It was for such reasons that *Ariel*'s owners ordered their next ship, the *Titania*, with two feet more beam to give her additional stiffness in carrying sail. *Ariel*'s fastest speed claimed by her master was 16 knots, which on a load line length of 195ft-0in gives a speed-length ratio of 1.15. He claimed her biggest 24-hour run to have been 340 miles.

The lines of the *Titania* were taken off the builder's half-model in the Science Museum, London, and show what an extreme form of clipper she was. The whole concept of her design was to achieve maximum speed, and cargo capacity had to take second place. 'Many of [the "heavily rigged China clippers" were] only yachts in disguise', commented James MacCunn, 'with their kentledge ballast, double crews and handsomely paid Captains.'[38]

318: The lovely bows and lean entrance of *Titania* can be judged from this photograph when she was dry-docked for repairs to her stem, part of which has been removed. *Nautical Photo Agency.*

317: A portrait of the celebrated master of *Ariel*, Captain John Keay. *MacGregor Collection.*

But although workmanship was of a high quality the cost of construction had still to bear the onus of competition in spite of MacCunn's remark that the cost was 'practically *carte blanche*'.[39] For example, in November 1861, Alexander Stephen was quoting prices to Philips, Shaw & Lowther of £18.18s per ton for a composite ship to class 15 A1, £18.10s for a composite 14 A1 ship and £17.9s for an iron 12 A1 ship. All prices included an East India outfit. Steele was also quoting in competition for an iron ship and a wood ship and his price was lower. Stephen later lowered his price for the iron ship to

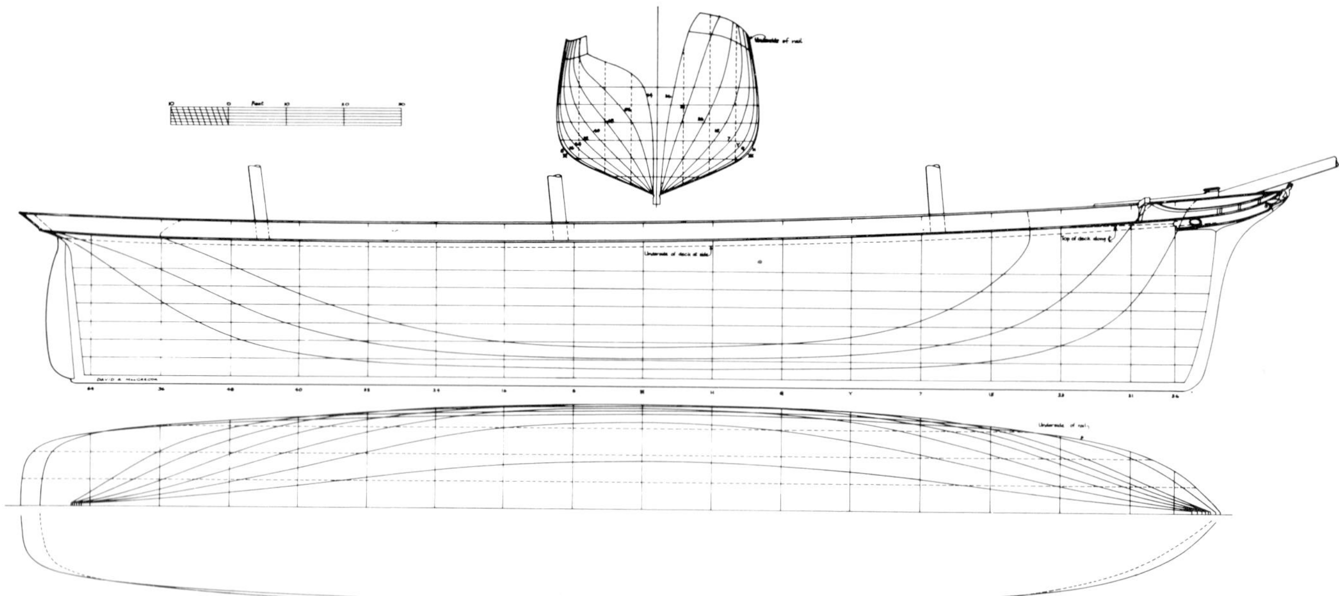

319: *Titania*. Lines: Built of composite construction in 1866 by Robert Steele & Co. at Greenock. Drawn from lines taken off builder's half-model in Science Museum. Dimensions for register: 200.0ft × 36.0ft × 21.0ft 879 tons. Reconstruction: mast positions; bowsprit; figurehead and trail boards.

£16.15s per ton if under one thousand tons, which was probably the approximate price quoted by Steele.[40] In the autumn of 1865 Stephen agreed to build a 15 A1 composite ship at £18 per register ton on 830 tons, and it is unlikely that Steele was quoting a higher price for *Titania*.[41]

The *Titania*'s lines are reproduced in figure 319 and show an exceedingly long, sharp entrance and run with great deadrise. The entrance, including the load line forward, is appreciably concave and much sharper than *Ariel*, but the run is only slightly finer and not so concave in the lowest two waterlines. There is considerably more deadrise than *Ariel* and the floors continue straight far longer before rounding up into firmer bilges with more tumblehome. *Ariel* has 15in tumblehome and *Titania* 20in. Although depth of hold is similar for each ship, *Titania* is 2.1ft broader and 2.6ft longer, according to register dimensions.

The *Titania*'s keel was 16in × 16in of American rock elm, and the stem and sternpost were of teak; the iron frames were 18in apart and composed of 4½in × 3½in × ½in angles with smaller reverse angles to each; the plate iron floors were 9/16in thick with a maximum depth of 24½in; the garboard strake was 9in thick, but the thickness from the adjacent plank up to the topsides was 5½in, the sheer strake being 4½in. Below a height equivalent to two-fifths the depth of hold, the outer planking was of American rock elm; above this it was East India teak. The decks were laid in yellow pine and the deck beams at approximately every third frame were composed of bulb iron plates with angles on the top edge.[42]

320: *Ariel*. General arrangement plan: It is considered that this general arrangement plan for *Ariel* is equally suitable for *Titania*, but allowance should be made for the fact of the slightly different dimensions of the two ships. Built of composite construction in 1865 by Robert Steele & Co. at Greenock. Entirely reconstructed. Dimensions for register: 197.4ft × 33.9ft × 21.0ft; 852.87 tons net. Sources for reconstruction: lines plan; longitudinal section and deckplan of *Sir Lancelot* for position of most fittings with exception of wheel, monkey poop, davits, windlass, forescuttle and catheads; Lloyd's Register survey report; log of ship printed in Basil Lubbock's *The China Clippers*; paintings of ship; contemporary illustrations and plans.

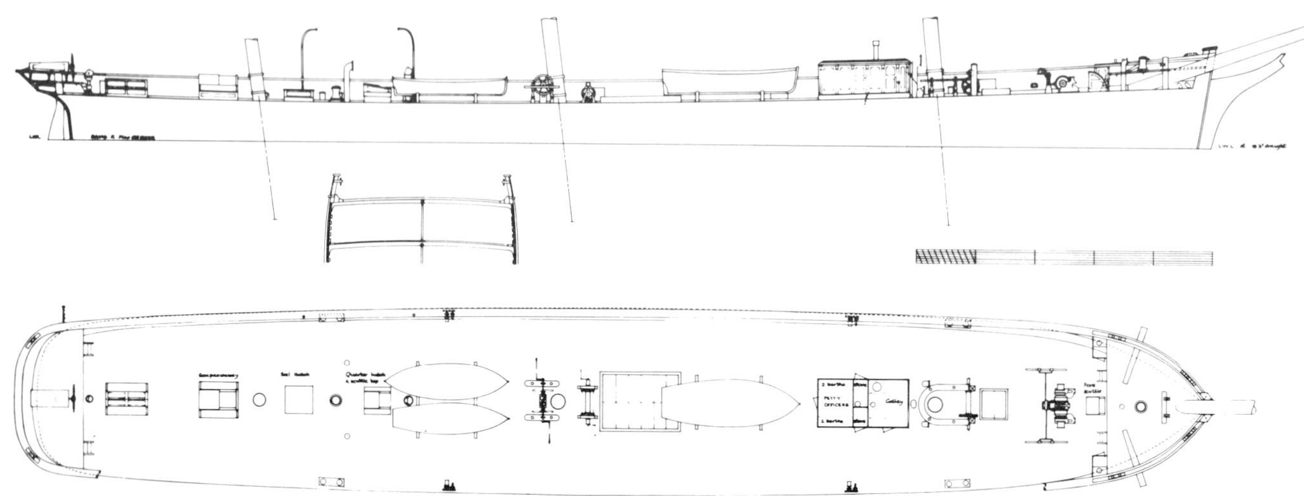

321: This watercolour painting confirms that *Titania* was built with flush decks as indicated by the hinged washport lids which are slightly open, owing to the roll of the ship. When loaded with cargo, these tea clippers had little freeboard and shipped a lot of water. The main skysail has been sent down.

A resumé on the back of *Ariel*'s survey report detailing the chief points of the composite construction, could apply equally well to *Titania*:

> 'This vessel, [ie *Ariel*] has been built under special survey as per order no 346. Is ship rigged and has a flush deck, with a small house on deck for galley &c forward. Is a composite ship — iron frames and wood planking; and fastened entirely with yellow metal screw bolts and nuts throughout; with the exceptions allowed as per Rule section 46; viz — fastened with galvanized iron for one-fifth the depth of hold below the upper deck. The keel is fastened with 1½ galvanized iron wood screw bolts, as shown in sketch herewith, 18in apart. The frames are doubled in the bottom for one half the length of the ship amidships from the keel upwards to the upper part of the bilges. Has a sheer belting plate at the gunwale 30in broad by ½in thick and another at the turn of the bilges all fore and aft 20in broad, the same being connected by double diagonals laid across each other 10in broad by ½in thick and spaced 8 feet apart on a square all fore and aft; has thick garboard strakes, the same being yellow metal bolted athwart ship through the keel as shown in sketch; is fitted with sister keelsons and a bulb iron to ditto 8in by 9/16in with double angle irons to ditto 5in by 4in by 8/16in. Has longitudinal tie plates on each side of hatchways to each deck, and diagonals very efficiently fitted all fore and aft on upper deck beams, with a substantial iron pillar fitted to every beam to each tier of beams.'[43]

The *Titania* was launched on 26 November 1866, and all evidence points to her and *Ariel* having virtually identical deck layouts. Accordingly, it is *Ariel*'s deck plan which is illustrated here, to save having to draw out another similar one on *Titania*'s slightly larger dimensions. The Lloyd's Register survey report for *Titania* also contains the statement quoted above in *Ariel*'s report: 'is ship rigged and has a flush deck with a small house on deck for galley &c forwd'. Accompanying the report is a sheer elevation which confirms the flush deck by showing a freeing port placed 23ft-0in abaft the mizen mast — which would have been impossible if there was a raised quarter-deck. A painting of *Titania*, reputedly done by the marine artist William Clark in 1867, confirms this.[44] So does a painting of *Ariel* by W B Spencer which is reproduced in *The Tea Clippers*. It is certainly unusual to find two ships of this size with practically all the accommodation situated below deck, and only a small house on the deck, thus affording virtually no shelter for anyone aboard, which in a wet ship like *Ariel* must have been a nightmare in bad weather. In addition, all the space in the 'tween decks aft was occupied by the after accommodation to the detriment of cargo capacity. It is hardly surprising that later illustrations show the two ships with a pair of large deckhouses which were probably installed in the early 1870s when the racing spars were shortened and other economies practised. A plan showing these two deckhouses is reproduced in *The Tea Clippers*.[45]

The plan reproduced here shows the *Ariel* when new, and the layout and fittings are identical with *Titania* except where stated. The deck fittings are typical of other ships which have raised quarter-decks: there is a small monkey forecastle for the men to stand on when working the anchors or the capstan; the windlass is Brown & Harfield's patent; there is a wooden barrelled winch across the mouth of the fore fife rails; the small deckhouse can be seen abaft the foremast; *Ariel* has a longboat standing in chocks on deck but *Titania* has none, just 'three life boats'; *Ariel*'s other two boats rest on the deck because no overhead skids are provided; the companionway and saloon skylight are no different to other ships. Right aft is a small 'monkey' poop for the helmsman to stand on, rather similar to that found in *Belle of Lagos*, and one of the few places where the master might keep his feet dry. The deck plan of *Sir Lancelot* was used extensively in this reconstruction, particularly for beam centres which give the fore and aft position of most deck fittings, although deckhouses do not always have their ends resting on beams. *Sir Lancelot*'s principal difference was in having a conventional raised quarterdeck.[46]

At first *Titania* was only classed at 14 A1, and in December 1867 her owners asked

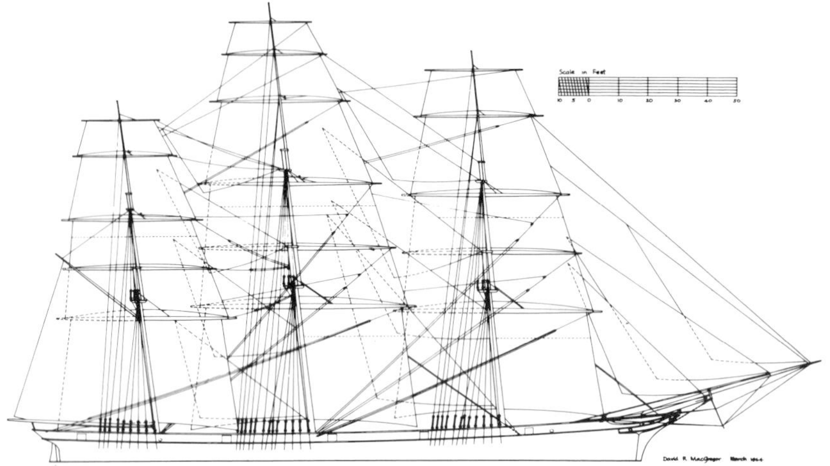

322: *Titania.* Sail plan: Redrawn from outline plan in Science Museum, signed and dated 'G C Watson 9 June 1873'. Reconstruction: yards mast-headed; sail outlines; running rigging; one extra topmast and topgallant backstay on fore and main masts; deadeyes, lanyards and chain plates.

and has been given as one reason which led to her dismasting on the maiden passage.[47]

The sail plan of *Titania* was traced from a spar and standing rig plan found in the Science Museum, London. This plan is signed and dated 'G C Watson 9 June 1873', suggesting that the later well known yacht designer traced the builder's plan in his appren-

Lloyd's Register to examine her specification and classify her at 16 A1 in conformity with the higher grade then being awarded to composite-built ships. *Ariel*'s lower masts and bowsprit were of iron: the 30in diameter bowsprit was stiffened inside with three 4in by 3in by $^{7}/_{16}$in angles, but the lower masts had no inside stiffening. *Titania*'s lower masts were of steel, made of plates ten feet long which had been manufactured in Prussia, but Robert Steele & Co had no test certificate from the manufacturer showing the tensile strength. A test was made in Greenock which gave 20 tons per square inch. The plate thickness of $^{5}/_{16}$in was below that usually adopted for masts which had no internal stiffening,

323: This spirited engraving appeared in the *Illustrated London News* on 22 September 1866 and pictures the tea clippers *Taeping* (nearest) and *Ariel* racing up Channel. The flying kites set by the two ships are presumably based on descriptions from actual observers of the scene, although they do not correspond entirely with Dutton's lithograph. However, wind and weather conditions must have changed somewhat during the time it took to traverse the Channel from end to end. *MacGregor Collection.*

324: An unidentified ship, probably photographed at Foochow, but bearing the unmistakable stamp of a British tea clipper. The absence of a main skysail rules it out as one of Robert Steele's creations. Suitable candidates could be *Taitsing* (1865) or *Leander* (1867). *Peabody Museum, Salem.*

tice days. It certainly represents the ship as built and not as later cut down. Reconstruction consisted of clothing the yards and stays with sails, because none is drawn, adding running, rigging, deadeyes and lanyards, and an extra topmast and topgallant backstay to the foremast and mainmast. Stunsails are not shown but would have been carried just as on the *Maitland*. The lower masts are very tall which was a hallmark of Steele's ships; the bowsprit projects a good way outside the knightheads, while there appears to be no separate flying jibboom; also, in place of inner and outer jibs, there is one large standing jib. A list of her spar dimensions in *Log of the 'Cutty Sark'* agrees fairly closely with this plan.[48] A list of sails carried aboard *Sir Lancelot* at the time of her dismasting includes square lower stunsails on the mainmast which are as big as those on the fore, and other flying kites are a 'Jamie Green', gaff topsail, ringtail and jib-o'-jib (usually called jib topsail and drawn on *Maitland*'s plan). It is interesting to note from this list that the flying jib is a larger sail than the main topmast staysail, whereas in many ships the latter is drawn as the biggest staysail.[49]

Captin Keay's private journals contain excellent accounts of handling a tender tea clipper and tell of some surprising sail combinations that were carried. One can read of the ringtail with its own watersail, of a mizen staysail laced to the outside of the lower stunsail, of large and small stunsails, foresail bonnet, 'Jamie Green', stunsail bonnets and save-alls.[50]

Titania was sold to the Hudson's Bay Company in 1885 and for them she rounded Cape Horn on six voyages to British Columbia. She was sold to Italy in 1894 and broken up in 1910.

A selection of the passage times made by *Ariel, Titania* and *Sir Lancelot* will show that they made some of the shortest runs ever accomplished to and from China.

Some record passages[51]

Ariel
London to Hong Kong: 83 days in 1866–67 (79 days 21 hours between pilots).
Foochow to London: 97 days in 1868 (95 days to off Falmouth).

Sir Lancelot
Foochow to London: 89 days in 1869 (84 days to off Lizard).
Shanghai to London: 100 days in 1867 (96 days, Woosung to Mizen Head)

Titania
Woosung to Deal: 96 days in 1869 (93 days land to land).
Foochow to London: 93 days in 1871.

All the above passages were made against the monsoon.

In one of his letters to Basil Lubbock, James MacCunn refers to a 24-hour run of 359 miles claimed on behalf of *Sir Lancelot* and thought it was correct.[52] This would be an average of 15 knots during which the ship must have often run at 16–17 knots.

In 1871 *Sir Lancelot's* 100 tons of specially cast iron kentledge — her 'racing ballast' — was removed to increase the deadweight capacity. In 1874 the main lower mast was reduced in height by eight feet and all the other masts and spars in proportion; simultaneously the rig was altered to that of barque, stunsails were abolished and the size of the crew reduced. Nevertheless, her fine hull form still enabled fast passages to be achieved under a good master, such as 95 days between Shanghai and New York in 1877.[53] When the ship was sold in 1886 to the Bombay merchant Visram Ibrahim, James MacCunn sent him the full hull model of the clipper which had been made and presented to him by Money Wigram & Son of Blackwall.

After recounting to W S Lindsay some of the particulars of *Sir Lancelot*'s construction and her fast passage home in 1869, James MacCunn summed up his feelings with this remark:

> '. . . I think that the most remarkable feature in the sailing of this ship was the maintenance of a comparative high speed in light winds, and the great power she had to beat dead to windward against a strong breeze.'[54]

Charles Connell and the *Spindrift*

When Charles Connell, who had been foreman shipwright and latterly yard manager in Alexander Stephen & Sons' Glasgow yard, left the firm to found his own shipyard in 1861, Alexander Stephen wrote in his diary, 'I do not think he will succeed.' But he was wrong, as Connell's business prospered, probably as a result of some of the training picked up in Stephen's yard. On his death in 1898 he left over £300,000.[55] In his yard at Scotstoun on the Clyde, Charles Connell produced many fine clippers during the 1860s, his first composite ship being *Wild Deer*, launched in 1863. Later came *Taitsing* (1865), *Spindrift* (1867), *Windhover* (1868), and *Duke of Aberdorn* and *Eme* (1869). He also produced many ships for Thomas Skinner which were named after various Castles, and which traded to the East.

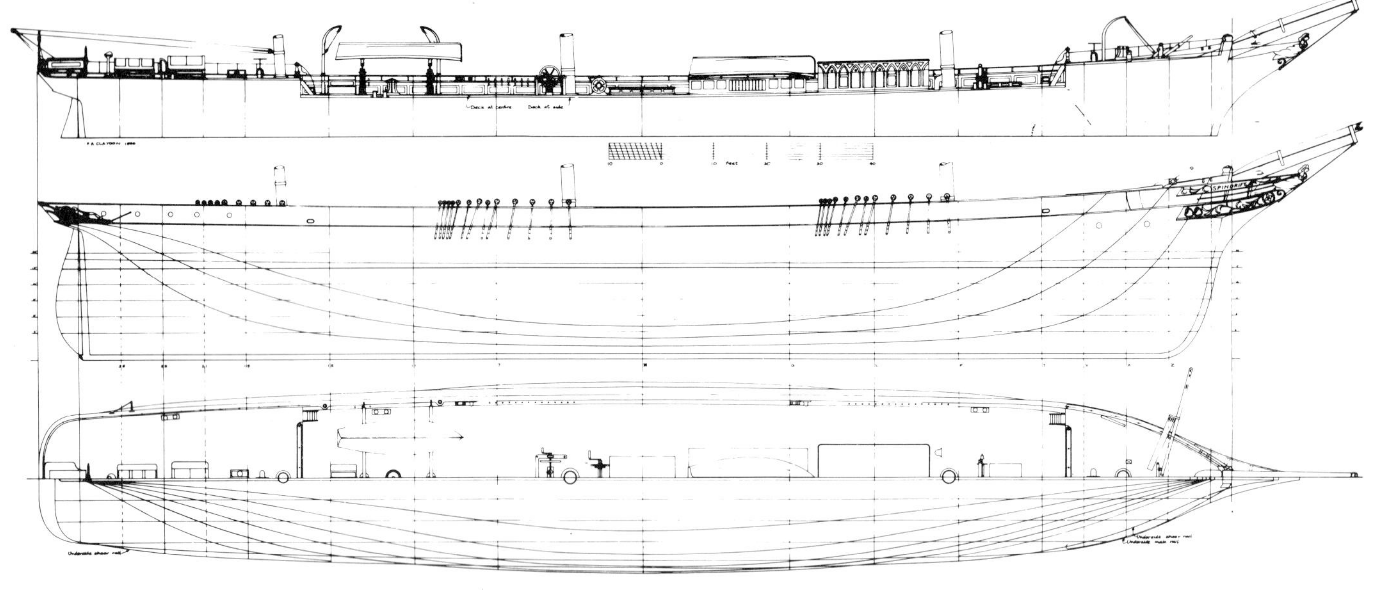

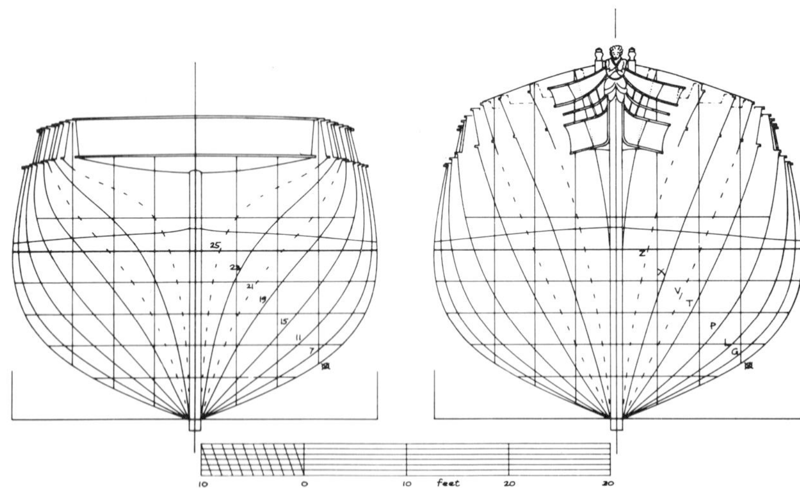

325a and b: *Spindrift*. Lines: 2 bodyplans, general arrangement. Built in 1867 at Glasgow by Charles Connell. Plans drawn by F A Claydon from lines and measurements he took off builder's rigged model in the Glasgow Museum and Art Gallery. Dimensions of ship for registry: 219.4ft × 35.6ft × 20.25ft; 899.43 tons net. No reconstruction. Left hand bodyplan shows stations on both sides of centre line for after body; that on the right shows stations for the fore body.

Taitsing had been built for James Findlay as an improvement on Robert Steele's *Serica*, and *Spindrift* was to be an improvement on *Taitsing*. In achieving this, Connell produced one of the most extreme clippers built on the Clyde in the 'sixties and one wonders whether he designed the ship himself or brought in outside help. Most of our knowledge of the ship stems from a superbly rigged model made to ¼in scale and now in the Glasgow Museum and Art Gallery. This model was carefully measured by Frederick A Claydon who has produced a fine set of drawings, and through his courtesy they are reproduced here.

The *Spindrift* has register measurements of 219.4 ft by 35.6 ft by 20.25 ft which makes her the longest tea clipper of the 'sixties and gives her 6.16 beams to length which, although a narrow proportion, was not as narrow as the long iron clippers of the early 'fifties. Her tonnage was 899.43 net register and under deck, which produces an under deck coefficient of fineness of .56.

Her lines are reproduced in figure 325 and provide an even more extreme version of a clipper than do those of *Titania*, her entrance and run being longer and much sharper, and the rise of floor steeper. *Spindrift*'s maximum

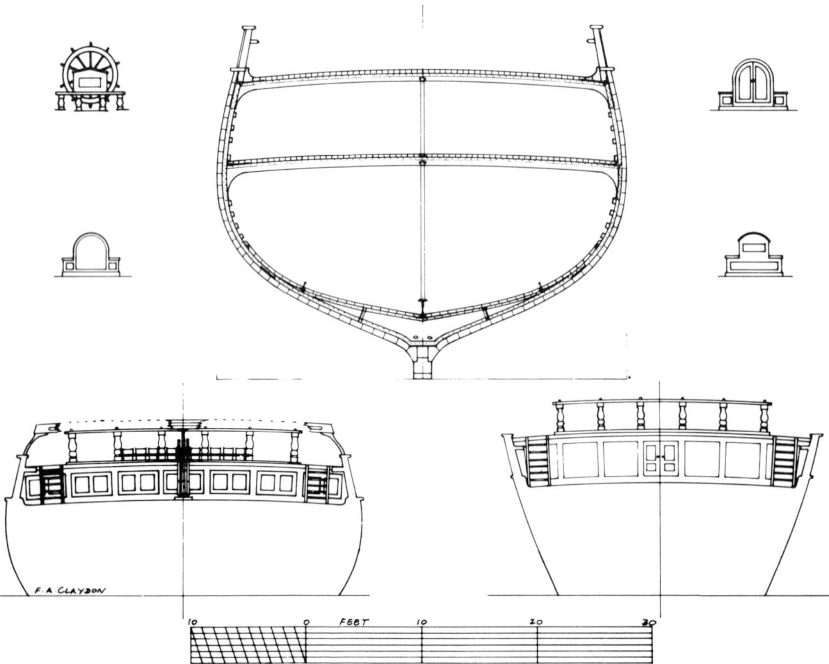

326: *Spindrift*. On topline: cross-section, end elevations of wheel and companionways at each side. On lower line: elevation at break of raised quarter-deck (left); end elevation at break of forecastle (right).

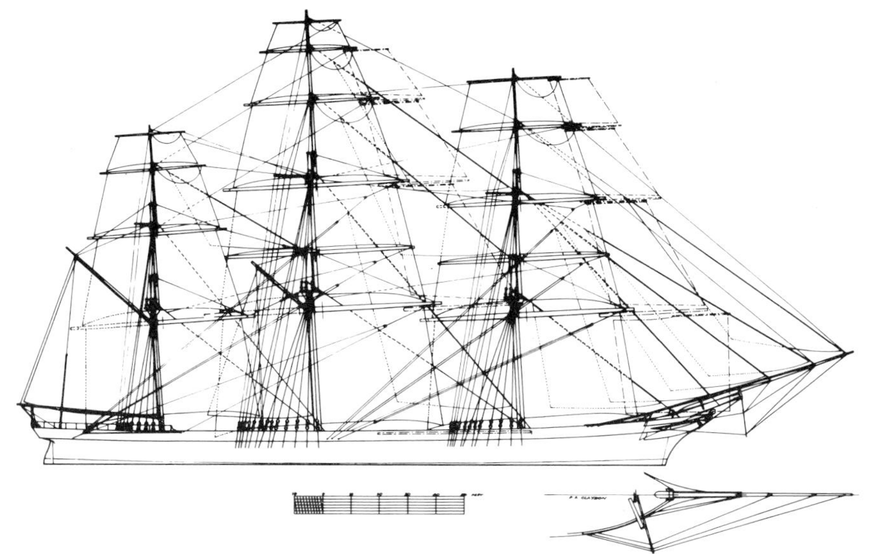

327: *Spindrift.* Sail plan: Measured and drawn out by F A Claydon from rigged model in Glasgow Museum and Art Gallery. Reconstruction: all sails, as there are none on model; stunsail booms, yards and their sails.

beam is situated at the height of her load line which might be nothing out of the ordinary for a 150-ton clipper schooner but is unusual for a 900-ton ship. *Leander* and *Thermopylae* also have their maximum beam at a similar height. *Spindrift*'s floors have no straight lengths in them but begin to curve right from the rabbet, and round up so steeply that bilge and side merge. A continuation of the outer planking line gives a tumblehome of 22in at the underside of the main rail. A constructional half midship section, drawn on a scrap of thin, yellow, brittle tracing paper was located at the National Maritime Museum, Greenwich, amongst one of the plans' boxes accompanying the Lloyd's Register survey reports, and although unnamed it bore Charles Connell's stamp and the yard no 48. The date and dimensions suggest that it refers to *Spinrift* and Frederick Claydon has redrawn it for his midship section; but it should be noted that this section has marked hollows at the garboards, slightly less deadrise, and a deeper, broader keel.

The load line at the entrance is straight rather than hollow, although in the run it is slightly concave, and the buttocks are extremely concave under the counter. In fact, this is just the type of hull which should have given cause for alarm when running before high following seas, rather than the *Ariel*'s. The *Spindrift*'s load line measures 216ft-6in on an even draught of 17ft-0in, and to achieve a speed-length ratio of 1.25, which is the maximum potential for many hulls, she would have had to reached a speed of 18.39 knots. No maximum speeds for *Spindrift* are known.

The deck layout is typical for a ship with a raised quarter-deck but one or two points can be mentioned. As there is no windlass barrel visible it can be assumed that the capstan was connected with Emerson & Walker's windlass which would have fitted tightly inside the low forecastle. The longboat is stowed upside-down on the pigsty and hen house; the capstan bars for the after capstan are stacked around the uprights supporting the boat skids; a small portable pump is placed on both forecastle and quarter-deck, where there were connections either to fresh water tanks or to the limbers; the fitting of the long whisker booms is clearly indicated here. An interesting point is the gothic headed panelling to the deckhouse instead of the usual classic, round-headed style. Considering that the Gothic Revival was much in vogue ashore, it is perhaps surprising that sailing ships did not adopt the style more often. Examples similar to *Spindrift* are very rare. Passenger steamers, on the other hand, seem to have been embellished extensively with the latest architectural fashions.

To produce the sail plan of *Spindrift*, Frederick Claydon measured the masts, yards and rigging of the Glasgow model and then added the sails, based on a sail plan published by Basil Lubbock, a lithograph by T G Dutton and a watercolour by Josiah Taylor. Basil Lubbock also lists the lengths of her masts and yards.[56] The only difference between the sail plan drawn here and the model is that the fore topmast has been lengthened 3ft-6in to agree with Lubbock's spar dimensions, and the topgallant mast shortened by a like amount in order to retain the foremast truck at the same height above deck. Before this reconstruction was adopted, the fore upper topsail had less hoist than the lower topsail, whereas the reverse was the case on the main. Now the proportions of upper and lower topsails on each mast are similar. This agrees with the pictures of her, and also allows space to accommodate two rows of reef points. At this date, the lower topsail yard had practically no arms and the foot of the upper topsail was almost straight.

The sail plan reproduced by Basil Lubbock shows the courses with vertical leeches as in the *Maitland*, although Frederick Claydon has drawn them with the sloping leeches one would expect to find on an extreme clipper. He has also given the foot of the courses very little roach in order to achieve the drop of 40ft at the slings on the main course, as specified by Lubbock.[57]

There are further points of interest in *Spindrift*'s sail plan. The mizen topsail is a roller-reefing sail and due to the absence of a vertical track down the centre, the gear must have been of Colling & Pinkney's type; there are two rows of reefs on the fore and main courses and one row on the crossjack; the bobstay on the model seems to be an iron rod and it is drawn thus here, although the pictures illustrate chain; there are running topsail lifts on the model and in Lubbock's sail plan, similar to early nineteenth-century practice, in which the lift goes through a block on the topmast cap in the same manner as the lower lifts; although absent from the model, a main royal stay is drawn on the sail plan; the topgallant braces are drawn single, as on the model, whereas Lubbock's sail plan and Dutton's lithograph indicate a brace pendant with a single block through which the running part of the brace reeves.

No stunsail booms or boom irons are shown on the model, and those drawn by Claydon are therefore reconstructed from contemporary practice. Basil Lubbock's sail plan of the ship shows the booms under the yards and this has been repeated here.

On her maiden passage, laden with tea, in 1868, *Spindrift* took only 95 days between Foochow and the Isle of Wight, and reached London two days later. She was wrecked off Dungeness outward-bound in November 1869, uninsured. Her crew numbered 35.

Bernard Waymouth and the *Thermopylae*

With one important exception, examples have now been given of designs by all the leading builders and naval architects who specialised in the production of fast sailing ships. But the story would not be complete without mention of Bernard Waymouth (1824-90) and the ships he designed: *Leander* (1867), *Thermopylae* (1868), *Shamrock* (1872), *Melbourne* and *Salamis* (both in 1875). The *Leander* was built at Glasgow by J G Lawrie; the *Thermopylae* was built at Aberdeen by Walter Hood & Co; the *Shamrock* was a schooner yacht built at Deptford by Walker for Sir Edward Sullivan, of 119 tons under-deck and 298 tons Thames Measurement; the *Melbourne*, later renamed *Macquarie*, was built by R & H Green at Blackwall for their own use as a passenger ship to Australia, and is said to have been an excellent combination of a clipper and a cargo carrier; the *Salamis* was a late attempt at a tea clipper and was constructed by the same yard that built *Thermopylae*. As yet, no further names of ships designed by Waymouth have been discovered.[58]

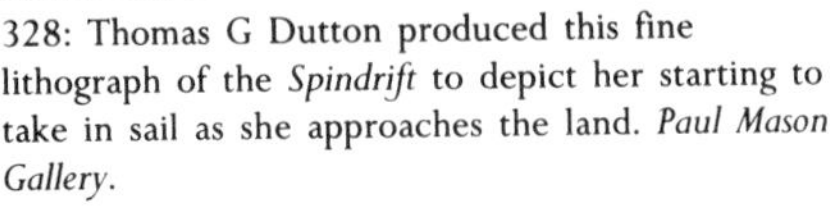

328: Thomas G Dutton produced this fine lithograph of the *Spindrift* to depict her starting to take in sail as she approaches the land. *Paul Mason Gallery.*

Little is known of Bernard Waymouth and it is not known where he trained as a naval architect. He obtained his first appointment with Lloyd's Register in 1854 as an assistant surveyor in London, having failed in his application to become a surveyor in Cumberland. His first position brought an annual salary of £200. One of his earliest surveys was in February 1854 on the brigantine *Earl of Mulgrave*. Four years later he became a senior surveyor. During the 1860s he became an authority on composite construction, visiting shipyards and inspecting vessels under construction. In this capacity he supervised the building of the composite ship *Shun Lee* in 1865–66 at Walker's yard, Rotherhithe. In 1869–70 he proposed new rules to a Lloyd's Register committee for the scantlings of iron ships, which were later adopted. He was advanced to the post of Principal Surveyor in 1871 and two years later he was appointed Secretary, at a salary of £1750, and held this important position until his death in November 1890.[59]

A mystery still exists as to how Waymouth achieved his knowledge of naval architecture which enabled him to produce such a sophisticated design as *Leander* at his first attempt,

329: This oil paining by William Clark of *Leander* shows that she had a large spread of canvas and that her main topgallant was fitted with Colling & Pinkney's roller-reefing mechanism, like *Thermoplyae*'s. There are also four buntlines to their sail. *Parker Gallery.*

330: The wooden ship *Christiana Thompson* was built in 1866 by Walter Hood & Co. and was fitted with Colling & Pinkney's roller-reefing main topgallant. The *Thermopylae*, built two years later, somewhat resembled her in appearance.

and indeed it is inconceivable that he could have produced her without having designed a number of earlier ships and studied their performance. The designs publicly acknowledged to him must have been carried out with the consent of Lloyd's Register but perhaps he suppressed his name prior to 1867. One characteristic of his clipper ship design was the shape of the midship section, and a similar shape in other clippers built prior to 1867 might be taken as evidence of his connection with their design or indicate how much he was influenced by it. Unfortunately, this turns out to be an unfruitful search because the only other British sailing ship bearing a like midship section occurs back in 1855, being the extreme iron clipper *Cairnsmore*, built on the Clyde by John Reid & Co.[60] But a well-known example can be seen in HMS *Warrior*, built on the Thames in 1860 as the first iron-clad. She was the joint design of Isaac Watts and John Scott Russell and her lines were published in 1865 by the latter in his monumental three-volume work, and in the following year by Prof W J M Rankine.[61] So Waymouth would have been fully conversant with the salient features of her design which consisted of great rise of floor, slack bilges and large tumblehome, with very sharp ends to the hull. The midship section closely resembles *Thermopylae* as do her fine ends, although the middle body is much longer than in the tea clipper. Writing of his design, Scott Russell says:

> 'One great characteristic of the "Warrior" class is its great length and the fineness of its lines. These two points were meant to give two qualities — high speed, especially high speed against strong head-winds and heavy seas; and, in similar circumstances, great stability of platform.'[62]

Thermopylae certainly possessed these fine qualities of sailing fast to windward although she was a much similar ship than the *Warrior*. The measurements of the latter were 380ft-2in (length between perpendiculars) by 58ft-4in (extreme breadth) by 21ft-1in (depth in hold), and 6109 tons om.

The form of midship section employed by Bernard Waymouth with its large deadrise, very rounded bilges and great tumblehome is traceable down from Chapman's designs for privateers, published in the eighteenth century in his *Architectura Navalis Mercatoria.*[63] It was employed in many of the Baltimore clippers such as the schooner *Grecian* or the ship *Hannibal* which had their maximum breadth at the level of the load line, whereas Waymouth's ships had theirs about three feet below it. It can be seen in the English cutter hulls reproduced here in chapter two. Another striking similarity to Waymouth's body plan appears in the design of the four French clippers *France et Chili*, *Paulista Carioca*, *Petroplis* and *Commerce de Paris*, built between 1850 and 1853 by Augustin Normand (senior) of Havre. This design has all the features to be found in Waymouth's body plans although the ships are not quite so long in proportion to beam, the ratio in this case being just over five to one.[64] The examples demonstrate how certain types of hull form are not restricted to a single decade but span the centuries.

Summing up the suggested examples which might have influenced Waymouth in his designs, one must observe that in his position as a senior surveyor at Lloyd's Register

331: *Thermopylae.* Lines: Built of composite construction in 1868 by Walter Hood & Co. at Aberdeen from a design by Bernard Waymouth of London. Drawn by James Henderson from builder's offsets given him by James R Melville. Dimensions for registry: 212.0ft—36.0ft—20.9ft; 947 tons net. Reconstruction: mast positions from sail plan.

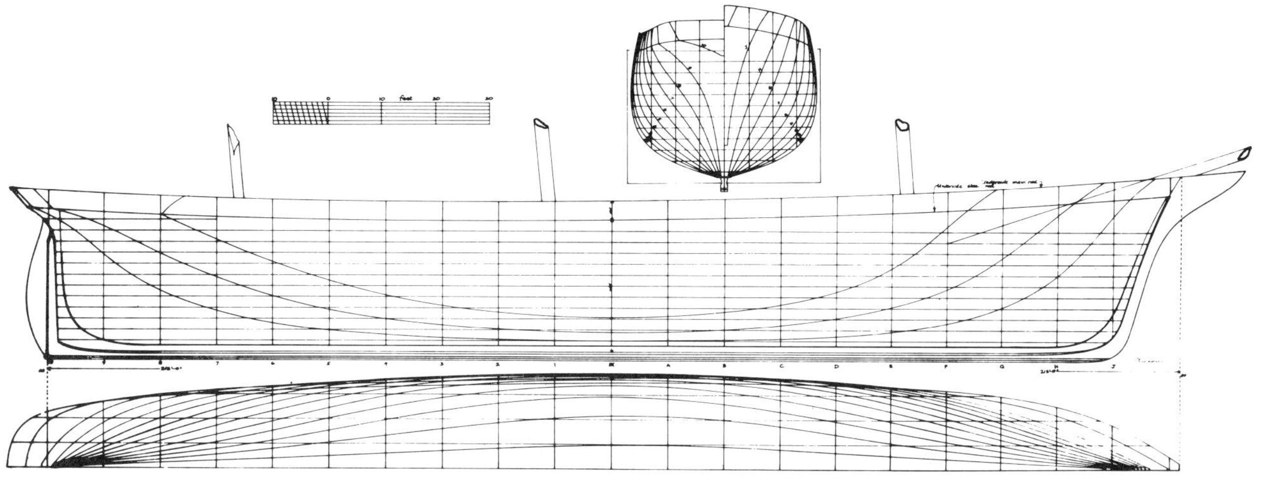

332: A stern view of *Thermopylae* to show her lovely counter and fine lines. Photographed c1895 at Bullin's Way, Esquimalt, British Columbia, when owned in Canada and converted to barque rig. *Provincial Archives, Victoria, BC.*

he had opportunities to study and compare the best designs being prepared for clipper ships in Great Britain during the 1860s, though to what extent this finally affected his designs it is impossible to tell.

Here are the dimensions for Waymouth's three clipper ships:

		Register dimensions	*Tonnage UD*	*Net*	*Coeff. of UD tons*
Leander	comp	215.5ft × 35.2ft × 20.7ft	848	883	.54
Thermopylae	comp	212.0ft × 36.0ft × 20.9ft	927	947	.58
Salamis	iron	221.6ft × 36.0ft × 21.7ft	1021	1079	.60

Up to and including 1874 in the case of *Leander*, and 1876 in the case of *Thermopylae*, *Lloyd's Register of Shipping* gave, annually, the length in their register books as 210.0ft for both ships, which was probably the length for tonnage. This difference was explained with a diagram in chapter five.

Although there are ¼in-scale plans of *Leander* and *Thermopylae* at the National Maritime Museum, Greenwich, both probably Bernard Waymouth's own drawings, the lines of *Thermopylae* reproduced here are taken from the builder's offsets, and thus portray the ship more accurately than ever before. These offsets were copied from Walter Hood's offset book by the Aberdeen naval architect, James R Melville, when he was an apprentice draughtsman with Hall, Russell & Co. During his long career, Melville worked in Beardmore's yard on the Clyde, designed hard-chine trawlers during the depression, became yard manager to Hall, Russell & Co, and a lecturer on naval architecture. He died around 1960. He was always keenly interested in the sailing ship era and allowed James Henderson to transcribe the offsets and trace the profile of *Thermopylae* which he had drawn out when an apprentice at the turn of the century. From the material provided by Melville, James Henderson has produced a beautiful lines plan and this is reproduced here through his courtesy.

This plan, figure 331, shows *Thermopylae* to have been an extreme clipper with very sharp ends. The entrance and run are exceedingly long and sharp, but without any hollow at the load line, and although the buttock lines are hollow under the counter, the quarter beam buttock has straightened up where it crosses the load line aft. Being drawn strictly to the inside of the planking, the lower ends of the sections in the body plan terminate at the floor plate which is 2ft-6in wide, and reference to the midship section will clarify this. Externally, the garboards are concave and there is hardly any straightness in the floors which round up steeply into very slack bilges with 20in of tumblehome above.

The result was a ship that hardly ever lost steerage way and could keep up a good average in light winds, that could beat to windward well and withstand hard driving, although extreme speeds might not be reached. These were some of the qualities claimed by J Scott Russell for HMS *Warrior*, as stated above, and which the shortest passage-makers among the tea clippers also possessed. *Thermopylae*'s longest 24-hour run

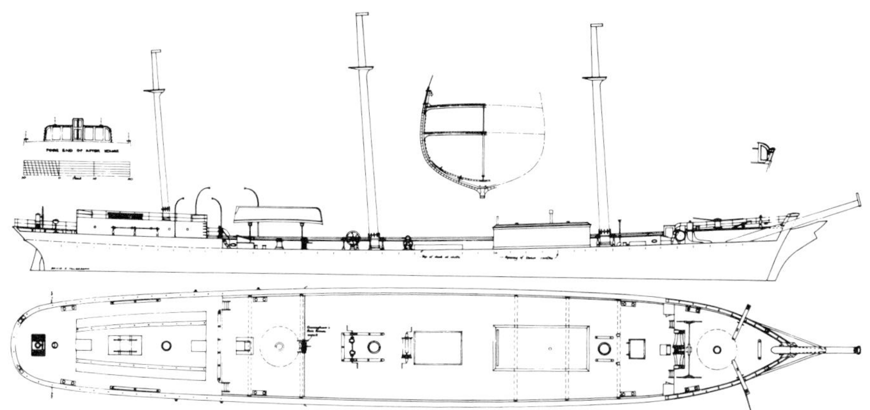

333: *Thermopylae.* General arrangement plan: Entirely reconstructed, with assistance of James Henderson. Sources: midship section from survey report in archives of Lloyd's Register; deck fittings based mostly on Cyril Hume's model of ship in Museum of Applied Science at Melbourne and from photographs of ship; spacing of deck beams from Bernard Waymouth's drawing at National Museum used to position principal fittings, forecastle, raised quarter-deck, etc.

was stated by Basil Lubbock to be 348 miles, giving an average of 14½ knots, during which time she must have attained 16 knots or a little more.[65] On a draught of 19ft-6in the load line length is 207ft-0in which results in a speed-length ratio of 1.11 at 16 knots, and 1.18 at 17 knots.

In the two plans at the National Maritime Museum, Greenwich, it was possible to make an accurate comparison between the lines of *Thermopylae* and *Leander* due to a tracing made of the former's plan which could be laid over the other. This indicated that *Leander* had finer lines. But in the present case an overlay is impossible as Henderson's plan is drawn to ³⁄₁₆in-scale. However, there appears to be little to choose between the two ships. A lines plan, midship section, and sail plan of an unnamed tea clipper were published by Admiral Paris in 1869 and can be identified from the dimensions as *Leander*; in any case, the body plan is unmistakably a Waymouth design.[66]

From dates on the Lloyd's Register survey report of *Thermopylae* when the special survey was made, one can gauge the rate of progress of building the ship in Hood's yard. The keel of elm, and the stem and sternpost of teak were erected by 16 September 1867; the iron frames at 18in centres with reverse angles to each were in place by 8 November; the iron beams to every third frame, the stringers, and the tie plates were rivetted in position by 15 November; the 6in bottom planking of American elm and the topsides of 4¾in by 5½in teak were laid on and fastened by 26 June 1868, but no caulking or cementing had begun so that the bolts and nuts could still be examined; the caulking was complete and the hull finished by 25 July; the ship was launched on 19 August; and she was finished and equipped by 17 September 1868. She was built of materials for the 14 years grade, but fastening the planking with yellow metal and galvanised iron bolts added two more years, and construction under a watertight roof another one, so that she ended up with a classification of 17 A1. The decks were planked with yellow pine and the ceiling was of teak. The scantling sizes adhered closely to those listed by Lloyd's Register in their rules for composite ships.

I have already commented on how, in the building of the auxiliary steamer *Sea King*, Alexander Stephen questioned the suitability of William Rennie's hull form, rejected his model, and obviously disliked being unable to build the ship to his own design. One can well imagine the same sort of thing happening in Walter Hood & Co's yard in Aberdeen, only in this instance the name of Cornelius Thompson, her owner's youngest son and a naval architect, is sometimes coupled with Bernard Waymouth's as assisting with the design.[67] Walter Hood had been drowned in 1862 in Aberdeen harbour, and the yard manager at this time was possibly Mr Greig. George Thompson himself was the principal shareholder in the shipyard, which explains why all his ships were built there. Waymouth's name does not crop up again in Aberdeen until the appearance of the *Salamis* in 1875. Of course, prior to *Thermopylae*, Hood's yard produced splendid ships which they designed entirely on their own.

The deck fittings indicated on *Leander's* plan at the National Maritime Museum were not fitted to her, but some are applicable to *Thermopylae*. There is a painting by a Chinese artist and another by William Clark to show that the former had a normal raised quarter-deck without the coach roof. There are several photographs in existence which show the basic features of *Thermopylae*'s deck fittings, and two important models: one model is in the Aberdeen Maritime Museum and was made by Walter Hood's model maker, although the spars, sails and rigging which were added in about 1930 when the Museum services acquired the model are not reliable. The other model was made by Cyril L Hume and is located at Melbourne in the Museum of Applied Science of Victoria. The latter model was made in about 1930 and was checked by men who had served in the ship: two mates, two apprentices and a bosun.

In reconstructing the deck layout, the first thing was to mark out the centres of the deck beams as given on the plan at the National Maritime Museum. These 42 beams are indicated on the deck plan in figure 333, including the closer spacing abaft the foremast. The mast spacing is in accordance with Bernard Waymouth's sail plan, and after this was settled the deckhouse, raised quarter-deck, pawl post and hatchways could be positioned with the help of the beam centres.

Many of the fittings on *Thermopylae's* decks can be seen in other ships, but some of the items are worthy of comment. The type of windlass is not specified in the Lloyd's Register survey report but the handles for the purchase mechanism can be discerned in photographs, and so it is obvious that the old-fashioned barrel type was fitted. The crew berthed in the large house abaft the foremast which would have also contained the galley. The employment of three skids over this house, particularly the foremost one, is unusual, but the latter provides better facilities for storing some of the spare spars. There was an ornamental upstand at the after end of the deckhouse roof for the spars to rest against. When photographed in Victoria, BC, in about 1892 this forward skid was not in position and the deckhouse seems much closer to the foremast than in the Aberdeen model. No longboat was specified in the survey report but there were 'four others': two

334: *Thermopylae.* Sail plan: Redrawn from plan by Bernard Waymouth found in archives of Lloyd's Register. Reconstruction: running rigging; stunsails with their booms and yards; figurehead; deadeyes and lanyards; chain plates; freeing ports. Based on Cyril Hume's model, photographs of the ship, and pictures of other ships built by Walter Hood & Co.

would have been above the deckhouse, two on the after skids, and no boat would have been stowed over the main hatchway. Two pumps are listed in the survey report and they were doubtless fitted with the usual flywheels. It should be noted that the starboard pair of davits is smaller and closer together than the port pair, but both pairs are mounted outside the bulwarks and terminate at the sheerstrake.

To avoid occupying valuable cargo space, the after accommodation is placed in an 'Aberdeen house' standing on the main deck, but surrounded on four sides with a quarter-deck raised 2ft-6in above main deck level. This gives a clear height inside the house of approximately 6ft-6in and the space under the raised quarter-deck was doubtless utilised to good advantage. An earlier example was the *Vision* (figure 236). The house runs parallel to the bulwarks and the top curves down on each side; at each end there is access to the house from the raised deck. Unlike some of George Thompson's earlier ships, such as *Ethiopian*, the binnacle and wheel are also mounted on the raised deck and there would probably have been room for hen coops and fire buckets. The steering gear is of the vertical pillar-box kind, to be seen in *Norman Court* and other ships. The figurehead of a Grecian warrior held a sword in his right hand, with the arm close to his side and the sword pointing downwards, and an up-raised shield on his left arm.

Like *Maitland*, the *Thermopylae* was fitted with Cunningham's patent brace winch, but on the foreyard only. The brace winch is placed abaft the pumps and the chain goes through it, across the deck, and out through a sheave in the bulwarks. Another of Thompson's ships to have it was the *Christiana Thompson*, built in 1866, and very similar in appearance to *Thermopylae*.

In ships such as *Thermopylae* and *Spindrift*, where the topgallant rail has been abandoned, a pin rail is normally fitted approximately 12 in below the main rail or on a level with the raised quarter-deck. In *Thermopylae*, a pin rail on turned supports is mounted on the quarter-deck abreast of the mizen rigging. The anchors first fitted were of Trotman & Rodgers type.

As to the colour scheme, the hull was painted the Aberdeen green to be found in all Thompson's ships; white was used on the figurehead, deckhouse panels, sides of the Aberdeen house, boats, lower masts, doublings, all the yards, bowsprit, spanker boom, and arms of varnished spars. The topmasts and topgallant masts between the cap and the hounds were varnished, as were the stunsail booms, spanker gaff, and jibboom.

In 1869, a Melbourne newspaper had this to say about her outfit:

> 'On the model of the *Leander*, somewhat modified and improved, the *Thermopylae* has been constructed . . . She has a raised poop on the quarter-deck, which gives increased accommodation in the cabin; her gear and arrangements aft generally, however, differ little from other ships of the same class. A light iron railing runs round the quarter-deck, and gives a neat finish to that part of her outline, resting as it does on what may be called a coping of polished brass. The men's quarters are forward as usual, and are arranged with due regard to their comfort and accommodation. The fore and main lower masts, and the two lower yards are of iron, while her main rigging is of galvanized wire. She has double topsail yards, with Pinkey's main topgallant sails and royals. She carries two jibs on one boom, with a flying jib.
>
> 'Cunningham's patent forebrace machine is used in swinging the foreyard. She has two swinging booms fifty feet in length, her lower studding sails having twenty-two cloths in the head. The length of the jibboom from the knight heads to the flying jibboom end is over eighty feet. With such a spread of canvas she goes, in even the lightest trades, with amazing speed. The fittings of the cabin are plain but substantial. The woodwork is of polished teak, relieved by gilt cornices. The cabins of many vessels may be more luxuriously furnished, but as she is not intended for the passenger trade under any circumstances, the arrangements are such as are found in vessels of her class. She carries 100 tons of pig iron ballast, which is placed under the ceiling . . . She carries twenty-two able seamen who with officers and boys, make up a crew of thirty-five.'[68]

This brings us on to the subject of the sail plan, which is reproduced in figure 334. Noticing that the survey report was missing from the files at the National Maritime Museum led to inquiries at Lloyd's Register of Shipping, and the eventual location of Bernard Waymouth's sail plan, and it is through the courtesy of the Society that this drawing is reproduced here for the first time. Waymouth's plan is drawn in ink on opaque tracing cloth to 3/16in-scale which is an unusually large scale for the sail plan. This drawing shows the complete hull profile with the load line marked, a female figurehead, spars, standing rigging, and all sail outlines with the exception of stunsails. The spar dimensions are also listed and a concluding note states: 'Main topgallant and mizen topsail Colling & Pinkneys Patent Rolling'. The sail plan has a single mizen topsail drawn, as for *Leander*, but a lower topsail yard has been added in red ink with the appropriate length. To judge from the photographs it may be that the bowsprit is drawn with a greater steeve than when the ship was built. This sail plan has an identical sheer to the lines plan, and there are only fractional differences in the stem and stern profiles. The spar dimensions from Waymouth's plan are tabulated in Appendix III.

The opportunity to use *Thermopylae*'s sail plan means that an authentic set of plans of this famous ship is available for the very first time. Some of the points to notice about this plan are the identical lengths of the fore and main lower and topsail yards, although above this level those on the main are longer; the main topgallant and royal are huge sails of great depth; the staysails between the masts are likewise large, and so are the headsails; the cap stay from the lower mast head is rarely seen in a China clipper. There is a strong similarity between *Leander*'s sail plan published by Admiral Paris and *Thermopylae*'s.

The Melbourne newspaper article, quoted above, confirms the roller-reefing main topgallant but does not make it clear whether the royal was so fitted or merely that the ship carried royals. The dimensions given by the article for the lower stunsails have formed the basis for reconstructing these sails, which have been drawn dotted on the plan. The photograph of the ships lying at Foochow (figure 295) shows every stunsail boom to have been under the yards – topmast, topgallant and royal. The dimension given of 'over eighty feet' from knightheads to end of the flying jibboom is over optimistic, because the length on the sail plan is just under 70ft.

The following table compares the lengths of the lower and royal yards of six China clippers, four of whose sail plans are given here.

Length of yards compared on six clippers[69]

	Length on load line	*Fore lower yard*	*Fore royal yard*	*Main lower yard*	*Main royal yard*
Maitland	179	73	37	73	37
Titania	197	71	33½	76½	36
Spindrift	216½	76	33	84	34
Thermopylae	207	81	35	81	37
Cutty Sark	211	78	38	78	38
The Caliph	208	80	35	85	38

All dimensions are in feet.

These figures illustrate how square *Maitland* and *Cutty Sark* are aloft, and how much the yards taper on *Spindrift*.

The naval architect, W H White, compared *Thermopylae*'s area of plain sail with that of the fast frigate HMS *Pique* in the following table:

Particulars	*Thermopylae*	HMS *Pique*
Length	210ft	162ft
Breadth	36ft	48¼ft
Displacement	1979 tons	1912 tons
Area of plain sail	17,520 sq ft	19,086 sq ft
Area of plain sail ÷ (displacement) ⅔	110	124

'The sail-spread of the *Thermopylae*', commented W H White, 'is, therefore, less proportionally than that of the *Pique*; but her greater length and fineness of form probably cause a considerable diminution in resistance, and give to the *Thermopylae* greater speed in making passages than the sailing frigate possessed.'[70] *Thermopylae*'s sailing qualities were amply demonstrated on her maiden voyage which made her one of the most celebrated clippers afloat, because she broke the record on every leg of her passage. Outward bound in 1868–69 she took only 60 days between passing the Lizard and sighting Cape Otway, from 8 November to 7 January, or 63 days between Gravesend and Hobson's Bay, Melbourne. Then she went round to Newcastle, New South Wales, and from there was 28 days to Shanghai with a cargo of coal, the time being reckoned between her pilots. Homeward-bound with tea from Foochow, she made her departure on 3 July 1869, sighted the Lizard 89 days out on 30 September, and was docked in London two days later, 91 days from Foochow. To her master's chagrin, the *Sir Lancelot* beat this magnificent passage by two days, only a fortnight later. Her outward passages were usually made to Australia and her first ten averaged 69 days between the Lizard and Melbourne, whilst her 11 tea passages averaged 106½ days.[71] In 1873 homeward-bound from Shanghai, she logged 2085 miles in seven days, from 14 to 20 November, with strong south-easterly trades in the Indian Ocean, a daily average of 297 miles.[72]

Most diaries belonging to masters of contemporary ships contain a newspaper cutting pasted inside which describes *Thermopylae*'s maiden passage to Melbourne, together with an abstract log, and their own logbooks sometimes contain references to what position they have reached by a cerain date in relation to *Thermopylae*'s record run, so it can be seen what a tremendous sensation she caused.

An article reprinted in the *Aberdeen Journal* in 1892 contained the following remarkable statement, which has not been verified:

> 'She [*Thermopylae*] then went back to Melbourne [ie in 1870–71 on her

335: Deep-laden, with bulwarks smashed and hull scarred, the clipper *Thermopylae* lies beside a wharf in a Canadian port. This photograph was taken after her sale to a Quebec owner in 1890. In spite of her masts being shortened in 1887, she was still a lofty ship. *A J Nesdall.*

336: An oil painting by a Chinese artist showing the *Thermopylae* in the 1870s after she had been fitted with double topgallants sails on the foremast and mainmast in place of the deep single sails. The change did not improve her looks. *Colin Denny Gallery.*

> second voyage], being but one day longer on the trip than her previous run, scoring in 24 hours the great distance of 414 miles, and report had it that in 17 consecutive days she logged 6300 miles.'[73]

J Edward McGill, apprentice aboard the iron ship *Rialto* (built in 1869 and 1166 tons) on a passage from Akyab to Queenstown, noted the following in his logbook for 30 September 1872:

> 'On Saturday [ie 30 September] a ship called the *Thermopolie* [sic] overhauled and passed us with royal stunsails set both sides, 98 days from Shanghai bound to London. She is celebrated for her sailing qualities. I fancy she is a tea clipper.'[74]

The wind was steady from the north-west and the following day the *Rialto* was in 33'.37'N; she took her pilot aboard on 20 October, 70 miles from the Irish coast, but *Thermopylae* had already docked in London on 11 October.

The Lloyd's Register surveys indicate that the following major repairs were carried out on the ship during her career:[75]

Survey dated London 9 November 1872: mizen mast replaced with spar of Oregon pine.

Survey dated London 13 May 1887: extensive examination made in dry dock and planks removed to expose frames, a few of which were corroded. Fore and main lower masts reduced in height by five feet. The following spars were renewed: fore, main and mizen topmasts, fore and main topgallant masts, main and mizen lower topsail yards, fore upper topgallant yard, crossjack yard.

Survey dated Victoria, BC, 11 May 1892 (when owned by Hall, Ross & Co of Victoria): one new bow port made on starboard side; one lower deck beam removed to admit lumber in lower hold, and thoroughly strengthened. Fore and main topmasts shortened two feet each; new fore and main topgallant masts; lower topgallant yards on fore and main removed; all yards stripped off mizen mast to make her a barque; new mizen topmast. Equipped with two suits of sails. Sixteen deck planks renewed; all woodwork around stern rotten, and so renewed; frames in excellent condition.

George Thompson had sold *Thermopylae* in 1890 to William Ross, and in 1897 her second Canadian owner sold her to the Portuguese for use as a training ship. Later she became a coal hulk on the Tagus, and was sunk at sea by a torpedo in 1907, with naval honours.

337: A group of petty officers aboard the *Sobraon*. Each is holding the tools of his trade: the carpenter is standing with his mallet and chisel; the bosun is holding a marlinspike; sitting on the right is the sailmaker with a 'palm' on his right hand; in front is the boiler man with his hammer. The first was usually nicknamed 'chips'; the third and fourth, 'sails' and 'engines' respectively. *MacGregor Collection.*

Some of Alexander Hall's clippers

Just as this firm had built, in the 1850s, the largest wooden merchant sailing ship ever constructed in the United Kingdom, the *Schomberg*, so now in the 1860s they produced the largest composite sailing ship ever built, the *Sobraon*. She was ordered by Gellatly, Hankey & Sewell, successors to Duncan Dunbar, and was given Dunbar's traditional figurehead of a lion rampant, but Gellatly's never took possession of her.[76] The builder's account, for a total of £43,965.3s.4d was settled by Robert Smith & Co of London, and the Lloyd's Register survey report lists them as her first owners, but Shaw, Lowther & Maxton soon bought her and resold her to Devitt & Moore in 1872. She was laid down as an auxiliary steamer but this idea was abandoned by Gellatly's and the screw aperture filled in. Her register measurements were given by Lloyd's Register as 272.0ft by 40.0ft by 27.0ft although the builder's certificate stated 272.1ft by 40.3ft by 27.85ft. Tonnage was 2089 under deck and 2131 net register. She had three decks and the 'tween decks were entirely devoted to passenger accommodation. Her life of 25 years under sail was entirely spent in the Australia trade, and she was not broken up until 1941, at Sydney, having been a stationary training ship there since 1891.

A whole model of the ship at $^3/_{16}$in-scale, which was owned by Captain J A Elmslie, her master for 22 years, was measured by Roderick W Glassford and Cyril L Hume. The lines show a long, fine, convex entrance and a long run, with appreciable hollow worked in near the sternpost. The fact that the ship had both sternpost and rudder post erected

339: The shapely bows of the *Sobraon* when the ship was dry-docked in Sutherland Dock, Cockatoo Island, Sydney, in 1891. *C L Hume.*

338: Aboard *Sobraon* on her last voyage, with the crew about to lower the anchor over the side where it will be held under the cathead, ready for dropping. It will then be in the position shown in figure 339. The massive size of the gear on such a ship is clearly indicated. *MacGregor Collection.*

340: In this photograph, the *Sobraon* is seen in the River Thames off Gravesend. The royal masts are fidded abaft the topgallant masts and her main topgallant sail has roller-reefing gear. The short poop looks incongruous. *Nautical Photo Agency.*

and framed up before it was decided to abandon the installation of a screw propeller, meant that the upper part of the immersed hull was faired out another four feet or so and this accounted for the concave form below. The quarter beam buttock is straight from the counter to three feet below the load line. The midship section is unlike Hall's other clippers in having no hollow at the garboards, and is really a deeper version of Barclay, Curle & Co's *Mermerus*; but she has more deadrise, with rounded floors, slacker bilges and less tumblehome. The form is probably dictated by the original need to provide adequate seating for the engines and boilers. She was a fine, powerful ship, loftily-rigged with double topsails and skysails on each mast, but due to her trade as a passenger ship, she was never driven hard, unlike the passenger clippers of gold rush days when washed-out cabins were tolerated if a short passage could be made. *Sobraon*'s longest day's run is said to have been 340 miles but speeds of 16 knots were regularly obtained.

The well-known ship photographer, F G Gould of Gravesend, took a splendid picture of her which is reproduced in figure 340. It shows that she crosses skysails on fidded royal masts, and that the main topgallant yard is equipped with roller-reefing gear. The lower masts are of iron, and the lower yards and topmasts of steel. The yards on the fore and main masts are of the same length: the lower yards measure 90ft-0in and the skysail yards 32ft-0in. Although royal masts were commonly fidded either before or abaft topgallant masts up to about 1830, they had become a rare sight, but were re-introduced in several ships in the early 1870s in an effort to overcome the severe strains which resulted in the dismasting of some of the larger over-canvassed iron ships. Basil Lubbock mentions the *Loch Garry, Loch Vennachar, Carlisle Castle, Romanoff* and the American *Manuel Llanguno* as five other ships which were so equipped.[77]

Another of Hall's clippers was the *Herradura*, built in 1868, the year after *Nicoya* and for the same owners. She had similar breadth and depth but was seven feet longer which increased the tonnage to 612. A lines plan in James Henderson's collection shows balanced, convex ends, a moderately sharp entrance but a longer run, and not much deadrise; the bow and stern profiles are similar to *The Caliph* which was launched the following year. The *Herradura* was composite-built and cost £17.10s per ton.

In 1865, the firm had built a barque of 296 tons for the London Missionary Society, for use among the Pacific islands. She was the second vessel to be named *John Williams* and was wrecked in 1867. A lithograph depicts her with an unusually long bowsprit and jibboom, and space to set skysails above her royals. An account of the ship at the time of her launch states:

> 'The ship is modelled to the finest lines of the Aberdeen clippers. Her entrance is sharp, and her run very clean; while the floor is long, and the sides so rounded that there is not an angular point about the hull . . . The main and fore-mast are of iron, and, having openings into the hold and at the top,[78] they form ventilating shafts . . .'

As no plans have survived in the London Missionary Society's archives, the description of the hull form cannot be verified.

The ship which was built to replace her is better documented and there are plans to support the descriptions, as reproduced here. A committee appointed by the Society in August 1867 reported that a smaller ship would be more manageable among the dangers of the islands, but they were not in favour of equipping her with a steam launch, nor of making her an auxiliary. 'Vessel with auxiliary screw would involve the additional outlay of £2,000 at first and a further increased charge of £1,000 per annum as working expenses, without taking into account the wear and tear.'[79]

The Society decided to ask Alexander Hall & Sons to build the new ship and three surviving letters from James Hall, who with his brother William ran the firm, describe the ship and how she was ordered. Unfortunately, the Society's replies have not survived.[80]

Aberdeen 13th Feby 1868

John Kemp Welch Esqre.,
Sir,
In accordance with your request I herewith enclose a copy of the letter you refer to and in order to point out the various proportions of vessel I subjoin the dimensions and prices leaving you to determine for yourselves John Williams *as measured by the Customs officer*
132 × 25 × 15 = 296 Price £7500
[this is the John Williams *built in 1865 by Hall]*
Ship agreed upon by Messrs. Bayley & Hall
115 × 25 × 14½ = 250 Price £6550
Ship proposed by James Hall while in London
100 × 24 × 13 = 200 Price £5000
This last vessel was proposed to be Composite hence her large Register measure in comparison to an oak framed ship but we consider an Wooden Framed Ship preferable for such a service where the vessel may receive Damage where Iron may not be found to repair it We are in the meanwhile preparing Drawings and Model for the Dimensions agreed upon by Messrs Bayley & ourselves. The vessel proposed will be rigged a Barque same as John Williams *the other was to be a three masted schooner. The proportions of the* John Wesley *were not determined by us and we considered her at least one foot too narrow I can only add that neither one nor other will more than compensate for the liberal manner in which we executed and intend to execute the former or proposed Ship and Am*
Sir Your Obt Servt
James Hall

15 College St
Dowgate Hill
London

The committee had consulted W A Bayley (they spelled it Bailey) and Captain Williams about the proposed replacement ship. The *John Wesley* was really a barquentine although Hall's refer to her as a schooner. She was built in 1867 for the Wesleyan Missionary Society with measurements of 118.0ft by 23.9ft by 13.5ft and 238 tons. The second letter is written from Aberdeen.

Aberdeen 20th Feby 1868

John Kemp Welch Esqre.
Sir In reply to yours of yesterday I state that the dimensions determined by Mr. Bayley and us must produce a more serviceable ship for your purpose and we would have given our reasons in our last had we not expected Mr Bayley to be in London. The first reason is she is two feet deeper in the Hold and will therefore contain more Cargo under the lower Deck leaving better Cabin Accommodation in twixt decks. Another reason is that the Barque Rig is thriftier than the three masted schooner and more as in bad weather When the last John Williams *was built we proposed dimensions for a Ship that would be safe in all weathers and sharp enough to beat off any lee shore and we think we succeeded and will do so again by reducing this one in proportion We have the Design ready but of course can make any other you may fix upon I also beg to point out that there is a very great difference in the price of a Ship last Augst and now, — We had just bought a Cargo of Teak at £8.15/- per load and today it is £12 — We have had more enquiries for ships within these four weeks than during these last two years — We have just laid down another kind of a Missionary from yours namely a* Gun Boat *for China and have a vessel of 890 to* Launch *next week besides a Steam Tug Boat for Chatham Dock Yard at same time we would be very much disappointed were we to lose your order for more reason than Profit. As I stated in my last the Rig and dimensions of* John Wesley *were not left to our approval neither had we the equipment of her*
I remain,
Yours very truly,
James Hall
'in haste for post)

From the remarks on the hull form of the *John William* (1865), it sounds as if she was an enlarged version of the lines shown in figure 342. James Hall's references to shipbuilding orders are full of interest: the gunboat referred to was probably the *Jho-sho-maru* launched in 1869 for the Japanese Navy and of 1459 tons; the vessel of 890 tons to be launched was the SS *Kwang Tung*, built of iron for Hong Kong owners; but the steam tug is not in the builder's yard list. The third letter was written by a clerk in Hall's office, and is punctuated.

Aberdeen 29 Febry 1868

John Kemp Welch Esqr
Dear Sir
In accordance with yours of 25th, we have reconsidered the various proposals, made in reference to the new vessel, and have fixed on the following Dimensions, which are in excess of those submitted formerly, for the smallest ship say, by six feet in length, and six inches in depth.

Dimensions

Length of Keel	*100 feet*	*Builder's*
Depth of Hold	*13½ feet*	*Tonnage*
Extreme Breadth	*24 feet*	*280 tons*
Fore rake	*6 feet*	*Register*
After rake	*1½ feet*	*Tonnage*
		210 tons

The vessel to have a raised Quarter Deck, of such length as the Cabin accommodation may require, and in every respect, fitted at least equal to the Late John Williams. *Plans of the vessel, and interior fittings to be submitted for approval. To be rigged a three masted schooner, with Yards on Fore & Main masts. The equipment to be as may be agreed upon between the Captain & ourselves. The vessel to be under the special inspection of Lloyds Surveyor, and Classed A.I. for 13 years on their Register. [Another hand has written here "Sheathed with Y Metal"].*
To be commenced forthwith, and delivered complete, first week of July.
We hereby make offer to build said vessel, and execute all the foregoing stipulations, for the sum of Five Thousand Pounds, to be paid on the following manner.
One fourth when the order is given
One fourth when all in frame
One fourth when Launched, and remainder when delivered complete.
Hoping the above may be satisfactory.
We are Sir
Your Obedient Servants
A. Hall & Co.

The manner of payment follows normal practice. The proposed rig of yards on fore and main masts would have produced a schooner similar to that proposed for Alexander Stephen's *Metero*, but in fact she was rigged as a barque with a main trysail. The above dimensions were agreed by the London Missionary Society and also the price. Her measurements were 106.0ft by 24.5ft by 13.5ft. Her tonnage worked out at 183 under deck and 17 for the raised quarter-deck, totalling 200 gross tons. The name decided on by the Board of Directors was *Samoa*, on which island the Society's principal Mission was situated, and she was named thus when launched in August 1868. However, at a Board Meeting on 21 October the same year, the Directors resolved 'that the name be *John Williams* as heretofore and not the *Samoa*', and so it was under the new name that she left London on 12 November. Her passage to Sydney took 108 days. The equator was crossed on 19 December and the meridian of the Cape of Good Hope passed on 21 January 1869. Commenting on the passage, the Rev T Powell wrote:

> 'Everyone who has seen the *John Williams* is enchanted with her. She has proved an admirable sea-boat, and will stand comparison with other ships in regard to speed. Captain Fowler is enthusiastic in his praise of both ship and crew, as well as the officers under his command. He never had such a ship before — would not change places with the Captain of the *Galatea*.'[81]

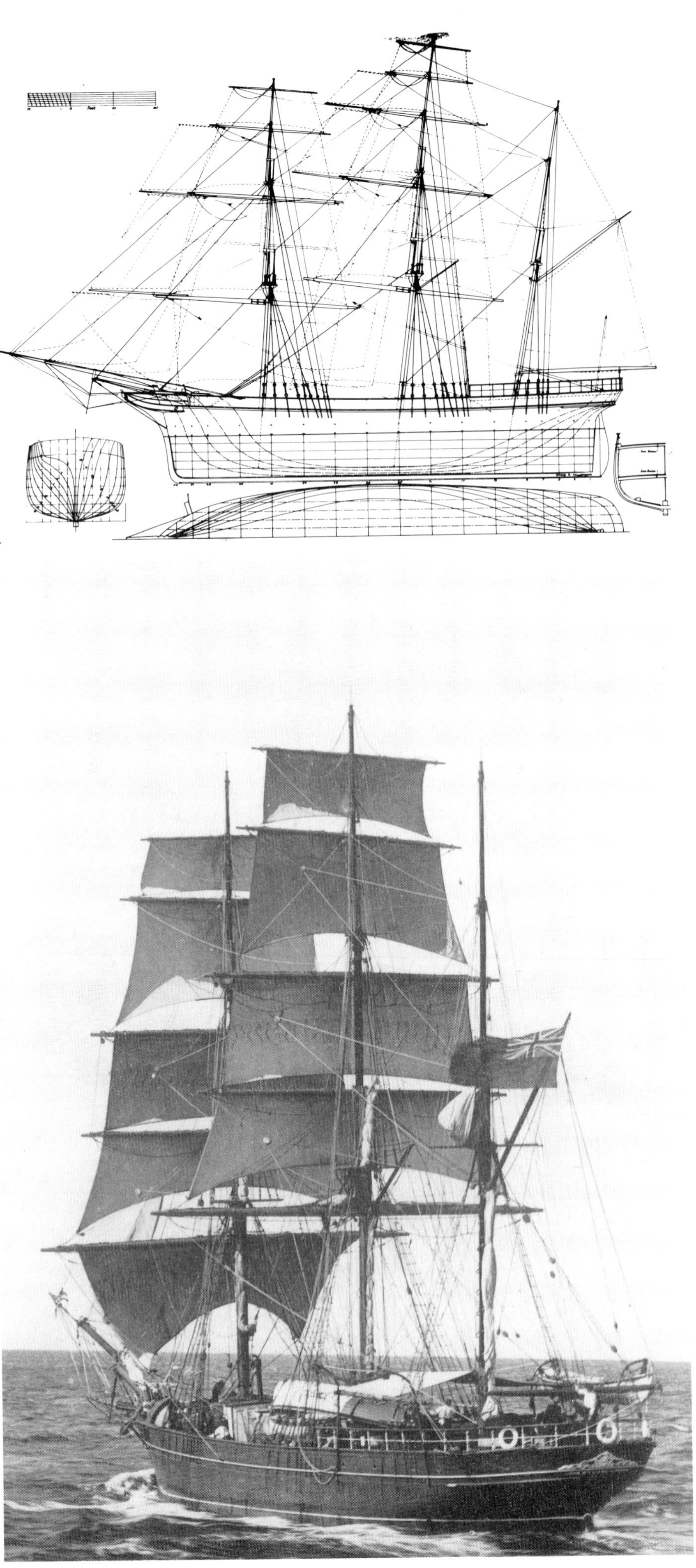

342: *John Williams.* ex *Samoa.* Built of wood in 1868 by Alexander Hall & Sons at Aberdeen. Redrawn from a small plan reconstructed by James Henderson. Dimensions: 106.0ft—24.5ft—13.5ft; 200 tons gross. Sources for reconstruction: lines from builder's table for offsets; spar dimensions from builder's cost account; rigging and sail outlines from pictures of ship and contemporary practice; midship section from Lloyd's Register survey report. Built as *Samoa* but renamed *John Williams* just prior to her maiden passage.

HMS *Galatea* was a very smart sailing frigate at that time on the Australian station. The *John Williams* remained successfully under the Society's employment, based on Australia and cruising amongst the Pacific islands, until sold in 1894 to other parties who renamed her *Kashgar*.

The plan of the ship in figure 342 has been redrawn from a plan prepared by James Henderson. The lines are from the builder's table of offsets; the sail plan is reconstructed from the builder's spar dimensions and mast spacings; and the rigging and sail outlines are according to contemporary practice and from the photograph reproduced in figure 341. No deck plan has been discovered, although photographs would permit an approximate deck layout to be worked out.

The lines plan of *John Williams* shows a fine-lined hull, formed in a manner similar to that employed by many schooners such as the *Fling* (figure 286), in which the entrance is long and predominantly convex, whereas the run is noticeable for the considerable concavity below the load line. Other small fine-lined ships and barques such as *Mansfield* had this form of hull. There is a fair amount of deadrise with straight floors, slack bilges and only slight tumblehome. No sailing speeds are known but with a fine hull and such a large spread of canvas she might easily have attained the fast speed-length ratio of 1.25 which would require a speed of 12½ knots.

She began life with Cunningham's roller-reefing topsails in which the stunsail booms are fitted below the yards. The shapes of the sails are reconstructed and have been drawn dotted. The main course is the conventional shape and causes considerable overlap, but

341: The *John Williams III* was originally equipped with single roller-reefing top-sails, and this photograph must have been taken some years later when they had been replaced with double ones. She was a small ship of only 200 tons. *Nautical Photo Agency.*

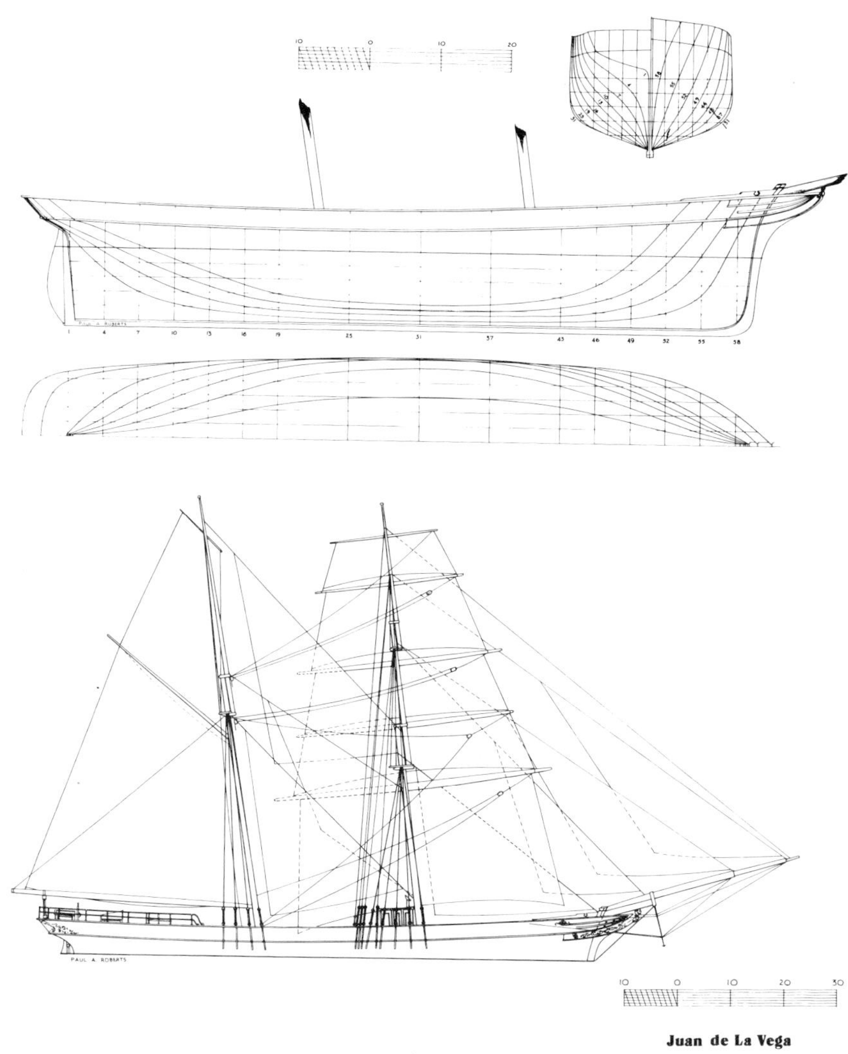

343: *Juan de la Vega.* Lines plan: Redrawn by Paul Roberts from draught prepared by James Henderson using the builder's offsets. Built in 1871 at Aberdeen by Alexander Hall & Sons for Spanish owners. Dimensions: 100.0ft–24.0ft–12.3ft and 172 tons. No reconstruction.

344: *Juan de la Vega.* Sail plan: Reconstructed by Paul Roberts from builder's plan loaned by James Henderson.

the foot of the fore course has been made shorter than the head to bring the tack nearer the cathead. The lengths of the stunsail booms and yards are listed by the builder.

A midship section has been reconstructed from the scantling sizes tabulated in the Lloyd's Register survey report, some of which are as follows: keel 12in by 12in, keelson 13in by 13in; floors 10in deep, first futtooks 8½in, second futtocks 8in, third futtocks and top timbers 7in; garboard strake 6in (American elm); planking from garboard to top of bilge 3in, from there to wales 3in and 4in, wales 4¼in, topsides 3¼in and 4in, plankssheer 3in. The frame was of British oak and the outer planking of teak. The upper and lower deck beams were of iron, 6½in sides with 2½in by 2½in angles along the upper edge. She was equipped with a longboat and two other boats.

Alexander Hall & Sons' last extreme clipper, *The Caliph*, is described in the next section.

Their wood brigantine *Juan de la Vega*, launched in 1871, was also fine-lined but with quite a different hull form to *John Williams* in spite of the fact that she was only 28 tons smaller. The lines plan shows that she has balanced ends, both of which are sharp but not extreme, with much more deadrise, firm bilges and little tumblehome. The two masts are stepped fairly close together with the foremast a long way aft.

Clippers of 1869–70

Sailing ship owners could have had no idea of the disastrous effects which the opening of the Suez Canal would have to freight rates nor to their ships' share of the market or they would never have placed so many orders for extreme clippers in 1868. Thus 1869 becomes one of the peak years for the production of China clippers and existing plans prove *Cutty Sark, Norman Court* and *The Caliph* to have been of this extreme clipper mould. Many other contestants for the clipper distinction were launched in 1869 but the absence of plans prevents confirmation of the fact, and although Basil Lubbock has listed 25 well known ships as built in this year in addition to the three named above, it is impossible to evaluate the hull form of the majority from verbal description alone.[82] Of the five ships in Lubbock's list which were built by Barclay, Curle & Co, plans show the *City of Lucknow, Loch Awe, Loch Ness* and *Loch Tay* to be fuller versions of *Mermerus* and therefore good medium clippers; the fifth ship, the *Golden Fleece*, was probably more along the lines of the *Mermerus*, although her plan has not been examined. A half-model of *City of Hankow* was measured in Alexander Stephen & Sons' offices, as no lines plan could be found, but she was not of the extreme clipper mould, just a sharpened medium clipper, nor was there any evidence on her sail plan of the numerous flying kites she is said to have carried.[83] Of other ships listed, it is more than likely that *Patriarch* and *Thomas Stephens* are likely candidates for clipper distinction and also some of the smaller ships. Some of the exuberance of clipper ship building spilled over into 1870 because of orders placed during the course of 1869, and the composite ship *Lothair* and the iron sisters *Blackadder* and *Hallowe'en* come under this heading.

If somebody closely connected with the shipping world had been asked in 1870 to name the best known clipper built during the

345: The white-hulled *Thomas Stephens*, photographed here at Gravesend, was built at Liverpool by Potter in 1869 and made some fast passages in the Australian trade. With a length of 263ft she had a tonnage of 1507. This picture was copied from one in an album.

previous year he might have paused for reflection, but today the name of *Cutty Sark* is unhesitatingly voiced by almost anyone. Nevertheless, it is her survival which has ensured her fame. As a China clipper she gave an average performance without making a passage from China in under 100 days; but in the Australian wool trade she was a star performer and gave an unbeatable record. Her owner, John Willis, owned a number of ships in eastern trades such as *Merse, Lammermuir* and *Whiteadder*, but *Cutty Sark* was probably his first extreme clipper. James MacCunn wrote in 1911: 'He was a fine affable sportsman and built his hopes in that ship — in vain.'[84]

Fortunately for us, however, *Cutty Sark* is an extreme clipper which affords an excellent opportunity to examine a ship of this rare breed in the twentieth century, 118 years after she was built. Looking at the ship in dry dock at Greenwich, where she is preserved by the Maritime Trust, one is immediately struck by the greath depth of hull, and then as the eye travels aloft one wonders how such a narrow and sharp-ended ship could have supported that cloud of canvas. The relationship of hull form to masts and spars is admirably demonstrated by this living example, and assists us in visualising all the other clippers which have been described in this work. Coming at the end of the 1860s, at the close of the second clipper ship boom, the *Cutty Sark* inherited all the skills and knowledge which had produced other successful ships and which, owing to her survival, may almost be said to be consumated in her.

Her lines have been published by Basil Lubbock in the best biography written of her, and more recently Cyril L Hume has produced a combined lines and sail plan.[85] These drawings show a very long, sharp entrance with slight hollow in the load line near the stem; a long, sharp run that is somewhat fuller on the load line than at the entrance; a quarter beam buttock which has some hollow where it crosses the load line aft; big deadrise in the body plan with hollow garboards, slack bilges and some tumblehome. Her register dimensions are 212.5ft by 36.0ft by 21.0ft, 892 tons under deck, 921 net and 963 gross. Various theories have been advanced as to whether *Cutty Sark* was a direct copy of *The Tweed* or stemmed entirely from the board of Hercules Linton, junior partner in Scott & Linton who built her at Dumbarton. *The Tweed* was built at Bombay in 1854 to designs by the naval architect Oliver Lang, and began life as the paddle steamer *Punjaub*; later John Willis bought her and removed the engines. As a sailing ship she proved very fast. It may be that *Cutty Sark*'s entrance was modelled on *The Tweed*, but her quarters were made fuller and the bottom was altered considerably from *The Tweed*'s flat floors and wall sides.[86] The resulting lines produced a fast, powerful hull which could go to windward well and could also stand driving in a heavy, following sea. *Cutty Sark*'s maximum recorded speed was 17½ knots, which on a load line length of 211 feet gives a speed-length ratio of 1.20, indicating a potentially fast vessel. Her coefficient of under deck tonnage is .55 which is the same as *Hallowe'en* and *Crest of the Wave*, and is .03 less than *Thermopylae*, but .04 more than the *Storm Cloud*. The *Cutty Sark* is said to have been designed with the intention of beating the *Thermopylae*, but this is open to question as her keel was laid in February 1869,[87] or a mere month after *Thermopylae* had reached Melbourne 63 days out from Gravesend. John Willis could, at the date Linton was designing the future *Cutty Sark*, have had no idea how fast *Thermopylae* would sail nor of her speed in the China tea trade. However, his imagination had been fired to have an extreme clipper built, in the same way that his fellow shipowners had caught this infectious enthusiasm, and no doubt the launching of any clipper ship was common knowledge at the time, so that her design would have been discussed and analysed by the leading *cognoscente*. However, the result of Willis' rivalry was an extreme clipper whose breadth and depth measurements were identical to those of *Thermopylae* while the length was a mere six inches longer.

William Ward's drawings of several of the

346: A drawing of the *Cutty Sark* with all the sails set, and the starboard side cut away to show the stowage of the tea boxes. *Cutty Sark Society*.

Small hand winch aboard *Cutty Sark*, mounted on the bulwarks (left). A variation on mounting a hand winch (right).

347: The fife rail on the foreside of the *Cutty Sark*'s main mast, showing the grooves in the timber worn by ropes.

deck fittings aboard *Cutty Sark* are typical of those in other contemporary ships. Owing to the mass of material already written about the ship and the detailed description of her deck fittings and sail plan, perhaps I may be excused for not repeating all this again here. However, the ship is well worth a visit where many aspects of her design and outfit can be examined at first-hand.

Another extreme Clyde-built clipper of 1869 was the *Norman Court*, reconstructed in the yard of A & J Inglis at Pointhouse, Glasgow, from designs by William Rennie. She was built to the order of Baring Brothers, the London merchants, who originally intended to name her *John o' Gaunt*. The builders acknowledged Rennie's involvement in their formal offer to build the ship when they wrote: 'we beg to say that we are prepared to undertake the contract for building said ship from the lines to be furnished by Mr Rennie'. The last paragraph reads: 'We quite understand that Mr Rennie is to inspect the lines when laid down and that his plan of masting is to be strictly adhered to.'[88] William Rennie's invoice, which was on plain paper with an account ruling, listed his services:

> 'To furnishing plans and finished model, with glass frame, of a composite

348: With a list to port, the *Ferreira* ex *Cutty Sark* lies at Muscogee Wharf, Pensacola, on 27 September 1906, after a hurricane had swept the town. The fore royal mast and its yard are hanging in the topgallant rigging; the dolphin striker is broken at its lower end and the chain stays leading to it are slack; but the gilded *Cutty Sark* can still be seen adorning the truck of the mainmast. *Smithsonian Institution.*

> clipper ship of about 800 tons Register and to several visits to Glasgow to inspect the same £123.10s.0d'

But in spite of the builders agreeing to follow Rennie's plan, Basil Lubbock records that they deviated slightly from his design in 'moulding the iron frames . . . in order to bring Rennie's measurements within Lloyd's scantlings for a thousand-ton ship'. This did not greatly reduce her speed but made her more tender.[90]

This ship has been called Rennie's masterpiece. According to her lines plan in figure 349 she has a very long, sharp entrance with slight hollow in the load line near the stem, and an equally sharp, long run; the quarter beam buttock runs in an almost straight line from the knuckle at the counter to 18in below the load line; there is a fair amount of deadrise above hollow garboards, with firm bilges and 15in of tumblehome. The original lines plan in the possession of Baring Brothers is not signed but the words 'W Rennie' are stencilled on it in Gothic characteris between the forefoot and the fore perpendicular.

The *Norman Court* measured 197.4ft by 33.0ft by 20.0ft, 796 tons under deck and 884 net register. On an even draught of 18ft-5in she displaced 1767 tons. Her coefficient of under deck tonnage is .61 which is the same as *Fiery Cross* (1860), another of Rennie's designs. The *Norman Court* excelled at going to windward and was very fast in light winds, both virtues being particularly important for a successful China clipper. She had a narrower sail plan than some of the ships and a mainyard which measured 74ft-0in. She had a monkey forecastle, a big

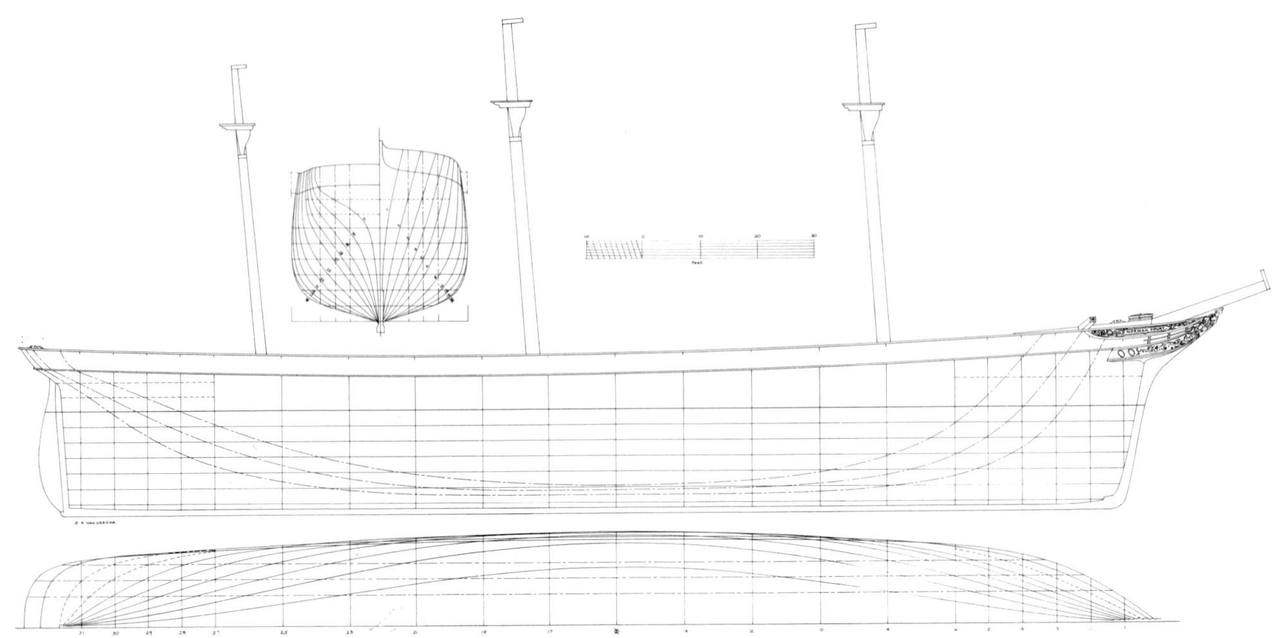

349: *Norman Court*. Lines plan: Redrawn from builder's plan (blueprint) loaned by Frederick Claydon. Built in 1869 at Glasgow by A & J Inglis. Dimensions: 197.4ft—33.0ft—20.0ft and 833.87 tons net. Reconstruction: lower masts, tops, and bowsprit to cap added from sail plan.

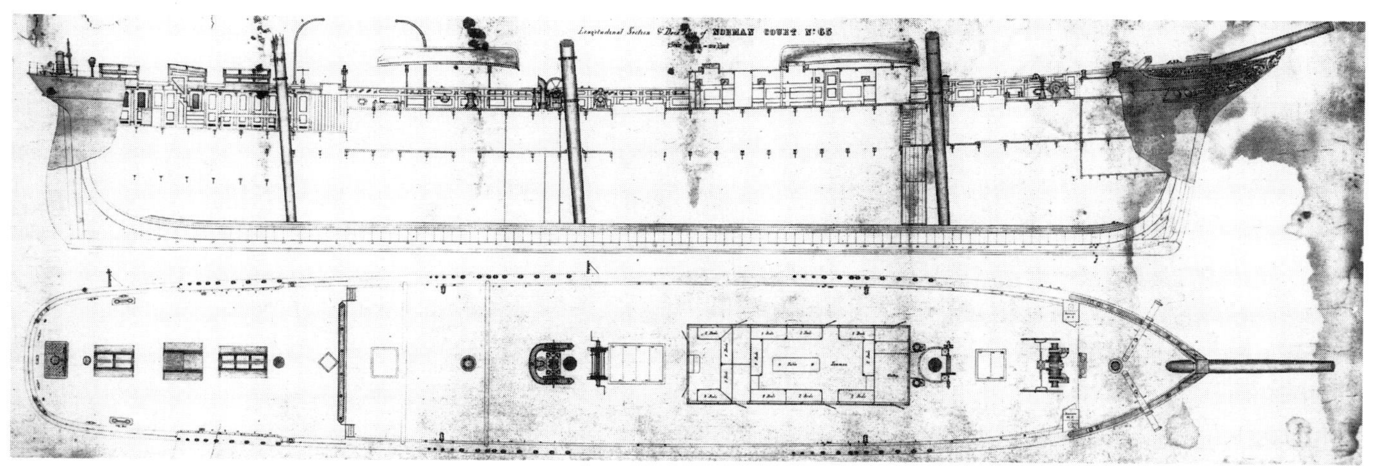

350: *Norman Court.* Longitudinal section and deck plan. Reproduced from photograph of builder's plan provided by Frederick Claydon.

deckhouse for the crew and a raised quarter-deck. She was equipped with Brown & Harfield's windlass and Kirkland's pumps; she had three boats — lifeboat, quarter boat, and gig. Her only passage from China in under 100 days was made in 1872 when she took 94 days between Macao and the Lizard, leaving on 14 September.

The third extreme clipper launched in 1869 was *The Caliph* which Alexander Hall & Sons built for a London merchant, Alexander Hector, a cousin of John Willis. Hall's had not produced such a sharp China clipper since the *Black Prince* which had appeared six years earlier, and with her they completed 30 years in the design of fast sailing ships that had begun with the *Scottish Maid. The Caliph* measured 215.1ft by 36.1ft by 20.4ft, 888 tons under deck and 914 net register. These figures give her a coefficient of under deck tonnage of .56 which is .02 less than *Thermopylae*.

Her lines plan was published in *The Tea Clippers*, as drawn by F A Claydon, and it shows a ship with extremely long and sharp ends in which the hollows in the waterlines are reduced to a minimum; there is a great rise of floor which is produced by extremely concave garboards and floors, with easy bilges but little tumblehome.[91] Her design closely follows that of the *Cairngorm*, built in 1853, with the same breadth and depth but 20ft more length. The sail plan is very lofty with skysails on each mast; skysail stunsails are listed by the builder for both her fore and main masts and the mainyard length is given

351: *Norman Court.* Sail plan: Reproduced from photograph of builder's plan provided by Frederick Claydon.

352: The last clipper built by Alexander Hall & Sons was *The Caliph*, seen here under full sail, with a jamie green set under her bowsprit and a ringtail abaft her spanker.

as 85ft-0in. The deck layout was similar to *Norman Court* except that she was also equipped with a steam engine of 8hp situated in the after end of the deckhouse. This drove the cargo winch, windlass, pumps and, like the *Ben Nevis*, could be used to rotate a small screw propellor amidships with which it was hoped to achieve 2½ knots in a calm. In addition to the builder's spar dimensions, a fully comprehensive list of sails, rigging sizes, inventory and description of construction are included in Chapman's *All About Ships*.[91] Her only tea-laden passage was a very fast one of 87 days between Foochow and New York, from 6 December 1870 to 3 March 1871. She went missing in the China Sea some time in the middle of August 1871.

No plans have been found of the sister ships *Hallowe'en* and *Blackadder*, but their low coefficients of under deck tonnage, namely .55, show that they must have been very fine-lined ships. Basil Lubbock says that in 1869 John Willis, owner of *Cutty Sark*, had the lines taken off his ship, *The Tweed*, by the naval architects Ritherdon & Thompson, and then contracted with Maudslay, Son & Field of Deptford to build *Blackadder* and *Hallowe'en* on these lines.[93] The influence of *The Tweed* was imputed in the case of *Cutty Sark*'s design, but if her lines were taken off for Linton's use it seems hardly feasible that Willis would go to the expense of having them taken off only a year later by another surveyor. It is possible that the lines of the iron ships were based to some extent on those of the *Cutty Sark* from which it could said that they might have inherited indirectly something from *The Tweed*. Both *Hallowe'en* and *Blackadder* were fast ships in the China and Australian trades, and the former's first three passages between Shanghai and London averaged only 91⅔ days, which is astonishingly quick even though they were all made in the favourable monsoon.

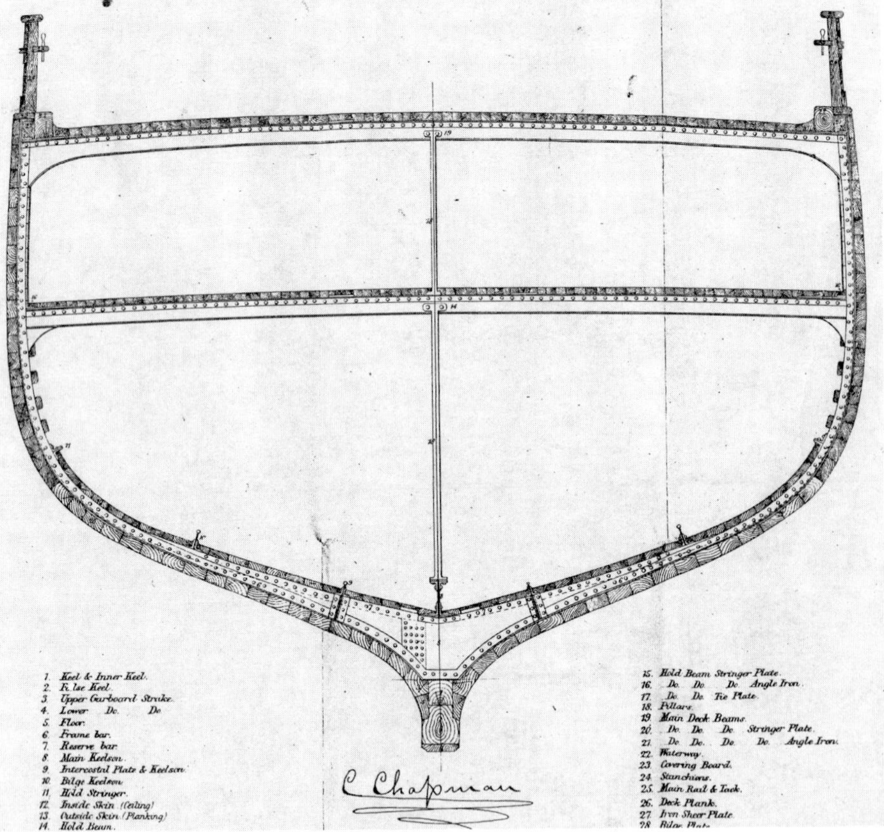

353: *The Caliph*. Midship Section: Reproduced from folding plate in *All About Ships* by Captain Charles Chapman (1869). No scale is drawn.

The *Mermerus* and other iron clippers of the 1870s

The *Mermerus* is representative of the numerous heavily-masted iron ships which were sent afloat in the early 1870s as the clipper ships' last bid against steam. Sailing ships were far from dead after 1875 but the majority tended to be constructed with a greater eye to economical cargo carrying and in this way were able to trade during the remainder of the century, often with good profit to their owners. There are many builders to be found associated with the big iron sailing ships of the early 1870s, but few produced anything better than the creations of Barclay, Curle & Co, of which *Mermerus* is the prime example. Her owners, A & J Carmichael of Greenock, ordered a whole series of beautiful iron ships from Barclay, Curle & Co for their 'Golden Fleece Line' in the Australian wool trade. Up until 1876, these consisted of the *Medea* (1868), *Golden Fleece* (1868), *Jason* (1870), *Mermerus* (1872), *Thessalus* (1874) and *Argonaut* (1876). The photograph of *Golden Fleece* running into Le Havre, reproduced in figure 355, is an excellent portrait of one of these magnificent ships in action and is the same picture that used to hang in her owner's

354: Photographed at Circular Quay, Sydney, on her maiden voyage in 1872, *Hallowe'en's* lofty spars were very prominent amongst the shipping. Her mainmast was 141ft high. There seems no sign of stunsail boom irons. *C L Hume.*

office. Barclay, Curle & Co produced a further seven ships for Carmichael's between 1877 and 1886.

The *Mermerus* was built in 1872 and her measurements indicate the rapidly increasing size for the larger class of iron ships. Her dimensions were 264.2ft by 39.8ft by 23.7ft with tonnages of 1588 under deck, 1750 gross, and 1671 net register. Compared with *Cutty Sark*, her measurements of breadth and depth only increased by 3ft-9in and 2ft-6in respectively, but the length increased by no less than 52ft-0in. This greatly increased length resulted in a far narrower and shallower hull, and the ratio of beam to length was 6.6 to 1 and of depth to length 11.1 to 1. For *Cutty Sark* the relative proportions were 5.9 to 1 and 10.1 to 1.

The plans of *Mermerus* reproduced here were redrawn from the originals found in Barclay, Curle & Co's plan store in 1961. The lines plan had had the stern torn off on both sheer elevation and half-breadth plans, and has been reconstructed from plans of other ships from the same yard; no general arrangement plan could be found except one showing the accommodation in plan and section for forecastle, deckhouse, and poop, and the missing detail comes from her sail plan and from plans of *Strathearn* (1871) and *Argonaut* (1876), assisted by photographs.

The lines of *Mermerus* are sharp enough to class her as a clipper but not as an extreme one. The ends are evenly balanced with a long, convex entrance and run, and the waterlines close to the sternpost show some concavity. Amidships there is 18ft of parallel body. There is very little deadrise and the maximum beam is kept low with firm bilges and appreciable tumblehome. The lines and form are fairly similar to most of Barclay,

355: The Glasgow shipbuilders, Barclay, Curle & co., built some beautiful ships in the sixties and seventies, and plans of their *Mermerus* are given here. This picture has caught the action of another of their iron ships, *Golden Fleece*, running into Le Havre with a following wind. There is no canvas on the mizen and the fore and main lower topsails have been taken in, which was frequently the custom in confined waters. The foresail is being clewed up and the main topgallant yard is being lowered to spill the wind from the sail. *A J Nesdall.*

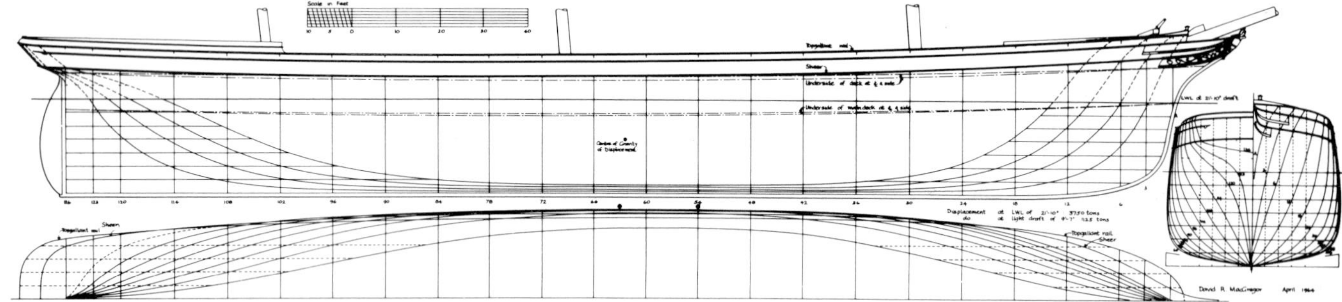

356: *Mermerus.* Lines: Built of iron in 1872 by Barclay, Curle & Co. at Glasgow. Redrawn from builder's plan. Dimensions for register: 264.2ft—39.8ft—23.7ft; 1671 tons net. Reconstruction: stern of ship (torn off original drawing) based on plans of other ships by same builder.

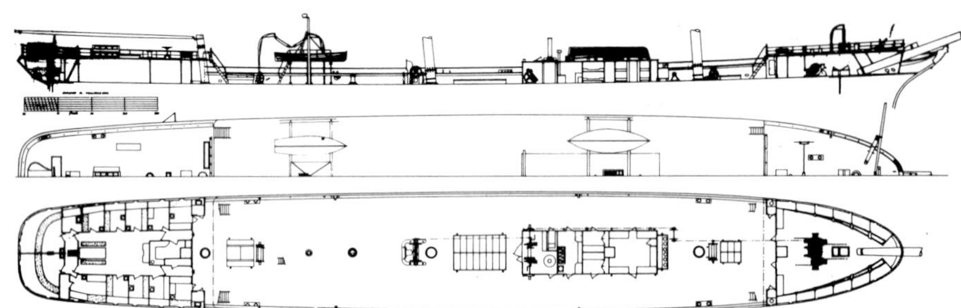

357: *Mermerus.* General arrangement plan: Entirely reconstructed. Sources: plans and sections of crew and passenger accommodation in poop, deckhouse and forecastle; lines plan; sail plan; plans of *Stratbearn* (1871) and *Argonaut* (1876) from same yard; photographs of ship.

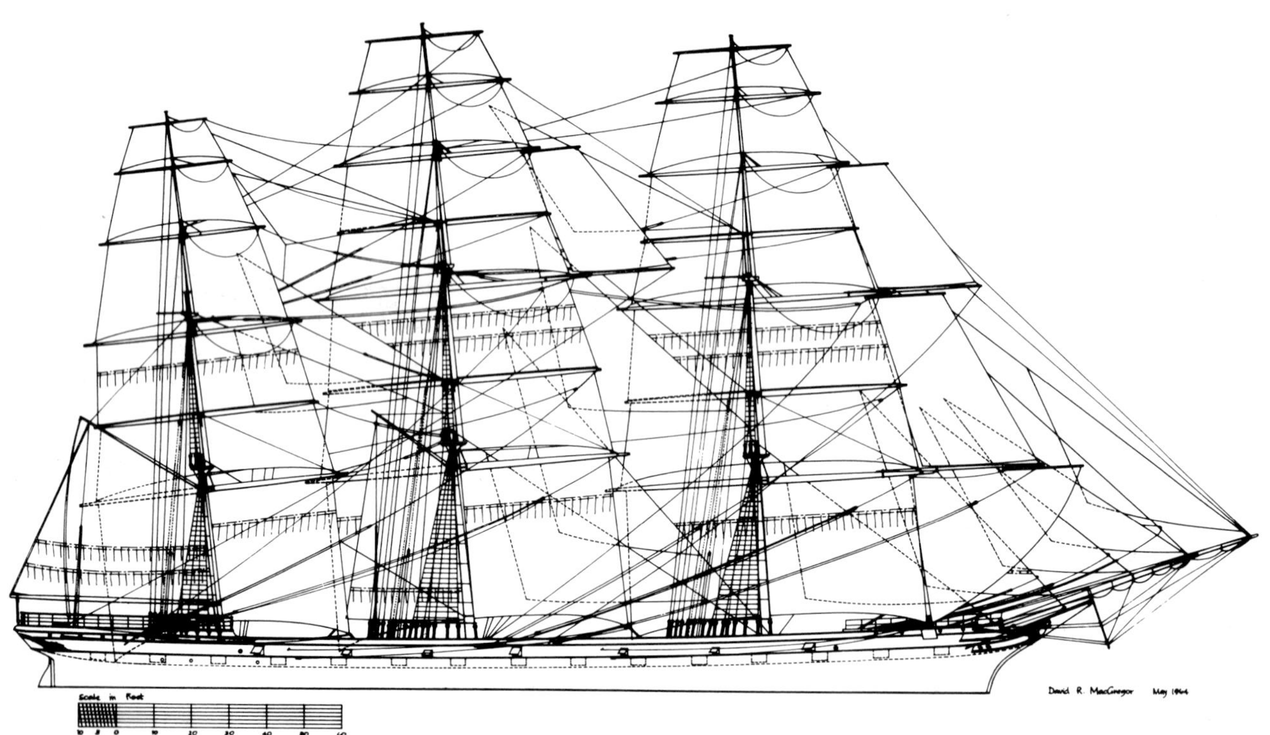

Curle & Co's ships built since 1860, and also to other iron clippers of the early 1870s such as *Timaru* (built 1874 by Scott & Co), and *Coriolanus* (1876 by A MacMillan & Son), whose plans have been published by Harold Underhill.[94] Although about nine feet longer than *Strathearn*, launched a year previously from the same yard, *Mermerus* is some 50 tons less under deck which indicates a finer hull form. On a load line length of 256ft-6in a speed-length ratio of 1.25 would have required a speed of 19.87 knots; only on examination of her logbooks could tell if she ever approached such a high rate, because when there was sufficient wind to drive a ship at this speed there was usually such a big sea running that the ship would be retarded by the waves. Several fast passages to and from Australia were recorded such as 66 days from Gravesend to Melbourne in 1876, and 71 days from Melbourne to the Lizard in 1877.

Barclay, Curle & Co, were not slow in providing steam power to assist their ships' crews and *Mermerus* had a boiler in the after end of the deckhouse to supply steam to the cargo winch. When in operation, doors in the after end of the deckhouse could be opened. There was also a belt or chain drive to the pumps by the mainmast and likewise along the deck to the windlass. Nevertheless, both windlass and pumps were also drawn with handles for operation by manpower, and Gould's photograph of the ship lying at anchor off Gravesend depicts the windlass handles in position. This suggests that the master found it simpler to raise the anchor by hand than by steam power. Bulwarks of over 5ft-6in in height, together with the usual deck camber, permitted the topgallant forecastle to be hidden behind the bulwarks and give an unbroken sheer forward; only aft was there a full poop to provide a headroom of seven feet inside.

There is a sheep or pig pen placed at the fore end of the deckhouse, and there are hen coops on the poop. The arrangement of the standard compass, accessible from a platform across the boat skids, is a detail so far not found in the ships illustrated here.

The sail and rigging plan of *Mermerus* reproduced in figure 358 is redrawn from the builder's plan, and all the running rigging, stunsails and reef points have been reconstructed from paintings and photographs of the ship, and plans of other vessels. The sail plan looks a tall one due to the presence of double topgallants on both foremast and mainmast and skysails on all three masts, but compared with many other iron ships she was not over-masted. Alexander Stephen's *Shenir* has a mainmast of equal height in proportion to hull length. The skysails on the fore and mizen masts of *Mermerus* were removed after a few voyages and the masts shortened, but the single topgallant on the mizen was never replaced with double yards. All the big iron ships continued to augment their sail plans with suits of stunsails, frequently on the mainmast as well as on the fore. A painting at the National Maritime Museum, Greenwich, depicts the ship with a triangular fore lower stunsail set, but the plan of *Strathearn* includes a lower swinging boom which measures 48ft-0in, thus indicating that this ship had square lower stunsails. *Mermerus* has a separate flying jibboom which could be dispensed with altogether for reasons of economy without having to alter much of the rigging or make a new spar.

Some ships such as *Macquarie*, ex *Melbourne*, had a bumpkin for the fore braces and the falls led through sheaves in the bulwarks, but the *Mermerus* has a plate drawn on her hull with four lugs for securing the standing part of the braces. The falling parts are led inside the rail through triple sister blocks mounted on the topgallant rail as shown in plans of *Strathearn* and *Argonaut*. There is the normal bumpkin for the main braces and the falls are led through sheaves in the topgallant rail, just forward of the poop; this was a fairly common practice and is depicted on the painting of the ship at the National Maritime Museum, although the sheaves are not drawn on the builder's sail plan.

The stunsail tacks on the foremast, which must act as a form of brace, are led through sheaves fixed on the topgallant rail. Perhaps

359: The lordly grandeur of a full-rigged ship is captured by this photograph of the *Mermerus*, taken at Melbourne in 1896. She still carries a main skysail yard, with bowsprit and jibboom, and does not appear to have been much cut down. *Nautical Photo Agency*.

360: This scene aboard *Marquarie* is well-known; nevertheless it portrays better than most the atmosphere aboard a passenger ship in fine weather on the poop. A three-sheave halliard is in the foreground. *Nautical Photo Agency*.

the sheet of the triangular stunsail, which has not been drawn, should also lead through one of these sheaves. Plans drawn by Alexander Stephen & Sons of their ships *William Davie* and *Shenir* have been consulted for the running rigging of stunsails, in addition to Harold Underhill's book on rigging.[95]

Basil Lubbock has made an interesting comparison between the sail plan of *Mermerus*, which works out to 34,997 yards, and that of the first four-masted ship, the *County of Peebles*, which at 30,610 yards is 4387 yards less. As both vessels emanated from the same yard the difference is at first surprising, particularly in view of the fourth square-rigged mast carried by the last named, but the four-master had much shorter masts in spite of possessing a hull of roughly similar size and tonnage.[95]

Prospects must have been considered fairly good for a hard-headed businessman like George Thompson Jnr to order an extreme clipper as late as 1874, yet this is what he did, modelling the new ship on the *Thermopylae* but building her ten feet longer, one foot deeper and constructing her of iron. This new ship, the *Salamis*, was 'built from Bernard Waymout's lines with a few minor alterations and improvements'.[97] Lines taken off in about 1938 from an unnamed half-model at Bangor Museum by William Salisbury almost certainly represent *Salamis*, the

361: Another scene aboard *Macquarie*'s poop with all the passengers' chairs deserted. The courses are full of wind and she must be making good progress. A Morrison photograph. *C L Hume*.

362: The iron ship *Harbinger* of 1506 tons is a splendid example of the beautiful clippers being produced during the first half of the 1870s. The missing fore and mizen skysail yards do not detract from this impressive sight. She was built by Robert Steele & Co. at Greenock. *Nautical Photo Agency*.

363: The sharp entrance and towering spars of an iron slipper are well portrayed in this photograph of the *Salamis* in the Alfred Graving Dock at Williamstown, Australia. She differed very little in hull-form from *Thermopylae*. *D M Little*.

breadth and depth being correct and the model's length being approximately two feet shorter. The whole hull model in the Liverpool Museum ascribed to her bears no resemblance to *Thermopylae* besides being much too short, and certainly cannot represent *Salamis* as built. Although designed for the China tea trade, *Salamis* only once managed to load a cargo of tea for London, but she proved a fast and successful ship in the Australian wool trade.

William Lund of London, owner of *Ambassador*, also thought the China tea trade could yield profits, because he ordered the 995-ton iron ship *Serapis* from Scott & Co of Greenock who delivered her in November 1876. Perhaps her lines were similar to those of *Timaru* which Scott also built. A photograph suggests she was fairly fine aft and a contemporary report states that she was 'designed for speed and elegance'.[98] In the autumn of 1878 she took 140 days to bring home her tea cargo, which was loaded at the miserably low rate of £1.15s per ton.

From the evidence of plans and models, other ships to possess clipper characteristics were the *Rodney*, built in 1874 by William Pile, and the *Coriolanus*, built in 1876 by Archibald McMillan at Dumbarton.

Clippers, brigs and schooners

Competition between smaller vessels either in the home trade or in the Atlantic and Mediterranean trades was just as keen as in larger ships, and many of the surviving plans show comparatively fine-lined craft. The fact that the majority had to take the ground in a reasonably upright position forced builders away from steep floors, and to make up for fullish midship sections the ends were often made very long and sharp. Many newspaper accounts of new schooners describe them as clippers and indeed there were a number of trades where the carrying of fruit, fish, animals and fresh vegetables required high speed.

Two basic hull forms had emerged by the beginning of the sixties for vessels of under about two hundred tons: in one of these the entrance was long and convex with almost vertical bow sections, but by contrast the run was very concave; in the other, the ends were more balanced and the lower part of the entrance could even be slightly hollow. The first type of hull form was certainly to be found in the south-west of England and the *Fling* is such an example, but the second type could be encountered in any part of the country. The south Cornish schooner *Rhoda Mary*, built in 1868 of 130 tons gross, is an example of the schooner with convex entrance and concave run. Her lines, which were taken off her decayed hull by Basil Greenhill and myself in 1949, are reproduced in *Merchant Sailing Ships 1850–1875*.[99]

An example of the schooner with balanced ends may be had amongst a collection of plans at the National Maritime Museum, Greenwich, formed by Henry W Lisslie (1859–1948), an Appeldore shipwright and draughtsman. The majority of the plans are as yet unidentified although some bear what might be yard numbers, and as he worked for Robert Cock, William Westacott and other builders it is probable that the plans relate to vessels built in yards on the Taw and Torridge Rivers.[55] One such plan is entitled 'No 5 A fruiter – good model' and portrays an extremely narrow hull of extreme clipper proportions as illustrated in figure 365. Dimensions written on the plan give 105ft-6in length 'under bowsprit for measurement', 18ft-0in maximum beam, 9ft-9in depth of hold and $163^{27}/_{94}$ tons BM. A short bowsprit is drawn but no mast centres and one would expect three masts to occupy this long hull. The above dimensions give a ratio of 5.86 beams to length which is very high for a wooden schooner, but John Westacott who preceded

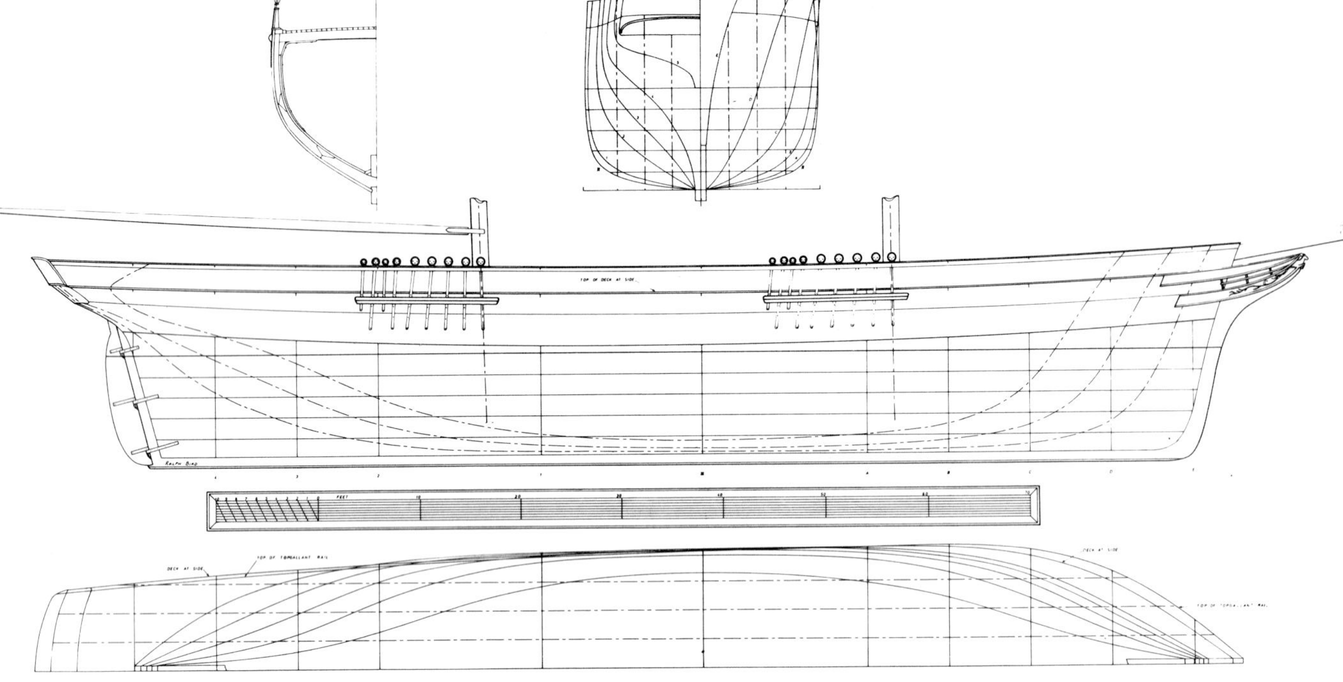

364: *Fawn*. Lines plan drawn by Ralph Bird from lines taken off builder's half-model by P Dalton in 1943. Built of wood at Dartmouth in 1866 by Phillips with dimensions of 109.1ft—23.2ft—12.9ft and 211 tons. Later, net tonnage given as 192, and when owned at Ramsgate by 1900, net tonnage is 178 and rig altered to brigantine. Trailboards, figurehead, masts and LWL as on model. Reconstruction by Bird: main boom; channels, chainplates and deadeyes; cross-section.

365: *Lisslie fruiter* Unidentified c1860-70. Plan entitled 'No 5 A Fruiter - good model'. Redrawn from Lisslie Collection in National Maritime Museum. Dimensions on plan: 101ft-3in (length of keel), 105ft-6in (length under bowsprit for measurement), 18ft-0in (beam, 17ft-6in (moulded beam), 9ft-9in (depth of hold); 153 27/94 tons om. Reconstruction: projection of buttocks in forebody.

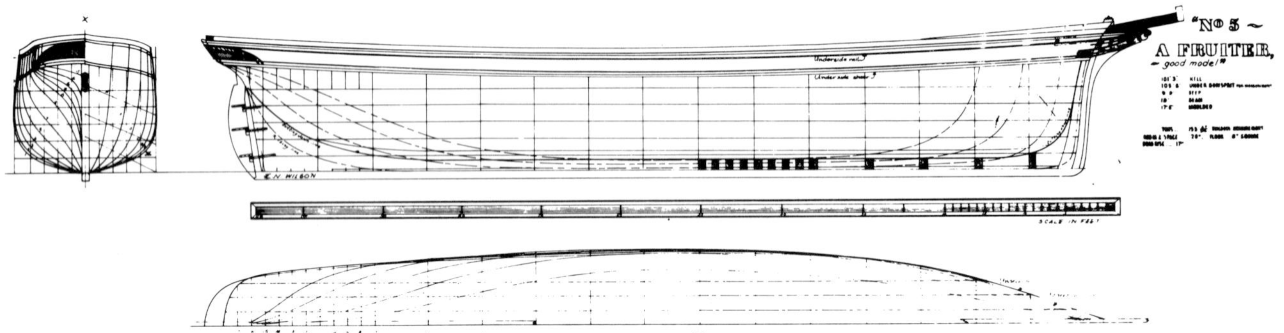

William built some small barques of these proportions and his *Spring Bok* (1853) and *Mary Anne Bruford* (1854) had ratios of 6.0 beams to length.

Other plans in the collection show fine-lined hulls, although usually with more beam.

The rig of these fine-lined schooners was little different from the *Scottish Maid* or *Caledonia*, and many possessed a main boom of immense length. A square topsail and topgallant were regularly carried on the foremast, although by 1870 a royal would rarely have been fitted to a new vessel. Although the square sails were regularly set, the gaff sails were the largest sails. Double topsails did not replace the single ones until the 1880s at

366: Three-masted schooners, such as the *Huntress*, were being heavily rigged with a large sail area including 3 or 4 yards on the foremast. She is here been painted entering Malta harbour. She was built in 1862 at Salcombe by Vivian with a tonnage of 176 and a length of 109ft. *F A L Fairweather*.

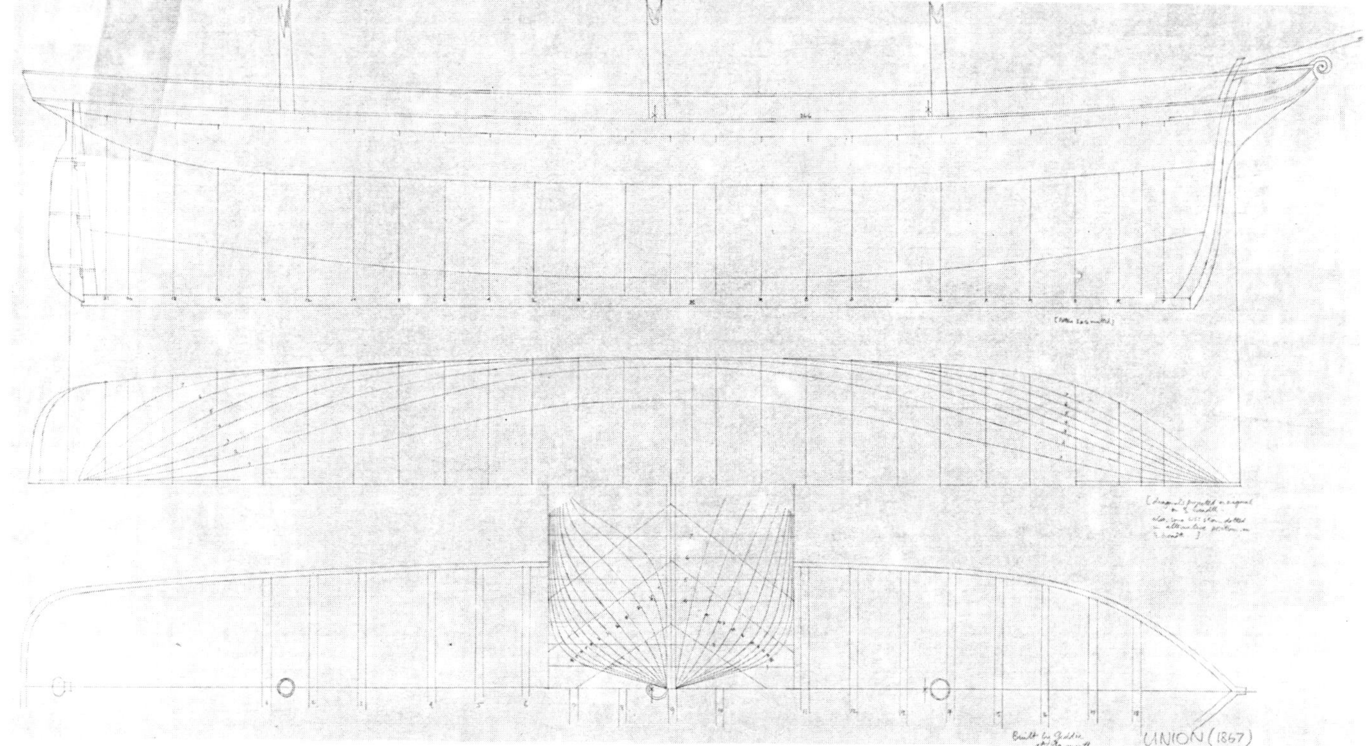

367: *Union.* Lines plan and deck beam plan traced from builder's plan in Science Museum. Built of wood at Garmouth in 1867 by James Geddie with dimensions of 113.4ft—24.5ft—14.3ft and 234 tons. Projected diagonals omitted and also some waterlines which were dotted on the half-breadth plan.

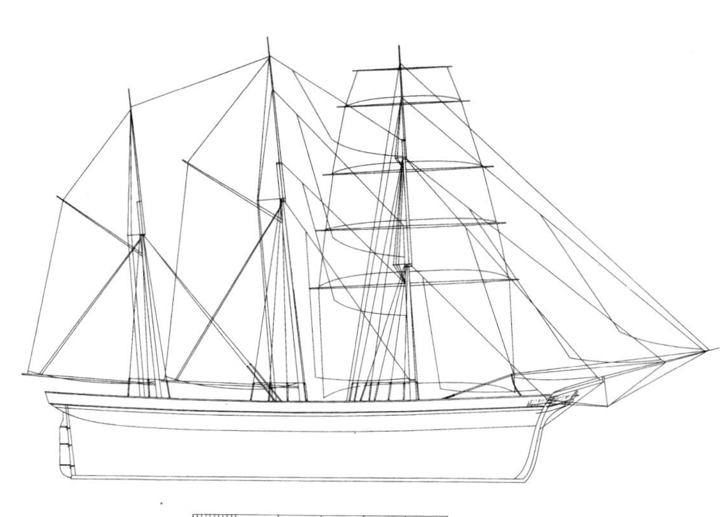

368: *Union.* Sail and standing rigging plan traced from builder's plan in Science Museum. Head was incomplete and so that of barquentine *Zephyr* (1869) was traced to complete hull. The rigging sizes written on the plan are listed in Appendix V.

which time older vessels often did away with the topgallant. A square sail was often set below the fore lower yard in favourable winds, and there were probably four head-sails; in addition, there was a fore-and-aft main topsail and a main topmast staysail. Stunsails were carried until the end of the seventies, although a few deepwater schooners retained them even later.

Schooners in Europe, both in Great Britain and on the Continent, almost invariably carried square sails on the foremast so that the term 'schooner' automatically assumes this fact; indeed, if square sails were absent, the term 'fore-and-aft schooner' had to be used to note the difference. Conversely, in America, a schooner was automatically deemed to be fore-and-aft rigged and so the presence of square canvas on the foremast drew the term 'topsail schooner'. Sometimes schooners in Europe that carried topgallants were called 'topgallant yard schooners'.

An interesting barquentine was built in Scotland in 1867. This was the *Union* which James Geddie launched at Garmouth in the same year that Alexander Hall & Sons produced the barquentine *John Wesley* at Aberdeen, so their relative measurements are of interest:

Union	234 tons 113.4ft × 24.5ft × 14.3ft	8 A1 wood
John Wesley	238 tons 118.0ft × 23.9ft × 13.5ft	15 A1 composite

The above figures show the two vessels to be very similar in size, and the lines plan of the *Union* and a builder's model of the *John Wesley*, both now in the Science Museum, London, indicate that the hull form is approximately similar too, although the *Union* is shorter and a little deeper.

The *Union*'s lines at ⅜-inch scale (figure 367) show a long, fairly shallow-draught hull with fine ends; the entrance is generally convex but some hollow is worked into the hull near the stem, rather as in an iron ship; the run has rather more concavity, but the hull does not taper much as it approaches the stern, which is rounded. There is a fair amount of deadrise with straight floors, slack bilges and vertical sides. The builder's plan has the deck beams drawn but no fittings are indicated, although the positions of the main and after hatchways are obvious from the wider beam spacing at these two places; however, the general arrangement plan could be reconstructed on the basis of the deck beams and the raised quarterdeck which is 21ft long.

A fine sail plan of the *Union* (figure 368) accompanied the lines plan and so enables us to gain a good idea of this lovely barquentine. As dimensions are written on the plan against each spar, and as the rigging is carefully drawn, the plan is undoubtedly a shipyard drawing and not a sailmaker's plan. No sail outlines were drawn on the original for any of the staysails, nor was the foot of the fore course or of any of the square sails

369: The barquentine *Lord of the Isles* lying in Peterhead harbour, possibly when new. She was built locally in 1869 and was then out in the China trade. A feature of her hull is the excessive rake of her stem and the elaborate carved trail board. *Peterhead Library and Arbuthnot Museum.*

370: *Planter.* Lines plan and midship section: Drawn by Peter Ferguson from lines taken off builder's half-model. Built in 1871 by John Cox at Cleave Houses, Bideford. Dimensions: 124.7ft—25.0ft—12.9ft and 267 tons register. She was rigged as a barque and built of wood. She has marked deadrise with a sharp entrance and a long line run. Reconstruction: midship section from Lloyd's Register survey report.

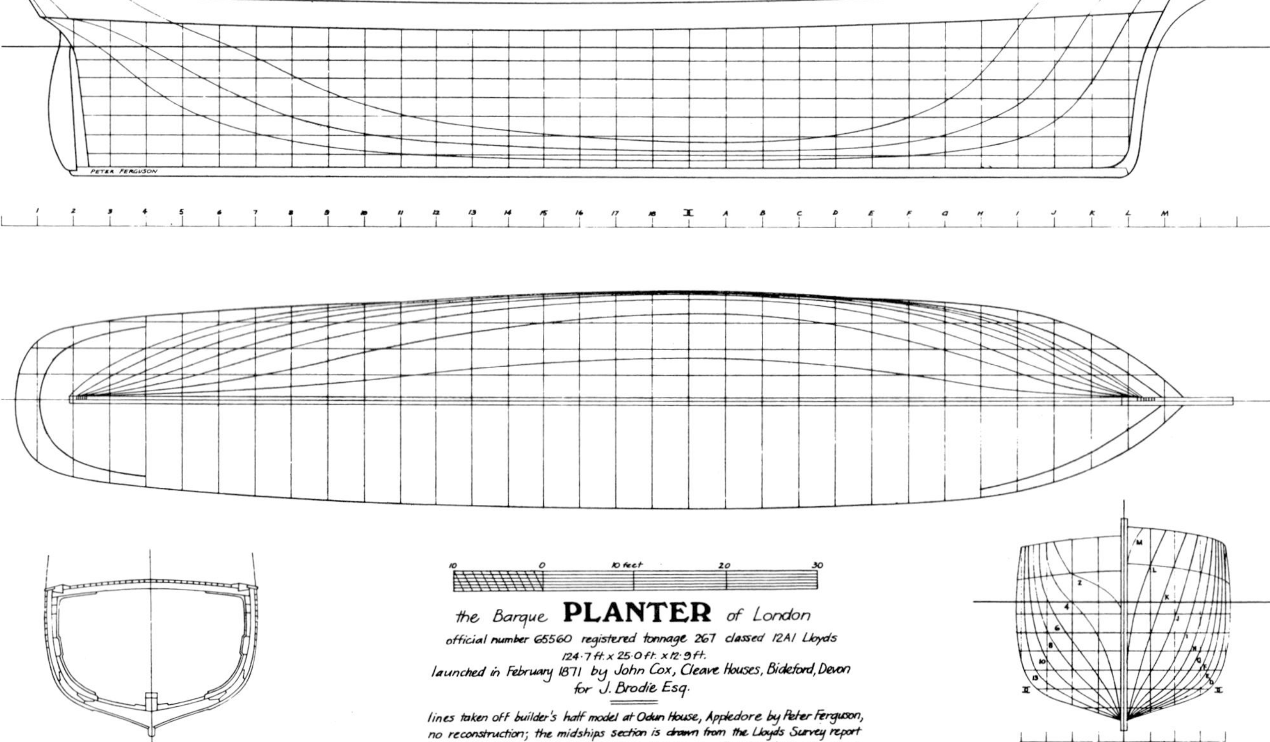

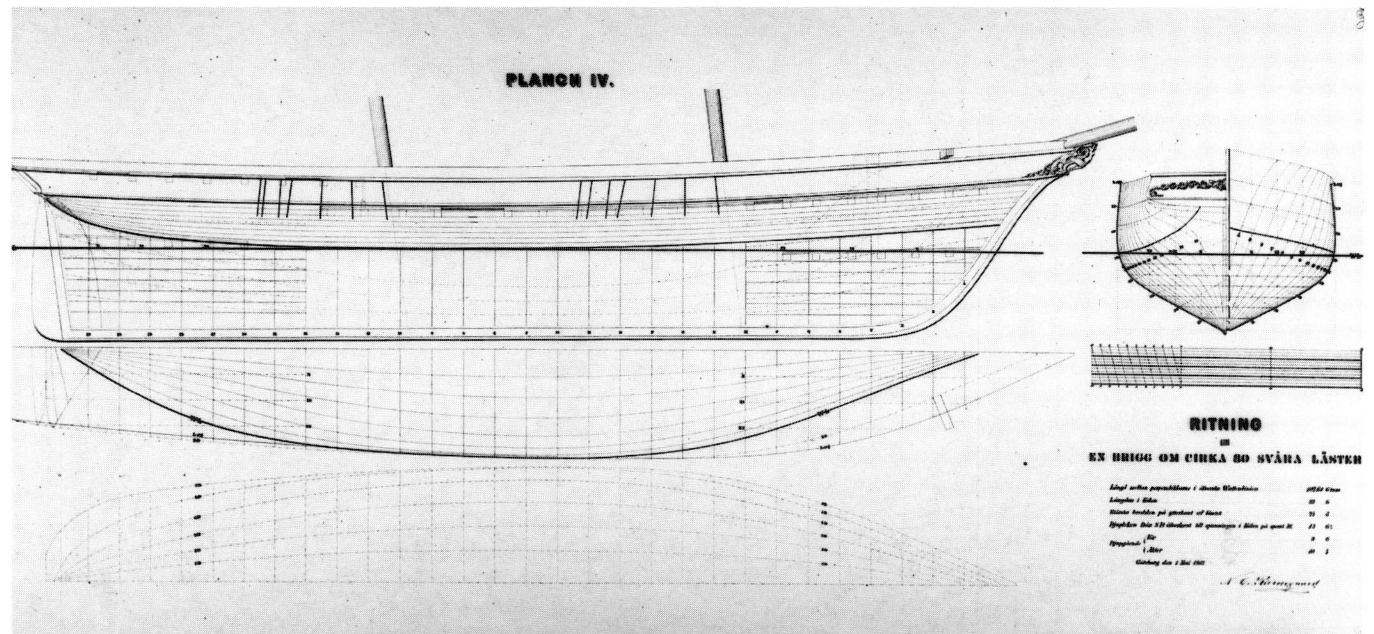

371: Clipper brig. Unidentified. Lines: Reproduced from plan drawn by N C Lierkegaard and dated Gothenburg 1 May 1862, and published as Plate IV in his portfolio of plans entitled *Plancher till Praktisk Skepps-byggnadskonst.* Dimensions on plan: 102 fot 6 tum (length on load line between rabbets)—24 fot 3 tum—13 fot 6 ½ tum; 80 lasts. (1 Swedish fot = .974ft.)

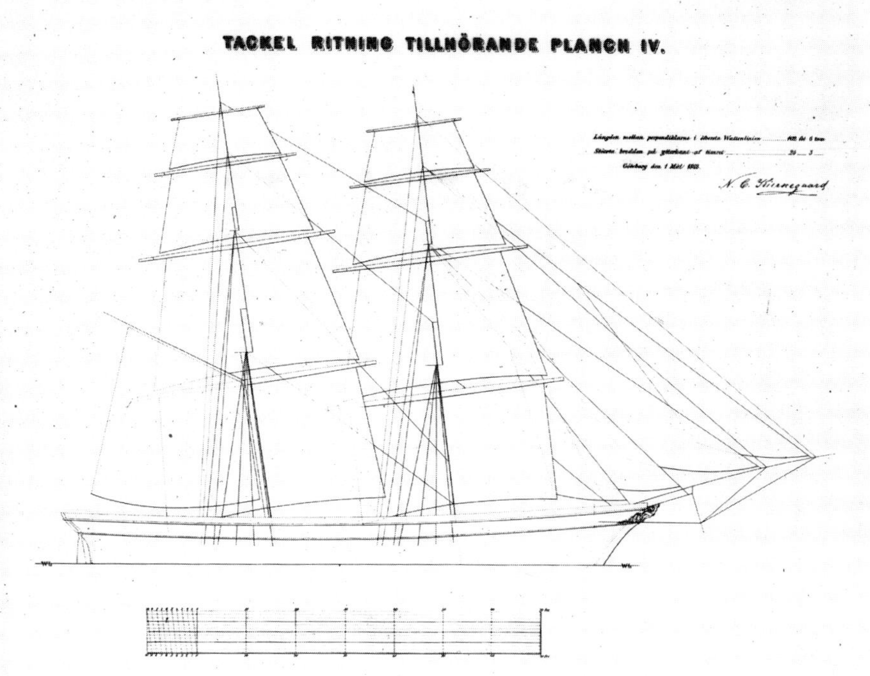

372: Clipper brig. Sail plan: Reproduced from same source as line plan.

indicated but these have been reconstructed here. The double mizen stays, one of which leads each side of the mainsail, were fairly common then, but were soon to be superseded by the arrangement in which the height of the main and mizen lower masts are made nearly equal, thus permitting a stay to the cap to clear the peak of the main gaff.

Because of the need to take the ground at low water, schooners and brigantines were not often given much deadrise, but this could be made up by sharp waterlines. At Glasson Dock, Matthew Simpson was building schooners such as the *Express* (1860) with flat floors but moderately sharp ends; on the Clyde, Alexander Stephen & Sons built the iron *Janette* (1867) of 82 tons under deck with big deadrise, slack bilges, tumblehome and fine ends; and at many other ports builders were producing splendid vessels combining fine lines with good cargo capacity.

Descriptions of schooners at sea are none too common and therefore Captain Chapman's remarks on a fruit schooner outward bound in the English Channel are welcome. His passage opens with comments on how pleasant a sight it is to see a large group of vessels get underway in the Downs, after a long wait for a change of wind, and how the larger ships stand well off the land. Then his eye lights on a schooner, which he describes more fully.

'Farther in shore, a pretty little fruiterer, painted all black, except a lady figurehead, which is pure white, with her pretty shaped cutwater, her well-proportioned overhanging stern, her fine clear lines, her spars all clean and varnished, her bowsprit only a few feet outside her figure-head, her jib and flying-jibboom just buckled down a little with the Martingale stays, which lead to the dolphin strikes of iron, with a harpoon point, and the galvanized wire back ropes set up to the catheads, with her heavy mainboom, and the sails of white canvass set to a nicety, going three points free, laying over slightly, and her spar just a little buckling to the breeze, the tops of her skylight and

376: The *Flower of the Fal* passing St Anthony's Point lighthouse as she sails into Falmouth harbour. The lower topsail has been clewed up and two of the crew are up aloft furling the upper topsail. She was built by Trewden at Padstow in 1870, and was of 139 tons with a length of 98ft. In 1871 she voyaged to the Mediterranean. *Basil Lavis Collection.*

> binnacle just in sight above the rail, and the inside of her weather-rail (white with blue beading) just visible over the lee — where it is not hidden by the longboat, the galley, or the masts; her sails only just bellying out a little, being set taut to their pretty cut; three hands standing in the way of the fore rigging, one in the way of the main rigging, a boy in the galley, the captain at the tiller — feeling proud of his pretty little craft, and he, with his four men and a boy, is going to face any wind or weather, blow high or blow low, he can hold his little vessel to windward.'[100]

Although the *Rhoda Mary* was never a fruiterer, this lively passage aptly describes both her and many of her contemporaries.

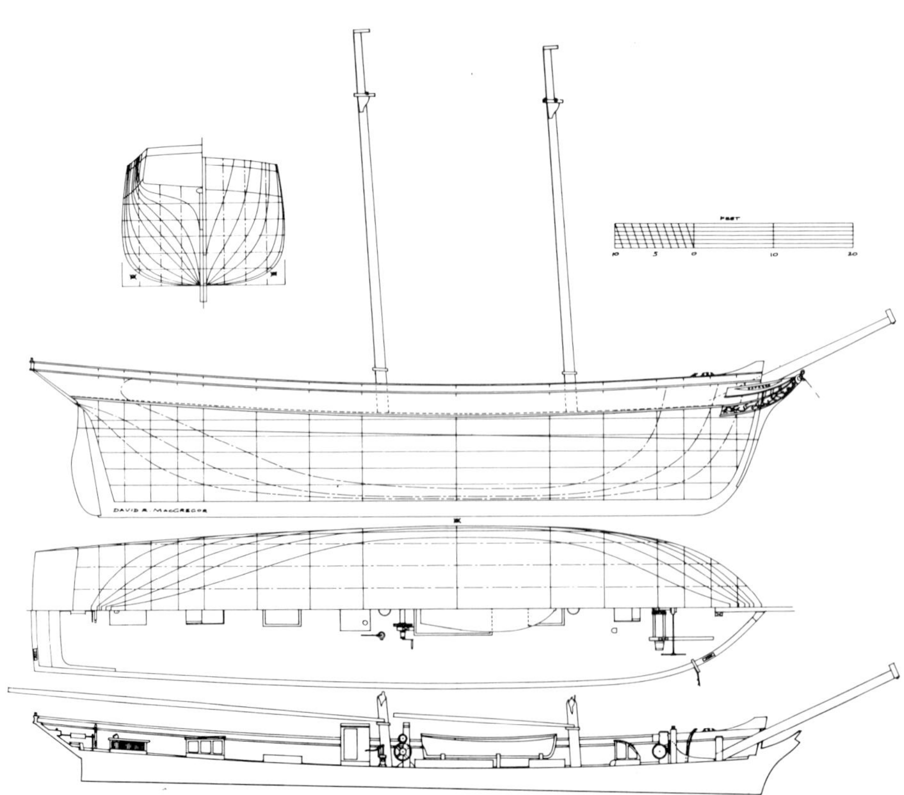

373: *Express.* Lines plan and general arrangement redrawn from material supplied by William Salisbury. Built in 1860 at Glasson Dock near Lancaster by Mathew Simpson with measurements of 86.5ft–21.0ft–11.1ft and 119 tons net.

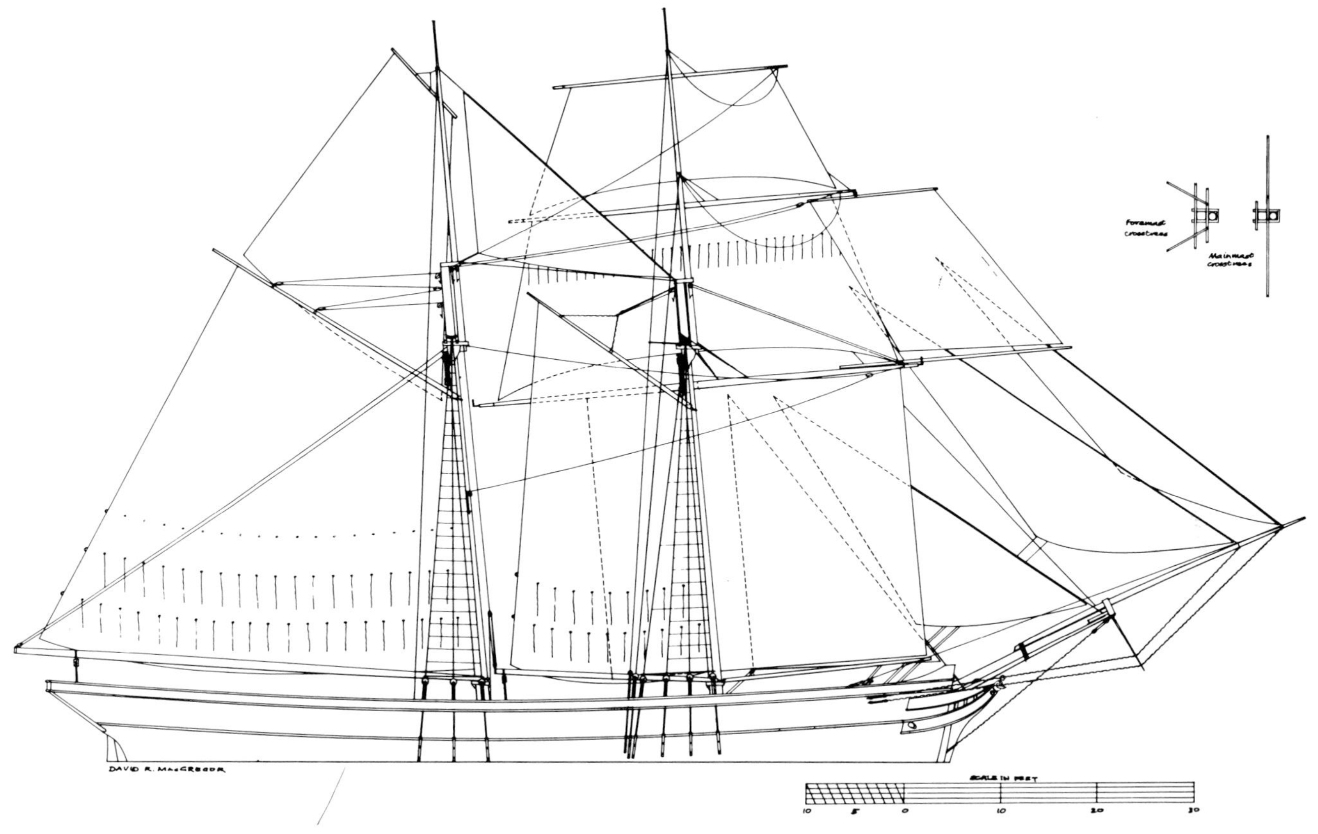

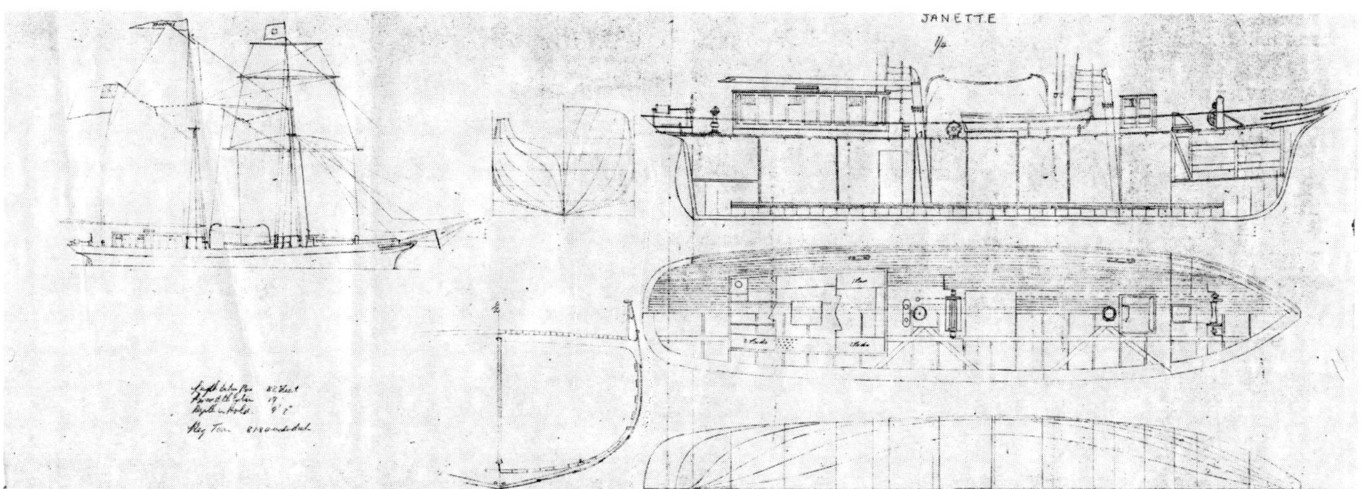

374: *Express.* Sail plan: Reconstructed from existing plan showing three masts. See *Merchant Sailing Ships 1850-1875* by David R MacGregor (p 98) for method of reconstructing sail plan.

375: *Janette.* Lines, general arrangement and sail plan. Traced by James Henderson from builder's plan. Built of iron in 1867 by Alexander Stephen & Sons at Glasgow. Dimensions: 87.7ft—19.0ft—8.9ft and 91 tons register. Her destined voyage in 1869 was given as 'Africa'. Reconstruction: some rigging added to sail plan.

CONCLUSIONS

A large number of ship plans have been reproduced here and it is hoped that the main lines of clipper ship development will have been sufficiently well described to permit a picture to be established of the types of fast sailing ships and the efforts of individual shipyards to produce them. Many ships have been omitted whose plans could have further illustrated the story, but over-embellishment might have rendered this account confusing. As far as possible the emphasis has been on the development of the ships, the design problems, and the factors which brought this about.

Ship design is probably one of the most intangible subjects touched upon here and yet it goes to the very root of the shipping industry. Books on naval architecture, for all their instruction on design, could never really solve the problems and it was only practical experience for the aspiring shipbuilder which could furnish him with adequate knowledge. Mathematical solutions were of little use to a practical man a century or more ago, and he was obliged to rely on the visual comparison of actual vessels with his own designs. The rise of the independent naval architect and consulting engineer coincided in the 1840s with the improvement of ship design, the wider use of iron and the growing awareness that steam power would have its uses. An effort has been made to mention specifically by name any naval architect concerned with the design of the ships described, but it is feared that many such individuals have been neglected while the work of others is very imperfectly recorded. William Rennie and John Grantham are at present the two consultants about whom most is known.

Before producing a design, the principal points to be considered can be briefly summarized in the following questions: What is the type of cargo to be carried and which is the principal trade for which the ship is intended? Will the ship remain afloat or must she be capable of taking the ground? Which is more important, cargo capacity or speed?

In answering these queries, shipbuilders usually deferred to the fashion of the day in respect of hull form, because the owners for whom they built had to obtain remunerative employment immediately and could not afford to experiment with a novel ship which might be a success but equally might not. Thus innovators received little encouragement, as we have witnessed in the case of Captain Richard Gower's *Transit*, so it is the more surprising that Alexander Hall & Sons' raking stem rabbet proved so successful. Lack of vision and indifference to new ideas may have restricted clipper ship design during the mania for speed in the early 1850s, and it undoubtedly was the reason why three shipbuilders — Alexander Stephen & Sons with the *Storm Cloud*, Benjamin Nicholson with the *Annandale* and Alexander Hall & Sons with the *Cairngorm* — risked their reputation by each building their concept of an ideal clipper without first receiving an order from an owner. Likewise, experimentation in ship construction usually lasted but a few years. Most examples we have cited refer to various forms of diagonal planking or framing, and we have described various systems, particularly those of Sir Robert Seppings, William Annesley, J & R White, Alexander Hall & Sons, and Bilbe & Perry. Innovations in ship fittings and rigging were also slow to be adopted and only the work of the successful inventors is acknowledged here, among the plethora of patents registered around the middle of the nineteenth century and onwards. Iron construction began as yet another innovation, but after much resistance and many disasters was finally the only satisfactory material for all sizeable vessels.

It has been shown how more satisfactory forms of ships began to evolve by the early 1840s and that it must have owed something to the new mode of tonnage measurement which took effect from 1836 in which depth was measured for the first time, because the new ships began to appear with longer, shallower hulls that carried as much cargo as before but which sailed better. It has been stated more than once that the wider use of iron permitted longer ships to be constructed without increasing the shell thickness, thus permitting a larger quantity of cargo to be carried in proportion to the area occupied by the structural framework.

It was a pleasure to write the chapter dealing with the clipper ship boom of the 1850s, because these splendid ships have been largely forgotten today in preference to the China clippers of the following decade, which by comparison were comparatively few in numbers. In discussing the development of ships built for speed and the research connected therewith, no strong American influences have been discovered in spite of much written this century to that effect. An effort has been made to trace the important effect which the British cutter had on hulls designed for speed, particularly in encouraging the use of great deadrise, and a number of illustrations have been provided. The myth of the 'first clipper' has also been exploded.

Shipyard records, statistical data and voyage account-books consulted by the Author may be examined by economic historians who can further analyse the facts and figures they contain and prepare exhaustive tables on shipbuilding and allied trades. This is to be welcomed. But it would have been advantageous if such analysis had already been undertaken prior to the compilation of material for this book because it would have simplified the preparation and presentation of this material. While not intending to cover the shipbuilding aspect in great economic details, it has, nevertheless, been necessary to state the basic particulars regarding costs and expenses to indicate the background against which the shipping industry operated. In certain cases it has been possible to complete the story by relating the profits attributable to certain contracts or voyages, and so suggest the rewards available to succesful shipbuilders and owners. Considerable data is becoming available in this field and it is highly desirable that conclusions be drawn concerning the profitability or otherwise of investing capital into shipbuilding and shipowning.

There is little doubt that this will be undertaken in increasing measure, but it is to be hoped that the advance in knowledge concerning the economic factors effecting ship design and management will be matched by equal advances in the study of what those ships were like, how they were designed and built, and exactly how they responded to the men who sailed them. The attainment of such knowledge must certainly be based on a thorough investigation of all the plans, models and illustrations known to exist, aided by the latest scientific techniques of ship research.

APPENDIX 1

Definitions of tonnage measurement and registration

The historical facts concerning the measurement of ships to determine their tonnage and registry are dealt with in the text in chapters one, three and five, but the following definitions of positions between which the measurements were taken will be found useful when comparing ships and models. Some additional terms met with on plans are also defined. The diagrams illustrating where tonnage measurements were taken should also be consulted.

Pre-1836 old measurement tonnage rule

That part of the 1773 Act which ascribed how tonnage should be measured stated:

'The length shall be taken on a straight line along the rabbet of the keel of the ship, from the back of the main-post to a perpendicular line from the fore part of the main-stem under the bowsprit; from which subtracting three-fifths of the breadth, the remainder must be esteemed the just length of the keel to find the tonnage; and the breadth shall be taken from the outside of the outside plank, in the broadest place in the ship, be it either above or below the main wales, exclusive of all manner of doubling-planks that may be wrought upon the sides of the ship; then multiplying the length of the keel by the breadth so taken, and that product by half the breadth, and dividing the whole by ninety four, the quotient will be deemed the true contents of the tonnage.'[1]

Definitions of measurements for tonnage, pre-1836 rule

Length for tonnage	Total length measured as the tonnage rule directs (see above), with no subtractions for rake of stem.
Keel for tonnage	Length as above *less* three-fifths of the breadth.
Length aloft	Length measured on deck from foreside of stem to afterside of sternpost.
Breadth of frame or 'Moulded breadth'	Maximum breadth inside the outer planking between the extreme outer edges of the frames. Most builder's lines plans are drawn to the inside of the planking, and this should be remembered when scaling the breadth. Lines taken off half-models and reproduced here will also be drawn to the inside of the planking.
Depth	Always depth of hold, *never* draught of water. Points of measurement vary, but frequently between underside of upper deck to top of ceiling beside the keelson. Beware small dimension in what are obviously big ships, which applies to the lower-hold only.
om or bom	Abbreviation for 'old measurement' or 'builder's old measurement'.

The above are liable to vary as shipbuilders gave their personal interpretation, and even though the tonnage law changed in 1836 many builders continued to give the old measurements for twenty or thirty years. It is necessary, therefore to establish when a vessel was built or approximately when the plan was drawn or the information assembled, to assess correctly the dimensions given.

Definitions of measurements for tonnage, 1836 rule[2]

Length	Measured internally at half the midship depth from the afterside of the stem to the foreside of the sternpost.
Breadth	Measured internally at the heights stated by the rule, between the inner faces of the ceiling.
Depth	Measured from underside of the upper deck to the ceiling at the limber strake (beside the keelson). The divisor was 3500.

Definitions of measurements for Registry 1836 Act[3]

Length	Measured along the upper deck from the foreside of the main stem to the afterside of the sternpost; measurements taken along the deck are often termed 'length aloft'.
Breadth	Maximum internal measurement, between inner faces of ceiling, at amidships.
Depth	Measured from under side of the upper deck to the ceiling beside the keelson; always refers to depth of hold, *never* to draught of water.
'nm'	Abbreviation for 'new measurement'.

Length	This is the distance between the extreme ends of the hold, below the tonnage deck. For the sake of convenience it is measured on top of the tonnage deck, and allowance has to be made at each end for the rake of the stem and sternpost, which if not deducted could increase the length somewhat. The transverse areas are set out along this length. It was found that in vessels with normal sheer, i.e. 3ft-0in in 250ft-0in, the length could be measured along the deck, rather than in a dead-straight line or chord between the extremities, and that the ultimate difference in the under deck tonnage was about .01%. But in vessels with great sheer, such as 5ft-0in in 100ft-0in the difference would be 1%, which meant that the length had to be measured 'by means of a tape or line stretched tightly from end to end of the deck'.[5]
Breadth	Taken at heights given in the rule, between inner faces of the ceiling, or battens in an iron ship; or to inner surfaces of frames if there is no ceiling or battens.
Breadth	Taken at heights given in the rule, between inner faces of ceiling, or battens in an iron ship; or to inner surfaces of frames if there is no ceiling or battens.
Depth	This is depth of hold, which is taken from below the underside of the deck to top of ceiling at the limber strake beside the keelson, from which is deducted one-third of the deck camber or 'round of beam'. If there is a water-ballast tank, the depth is measured to the upper edge of the ordinary floor plate.
Under deck tonnage	This is the figure obtained from all spaces below the tonnage deck. No deductions are made from it. It is sometimes used as a basis for block coefficients of fineness.
Gross tonnage	The volume of all enclosed spaces above the tonnage deck was added to the under deck tonnage, to produce this gross figure and it is from this total that deductions can be made for the various crew and store-room allowances. Before 1867 when crew accommodation *above* the tonnage deck was exempted from measurement, small flush-decked vessels with only a deckhouse for the crew had similar figures for under deck and gross tonnage, and as there was nothing to deduct, the net tonnage was also similar.
Net Register tonnage	Any allowances were deducted from the gross tonnage to give the net tonnage. Before 1867, the only allowable deduction was the engine room in steamships, but after that year crew accommodation was *deducted* from the gross total rather than *exempted* from it. Other allowances have since been added. The net tonnage is also the 'register tonne' (never

'registered') on which is assessed light, pilot and harbour dues and which is the official tonnage entered for registry.

BM or BOM tonnage

Builder's Measurement or Builder's Old Measurement tonnage. These were synonymous terms for the pre-1836 old measurement rule which many builders used until the mid-sixties for quoting the price for a new ship, as it only required a simple calculation to obtain the tonnage figure. Due to the divisor of 100, easy arithmetical sums resulted without any of the awkward fractions that occurred when 3500 was the divisor, as in the years 1836–54.

Definitions of measurement for Registry, 1854 Act

These are the dimensions normally seen in descriptions of ships which appeared in the Certificate of Registry and survey reports. The length is often the most difficult to measure for the layman when confronted by a sheer elevation, and it is hoped that this description and sketch will elucidate the matter. (See figure 206.)

Length

'Length from the forepart of the stem under the bowsprit to the aftside of the head of the sternpost'. So runs the description in the Certificate. The length was measured along the deck, although in craft with considerable sheer it was probably taken in a dead-straight line. (See above under 'tonnage length' for 1854.) The aftside of the sternpost at deck level is easy to locate, but the forward point presents difficulties, which are intensified in iron ships. In wooden ships, it is frequently necessary to project the line of the stem parallel to the stem rabbet to a point below the bowsprit, to obtain the forward termination of the length. But in iron ships, the stem and cutwater are the same and the stem curves away rather as in an Aberdeen bow until it is running almost parallel with the steeve of the bowsprit. A practical article in the magazine *Naval Science* contained an explanatory drawing upon which figure 161 is based, which shows that in iron ships the length was measured from the stem where it stopped against the bottom block of the figurehead.[6] It will be obvious from the drawings that length for registry will often be longer in sailing ships of normal design than length for tonnage. The forward termination of the length reverted to that in use before 1836, which some shipyards had continued to use.

Breadth

'Main breadth to the outside of plank'. This was the maximum external bradth sometimes called 'extreme breadth outside'.

Depth

'Depth in hold from tonnage deck to ceiling at midships'. This is fairly straightforward, the upper point of measurement being the underside of the deck and the lower point being taken beside the keelson; it is *never* the draught of water.

Other measurements encountered:

Length between perpendiculars

This is a term used by shipbuilders and varied from yard to yard, but in many cases it lay between the afterside of the stem at deck level and the afterside of the heel of the sternpost, perpendiculars being drawn through these points and projected down to the half-breadth plan.

Length aloft

'Aloft' indicates a length measured along the deck as opposed to the keel and probably lies between the same points as for the register length.

Length overall

Usually measured from foreside of figurehead to afterside of taffrail.

Moulded breadth

This is identical to the description for the old measurement rule.

The above detailed comments, if read in conjunction with the drawings, will go some way to prevent those anomalies which frequently cause confusion over a ship's length and tonnage.

APPENDIX 2

Ships built by Alexander Hall & Sons, Aberdeen, 1811–1875

From cost account of each ship transcribed by James Henderson.

The 'tons for contract' is often an average between om and nm tons or between om and gross register. The LR class also affects the price, as does the type of contract, ie whether the ship is built with 'hull and spars' only or 'complete ready for sea' &c. There is not space here to include all the variations listed in the accounts. Where no cost per ton is given in the contract, the lump sum is listed here; cost per ton can then be calculated, if necessary by using the contract tonnage figure when stated. All ships are built of wood, unless otherwise stated.

Yard No	*Date*	*Name*	*Rig*	*Tons om*	*Contract price per ton*	*lump sum*
1		[not stated]		87¾	[not stated]	
2	1811	*Glasgow Packet*	—	83	[not stated]	
3	1811	*Plough*	sch	86	£10	
4	1812	*Edinburgh Packet*	smk	86	£12	
5	1812	*Twins*	slp	?		£400 'as agreed'
6	1813	*Minerva*	bg	202	£13	
7	1813	*Inverness and Cromarty Packet*	smk	63	£11.11s	
8	1813	*Britannia*	bg	132	£11.10s	
9	1814	*Don*	S	332	£15.10s	
10	1814	*Brilliant*	S	332	£15.10s	
11	1815	*Nicholas*	bg	212	£13	
12	1815	*Nautilus*	bg	130	£12.5s	
13	1815	*Oak*	bg	119	£11	
14	1815	*Prince of Waterloo*	S	287	£14.14s	
15	1815	*Dolphin*	smk	55	£13	
16	1816	*Orange*	bg	137	£11.11s	
17	1816	*Rotterdam Packet*	smk	112	£12.12s	
18	1816	*Lady Hood McKenzie*	bg	117	£11.15s	
19	1817	*Reliance*	slp	64		£490
20	1816	*Abundance*	bg	112	£1.5s labour for hull only	
21	1817	*Barbara*	bg	164	£9.6s	
22	1817	*Lively*	slp	46	£7.7s	
23	1817	*Lady Saltoun*	slp	38	£6.17.6	
24	1817	*Expedition*	bg	180	17s 6d labour only	
25	1818	*Resolution*	bg	121	£8	
26	1818	*Agnes*	bg	144	£10.10s	
27	1818	*Asia*	S	532	£13	
28	1819	*Hannah Moore*	bg	202	£1 labour for hull only	
29	1820	*The Bruce*	bg	240	£10	
30	1819	*Philorth*	slp	36		£230
31	1819	*Sophia*	slp	43	£7	

Yard No	Date	Name	Rig	Tons om	Contract price per ton	lump sum	
32	1820	*Palladium*	bg	120	£9.10s		
33	1820	*Mary*	slp	49	£8		
34	1821	*Mountaineer*	bg	106	£8.15s		
35	1821	*James*	sch	66	£8		
36	1822	*Osborn*	sch	86	£7.14s		
37	1822	*Thane of Fife*	slp	62	£8.5s		
38	1823	*Jean Steuart*	bg	114	£8		
39	1823	*Andrew Forbes*	smk	43	£7.5s		
40	1823	*Harmony*	slp	74	£8.8s		
41	1823	*Radiant*	bg	167	£9.9s		
42	1824	*Sir Charles Forbes*	S	363	£11		
43	1825	*Caledonian*	bg	236	£11.12s		
44	1825	*Banchory*	bg	129	£11		
45	1825	*Craigievar*	bg	262	£12.12s		
46	1826	*Albion*	bg	266	£12.12s		
47	1826	*Marmion*	sch	78	£9		
48	1826	*Union*	smk	79	£12.12s		
49	1826	*Aultnaskiach*	smk	63	£8.5s		
50	1827	*Helens and Eleonara*	sch	84	£8.15s		
51	1827	*Corsican*	bg	87	£2.2s labour hull and spars only		
52	1827	PS *Paul Jones*	tug	29		£800 excl engines &c	
53	1827	*John Pirie*	sch	105	£9		
54	1828	*Childe Harold*	bg	115	£8.15s		
55	1828	*Warren Packet*	smk	48	£6		
56	1829	*Visitor*	bg	136	£8.12.6		
57	1829	*Matilda*	bgn	109	£8.12.6		
58		*Hannah Moore*	[not stated; possibly repairs to no 28]				
59	1830	*Magnus Troil*	sch	124	£9		
60	1831	*Walter Hamilton*	bg	127	£8.5s		
61	1833	*Adventure*	bg	149	£7.9s		
62	1833	*Sisters*	bg	137	£7.9s		
63	1833	*St Nicholas*	bg	140	£7.7s		
64	1834	*Jack Tar*	bg	195	£8.15s		
65	1834	*Harmony*	bg	155	£9.5s		
66	1834	*Europa*	bk	224	£8.15s		
67	1835	*Osprey*	smk	40	£8.8s		
68	1835	PS *Jardine*	sch	58		£600 hull only (yacht)	
69	1835	*Cock of the North*	smk	59	£8.12.6		
70	1835	*Sir William Wallace*	bg	183		£1500 'as agreed'	
71	1835	*Buchan*	bgn	116	£8.16s		
72	1836	*Earl of Fife*	bgn	82	£9.2.6		90 om
73	1836	*Duke of Sutherland*	smk	69	£8.12.6		69 om
74	1836	*Violet*	bg	168	£8.10s		160 average
75	1836	*Hawk*	sch	80	£9.2.6		92½ 'as agreed'
76	1836	*Samson*	bgn	120	£8.11s		126 om
77	1836	*Barbara Allen*	bg	143	£9.10s		149½ om
78	1836	*Joseph*	smk	30	£8.15s		45 om
79	1837	*Commodore*	bg	149	£10.16.6 for 145 tons; £5.8.3 for 11½ tons		
80	1837	*Alert*	bg	118	£8.5s		121 om
81	1837	*Orlando*	bg	158	£11		157 'as agreed'
82	1837	*Catherine*	bk	247	£11		225
83	1837	*Victoria*	bg	109	£9.5s		115 'as agreed'
84	1837	*Ythan*	sch	84	£8.10s		103 om
85	1838	*Mary and Ann*	bk	262	£11		238½ om
86	1838	*Ceres*	bg	134	£7		132½ om
87	1838	*Queen Victoria*	bgn	110	£10.10s		117 om
88	1838	*Commerce*	bgn	140	£7		142 om

* *nm and om tons first appeared in 1836 because of tonnage rule.*

Yard No	Date	Name	Rig	Tons nm	Contract price per ton	lump sum	Tons for contract
89	1838	*Venilia*	bg	207	£9.10s		208½
90	1838	*Minerva*	bg	153	£10		153
91	1838	*Falcon*	sch	85	£11		90 average
92	1838	*Harmony*	bg	142	£7		142
93	1839	*Sarah*	bg	232		£2000	
94	1838	*Wanderer*	bg	155	£7		155
95	1839	*Mendora*	bg	152	£6.15s		151½ average
96	1839	*Fortitude*	bk	251	£11.10s		230
97	1839	*Angler*	bgn	92	£8.5s		104
98	1839	*Bessy Robertson*	bg	150	£11.15		155
99	1839	*Gem*	bg	188	£7.7s		180 'as agreed'
100	1839	*Enchantress*	bk	241		£2800	
101	1839	*Scottish Maid*	sch	143		£1700	
102	1840	SS *Gazelle*	sch	121		£1000 hull only (yacht)	
103	1839	*Ann Smith*	bk	292	£9.15s		258 om
104	1839	*Columbine*	bg	176		£2400	
105	1840	*Lord Western*	bk	530		£7300	
106	1840	*Crusader*	bk	224	£10.5s		205 om
107	1840	*Tartar*	bg	203		£2100	
108	1840	*Rover*	sch	139	£11.10s for 134 tons; £5.15s for 5 tons		
109	1840	*Aberdonian*	sch	146		£1770	
110	1840	*Elizabeth*	sch	136		£1500	136
111	1840	*London*	sch	142		£1700	
112	1840	*Port Fleetwood*	sch	162	£16.10s		171 average
113	1841	*Resource*	bg	146	£9.10s		152 average
114	1840	*Western Isles*	sch	83	£8		91 om
115	1841	*Thomas Arbuthnot*	S	621	£18.5s for 507 tons om; £9.2.6 for 14 tons		
116	1842	PS *Iris*	sch	280	£12		280 om 'as agreed'
117	1841	*Trio*	bk	388	£15		355 om
118	1841	*Flora*	bg	148	£11		157 'as agreed'
119	1841	*Maid of Aln*	sch	108		£1400	
120	1841	*Wave*	bgn	95		£1200	
121		barge				£55	
122	1842	*Queen of the Isles*	bk	278	£13		255 'as agreed'
123	1842	*Glentanner*	S	610	£10.10s		510 'as agreed'
124	1841	*Union*	bgn	94		£1400	
125	1841	*Rambler*	sch	110	£10		121½ average
126	1842	*Humayoon*	S	530	£18.2.6		440 om
127	1841	*Lightning*	sch	177		£2000	
128	1842	*Rapid*	sch	149	£12.7.6		205 'as agreed'
129	1842	*Non-Such*	sch	151	£12.7.6 for 205 tons om; £6 for 5 tons om		
130	1842	*Fairy*	sch	150		£1250	
131	1842	*Annabella*	sch	156	£10.2.6		166 average
132	1842	*Mountain Maid*	bg	192		£1710	192
133	1842	*Alnwick Castle*	sch	54		£700	
134	1842	*Cynthia*	bk	251		£2300	
135	1843	*Border Maid*	sch	91		£1562	
136	1843	*Waterwitch*	sch	92		£1562	
137	1843	*Pera*	sch	191	£12		220 average
138	1843	*Ebenezer*	sch	67		£528	67
139	1843	*Swift*	sch	183		£2688	
140	1843	*Hope*	bg	126		£800	
141	1843	*Strathbogie*	sch	45	£10.10s		65 om
142	1843	*Hero*	sch	52	£12		83 'as agreed'
143	1844	*Colloony*	bk	287		£3600	
144	1844	*Heroine*	sch	75	£10.10s for 102 tons; £5.5s for 7 tons		
145		*Queen*	sch	?		£2636 hull and woodwork	

Yard No	Date	Name	Rig	Tons nm*	Contract price per ton	lump sum	Tons for contract
146	1844	*Dart*	sch	88	£12.10s		118 'as agreed'
147	1845	*Acasta*	bk	327		£3800	
148	1845	*William Punton*	bg	170		£2268	
149	1845	*Prince of Wales*	sch	178		£2268 spars and woodwork	
	(Hull built of iron by Wm Simpson of Aberdeen)						
150	1845	*Torrington*	sch	144		£3877	
151	1845	*Alexander Hall*	bk	403		£2800	
152	1845	*White Mouse*	sch	72		£1450	
153	1845	*Bon Accord*	S	380	£18.5s		388½ average
154	1846	*Wizard*	sch	93		£1200	
155	1846	*Sir William Wallace*	sch	105		£1900	
156	1846	*Matchless*	sch	107		£2000	
157	1846	*Gitana*	sch	92		£1300	
158	1846	*Electra*	bk	306		£5400	
159	1847	*North Star*	S	384	£18.5s		430 om
160	1847	*Amelia*	sch	150	£16.10s		240 om
161	1847	*Victoria*	sch	65		£1500	
162	1847	*Curlew*	sch	116		£1800	116 nm
163	1848	*Pilot Fish*	S	302		£6119	
164	1848	*Ben Muick Dhui*	bk	244		£3300	
165	1848	*Bonita*	S	299		£4850	
166	1848	*Guide*	sch	132	£16		153 om
167	1848	*Peruvian*	bk	413		£3000	361 om
168	1848	*Reindeer*	S	328	£10		375 average
169	1849	*Princeza*	bg	149		£2020	
170	1849	*Benjamin Elkin*	S	367	£15		396 average
171	1850	*City of Hamilton*	S	517	£11 for 500 tons; £5.10s for 24 tons		
172	1849	*Emperor*	bk	368		£4600	
173	1850	*Conqueror*	S	457	£14		472½ average
174	1850	*Princess Royal*	sch	172		£2800	
175	1850	*Stornoway*	S	527	£17		562 average
176	1851	*John Taylor*	S	787	£18.18s		763½ average
177	1851	*Chrysolite*	S	440	£17.17s		505 average
178	1851	ss *Juno*	sch	213		£3330 hull and woodwork	
179	1851	*Dunrobin Castle*	S	545	£9		464 'as agreed'
180	1852	*Hannibal*	S	576	£15.15s		577 average
181	1852	*Francis Henty*	S	432	£11.10s		505 average
182	1852	*Julia*	S	475	[£11.19.1]	£6300	550 average
183	1853	*Cairngorm*	S	939	£14		1094 average
184	1852	*Enterprise*	sch	76	£12.10s		95 average
185	1852	*Velocidade*	S	280	£15 for 290 tons; £7.10s for 10 tons		
186	1853	*Leichardt*	S	589	£15		611¾ average
187	1853	*Mimosa*	S	447	£12		493 average
188	1853	*Marion*	bk	191	£14.14s		250 average
189	1854	*Vision*	S	563		£9400	
190	1854	*Oribe*	bk	220	£18.10s		245 average
191	1854	*Undaunted*	S	314		£6000	
192	1854	*Woodland*	bg	203	£15		246 average
		[? *Woodlark* as spelt in LR]					
193	1855	*Charles Horsfall*	S	798	£15.5s		860 om
194	1854	*Harriet Armitage*	bk	199	£16.13s		300 average
195	1855	*Schomberg*	S	2284	£14		2492 om
					tons gross*		'as agreed'
196	1855	*Sea Star*	S	591	£16		707½ average
197	1856	*Sunshine*	S	549	£15		645 om
198	1855	ss *Fox*	3-sch	177		£5000 incl engines	
199	1856	*Dorothy*	S	761	£15		882 om
200	1855	*Kelpie*	bkn	118		£3000	
201	1855	*Vindex*	sch	179	£18.10s		264 om

**change in tonnage because of 1854 tonnage rule.*

Yard No	Date	Name	Rig	Tons om	Contract price per ton	lump sum	Tons for contract
202	1856	*Star of Tasmania*	S	632	£17		778 om
203	1856	*Kitta Wake*	sch	150		£3500	(yacht)
204	1857	*Friar Tuck*	S	662	£13.10s		863 om
205	1856	*Robin Hood*	S	853	£18 for 1166 tons om; £9 for 18 $^{54}/_{94}$ tons om		
206	1856	*Salamander*	sch	115		£5000	(yacht)
207	1856	*Martinet*	sch	72		£1600	123 om
208	1857	*The Oak*	sch	155		£2600	
209	1857	*Bon Accord*	bk	290	£13		321 om
210	1857	*Recruit*	sch	53		£1050	
211	1857	*Artizan*	bg	170		£2600	
212	1857	*Agricola*	bg	159	£15		158
213	1859	*MacDuff*	S	1136		£20,000	
214	1858	*Mary*	bk	316		£5000	
215	1858	*Ziba*	bkn	497		£8835	570 average
216	1859	*Asterope*	S	602	£15		638½ average of om, bm and reg tons
217	1860	*Chaa-sze*	S	556	£17		605 average
218	1859	*Ocean Mail*	S	630	£17.10s		754 average
219	1860	*Flying Spur*	S	735	£16.10s		805¾ average
220	1860	*Chepica*	S	446	£16		465 average
221	1861	*Pegasus*	S	525	£17		542½ 'as agreed'
222	1861	*The Murray*	S	902	£17		961 average
223	1861	*Adam Sedgwick*	S	458	£16		482 average
224	1861	*The Colleen Bawn*	bk	386	£14		399¼ average
225	1862	*Clara Sayers*	bk	294		£4300	
226	1862	*Star of China*	S	794	£17.5s		840¾ average
227	1862	*Emily*	bg	177		£3800	
228	1862	*Coulnakyle*	S	579	£18		650 'as agreed'
229	1862	*Vanda*	bk	353	£16.10s		370 average
230	1862	*Natal Star*	S	366		£5850	
231	1863	*Reindeer* (comp)	S	965	£18.15s		934 average
232	1863	*Fy-Chow*	S	710	£18.10s		853 $^{22}/_{94}$ om
233	1863	*Celaeno*	S	702	£18		
234	1863	*Black Prince* (comp)	S	751	£18		919½ om
235	1863	*Yang-tsze* (comp)	S	688	£19		772 om
236	1864	*Tugela*	S	475	£17		494 average
237	1864	*The Goolwa* (comp)	S	717	£20		717 gross
238	1864	*Edward P Bouverie*	S	997	£18.10s		1028 om
239	1866	*Sobraon* (comp)	S	2131	£19		2273 om
240	1864	*Devana*	S	795	£18.7.6		855 om
241	1865	*Darra* (comp)	S	999	£17.10s		1000 'as agreed'
242	1864	ss *Admiral* (comp)	sch	665		£22410	incl engines
243	1865	*John Williams* (wd)	bk	296		£7500	537.39
244	1866	ss *Douglas* (iron)	bk	873		£12350; engines & boilers £9000 extra	
245	1865	*Ada* (comp)	S	687	£16.10s		
246		barge (iron)	—	392		£1250 (dismanted for shipment to China)	
247	1867	*Brucklay Castle* (comp)	S	1014		£16000	
248	1866	*Electra* (comp)	S	788	£16.15s		728 average
249	1866	ss *Taiwan* (iron)	bg	338		£6500 without engines &c £11700 incl engines	
250	1867	ss *Eclipse* (wd)	S	435			
251	1867	*John Wesley* (comp)	bkn	238		£3480	
252	1867	*Nicoya* (comp)	S	593	£18.5s		644¾ average
253	1868	*Commissary* (wd)	S	941		£15000	

Yard No	Date	Name	Rig	Tons nm*	Contract price per ton	lump sum	Tons for contract
254	1867	*Illovo* (wd)	S	397	£15.15s		
255	1867	*Whalsey* (wd)	sk	15		£300	
256	1868	ss *Kwang Tung* (iron)		860		£21358	Some work by Hall, Russell (?)
257	1868	*Helen Black* (wd)	bk	305		£4000	
258	1868	*Samoa*, later *John Williams* (wd)	bk	200		£5000	
259	1868	ss *Ho-Sho-Maru* (wd)	bk	173		£9238	
260	1868	*Herradura* (comp)	S	612	£17.10s		682 average
261	1869	ss *Jho-Sho-Maru* (wd)	bk	1459		£45000 incl engines	
262	1869	*May Queen* (iron)	S	780	£15.10s		732.13 net
263	1869	*The Caliph* (comp)	S	961	£17		900 average
264	1869	*Barranca* (comp)	S	677	£17		
265	1870	*Lufra* (comp)	S	704		£10000	
266		lighter (wd)		[not stated]			
267	1871	ss *Richmond* (iron)	?	191		£3730	
268	1871	*Hokitika* (iron)	bk	292		£3950	
269	1871	*Juan de la Vega* (wd)	bgn	172		£2780	
270	1872	ss *Greenland* (wd)	bk	448		£12800	
271	1872	ss *Graphic* (iron)	?	1029	[not stated]	£17586 completed	
272	1873	ss *Hope* (wd)	S	452		£13500	(whaler)
273	1872	*Elizabeth* (wd)	sch	99	[not stated]	£1846 completed	
274	1872	*Robert Miller* (wd)	smk	81	[not stated]	£1338 completed	
275	1872	ss *Lily* (iron)	?	213		£3500	hull only
276	1872	ss *Vanguard* (wd)	?	559	£18		559.32 gross
277	1873	*John Walker* (wd)	smk	77		£3000	
278	1873	Robert Kirkwood (wd)	smk	78		£3000	
279	1873	ss *Princess Louise* (comp)	?	30		£650	
280	1873	ss *Dee* (iron)	?	304		£14000	
281	1873	ss *Don* (iron)	?	304		£14000	
282	1873	ss *Alexander Pirie* (iron)	?	514	[not stated]	£14170 completed	
283	1874	*Calypso* (iron)	S	1061	£18.12.6 for 1013 tons; £9.6.3 for 6½ tons		
284	1875	*Alive* (iron)	bk	313		£4950	
285	1874	*Avalanche* (iron)	S	1210		£19973 completed	
296	1875	*Bay of Naples* (iron)	S	1676		£27458 completed	
287	1875	*Ullock* (iron)	bk	815	£17.7.6		776

APPENDIX 3

Spar dimensions of *Thermopylae*

Dimensions of *Thermopylae* from list on Bernard Waymouth's sail plan

			Diameter
Fore mast deck to hounds	45ft	head 15½ ft	29in
Fore topmast, heel to stop	42ft	head 10ft	17½in
Fore topgallant mast	28ft	—	12½in
Fore royal mast	18ft	pole 1ft	[not stated]
Main mast, deck to hounds	49ft	head 15½ft	30in
Main topmast, heel to stop	42ft	head 10ft	17½in
Main topgallant mast	32ft	—	12½in
Main royal mast	23ft	pole 1ft	[not stated]
Mizen mast, deck to hounds	42ft	head 11½ft	23in
Mizen topmast, heel to stop	32ft	head 8ft	14in
Mizen topgallant mast	23ft	—	9in
Mizen royal mast	15ft	pole 1ft	[not stated]
Foreyard, extreme length	81ft	arms 3½ft	19in
Fore lower topsail yard, extreme length	66ft	arms 1ft	15½in
Fore upper topsail yard, extreme length	65ft	arms 3½ft	14½in
Fore topgallant yard, extreme length	47ft	arms 2½ft	11in
Fore royal yard, extreme length	35ft	arms 1½ft	8in
Main yard, extreme length	81ft	arms 3½ft	19in
Main lower topsail yard, extreme length	66ft	arms 1ft	15½ in
Main upper topsail yard, extreme length	65ft	arms 3½ft	14½in
Main topgallant yard, extreme length	50ft	arms 2½ft	11in
Main royal yard, extreme length	37ft	arms 1½ft	8in
Crossjack yard, extreme length	65ft	arms 3½ft	[not stated]
Mizen lower topsail yard, extreme length	53ft	arms 1ft	[not stated]
Mizen upper topsail yard, extreme length	50ft	arms 2½ft	[not stated]
Mizen topgallant yard, extreme length	37ft	arms 1½ft	[not stated]
Mizen royal yard, extreme length	28ft	arms 1ft	[not stated]
Mizen boom, extreme length	52ft	—	[not stated]
Mizen gaff, extreme length	39½ft	pole 4½ft	[not stated]
Bowsprit, outside knightheads	20ft		[not stated]
Jibboom, first stop from cap	16½ft		[not stated]
Jibboom, second stop	18ft		[not stated]
Jibboom, third stop	13ft		[not stated]

Rake of masts: Fore ⅞in; Main 1in; Mizen 1⅛in per foot

"Storm staysails to be fitted to each mast"

"Main topgallant and mizen topsail Colling & Pinkneys Patent Rolling"

(As described in text, mizen roller-reefing topsail was replaced with upper and lower topsails)

APPENDIX 4

Specification of Iron Sailing Ship *Sarah Palmer*

Specification of Iron Sailing Ship "Sarah Palmer," 1462 53/94 *tons, OM. Built at the Bank Quay Works, Warrington, by Messrs C Tayleur & Co.*

Dimensions.—Length between the perpendiculars, 225½ft; beam extreme outside, 36½ft; depth of hold, from underside of deck to the top of ceiling amidships, 23ft; rake of stern post 3ft.

Keel to be of best hammered scrap-iron, 9in deep, 3in thick, welded in lengths as long as possible, say 50ft, and scarphed with 2ft-6in scarphs, riveted with a double row of 1⅛in rivets from end to end to the garboard strake.

Stem.—Best hammered scrap-iron, 12 × 3in at heel, 9 × 2½in at load line, 7 ×2¼ upper end. Riveted with a double row of 1in rivets, the fore-part to be rounded.

Stern Post.—Best hammered scrap-iron, 9 × 3in at heel, 7 × 4in at load line, 6 ×in at top; solid eyes to be welded on for rudder, to project at heel for rudder foot, with steel cap, and elbowed at least 6ft on the line of keel; the fastenings on both stem and stern post to be the same as keel and garboard strake, riveted same as stem.

Plates.—None to exceed 30in wide, lapped, the plates being alternately in and outside; horizontal and vertical joints to be double riveted. Garboard strake, for 120ft amidships, ⅞in, ends, 13/16in; first row of bottom plates, 120ft do ¾in, ends, 11/16in, remainder of bottom up to turn of bilge, do ⅝in, ends, 9/16in; two strakes at turn of bilge, do ¾in, ends, 11/16in; one strake at turn of bilge next above, do ⅝in, ends, 9/16in; top of bilge to lower deck do 9/16in, ends, ½in; lower deck binding strake, 2½ft wide for 180ft amidships, 11/16in, ends ⅝in; top sides, ½in ends, ½in; gunwale or binding strake, 2½ft wide for 180ft amidships, 11/16in, ends, ⅝in. To be strengthened in the way of the channel, and hawse pipes as the superintendent will point out; all plates to be best iron, free from flaws and cracks, and to be sound round each hole when punched; no filling in pieces in any of the seams or butts. Poop and forecastle to be plated up with ⅜in plates. Plates to overlap stern post, so as to make a recess for the rudder to work in. To be plated solid round mastholes on all decks, with deep iron rings for masts to wedge against on all the decks they pass through.

Frames to be of angle-iron, 5 × 3 × ⅝in at centre to ½in at ends, and spaced 18in throughout, with reversed angle-iron, 3 × 3 × ½in on every alternate frame up to the top, the reversed frames on every intermediate frame, to be carried up to an average 5ft above the turn of the bilge, but to be shifted, say alternately, 2½ft and 7½ft above the bilge, in as great lengths as possible, and well secured at the joinings; to have filling pieces at back of frames for the alternate strakes. The frames for the poop and forecastle to be main frames carried up, and reversed frames on them alternately, 2½ × 2½ × ⅜in. All the frames and reversed angle-irons to be either welded in one length up to the top, or secured at joinings by back pieces at least 4ft long and well riveted, these joinings or back pieces to be put in independently of the frames or reverse angle-iron, as the case may be, passing and securing such joining.

Floorings to be of plate-iron in every frame, 24in deep in centre × 7/16in thick, riveted to frames, and carried well up round turn of bilge, with an angle-iron on top, 3 × 3 × ½in running up above bilge, and joining reverse angle-iron on frames, short pieces of angle-iron in addition on top of the all floors in way of keelsons, and in order to connect them by four rivets to each floor.

Main Keelson to be box-shaped, 2ft-6in deep and 1 foot 9in wide, plates ⅜in thick, stiffened inside as the superintendent may point out; angle-iron for corners, 3 × 3 × ⅜in, and for connection to floorings, 3 × 3 × ½in; well secured, and extra strengthened in wake of masts; to be water-tight, and suitably finished for a water-tank, with wash plates and man holes as may be wanted; pipe leading to deck, with brass socket on deck. Keelson to be carried as far forward and aft as possible, and secured if necessary to ends.

Bilge Keelsons.—To have four, two formed of two plates, ⅜in thick, 10in deep, placed on edge, 4in apart, and one overlap of 4in at top, riveted together, and secured at the bottom by angle-irons on each side, 3× 3 × ⅜in, to every flooring, also two formed of two angle-irons, 7½ × 4 × ¾in, back to back riveted together and to every floor; all the keelsons extending right fore-and-aft, and not broken by bulkheads, but the latter made to fit water-tight round them.

Beams to be placed on every alternate frame, both in lower and upper deck, poop, and forecastle. The lower deck to be 9in deep × ½in in centre; upper deck to be 8in deep × ½in do; poop deck to be 6in deep × ⅜in do; forecastle to be 5 × 3 × ⅜in; double-angle irons back to back, to have plates riveted to them, so as to form ends extending along the beams 18in, and down the sides 20in from top of the beams, and to have double angle-irons on top, for lower and upper deck, 3 × 3 × 7/16in wide and for poop, 2½ × 2½ × ⅜in, and to be carried down the corner part of the beam arms; all beams furnished with two half-round irons, riveted to the lower edge; additional beams at the break of the poop and forecastle, and to have carlings where necessary, and all hatchways, partners, and openings to be framed with iron of the same size, make, and strength as the beams.

Gunwale.—Angle-iron, 5 × 3 ⅝in, riveted the whole length of the ship, and going entirely round her.

Gunwale Box-Beam, between poop and forecastle, to be made water-tight, to be formed of two ⅜in plates, 15in deep, 7 or 8in apart, with an angle-iron outside, back to back to gunwale angle-iron, 5 × 3 × ⅝in, and one inside on stringer-plate, 3 × 3 × ½in; the wooden stanchions to be fitted into the box, and bolted with two bolts in each end; the intermediate space filled up with wood, bedded with felt and caulked; the inner plate of the box-beam to be carried round the poop and forecastle together with the angle-iron.

Stringers placed on their flat on top of beams; lower deck to be 21in wide × ⅝in; upper deck to be 21in wide × ½in; poop and forecastle, 15in wide ⅜in. The lower deck beams to have in addition a stringer on edge, 18in deep × ⅝in, to be riveted to every frame; a short piece of angle-iron to be placed on every alternate frame to receive this, and to be secured to flat stringers and beams, by an angle-iron, 4 × 4 × ½in, riveted all along. The poop and forecastle to have angle-irons to secure stringers, 3 × 3 × ½in.

Stanchions to be rod-iron in lower hold, 3¼in diameter; 'tween decks, 3in do; in poop, forecastle, and house, as purchasers may wish; placed under every beam throughout ship, and riveted to them, and secured to box-keelson by two angle-irons across top, 5 × 3 × ⅝in.

Breastplates and Crutches, as many as purchasers may want, forward and aft, to be 24in deep in the throat, with arms, 30ft long, and tapering to ends, the lower ones to be 9/16in thick, and the upper ones ½in, with suitable angle-irons.

Bulkheads.—To be four in number, and water-tight, placed as purchasers shall direct, extending up to the lower deck, the forward ones to be 5/16in plates, with vertical bars, 3 × 3 × ⅜in, 2ft apart, extending up to main deck; the others to be 5/16in plates, stiffened with vertical bars, 3 × 3 × ⅜in, 3 feet apart, well secured to the beams.

Rudder.—Rudder and frame 7in diameter to the throat, and there flattened out to 9 × 4in, then tapering down to 7 × 3in; the keel to have a steel pin inserted to work on the stern post cap, the outer frame to taper 6 × 4in at top, 6 × 3in at heel, and 4 × 2in at the outside edge, cross bars welded on 4in wide; the upper part of the rudder to be recessed, to receive the ⅜in plates, single riveted to the frame, clean and made flush as by the drawing to be furnished by the purchasers.

Beam Bracings.—To have diagonal riders on top of upper and lower beams, 6in wide × ⅜in thick, placed about 10ft apart, riveted to stringers, beams, and to themselves at crossings, to be carried right fore-and-aft.

Chain Plates.—Chain plates of length and strength as shall be approved by purchasers, very securely riveted to the sides, and long enough to take hold of two plates, finishing through rails with extra stringers to receive dead eyes.

Channel Boards of hard wood; size, length, and to be fastened as purchasers will point out, with plate-iron knees to support them, with strong iron band outside edge to protect from chafing.

Ballast or Cargo Ports.—To have four into 'tween decks, the size will be pointed out, substantially framed, hinged, and secured in the most approved manner.

Side Lights, for the 'tween decks, of brass to be found by owners, builders fitting them in.

Rudder Trunk to be formed of ⅝in plates, well secured to stern post and shell, and about 22in diameter inside, with cap on lower part to make a finish.

Rivets to be the very best quality and full size, to suit plates, and to be placed as close as purchasers may point out: particular care must be paid to the riveting and the quality of the rivets.

Reprinted from *Iron Ship-building with Practical Illustrations* by John Grantham (London 1868, 5th edition) pp 230-33.

SOURCES AND BIBLIOGRAPHY

Abbreviations used in the references

A S & Sons	Alexander Stephen & Sons
CH	Custom House
LR	Lloyd's Register
MM	The *Mariner's Mirror*
NMM	National Maritime Museum
PP	Parliamentary Papers

Ships plans and models

The structure of the book depends on the plans, which have been redrawn or photographed from old originals, or which have been prepared from measurements taken from models. In a majority of cases, the source of the plan is fully described in the text, and the scope of any large collection is referred to, so it is not proposed to repeat such information here. The following list comprises collections consisting of more than one model or plan which have been consulted.

National Maritime Museum. Admiralty Collection of Draughts; plans of merchant ships embodying drawings from various shipbuilders and collectors, including the Croad Collection, Denny Collection, Hilhouse Collection, Lisslie Collection and Longstaff Collection; also numerous models.

Alexander Stephen & Sons. Plans and half-models from 1852 onwards for almost all vessels launched at the Glasgow yard; plans now housed at National Maritime Museum. Nothing located from Dundee yard except two plans and one half-model which were found in the Glasgow yard.

Barclay, Curle & Co. From about 1850 onwards, plans of almost all vessels; now housed at National Maritime Museum.

Science Museum. Geddie Collection of plans; sail plans drawn by G C Watson; photographic negatives of Hilhouse Collection and vessels from other sources.

Liverpool Museum. Many models, including Kellock Collection.

Whitehaven Museum. Some half-models; sail plans from William Kennaugh.

Glasgow Museum. Half-models of clippers built by Alexander Hall & Sons; also of ships by John Reid; many other models.

Sunderland Museum. Half-models of ships built by Robert Thompson; other models of locally-built ships.

Whitby Museum. Plans of locally-built ships.

Brixham Maritime Museum. Half-models of locally-built vessels.

Bristol Museum. Half-models of ships built by G K Stothert from 1851; other models, some of locally-built vessels.

Thos & Jno Brocklebank. Plans of ships built in Whitehaven.

Smith's Dock Co. Models at N Shields and Middlesbrough offices.

The late James Steele. Half-models of ships built by Robert Steele & Co. Their whereabouts are now unknown.

J W & A Upham. Half-models of ships built in their yard.

B E Nicholson. Half-models of ships built at Annan 1853–65.

Howard I Chapelle. Various plans; lines taken off half-models.

James Henderson. Models of Aberdeen-built ships; plans drawn from models or redrawn from originals.

William Salisbury. Some models; plans drawn from models or redrawn from originals.

Author's Collection. Some models; plans drawn from models or redrawn from originals.

F Holm-Petersen Coll. Models and plans of Danish-built vessels.

Mariners Museum, Newport News. G Hillman Plans (c 1850–65) and eighteenth-century plans of French vessels.

Francis Russell Hart Nautical Museum, Massachusetts Institute of Technology. Some models; original plans of McKay's clippers.

Peabody Mus, Salem. Some models; plans from various sources.

Manuscripts

It is a harder task to establish lists of ships according to their builder rather than their owner, perhaps because most research in the past has been directed towards shipowning. This has been accentuated by the material readily available in such publications as *Lloyd's Register of Shipping* where the builder's name was never published prior to 1859 and the place of building was often inaccurately named. Shipowning-research has been further assisted in the past by the detailed information as to division of shares in a ship, obtainable in the Custom House registers, and by the fleet lists given in *Lloyd's Register* as from 1878. By contrast, particulars on shipbuilders require more research.

A valuable source of shipbuilders' lists is that formed by Arthur C Wardle at the Liverpool Museum. In addition, I have located others at shipbuilder's offices, in the Museums and Libraries of shipbuilding towns, and in private collections. A systematic transcription of the Custom House registers would eventually provide complete lists of vessels constructed by every builder, but this is a time-consuming occupation. In the case of a small port whose ships are almost entirely locally-built, the Custom House records at that port alone can provide a fairly complete list of ships built there; but in larger ports, this is impossible. A very valuable way of obtaining data on shipbuilders and their ships is by consulting the Lloyd's Register survey reports, now at the National Maritime Museum. Although many ships were never classed by Lloyd's Register, these reports provide the surest way to obtain an accurate sample of any shipbuilder's activities, together with a surveyor's coments on the ships produced.

The principal manuscript sources consulted are listed below:

Barclay, Curle & Co. List of ships built.

Baring Brothers. Specification and operating costs of the clippers *Black Prince* and *Norman Court*; letters and specification about the *Falcon* (1824); and Captain Andrew Shewan's writings.

Blyth, Greene, Jourdain & Co. Letters from James Blyth and list of ships owned.

Custom House registers: consulted at London and Glasgow.

Dr and Mrs Donald. Log-books and letters of Captain Thomas Mitchell, master in the Aberdeen White Star Line.

L E Evans. Log books and documents of Captain Joseph E McGill and his son Captain J Edward McGill.

Grahame Farr. Lists of ships built in the Ports of Bideford, Barnstaple &c, compiled from Custom House registers and other sources.

Glasgow Museum. List of ships built by William Simons, including spar dimensions.

India Office Library. Log-books of *Farquharson* and *St Helena*.

James Henderson Collection. Cost accounts of ships built by Alexander Hall & Sons.

Sir James Laing & Co Ships built, with spar and rigging dimensions.

Liverpool Museum, Shipping Collection. List of ships built by Jones, Quiggin & Co; MS lists compiled by Arthur C Wardle of shipbuilders in the British Isles together with lists of ships built.

Lloyd's Register. Visitation Committee Reports to shipbuilding centres from 1851; Surveyor's Committee Reports 1838–74; survey reports of some ships.

London Missionary Society. Papers relating to ships *John Williams II* and to *Samoa*, later *John Williams III*.

National Maritime Museum. Lists of ships built at the Blackwall Yard, London; Lubbock Collection, letters from James MacCunn; various log-books; Lloyd's Register survey reports from c 1834.

B E Nicholson. Voyage account books of ships owned by John Nicholson & Co.

W Salisbury Collection. MS lists of ships built and owned in north-west England and compiled by W Stewart-Rees.

Alexander Stephen & Sons Ltd. Diaries kept by Alexander Stephen Snr 1824–51, and by Alexander Stephen Jnr 1856 onwards; also note books kept by the latter 1851–56. Letter books for Clyde-side yard from 1856. (All now deposited with Department of Economic History, Glasgow University, since I examined them.)

Tower Hamlets Borough Council (formerly Poplar). Collection of records compiled by Daniel R Bolt, including individual sailing ship histories.

J W & A Upham. List of ships built, 1856 onwards.

Whitehaven Library and Museum. Lists of locally-built ships and particulars of shipbuilders, compiled by Daniel Hay; also account books.

Author's Collection. Lists of ships built by William Pile of Sunderland, beginning at no 52 (1858); and of Robert Steele & Co (complete); also log-books and voyages accounts.

NEWSPAPERS AND PERIODICALS

This list comprises those most frequently consulted.

Aberdeen Journal
Albion (Liverpool)
American Neptune (Salem, Mass, from 1941)
Argus (Melbourne)
Artizan (London)
Australia and New Zealand Gazette (London, from 1851)
Canton Register
Chronicle of London Missionary Society
Cornwall Chronicle (Launceston, Tasmania)
Economic History Review (Cambridge)
Glasgow Herald
Illustrated London News (London, from 1841)
Lloyd's Lists
Log Chips (Washington, 4 vols, 1948–59)
London and China Telegraph (London, from 1859)
Marine Models (London, c 1927–39)
Mariner's Mirror (London, from 1911)
Mechanics' Magazine (London)
Mercantile Marine Magazine (London, 1856–64)
Monthly Nautical Magazine and Quarterly Review (New York)
Nautical Magazine (London)
Nautical Research Journal (USA, from c 1948)
Norfolk Sailor (Norwich, from 1959)
North British Daily Mail (Glasgow)
Sea Breezes (Liverpool, from 1919)
Ships and Ship Models (London, from 1931)
Ships Monthly (London, from 1966)
Smith's Dock Monthly (North Shields)
Sunderland Echo
Sydney Morning Herald
The Times (London)
Transactions of the Institution of Naval Architects (London, from 1860)

PRINTED WORKS

The following are the principal books and articles referred to, but the Notes, Queries and Answers in the *Mariner's Mirror* are too numerous to list here, with one or two exceptions, although they are given fully in the References.

Abell, Sir Westcott, *The Shipwright's Trade*, Cambridge 1948.

'The "Aberdeen Bow"', *Aberdeen Journal*, 12th July 1848, p5.

Albion, Robert G, *Forests and Sea Power 1652–1862*, Cambridge, Mass 1926.

— *Square-riggers on Schedule*, Princeton, NJ 1938.

Anderson, R C, 'Eighteenth-Century Books on Shipbuilding, Rigging, and Seamanship', *MM*, 1947, vol 33, pp 218-25.

— *Catalogue of Ship-Models at the National Maritime Museum*, London 1952.

Annesley, William, *A New System of Naval Architecture*, London 1822.

Ansted, A, *A Dictionary of Sea Terms*, Glasgow 1933.

Baker, William A, *From Paddle Steamer to Nuclear Ship*, London 1965.

— *Sloops and Shallops*, Barre, Mass 1966.

Baugean, *Collections de toutes les espèces de bâtiments de guerre et de bâtiments marchands*, Paris 1814.

Benham, Hervey, *Last Stronghold of Sail*, London 1948.

— *Once upon a Tide*, London 1955.

Bennett, J, 'Observations on the Effects Produced by Iron Masts. . .', *Papers on Naval Architecture* (edited by William Morgan and Augustin Creuze), vol I, London 1826, pp 100-9.

Biddlecombe, George, *The Art of Rigging*, London 1848.

Blake, George, *Lloyd's Register of Shipping 1769–1960*, London c 1961.

— *Gellatly's 1862–1962*, London 1962.

Bouquet, Michael R, *No Gallant Ship*, London 1959.

Bowen, Frank C, *The Golden Age of Sail*, London 1925.

— *The Sea, its History and Romance*, 4 vols, London 1926.

— *The Flag of the Southern Cross: Shaw Savill Albion Co., 1858–1939*, London c 1939.

Brett, Henry, *White Wings*, 2 vols, Auckland 1924 and 1928.

Brewington, M W, *Shipcarvers of North America*, Barre, Mass 1962.

— and Dorothy Brewington, *The Marine Paintings and Drawings in the Peabody Museum*, Salem, Mass, 1968.

British Association, *Report from a Committee. . . to Inquire into the Defects of the Present Methods of Measuring and Registering the Tonnage of Shipping*, London 1857.

Burstall, Aubrey F, *A History of Mechanical Engineering*, London 1965.

Bury, J P T (editor), *The New Cambridge Modern History*, vol X, Cambridge 1960.

Cable Boyd, 'The World's First Clipper', *MM*, 1943, vol 29, pp 66-91.

Cammell Laird & Co, *Builders of Great Ships*, Birkenhead 1959.

Campbell, G E, *China Tea Clippers*, London 1954.

Carr, Frank, G G, 'The Restoration of the *Cutty Sark*', *Transactions of the Royal Institution of Naval Architects*, 1966, vol 108, pp 193-216.

— *The Story of the* Cutty Sark, London 1969.

Chapelle, Howard I, *The Baltimore Clipper*, Salem, Mass, 1930.

— 'The Bermuda Sloops and Dinghies', *Yachting*, April 1933, pp 57-60.

— *The History of American Sailing Ships*, New York 1935.

— *Yacht Designing and Planning*, New York 1936.

— 'The First Clipper', *MM*, 1948, vol 34, pp 26-33.

— *The History of the American Sailing Navy*, New York 1949.

— *The National Watercraft Collection*, Smithsonian Museum, Washington 1960.

— *The Search for Speed under Sail*, New York 1967.

Chaplin, W R, 'The Four-Masted Ship *Transit*', *MM*, 1933, vol 19, pp 312-26.

Chapman Charles, *All About Ships*, London c 1869.

Chapman, Fredrik H, af, *Architectura Navalis Mercatoria* (half-size reprint of 1768 eds), Magdeburg c 1956.

Chatterton, E Keble, *Fore and Aft: the Story of the Rig*, London 1912.

Cheal, Henry, *The Ships and Mariners of Shoreham*, London 1909.

Clark, Arthur H, *The Clipper Ship Era 1843–1869*, New York 1910.

'Clipper Ships', *Naval Science*, July 1873, vol II, pp 265 *et seq.*

Clowes, G S Laird, *Sailing Ships*, Science Museum, 2 vols, London 1932.

Coates, W H, *The Good Old Days of Shipping*, Bombay 1900.

Cooke, E W, *Fifty Plates of Shipping and Craft*, London 1829.

Cotton, Sir Evan, *East Indiamen*, London 1949.

Course, A G, *Painted Ports*, London 1961.

Court, W H B, *A Concise Economic History of Britain from 1750*, Cambridge 1954.

Craig, Robert S, 'The African Guano Trade', *MM*, 1964, vol 50, pp 25-55.

Creuze, Augustin F B, *Theory and Practice of Naval Architecture*, Edinburgh 1841.

Crowe, Austin M, *Warrington: Ancient and Modern*, Warrington 1947.

Cunningham, H D P, 'On Working Ships' Yards', *Transactions of the Institution of Naval Architects*, 1867, vol VIII, pp 183-6.

— *Cunningham's Patent Mode of Reefing Topsails &c*, (instructions), 1854.

HM Customs, *Instructions to Measuring Surveyors*, London 1861.

Cutler, Carl C, *Greyhounds of the Sea*, New York 1930.

— *Five Hundred Sailing Records of American-Built Ships*, Mystic, Conn 1952.

— *Queens of the Western Ocean*, Annapolis Maryland 1961.

Danish Maritime Museum, Maritime History in Pictures, Helsingor 1967.

Davis, Charles G, *The Ways of the Sea*, New York 1930.

— *The Ship Model Builder's Assistant* (1926 ed), New York 1955.

— *The Built-up Ship Model* (reprint of 1933 ed), New York 1960.

Davis, Ralph, *Rise of the English Shipping Industry*, London 1962.

Dingley, E A, 'Gwyn's Book of Ships', *MM*, 1921, vol 7, pp 46-52.

Edye, John, *Calculations Relating to Equipment &c of Ships and Vessels of War*, London 1832.

Encyclopedie Methodique: Marine, vol V, plates only, Paris 1787.

Evans, James, *Recollections: or Incidents from the Lives of our Sea-Faring Men*, Berwick-on-Tweed 1908.

Facts versus Fiction: Sir Wm Symonds' Principles Vindicated, London 1845.

Fairbairn, William, *Treatise on Iron Ship Building*, London 1865.

Falconer, William, *An Universal Dictionary of the Marine*, London 1780.

— (editor William Burney), *A new Universal Dictionary of the Marine*, London 1815.

Farr, Grahame, *Records of Bristol Ships 1800–1838*, Bristol 1950.

— *The Steamship Great Britain*, Bristol 1965.

Fayle C Ernest, *A Short History of the World's Shipping Industry*, London 1933.

Finberg, H P R (editor), *Approaches to History*, London 1965.

Fincham, John, 'Dimensions and Calculated Elements of some of the Vessels of the Royal Yacht Club', *Papers on Naval Architecture* (edited by William Morgan and Augustin Creuze), vol 1, London 1826, pp 208-17.

— *A History of Naval Architecture*, London 1851.

— *An Outline of Shipbuilding*, 2 vols (text and plates), London 1852.

— *A Treatise on Masting Ships and Mast Making*, 2 vols (text and plates), London 1st ed 1829 and 3rd ed 1854.

Fishbourne, E Gardiner, *Lectures on Naval Archirecture*, London 1846.

Forfait, *Traite elémentaire de la mature des vaisseaux*, Paris 1815.

Gavin, C M, *Royal Yachts*, London 1932.

Gibson, John F, *Brocklebanks, 1770–1950*, 2 vols, Liverpool 1953.

Goodwin, S [= Carr Laughton], 'Cutter and Sloop', *MM*, 1911, vol I, pp 306-12, and 1912, vol II, pp 20-1.

Gower, Richard Hall, *Supplement to the Practical Seamanship*, London 1807.

— *Improvements in Naval Architecture*, London 1811.

— *Original Observations . . . as Practised on brd the* Transit, Ipswich c 1835.

Graham, Gerald S, 'The Ascendancy of the Sailing Ship 1850–85', *Economic History Review*, vol IX, no 1, pp 74-88.

Grant, Gordon and Henry B Culver, *The Book of Old Ships*, New York 1936.

Grantham, John, *Iron, as a Material for Ship-Building*, London 1842.

— *Iron Ship-Building*, 2 vols (text and plates), London text 1st ed 1858 and 5th ed 1868, plates 2nd ed 1859.

— 'On the *Richard Cobden* Iron Sailing Ship', *Transactions of the Institution of Naval Architects*, 1871, vol XII, pp 252-9.

Greenhill, Basil, *The Merchant Schooners*, 2 vols, London 1951 and 1957.

— 'Note on the Lisslie Collection of Ships' Draughts, *MM*, 1961, vol 47, pp 58-60.

Gregory, Dickson, *Australian Steamships, Past and Present*, London 1928.

Griffiths, John W, *A Treatise on Marine and Naval Architecture*, New York 1853.

Grimwood, V R, *American Ship Models*, New York 1942.

Groenwegen, G, *Verzameling van . . . Hollandsche Schepen* (reprint of 1789 ed), Rotterdam 1967.

Guest, Montague, *List of Members of the Royal Yacht Squadron and their Yachts: from its Inception in 1815 to 1897*, London 1897.

— and William B Boulton, The Royal Yacht Squadron, London 1903.

Halldin, Gustaf (editor), *Svenskt Skeppsbyggeri*, Malmô, Sweden 1963.

Hardy's Register of Ships Employed by the East India Co, London 3rd ed 1820 and 4th ed 1835.

Harper, Lawrence A, *The English Navigation Laws* (reprint of 1939 ed), New York 1964.

Hasslöf, Olof, 'Wrecks, Archives and Living Tradition', *MM*, 1963, vol 49, pp 162-77.

— 'Sources of Maritime History and Methods of Research', *Mm*, 1966, vol 52, pp 172-44.

Heaton, Peter, *Yachting; a History*, London 1955.

Heckstall-Smith, B, *Yachts and Yachting in Contemporary Art*, London 1925.

Hedderwick, Peter, *A Treatise on Marine Architecture*, 2 vols (text and plates), Edinburgh 1830.

Henderson, Andrew, 'On Ocean Steamers and Clipper Ships', *Report of British Association*, 1854.

Hidy, R W, *The House of Baring in American Trade and Finance, 1763–1861*, Harvard 1949.

Hill, John C G, *Shipshape and Bristol Fashion*, Liverpool c 1955.

Holland, A J, 'The Beaulieu River: its Rise and Fall as a Commercial Waterway', *MM*, 1963, vol 49, pp 275-87.

Holm-Petersen, F, *Skibsportraetmalere*, Denmark 1867.

Höver, Otto, *Von der Gallito zum Fünfmaster, 1780–1930*, Bremen 1934.

Howe, Octavius T and Frederick C Matthews, *American Clipper Ships 1833–1858*, 2 vols, Salem, Mass 1926 and 1927.

Hutchinson, Will, *A Treatise on Naval Architecture*, London 1794.

Jardine, Matheson & Company, London 1965.

Kemp, Dixon, *A Manual of Yacht and Boat Sailing*, London 1895.

— *Yacht Architecture*, 2 vols (text and plates), London 1897.

Kierkegaard, N C, *Plancher till Praktisk Skeppsbyggnadskonst*, plates, Gothenburg 1864.

Kipping, Robert, *The Elements of Sailmaking*, wnd ed, London 1851.

— *Sails and Sailmaking*, 1st ed, London 1858.

— *Masting, Mast-Making and Rigging of Ships*, 10th ed, London 1866.

Kirkaldy, Adam W, *British Shipping*, London 1919.

La Roërie, G and J Vivielle, Navires et marins de la Rame de l'Helice, 2 vols, Paris 1930.

Laing, Alexander, *American Sail*, London 1961.

Landström, Björn, *The Ship*, London 1961.

Laughton, L G Carr, *Old Ship Figure-heads and Sterns*, London 1925.

Learmont, J S, 'Speed under Sail', *MM*, 1957, vol 43, pp 225-231.

Leather, John, 'The Shipbuilding Bayleys', *MM*, 1965, vol 51, pp 131-45.

Lescallier, Antoine, *Vocabulaire des termes de marine*, Paris 1777.

— *Traité pratique de gréement des vaisseaux*, 2 vols, Pars 1791.

Leslie, Robert C, *Old Sea Wings, Ways, and Words* (with notes by L G Carr Laughton), London 1930.

Lever, Darcy, *Young Sea Officer's Sheet Anchor*, London 1808 and 2nd ed 1819.

Lewis, Michael, *The Navy of Britain*, London 1948.

Lindsay, W S, *History of Merchant Shipping 1816–1874*, 2 vols, London c 1874. Identical to vols 3 and 4 of larger work, pub'd 1876 in 4 vols.

Lissignol, E, *Navaires en fer à voiles*, Paris 1866.

List of the Shipping Registered in the Ports of Scotland, 3rd ed, Glasgow 1828.

Lloyd, Christopher, *The Navy and the Slave Trade*, London 1949.

Lloyd's Register, *Report on Dismasting of Large Iron Sailing Ships*, London 1886.

— *Register of Shipping*, annually, London. Since 1834 entitled *Lloyd's Register of British and Foreign Shipping*.

— *Annals of Lloyd's Register*, London 1934.

Longridge, C Nepean, *The* Cutty Sark, 2 vols, London 1949.

Lubbock, Basil, *The Blackwall Frigates*, Glasgow 1922.

— *The China Clippers*, Glasgow 1922.

— *The Colonial Clippers*, Glasgow 1924.

— *The Log of the* Cutty Sark, Glasgow 1924.

— *Last of the Windjammers*, 2 vols, Glasgow vol I 1927 and vol II 2nd ed 1935.

— *The Opium Clippers*, Glasgow 1933.

Lyman, John, 'The *Scottish Maid* as the World's First Clipper, *MM*, 1944, vol 30, pp 194-9.

— 'Register Tonnage and its Measurement', *American Neptune*, 1945, vol V, pp 223-33 and 311-25.

— 'Composite and Diagonal Building', *Log Chips*, 1951, vol 2, pp 77-80 and 82.

— 'The Cutter Brig', *MM*, 1969, vol 55, pp 17-21.

Lythe, S G E, *Gourlays of Dundee*, Abertay Historical Society, Dundee 1964.

MacGregor, David R, 'Some Early British Tea Clippers', *MM*, 1948, vol 34, pp 67-82, 184-98 and 280-293.

— *The Tea Clippers*, London 1952 and 1983.

— *The China Bird*, London 1961 and 1986.

— *Merchant Sailing Ships 1775–1815*, London 1985.

— *Merchant Sailing Ships 1815–1850*, London 1984.

— *Merchant Sailing Ships 1850–1875*, London 1984.

— 'Tendering and Contract Procedure in Merchant Shipyards in the Middle of the Nineteenth Century', *MM*, 1962, vol 48, pp 241-64.

Mackrow, Clement, *The Naval Architect's and Shipbuilder's Pocket Book*, London 1889.

MacLean, Duncan (Editor John Lyman), *Clipper Ships and Packets 1851–1853*, Washington 1952.

Marriett, P R, *Yachts and Yacht Building*, London 1865.

Marryat, Captain, *Code of Signals for Use of Vessels in the Merchant Service*, London 1841, 1854 and 1856.

Maudslay, Joseph, 'An Improvement in the Form of Ships', *Transactions of the Institution of Naval Architects*, 1860, vol I, pp 54-6.

McEwen, W A and A H Lewis, *Encyclopedia of Nautical Knowledge*, Cambridge, Maryland 1953.

McKay, Richard C, *Some Famous Sailing Ships and their Builder Donald McKay*, New York 1928.

McLellan, R S, *Anchor Line 1856–1956*, Glasgow 1956.

Mitchell, B R, and P Deane, *Abstract of British Historical Statistics*, Cambridge 1962.

Montagu, Lord, *Buckler's Hard and its Ships*, London 1909.

Moorsom, George, *A Brief Review and Analyses of the Laws for the Admeasurement of Tonnage*, London 1852.

Morgan, William, and Augustin Creuze (editors), *Papers on Naval Architecture*, 4 vols, London, 1826, 1828, 1830, 1832–65.

Morris, E P, *The Fore-and-Aft Rig in America*, New Haven, Conn 1927.

Moses, Henry, *Sketches of Shipping and Craft*, London 1824.

Munro, G W, 'East Indiamen', *Marine Models*, June 1934, vol 7, no 3, pp 64-5.

Murphy, John M'Leod, and W N Jeffers Jnr, *Spars and Rigging from Nautical Routine* (reprint of 1849 ed), Providence, RI 1933.

Murray, Andrew, *Theory and Practice of Ship-Building*, Edinburgh 1861.

Murray, Mungo, *A Treatise on Ship-Building and Navigation*, London 1765.

Naish, G P B, *Royal Yachts*, Nat Maritime Museum, London 1953.

Napier, James, *Life of Robert Napier*, Edinburgh 1904.

Nares, George S, *Seamanship*, Portsea 1862.

Norway, Arthur, *History of the Post-Office Packet Service, 1793–1815*, London 1895.

Paasch, Capt H, *From Keel to Truck*, Antwerp 1985.

— *Illustrated Marine Encyclopedia*, Antwerp 1890.

Paris, Vice-Adml Edmond, *L'Art naval jusqu'en 1769*, Paris c 1870.

— *Souvenirs de marine* (second selection), Rostock 1962.

Parker, Capt H and Frank C Bowen, *Mail and Passenger Steamships of the Nineteenth Century*, London 1928.

Parkinson, C Northcote, *Trade in the Eastern Seas, 1793–1813*, Cambridge 1937.

— (editor), *The Trade Winds: British Overseas Trade, 1793–1815, London 1948*.

Parliamentary Papers, *Fifth Report from the Select Committee on the Road from London to Holyhead*, July 1819.

— *Report on the Admeasurement of Shipping*, 21st February 1834.

— *First to Fifth Reports from the Select Committee on Navigation Laws*, 26th March to 17th July 1847.

— *Mortality on Emigrant Ships*, 1852–3, XCVIII.

— *Liverpool Compass Committee*: First and Second Reports 1857, Third Report 1862.

— *Royal Commission on Unseaworthy Ships*: Preliminary Report 1873, Final Report 1874.

Patent Office, *Abridgements of Specifications Relating to Ship Building, Repairing, Sheathing, Launching, &c, 1618–1860*, London 1862.

— *Abridgements of Specifications Relating to Masts, Sails and Rigging, 1625–1866*, London 1874.

— *Abridgements of Specifications Relating to Steering and Manoevring Vessels, 1763–1866*, London 1875.

Payne, Peter L (editor), *Studies in Scottish Business History*, London 1967.

Peake, James, *Rudiments of Naval Architecture; or, an Exposition of the Practical Principles of the Science*, London 1851.

— *Rudiments of Naval Architecture; or, an Exposition of the Elementary Principles of the Science*, London 1855.

Petrejus, Door E W, *Model van de Oorlogsbrik* Irene, Hengelo, Holland 1947.

Philips-Birt, Douglas, *Ships and Boats: the Nature of their Design*, London 1966.

Phipps, John, *Ship Building in India*, Calcutta 1840.
Pinckney, Pauline A, *American Figureheads and their Carvers*, New York 1940.
Plimsoll, Samuel, *Our Seamen*, London 1873.
Powell, J W Damer, *Bristol Privateers and Ships of War*, Bristol 1930.
Prouty, Roger, *The Transformation of the Board of Trade, 1830–1855*, London 1957.

Rankine, W J MacQuorn (editor), *Shipbuilding, Theoretical and Pracical*, London 1866. The plates are sometimes bound separately.
Reed, E J, *Shipbuilding in Iron and Steel*, London 1868.
Rees, Abraham, 'Naval Architecture', *Cyclopedia*, London 1820.
'Register Tonnage in Practice', *Naval Science*, July 1873, pp 370-4.
Registrar-General of Shipping and Seamen, *Mercantile Navy List*, London, annually since 1857.
Richardson, Pelham, *A Practical Digest of the Law of Merchant Ships and Seamen*, London 1847.
Richardson, Thomas, *Mercantile Marine Architecture*, London 1833.
Robinson, H, *Carrying British Mails Overseas*, London 1964.
Rogers, Inkerman, *Record of Ships Built in the Port of Bideford 1568–1938*, Bideford 1947.
Rostow, W W, *British Economy of the Nineteenth Century*, Oxford 1963.
Russell, John Scott, *The Modern System of Naval Architecture*, 3 vols London 1865.

Salisbury, W, 'A Post Office Packet of c 1800', *MM*, 1943, vol 29, pp 57-8.
— 'Hollow Water-lines and Early Clippers', *MM*, 1946, vol 32, pp 237-41.
— 'Early Tonnage Measurement in England', *MM*, 1966, vol 52, pp 41-51, 173-80 and 329-40; 1967, vol 53, pp 251-64; 1968, vol 54, pp 69-76.
Seppings, Sir Robert, 'On a New Principle of Constructing His Majesty's Ships of War', *Philosophical Transactions*, 10th March 1814.
— 'On a New Principle of Constructing Ships in the Mercantile Navy', *Philosophical Transactions*, 9th March 1820.
Sharp, James A, *Memoirs of the Life and Serivces of Rear-Admiral Sir William Symonds*, London 1858.
Shewan, Capt Andrew, *The Great Days of Sail*, London 1927.
Shields, John, *Clyde Build*, Glasgow 1949.
The Shipbuilder's Repository; or, A Treatise on Marine Architecture, London, nd, but assigned to 1788.
'Ships and Shipbuilding', *Encyclopaedia Britannica*, Edinburgh, 1815.
Smith, Edgar C, *A Short History of Naval and Marine Engineering*, Cambridge 1937.
Smith, John, *Rise and Progress of the City Line*, Glasgow 1908.
Smith, J W, and T S Holden, *Where Ships are Born: Sunderland 1346–1946*, Sunderland 1947.
Smyth, Herbert Warrington, *Mast and Sail in Europe and Asia*, London 1929.
Smyth, Adml W H, *The Sailor's Word-Book*, London 1867.
Sommer, Graeme, 'The London and Edinburgh Shipping Co, Ltd of Leith', *Sea Breezes*, 1963, vol 36, pp 139-46.
Spurling, J, and Basil Lubbock, *Sail*, London, vol I 1927, vol III 1936.
Steel, David, *The Elements and Practice of Rigging and Seamanship*, 2 vols, London 1794.
— *Elements and Practice of Naval Architecture*, 2 vols (text and plates), London 1822 (ed John Knowles).
— *The Ship-Master's Assistant and Owner's Manual*, London 6th ed 1795 and 21st ed 1834.
— *The Shipwright's Vade-Mecum*, 2 vols (text and plates), London 1805.
[Stephen, Sir A Murray], *A Shipbuilding History 1750–1932*, Glasgow c 1932.
Stevens, John R, *Old Time Ships*, Toronto 1949.
Stevens, Robert W, *On the Stowage of Ships and their Cargoes*, London 1869.
Stewart-Brown, R, *Liverpool Ships in the Eighteenth Century*, Liverpool 1932.
Sutherland, William, *The Ship Builder's Assistant or Marine Architecture*, London 1794.
Szymanski, Hans, *Deutsche Segelschiffe*, Berlin 1934.

Tables of Dimensions of Masts, Yards &c for Naval Vessels, c 1845. No title page.
Teenstra, Anno, *De Clippers*, Amsterdam 1945.
Thearle, Samuel J P, *Naval Architecture: Laying off and Building, Wood, Iron and Composite Ships*, 2 vols, London text 1876, plates 1874.
— *Shipbuilding in Iron and Steel*, 2 vols (text and plates), London 1886.
Tweedie, Francis, 'The Era of Shipbuilding at Annan', *MM*, 1951, vol 37, pp 128-42.
Tryckare, Tre, and Ewert Cagner (editors), *The Lore of Ships*, London 1964.

Underhill, Harold A, *Sailing Ship Rigs and Rigging*, Glasgow 1938.
— *Masting and Rigging, the Clipper Ship and Ocean Carrier*, Glasgow 1946.
— *Deep-Water Sail*, Glasgow 1952.
Underwriters' Registry for Iron Vessels, Liverpool 1865; re-titled as *Underwriter's List of Iron Vessels Surveyed by the Liverpool Registry*; Liverpool 1872, 1875, 1878.

Villiers, Alan J, *The Way of a Ship*, London 1954.

Wallace, Frederick William, *Wooden Ships and Iron Men*, London 1924.
— *In the Wake of the Wind-Ships*, London 1927.
— *Record of Canadian Shipping*, Toronto 1929.
Warner, Oliver, *An Introduction to British Marine Painting*, London 1948.
White, John, 'On an Improved Method of Building Diagonal Ships', *Transactions of the Institution of Naval Architects*, 1860, vol I, pp 112-120.
White, J Samuel, & Co, Ltd, *Shipbuilding—From Smack to Frigate*, London c 1930.
White, Thomas Jnr, *Theory and Practice of Shipbuilding*, London 1851.

White, W H, *A Manual of Naval Architecture*, London 1882.
Williams, Peter J, and Roderick Serle, *Ships in Australian Waters*, Sydney 1968.
Wilson, Theodore D, *An Outline of Shipbuilding*, New York 1878.
Winchester, Clarence (editor), *Shipping Wonders of the World*, 2 vols, London c 1936.
Woodward, Sir Llewellyn, *The Age of Reform, 1815–1870*, Oxford 1967.

Young, Arthur, *Nautical Dictionary*, Dundee 1846, 2nd ed, London 1863.
Young, Ch F T, *Fouling and Corrosion of Iron Ships*, London 1867.

ACKNOWLEDGEMENTS

The acquisition of knowledge when undertaken on a part-time basis can be a lengthy affair and much of the material for this book has been collected over a period of fifteen years, and a few persons who assisted me in the mid-fifties may no longer be alive to see the fruits of their help. I refer, in particular, to James Steele whose father, Robert Steele, closed down their celebrated shipyard at Greenock in the 1880s. Mr Steele encouraged my youthful interest in his father's clipper ships and allowed me to measure his half-models and copy his comprehensive list of ships built by the firm.

But there are other friendships from this period and earlier which have been very productive during the years and still flourish. I refer especially to Howard I. Chapelle, that great exponent of how best to combine the rôles of naval architect and author, from whose work I have derived great inspiration and pleasure. His books have been a model on how to draw ship plans and present the written word. In long discussions on both sides of the Atlantic, his advice and suggestions have proved of inestimable value.

The history of shipbuilding at Aberdeen with all the technical details of the ships themselves could not have been written without the generous help of James Henderson who has placed all his material at my disposal and supplemented this with his wide knowledge of nineteenth-century ships. He has drawn several plans which are reproduced here and his co-operation with a lines plan of *Thermopylae* has been especially welcome. I should like to acknowledge the accuracy of his draughtsmanship and all the generous help contributed over the last twenty-two years. Captain John Henderson, who commanded *Thermopylae*, was his great-great-uncle.

For shipbuilding history and methods of construction, I have greatly benefited by the advice and encouragement of William Salisbury over many years. Much profitable knowledge has been obtained during numerous discussions, and we have have made several expeditions together to measure models and copy plans. Several plans drawn by him are reproduced here and others are based on his take-offs.

I also owe a deep debt of gratitude to William Ward for the excellent drawings he has made at my suggestion of some of the ships described here. He has gone to great pains to ensure the highest accuracy and we have carefully checked contemporary illustrations. Some of his drawings are of museum models but most are worked up from my plans, with additional detail inserted where appropriate.

The plans from the Glasgow shipbuilders, Alexander Stephen & Sons Ltd, are now deposited with the National Maritime Museum but when they were still lodged with the firm I spent much time examining and tracing them over a period of years, and I am most grateful to the Directors for their kind permission to undertake this research. During much of this time, my fellow-clansman, Robert W McGregor, was chief draughtsman, and I wish to acknowledge the generous assistance and the warm welcome he gave.

Much useful material has been received from Karl Kortum, Director of the San Francisco Maritime Museum, relating to ship fittings and ship construction, and he has suggested many profitable lines of inquiry.

The National Maritime Museum is one of the principal storehouses for maritime knowledge which I have consulted and all the staff have given generously of their time and knowledge over many years and greatly facilitated my search for material on merchant ships. In particular, the Director, Basil Greenhill, has stimulated interest in shipping matters and encouraged research into schooners and fore-and-aft rigged vessels; George P B Naish, Arthur H Waite, Arthur L Tucker and David J Lyon have assisted me in my search for plans and models; Michael S Robinson and George A Osbon have enabled me to obtain excellent illustrations of paintings, drawings and photographs; Alan W H Pearsall has advised on manuscripts and Michael W B Sanderson on printed books.

The Curator of the Sailing Ship Collection at the Science Museum, Basil W Bathe, has generously provided facilities for research and the measuring of models in the collection. He has also given good advice and sound encouragement, and kindly read through some of the manuscript.

At the Glasgow Museums and Art Galleries, I have received every assistance from A S E Browning, Curator, Department of Technology, in measuring half-models and obtaining other information.

For permission to examine their records and copy plans, I am grateful to the Committee of Lloyd's Register of Shipping and their archivist, R P Tonkin; also to the Directors of Baring Brothers and their archivist, T Ingram. The shipbuilders, Barclay, Curle & Co kindly allowed me to examine their old plans and make copies, and their chief draughtsman, R Campbell, was most helpful. John C G Hill of Charles Hill & Sons provided full access to their old plans, and so did Thos & Jno Brocklebank. I am grateful to the following firms who let me take lines off their models: Joseph L Thompson & Sons Ltd, and J W & A Upham. Wm Thomson & Co. kindly allowed me to examine their voyage accounts.

I should like to thank the following persons for their generous assistance in many ways: Robert S Craig for his advice and comment on the economic aspects of the shipping industry and for reading part of the manuscript; Dr Peter L Payne for assistance with business history in Glasgow; Benjamin E Nicholson for allowing me to measure his grandfather's half-models and providing other data; Mrs Boyle for allowing me to measure a half-model; Peter Barton for data on shipbuilding on the north-east coast of England; J G M Stamp for providing a list of ships built by William Pile; John Leather for comments on naval architecture; Mrs Rowland, formerly Librarian at the Royal Institution of Naval Architects; Michael B Stevens for literary advice; and Frank G G Carr for his encouragement over many years. Grahame Farr has provided much useful information on ships and shipbuilders in the West Country, and so has Michael Bouquet; Richard H C Gillis, F A L Fairweather and J D Attwood have likewise assisted with data and illustrations. Several persons have kindly loaned or allowed me to examine manuscripts in their possession including Dr and Mrs Donald, and L E Evans. Further acknowledgement is given in the text and references for assistance rendered.

I am indebted to the following Museums, Libraries and their Staff for assistance in making plans, models, illustrations and documents available to me: Ian McKenzie Smith of the Aberdeen Art Gallery and Museum; James D Boyd of Dundee Art Gallery and Museum; Sunderland Musuem; Miss Dora M Walker of Whitby Literary and Philosophical Society which maintains the Whitby Museum; the Maritime Museum at Pickering Park, Hull; the Librarian, Tower Hamlets Borough Council (formerly Poplar); the Royal Institution of Naval Architects, London; John E Horsley of Brixham Maritime Museum; the City Museum, Bristol; E W Paget-Tomlinson, formerly Curator of the Shipping Collection, City of Liverpool Museums; Daniel Hay of Whitehaven Public Library and Museum; Bertram Newbury of the Parker Gallery, London.

Similar expressions of thanks for their generous help go to museums and their staff in America: John Lochhead of the Mariners Museum, Newport News; William A Baker of the Francis Russell Hart Nautical Museum at the Massachusetts Institute of Technology; the Marine Historical Association and staff at Mystic Seaport; and the Peabody Museum. In Canada to Dr George MacBeath of the New Brunswick Museum, and to John R Stevens, formerly curator of the Maritime Museum of Canada at Halifax.

Individual collectors and authorities on shipbuilding history abroad have been most helpful, and among these in the USA are Dr John Lyman, who advised on some of the earlier chapters and read through parts of the manuscript; Michael Costagliola; Winston V Langdon; Andrew Nesdall; Robert A Weinstein. In Australia, Roderick W Glassford, Cyril Hume, the late Arthur D Edwardes, and the late David M Little have given valuable assistance on British ships over many years. In Denmark, Frode Holm-Peterson has made his collection of ship plans available, in addition to providing information on ship-portrait painters and north European ship types. In the Netherlands, J J van Griethuysen has advised on Dutch clipper ships.

A final word of thanks to those who have helped in checking the proofs and to my wife's kindly tolerance as she has watched my collection slowly spread through our house.

REFERENCES

Chapter One

1 N M M, Admiralty Draughts, ship *Cupid*, plan 3730 box 53.
2 R Stewart-Brown, *Liverpool Ships in the Eighteenth Century* (Liverpool 1932), p 48.
3 C Ernest Fayle, *A Short History of the World's Shipping Industry* (London 1933), p 217.
4 34 George III, c 47, was the first of several smuggling Acts. For summary of these Acts see David Steel, *Shipmaster's Assistant* (London, 6th ed, 1795), pp 301 *et seq*.
5 His address to the Royal Society was quoted in *Mechanics' Magazine*, 1823, vol 4, pp 419-21.
6 3 and 4 William IV, c 53.
7 For a fuller list of eighteenth century books on naval architecture, see R C Anderson, 'Eighteenth-Century Books on Shipbuilding, Rigging and Seamanship', *MM*, 1947, vol. 33, pp 218-25.
8 John Fincham, *An Outline of Ship Building* (London, 3rd ed, 1852), p 28. The first edition appeared in 1825.
9 Howard I Chapelle, *The Search for Speed under Sail, 1700–1855* (New York 1967), pp 100 and 139.
10 *The Shipbuilder's Repository; or, A Treatise on Marine Architecture* (London, nd but assigned to 1788), p 114.
11 *Ibid*, pp 115-16.
12 Chapelle, *Search for Speed under Sail, op cit*, p 9.
13 [David Steel], *The Elements and Practice of Naval Architecture: or, A Treatise on Ship-Building*, revised by John Knowles (3rd ed, London 1822), p 143.
14 The English edition of 1820 was translated from the French version by the Rev James Inman and was entitled *A Treatise on Ship-Building*; it contained some comments on the magnificent plates of Chapman's *Architectura Navalis Mercatoria* (1768–9) which did not have any accompanying text.
15 [David Steel], *The Shipwright's Vade-Mecum* (2nd ed, London, 1822), p 165
16 George Bayley, 'Merchant Yards v HMS Yard's, *Mechanics' Magazine*, 1827, vol 8, p 250.
17 Fincham, *Outline of Ship-Building, op cit*, pp 21-2 and 32-3.
18 *Ibid*, pp 33-4.
19 Chapelle, *Search for Speed under Sail, op cit*, p 150.
20 *Ibid*, pp 29-30.
21 *Ibid*, pp 43-5 and 404-7.
22 David R. MacGregor, *The Tea Clippers: their History and Development 1833–1875* (London 1983), pp 88 and 247.
23 Sir Westcott Abell, *The Shipwright's Trade* (Cambridge 1948), p 96.
24 *Ibid*, pp 104-5.
25 George Moorsom, *A Brief Review and Analyses of the Laws for the Admeasurement of Tonnage* (London 1852), p 82.
26 John Fincham, *A History of Naval Architecture* (London 1851), pp 107-15. On p 107, Fincham gives date of letter as 1776, but other authorities give year as 1796.
27 [Steel], *Elements and Practice of Naval Architecture, op cit*, Appendix, pp 1-24. See also Robert Seppings, 'On a new principle of constructing His Majesty's ships of war', *Philosophical Transactions of the Royal Society*, read 10th March 1814.
28 Robert Seppings, 'On a new principle of constructing ships in the mercantile navy', *Philosophical Transactions of the Royal Society*, read 9th March 1820. Reprinted in [*Steel*], *Elements and Practice of Naval Architecture, op cit*, Appendix, pp 52-62.
29 *Ibid*, p 52.
30 *Mechanics' Magazine*, December 1831, vol 16, p 250; being evidence taken before Committee of House of Commons.
31 Basil Lubbock, *The Opium Clippers* (Glasgow 1933), pp 118-19.
32 William Annesley, *A New System of Naval Architecture* (London 1822). He describes the construction and lists the vessels built.
33 C M Gavin, *Royal Yachts* (London 1932), pp 121 and 127.
34 Oliver Lang, *Improvements in Naval Architecture* (Woolwich 1853), esp p 26, item XCIV.
35 Letter to the *Merchants' Magazine*, 1832, vol 16, p 294, signed 'Junius Redivious'.
36 13 George III, c 74; see also William Salisbury, 'Early Tonnage Measurement', *MM*, 1966, vol 52, part III, pp 333-4.
37 Moorsom, *Review and Analyses of Laws for Admeasurement of Tonnage, op cit*, pp 149-51, quoting report of the Commission.
38 *Ibid*, p 8.

Chapter Two

1 John Charnock, *History of Marine Architecture* (London 1802), vol 3, pp 268-9.
2 F H AF Chapman, *Architectura Navalis Mercatoria* (Stockholm 1768–9, reprint 1957), pl LX, no 6.
3 NMM, Admiralty draughts, plan no 6802, box 65.
4 Howard I Chapelle, *The Search for Speed under Sail 1700–1855* (New York 1967), p 131.
5 Howard I Chapelle, *National Watercraft Collection* (Washington 1960), United States National Museum Bulletin 219, pp 17-18.
6 *Ibid.*
7 *Ibid*, p 18.
8 See Chapman, *Architectura Navalis, op cit*, pl LVII, No 15; and fo 40 in Hilhouse Collection.
9 Hilhouse Collection, fo 49.
10 W A Baker, *Sloops and Shallops* (Barre, Mass 1966), p 121.
11 Howard I Chapelle, 'The Bermuda Sloops and Dinghies', *Yachting* (USA), April 1933, p 58. These lines were taken off by the Admiralty in 1804, but the connection with Hilhouse set of lines dated 1792 is unknown.
12 Adml W H Smyth, *The Sailor's Word-Book* (London 1867), p 230.
13 David Steel, *Naval Architecture; or a Treatise on Ship-Building* (London 1805), p 12.
14 John Lyman, 'The Cutter Brig', *MM*, 1969, vol 55, pp 17-21.
15 *Ibid*, p 20.
16 NMM, Admiralty Draughts, *Busy*, plan no 6797, box 65.
17 *Ibid, Camelion*, plan no 3259, box 48.
18 *Ibid, Helena*, plan no 4523, box 64.
19 J W Damer Powell, *Bristol Privateers and Ships of War* (Bristol 1930), p 251.
20 *Ibid*, p 278.
21 Chapman, *Architectura Navalis, op cit*.
22 Chapelle, *National Watercraft Collection, op cit*, pp 20-21.
23 Chapelle, *Search for Speed under Sail, op cit*, pp 176-78.
24 William James, *The Naval History of Great Britain*, (London 1859), vol III, pp 141-42.
25 NMM, Admiralty Draughts, *L'Invention*, plan no 6147, box 44 (part 2).
26 Chapelle, *National Watercraft Collection, op cit*, p 163, which also gives their lines.
27 See Howard I Chapelle, *The Baltimore Clipper* (Salem, Mass, 1925) and *Search*

for Speed under Sail, op cit, for plans of these ships.

28 James A Sharp, *Memoirs of the Life and Services of Rear-Admiral Sir William Symonds Kt* (London 1858), p 131.

29 Basil Lubbock, *The Opium Clippers* (Glasgow 1933), p 71 *et seq*; lines of the *Prince de Neuchâtel* appear in Howard I Chapelle, *History of American Sailing Ships* (New York 1935), pl V.

30 David R MacGregor, *Merchant Sailing Ships 1775–1815*, (London 1985), p 80.

31 J F Gibson, *Brocklebanks 1770–1950* (Liverpool 1953), vol I, pp 23-24.

32 I traced *Jupiter*'s lines plan from original in the Brocklebank archives.

33 William Hutchinson, *A Treatise on Naval Architecture* (Liverpool 4th ed 1794), pp 22-23.

34 *Ibid*, p 42.

35 *Ibid*, pp 43-44.

36 David R MacGregor, *Merchant Sailing Ships 1775–1815, op cit*, pp 109-14.

37 David Steel, *Elements and Practice of Rigging and Seamanship* London 1794), vol I, p 52.

38 Data on James Spencer from Director of Hull Museums 11th March 1965. No birth and death dates are known.

39 John C G Hill, *Shipshape and Bristol Fashion* (Liverpool, 2nd ed, *c* 1958), p 3 *et seq*. Photographs of many of the plans can be examined at the Science Museum, London.

40 Examined in office of Charles Hill & Sons, Bristol.

41 Hilhouse Collection, fo 113. It should be noted that the numbering of the Hilhouse plans in the Science Museum's list does not agree in most cases with the numbering on the originals.

42 A H Norway, *History of the Post Office Packet service* (London 1895), p 38.

43 This plan is now at the NMM.

44 H D Blyth, *History of Falmouth as a Packet Station* (1863), 4 pp monograph in copper plate printing. A typewritten copy in GPO Archives states it was written by H D Blyth of London and dated 1st January 1863.

45 For further details see W Salisbury, 'A Post Office Packet of *c* 1800', *MM*, 1943, vol 29, pp 57-8.

46 William Salisbury has not projected the waterlines in his half-breadth plan, but this is easily done.

47 From contemporary issues of *Lloyd's List* 1821.

48 I should like to acknowledge William Salisbury's generosity in loaning me his unpublished MS on the *Transit*'s and for his appraisal of their designs.

49 Capt W H Chaplin, 'The Four-Masted Ship *Transit*', *MM*, 1933, vol 19, p 316. Capt Chaplin's article covers the first ship of this name.

50 R H Gower, *Supplement to Practical Seamanship* (London 1807), p 11, pl I; and John Fincham, *History of Naval Architecture* (London 1851), p 181, pl 22.

51 Gower, *Supplement to Practical Seamanship, op cit*, p 91.

52 See lines plan in Basil Lubbock, *Last of the Windjammers* 2nd ed (Glasgow 1935), vol II, p 12.

53 George Bayley, 'His Majesty's Ship *Transit*', *Mechanic's Magazine*, 1828, vol 10, p 120.

54 Gower, *Original Observations, as Practised on board the Transit* (Ipswich *c* 1835), p 47.

55 *Ibid*, p 49.

56 Chapelle, *Search for Speed under Sail, op cit*, p 151.

57 'Noah', 'On ship-Building', *Mechanics Magazine*, 1826 vol V, p 304.

58 David Steel, *Naval Architecture*, revised by John Knowles (3rd ed, London 1822), p 180 (footnote).

59 William Sutherland, *The Ship Builder's Assistant, or Marine Architecture* (revised ed London 1794), p 57. For comments on varying editions of this work, see chapter one.

60 Chapelle, *Search for Speed under Sail, op cit*, p 133.

61 Vice-Admiral Edmond Paris, *Souvenirs de Marine* (Paris *c* 1875), plate 29.

62 *Exeter Flying Post*, 27th January 1791. Seen in collection of R H C Gillis, May 1966, but not verified.

63 US National Archives no 81-10-100, Records of the Department of the Navy, Bureau of Construction and Repair.

64 Letter to the Author from Howard I Chapelle, dated 8th April 1969.

65 Chapelle, *Search for Speed under Sail, op cit*, plate 50.

66 NMM, Admiralty Draughts, plan no 4557, box 64.

67 India Office Library, log book no 327(a) covering years 1819-22.

68 *Ibid*.

69 India Office Library, Marine Records, ledger no 327(c).

Chapter Three

1 See Chapter Two.

2 NMM, plan no 4148, box 59.

3 D W Privett and J R D Francis, 'The Movement of Sailing Ships as a Climatological Tool', *MM*, 1959, vol 45, p 297.

4 PP, 'Fifth Report from the Select Committee on the Road from London to Holyhead &c', printed 6th July 1819, appendices 23 to 26.

5 NMM, Admiralty Draughts, plan no 6635, box 65, named *Sylph* to a scale of ⅜in to 1ft-0in; she has identical dimensions to the design in Select Committee's report and confirms that Sainty's proposed design was actually built.

6 Dixon Kemp, *Yacht Architecture* (3rd ed, London 1897), vol I, p 8.

7 PP, 'Select Cttee - London to Holyhead', *op cit*, p 61.

8 Hervey Benham, *Last Stronghold of Sail* (London 1948), p 52.

9 James Ballingall, *The Mercantile Navy Improved* (London 1832), pp 124–7.

10 *Lloyd's List*, 2nd May 1826, for date of arrival.

11 David Steel, *The Elements and Practice of Naval Architecture* (London 1805), plate XX.

12 Abraham Rees, *The Cyclopaedia; or, Universal Dictionary of Arts, Sciences, and Literature* (London 1820); the plans of ships appear in vol III of the plates under 'Naval Architecture', plate XII.

13 G W Munro, 'East Indiamen', *Marine Models*, June 1934, vol 7, no 3, pp 64–5. I am grateful to B W Bathe when he was curator of Shipping at the Science Museum for drawing my attention to this article and loaning me his copy of it.

14 India Office Library, log-books nos 40 A-H.

15 David Steel, *Art of Making Masts and Yards* (2nd ed, London 1816), p 100.

16 India Office Library, logbook no 40E.

17 John Edye, *Calculations of Ships and Vessels of War* (London 1832), esp pp 100-1.

18 India Office Library, logbook no 40C.

19 David Steel, *The Elements and Practice of Rigging and Seamanship*, vol I (London 1794), p 37.

20 Carl C Cutler, *Queens of the Western Ocean* (Annapolis, Maryland 1961), p 67.

21 Hilhouse Collection, fo 34. I am grateful to John C G Hill of Charles Hill & Sons Ltd for his assistance in making this plan available to me. The dimensions and

extracts of the CH Registers were kindly furnished by Grahame Farr.

22 Extracts of advertisement supplied by Grahame Farr.

23 John C G Hill, *Shipshape and Bristol Fashion* (2nd ed, Liverpool c 1958), p 94.

24 NMM, Admiralty Draughts, plan no 6457, box 53.

25 Science Museum, neg no 5955 for fo 42 and no 6101 for fo 51.

26 John Fincham, *Treatise on Masting Ships* (3rd ed, London 1854), volume of text, p 28.

27 Howard I Chapelle, *National Watercraft Collection* (Washington 1960), United States National Museum Bulletin 219, p 24.

28 Montague Guest and William B Boulton, *The Royal Yacht Squadron, Memorials of its Members* (1903), p 137.

29 James A Sharp, *Memoirs of the Life & Services of Rear-Admiral Sir William Symonds Kt* (London 1858), p 68.

30 John Fincham, 'Dimensions and Calculated Elements of some of the Vessels of the Royal Yacht Club', in William Morgan and Augustin Creuze (editors), *Papers on Naval Architecture* (London 1826), vol I, Article XXVIII, pp 208-17. Fincham later reprinted some of the particulars in his *History of Naval Architecture* (1851).

31 *Ibid*, p 214.

32 Plans of model in Science Museum are reproduced in David R MacGregor, *The Tea Clippers, their History and Development 1833–1875* (London 1983), p 37.

33 Fincham, 'Dimensions . . . of Vessels of Royal Yacht Club', *op cit*, p 217.

34 Guest and Boulton, *The Royal Yacht Squadron, op cit*, p 170.

35 Baring Bros Archives, Letter Book 5D, fo 470-3 (6th October 1986).

36 Basil Lubbock, *Opium Clippers* (Glasgow 1933), p 187.

37 John Fincham, *History of Naval Architecture* (London 1851), p 294.

38 Baring Bros Archives, Letter Book 9, fo 55.

39 *Ibid*, HC, 3.35, Pat V, dated 4th May 1839.

40 *Ibid*, Letter Book 9, fo 217-8.

41 John F Gibson, *Brocklebanks 1770–1950* (Liverpool 1953), vol I, pp 84 and 233.

42 David R MacGregor, *Merchant Sailing Ships 1815–1850* (London 1984), p 77, fig 78.

43 Thomas Brocklebank's notebook deposited with Brocklebank archives in Liverpool Maritime Museum.

44 Gibson, *Brocklebanks, op cit*, p 114.

45 *Ibid*, p 80.

46 Peter Hedderwick, *A Treatise on Marine Architecture* (Edinburgh 1830), p 178.

47 David Steel, *The Elements and Practice of Naval Architecture* (London 1805), folio volume of plates, pl. XXVI.

48 PP, 'Select Cttee . . . London to Holyhead', *op cit*, pp 59-60.

49 *Ibid*, appendix no 24.

50 *Ibid*,

51 Hedderwick, *A Treatise on Marine Architecture, op cit*, p 147.

52 *Ibid*, p 242.

53 Science Museum, plan no A/6/29.

54 A Hall & Sons Yard Book, transcribed by James Henderson.

55 John Leather, 'The Shipbuilding Bayleys', *MM*, 1965, vol 51, p 138.

56 James Evans ('Quaysier'), *Recollections* (Berwick-on-Tweed, 1908), p 25.

57 I am grateful to W Caufield of Morpeth for information on the smacks, their crews and accommodation.

58 Baring Bros Archives, DEP 11 4 (viii), Capt Shewan, 'East Coast Ships and Seamen' (MS).

59 Query by Michael Bouquet, 'English-built Smacks in Scottish Packet Trades', *MM*, 1963, vol 49, p 75; replies by Robert Craig, *MM*, 1963, vol 49, pp 232-3, W Salisbury and John Leather, *MM*, 1964, vol 50, pp 66-8.

60 Data supplied to me by W Caufield, based on figures in the *Leith Commercial List* 1832-3, which recorded movements of ships sailing in and out of Leith.

61 W Caufield, 'English-built Smacks in Scottish Packet Trades', *MM*, 1964, vol 50, p 236.

62 'The "Aberdeen Bow"', the *Aberdeen Journal*, 12th July 1848.

63 See Basil Greenhill, *The Merchant Schooners* (London 1951), vol I, esp pp 9-11; Michael R Bouquet, *No Gallant Ship* (London 1959), pp 70-80; Hervey Benham, *Once Upon a Tide* (London 1955), pp 49-54; and Basil Lubbock, *Last of the Windjammers*, vol I (Glasgow 1927), pp 437-45.

64 Henry Cheal, *The Ships and Mariners of Shoreham* (London 1909), p 62 *et seq*. A picture of the schooner *Parga* appears in Basil Lubbock, *Last of the Windjammers*, vol I, *op cit*, p 440.

65 T J Ditchburn in discussion to paper by Joseph Maudslay, 'An Improvement in the Form of Ships', *Transactions of the Institution of Naval Architects*, 1860, vol I, p 56. Ditchburn gave the *Time*'s date of building as 1835, but a slip like this is easily overlooked when the builder is speaking from memory about a vessel constructed thirty years earlier.

66 Basil Lubbock, *The Opium Clippers, op cit*, p. 126.

67 Basil Lubbock, *Last of the Windjammers* (2nd ed, Glasgow 1935), vol II, p 358.

68 Thos. Golding, 'Rantipike Schooner', *MM*, 1929, vol 15, p 202.

69 NMM, Admiralty Draughts, plan no 6439E, box 65.

70 Howard I Chapelle, *Search for Speed under Sail 1700–1855* (New York 1967), pp 304-5.

71 R W Hidy, *The House of Baring in American Trade & Finance, 1763–1861* (1949), notes to Chapter VII, pp 524-5.

72 Typed extracts of letters bound in book form and preserved in the office of Blythe, Greene, Jourdain & Co Ltd, London, fo 301, dated 20th April 1834.

73 *Ibid*, fo 382, dated 6th October 1834.

74 *Ibid*, fo 555, dated 28th September 1835.

75 *Ibid*, fo 430, dated 5th January 1835.

76 *Ibid*, fo 769, dated 18th October 1836.

77 *Ibid*, fo 785.

78 *Ibid*, fo 914, dated 19th July 1837.

79 1837 edition of *Lloyd's Register* shows destined voyage as Mauritius, and no other vessel named *Rapid* has a similar voyage assigned.

80 Sharp, *William Symonds, op cit*, pp 128-9.

81 Thomas White Jnr, *The Theory and Practice of Ship Building* (London, 2nd ed, 1851) pp 29-30.

82 Sharp, *William Symonds, op cit*, p 614.

83 *The Canton Register*, 3rd February 1835, vol 8, no 5, p 19.

84 Lubbock, *Opium Clippers, op cit*, pp 77-8.

85 Andrew Henderson, 'On Ocean Steamers and Clipper Ships', reprint of *Report of British Association for the Advancement of Science*, 1854, p 2.

86 Lubbock, *Opium Clippers, op cit*, pp 382-4.

87 Andrew Henderson, 'On the "Descriptive Measurement" of Ships and Steamers', reprint of *Journal of the Society of Arts*, 17th August 1855, p 3.

88 Lubbock, *Opium Clippers, op cit*, pp 93-4 and 382.

89 NMM, Admiralty Draughts, lines plan no 4574, box 64.

90 Lubbock, *Opium Clippers, op cit*, p 119.

91 NMM, Admiralty Draughts, plan no 3957, box 56. A composite outline sail plan for the brigs *Pantaloon, Waterwitch* and *Rapid*, the respective sails and spars

being differentiated by coloured inks.
92 Frank C Bowen, *The Golden Age of Sail* (London 1925), pl 22. This brig was built in 1833.
93 John Phipps, *Ship Building in India* (Calcutta 1840), pp 113-15.
94 Lubbock, *Opium Clippers, op cit*, p 134.
95 Phipps, *Ship Building in India, op cit*, pp 134-5.
96 Lubbock, *Opium Clippers, op cit*, pp 382-4.
97 Henry Hall, *Report on the Ship-Building Industry of the United States* (Washington, DC, 1884; reprint New York 770), p 72. This is the popular title of this report, but it originally appeared as the final section of vol 8 of the Tenth Census published by the Department of the Interior, Census Office.
98 Hidy, *The House of Baring in American Trade, op cit*, p 190.
99 Baring Bros Archives, HC 3.35. Letter dated 19th September 1845 shows that Baring's asked £5000 for ship but that an offer of £4500 was received. Letter dated 27th September 1845 states that ship delivered to purchasers, but no price mentioned and letter from London letter book (LB 15 fo 318), which might have commented on price, is missing.
100 MS list of Liverpool shipbuilders compiled by W Stewart Rees, dated 23rd November 1947.
101 *The Times*, c 1944, quoting 'a Liverpool Paper' dated 20th September 1844.
102 See David R. MacGregor, 'Some Early British Tea Clippers', *MM*, 1948, vol 34, p 74.
103 Chapelle, *Search for Speed under Sail, op cit*, pp 286-87.
104 *Ibid*, p 288.
105 Hall, *Report on Ship-Building Industry, op cit*, p 84.
106 Carl C Cutler, *Greyhounds of the Sea; the Story of the American Clipper Ship* (New York 1930), pp 92-3 and 107.
107 George Moorsom, *A Brief Review & Analyses of the Laws for the Admeasurement of Tonnage* (London 1852), p 152, quoting report of the Commission.
108 5 and 6 William IV, c 56.
109 Moorsom, *Laws for Admeasurement of Tonnage, op cit*, pp 154-7; also quoted in David R MacGregor, *The Tea Clippers, op cit*, p 248.
110 John Lyman, 'Register Tonnage and its Measurement', *American Neptune*, 1945, vol 5, p 229. For a fairly similar drawing, see Pelham Richardson, *Practical Digest of the Law of Merchant Ships and Seamen* (London 1847), p 18.

Chapter Four

1 Graeme Sommer, 'The London & Edinburgh Shipping Co Ltd of Leith', *Sea Breezes*, 1963, vol 36, pp 144 and 146.
2 John Lyman, 'Register Tonnage and its Measurement', *The American Neptune*, 1945, vol 5, pp 228-9.
3 'The "Aberdeen Bow"', the *Aberdeen Journal*, 12th July 1848, p 5.
4 *Ibid*.
5 Builder's cost account, transcribed by James Henderson.
6 NMM, LR survey report, Aberdeen, no 560.
7 Boyd Cable, 'The World's First Clipper', *MM*, 1943, vol 29, pp 66'91.
8 John Lyman, 'The *Scottish Maid* as the World's First Clipper', *MM*, 1944, vol 30, pp 194-9; W Salisbury, 'Hollow Water-Lines and Early Clippers', *MM*, 1946, vol 32, pp 237-41; Howard I Chapelle, 'The First-Clipper', *MM*, 1948, vol 34, pp 26-33.
9 Boyd Cable, 'The World's First Clipper', *MM, op cit*, p 68.
10 Howard I Chapelle, 'The First Clipper', *MM, op cit*, esp pp 26-8.
11 Boyd Cable, 'The World's First Clipper', *MM, op cit*, pp 76-7.
12 James Sellar, 'Hall's of Aberdeen', *Sea Breezes*, 1924, vol VI, p 57.
13 Science Museum, sailing ship collection; plan press B, drawer 2.
14 Howard I Chapelle, *The Search for Speed under Sail, 1700–1855* (New York 1967), p 151 and footnote.
15 Howard I Chapelle, 'The First Clipper', *MM, op cit*, p 33.
16 'The "Aberdeen Bow"', *Aberdeen Journal, op cit*.
17 Basil Lubbock, *The Opium Clippers* (Glasgow 1933), p 322.
18 'The "Aberdeen Bow"', *Aberdeen Journal, op cit.*.
19 *Ibid*.
20 I am grateful to James Henderson for the loan of a copy he obtained from Alexander Hall & Sons Ltd. This diagram was also reproduced in the *Artizan*, June 1850, vol VIII, plate 10.
21 'The "Aberdeen Bow"', *Aberdeen Journal, op cit*.
22 *Ibid*.
23 See 'Aberdeen Clipper Bow', the *Artizan*, June 1850, vol VIII, p 126.
24 Boyd Cable, 'The World's First Clipper', *MM, op cit*, p 82 *et seq*.
25 William Skene, *East Neuk Chronicles* (1905). This extract was transcribed by

James Henderson. 'East Neuk' is the local name for the eastern end of Aberdeen.

26 NMM, LR survey report, Aberdeen, no 1227.

27 'The "Aberdeen Bow"', *Aberdeen Journal, op cit.*

28 Lines taken off half-model of *Benjamin Elkin* by James Henderson, when in possession of Mr Smith, late managing director of Alexander Hall & Sons Ltd.

29 NMM, R C Anderson, *Cataloguing of Ship-Models* (London 1952), p 71, referring to item no 1845-5.

30 Builder's cost account, transcribed by James Henderson.

31 *Sydney Morning Herald*, 14th January 1854.

32 NMM, LR survey report, Aberdeen no 1064.

33 'The "Aberdeen Bow"', *Aberdeen Journal, op cit.*

34 See Basil Greenhill, *The Merchant Schooners* (London 1951), vol I, p 13.

35 Diaries in possession of Alexander Stephen & Sons Ltd, Glasgow.

36 John Fincham, *Outline of Ship Building* (3rd ed, London 1852), plate 20. No schooner built by A Hall agrees exactly with the dimensions given by Fincham, although several schooners such as the *Torrington* or the *Amelia* closely approximate the dimensions. The tonnage he gives is probably old measurement.

37 Photostat of lines plan from a Dutch Museum, in possession of Howard I Chapelle; examined October 1964.

38 Lines plan in possession of F Holm-Petersen, Denmark.

39 Data supplied by John Stevens, Maritime Museum of Canada.

40 *Illustrated London News*, 21st February 1852.

41 *Ibid.*

42 Painting in possession of Alan Stinchcombe of Okehampton, who loaned it to me in 1952.

43 David R MacGregor, *The Tea Clippers their History and Development 1833–1875*, (London 1983), pp 49-50.

44 James Evans ('Quaysider'), *Recollections* (Berwick-on-Tweed, 1908), pp 28-9 and 40.

45 Tower Hamlets Borough Council (formerly Poplar Borough Council), Central Library; data on Duthie family compiled by Boyd Cable.

46 From a lines plan of the schooner *Proto* in my possession, being a tracing of the original done in c 1935.

47 Glasgow University, Register of Business Archives, William Denny Brothers, private ledger, fo 419.

48 *Stockton Herald*, 1st November 1850. I am grateful to Peter Barton for this quotation, and for information on the *Caledonia* when owned in Stockton. Also to David I Moor for contract price and letter of acceptance.

49 Michael R Bouquet, *No Gallant Ship* (London 1959), p 113.

50 George Moorsom, *Brief Review and Analyses of the Laws for the Admeasurement of Tonnage* (London 1852), p 94.

51 NMM, lithograph by T G Dutton dedicated to the merchants of Mexico; neg no 7413.

52 *The Times*, 10th January 1846. p 7, quoting *Liverpool Mercury*, nd.

53 'Memoir of the late T.J. Ditchburn', *Transactions of the Institution of Naval Architects*, 1870, vol XI, pp 241-6. The *Swordfish* does not figure in the list of ships, presumably because she was not built in his yard.

54 NMM, Admiralty Draughts, lines of HMS *Recruit*, plan no 3740, box 53.

55 P R Marett, *Yachts and Yacht Building: being a Treatise on the Construction of Yachts* (London 1865), p 85. Plate 5 gives her lines plan.

56 John Grantham, 'On the *Richard Cobden* Iron Sailing Ship', *Transactions of the Institution of Naval Architects*, 1871, vol XII, p 254 and plate IX. The article and discussion on its have been used for describing the ship.

57 NMM, LR survey reports for iron ships.

58 W H Webb, *Plans of Wooden Vessels... Built by William H Webb in the City of New York* (1958) 2 vols.

59 Howard I Chapelle, *The Search for Speed under Sail 1700–1855* (New York 1967), p 290, fig 84.

60 *Ibid*, p 321.

61 *Ibid*, pp 322-6.

62 *Ibid*, pp 327-30.

63 Carl C Cutler, *Five Hundred Sailing Records of American Built Ships* (Mystic, Conn, 1952), pp 84-5.

64 See David R MacGregor, *The China Bird: the History of Captain Killick and the Firm he Founded, Killick Martin & Co* (London 1986), pp 105 and 107 for quotations and summary from M F Maury's *Sailing Directions* (1859 8th ed).

65 Lloyd's Register of Shipping, Visitation Committee Reports, annual visit of 1851.

66 *The Whitehaven Herald*, Saturday, 19th August 1848. Extract made for me by Daniel Hay, Borough Librarian, Whitehaven.

67 Duncan MacLean, *Clipper Ships and Packets, 1851–1853* (Washington, DC, 1952). Thirty-nine of MacLean's reports were collected and reprinted in facsimile by John Lyman to form this valuable source material.

Chapter Five

1 J Scott Russell, *The Modern System of Naval Architecture* (London 1865), vol I, p 352.
2 John Grantham, *Iron Ship-Building* (London 1858), p 96.
3 Grantham, *Iron Ship-Building, op cit*, pp 86-7.
4 A S & Sons, Letter Book A, letter to William Duthie Esq, London, dated 18th November 1858.
5 Grantham, *Iron Ship-Building, op cit*, p 98.
6 George Moorsom, *A Brief Review and Analyses of the Laws for the Admeasurement of Tonnage* (London 1852), pp 71 *et seq*. Moorsom was trained as a naval architect.
7 *Ibid*, p 78. The calculations on which this table is based are explained earlier in the same chapter.
8 See Grantham, *Iron Ship-Building* (5th ed, London 1868), supplement, pp 237-41. Also Charles F T Young, *The Fouling and Corrosion of Iron Ships* (London 1867), esp chapter V; and W H White, *A Manual of Naval Architecture* (2nd ed, London 1882), pp 415-24.
9 White, *Manual of Naval Architecture, op cit*, p 416.
10 A S & Sons, Letter Book A, letter to Thomas Hood Esq, Hull, dated 23rd October 1858.
11 Young, *Fouling and Corrosion of Iron Ships, op cit*, p 66.
12 Booklet issued c 1960 by Peacock & Buchan Ltd, Southampton.
13 See White, *Manual of Naval Architecture, op cit*, pp 416-24 and Young, *Fouling and Corrosion of Iron Ships, op cit*, chapter VII.
14 *LR*, Visitation Committee Reports, year 1853.
15 *Ibid*.
16 *Ibid*.
17 *Annals of Lloyd's Register* (London 1934), p 83.
18 *Lloyd's Register of British and Foreign Shipping, 1 July 1855 to 30 June 1856* (London 1855), p 29.
19 LR, Visitation Committee Reports, year 1855.
20 Andrew Murray, *Theory and Practice of Ship-Building* (reprinted from *Encyclopaedia Britannica*, Edinburgh 1861), p 104.
21 J Scott Russell, *Modern System of Naval Architecture, op cit*, pp 372 and 380.
22 *The Times*, 7th January 1846, p 7, column 1, quoting *North British Railway and Shipping Journal* (nd)
23 AS & Sons, Diary, 'Remarks on 1851'.
24 AS & Sons, Letter Book A, fo 259, c 30th September 1858.
25 I am very grateful to Winston V Langdon of Hornersville, Missouri, for placing at my disposal his research into the building of iron ships before 1865.
26 John Grantham, *Iron Ship-Building* (1858), *op cit*, pp 221-33.
27 W J Macquorn Rankine, *Shipbuilding, Theoretical and Practcial* (London 1866), plates F 1-5.
28 Capt H Parker and Frank C Boven, *Mail and Passenger Steamers of the Nineteenth Century* (London 1928), p 193.
29 Data supplied by Peter Barton, then residing at Middlesbrough, 15th December 1966.
30 Liverpool Museum, Sailing Ship Collection, MS list of ships built by Jones, Quiggin & Co.
31 AS & Sons, Diary, 29th September 1862.
32 *Log Chips*, May 1951, vol 2, p 72. John Lyman was the publisher and principal contributor.
33 Basil Lubbock, *The Blackwall Frigates* (Glasgow 1922), pp 300-2.
34 Frederick W Wallace, *Wooden Ships and Iron Men* (London 1924), p 71.
35 *Ibid*. See also Wallace's other books, *In the Wake of the Windships* (London 1927), and *Record of Canadian Shipping* (Toronto 1929).
36 Carl C Cutler *Greyhounds of the Sea* (New York 1930), pp 412-47.
37 *Ibid*; three ships in the 1854 total taken from Richard C McKay, *Some Famous Sailing Ships and their Builder Donald McKay* New York 1928), p 371.
38 Patent no 14,034, dated 24th 1852. See also description by John White, 'On an Improved Method of Building Diagonal Ships', *Transactions of the Institution of Naval Architects,* 1860, vol 1, pp 112-20 and plate IV. An informative set of plans of White's steamer *Vectis*, are to be found in Scott Russell, *Modern System of Naval Architecture, op cit*, vol III, pl 125.
39 White, *Manual of Naval Architecture, op cit*, p. 117. The dates of building and rigs have been added from *Lloyd's Register*, the *Illustrated London News*, and other sources.
40 Murray, *Theory and Practice of Ship-Building, op cit*, pp 92-3.
41 NMM, LR survey reports, Aberdeen, no 1647.
42 NMM, LR survey reports, London, plans case.
43 *Official Descriptive and Illustrated Catalogue of the Great Exhibition* (London 1851), 3 vols; class 2, item 141.
44 NMM, LR survey class reports, London, no 18764.
45 *Ibid*, from examination of London boxes nos 17051 to 19100. The half-model was returned to Lloyd's Register prior to 1939 and now cannot be found.
46 Commissioners of Patents, *Abridgements of Specifications Relating to Shipbuilding, Repairing, Sheathing, Launching &c* (London 1862), pp 59-60, 106-7, 114.
47 John Jordan, 'On Composite Ships', *Proceedings of the Scottish Shipbuilders' Association* (Session 1863-64), p 39, statement in discussion made by John D Napier.
48 *Ibid*, statement by John Jordan in discussion.
49 AS & Sons, Diary, 23rd July 1961, copy of letter from L H Macintyre & Co.
50 The *Albion* (Liverpool), 10th October 1853, p 9.
51 Some of the ships' names from A C Wardle's MS list in Liverpool Museum, Shipping Collection (vol 3, p 28); description of building from appropriate volumns of *Lloyd's Register*.
52 John Jordan, 'On Composite Ships', *op cit*, p 41.
53 Patent no 517, dated 26th February 1862.
54 AS & Sons, Letter Book 'A', fo 191, letter to William Stephen dated 7th June 1861.
55 AS & Sons, Diary, 31st July 1861.
56 *Ibid*, 10th October 1861.
57 *Ibid*, 11th October 1861.
58 *Ibid*, 10th and 12th October 1861.
59 *Ibid*, 16th January 1862.
60 Lloyd's Register, Surveyors Committee Reports, May 1838 to June 1874, report dated 31st January 1863.
61 AS & Sons, Diary, 24th and 25th March, 1863.
62 *Ibid*, 16th October 1863.
63 *The Times*, 6th December 1865, p 11.
64 *Ibid*, 30th April 1866, p 11.
65 John Lyman, 'Composite and Diagonal Building', *Log Chips*, 1951, vol 2, no 7, p 78.
66 Alexander Hall & Sons, cost account transcribed by James Henderson.
67 J. Bennett, 'Observations on the Effect Produced by Iron Masts . . .', *Papers on Naval Architecture*, conducted by William Morgan and Augustin Creuze (London 1826), vol I, p 106.
68 *Ibid*, p 101. See also report from Deptford signed 'CP' and dated 15th March

1825 in *Mechanics Magazine*, 1825, vol 3, p 432.

69 Patent dated 15th May 1820, no 4461.
70 *The Times*, 31st January 1851.
71 Robert Kipping, *Elementary Treatise on Sails and Sailmaking* (London 1858), pp 171-3.
72 Patent dated 30th November 1850, no 13,368.
73 Letter from H D P Cunningham, *Nautical Magazine*, May 1853, vol 22, pp 261-6.
74 *The Liverpool Telegraph and Shipping Gazette*, 18th May 1855.
75 Oil Painting of ship seen at the Parker Gallery, London, on 5th November 1965.
76 AS & Sons, Letter Book 'A', dated 5th April 1858; quotation to George Smith & Sons, Glasgow.
77 See W A McEwan and A H Lewis, *Encyclopaedia of Nautical Knowledge* (Cambridge, Maryland 1953), pp 179 and 565; also Kipping, *Treatise on Sails and Sailmaking, op cit*, pp 174-5.
78 *Illustrated London News*, December 1855; description and engraving of the ship.
79 *Ibid*, August 1862, description and engraving of the ship; also contemporary lithograph by T G Dutton.
80 Basil Lubbock, *Last of the Windjammers* (Glasgow 1927), vol I, p 141.
81 Wallace, *Wooden Ships and Iron Men, op cit, pp 150* and *155*.
82 H D P Cunningham, 'On Working Ships' Yards', *Transactions of the Institution of Naval Architects*, 1867, vol VIII, pp 183-6, and plate VII, figs 7 and 8.
83 George Moorsom, *A Brief Review & Analyses for the Laws for the Admeasurement of Tonnage* (London 1852), p 180.
84 *Ibid*, pp 12 and 78.
85 HM Customs, *Instructions to Measuring Surveyors* (London 1861), pp 42-6, quoting from the Act.
86 Moorsom, *Laws for Admeasurement of Tonnage, op cit*, p 70.
87 17 and 18 Vict, c 104, sec 20-29.
88 John Lyman, 'Register Tonnage and its Measurement', *American Neptune*, 1945, vol 5, p 231.
89 Thomas H Farrer was appointed assistant secretary to the Marine Department of the Board of Trade in 1850 and later became chief secretary. See Roger Prouty, *Transformation of the Board of Trade 1830–1855* (London 1957), p 93; and W S Lindsay, *History of Merchant Shipping and Ancient Commerce* (London 1876), vol III, pp 298-9.
90 Lindsay, *History of Merchant Shipping, op cit*, vol III, p 309, note 1.

Chapter Six

1 See *Cornwall Chronicle* (published in Launceston, Tasmania), 1st September 1855.
2 *Australia and New Zealand Gazette*, 11th February 1854, quoting *Southern Cross* of Auckland (nd).
3 *Sydney Morning Herald*, 2nd April 1851, p 2, quoting an 'Adelaide paper'.
4 Carl C Cutler, *Queens of the Western Ocean* (Annapolis 1961), p 294.
5 *Australia and New Zealand Gazette*, 10th April 1852, p 116.
6 *The Times*, 13th September 1851, p 6.
7 *Australia and New Zealand Gazette*, 1st May 1852, p 149.
8 *Illustrated London News*, 12th April 1851.
9 NMM, LR survey report, Aberdeen box.
10 *Ibid.*
11 *Ibid.*
12 David R MacGregor, 'Some Early British Tea-Clippers', *MM*, 1948, vol 34, plate 4 (facing p 81).
13 Andrew Murray, *Theory and Practice of Ship-Building* (Edinburgh 1861), plate IV; and Basil Lubbock, *The China Clippers* (5th ed, Glasgow 1922), p 128.
14 AS & Sons, Alexander Stephens' Notebook 'C', beginning 7th January 1852.
15 *Ibid.*
16 *Glasgow Herald*, 23rd August 1852.
17 *Glasgow Herald*, 4th April 1853, quoting the *Mail* [probably *North British Daily Mail* published in Glasgow], nd.
18 *Ibid.*
19 *Argus* (Melbourne), 3rd August 1854.
20 AS & Sons, Alexander Stephen's diary, 1856: various entries commencing with 'work in hand on 1st January 1856'.
21 See Howard I Chapelle, *Search for Speed Under Sail, 1700 to 1855* (New York 1967), p 409.
22 *Sydney Morning Herald*, 2 Feb 1854, letter to the Editor.
23 Dimensions from LR survey reports at NMM. The iron ships are filed separately.
24 R S McLellan, *Anchor Line 1835–1956*, (Glasgow 1956), p 161.
25 Basil Lubbock, *Last of the Windjammers*, vol II (2nd ed, Glasgow 1935), pp 10-11.
26 NMM, LR survey reports, Aberdeen no 749.
27 *Illustrated London News*, 1853.
28 *The Albion* (Liverpool), 10 Oct 1853, p 9 (second edition).
29 NMM, LR survey reports, iron ships, box 2, *Sappho*.
30 *Glasgow Herald*, 8th September 1854.

31 I have lost the reference to this quotation, but it was probably from a shipping advertisement in a Glasgow paper.
32 *Gore's General Advertiser* (Liverpool), 30th January 1855, and the *Liverpool Mercury*, 26th June 1855. The information and references were obtained from the Shipping Collection at Liverpool Museum, MS Notebooks kept by Arthur C Wardle (vol I, p 104).
33 *Liverpool Chronicle*, 4th August 1855, p 5.
34 Lubbock, *The China Clippers*, *op cit*, p 132.
35 The *Albion* (Liverpool), 8th April 1856.
36 Lubbock, *The China Clippers*, *op cit*, p 132.
37 *Argus* (Melbourne), 31st December 1855, p 4.
38 Many of the vessels, including those not listed in volumes of *Lloyd's Register of Shipping* are from the MS list prepared by Arthur C Wardle, *op cit*.
39 The first edition was dated 1850, published in New York. This third edition was published in New York and also by John Weale in London.
40 J Scott Russell, 'The Wave' Line Principle of Ship-Construction', part II, *Transactions of the Institution of Naval Architectus*, 1860, vol I, p 205. See also comments and explanations in Dixon Kemp, *Yacht Architecture: a Treatise* (3rd ed, London 1897), chapter VIII.
41 The *Artizan*, 1855, vol XIII, p 199.
42 *Cornwall Chronicle* (Launceston, Tasmania), 1st September 1855.
43 AS & Sons, Alexander Stephen's Jotting Book (including summaries of sermons). These remarks were written at Edinburgh.
44 *North British Daily Mail* (Glasgow), 15th July 1854.
45 The dimensions have intentionally been taken by this Act, because they relate more correctly to the under deck tonnage figure.
46 Chapelle, *Search for Speed under Sail*, *op cit*, plate 112.
47 NMM, LR survey reports, Iron Ships no 655.
48 CH register, no 115 in 1854 at Glasgow. The certificates cover the period 3rd July 1856 to 7th August 1862.
49 AS & Sons, Letter Book 'A', letter dated 26th February 1856 to Robinson & Majoribanks, Glasgow.
50 *Ibid*.
51 AS & Sons, Alexander Stephen's diary 26th October, 2nd November and 19th November 1859.
52 *Ibid*, 13th April 1860.
53 *The Tasmanian Daily News* (Hobart), 1st September 1855.
54 Cmdr Francis Tweedie, 'The Era of Shipbuilding at Annan', *MM*, 1951, vol 37, pp 128-42. This lists the larger ships and their voyages in detail and also gives names and dates of ships built prior to 1853.
55 *Dumfries and Galloway Standard and Advertiser*, 16th August 1854.
56 NMM, LR survey reports, Whitehaven, no 1415.
57 Letter dated 22nd November, but no year given. Newspaper cutting in collection of Dr R C Anderson whose grandfather, Thomas Anderson, held four shares in the ship.
58 Earnings from figures in possession of Benjamin E Nicholson, Carlisle.
59 See Tweedie, 'The Era of Shipbuilding at Annan', *MM*, *op cit*, p 139.
60 As no 58.
61 David MacGregor, *The Tea Clippers, their History and Development 1833–1875* (London 1983 revised edition),pp 53, 56, 60.
62 *Ibid*, p 57, caption to plan.
63 William H Webb, *Plans of Wooden Vessels* (New York, 1895).
64 'The Aberdeen Clipper Ship *Chrysolite*', *Monthly Nautical Magazine and Quarterly Review*, New York, 1855, vol II, pp 40-4.
65 *Illustrated London News*, 3rd January 1852.
66 NMM, LR survey reports, Aberdeen no 1470.
67 Baring Bros archives, Dep 11.4 (vii), fols 12-23, Capt Andrew Shewan's reminiscences.
68 NMM, LR survey reports, Aberdeen no 1550.
69 *Aberdeen Journal*.
70 *Illustrated London News*, 5th March 1853.
71 Chapelle, *Search for Speed under Sail*, *op cit*, plates 100 (*Samuel Russell*) and 105 (*Nightingale*).
72 MacGregor. *Tea Clippers*, *op cit*, p 60.
73 As no 67.
74 William Salisbury, 'Hollow Water-Lines and Early Clippers', *MM*, 1946, vol 32, plate 7 facing p 240.
75 NMM, LR survey reports, plan kept in Aberdeen plans case, report no 1584.
76 Patent no 1482 dated 18th June 1853.
77 Murray, *Theory and Practice of Ship-Building*, *op cit*, p 93.
78 NMM, LR survey reports, Aberdeen, box 3.
79 The *China Mail*, 5th March 1857, no 629, p 39.
80 See Chapelle, *Search for Speed under Sail*, *op cit*, for lines of *Sweepstakes*, late XIV.
81 *Illustrated London News*, 4th November 1854.
82 Notes by Peter Barton. See also R. Martin, *Historical Notes of West Hartlepool and its Founder* (West Hartlepool 1924).
83 David R MacGregor, *The China Bird* (London 1961), pp 9-11.
84 Glasgow Museum and Art Gallery, Shipping Collection, William Simon's 'Spark Book'.
85 AS & Sons, Alexander Stephen Jnr, Notebooks C and D.
86 Webb, *Plans of Wooden Vessels*, *op cit*, for plans of *Challenge* and Webb's comments on design.
87 Carl C Cutler, *Five Hundred Sailing Records of American Built Ships* (Mystic 1952), p 71.
88 Chapelle, *Search for Speed under Sail*, *op cit*, p 368.
89 F W Wallace, *Wooden Ships and Iron Men*, (London 1924), p 45.
90 F W Wallace, *In the Wake of the Windships*, (London 1927), p 45.
91 Wallace, *Wooden Ships and Iron Men*, *op cit*, p 45.
92 For description of stern decoration, see Wallace, *Wake of Windships*, *op cit*, p 47.
93 *Illustrated London News*, 19 February 1853.
94 *Argus* (Melbourne), 1 February 1854.
95 PP, *Mortality on Emigrant Ships*, 1852-3 XCVIII, pp 329-45.
96 *Ibid*; see also report on arrival in *Morning Herald* (Melbourne), 21 September 1852.
97 *Aberdeen Journal*, 11th April 1856.
98 *Australian and New Zealand Gazette*, 1st January 1853, p 1.
99 Chapelle, *Search for Speed under Sail*, *op cit*, pp 359-61.
100 Clark Collection housed in Francis Russell Hart Nautical Museum at Pratt Institute of Naval Architecture, Massachusetts Institute of Technology, Cambridge, Mass.
101 Cutler, *Five Hundred Sailing Records*, *op cit*, pp 9-20.
102 James S Learmont, 'Speed under Sail', *MM*, 1957, vol 43, pp 225-31; notes by Alan Villiers, E Bowness and David R MacGregor, *ibid*, pp 341-2; further notes by H Daniel and H I Chapelle, *ibid*, 1958, vol 44, pp 64-9; John Lyman, E Bowness and R M Bousefield, *ibid*, pp 141-5; R C Anderson, Alex A Hurst and A Lamont, *ibid*, pp 328-31; D L Dennis, *ibid*, 1963, vol 49, p 306.

103 *Australia and New Zealand Gazette*, 16th June 1855, p 485, quoting *Argus* (Melbourne), nd.
104 Source not recorded; must have been a Liverpool paper.
105 Builder's cost account transcribed by James Henderson. In the original, the items for Day Book extras and for Tanks are both £3,463.0.10 which makes it impossible to achieve the total given. Henderson suggests that the Day Book's extras should be £128.15.1, which is the difference between the grand total and the sum of the other items.
106 Murray, *Theory and Practice of Ship-Building*, *op cit*, plate III.
107 'Launch of the Australian Clipper ship *Schomberg*', the *Aberdeen Journal*, 11th April 1855.
108 *Ibid*, and 27th June 1855.
109 Murray, *Theory and Practice of Ship-Building*, *op cit*, p 92.
110 MacGregor, *The Tea Clippers*, *op cit*, p 89; and MacGregor, *The China Bird*, *op cit*, plate I, facing p 16.
111 NMM, LR survey reports, London, box 38, no 17,194.
112 *Sydney Morning Herald*, 23rd March 1854.
114 Vernon C Boyle died 1954 and so the source of the model can no longer be cheked. I took off the lines in 1957 or 1958.
115 NMM, LR survey reports, Bideford box.
116 *Argus* (Melbourne), 2nd February 1854, in describing building of *Tayleur* (quoted from *Liverpool Standard*, nd). Also notes in Warrington Public Library.
117 Names, dimensions and tonnages principally from LR survey reports; additional names from Liverpool Museum, Shipping Collection, MS Notebooks kept by A C Wardle (vol I, p 130).
118 *Argus* (Melbourne), 2nd February 1854 quoting *Liverpool Standard*, nd.
119 *Ibid*, and the *Albion* (Liverpool), 10th October 1853, p 9.
120 *Argus* (Melbourne), 27th April 1854.
121 The *Liverpool Telegraph and Shipping and Commercial Gazette*, 17th May 1855.
122 The *Liverpool Chronicle*, 4th August 1855, p 5.
123 John Grantham, *Iron Ship-Building* (5th ed, London 1858), pp 130-1, 223-5, 227-33.
124 The *Liverpool Chronicle*, 4th August 1855, p 5.
125 Liverpool Museum.
126 Chapelle, *Search for Speed under Sail*, *op cit*, plate 90.
127 MacGregor, *The Tea Clipper*, *op cit*, p 118.
128 *Ibid*.
129 *Illustrated London News*, 17 April 1858.
130 NMM, LR survey reports, Aberdeen box no 3.
132 W S Lindsay, *History of Merchant Shipping and Ancient Commerce* (London 1876), vol IV, p 418.
133 Hervey Benham, *Once Upon A Tide* (London 1955), p 50.
134 *Ibid*, p 52.
135 Chas G Davis, '*Peri*, an English "Butterman" Schooner', *Yachting* (published USA), January 1925, pp 51-2.
136 Robert W Stevens, *On the Stowage of Ships and their Cargoes* (5th ed London 1869), p 180.
137 Henry Cheal Jnr, *The Ships and Mariners of Shoreham* (London 1909), pp 65-6.

Chapter Seven

1 A & S Sons, Alexander Stephen's Diary, 31 Oct and 4 Nov 1863.
2 'Clipper Ships', *Naval Science*, July 1873, vol II, no 6, pp 265–70. No volumes were published after no IV.
3 A S & Sons, Alexander Stephen's Diary, 9 Sept 1962.
4 *Ibid*, 11 Sept 1862.
5 David R MacGregor, *The Tea Clippers, their History and Development 1833–1875* (London 1983), pp 121 and 122.
6 *Ibid*, p 159, for photograph; oil painting in possession of Gilbert Floyd, Blackheath, in 1957, when I inspected it.
7 A S & Sons, Alexander Stephen's Diary, 15 Nov 1861, and loose scrap of paper dated Liverpool 11 Sept 1862 beside entry of that date.
8 Baring Brothers Archives, Capt A Shewan's MS Notes, DEP 11.4. (vi), 'Voyage in *Black Prince* 1866–67'.
9 William Rennie cited as the designer of *Chaa-Sze* in A G Course, Painted Ports, (London 1961), p 44.
10 Baring Bros Archives, class HC. 18.1.4 (i) for contract figure; and Voyages 1863–67 HC. 18.1.2 for cost ready for sea.
11 Baring Bros Archives, Shewan's MS Notes, *op cit*.
12 *Ibid*.
13 *Ibid*.
14 Baring Bros Archives, class HC. 18.1.2, voyages of *Black Prince* 1863–67.
15 AS & Sons, Alexander Stephen's Diary, 4 Sept 1862.
16 *Ibid*, 6 Sept 1862.
17 *Ibid*, 12, 16, 22 and 23 Sept 1862.
18 *Ibid*, 23 Sept 1862.
19 *Ibid*, 21 and 22 Oct 1862.
20 *Ibid*, 6 Nov 1862.
21 *Ibid*, 20 Oct 1863.
22 *Ibid*, 10 Oct 1863.
23 *Glasgow Herald*, 15 Sept 1865.
24 *The Times*, 23 March 1866.
25 Basil Lubbock, *Coolie Ships and Oil Sailers*, (Glasgow 1935), p 85.
26 *Glasgow Daily Herald*, 16 Feb 1866. This newspaper cutting was loaned me by George R Worcester, a descendant of her first owner.
27 Letter written by Captain James Cawse to his wife, dated 18 July 1875. Extract sent me by J C Cawse of Uxbridge in 1954.
28 David R MacGregor, *The Tea Clippers* (1st ed, London 1952), pp 118-19 and 155-6.

29 Basil Lubbock, *The China Clippers* (5th ed, Glasgow 1922), p 246.
30 H D P Cunningham, 'On Working Ships' Yards', *Transactions of the Institution of Naval Architects*, 1867, vol VIII, p 185.
31 NMM, LR survey reports, Sunderland box, nos 880 (*Maitland*) and 9234 (*Undine*).
32 David R MacGregor, *The Tea Clippers 1833–1875, op cit*, pp 110 and 153.
33 NMM, Basil Lubbock Collection, letter from James MacCunn dated 7 July 1911.
34 *Ibid*, letter dated 20 July 1911.
35 Andrew Shewan, *The Great Days of Sail* (London 1927), p 223.
36 NMM, Lubbock Coll, *op cit*, letter from James MacCunn dated 18 June 1911.
37 Letter from James Steele to the Author dated 20 Feb 1950. James Steele died 1955.
38 NMM, Lubbock Coll, *op cit*, letter from James MacCunn dated 23 June 1911.
39 *Ibid*.
40 AS & Sons, Alexander Stephen's Diary, 14, 15 and 18 Nov 1861.
41 *Ibid*, 1 Nov 1865; the ship built by Stephen was the *William Davie*.
42 NMM, LR survey reports, Greenock box, no 5768.
43 *Ibid*, Greenock box, no 4954.
44 See Lubbock, *The China Clippers, op cit*, plate facing p 236.
45 David R MacGregor, *The Tea Clippers 1833–1875, op cit*, p 172.
46 David R MacGregor, *The Tea Clippers (*1st ed), *op cit*, vol VII.
47 Mast particulars from LR survey reports.
48 Basil Lubbock, *Log of the 'Cutty Sark'* (Glasgow 1924), pp 396-7.
49 Lubbock, *The China Clippers, op cit*, Appendix B, p V. This list accompanied the average statement concerning her dismasting.
50 *Ibid*, Appendix H, pp xvii-xxxiii.
51 David R MacGregor, *The Tea Clippers 1833–1875, op cit*, Appendix II, including departure and arrival dates.
52 NMM, Lubbock Coll, *op cit*, letters dated 11 and 17 July 1911.
53 *Ibid*, letter dated 27 Feb 1913.
54 W S Lindsay, *History of Merchant Shipping and Ancient Commerce* (London 1876), vol III, p 419 (footnote).
55 [Sir A Murray Stephen], *A Shipbuilding History 1750–1932* (privately printed c 1932), p 38.
56 Lubbock, *Log of the 'Cutty Sark', op cit*, p 58 for sail plan; and Appendix III, pp 396-7 for spar dimensions.
57 *Ibid*, p 37.
58 For names of ships designed by Waymouth, see 'Clipper Ships', *Naval Science*, July 1873, vol II, no 6, p 275; and W H White, *A Manual of Naval Architecture* (2nd ed, London 1882), p 513.
59 Information on Waymouth from Lloyd's Register of Shipping; also George Blake, *Lloyd's Register of Shipping 1760–1960* (London c 1961).
60 Lines reproduced in Basil Lubbock, *Last of the Windjammers* (2nd ed, Glasgow 1935), vol II, facing p 10.
61 J Scott Russell, *The Modern System of Naval Architecture* (London 1865), vol III, plate 146; and Prof W J M Rankine, *Shipbuilding, Theoretical and Practical* (London 1866), plate D/1.
62 Russell, *Modern System of Naval Architecture, op cit*, vol I, p 652.
63 Plates XXI to XL.
64 Vice-Admiral Edmond Pâris, *Souvenirs de Marine*, (Paris 1889), vol III, plate 176.
65 J Spurling and Basil Lubbock, *Sail* (London 1927), vol I, p 97. This occurred when running her easting down in 1875.
66 Vice-Admiral E Pâris, *L'Art Naval* (Paris 1869), plate XXVII, figs 3, 4 and 5.
67 From information supplied by James Henderson of Aberdeen.
68 Name and date of newspaper has been mislaid, but it is not the Melbourne *Argus* of 11 Jan 1869.
69 *Cutty Sark*'s spar dimensions given by Lubbock, *Log of the 'Cutty Sark', op cit*, pp 396-7; *The Caliph*'s are from A Hall & Sons' cost account, transcribed by James Henderson.
70 White, *Manual of Naval Architecture, op cit*, p 513.
71 MacGregor, *The Tea Clippers 1833–1875, op cit*, p 190.
72 Typed copy of abstract log in my possession.
73 'Tea Clippers', *Aberdeen Journal*, 9 Nov 1892, p 3, quoting *San Francisco Commercial News and Insurance Record* (nd).
74 Logbook owned by L E Evans of Bray, Co Wicklow.
75 Inspected in archives of Lloyd's Register of Shipping.
76 George Blake, *Gellatly's 1862–1962* (London 1962), p 64.
77 Basil Lubbock, *Last of the Windjammers* (Glasgow 1927), vol I, p 186.
78 'Launch of the *John Williams', Chronicle of the London Missionary Society*, Nov 1865, p 304.
79 London Missionary Society, Summary of Board Minutes relating to Mission Ships, meeting of 25 Nov 1867, fo 7.
80 London Missionary Society, Home Letters, Box 12, Folder 5, Jacket A.
81 *Chronicle of the London Missionary Society*, 2 Aug 1869, p 181.
82 Lubbock, *Log of the 'Cutty Sark', op cit*, p 395.
83 Lubbock, *Last of the Windjammers*, vol II, *op cit*, pp 14-15.
84 NMM, Lubbock Coll, *op cit*, letter dated 7 July 1911.
86 Lubbock, *Log of the 'Cutty Sark', op cit*, facing p 31; Cyril L Hume's plan reproduced in MacGregor, *The Tea Clippers 1833–1875, op cit*, p 196.
86 For midship section of *The Tweed* see Basil Lubbock, *The Blackwall Frigates* (Glasgow 1922), facing p 212.
87 Robert E Brettle, *The Cutty Sark: her Designer and Builder, Hercules Linton* (Cambridge 1969), p 18.
88 Baring Bros Archives, class HC 18.2.1, letter to William Walkinshaw, one of the partners, dated 27 Nov 1868.
89 *Ibid*, HC 18.2.12, invoice dated 21 Sept 1869.
90 Lubbock, *The China Clippers, op cit*, pp 297-8.
91 MacGregor, *Tea Clippers 1833–1875, op cit*, p 205.
92 Capt Charles Chapman, *All About Ships* (London c 1869), pp 369-92.
93 Spurling and Lubbock, *Sail*, vol I, *op cit*, p 105.
94 Harold A Underhill, *Deep-Water Sail* (Glasgow 1952), plates 47 and 50.
95 Harold A Underhill, *Masting and Rigging: the Clipper Ship and Ocean Carrier* (Glasgow 1946), p 179.
96 Spurling and Lubbock, *Sail*, vol I, *op cit*, p 113.
97 Basil Lubbock, *The Colonial Clippers* (3rd ed, Glasgow 1924), p 265.
98 *London and China Telegraph*, 7 Nov 1876.
99 David R MacGregor, *Merchant Sailing Ships 1850–1875: Heyday of Sail* (London 1984), figure 277.
100 Chapman, *All About Ships, op cit*, p 83.

INDEX

Page numbers in italics refer to captions of illustrations

Vessels are British, except where stated

Abeona, smuggling cutter, 54
Aberdonian, schooner, 107; costs, 276
Aberdeen, photographs of ships at, *195*, *220*, *230*; schooners replace Leith smacks, 99
Aberdeen bow, *108*, *181*; copied abroad, 116, 124, *209*, *267*; development of, 105 et seq, 216; extreme forms, 109-10, 113-14, 173; first appearance, 100; first three-masted square-rigged vessel, 106, 108; fitting of bowsprit, 105; influence of, 115-21, 134; list of vessels having it, 107; reduces new meausurement tonnage, 106-07, 114-15; use in Holland, 116, 118; variations adopted in many schooners, 85
'Aberdeen' house, 111, 246
Aberdeen Journal, copying of Aberdeen bow, 116, describes launches, 159, 225; describes *Cairngorm* 178, *Robin Hood* 182, *Schomberg*, 195; *Scottish Maid*, 100, lists vessels with Aberdeen bow, 107; reports on *Bon Accord*, 111; *Thermopylae*'s fast speed, 247-48
Aberdeen & London Steam Navigation Co, 99
Aberdeen Public Library, 182
Aberdeen Maritime Museum, 177, 182, 230, 245
Aberdonian, schooner, 101, 107
Abundance, brig, cost, 274
Acadia, ship, 139
Acasta, barque, *109*, *110*; compared with ordinary vessel, 106-07; with other clippers, 109-10, 116; with unknown barques, 108-111; costs, 277; deck layout and sail plan, 110-11; extreme raking stem, 109; hull-form, 107, 109-10, 119; listed, 106-07; reconstruction of lines plan, 109-10; sliding gunter masts, 65, 111
Actaeon, wood construction illustrated, *137*
HMS *Active*, flying kites set, 221, 233, *233*
Acts of Parliament, against smuggling, 14-15; Merchant Shipping Act 1854, 23, 114, 151-52, 154; Navigation Acts, 24; Plantation Registration Act, 24; 'Registry Act' 1786, 24; Registry Act for New Measurement tonnage, 97-98
Ada, ship, 224; costs, 278
Adam Sedgwick, ship, costs, 278
Adams, Balthazar and Edward, builders of *Mary*, 62, 68, of *Thalia*, 62, 68; hull-form of their ships compared, 62, 68
Adams, Edward, builder of *Australia*, 65-66, of *Friendship*, 63, of *Neilson*, 68-69
Adams, Henry, shipbuilder, 62
Adams, Capt James, 172
Admiral (1850), ship, 160
SS *Admiral* (1865), schooner, costs, 278
Admiral Collingwood, barque, 141
Admiralty, commissions building of second *Transit*, 51; declines to buy first *Transit*, 50; lines taken off vessels, 38, 168; takes over Post Office packets, 14, 48, 59
Admiralty draughts, of *Anonyma*, 101, of *Britannia* and *Cupid*, 40, of HMS *Fly*, 26, of French ships, 38, of HM *Helena* 31; of HMS *Lyme*, 28; of *Nightingale* ex *Marchioness of Salisbury*, 62, of HMS *Rambler*, 29, of *Shamrock* 55; of ships bought into Navy 13, 40
Adventure, brig cost, 275
Aerolite, ship, described, 201; passages 201
Agamemnon, ship, 137-38, beam-to-length ratio, 164
Agda ex *Waitangi*, capstan, 147
Agnes, brig, costs, 274
Agnes Rose, ship, *230*, 230
Agricola, brig, costs, 278
Aimwell, brig, 83
Albion, brig, costs, 275
Albion, (Liverpool), describes *Fiery Cross* (1855), 188; describes *Margaret Deane*, 166
Aldous of Brightlingsea, 19
Alert, brig, costs, 275
Alexander (*c*1770-80), Science Museum model, 33; compared with *Jupiter*, 44, hull-form and deck layout, 32, 34
Alexander (rebuilt 1777), Bristol privateer, 32
Alexander (1785), cutter brig, 24
Alexander (1833), schooner, 80, 84, *84*
Alexander Baring, ship, 95-96
Alexander Hall, barque, costs, 277, half-model, 104, *104*; hull-form, 104, 107; listed 109
SS *Alexander Pirie*, costs, 279
Alfred Graving dock, Williamstown, *263*
Alhambra, ship, 141
Alive, barque, costs, 279
All About Ships (Chapman), 258, *258*
Alma, iron schooner, 214
Alnwick Castle, schooner, costs, 276
Altcar, ship, 135
Ambassador, ship, *145*, 263
Amelia, schooner, 107; costs, 277
America, operates packet ships, 97, 123; War of Independence, 13, 28-29, 38
America, schooner yacht, 55; compared with *Storm Cloud*, 167-68; with *Mosquito*, 122, with *Sunny South*, 169; hull-form, 167, 169
American Revolution, *see* America, War of Independence
Amur, barque, 161, 143
Anderson, Dr R C, 114, 164
Andrew Forbes, smack, costs, 275
Andromeda, ship, 146
Angler, brigantine, costs, 276
Anglesea, Marquis of, 73
Anglo-Chinese War, 74, 95
Ann Duthie, ship, 230; described, 229-30
Ann McKim, 96, 97, American ship, compared with *Falcon*, 72; hull-form 97; not the first clipper, 72; prismatic coefficient, 20; lines and sail plans redrawn 97; passages 97
Ann Smith, barque, 109; costs, 276
Annabella (1834), barque, 88
Annabella (1842), schooner, costs, 276
Annan, shipbuilding at, 173-74
Annandale (1827), 173
Annandale (1854), 173, 174; compared with *Thermopylae*, 175, with *Chariot of Fame*, 136-37, with *Storm Cloud*, 170, 172; deck layout, 175; design not dictated by owner, 172, 174, 270; dimensions analysed, 173; extreme clipper, 155, 172, 174; hull-form, 174-75; beam-to-length ratio, 164, 175; journalist's description, 173-74; timber construction, 131, 137, 175, 194; passages, 175; sail plan, 175; scantlings, 137, 200, 217; speed, 199-201; two partial dismastings, 174-75
Annesley, William, diagonal construction, 23, 140
SS *Annette*, auxiliary, 133
Annie Dixon, brig, 183
Annsbro', schooner, 120
Anonyma, brig yacht, 93, 94; becomes opium clipper, 92-93, 95; compared with *Scottish Maid*, 105, with *William Punton*, 111; development of cutter hull, 55, 59, 92; hull-form, 92; reconstructed sail plan, 93-94
Anstruther, Captain, 88
HMS *Ant*, Bermudian schooner, 16
Antiope, ship, 150
Aphrodita, ship, 134-35, 150
Arabia, ship, *96*
PS *Arabia*, 138
Aracan, ship, described, 201
Archduke, steamer, 142
Archer, American clipper, *153*
Architectura Navalis Mercatoria, 32, 243
Arctic, American packet, *139*
Ardaseer, opium clipper, 94
HMS *Arethusa* (1781), frigate, 37
Argonaut (1858), Dutch ship, *179*
Argonaut (1876), ship, 258-59, *260*, 261
Argus (Melbourne), detailed reports of ships, 190, 215
Ariel (1837), opium clipper barque, 94
Ariel (1865), ship, *235*, *236*, *238*; compared with *Maitland* *231-32*, with *William Le Lacheur* 228; hull-form and deck layout compared with other ships 234-38, 241; speed and fast passage, 335; type of windlass, 147; photograph, *216*; measurements, 234; scantlings, 237
Ariel (1870), schooner, *279*
Arima, ship, 144
Armament, of Bristol privateers, 32-33; of *Cupid*, 41; of HMS *Dolphin*, 89; of East Indiaman, 71; French privateer, 38; opium clipper *Time*, 95; regulated by Smuggling Acts, 14; of smuggler (1791), 54
Armstrong patent windlass, *146*, 146
Artizan, brig, costs, 278
Artizan (London), 142; technical description of *Storm Cloud*, 167-68, 193
Asia, ship, costs, 274
Assam, steamer, 91, 142
Assam Co, 91
Asterope, ship, costs, 278
Atkins, George, draughtsman, 93
Atkinson, Capt John A, 57
Atlas (Boston), detailed reports of ships, 126, 184, 190
Aultnaskiach, smack, costs, 275
Aurora, ship, 183
Australia, gold rush to, 157, 159

Australia, ship, hull-form, 62
Auxiliary ships, *Annette*, 133; boom in building, 216; extra expenses involved, 250; SS *Euphrates*, 169; *Highflyer* designed as one, 226; *Hurricane* converted, 162-63. *Q.E.D.* 148; *Sea King*, 220, 221-25; *Sobraon* designed as one, 224, 249; *Tempest*, 164
Avalanche, ship, costs, 279

SS *Bahama*, tea steamer, 223-24
Baines, James, buys *Marco Polo*, 187; charters *Startled Fawn*, 199; orders clipper from Aberdeen, 215-16, 219; orders clippers from America, 189; owner of *Donald McKay*, 150, of *Schomberg*, 137, 193, 196, of other ships, 192
Baker, William A, 28
Ballarat, ship, *158*; compared with *Chrysolite*, 177, with *James Booth*, 158, with *Marco Polo*, 211, with *Three Bells*, 155; hull-form, 158
Ballast, permanent iron, 202, 235, 246
Balley, James B, ships built by, 83-84, 214
Ballingall, Capt James, 62-63
Balmoral, ship, 159
Baltimore clippers, 38-40, 42; *Ann McKim*, 72; examples described, 38-40; extreme models, 20, 39, 79; *Fly*, later HMS *Sea Lark*, 39; hull-form, 102; influence on fast sailing vessels, 27, 243, on opium clippers, 40; *Musquidobit*, 39, 40; *Nonpareil*, 20, 39; refers to any fast schooner, 38
Banchory, brig, costs, 275
Bank Quay Foundry Co, builders of *Lady Octavia*, *Sarah Palmer*, *Startled Fawn*, and *Tayleur*, 134; list of ships built at, 198
Banian, ship, 201
PS *Banshee*, blockade runner, 135
Barbara, brig, costs, 274
Barbara Allan, brig, costs, 275
Barclay, Curle & Co, build big iron clippers, 258-61; builders of *City of Nankin*, 134, of *Mermerus*, 130, 230, 258-59, of *Montrose*, 150, of *Shandon*, 165; names of medium clippers built 1857-60, 204, names of ships built 1869, 233; style of ships built, 224-26, 230, 250, 253, 258; steam donkey engines, 260
Baring Brothers, owners of *Alexander Baring*, 95, of *Falcon*, 74, of *Norman Court*, 255-56; require fast ships, 87
Barquentines, 265-67; *Transit*, an early example, 50-51, *51*; *Bonanza* (1830), 77, *78;* rig development, 78
Barquetta, *see* Jackass Barques
Barranca, ship, costs, 279
Bates, Joshua, 74
Bates Family, ship, large tonnage, 134-35, 198
Baugean, Jean, artist, *15*, 31
Bay of Cadiz, ship, 135
Bay of Naples, ship, costs, 279
Bayley, George, shipbuilder, 17, 51, 80
Bayley, W A, 251
Beale, John H, draughtsman, 36, 63
Beam-to-length ratio, clipper barques, 264; cutters in 1763, 29; high ratio did not make a clipper, 155; increases for vessels of cutter-build after 1815, 59; privateer, 37; reduced by smuggling Acts, 14-15, 52; sloop 1745, *28*; very high examples, 50-52; tabulated 1825-52, 18; two ships by A Hall & Sons, 108; vessels listed with more than 6½ beams to length, 164
Beaufoy, Col, 14
Beazley, James, owner of *Robin Hood*, 182, of *Vision*, 182, of *Star of the East*, 191
Belfast, Lord, 73, 89, 94
Bell, Jacob, shipbuilder, 126
Bell, John, shipowner, 156, 172
Bell, William and Findlay, shipowners, 156
Belle of Lagos, deck layout, 237
Belle of the Clyde, brig, *132*, 149
Belmore, Earl of, 74
Belted Will, ship, described, 201-02
Ben Avon, ship, 159
Ben Muick Dui, barque, costs, 277; listed, 107; possible picture, 110, *110*
Ben Nevis, ship, 258
Ben Voirlich, ship, 151
Benham, Hervey, author, 212
Benjamin Elkin, barque, compared with *Reindeer*, 113, 114; costs, 114, 277; extreme raking stem, 108-09; half-model, 113, 154; listed 108
Bentham, Sir Samuel, 21
Bentinck, ex-pilot brig, 94
Beraza, barque, 121, 165
Bermudian model, influence on design, 27-28; schooners, 16; sloops, 27-28, 68
Berwick Shipping Co, 118
Berwick smack, 79, 82
Bessemer steel, 135
Bessy Robertson, brig, costs, 276
Bilbe & Perry, composite construction, 142-43; diagonal construction, 140-41, 281; lists of ships built, 144-42
Bilbe, Thomas, takes out patent, 142-43
Bilbe, Thomas & Co, *see under* Bilbe & Perry
Bill, Robert, patentee of iron spars, 147-48
Bird, Ralph, draughtsman, 264
Blackadder, ship, 273; clipper status, 253, 258
Black Ball Line, of trans-Atlantic packets, 66
Black Ball Line (James Baines), 187, 190-92
HMS *Black Joke*, ex *Henriquetta*, brig, *87*
Black Prince, ship, 220; compared with *Fiery Cross*, 200-21; with *Maitland*, 231-32; cost of building, 221, 278; described by Capt Shewan, 221; designed by Rennie, 167, 220; low forecastle, 155, 221, 231; passages and earnings, 221; spar dimensions, 221; compared with *The Caliph*, 257
Blackwall Frigates, 137
Blackwall Yard, 126, 184
Blenheim, ship, 137
Block Coefficient, explained, 20
Blockade runners, American, 135
Blyth, Greene, Jourdain & Co, 87-88
Blyth, James, merchant, 84, 87-88
Bon Accord (1846), ship, 108; costs, 277; described at sea, 111, 124; listed, 107
Bon Accord (1857), barque, costs, 278
Bonanza (1830), barquentine offsets, 77; plans, 77, 78; reconstruction, 77-78; sail plan, 77-78; record passage, 96-97
HMS *Bonetta*, ex *Les Huits Amis*, ex-privateer, 37
Bonita, ship, *113;* compared with *Reindeer*, 113, 114; costs, 277; listed, 107; painting by Smith, 111, 114
Bonnie Dundee, steamer, 107
Boolds, H J, draughtsman, 141
Border Maid, schooner, 107; costs, 276
Bouguer, Pierre, author, 15-16
Bouquet, Michael, 83, 120
Bowman & Vernon, windlass makers, 146
Boyle, Vernon, 197
Boyd, M F, 231
Brazils Packet, brig, 70
Bridge Foundry Co, shipbuilders, 197
Brierly, Sir Oswald W, artist, 86
Brig-cutters, *see* Cutter-brigs
Brilliant (1814), ship, costs, 274
Brilliant (1850), ship, 158
HMS *Brisk*, *168*
Bristol, privateers fitted out, 32-33; ships built by J M Hilhouse, 47, 73-74
Bristow, barque, *115;* composite construction, 142; had Aberdeen bow, 115, *181*, 182
Britannia, ship, bought 1781 by Navy, 40
Britannia (1813), brig, costs, 274
Britain's Glory, or Ship-Building Unvail'd, *15*
British Ambassador, ship, 196
British Association, 97, 168
Brockbank, John, builder of *Thetis*, 34; possible designer of privateer, 34; tonnage formula, 23
Brocklebank, Daniel, builder of *Jupiter*, 20, 42, 44
Brocklebank, T. & J., builders of *Bonanza*, 97, of *Dash*, 75-78, of *Everest*, 225-26, of *Rajmahal*, 138, of *Susanna*, 85; some ships described, 76-77; two of their clippers, 201
Brooklands, ex *Susan Vittery*, schooner, 214, *215*
Brown, Walter, shipbuilder, 186, 192
Brown & Bell, shipbuilders, 126
Brown & Harfield, patent capstan replaces windlass, *146*, 147, 162; windlass, 146-47, *259*
Browning, A S E, 102
Browning, Drew & Co, owners of *Fling*, 211
Brucklay Castle, ship, costs, 278
Bruhn, Jôrgen, builder of *Cimber*, *205*, 206
Brunel, Sir Marc, 22
Buchan, brigantine, costs, 275
Buckle, Capt, 111
Budge, Capt, 159
Burney, Dr William, 15
Burns, ship, described, 173; half-model, 174
Burnswark, ship, listed, 173
HMS *Busy*, cutter, 29-30
Butterman, defined, 212
Buttersworth, Thomas, artist, 67

Cable, Boyd, article on *Scottish Maid*, 102-04; on first square-rigged clipper, 118; 'World's First Clipper', 102

Cairngorm, ship, *178*, *179;* colour of hull, 182, compared with *The Caliph*, 257; costs, 140, 179, 277; described by 2 journalists, 178-79; design not dictated by owners, 178-79, 270; dimensions, 176; fast passages, 179; half-model, 103, 154, 176, *177;* hull-form, 178-79; larger version of *Vision*, 179; new lines plan, 178, 179; very steep dead-rise, 178-79
Cairnsmore, ship, compared with *Thermopylie*, 243; hull-form, 165, 243; listed, 134, 164
Caledonia, schooner, *119*, *120;* Aberdeen bow, 116; costs, 120; hull-form, 119; plan survives, 206; reduced version of *Three Bells*, 155; sailplan, 119-20, 264
Caledonian, brig, costs, 275
Calypso, ship, costs, 279
Cambalu, ship, 201
HMS *Camelion*, brig, 29-30
Camertonian, ship, *126-29;* compared with *Three Bells*, 155; deck layout, 128-29; sail plan, *128*, 129; model and hull-form, 126-29; newspaper description, 126; whisker booms, *25;* windlass, 128, *128*, 146; scantlings, 127
Cammell, Laird, 118
Campbell, John, shipowner, 135, 166, 219
Camper, William, shipbuilder, 92
Canada, large wooden ships constructed, 138-39
Canada Works, builder of *Simla*, 134
Canton Register, 90, 94
Cape Town, *St Helena* sails into harbour, 57
Capstan, being operated, 147; geared to windlass, 162; *see also* Brown & Harfield
SS *Carbon*, listed, 166
Cargo capacity, greater in iron than in wooden ships, 131, 150, 173, 270
Carlisle Castle, ship, 250
Carmichael, A & J, shipowners, names of ships owned, 258-59
Caroline, barque, 165
Carpenters Society, 199
Catherine, barque, costs, 275
Cato, Miller & Co, builders of *Conflict* and *Talavera*, 134
Cecile, schooner yacht, 140
Celaeno, ship, costs, 278
Celestial, ship, 220, 141
Centreboard, 120
Ceres, brig, costs, 275
Chaa-sze, ship, costs, 278; designed by Rennie, 167, 220; diagonal build, 140, 181; windlass, 147
Challenge, Baltimore clipper schooner, 38
Challenge, American ship, 185, 186; hull-form, 185; listed, 139; lines to be taken off, 184; passages 185-86; sail plan, 185, 186
Challenger, ship, 196; tea clipper, 183, 185; hull-form, 196
Chaloner, shipbuilder, 166, 219
Champion of the Seas, ship, bows sketched, 184; compared with other clippers, 139, 189, speed, 190
Chapelle, Howard I, comments on Bermudian model, 28 on design of *Shamrock*, 55; defines clipper characteristics, 102; finds sail plan of English cutter, 27; hull analysis, 20; on evolution of British and American clippers, 179, 186; reproduces plans, 86, 97, 123; reconstructs sail plan of *Lady Hamond*, 28, of HMS *Sea Lark*, 39;
Chapman, partner in Gladstone & Co, 222
Chapman, Capt C, author, 258, *258;* quoted, 267-68
Chapman, af, F H, 16, 26, 28, 105; privateer plans, 32, 34, 35, 36, 243; packets, 50
Chariot of Fame, ship, *136*, 136-37, 139
Charlemagne, ship, 134, 171-72
Charles Horsfall, ship, 141; costs, 277
Charlotte (1808), pilot cutter, 48
Charnock, John, 26
Chepica, ship, costs, 278
Chesapeake model, bought by Royal Navy 1745, 27
Childe Harold, brig, costs, 275
Childers, ship, described, 226; listed 225
China Bird (MacGregor), 183, 196
China Clippers (Lubbock), 218, *236*
Chinaman, ship, 221, 234
China trade, American competition, 95-96, 154; in 1860s, 216-19; fast ships in 1830s, 74, 95-97; packet ship design, 123-26; new clippers, 154
Chowringhee, ship, 182
Christiana Thompson, ship, *243;* brace winch, 151, 246; resembles *Thermopylae*, 246; roller-reefing topgallant, 149, *264*
Chrysolite, ship, 225; costs, 277; famous captain, 114; half-model, 103, 134, 176, *177;* hull-form, 177-78, 182; speed, 177-78; article by Griffiths, 177
Cimber, Danish ship, *205*, *205;* hull-form, 205; described, 205
Circular Quay, Sydney, *159*
City Line (G Smith & Sons), 204
City of Bombay, ship, 144
City of Calcutta, ship, 143
City of Canton, ship, 134
City of Hamilton, ship, costs, 277
City of Hankow, ship, 146, 253
City of Lucknow, ship, 253
City of Madras (1855), ship, 134
City of Madras (1859), ship, 134
City of Nankin, ship, 134, 204
City of Perth, ship, described, 204
City of Shanghai, ship, described, 204
Clara Sayers, barque, costs, 278
Clark Collection, of plans, 189
Clark, William, artist, 237, *242*, 245
Claydon, F A, draws plans, *240*, 240-41, *241*, 257
Clinker build, 14, *29*, 31
Clippers, Aberdeen bow, 99 et seq, 154; American clippers of over 1500 tons listed, 139; Australia trade, 218; British did not copy American, 184-85, 214, 270; boom in building for China trade 1865-69, 154, 218, 253, 282; building boom 1853-55, 138-39, 154, 270; building boom in America, 154; compared with French privateers, 37; design evolved from cutter, 29, 58, 61, 270; development, 34, 58, 61; ideal form of clipper, 168-69, 174, 214, 270; early, 236; early use in tea trade, 74, 124-25; extreme, 154, 174; extreme British as sharp as American, 214; extreme clippers needed high freights, 172, 217; extreme form in ships, 159 *et seq;* and 235 *et seq; Spindrift*, 240; large iron built, 15 *et seq;* large size of American and Canadian, 138-39, 186; listed with Aberdeen bow, 107-08; long sharp entrance of *Storm Cloud*, 170; loss of cargo capacity in extreme vessels, 131, 172, 202, 217; Mauritius trade in 1830s, 87-88; new American style in *Sea Witch*, 124-25; compared wit *L'Invention* (1801) 37; naval, 90; no first clipper, 72, 153, 270; opium trade, 91-95; *Reindeer* one of sharpest built before 1848, 113; schooners of new style in 1840s, 82-86; terminology, 26, 154; unidentified fruiter 1860-70, 263-64, *264;* use of word in 1819, 52, 53 'World's First Clipper', 112; *see also* Baltimore Clipper
Clyde and Australian Shipping Co, names of ships owned, 160
Clytemnestria, ship, 135
Coalbrookdale iron, 122
Coats & Young, shipbuilders, 155
Cock of the North, cutter, costs, 80, 275
Cock, Robert, shipbuilder, 263
Cod's head and mackerel tail, 47-48, 122
Coefficient of Under Deck Tonnage, explained, 20; tea clippers compared, 234
Colliers, 81
Colling, John, 148
Colling & Pinkney, roller-reefing gear, 148-49, *149*, 241; roller-reefing gear in *Thermopylae*, *242*, 247
Colloony, barque, 107-08; costs, 276; hull-form, 109
HMS *Columbine* (1826), 12-gun sloop, 88
Columbine (1839), brig, costs, 276
Colonial Empire, ship, 151
Comet (1810), Leith smack, 79, 80, 82; model, *80*
Comet (1851), American ship, 214, *184*
Commerce, brigantine, costs, 275
Commerce de Paris, French clipper ship, 243
Commissary, ship, costs, 279
Commodore, brig, costs, 275
Compass deviation, 162, 199
Composite construction, 142-43; advantages, 132; last in UK, 146; history of, 144-46; largest ships, 146, 267; royalties paid on Jordan's patent, 160-1; A Stephen obtains Lloyds consent, 143-44 variations built, 146
Confederate Government of America, blockade runners, 135, 223; cruiser *Shenandoah*, 221
Conference, ship, 198-200
Conflict, ship, 134
Connell, Charles, 218; names of ships built, 239-40;
Conqueror, ship, 181; costs, 277
Constance, barque, 188, 192
Construction, Annesley's laminated, 23; comparison of British and American in wood, 136-37, 139; corrosion between copper and

iron, 132; diagonal planking, 140-41; Hall's diagonal, 22; innovations before 1850, 21-23; number of iron plates in *Typhoon's* hull, 160; timber consumed in a ship, 20; under a roof, 160; *see also* Diagonal, Scantling sizes, Wood Shipbuilding
Contract, in form of letter, 257
Copper sheathing, 132
Coquette, brig yacht, 73, 74
Coral Nymph, ship, 233
Coriolanus, ship, 260, 263
Corsican, brig, costs, 275
Cornwallis, ship, 150, *150*
Cossipore, ship, *226*
Costagliola, Michael, draws plan, *190*
Costs of building *Annabella*, 88, of *Black Prince*, 231, of *Caledonia*, *120*, *of Cairngorm* and *Stornoway*, 179, of *Falcon* (1824), 74, of *Fling*, 212, of *Hurricane*, 160, of *Irt*, 76, of *John Lidgett*, 144, of Leith smacks, 80, of *Reindeer* itemised, 125, of *St Helena*, 55, of *Salamander*, 204, of *Schomberg*, 193, of *Scottish Maid* itemized, 101, of SS *Sea King*, 221-24, of *Sobraon*, 250, of *Storm Cloud*, 172, of *Tayleur*, 199 of *Transit* (1800), 51, of *Typhoon*, 160; building in steel, 135; of diagonal construction, 140; of early composite ships, 142; Emerson & Walker windlass, 147; estimate of composite ship (1861), 143; estimate for *Samoa* and periods of payment, 251; fitting propellor to *Hurricane*, 162-63; of iron shipbuilding, 130; list of vessels built by A Hall & Sons 1811-75, 274-80; of roller-reefing gear, 148, 208; royalties on composite construction patent, 144-46; of scraping and painting bottom of iron ship, 132; of tea clippers in 1860s, 235; of White's diagonal construction, 140; of wooden ships in 1850s, 136
Coulnakyle, ship, costs, 278
Coulson, Capt, 233
Countess of Chichester, packet, 60
Countess of Seafield, ship, 117
County of Peebles, 262
Courant, schooner of Kiel, 209
Courier, schooner, 77
Courier de St Paul, 87
Coutts & Co, builders of *Q.E.D.*, 148
Coutts, John, 23
Coutts & Parkinson, 133; builders of *Sir Charles Napier*, *Swarthmore* and *W S Lindsay*, 134
Cowasjee Family, opium clipper, 23, 91-92, 94
Cowasjee Jehangeer, later *Ranee*, *133*
Cowasjee, Rustomjee, merchant, 91
Cox, George, of Bideford, builder of *Jane Leech*, *Shuttle*, and *Sarah Neumann*, 198
Cox, John, shipbuilders, 266
Cox & Con, of Bridport, shipbuilders, 197
Cradock H, naval architect, 97
Craigievar, brig, costs, 275
Cram H, builder of *Winefred*, 134
Crest of the Wave, ship, 182, 254
Creuze, Augustin F B, 17, 132
Crew, of *St Helena*, 57; of *Schomberg*, 195; smuggler (1791), 54; of *Thermopylae*, 245; wages during Australian gold rush, 157, 189; Crimean War, clipper carries news, 191; effect on shipping industry, 154, 202, 204
Crockett, Capt William, 174-75
Crusader, barque, 109; costs, 276
Cuirassier, steamer, 135
Cunard, Joseph, shipbuilder, *121*, 121-22
Cunningham, H D P, brace winch and list of ships fitted, 150-51, *154;* brace winches in *Maitland*, 51, 232-33, 246, in *Thermopylae*, 151, 246; stunsail booms fit below his yards, 270; roller-reefing gear to topsails, *148*, 148-50, *150*, *208*, 221; roller-reefing topgallants, 148
Cupid, ship bought by Navy, 40; hull-form 40-41; plans *41*, 46; spar dimensions, 41; compared with other ships, 40-41
Curlew, schooner, 106; costs, 277; listed, 107
Custom House Registers, commencement date, 24
Cutler, Carl C, 139, 190
Cutters, *Abeona*, 54; compared with French lugger, 39; with sloop, 15; development of hull-form in larger vessels, 32, 53, 59, 92, 110, 243; Dutch naval, *31*, HMS *Dwarf*, 26; eighteenth-century sail plan described, 27; favoured by British, 13, 28; HMS *Fly*, 26-27; HMS *Hawke*, *28;* inspired design of fast ships, 20, 26-32, 53, 55, 59, 66, 92, 101, 243, 270; lengthened and rigged as schooners, 66; mizen mast, 29,30; Naval *c*1800, *29;* HMS *Pitt*, 26, *Rebecca*, 48; rerigged as brigs or schooners, 29, 97; as smuggler, 14; square sails listed, 28; *Sylph*, 60-61, HMS *Viper*, 28; *see also* Leith smacks
Cutter brigs, 29, 47, 55, 58; *Alexander*, 29; HMS *Rambler*, 29; *Shamrock*, 55
Cutter-build (cutter-built), definition, 27; equivalent to clipper-built, 29; examples listed, 29, 55
Cutty Sark, ship, *255*, *256;* an extreme clipper, 253-54; compared with *Mirzapore*, *226;* compared with other ships, 182, 228-29, 234, 253-54; dimensions compared with *Mermerus*, 259; hull-form, 254; influences affecting her hull-form, 254, 258; spars and sail plan compared, 247, 255; speed, 254; unique survival described, 254; spar dimensions listed, 247; was she designed to beat *Thermopylae?* 254
Cyclone, ship, 159
Cyclopaedia (Rees'), 63, 64
Cynthia, barque, 109; costs, 276

Damier Powell, J W, 32
Dandridge, C, draughtsman, 63
Dandy rig, 29
Danish Royal Archives, 27
Darby & Sim, shipowners, 123
HMS *Daring*, brig, 89
Darra, ship, costs, 278
Dart, schooner, 107; costs, 277
Dash, brigantine, 75, *76;* compared with *Neilson*, 75-76; hull-form, 75-76; old-fashioned design, 76; retains rounded body form, 53; sail and rigging plan, 76
Davis, Charles G, plan of *Peri*, 212, *213*
Davy, Robert, shipbuilder, 82
Deadrise, as steep in British vessels as in American, 39, 179; enormous in *Cairngorm*, 179; reasons for steepness in American ships, 44; steep in Hilhouse vessels, 48, 66, 68; in *Richard Cobden*, 122; in *Spindrift*, 240-41; in all Symondites, 89; steep in Post Office packets, 48
Deck fittings, improvements to, 146-47, 150-51; Cunningham's brace winch, *see* Cunningham; mechanical gear on *Pride of Canada*, 165; *see also* Aberdeen house, Anchors, Boats, Capstan, Windlass
Deck layouts, distinguishing merchantmen from navel ships, 37, 64; East Indiamen, 64; *Neilson*, 69-70
SS *Dee*, costs, 279
Deerhound, ship, 233
Deerslayer, barque, listed, 198, 200; specification, 135, 200
Defiance, ship, 134
Demerara, ketch, for Demerara pilot company, 142
Denny, Alexander, 155
Denny, James, 155
Denny, Peter, 143, 155, 165
Denny, William, shipbuilder, 155, 206
Denny, Wm & Bros, builders of *Caledonia*, 119-20, 155, 207; of *Three Bells*, 155; iron schooners described, 119-20; tank tests, 105
Denny & Rankin, 133; builders of *Gauntlet*, 162, 165, 166; of *Glen Roy*, 134,187
Denton, Gray & Co, 183
Depth in hold, defined, 283-4
Derwent, barque, described, 230
Design, Aberdeen bow variations, 124; at A Stephen & Sons' yard, 160, 168-70; by arcs of circles, 16, 18, 32-33, 44, 52-53, 76; British did not copy American and Canadian clippers, 214; Baltimore clippers not restricted by rules, 38; coastal craft, 14; described by Fincham, 16-18; by Hedderwick (1830), 18; by *shipbuilder's Repository*, 16; by Steel, 16; by Sutherland (1794), 53; of East Indiamen, 64; eighteenth century, 15, 16, 42, 52-53; favoured by Ditchburn, 122; freedom from owners' restrictions yields extreme clippers, 168-69, 174, 179; foreign influence over-emphasised, 20, 32, 41; of *Hall*, 44-45; influence of Bermudian model, 27-28; of cutters, 28, 29, 53; of wave form theory, 190, 193. J W Griffiths' theories for fast ships, 124, 168, 189; Leith smacks, 79-80; midship section, 52-53; naval brigs, 39, 88-89; one plan applicable to many vessels, 81, 89; opium clippers, 91-95; Post Office packets 1793, 48; raking midsection, 84-85, 202; schooners, 66; slavers, 14, 36; Steele's tea clippers, 234-39; three *Transit's* compared, 50-11; tonnage reduction, 99-100, *106;* Waymouth's skill in clippers, 243
Devana, ship, costs, 278

Devitt & Moore, shipowners, 249
Diagonal construction, Bilbe & Perry, 140-41; Fearnall and Fletcher, 23; Hall, 23, 140-41, 181, 195; Seppings, 22-23, 140; in Royal yachts, 23; White, 23, 140; other builders, 141; radiating frames, 141
Diagonal iron trussing, *22*, 22
Diagonal wood trussing, in *Renown*, *25*, 151
Dickie, James, collector, *219*
Dickinson, Robert, engineer, 147
Die Sciffbankunst, *228*
Dilawar, ship, 146
Dilbur, ship, 146
Diligente, slaver brig, 202
Dilpussund, ship, 146
Dinapore, ship, *226*
Directions for Laying off Ships, 17
Ditchburn, Thomas J, naval architect, career, 122; describes design of vessel, 84, *85*; designer of *Swordfish*, 121-22; methods of design, 132; patent for composite construction, 141-42, 161
Dodgson, Thomas, shipbuilder, 32
Dolphin (1815), smack, costs, 274
HMS *Dolphin* (1836), true brigantine, 89; hull-form, deck fittings, and sail plan, 89; sail plan compared with *Psyche*, *94;* slave chaser, 14, *90;* outsails *Waterwitch*, 90
Dolphin striker, in use by 1794, 47
Domitila, schooner, 135
Donald McKay, American ship, double topsails, 150; hull-form, 189; listed 139; medium clipper, 189, speed, 190, very long lower yards, 196
Don (1814), ship, costs, 274
SS *Don* (1873), costs, 279
Donegal, Marquis of, 89
Donietta, schooner, 135
Dorothy, ship, costs, 277
SS *Douglas*, schooner, costs, 278
Dove, iron schooner, 23
Dragon, ship, 151
Druid, schooner, later *Susanna*, 84
du Monceau, Duhamel, 15
Duke of Abercorn, ship, 239
Duke of Marlborough, Falmouth packet, 49
Duke of Sutherland, smack, costs, 275
Duke of York, packet brig, 59
Dunbar, Duncan, shipowner, 158, 249
Dunbar, ship, 138, 174
Duncan Dunbar, ship, 138
Dunmail, ship, described, 201-02; painting, 202, *203*
Dunrobin Castle, ship, costs, 277
Dusty Miller, schooner, 83
Duthie, Alexander & Co, shipbuilders, 130, 158-59
Duthie, George, shipwright, 118
Duthie, John, description of ships built, 117-18
Duthie, John, jnr, shipwright, 118, *118*, *141*
Duthie, John, Sons & Co, shipbuilders, 118, 229
Duthie, Robert, shipwright, 118
Duthie, Wm Bros, shipbuilders, 118, 158
Dutton, T G, artist, 74, *204*, *231*, *233*, *238*, 241
HMS *Dwarf*, cutter, 28
Dyer, Capt Samuel, 148

Eagle, Leith smack, 79
Earl of Eglinton, ship, 138, 166
Earl of Fife, brigantine, costs, 275
Earl of Mulgrave, brigantine, 242
Earle, C & W, shipbuilders, 134
Earnings, of *Hurricane*, 162; of *Storm Cloud*, 172
East India Company, abolition of monopoly, 95; builds packet schooner *St. Helena*, 55; declines to buy first *Transit*, 51; grants trade licences, 62; experts in transporting troops, 73; its surveyor, 21
East India outfit, cost of, 235
East Indiamen, calling at St Helena, 55; *Farquharson*, 63-66; *London*, 66; of 1200-ton class, 63-65
Eastern Monarch, ship, 135, 137-38
Ebenezer, schooner, 107; costs, 276
Echo, Emsworth smack, 109
Eckford, Henry, shipbuilder, 123
Eckford Webb, American schooner, 185
SS *Eclipse*, ship, costs, 278
Edinburgh Packet, smack, costs, 274
Edith Moore, ship, 134
Edward P. Bouverie, ship, costs, 279
Edward, Thomas, shipbuilder, 103
Edwards & Balley, shipbuilders, 83
Edwards, John, shipbuilder, 83
Edye, John, 65
Electra (1846), barque, 107; costs, 277
Electra (1866), ship, costs, 278
Electric Telegraph, barque, 121, 197
Elements de l'Architecture Navale (du Monceau), 15
Elements and Practice of Naval Architecture (Steel), 16, 49, 63
Elfin, steam yacht, 23
Elinor, schooner, 212
Eliza Shaw, ship, described, 172, 218, 226; royalty fee, 145; listed, 225
Elizabeth (1840), schooner, 107; costs, 276
Elizabeth (1872), schooner, costs, 279
Elizabeth Barter, barque, listed, 166
Elizabeth Nicholson, ship, listed, 173; hull-form, 174; roller-reefing topgallant, 148
Elien Bates, ship, 134
Ellen Rodger, ship, 202, 234
Ellen Stuart, ship, 134
Elliot Joseph, ship draughtsman, 44-45
Elmslie, Capt J A, 249
El Zeide, schooner, 120, 206
Eme, ship, 239
Emerald, cutter yacht, 73
Emerson & Walker, modernise windlass, *147*, 147, 241
Emigrant, barque, 181
Emigration, to Australia, 187-88
Emily, brig, costs, 278
Emma (*c*1810-20), schooner, Science Museum model, 84
Emma (1824), brig, 67
Emma (1826), built by Hilhouse, 67
Emma (1830), schooner, built by James Balley, 83
Emperor, barque, 108; costs, 277; painting, *114;* compared to *Reindeer*, 114
Empress, ship, 140
SS *Empress Eugenie*, 166
Empress of the Seas, American ship, 139
Emsworth smacks, 109
Enchantress (1839), barque, costs, 276
HMS *Enchantress*, ex *Manuela*, ex *Sunny South* (1854), *168*
Encyclopaedia Britannica (1841), article 'Shipbuilding', 17
Encyclopaedia Britannica (1861), article 'Shipbuilding', 133, 140, 181, 193
Enoch Train, American ship, 184
Enright, Capt Anthony, 114
Enterprise (1852), schooner, costs, 277
Enterprize (1846), schooner, 198
Esther, barque, 166
Ethiopian, ship, 149, 226, 246
Euphrates (1834), ship, 95-96
SS *Euphrates* (1855), auxiliary ship, hull-form, 169; sail plan, 171; measurements, 169
Europa, barque, costs, 275
Evangeline, ship, 134
Everest, ship, *226;* described, 226; listed, 225
Excelsior, schooner, 141-42
Expedition, brig, costs, 274
Express, schooner, plans, 267, *268*, *269*

Fairfax, Capt James, 57
Fairlight, ship, 148, 164
Fairy (1833), brig, 91
Fairy (1842), schooner, 107; costs, 276
Fairy (1845), steam yacht, 122
Falcon (1815), brig yacht, 71, 74, 195
Falcon (1824), ship, yacht, *72*, *73*, *75;* altered in 1839, 74; as tea clipper, 71, 74, 96; becomes opium clipper, 74, 95; bought by Baring's, 74, 87; cost of building and sale price, 74; cutter-built hull, 55; discrepancies between model and Fincham's measurements, 71, 74; engravings, *72*, *75;* hull-form, 71-74; passages, 74; plans found, 71, 73; spar dimensions listed, 73
Falcon (1838), schooner costs, 276
Falcon (1859), ship, 202; dimensions, 234; hull-form, 234-35; in tea trade, 218-19; compared with other ships, 220-21
Falconer's Dictionary (1815), 15-17
Falconer, William, 17-18
Falmouth packets, 49, 63
Fanny (1850) of Bremen, 77
SS *Far East*, tea steamer, 224
Farewell, brigantine, 122
Farquharson, East Indiaman, *64*, *65;* compared with warship, 64-65; hull-form and deck layout, 63-64; sail and rigging plan, 64-66; speed, 63; passages from China, 63; plans analysed, 63-65
Farrer, T H, 152
Fast ships, absence of design rules, 20; design factors, 14-16, 18, 88; inference from ships'

names, 42, 75; influence of English cutter, 27, 58-59; needed in competitive commerce, 85, 87, 172; *see also* Clippers
Fast-sailing ships, *see* Fast ships
Favourite, schooner, 115
Fawn, brig, *264*
Feathers, inside iron masts, 201
Fearnall, William, shipbuilder, 23, 140
Fedi, Guiseppi, artist, *71*
Fell, Jonathan, shipbuilder, 126, 128; shipbuilder career and ships designed, 201-02
Ferguson, Peter, draughtsman, *266*
Ferme, French ship, 32
Ferreira, ex *Cutty Sark* photographed at Pensacola, *256*
Ferrett, smuggler, 68
Ferris, William, shipbuilder, 19
Fiery Cross (1855), ship, compared with *Reindeer*, 167; dimensions, 166; hull-form and passages, 166-67
Fiery Cross (1860), ship, *219;* compared with *Black Prince*, 219-21; with *John R. Worcester*, 228; with *Norman Court*, 272; designed by Rennie, 167, 219-21; model and hull-form, 220, 222-23, 256; roller-reefing sails, 148; sailplan, 220
Fincham, John, analyses five yachts, 73; compiles tables of spar dimensions, 93; his books, 16-17, 51; on how to design a ship, 17-18; plan of clipper schooner, 116; recommendations on sails, 71
Findlay, J, owner of *Serica*, of *Spindrift* and *Taitsing*, 240
Fisher, John, shipbuilder, 45
Flash, iron schooner, 23
Fletcher, Joseph, shipbuilder, 23, 154
Fletcher & Fearnall, shipbuilders, 23, 140
Fletcher, Son & Fearnall, builders of *Time*, 84, 122
Fling, schooner, *211;* hull-form, 211, 263; sail plan, 212; hull-form compared with *John Williams*, 252; half-model, *19;* 212
Flora, brig, costs, 276
Florence, schooner, 165
Flower of the Fal, schooner, *268*
Flush decks, *see Ariel*, *Titania*
HMS *Fly*, bought 1763, cutter, *26, 27;* hull-form, 26; sail plan and square canvas, 26, 27, 31, 53, 84
Fly, captured 1811, American schooner, 39, 57
Flying Dragon, barque, 182, *183*
Flying Fish (1802), pilot cutter, 48
Flying kites, Aberdeen schooners, 102; clipper ships, 202, *203*, 221, 233, *238*, 239; cutters, 28; East Indiamen, 65-66; *Midas*, 40; opium clipper barque, *91;* photographed, *233*
Flying Scud, American ship, 190
Flying Spur, ship, 224; costs, 278
Flying Venus, ship, 134
Foam, ship, 95
Foig a Ballagh, iron schooner, 23
Forbes, Capt J N, 188-89
Forbes, Robert B, double topsails, 148-49
Formby, ship, cost, 135; plans, 135; windlass, *147*
Fortitude, barque, costs, 276
Fouling of iron ships' bottoms, 131-32
Four-masted ship, 276, *37*, 37-38
Fowler, Capt, 251
SS *Fox*, schooner, costs, 277
France, composite shipbuilding, 157
France et Chili, French clipper ship plan, 243
Francis Henty, ship, 181; costs, 277
Freak, schooner, 83
Freights, from China in 1834, 96; from China in 1850s, 154; from China in 1860s, 217-18; from China in 1878, 263; to and from Australia in 1850s, 162, 172; effect of Suez Canal, 253
Friar Tuck, ship, costs, 278
Friendship, schooner, 68-70
Fruit trade, fast schooners, used, 83-86, 209, 211-12; Hilhouse schooners, 66-67; unidentified clipper, 263; schooner described, 267-68
Furnaux, shipbuilder, *277*
Fusi Yama, tea clipper, *228;* hull-form, 227
Fusilier, ship, listed, 166
Fy-Chow, ship, costs, 278; tea clipper, 221
HMS *Galatea* (1859), frigate, 252
Ganges, ship, compared with *Maitland*, 253; hull-form, 225-26; half-model, 183, 226; listed, 225
Gauntlet, ship, *163;* coefficient of UD tons, 165; compared with *Hurricane*, 162; described, 163, 165; designed by Rennie, 166-67
Gazehound, barque, 141
SS *Gazelle*, schooner, costs, 276
Geddie, James, shipbuilder, 207, 265
Geelong, ship, 160
Gellatly, Hankey & Sewell, owners of *Sobraon*, 249
Gem, brig, costs, 276
Genoese pink (1800), lines plan, *42*
George Jordan, schooner, 142
George Marshall, ship, 138
Getty, John, shipbuilder, 142
Getty, John, & Co, builders of *James Pilkington*, 134
Getty Jones & Co, builders of *Ellen Stuart*, 134
Gitana, schooner, 107; costs, 277
Gladstone & Co, 222
Glasgow, schooner, 79, 80
Glasgow Herald, describes *Hurricane*, 160, 162; describes *Typhoon*, 160, reports on clipper *Storm Cloud*, 167-68; reports on shipbuilding, 134
Glasgow Museum and Art Gallery, half-models of Aberdeen clippers, 102-04, 176, 179, 194, model of *Helen Nicholson*, 225, model of *Spindrift*, 240-41; model of *Vision*, 180, 206; paintings by R Salmon, 71
Glasgow Packet, costs, 274
Glassford, R W, 249
Gleam, barque, 142
Glen Roy, ship, 134, 164; speed, 165
Glentanner, ship, 108; costs, 276; listed, 109
Gold, discovered in Australia, 129, 153, 157; discovered in California, 129, 153; problems arising, 157
Gold rush, demand for large clippers, 139, 159; to Australia, 157, 159
Golden Fleece, ship, *259;* photographed, 253
Golden Fleece Line, 258
Goliath, ketch, 132
Gondola, barque, 142
Good, shipbuilder, 81
Gore, Charles, 52
Gordon, shipbuilder, 63
Gould, F G, photographer, 250, 260
Gourlay Brothers, shipbuilders, 214
Gourock Rope Co, 198
Governor MacLean, brig, 94
Gowan, A B, & Sons, shipbuilders, 118
Gower, ketch, 50
Gower, Richard Hall, designer of *Transit*, 281
Gracie, Beazley & Co, 180
Grand Banks, schooners, 109
Granite, brig, *116*
Grantham, John, consulting naval architect, 270; on iron ships, 122, 130-31; specifications of iron clippers, 135, 224
SS *Graphic*, costs, 279
HMS *Grasshopper*, ex *London* (1770), 40-41
Gray, John, builder of *Electric Telegraph*, 121, 197, of *Lewes*, 121, of *Watkins*, 120-21, 220
SS *Great Britain*, saved by iron construction, 130; shape of midship section, 122; surveyed, 132
Great Exhibition 1851, 130, 141
Great Republic, American ship, *188;* huge size, 139-40, 193; photograph, *188*
PS *Great Western*, 122
HMS *Grecian*, brig, *95*
Green, Capt, 166
Green, Richard, builder of *Agamemnon*, 137-38; of *Challenger*, 183, 196; owns Blackwall Yard, 183
Green, R & H, builders of *Childers* and *Highflyer*, 225-26, of *Melbourne*, 242
Greenhill, Basil, 83, 263
SS *Greenland*, barque, costs, 279
Greenock, ship, 164
Greig, Hood's yard manager, 245
Greville, Hon R F, 86, 92
Greyhounds of the Sea (Cutler), 139
Griffiths, J W, apprenticed 123; design theories for fast ships, 124-25, 168, 189; his book known in Britain, 168, 184; publishes lines of *America*, 168; writes about *Chrysolite*, 177
Griswold, N L and Co, shipowners, 185
Guibert Collection of Plans at Mariner's Museum, *35*, 36, *36*, 38, *38*, 43, 86
Guide, schooner, costs, 277
Guiding Star, ship, 139
Guinevere, ship, 234; hull-form, 234
Gun Brigs, plan of 18-gun, 18; *Rolla* class, 41; 10-gun, 41, 95; 12-gun *Recruit*, 135
Guns, *see* Armament
Guppy, T R, shipbuilder, 122-23
Gwyn, Edward, artist, 31

Half-models, bird's nest type, 19, 212; bracket

type, 19, 212; lift model, 19-20; *Robin Hood,* 182; *Scawfell,* 202; ships built by A Hall & Son, 154, 176; survival of some of Hall's, 176
Hall (1785) West Indiaman, design of, 44-45; hull-form, 45-46; plans, *45*
Hall, Alexander, & Sons, build *Cairngorm* as ideal clipper, 179, 270; build clippers in 1850s, 154; build clipper schooners in 1890s, 207-08, *208;* build composite ships, 144; builders of *Black Prince,* 220-21; *Acasta,* 106-07; of *Nicoya* and *Herrandura,* 228, 250; of *Reindeer* (1863), 150; of packets, 80; of *Schomberg,* 138, 193-96; of *Scottish Maid,* 99; of *Sobraon,* 196, 249-50; of other ships, 51, 205, 218, 221, 225, 249-53, 257, 265; building costs compared, 84, 114; carpenter's tonnage formula, 25; comparison of their clippers, 108 *et seq,* 176-82; copies of their Aberdeen bow, 115-21; diagonal construction, 23, 140-41, 180-81, 217, 281; diagram comparing clipper and traditional hulls, *106;* evasion of tonnage laws with clipper bow, 98, 99-100, 106-07, 114-15; their half-models, 102-04, 176; hollow lines, 102, 104; list of non-clipper ships, 108-09; list of ships built by diagonal construction, 140; list of ships built 1811-75, 274-80; launch problems of ships with sharp bottoms, 178, 182; list of 36 vessels built with Aberdeen bow, 117; models and plans burnt, 104, 176; offer to build auxiliary steamer, 222; offer to build *Samoa,* 250-52; port side of half-model, 20; raking stem rabbet a success, 100, 270; tank tests, *104,* 104-05; windlass, 147; *see also ships by name.*
Hall, Henry, 95, 97
Hall, James, 79, 100, 104, 116, 134, 144, 222, 251
Hall, James and William, managed A Hall & Sons, 94, 250; visit Liverpool to secure orders, 193-94
Hall, Ross & Co, shipowners, 248
Hall, Russell & Co, 244, 289
Hall, William, 99, 100, 104, 116, 134, 181; disliked a hollow entrance, 114; patented screw treenails, 206
Hallowe'en, ship, 253; fast passages, 258; clipper status, 254, 258; at Sydney, *259*
Handyside & Co, 164
Handyside & Henderson, 172
Hannah More, brig, costs, 274-75
Hannibal, ship, 181; costs, 272
Hanscomb, Samuel, jnr, shipbuilder, *185*
Harbinger, ship, *262*
Harlaw, ship, described, 231
Harmonie, Danish brigantine, 116
Harmony (1823), cutter, costs, 275; sail plan, *82*
Harmony (1834), brig, costs, 275
Harmony (1838), brig, costs, 276
Harratt, Charles, shipbuilder, 141
Harrier (1816), schooner, 68
Harriet, cutter yacht, 89
Harriet (1834), schooner, *83*
Harriet Armitage, barque, costs, 83, 277
Harvey, Thomas, & Son, shipbuilders, 61, 212, *213*
Hawk, schooner, costs, 275
HMS *Hawke,* cutter, *27*
Hay, John, shipowner, 233
Heard, Joseph, artist, *130, 221*
Heathcote, shipyard manager, 199
Heaton, Capt G H, 157
Hebe, Norwegian ship, lines and sail plan, *206*
Hector, Alexander, owned *the Caliph,* 257
Hedderwick's 500-ton ship, sail plan, 63, 109
Hedderwick, Peter, designer of Leith smack, 17, 79, 80, 82; evidence before Select Committee, 79, 82; naval architect and author, 18; sail plan of 500-ton ship, *63;* ship curves, *19;* submits plan of cutter, 60
Helen Black, barque, costs, 279
Helen Nicholson, ship, described, 225; listed 225
HMS *Helena* (1778), schooner, hull-form, 31; lines plan, 30; measurements, 29-31; sail plan, *30,* 31-32; spar dimensions, 31-32
Helena (1841), American ship, 123, *123*
Helena Mena, barque, 146
Helens and Eleonora, schooner, costs, 275
Hellas, brigantine, *86;* bought for opium trade, 84, 85, 95; rig described, 76, 86
Hely, F G, artist, 91, *94*
Henderson, Capt Andrew, builds with composite construction, 142; designer of *Kelpie,* 91; of *Waterwitch,* 91, names of ships designed, 91
Henderson, James, draws new lines plan of *Cairngorm, 178,* 179; draws lines plan of *Thermopylae, 243,* 244-45; draws line plans of *Ann Duthie,* 230; makes model of *Stornoway,* 154, *154,* 177; model of *Vision, 180; reconstructs sail plans, 111, 114; research into Aberdeen clippers, 102, 104; research on John Williams,* 252; on *Schomberg,* 194; takes lines off half-models, 158, *182,* 229
Henderson, Patrick, shipowner, 172
Henriequetta, slaver brig, *87*
Henry Moore, ship, 134
Henslowe, Sir John, surveyor to the Navy, 52
Herald, ship, 233
Hero, schooner, 107; costs, 276
Heroes of Alma, ship, 140
Heroine, schooner, 107; costs, 276
Herradura, ship, built for coffee trade, 228; costs, 279; hull-form, 250
Hickson, R, & Co, builders of *Mary Stenhouse,* 134; of *Norah Greame,* 134
Highflyer, ship, described, 226; listed, 225
Hilhouse Collection of Plans, 28, 38, 47, 66-68
Hilhouse, George, 28, 47
Hilhouse, Hill & Co, successors to J M Hilhouse, 47
Hilhouse, J M, builder of 'Beal's Schooner', 68; of *Charlotte,* 48; of 'Cunningham schooner', 48; of *Flying Fish,* 48; of *Harrier,* 68; of *Maris,* 32-33; of Post Office packet, 47-48, 53, 55, 58, 68; of *Rebecca,* 48; of *Renown,* 137; of *Sappho,* 66-68; of steep-floored schooners, 66-68, *68;* collects plans, 28, 38; design of privateer, 33-34; list of vessels built, 48
Hill, Charles, & Sons, 33, 47
Hill, John C G, 49
Hill, Laurence, & Co, builders of *Pride of Canada,* 165
Hillmann, G, draughtsman, *111, 185, 188, 204, 210;* copying plans, 205
History of Naval Architecture (Fincham), 19, 51
Hoang Ho, clipper, *227*
Hodgson, James, shipbuilder, 122, 166
Hoksitika, barque, costs, 279
Holland, composite construction liked, 162
Hollow, lines, 18, 112-14; entrance in *Jupiter,* 42-43; lines, 166, 168, 174
Holmsdale, ship, 138
Honduras, takes first gold from Melbourne, 157
Hood, Walter, drowned, 247
Hood, Walter, & Co, absence of models and plans, 116, 159, 230; builder of named ships, 150, 159, 162; builds clippers, 218, 245; builds *Thermopylae,* 242, 244-45; description of vessels built with Aberdeen bow, 115-17; three of his clippers compared, 116-17; roller reefing gear, 149
Hope (1843), brig, costs, 276
SS *Hope* (1873), ship, costs, 279
Horsfall & Co, shipowners, 135
Ss *Ho-Sho-Maru,* barque, costs, 279
Hotham, Capt Henry, 37
Hotspur, ship, 147
House of Commons, Select Committee, 60-61, 79, 81-82; Parliamentary Papers, 184
Howden, ship, 134
Howes, Capt F, double topsails, 149-50, *210*
Howland & Aspinall, shipowners, 124
Huggins, W J, artist, *72, 83, 90*
Hull, Maritime Museum, 47
Hull-form, American schooners and British cutters compared, 28; Aberdeen clippers, 99-102. 113-14; Baltimore clippers described, 38-39; basic types after 1860 for smaller vessels, 263; cutters, 29; eighteenth century described, 42; clippers built by McKay, 189; Hall described by designer, 44-45, 182, 190, 194; hollow lines, 42-43, 102, 104, 124, 166, 170; influenced by ships having to take the ground, 44, 51, 79, 263, 267; influence of cutter, 92; iron clippers 1853-55, 160-64, 167-70; *Jupiter* described by her builders, 42-3; Leith and Berwick smacks, 79-82; pear-shaped mid-section, 36; privateers, 34-38; raking mid-section, 202, 212; raking stem rabbet, 109-10, 113-15, 24, *267;* recommended by J W Griffiths for maximum speed, 24, 168; schooners in Britain after 1850, 207-08, 211-12, 214, 263-65,; shape affected by timber storage, 21-3; ships bought into Navy 1775-83, 40; steep deadrise makes launching difficult, 178, 182; Symondites, 89; *see also* Deadrise
Humayon, ship, 109; costs, 276
Hume, Cyril, *245,* 245, 249, 254

Huntress, three-masted schooner, *264*
Hurricane, ship, *160, 161;* Brown & Harfield windlass, *146,* 162; compared with *Storm Cloud,* 162, 169-71; with other iron clippers, 160, 164-65, 197, 224; converted to auxliary screw, 162-63; cost, 160; deck layout, 162; earnings, 162; extreme clipper, 222; hull-form, 161, 200; iron construction absorbs little cargo space, 131; listed, 134; passages to Melbourne, 162; plans compared, 162; sail plan with pole masts, *161,* 162, 171; speed, 163
Hutchins, William, *22*
Hutchinson, William, author and mariner, 44-46

PS *Iberia,* 148
Ibrahim, Visram, Bombay merchant, 239
Idea, half-model, 198
Ignis Fatuus, barque, 141
Illovo, ship, costs, 279
Illustrated London News, describes *Cairngorm,* 178; describes *Gauntlet,* 163; describes *James Booth,* 158; describes *Phoenician,* 117; describes SS *Royal Charter,* 149; describes *Cimber,* 206; engravings of *Flying Dragon,* 183; engraving of *Speedy,* 197; describes *Marco Polo,* 187; engraving of *Taeping,* 233, *238*
Illustrated Times, 196
HMS *Immortalité,* frigate, 37
HMS *Imperieuse,* steam frigate, *15, 232*
Inch, Philip, draughtsman, 55
Indagador, spanish slaver, *94*
India, shipbuilding, in, 94; trade restrictions lifted, 65
India, barque, 146
India Office Library, 64
Indian Chief, ship, 151
Indianer, barque, *111*
Inglis, A & J, builders of *Norman Court,* 255, *256;* built engines for SS *Sea King,* 222
Inglis, Capt W, 220-21
Institution of Naval Architects, 84, 135, 202, *206*
Inverness and Cromarty Packet, smack, costs, 274
PS *Invincible,* listed, 198
PS *Iris,* 107; costs, 276
Iron Duke, 132
Iron, ballast, 81, 227, 240, 256, 265; corrosive action of copper, 144; used as structural members in wooden ships, 24, 148-51, *137; see also* Spars
Iron ships, fouling and anti-fouling, 131-32; greater cargo capacity, 131; of sailing ships over 900 tons listed, 134; size increases after 1860, 135
Iron shipbuilding, advantages and disadvantages, 130-32; boom years 135; costs of, 130; concentration on vessels of over 100 tons, 134; comparison of ships built at Warrington, 135, 198-201; construction of *Richard Cobden,* 122; Lloyd's Register rules, 132-34; longitudinal system, 133; shell expansion plan, *132;* skills required in its infancy, 130; speed of construction, 199; sharp schooners, 23; survivals encourage it, 142-43; weight of metal hull, 199
Irt, barque, cost of, 78
Isis, three-masted schooner, 141

Jack Tar, brig, costs, 275
Jackass barques, *Matchless, 204,* 205; *Ziba,* 205
HMS *Jackdaw,* schooner, *85,* 85-86
James, schooner, costs, 275
James, William, naval historian, 37
James Livesey, ship, 134
James Matheson, ship, 96
James Pilkington, ship, 134
James Baines, American-built ship, *191;* listed, 139; hull-form, 189; 100-feet mainyard, 196; speed,190
James Booth, ship, *158,* 158
Jane Leech, ship, 198
Janette, iron schooner, 267; plan, *269*
PS *Jardine,* schooner, costs, 275
Jardine, Matheson & Co, owners of *Anonyma, 93, of Cairngorm,* 178-79, of *Falcon* (1824), 74, 75
Jason, ship, 258
Jean Steuart, brig, costs, 275
Jeanne Richard, French privateer, *48*
Jhelum, construction of interior, *137*
SS *Jho-Sho-Maru,* barque, 251; costs, 279
John Bell, ship, an extreme clipper, 172, 222; arrival in Tasmania, 190; beam-to-length ratio, 164; compared with *Tempest,* 186, converted into steamer, 172; hull-form, 169-70; listed, 134, 169; long mainyard, 196
John Bright, schooner, 123
John Bunyan, ship, 116-17, 159; passages, 117
John Campbell, ship, 166
John Garrow, ship, 132
John Gilpin, brig, 91
John Knox, barque, 159
John Lidgett, ship, cost of, 144; quickly built, 144; sail plan, 150
John Nicholson, ship, 173, *176*
John o'Gaunt, ship, 95-96, 178
'John o'Gaunt', provisional name for *Norman Court,* 255
John Pirie, schooner, costs, 275
John R. Worcester, ship, *229;* described, 228; designed by Rennie, 167, 220, 228; passage, 228-29
John Taylor, ship, 141, 181; costs, 277
John Walker, smack, costs, 278
John Wesley, barquentine, 251, 265; costs, 279
John Williams (1865), barque, 250-51; costs, 278
John Williams, ex *Samoa* (1868), barque, *252;* compared with *Mansfield, 252; hull-form, 252-53; spar and rigging plan, 251-53; performance, 251-52; dimensions, 251; scantlings, 253*
Johnson, John, shipbuilder, 166
Joly (1776), French slaver, *35;* hull-form, 36-37
Jones, Calvert, photographer, *25, 89*
Jones, Josiah, jnr, builder of *Aphrodita,* 134, 150; of *Khimjee Oodowjee, 134;* names of ships built, 135
Jones, Palmer, & Co, shipowners, *199*
Jones, Quiggin & Co, builder of *Andromeda,* 161; employ steam power aboard, 224; names of ships built, 135
Jordan v Moore, 145-46
Jordan, George, royalties for composite construction, 145-146
Jordan & Getty, builders of *Evangeline,* 134; names of composite ships built and costs, 142; shipyard, *142*
Jordan, Henry, royalties for composite construction, 145-46
Jordan, John, shipbuilder, patent for composite construction, 141-45; lecture, 143; royalties on his patent, 144-45
Joseph, smack, costs, 275
Joseph Fletcher, ship, 154
Josephine, specification, 135
Joy, William, artist, *61*
Juan de la Vega, brigantine, described, 253, *253;* costs, 279
Jubilee, ship, described, 201-02
Julia, ship, compared with *Chrysolite,* 182; costs, 277
SS *Juno,* schooner, costs, 277
Jupiter, ship, *43;* compared with clippers, 43-44; compared with *Venus,* 47; described by builder, 42-43; designed by arcs of circles, 44, 52; hull-form, 43-44, 58; speed-length ratio, 20

Kagosima, ship, 149
Kaisow, ship, listed, 234; hull-form, 234
Kashgar, ex *John Williams,* ex *Samoa,* 252
Kate Carnie, ship, listed, 234
Keay, Captain, master of *Ariel, 235,* 239
Keel for tonnage, defined, 283
Kelly, W, builder of *Teazer, 208,* 214
Kelpie, captured 1836, ex-slaver, 91
Kelpie (1842), designed by Henderson, 91; hull-form, 91
Kelpie (1855), barquentine, costs, 277
Kelvinhaugh, Stephen opens shipyard, 181
Kelso (1855), ship, 183, 233
Kelso (1861), ship, 233
Kelso, John R, names of his tea clippers, 233; owner of *Maitland,* 231-33
Kemp, Dixon, pear-shaped curves, 109
Kennard & Williamson, shipbuilders, 97
Ketches, 144, 157; square-rigged, 50, 52
Kettle bottom hull, 242, 253
Khimjee Oodowjee, ship, 134
Kierkegaard, N C, folio of plans, *136, 267*
Killick, Capt James, 197, 218, 224
Killick, Martin & Co, shipowners, 218, 233-34
King, shipbuilder, 29
King and Queen Dock, Rotherhithe, 189
King Arthur, ship, 234
King of Tyre, schooner, *82,* 83-86
King William, Leith smack, 81
Kipping, Robert, author, 148-49
Kirkaldy & London Shipping Co, 63

Kirkham, ship, 134
Kitta Wake, schooner yacht, 181; costs, 278
Kitty, slaver, *14*
Knight Errant, ship, 134
Knowles, John, 18, 25
Koh-i-noor, mentioned, 141
Kortum, Karl, *147*
Kosciusko, ship, sail plan, 150
SS *Kwang Tung*, 251; costs, 279
Kyd, J, & Co, shipbuilders, 91

La Hogue, ship, 138
PS *La Perlita*, listed, 198
La Vengeance, French privateer, 37
Lady Clarke, ship, 157
Lady Grant, opium clipper, 94
Lady Hamond, Bermudian sloop, hull-form, *28*, 28
Lady Hood McKenzie, brig, costs, 274
Lady Octavia, ship, listed, 134, 198, 201; specification, 135, 200
Lady Saltoun (1817), sloop, 274
Lady Saltoun (1854), brig, 208
Lady William Bentinck, pilot brig, 94
Labloo, ship, listed, 234
Laing, J, builder of *Dunbar, Duncan Dunbar* and *La Hogue*, 138
Laird, John, builder of *Dove*, 23; of *Kirkham*, 134, of *Ma Lucy*, 148; of *Proto*, 118; of *William Fairbairn*, 134
Lammermuir, claim to clipper status, 183, 234; race with *Cairngorm*, 179
Lamport, Charles, ships he built listed and described, 201-02, *201*
Lancaster Museum, model of *Thetis*, 13, 34
Lang, Oliver, naval architect, 186, 192, 254
HMS *Lapwing*, captures slaver, 58
Lardner, Dr D, 168
Largest wooden merchant sailing ship built in UK, 186
Lark, taken into Danish Navy 1790, three-masted lugger, 53
HMS *Lark* class (1829-30), cutters, 85
Larken, ex *Lark*, taken into Danish Navy 1790, lugger, 53
Lattery, smuggler, 68
Lauderdale, ship, 142
Laurence, Hill & Co, builder of *Pride of Canada*, 134
Lavinia, jackass barque, *204*
Lawrie, J G, builder of *Leander*, 242
Le Couveur (1775), French lugger, 53; plan, *53*
Le Havre, ship entering under sail, *271*
Leander, ship, *242*; candidate for identification, *239*; compared with *Thermopylae*, 244-47; with other ships, 241-42; one of six fastest tea clippers, 234; plans of, 244-45; roller-reefing topgallant, 149, 242; hull-form, 242-43; dimensions, 244; sail plan, 247
Leech, John, shipowner, 198
Liechardt, ship, 181; costs, 277
Leith & London Shipping Co., 82, 106
Leith smack of 173 tons, *79, 80;* designed by Hedderwick, 79-82; hull-form, 79, 80; sail and rigging plan, 80-81; speed-length ratio, 80
Leith smacks, *Comet*, 79-80; compromise design, 79; *Matchless*, 80; *Queen Charlotte*, 80, 81; reasons for construction in south-west England, 81-82; replaced by schooners, 82, 99
Les Huits Amis, French privateer; hull-form, 37
Leslie, G, shipowner, 159
Lever, Darcy, author, 47
Lewes, barque, 121
Lidgett, John, & Co, order composite ship, 143-44
Light Brigade, ex *Ocean Telegraph*, American ship, *183*
PS *Light of the River*, 135
Lightning (1841), schooner, 107; costs, 276
Lightning (1852), schooner, 212
Lightning (1854), American-built ship, *189*, *190;* deck layout and sail plan, 190, famous Captain, 114; fast passages, 191-92; hollow bow filled in, 186; hull-form, 189-90, 194; listed, 139; model, *215;* prismatic coefficient, 20; probable sail plan, 190; speed, 190; speed-length ratio, 163
SS *Lily*, costs, 279
Lindsay, W S, 152, 209, 239
Linton, Hercules, designer of *Cutty Sark*, 254
L'Intrepide (*c*1800), French privateer, hull-form, *36*, 36-37, 53, 71
L'Invention (1801), French privateer, captured, *37*, 38; dimensions, *37;* hull-form, 38; sail plan, *37*, 37, 38
Lisslie, H W, collection of plans, 263, *264*
List, builder of *Falcon*, 71-73
Little Lucy, steamer, 135
Little Western, steamer, 142
Lively, sloop, costs, 274
Liverpool, mail packet pictured at, *49;* privateers fitted out, 15; shipbuilding at, 147, 187-89; wet dock in use pre-1800, 44
Liverpool Compass Committee, 199
Liverpool Museum, model of *Salamis*, *263;* of *Scawfell*, 201; of *Vision*, 180, 205; painting of *Rapido*, 207
Liverpool Standard, describes Tayleur, 199
Liverpool Underwriters' Association, 133, 160
Liverpooliana, ship, 198-200
Livestock, carried on *Marco Polo*, 211
Livingstone, Dr, 135
Lizzie Webber, brig, 183
Llewellyn, shipowner, 67
Lloyd's Register (annual volumes), describes ship as 'sharp', 83
Lloyd's Register of Shipping, composite construction, 143-44; describe composite ships as experimental, 144; many iron ships not classified, 133, 135; model of ship mislaid, 141; rules for building iron ships, 132-34; rules for wood shipbuilding, 135-36; rules for composite ships, 144; survey reports, 122; survey reports for *Ariel* and *Titania*, 236-37; reclassify *Titania*, 238; surveyor of Aberdeen describes clippers, 112; surveys first iron vessel, 132; *Thermopylae*'s sail plan, 247; Visitation Committee, 126, 132-33, 143
Loch Awe, ship, 253
Loch Garry, ship, 250
Loch Ness, ship, 253
Loch Tay, ship, 253
Loch Vennachar, ship, 250
Lodore, ship, 201
Log of the 'Cutty Sark' (Lubbock), 239
London (1770), American ship, 40
London (1817), East Indiaman, 66, *66*
London (1840), schooner, 101, 107; costs, 276
London, shipbuilding at, 25, 67, 156-57, 219-20
London & Edinburgh Shipping Co, 99, 103
London and Leith Smack and Steam-Yacht Guide (1824), 81
London & Liverpool Shipping Co, 118
London Missionary Society, orders ships from A Hall & Sons, 250-53; renames new ship, 251
London & Waterford Shipping Association, 84
Longboat, made of iron, 124; on rollers, 180
Lord of the Isles, (1853), ship, *164;* compared with *Hurricane*, 161, 163, 165; fast passage to Sydney, 164; plans published, 159; speed, 164; speed-length ratio, 163
Lord of the Isles (1869), barquentine, *266*
Lord Saumerez, brig, 88
Lord Western, barque, 109; costs, 276
Lothair, ship, clipper status, 253
Louisa (1834), brig, 88
Louisa (1858), schooner, 141
Lowther Castle, East Indiaman, 63
Lubbock, Basil, author of *China Clippers*, 218, *236;* compares 3- and 4-masted ships, 262; describes *Cairnsmore*, 165; lists Blackwall frigates, 137; lists ships built in 1869, 253; on double topgallants, 150; on *Maitland*, 232-33; on ships in China and opium trades, 40, 74, 91, 95; plan of *Fiery Cross* (1855), 166; plan of *Lord of the Isles*, 159; sail plan of *Spindrift*, 241; source material for China clippers, 218, 241, 245, 254, 256; quoted, 226; letters to MacCunn, 234-235, 239; royal masts, 250
Lufra, ship, costs, 279
Luggers, experimental, 52; French, 32, 39, 54, *55;* long in proportion to breadth, 52; three-masted used for smuggling and privateering, *53*, 53
Lund, William, shipowner, 263
Lungley, Charles, shipbuilder, 161-62
Lyman, John, comment on cutter-built, 29; finds plan of cutter brig, 29; on tonnage measurement, 104
HMS *Lyme*, 24-gun ship, 28
Lynn, John engraver, 84
Lynx, Baltimore clipper, *40*

Ma Roberts, 135
McCalmont, shipowner, 121
McCatcheau, Capt, 88
McClellan, Capt, 225
MacCunn, James, names of tea clippers owned, 234; letters to Lubbock on clipper

ship design, 234-35, 239; John Willis commented on, 254
McDiarmid & Greenshields, shipowners, 234
MacDonnell, Capt Charles, 188
MacDuff, ship, costs, 278
Macfarlane, J G, shipowner, 172
McGee, Paddy, 187
McGill, J Edward, aprentice, 248
Macintyre, L H, & Co, shipowners, 142-43
McKay, Donald, apprenticed, 123; builds clippers for Baines, 189, 193-94; names of ships built, 184, 211; shipbuilder's yard, *139*
Mackinnon, Frew & Co, shipowners, *242*
McLean Museum, Greenock, 234
MacLean, Duncan, seaman-journalist, 136
McMillan, A, & Son, shipbuilders, 260, 263
McMinnis, partner in Robertson & Co, 221-22
Macquarie, ex *Melbourne*, *261*, *262;* clipper, 242; sail plan, 261
McTear, Thomas, shipowner, 114
Madge Wildfire, ship, 148
Magnus Troil, schooner, costs, 275
Maid of Aln, schooner, costs, 276
Maid of Judah, ship, 159
Mail packets, clippers supersede steamers in Crimean War, 215; *see also* Post Office packets
Maitland (1851), ship, 233
Maitland (1865), ship, *231*, *232;* compared with *Ariel*, 231-32; brace winch, 151, 232-33, 246; compared with *William le Lacheur*, 220; deck layout, 221, 232; fast passages, 231; half-model, 183, 231; hull-form, 232; iron and steel spars, 233; plans now complete, 231; sail plan, 232-33, 241; speed, 232; stunsails compared with *Titania*, 239; *Undine* similar, 232; spar dimensions, 232-247
Malek-Adhel, American brig lines and sail plans, *88*
Manchester, barque, 87
Mangles, ship, 96
Mansfield, barque, hull-form, 174; hull-form compared with *John Williams*, 225, 252; listed, 173, 225
Manuel Llanguno, American ship, 250
Manuela, ex *Sunny South*, captured, *168*
Marchioness of Salisbury, Post Office packet brig, *59;* bought by Royal Navy and renamed *Nightingale*, 59; compared with *Neilson*, 69; with *St. Helena*, 59; hull-form and deck layout, 59; mentioned, 50; passages, 59
Marco Polo, ship, 186, *187*; compared with *Storm Cloud*, 172; design not copied in Britain, 186; deck fittings, 187-88; hull-form, 187, 211; speed, 190; passages, 187-89; passengers, 188
Mare, Charles & Co, 122, 134
Margaret Deane, ship, 166; hull-form, 166
Marine Investment Co, shipbuilders, 228
Marine Models, 64
Mariner's Mirror, cutter-brigs, 29; Leith smacks, 81; painting of *John Knox*, 159; plan of *Vision*, 179; 'Speed under Sail', 190; 'The World's First Clipper', 102
Mariner's Museum, Newport News; model of *Marco Polo*, 186
Marion, barque, 141, 181; costs, 277
Marion Macintyre, barque, *142*, 142-43
Marlborough, ship, 137
Marmion, schooner, costs, *275*
Marpesia, ship, 150
Marquand & de la Mare, shipbuilders, 204
Mars, privateer, armament and hull-form, 32-33
Marshall, George, builder and owners, 138, 143
Marshall, John, draughtsman, 55
Martaban, ship, described, 201
Martha, schooner, 84, *84*
Martin, J H, surveyor, 133
Martinet, schooner, costs, 278
Mary, (1818), brig, 62, 68-70
Mary, (1820), sloop, costs, 275
Mary, (1858), barque, costs, 278
Mary and Ann, barque, costs, 275
Mary Anne Bruford, barque, 264
Mary Moore, ship, 151
Mary Stenhouse, ship, 134
Massey's log, 164
Masts, *see* Spars
Matchless (1810), Leith smack, 79, 80, 82
Matchless (1846), schooner, 107; costs, 277
Matchless (1859), barquetta, *204*, 205
Matheson, Alexander, 74
Matilda, brigantine, costs, 275
Matilda Wattenbach, ship, 138
Maudslay, Joseph, shipbuilder, 85, 202
Maudslay, Son & Field, shipbuilders, 258
Mauritius, trade with, 87-88
Maury, M F, 125, 214
Maypo (1829), barque, hull-form and offsets, 77
Maxton, Capt Peter, 164
May queen, ship, costs, 279
Mechanic's Magazine, 17, 23, 51-2, 142
Medea, ship, 258
Mediator, Bermudian sloop, 27-28
Medina, ship, 140
Mediterranean, fruit trade, 211, 212, 214
Medora, ex *Liverpooliana*, ship, 198
Melbourn (1847), ship, 160
Melbourne (1875), ship, described, 242; sail plan, 261
Melville, James R, naval architect, 244
Memorials of Royal Yacht Squadron, 73
Mendora, brig, costs, 276
Mercantile Navy Improved, 62
Merchant Sailing Ships 1775-1815 (MacGregor), 47
Merchant Sailing ships 1815-1850 (MacGregor) 76, *98*
Merchant Sailing Ships 1850-1875 (MacGregor) 263
Mermaid, pilot brig, 94
Mermerus, ship, *260*, *261;* compared with *Cutty Sark*, 259; with other Barclay, Curle ships, 230, 253, 258-61; deck layout, 260-61; double topgallants, 150, 261; example of large iron clipper, 258; hull-form, 259; hull-form compared with *Sobraon*, 250; sail plan and rigging details, 261-62
Merse, ship, 254
Metero, schooner, 270
Miako, barque, 233
Midas, Baltimore schooner, *40*
Middlemist, Capt 74
Midship section, importance in hull design, 19-20, 38, 53
Miles Barton, Canadian ship, 192
Millar, Capt W, 84
Miller, W C, shipbuilder, 134
Miller and Thompson, shipowners, 192
Mimosa, ship, *179;* costs, 277
Min, ship, 221, 234; hull-form, 234
Minerva (1813), brig, costs, 274
Minerva (1838), brig costs, 276
Minstrel Boy, brig, 83, *83*
Mirage, ship, 183
PS *Mirage*, steamer at Shanghai, *218*
Mirzapore, ship, *226*
Missionary ships, 267-70
Mosfussilite, ship, described, 226-27
Monarch, ship (1840) or barque (1844), 95-96
Monarch (1844), ship, Blackwall frigate, 137
Money, Wigram & Son, 239
Monkey forecastle, 237
Monkey poop, 237
Monsoon, ship, 161
Montauk, American ship, 123, *124*
Monthly Nautical Magazine (New York), 177
Montrose, ship, 150
Moonsails, *see* Sails, moonsails
Moore, Charles & Co, shipowners, 199
Moore, G S, shipbuilder, 145
Moore, H, shipowner, 222
Moorsom, George, America adopts his system, 154; book on history of tonnage, 97; compares capacity of wood and iron ships, 131; describes a barque, 121; his proposals for tonnage measurement, 151; his tonnage system, 23, 98, 151-52; on 1821 tonnage recommendations, 25
Morgan, William, editor, 17
Morning Light, Canadian ship, 139
Morning Star, ship, Canadian, *2* (frontispiece)
Moseley, Ebenezer, shipbuilder, 116
Mosquito, iron yacht, 122
Moulded breadth, defined, 283-8
Mountain Maid, brig, 107, 114; costs, 276
Mountaineer, brig, costs, 275
Munro, George, shipowner, 101
Munro, G W, 64
Murray, Andrew, 133; diagonal construction, 140; reproduces plan of *Lord of the Isles*, 159; reproduces plan of *Schomberg*, 194-5; reproduces section of *Vision*, 181
Murray, Mungo, 15, 52
Museum of Applied Science, Melbourne, 245
HMS *Musquidobit*, ex *Lynx*, ex-privateer, 39, *40*
Mystery (1841), iron yacht, 122
Mystery, ex *Retriever* (1855), barque, 198

Naga, steamer, 91
Nairac, Elizé, shipowner, *36*, 37

Napier, Robert, shipbuilder, 133, 155, 221
Napier, W, artist, 224, *225*
Napoleonic Wars, 24, 27, 56, 67
Natal Star, ship, costs, 278
Natchez, American ship, 124
National Maritime Museum, Greenwich, drawings and paintings examined at, 91; Lisslie plans, 263; Lloyd's Register survey reports, 111, 241, 247; model with Aberdeen bow cost, 113-14; model of *Fling*, 212; painting of *Hurricane*, 162; painting of *Mermerus*, 261; plans examined at, 26-27, 56, 59, 62, 63, 76, 89, 93, 150; plans of Denny's ships, 119, 207; plans of *Leander* and *Thermopylae*, 244-45; preservation of Admiralty draughts, 37
National Watercraft Collection, 27
Nautical Magazine, 148
Nautical Photo Agency, 194
Nautilus (1762), ship, privateer, *32;* hull-form, 32
Nautilus (1815), brig, costs, 274
Nautilus (by *c*1827), cutter yacht, 73
Nautilus (*c*1840-50), steamer, 91
Naval architects, rise of, 121, 270; see under individual names
Naval architecture, books on, 15, 270; in eighteenth century, 15-18; *see also* Design, Hull-form
Naval Architecture (Stalkartt), 16, *17*
Naval Science, 218
Navigation Acts, repeal of, 129, 153-54, 184; *see also* Acts of Parliament
Neath Abbey Iron Co, builders of *Ellen Bates*, 134
Neilson, brig, *68, 70;* compared with *Dash*, 75, 76; deck layout, 69-70; hull-form, 68-69; list of spar dimensions, 69; sail and rigging plans, 69-71; style of plans, 62
Nelson, ship, 148
Nelson, T, & Co, shipowners, 212
Neptune, schooner, 198
New York Tribue, 184
New Zealand Shipping Co, 172
Newall, Robert S, wire rigging, 148
Nicholas, brig, costs, 274
Nicholson, Benjamin, collects grandfather's half-models and paintings, 174-75, 225
Nicholson, Benjamin E, (*d*1913), builder of *Mansfield*, 225; designs extreme clippers, 172-74, 270; his ships described, 172-76; list of ships built, 173; took charge at shipyard, 173
Nicholson, John, shipbuilder, 173
Nicholson, John & Co, builders and owners, 172, 175
Nicholson & McGill, shipowners, 173
Nicol, Alexander, shipowner, 101
Nicoya, ship, 228, 250; costs, 278
Nightingale, ex *Marchioness of Salisbury* (1816), brig, 59
Nightingale (1851), American ship, *184, 185;* deadrise, 179
Noble, Capt., 199
Nonpareil, Baltimore schooner, extreme model, 390; prismatic coefficient, 20
Non-Such (non-such), schooner, *100, 101, 105;* costs, 276; deck plan, 101; half-model, 103; listed, 107; passages, 106; replaces Leith smacks, 82, 107; sail plan, *102*
Norah Greame, ship, 134
Norman Court, ship, *256, 257;* deck layout, 256-58; dimensions, 223, 258; designed by Rennie, 157, 220; extreme clipper, 253, 255; Rennie's lines plan, 255-56, steering gear, 246; young captain, 234
Normand, Augustin, shipbuilder, 243
Norna, ship, 183
North British Daily Mail, describes *Storm Cloud*, 167-68
North Star, ship, 107, 113; costs, 277
Norway, Arthur H, author, 48
Nourse, James, shipowner, 226
Novidade, ex *Electric Telegraph*, 121
Nymph, opium clipper, 94

Oak, brig, costs, 274
Oberon, brigantine, 76-78
Observations on Naval Architecture, 73
Ocean Bride, schooner, 214
Ocean Mail, ship, costs, 278
Ocean Queen, barque, *117*, 117-18
Ocean Telegraph, American ship, *183*
Oceanography, its contribution, 237
Offsets, plans drawn from, 49, 77, 244
Old England, ship, privateer, 32
Oliver Cromwell, ship, 186, 192
Oliver Lang, Canadian ship, 186, 192
Olivier van Noord, Dutch ship, 148
Omar Pasha, ship, 138; described, 159
On the Stowage of Ships and Their Cargoes, (Stevens), quoted, 212
Opium clippers, American influence in design, 40, 91; built by A. Hall & Sons, 106, 207, 209; described, 23, 90-95; *Falcon* (1824), 74; fruiters bought, 85-86; rig of, 85, *98, 99*
Opium Clippers (Lubbock), 106
Opium trade, 90-95
Orange, brig, costs, 274
Orange Grove, barque; deck layout compared with *Ariel*, 259; described, 226; listed, 225
Oribe, barque, costs, 277
Orient, ship, construction, 141
Oriental, American ship, *126;* lines taken off in London, 126, 183; passage from China, 117, 126, 154
Orlando, brig, costs, 275
Orwell, ship, 138
Osaka, barque, 233
Osborn, schooner, costs, 275
Osprey, schooner, 214
Osprey, smack, costs, 275
Osprey, yacht, 74
Outline of Ship Building (Fincham), 15-17, 116
Overend, Gurney & Co, 183

P & O (Peninsular & Oriental Steam Navigation Co), 164
Pacific Steam Navigation Co (PSNCo), 222
Packet Ships, for East India Company, 55; trans-Atlantic, 66, 123
Pagoda Anchorage, Foochow, *216*
Palladium, brig, costs, 275
Palmer, Miss Sarah, 199-200
Panama, American ship, 123
Pantaloon, brig, 88
Papers on Naval Architecture, 17, 73
Pareora ex *White Eagle*, *170*, 172
Parga, schooner, 83, *83*
Paris, Adml Edmon, 53, 245, 247
Paris Exhibition 1855, 183
Park Bros, shipowners, 234
PS *Parramatta*, 166
Parsons, William, naval architect, 151
Passages, Azores fruit trade, 212; record from China to New York, 125; Brazil to Liverpool, 122; by Falmouth packets, 49, 59; 'Great Ocean Regatta', 191; to and from Australia in 1850s, 162, 164, 172, 188-89, 191; record from Macao to Liverpool, 202; to Australia, 162; passages to and from China in 1830s, 96, 97; before 1845, 95-97; in 1850s, 167, 175, 179; in 1860s, 218, 239; to Melbourne by *Hurricane*, 162; *Virginia*'s trans-Atlantic, *123*
Passengers, aboard Post Office packets, 81; aboard *St. Helena*, 57; accommodation *Marco Polo*, 187-88
Patriarch, ship, clipper status, 253; pole masts, 162
Patricia, barque, 140
Patten, J Wilson, 198
Patton, John, shipowner, 228, *229*
PS *Paul Jones*, tug, 113; costs, 275
Paulista de Carioca, French ship, 243
Peabody Museum, Salem, 136
Peacock & Buchan, 132
Peake, Sir Henry, naval architect, 39, 52, 59
Pearl (1820), cutter yacht, 61, 73
HMS *Pearl* (1828), sloop, 61
Pearse, M, shipbuilder, 135
Pegasus, ship, costs, 278
Peile, Scott & Co, 202; builders of *Banian*, 201; of *Camertonian*, 126
HMS *Pelorus*, brig, 86
Pera (1831), schooner, 84
Pera (1843), schooner, 105; costs, 276; listed, 107; sail plan, 102, *102*
Peri, schooner, *213;* hull-form, 212; sail plan, 212, *213*
Persian, schooner-brigantine, *214*
Peruvian, barque, 109; costs, 277
Petersen, Jacob, artist, 75, *76*
Petropolis, French clipper ship, 243
Phillips, Shaw & Lowther, shipowners, 157, 234, 235
Philort, sloop, costs, 274
Philosopher, ship, 134, 135
Phipps, John, author, 94
Phoenician, barque, *117;* carries gold, 157; comapred with other ships, 116-17; dimensions compared, 116-17; hull details, 110, 117, 159; tonnage, *116*, 117
Pike, Capt, 74
Pile, John, names of ships he built, 183, *203*

Pile, John and William, few plans of their clippers, 182-83; shipbuilders, 183
Pile, Spence & Co, shipbuilders, *242*, 183
Pile, William, builder of *Ganges*, 225; of *Lammermuir*, 179, 208; of *Maitland*, 231-33; of *Rodney*, *131*, 263; names of ships he built, 183, 233, 255; builds clippers, 218, 233
Pilgrim, American brig, *231*
Pilot boat, Virginia-built, 18, *42*
Pilot brig, Bengal, 94
Pilot cutters, 179, 236; built at Bristol, 47
Pilot Fish, ship, 107; costs, 277; described, 111
Pinkney, D G, 148
HMS *Pique*, frigate, compared with *Thermopylae*, 247
Pitcher, shipbuilder, 65
HMS *Pitt*, cutter, 26
Planter, barque, 266
Plough, schooner, 23; costs, 274
Plover, ex *Bentinck*, survey ship, 94
Pocock, Nicholas, artist, 32, *33*
Polly, brigantine, *277*
Pook, Samuel, H, designed *Red Jacket*, 184, 191
Pope & Co, shipowners, 84
Port Fleetwood, schooner, 107; costs, 276
Port Jackson (1854), ship, 183
Portland, Duke of, 73, 89
Portland Shipbuilding Co, 166
Post Office packets, 14, 47-50, 59-61; accommodation on Holyhead route, 81; design of packets 79, 82; *Duke of Marlborough*, 49; example of cutter-build, 58; Hilhouse-built ship, 48, 49; Holyhead to Dublin, 79; Mail Packet off Liverpool, *49*; *Marchioness of Salisbury*, 50, 59; organisation of packets, 48, 59; plan from Steel's offsets, 49, 50; 1793 design analysed, 48
Post Office packet of 179 tons, *49*; example of cutter-build, 55, 58; hull-form, 48, 68; identification, 48
Potter, Alexander, 160
Potter, Lewis, 160
Potter, Wilson & Co, shipowners, 159-60
Pow & Fawcus, windlass makers, 146
Poyser, Capt F C, 193, 194
Present Imperfect State of British Naval Architecture, 17
Preston (1823), brig, 70, 71
Pride of Canada, ship, 134, equipment, 165
Prince Alfred, barque, *141*
Prince de Neuchatel, brigantine, 91; American privateer, 40
Prince of Wales, schooner, 106, 107; costs, 277
Prince of Waterloo, ship, costs, 274
Prince Regent, Royal yacht, 52
Prince Royal of Denmark's yacht, 16
Princess Augusta, Royal yacht, 52
SS *Princess Louise*, costs, 279
Princess Royal, schooner, costs, 277
Princeza, brig, 108; costs, 277
Prismatic Coefficient, explained, 20
Privateers, 13, 32-39; *Alexander* (rebuilt 1777), of Bristol, 32; *Alexander* (Science Museum model), 32, *33;* characteristics of French 1795-1803, 37; *Nautilus*, 32; *Old England*, 32; *Rackoon*, 36; *Ranger*, *33; Thetis* (by Brockbank), 34; Virginia-built, 16
Propellor, lifting-gear, 224
Proto, schooner, *118, 119;* Aberdeen bow above waterline, 116, 118; hull-form, 118; compared with *Scottish Maid*, 118
Prowse, J, & Co, shipowners, 197
Psyche, ex *Indagador*, true brigantine, *92, 94*
Pumps, insufficient number in a ship, 62
PS *Punjaub*, later *The Tweed*, 254
Punton, T W, & Son, mast makers, 233

Q.E.D., auxiliary barque, 148
PS *Queen*, steamer, 107; costs, 276
Queen Charlotte, Leith smack, 80, *81*
Queen of Clippers, American ship, 139, 184
Queen of the Isles, barque, 119; costs, 276
Queen of the Tyne, schooner, 115
Queen of the West, schooner, 85, 212, *212*
Queen Victoria, brigantine, costs, 275
Queensbury, ship, beam-to-length ratio, 164; compared with *Annandale*, 174-75; dimensions, 173; half-model missing, 174-75; hull-form, 179; painting of, *173, 174, 175;* passages and earnings, 175

Rackoon, French corvette, *36*, 68
Radiant, brig, costs, 275
Rainbow, American ship, 124
Rajmahal, ship, 138
Raking midsection, 226-27, 236
Raking stem, *see* Hull-form
HMS *Rambler* (1796), cutter converted to brig, 29
Rambler (1841), schooner, costs, 276
Ranee, ex *Cowasjee Jehangeer*, under repair, *133*
Ranger, privateer, *33*
Rankin, Daniel, 165-66
Rankine, William, shipbuilder, 165
Rankine, Prof W J M, publishes plans, 135, 243
Ranterpike (rantipike), 85
Raphael (1846), barque, 121, 165
Raphael (1854), 158
Rapid (1833), schooner, *84;* described, 84; fast passage to Mauritius, 87
Rapid (1842), schooner, her hull-form copied, 116; costs, 276; listed, 107; passages, 82, 106
Rapido, barque, 182
Rats, destruction of, 59
Rebecca (1791), cutter, 48
HMS *Recruit* (1846), iron brig, 122
Recruit (1857), schooner, costs, 278
Red Jacket, American ship, *191;* earnings, 191; fast passages, 191; listed, 139; spar dimensions, 184
Red Riding Hood, ship, 142-43
Red Rover, opium clipper, *90*, 94; passage as opium clipper, 91; source of design, 40, 91
Reed, J, shipbuilder, 138
Rees, Abraham, editor, 63, 64
Regina Maris, barquentine, 233
Registry, measurements pre-1836, 271; measurements by 1836 Act, 103, 272; measurements by 1854 Act, 273
Reid, John, & Co, builders of *Antiope and Marpesia*, 150; of *Cairnsmore*, 134, 165, 243; of *Helen Nicholson*, 225; of *Vanguard*, 165; of *Weymouth*, 204
Reindeer (1848), ship, *112, 113;* compared with *Bonita*, *113*, 114; with other ships, 116, 118, 166; costs, 114-15, 277; extreme raking stem, 108, 114, 130; half-model, 102, 114, 154, 176; hull-form, 113-14, 177; passages, 114
Reindeer (1863), ship, 144-45, 150; costs, 278; moonsail, 221; launch account, 225
Reliance, sloop, costs, 274
Rennie, George, engineer, 166
Rennie, Johnson & Co, shipbuilders, 166
Rennie, Johnson & Rankine, description of ships built, 166-67; firm founded, 166
Rennie & Marshall, naval architects, 167, 223
Rennie, William, builds at Aberdeen and in Canada, 121, 165; consulting naval architect, 270; designs *Beraza* and *Raphael*, 121, 166; designs *Black Prince*, 167, 220, 224; designs *Earl of Eglinton*, 186; designs *Fiery Cross* (1855), 166-67; designs *Fiery Cross* (1860), 219; designs *Gauntlet*, 165; designs *John R. Worcester*, 228; designs *Margaret Deane*, 166; designs *Norman Court*, 255-56; designs PS *Parramatta*, 167; designs SS *Sea King*, 222-24, 245; designs *Strathmore*, 167; designer's fee, 256; moves to London, 167; names of six ships designed in 1860s, 167, 220; partner in Rennie, Johnson & Rankine, 166; model of SS *Sea King*, *222*, 222-23; remarks on hull-form of SS *Sea King*, 222-23; starts building in Liverpool, 166
Renown, ship, 121, 137
Resolution, later *Shamrock* (1805), *55*, 56
Resolution (1818), brig, costs, 274
Resource, brig, costs, 276
Retriever, barque, 198, 200
Revenue cutters, 15; described, 53-55
Rhoda Mary, schooner, 268; hull-form, 263
Rialto, ship, 248
Richard Cobden, barque, *122*, 123; hull-form, 122
Richardson, Duck & Co, shipbuilders, 135
Riddle, Edward, 97
SS *Richmond*, costs, 279
Rigging, lead of braces in 1870s, 261; old methods of leading braces persist, 177; rigging screws, 148; running topmast backstay, 201; wire introduced, 148; stunsail running rigging, 261-62
Rigging and Seamanship (Steel), *45*
Riley, Capt, 88
Rimac, brig, *78*
Ritchie, Capt, 82, 106
Ritchie, J H, surveyor, 133, 143
Ritherdon & Thompson, naval architects, 258
Rob Roy, opium clipper, 94
Robert Bruce, Leith smack, 82
Robert Kirkwood, smack, costs, 279
Robert Miller, smack, costs, 279

Robertson, Capt John, 96, 178
Robertson, William, draughtsman to A Stephen & Sons, 144, 160, 171, 223
Robertson & Co, owners of SS *Sea King*, 221-22, 224
Robin Hood, ship, *182*, beautiful half-model neglected, 182; compared with *Cairngorm*, 179; costs, 278; described, 182; dimensions, 176; half-model, 115, 134; hull-form and speed, 182; model for preliminary design, 182, 202
Robinson, R surveyor, 111
Rodger, A, names of six tea clippers owned, 234
Rodney, ship, *131;* clipper status, 263
HMS *Rolla*, 10-gun brig, 39
Romanoff, ship, 250
Roseneath, ship, 151
Ross, William, shipowners, 248
Rotterdam Packet, cutter, 80; costs, 274
Round sterns, early use in India, 94; when first used, 94, 113
Rover, schooner, costs, 276
Row, Gilbert, designer of *Stonehouse*, 229
Roxburgh Castle, ship, 182
Royal Blue Jacket, schooner, 140
SS *Royal Charter*, auxiliary ship sail plan, described, 149-50
Royal George, Royal yacht, hull-form, 52
Royal Mail Steam Packet Co, 166
Royal Navy, adoption of new constructional methods, 22; builds two sharp schooners at New York, 38; buys cutters, 36; buys merchant ships, 13, 32, 40; buys Chesapeake sloop 1745, 27; fights slave trade, 14, 89-90; influence of yachts, 89; iron ships planked with wood, 132; plans of purchased vessels, 29; quantity of timber used in construction, 20; Sir William Symonds appointed Surveyor, 88-89
Royal Society, 22
Royal Sovereign, Royal yacht, described, 52; hull-form, 52; plans, 16, *52, 53*
Royal Thames Yacht Club, 52
Royal Yachts, 23, 52-53
Royal Yacht Squadron, 71, 73
Rubens, ship, 158
Rudder, round-headed, 21
Rumford, Count, 16, 17
Russell, J Scott, on iron shipbuilding, 130, 133; wave form theory, 168; design of HMS *Warrior*, 243-44
Russell & Co, merchants, 74
Rustomjee Cowasjee, ship, 91

Sail plans, Aberdeen schooners, 106; schooners 1860-75, 264-65; cutters, 26-28; early barquentine, 77-78; late-eighteenth century merchant ship reconstructed, 46-47, *46;* Leith smack, 80-81; squarer plan evolving by 1850, 129, 247; *Thermopylae*'s found, 247
Sailor's Word-Book, 28
Sails, crossjack omitted in 1855, 201; brig's single topsails, *108;* early examples of double topgallants, 150, 261; early examples of double topsails, 149-50; four headsails from fore topmast, 160; jamie green, 202, 203; list of sails aboard *Sir Lancelot*, 239; main lower stunsail, 233, 239; mizen stunsails, 66, 73, *91, 190,* 221, 233, *233;* moonsails, 65, 124, *156,* 190, *191, 203,* 221, 233; ringtail, *203,* 233; roller-reefing, 148-49, 165; schooner or cutter's square sail with head yard, 26, 31; skysail stunsails, *191,* 229, 233; spindle staysail, 65; stunstails, unusual for builder to draw them on plan, *227;* watersail, *233,* 233; *see also* Flying Kites
Sails and Sailmaking, (Kipping), 149
St Helena, 55-57
St Helena (1776), American-built ship, *44*
St Helena (1814), brigantine, 55, *56;* compared with *Marchioness of Salisbury*, 59; compared with HMS *Sea Lark* ex Fly, 39, 56; hull-form and deck layout, 55-56; passages described, 56-57, 97; sail plan, 56-57; speed, 57
St Nicholas, brig costs, 275
St Peter Port, Guernsey, *245*
Saint Vincent, ship, 151
Sainty, Philip, *60;* names of ships built, 61; submits plan of cutter, 60, 101
Salamander, schooner yacht, *208, 209;* costs, 207, 278; diagonal build, 140, 181, 207; photographed, 207, 208; sail plan, 207, 208; opium clipper, 207-09
Salamis, ship, *263;* brace winch, 151; compared with tea clippers, 263; dimensions, 244; indentification of models, 263; possible half-model, 116-263, similar to *Thermopylae*, 244, 262-63, *263;* tea clipper, 242, 245, 263
Sales prices of, *Alexander Baring*, 103; *Annandale*, 201; *Hurricane*, 185; *Lord Saumarez*, 95; SS *Sea King*, 252; *Storm Cloud* and *White Eagle*, 196
Salisbury, William, draws plan of Post Office packet, 49; measures model of *Vision*, 180; model of *Camertonian*, 127, takes lines off models, 32-34, 262-63
Salmon, Robert, artist, *14,* 49, *49,* 71
Salthouse Dock, Liverpool, 164
Samoa, later *John Williams*, barque, *252;* costs, 251, 279; description by builder in letters, 251; renamed *John Williams*, 251; *see also John Williams*
Samuel Russell, American ship, 126, 179
Samuelson & Co, builders of *Bates Family*, 134
Samson, brigantine, costs, 275
San Francisco, American steamer, 156
San Francisco Maritime Museum, 215
Sancho Panza, schooner, 83
Sandeman & McLaurin, builders of *Tempest*, 164; of *Vision* (1854), 166
Sanderson, George S, engineer, 198
Sandridge Railway Pier, *157*
Sappho (1821), schooner, *67;* compared to other schooners, 68; hull-form, 66-68; influence of cutter hull, 55, 59, 66; passages, 67
Sappho (1854), barque, described, 166
Sarah, brig, costs, 276
Sarah Neumann, ship, 197; compared with *Tayleur*, 199; half-model identified, 198; hull-form, 198; size compared, 138
Sarah Nicholson, ship, 173
Sarah Palmer, ship, 200; compared with Tayleur, 200; dimensions, 198; hull-form, 200; listed, 134, 198; premature launching, 199-200; sail plan, 200-01, specification, 135, 200, 281-82
Saucy Jack, brig, 83
Savin-Taylor, Brian, 118
Scantling sizes, *Annandale*, 137; *Chariot of Fame*, 136,37; *Storm Cloud*, 170; *Sarah Palmer*, 281-82
Scawfell, ship, *201, 202;* compared with others, 127, 201; half-model identification, 201-02; hull-form, 202; record passage from Macao, 202; listed, 201
Scheepvaart Museum, Amsterdam, 118
Schetky, J C, artist, *81,* 84, 90
Schomberg, ship, *193, 194, 195, 196;* big press coverage, 190, compared with Charles Tayleur's clippers, 200; costs listed, 193, 277; deck layout, 195; diagonal build, 40-41; dimensions, 176, 193; equal in size to largest American clipper, 137, 140, 186, 193; half-model, 103, 115, 154, 201; half-model and lines plan compared, *193,* 194; hull-form, 194; largest ship of 1850s built in UK, 135, 137-38, 249; passage, 196; photographed, 195; plank thickness, 195; sail plan, 195-96; speed, 194-95
School of Naval Architecture, Portsmouth, 17-18, 73
Schooner-brigantine, *67,* 56
Schooners, American, 32, 38-40, 86; built of iron, 23, 85, 116, 118-21, 134-35; *Caledonia*, 131-32; clipper style emerges in 1840s, 83-86; design by Henry Steers in 1805, 56; *Fling*, *235; Helena* 30-32; Hilhouse, 68; main topsail or two topsail, *30,* 31, of clipper model, 1860-75, 263-65; photographed at Swansea, 87; replace smacks, 82; ranterpike rig, 85; relation to shallop, 15; *Sappho*, 66-68; *Scottish Maid*, 99-105; slaver, 58; smuggling, 15; sufficient square canvas equivalent to brigantine, 83, *83;* survivor from past at Havana, *207;* three-masted, 86, *93;* 214, 264; yards on fore and main masts, 30, 32, 38; *see also* Baltimore clippers
Science Museum, model of *Alexander*, 32, *33;* model of *Comet*, 79, *80,* 82; model of *Emma*, 84; model of *Falcon*, 71, 74; model of *Fiery Cross* (1860), 220, 222; model of SS *Sea King*, 221, *222;* model of *Stonehouse*, 229; model of *Titania*, 235, *236;* plans of *Maitland, 231-233; plan of Titania*, 238
Scott & Co, builders of *Lord of the Isles*, 164; of *Serapis*, 263; of *Timaru*, 260, 263; builders of other ships, 22
Scott, Isaac, shipowners, 126
Scott, J, & Sons, builders of *Henry Moore*, 134
Scott & Linton, shipbuilders, 254
Scottish Maid, schooner, *100, 102, 103;* begins

Hall's clipper period, 134, 257; compared with schooners from other yards, 118-19; costs, 101, 276; deck layout, 101; dimensions from various sources compared, 103; first of Hall's ships with Aberdeen bow, 107-08; fitting of bowsprit, 105; half-model, 102-04, 105, 176; hull-form, 100-105, 107, 139; influence of cutter hull, 59, 101; order to build, 99, 104-05; scantlings, 101; sail plan, 102, 264; 'world's first clipper', 102; tank tests, 104-05; tonnage reduced, 99-100, 107
Scottish Shipbuilders Association, 141, 143
HMS *Scout*, ex *La Vengeance*, ex-French privateer, 37
Sea Breezes, 114
Sea Gull, Canadian brigantine, 150
HMS *Seagull*, 92, *92*, 93, *93*
HMS *Sea Lark*, ex *Fly*, American-built schooner, prismatic coefficient, 20; compared with *St Helena*, 39, 56; hull-form and deck layout, 39; plans, 39
SS *Sea King*, auxiliary ship, 222, 223, 225; costs itemised, 224; deck layout, 224; designed by Rennie, 167, 220, 222-23, 245; engines, 222; hull-form, 222-23; model, 222; negotiation of price and contract, 221-22; passages, 224; Rennie's lines plan, 223; rigging compared with *Maitland*, 255; royalty fee, 145; sail plan, 224, *225;* sold 224
SS *Sea King*, ex *Shenandoah*, ex *Sea King*, 225
Sea Queen, ship, 172
Sea Snake, ship, 198
Sea Star, ship, costs, 277
Sea Witch, American ship, *124*, 125; hull-form, 124-25; record passages, 125; master, 185
HMS *Seagull*, schooner packet, 59; hull-form, 100-1
Search for Speed under Sail, 20, 86, 123, 179, 204
Sebastion Cabot, ship, 201
Sebire, James, shipbuilder, 227
Sellar, James, 104
Selkirk, Earl of, 207, *209*
Seppings, Sir Robert, designer of *Cowasjee Family*, 23, 91-92; of *Rustomjee Cowasjee*, 91; of *Sylph*, 23, 91-92; diagonal construction, 22, 140, 281; employed cutter hull in fast ships, 71, 92; submits plan of cutter, 60; Surveyor to Royal Navy, 88
Serapis, ship, described, 276
Serica, ship, 218; compared with *Taitsing*, 240; dimensions, 234; hull-form, 234
Serringapatam, ship, retains rounded body form, 53
Seven Years War, 37
74-gun ship, *17*, 23
Seyfang, G B, 143
Shallcross & Co, shipowners, 222
Shallop, 15, *42*
Shakspere, ship, *176;* compared with *Annandale* 174-76; dimensions, 173; hull-form, 174-76; passage, 176
Shamrock, ex *Resolution* (1805), Revenue cutter brig, *54;* hull-form and sail plan, 55; influence of cutter hull, 55, 58
Shamrock (1849), schooner, 120
Shamrock (1872), schooner yacht, 242
Shandon, ship, hull-form, 163; roller-reefing gear to sails, 148, 165
Shanghai, photograph of Woosung River, *218*
PS *Shannon*, 22
Sharp, James, A, author, 39, 73
Sharston, barque, 167
Shaw, Lowther & Maxton, owners of *Ariel* and *Titania*, 234; of *Sobraon*, 249
Sheers & Co, shipowners, 214
Shenandoah, ex *Sea King*, 167; Confederate cruiser, 221, *223*, 223-25; *see also Sea King*
Shenir, ship, 261-62
Shewan, Capt Andrew, describes Aberdeen clippers, 78-79, 221; describes *Black Prince*, 220-21; describes Capt W Inglis, 221; lists six fastest tea clippers, 234; on Leith smacks versus colliers, 81; remarks on clippers, 233
Shepherdess, barque, 118
Ship-handling, clippers lacked knowledge of winds, 214; on *Black Prince*, 220-21
Ship Builder's Assistant (Sutherland), 15-16
Shipbuilders, shipbuilders of the 1860s, 218; critical of Lloyd's Register, 139; listed with iron ships of over 900 tons, 134
Shipbuilder's Repository, 16
Shipbuilding, *see* Composite Construction, Construction, Iron Shipbuilding, Wood Shipbuilding
Shipwright's Vade-Mecum (Steel), 16, *17*, 22, 47, *45*
Shoreham, ships built at, 83-84, 214
Shun Lee, ship, 242
Shuttle, barque, *197*, 198
Sibbald, John, 90
Siemens-Martin steel, 135
Simla, ship, 134
Simpson, Matthew, shipbuilder, 267
Simpson, William, shipbuilder, 288
Simons, William, shipbuilder, 134, 184
Sir Charles Forbes, ship, costs, 275
Sir Charles Napier, ship, 134
Sir Lancelot, ship, compared with *William le Lacheur*, 228; dimensions, 234, 228; in fast passages, 239; hull-form, 234-235; iron ballast, 202, 239; plans, *236*, 237; record passage from China, 239; photograph, *216;* list of sails carried in 1866, 239
Sir William Wallace (1835), brig, costs, 275
Sir William Wallace (1846), schooner, 107; costs, 277
Sisters, brig, costs, 275
Sjôhistoriska Museum, 71, 73
Skene, William, 110
Skillott, S D, artist (Skillett), *105*, *196*
Skinner, Thomas, shipowner, 239
Slade, Sir Thomas, 16
Slave trade, 14, 15, 86-87
Slavers, *Henriquetta*, *87; Joly*, 35, 36-37; *Kitty*, *14; Manuela*, *168;* rig of true brigantine, 84, 97, *100;* schooner, *58*
Slieve Donard, ship, 134
Sloops, defined 1815, 15
Smacks, 14-15; *see also* Berwick Smacks, Leith Smacks
Smith, Andrew, wire rigging, 148
Smith, Arthur, artist, *110*, 110-11, *128*, 129
Smith, George & Sons, cost of scraping and painting hull, 132; names of ships owned, 144, 204-05
Smith, James, shipbuilder, *186*, 186
Smith, Roberts, & Co, 249
Smith, T & W, shipbuilders, 147
Smith, W T, 104
Smith & Dimani, shipbuilders, 124, *124*
Smith & Rodger, shipbuilders, 133, 164
Smithsonian Institution, Washington, 27
Smugglers, built by Sainty, 61; fast cutters used, 53-54; plans in Hilhouse Collections, 68; regulations against likely vessels, 14-15
Smuggling, Acts to prevent, 14-15; fast craft required, 14, 52, 53
Smurthwaite, John, shipbuilder, 229
Smythe, Adml W H, 28
Snodgrass, Gabriel, surveyor, 21
Sobraon, ship, *249*, *250;* compared with *Schomberg*, 196; costs, 249, 278; described, 249-50; hull-form, 249-50; largest composite sailing ship, 146, 249; petty officers, *249;* designed as auxiliary, 224, 249-50; sail plan and spars, 250, *250*
Society for the Improvement of Naval Architecture, 14, 17, 52, 105
PS *Solent* (1853), 140
Solent (1857), ship, 140
Solway Queen, brig, 173
Somes, Frederick, shipowner, 143
Sophia, sloop, costs, 274
Souvenirs de Marine Conservées (Paris), 53
Sovereign of the Seas, American ship, British builder's interest, 184; listed, 139; speed, 190; clipper, 205
Spanish schooner, *234*
Spars, alterations in *St. Helena*, 57; spars for *Falcon* tabulated, 73; comparison of three eighteenth-century ships, 41; comparison of six clippers tabulated, 247; crossjack yard in cutter, 26; cutters, 26-27, 55; cutter-built vessels compared 1778-81, 28, 29; East Indiaman, 64-65; eighteenth-century ships, 46-47; eighteenth-century sloops, 28; Forbes' double topsail, 149; *Helena*'s spars, listed, 31; iron masts and yards, 147-48, 238; Howes' double topsails, 149; passaree boom, 82, 84; pole masts, *161*, 162; roller-reefing gear, 148-49; spread yard, 26, 31, 34; royal masts fidded abaft, 72, *250;* steel masts, 238; stunsail booms under yards, 241, 247; sliding gunter masts, 65, 111, 190, 221; spike bowsprit on *Vision*, *180;* telescopic bowsprit and jibboom, 160, 162; *Thermopylae*'s listed, 280; yards more than 100 feet long, 195-96; thickness of iron and steel, 238
Specifications for six ships, 200
Speed, days' runs over 400 miles, 164, 190, 248; days' runs over 350 miles, 164, 168, 172, 174, 239; high rate in knots, 164, 190; *Lord of the Isles*, 164

Speed-length ratio, explained, 20; examined for clippers, 163, 168, 174
Speedy, ship, described, 197-98
Spence, Joseph, 183
Spencer, James, shipwright, 47
Spencer, W B, artist, 237
Sphynx, ship, 141
Spin, J, artist, *156*
Spindrift, ship, *240, 241, 242;* compared with other tea clippers, 234, 239-41; deck layout, 241, 246; extreme clipper, 240-41; hull-form, 240-41; sail plan, 241; sail plan compared with *Maitland*, 232, 241; photograph, 216; spar dimensions listed, 241, 247; speed 241-42; wrecked, 242
Spirit, schooner, 83
Spirit of the Age, barque, 182
Spirit of the North, barque, 182
Spray of the Ocean, ship, 183
Spring Bok, barque, 198, 264
Stag, Canadian barque, *119*
Stalkartt, Marmaduke, author, *16, 17*
Standard, ship, 233
Star of China, ship, costs, 278
Star of Empire, American ship, *136*, 136-37, 139, 184
Star of Peace, ship, *159;* compared with *Ballarat*, 159
Star of Tasmania, ship, costs, 278
Star of the East, Canadian ship, *192;* description, 192-93
Startled Fawn, ship, chartered by James Baines, 199; dimensions, 198, 224; listed, 134, 201; hull, 199-200
Steel shipbuilding, advantages for spars, 148; Bessemer steel expensive, 135; history of, 135; named ships, 135; Siemens-Martin process, 135
Steel, David, author, his books listed, 16, 47; on cutter-brigs, 29; plan drawn from his offsets, 49; post office packet, 48, 55; publishes plans, 16, 47, 63, 77; sail plan of ship of 330 tons, *46*, 47; tables of spar dimensions, 41, 47, 64, 65
Steele, James, 235
Steele, Robert (1821-90), built clippers, 235
Steele, Robert (1745-1830), founder of shipyard, 235
Steele, Robert, & Co, shipbuilders, 221; bracket half-model, 19; builders of *'City'* ships, 13; builders of clippers, 240; clipper designs listed and analysed, 202, 218, 234-39; prices for tea clippers, 235-36; royalty fees, 146;
Steele, William, shipbuilder, 235
Steering gear, 246
Steers, George, naval architect, designer of *America*, 55, 169; of *Sunny South*, 194, *168*, 169
Steers, Henry, shipwright, 55
Steinhaus, C F, author, *228*
Stephen, Alexander, jnr, shipbuilder, advantages of iron shipbuilding, 130; begins designing ships, 160; conversation with James and William Hall, 134; cost of scraping hull, 132; influenced by wave form theories, 168; interest in American ships, 169, 184-85; joins Glasgow shipyard, 160; knows Griffiths' book on naval architecture, 185; obtains class for composite ships, 143-44; obliged to build from Rennie's design, 224, 245; offers to build auxiliary steamer in 1862, 221-22; pays Jordan royalties, 144-46; promotes composite construction, 143-46; quotes prices 1862, 135, 144; quotes prices for tea clippers, 219, 235-36; remarks on sharpness of hull, 219; seeks orders for new ships, 116, visits to ports and shipowners, 218
Stephen, Alexander, snr, begins iron shipbuilding, 134, 159; builder of *Eastern Monarch*, 137-38; shipbuilding activities, 159-60; attitude to son, 168
Stephen, A, & Sons, 261-62; build for G Smith & Son, 205; builders and owners of *Storm Cloud*, 168-69, 172; builders of *Charlemagne*, 134; of *City of Hankow*, 233; of *City of Madras*, 134; of composite ships, 143-44; of *Eliza Shaw*, 225-26; of SS *Euphrates*, 169; of extreme iron clippers, 222; of *Hurricane*, 134, 162, 222; of Janette, 267; of *John Bell*, 134, 169, 222; of *John Lidgett*, 150; of *Mofussilite*, 226; of SS *Sea King*, 22-24; of *Storm Cloud*, 134, 167-172, 222, 270; of *White Eagle*, 134, 222; Connell was yard manager, 239; never built another extreme clipper, 172; prices of wooden ships, 136; rules for iron ships, 133; roller reefing gear, 148; typical ship of 1860s, 227
Stephen, James, shipbuilder, 160
Stephen, William, shipbuilder, 143, 160
Stevens, John R, draws plan of *Marco Polo, 186*
Stevens, Robert, engineer, 105
Stevens, R W, author, 212
Stobart, John, artist, *184*
Stockton & London Shipping Co, 119-20
Stoddard Brothers, 225
Stonehouse, ship, described, 229-30
Storm Cloud, ship, *167, 169*, 170, *171;* beam-to-length ratio, 164; *big press coverage*, 167; compared with *Annandale*, 172; with *Cutty Sark*, 272; with *Marco Polo*, 172; costs and earnings, 172; deck layout, 162, 171; design not dictated by owner, 168-69, 281; extreme clipper, 135, 170, 222; hull-form analysed, 167-70, 254, journalist's description, 154, 167, 190; listed, 134, 161; passages, 154, 172; sail plan, 162, 172; speed, 168
Stornoway, ship, *154*, compared with *Three Bells, 156*, with *Vision*, 181; continually named by newspapers, 178; costs, 179, 277; half-model, 103, 154, 176; hull-form, 109, 176-77
Stowage capacity, iron and wood ships compared, 143
Stratford ex *Arctic*, ex-Atlantic packet, *139*
Strathbogie, schooner, costs, 276
Strathearn, ship, 259-60, 260, 261
Strathmore, barque, designed by Rennie, 167
Stuart & Douglas, shipowners, 175
Stuart Hahnemann, ship, 196
Suez Canal, effect on clippers, 253
Sullivan, Sir Edward, yacht owner, 242
Summer Cloud, painting, *203*
Sunderland, wooden shipbuilding beside River Wear, 138, *138*
Sunderland Museum, model of *Ganges*, 226
Sunny South, American clipper, *168*, 169
Sunshine, ship, costs, 277
Surveyors to Royal Navy, Sir John Henslowe, 52; Sir Henry Peake, 52; Sir Robert Seppings, 88; Sir William Symonds, 89
Susan Vittery, schooner, 214, *215*
Susanna, schooner, ranterpike rig, *84*, 85; sliding gunter masts, 65, 85
Sutherland, William, author, 15-16, 52
Swarthmore, ship, 134, 186
Swayne & Bovill, engineers, 162-63
Sweepstakes, American ship, 194; compared with *Robin Hood*, 182
Swift, schooner, *106;* Aberdeen clipper, 101, 105; costs, 276; faster than smacks, 82, 106; listed, 107; passages, 106
Swordfish (1845), ship described, *121*, 121-22, 166; speed 122
Swordfish (1851), American clipper, 177, *203*
Sydney, early effects of gold rush, 177-78
Sydney Daily Telegraph, 175
Sydney Morning Hrald, 157, 197
Syed Khan, opium clipper, 94
Sylph (1821), cutter, *60, 61;* compared with Leith smack, 79; with *Sappho*, 66-67; with *Scottish Maid*, 101; hull-form, 60-61; sail plan, 60
Sylph (1831), ship, 23, *92;* hull-form, 25, 91-93; sail plan, 92; specially built for opium trade, 94
Sulphiden, Danish schooner, lines and sail plans, *210*
Symmetos, 88
Symmetry, ship, 88
Symonds, Sir William, advocates steep deadrise, 39, 63, 73, 97; as designed, 59, 73, 88-90; designer of HMS *Columbine*, 93; of HMS *Dolphin*, 89; of *Pantaloon*, 93; surveyor to Royal Navy, 88-89
Syren (1838), opium clipper, 94
Syren (1856), schooner, 173

Taeping, ship, *234, 238;* compared with *Ganges*, 225; with other tea clippers, 220, 234; flying kites set, 233; dimensions, 234; hull-form, 234-35; half-model, 234
Tait, Capt R, 162
Taitsing, ship, compared with *Serica*, 240; candidate for identification, *239;* compared with other clippers, 239-40
SS *Taiwan*, brig, costs, 278
Talavera, ship, 134
Talpore, troopship, 135
Tank tests, early use of, 16, 105; by A Hall & Sons, *104*, 104-05
Tartar (by 1779), privateer, 32
Tartar (1840), brig, costs, 276
PS *Tartar* (1853), 140
Tasmanian Daily News, 190

Tayleur, ship, *199;* compared with other iron ships, 134-35, 199-200, 202; cost of building, 199; half-model and ship as built, 198-99; wreck, 199; listed, 198
Tayleur, Charles, shipbuilder, 198-99
Tayleur, Charles, & Co, ships they built listed and described, 198-201, 281
Tayleur, Edward, 198
Tayleur, Sanderson & Co, 198
Taylor, Josiah, artist, 241
Tea clippers, early use of, 74; fastest in 1860s, 219-20; recognisable type, 218, 221; principal builders of, 218
Tea Clippers (MacGregor, revised 1983 edition), Block Coefficient explained, 20; paintings, 237; plans of clippers, 176, 177, 179, 204-05, 220, 234, 257; of *Maitland*, 231; *Oriental*'s passage, 117; *Challenger*'s lines plan, 196, 219
Teazer, brig, setting single topsails, *208*
Tempest, ship, converted to auxiliary screw, 86; listed, 161, 164
Ternate, Dutch ship, *156*
Teupken, D A, artist, *114*, 114, *122*
PS *Teviot*, mail steamer, 157
Tebiot, schooner, 118
Thalia, ship, *62;* builder's plan, 62; calls at St Helena, 59; compared with *Neilson*, 68; hull-form and deck plan, 62; maiden passage described, 62-63
Thames, schooner, 118
Thames Iron & Shipbuilding Co, 166
Thane of Fife, sloop, costs, 275
The Bruce, brig, costs, 274
The Caliph, ship, *258;* auxiliary screw, 258; compared with other ships, 250; with *Transit*, 51; costs, 279; Hall's last extreme clipper, 253, 257; hull-form, 257; spar dimensions compared with other clippers, 247, 253, 257-58
The Colleen Bawn, barque, costs, 278
The Goolwa, ship, costs, 278
The Murray, ship, 278
The Oak, schooner, costs, 278
The Times, reports first news of gold discovery, 157
The Tweed, ship, ex PS *Punjaub;* influence on *Cutty Sark*, 254, 258
Theory of the Wave System of Naval Architecture, 168
Theresa Secunda, slaver, 86
Thermopylae, ship, *243, 244, 245, 246, 248;* brace winch, 151, 246; compared with *Annandale*, 175; with *Cutty Sark*, 254; with *Gauntlet*, 165; with other ships, 246-48; barque rig, 248; dimensions, 244, 247, 254; deck layout, 245-46; designed by Waymouth, 242-245; Double topgallants, 150, *248;* hull-form, 241, 243-45; hull-form similarities with other ships, 243-44, 254, 257, 262; record passages and career, 247-48; plans survive, 116, 232, 244; resemblance to *Christiana Thompson*, *243*, 246; roller-reefing sails, 149, *242;* sail plan and spar dimensions, 246-48; sail plan compared with *Maitland*, 232; spar dimensions listed, 247, 280; speed, 234, 254-55; Waymouth's original plans, *246*, 280; photograph, *216;* UD tons coefficient, 231
Thessalus, ship, 258
Thetis (*c*1780), unidentified fine-lined ship, 34
Thetis (1801), privateer built by Brockbank, 34
Thibaut, French master, 37
Thomas, shipwright, 55
Thomas, George, shipbuilder, *191*
Thomas Arbuthnot, ship, half-model, 104, *104*, 108; costs, 276; hull-form, 104, 107-08; takes first Australian gold to England, 157
Thomas Hamlin, ship, 135
Thomas Stephens, ship, *254;* clipper status, 253
Thompson, Benjamin, (Count Rumford), 16, *17*
Thompson, Cornelius, naval architect, 245
Thompson, George, interest in Hood's shipyard, 245; names of ships owned, 150-59, 246; orders clipper 1874, 262; owners of *Phoenician*, 128; owner of *Thermopylae*, 150, 245, 248
Thompson, Joseph, L, & Sons Ltd., shipbuilders, 231
Thompson, Robert, jnr, builder of *Helena Mena*, 146
Thomson, J & G, builders, of *Bay of Cadiz*, 135
Thorald, yacht owner, 74
Three Bells, ship, 155, 156; hull-form, 155; ownership, 156; passages, 156; speed, 156; sail plan, 156
Three Sisters, ship, *46*, 46-47
Ticonderoga, ship, 187
Tide, rise and fall affects hull-form, 44
Tiller, on schooner *c*1869, 279
Timaru, ship, 260, 263
Time, schooner, bought for opium trade, 84, 93, 95; designed with raking midship section, 84-85, 122; ranterpike rig, 85
SS *Tintern*, 123
Titania, ship, *235, 236, 237, 238;* deck layout similar to *Ariel*, 235, 237; dimensions, 234; compared with *Gauntlet*, 165; with *Harlaw*, 231; with *Scawfell*, 202; extreme clipper, 235-36, 240; fast passages, 239; hull-form compared with other clippers, 234-36; sail plan, 238-39; UD tons coefficient, 202, 231, 234; speed, 235; scantlings, 236-37; spar dimensions listed, 247
Titus, A, shipbuilder, *123*
Todd, Capt, 79
Tonnage, Aberdeen bow reduces new measurement, 99-100, 106-07, 114-15; builder's old measurement defined (BM or BOM), 271; as measured in America, 138, 154; carpenter's measure formula, 24; evasion of New Measurement produces fine-lined hulls, 104, 100, 106, 154, 270; gross defined, 272; guide to fineness of hull, 20, 107, 155; history of measurement rules before 1836, 23-25; internal measurement proposed, 151-52; Old Measurement, 23-55, 98; Old Measurement dimensions, 271; New Measurement, 23, 25, 97-98, *98*, 99; New Measurement dimensions, 272; 1854 Rule Measurements, 272-73; net register defined, 272; under deck defined, 272; rules defined, 271-73
Tonnage, 1821 Commission, 24-25, 97; 1833 Commission, 25, 97; 1849 Commission, 151; 1854 rules outlined, 151-52
Tornado, ship, 134, 161, 164, *165*
Torrington, schooner, 107; as opium clipper, 106; costs, 277
Trade Wind, American ship, 139
Tractat om Skepps-Byggeriet, *16*
Traité du Navire (Bouguer), 15
Transactions of the Institution of Naval Architects, *229, 234*
Transit (1800), as first rigged, *51;* cost, 51; design, 50-51, 110, 270; hull-form, 101; sail plan, 50-51, 77
Transit (1809), compared with Post Office packet, 48; described, 50-51, 110; plan, *51*
Transit (1819), described, 50-52; a clipper, 58
Treatise on Marine and Naval Architecture (Griffiths), 168
Treatise on Marine Architecture (Hedderwick), 18
Treatise on Masting Ships and Mast Making (Fincham), 17, 92
Treatise on Naval Architecture (Hutchinson), 44, *45*
Treatise on Ship-Building and Navigation (Murray), 15
Tredwen, shipbuilder, *268*
Treenails, with screw threads, 140, 206
Trevithick, Richard, engineer, 147
Trial trips, 223, 250
Trio, barque, 109; costs, 276
Trotman & Rodgers, anchors, 265
SS *Tsz'ru* 146
Tubal Caine, ship, 142-43
Tugela, ship, costs, 278
Turnbull, Gregor, & Co, shipowners, 144
Tweedie, Cmdr Francis, 173
Twins, sloop, costs, 274
Tyburnia, ship, compared with *Mofussilite*, 227; model for Stephen's designs, 172, 227
Tynemouth, barque, 135
Typhoon, ship, compared with *Hurricane*, 160-62; cost, 160; described, 159, 161, 197; dismasted, 160, 162; spar dimensions, 160, 184; sharp hull, 172
Tyzack & Dobson (Dobinson), 111, 121, 146

Uitenhague, schooner, 57
Ullock, barque, costs, 279
Undaunted, ship, costs, 277
Underhill, Harold, 260, 262
Undine, ship, sister to Maitland, 232-33
Union (1826), smack, costs, 275
Union (1841), brigantine, costs, 276
SS *Union* (1854), 142
Union, barquentine, *265;* hull-form, 265; sail plan, 265-67
United States National Archives, 55
United States Nautical Magazine and Naval Journal, 191

Universal Dictionary of the Marine (Falconer's), 15
Upham, J A & W, shipbuilders, 19, 211, *211*

Vanda, barque, costs, 278
Vanguard (1852), ship, 165
Vanguard (1857), ship, 233
SS *Vanguard* (1872), costs, 279
PS *Vectis*, 140
Velocidade, ship, 181; costs, 277
Venilia, brig, costs, 275
Ventilation, in wood ship, 195
Vernon, Hon George, 52, 73, 89
Vernon, H J, artist, *90*
Vernon, T, & Son, builder of *James Livesey*, *Philosopher*, and *Slive Donard*, 134; takes over yard of Rennie, Johnson & Rankine, 166
Venus (1807), ship, *47;* hull-form, 47
Victoria (1837), brig, costs, 275
Victoria (1847), schooner, 107; costs, 277
Victoria (*c*1855), 141
PS *Victoria and Albert*, Royal yacht, 23
Victory, ship, 148
Vimeira, ship, 157
Vindex, schooner, described, 207; costs, 207, 277
Vining, Robert, shipowner, 114
Violet, brig, costs, 275
HMS *Viper*, cutter, 28
Virginia, plans of vessels built in, 16
Virginia, ship, *123*
Vision (1854), Aberdeen ship, *180;* Aberdeen house, 180, 246; costs, 277; deck layout, 181; cost of diagonal build, 140; diagonal construction, 140, 180-81, 194; dimensions, 176, 202; half-models, 103, 154, 176, 180; hull-form, 107, 179-81; moderate rake to stem, 115; passages, 181-82; sail plan, 181
Vision (1854), iron ship, 166
Visitor, brig, costs, 275
Volant, American brig, lines plan, *211*
Vulcan, ship, 132
Vulcan Foundry, 198

W. S. Lindsay, ship, 134
Wade, partner in Robertson & Co, 221
Waddell, Lieut, captain of *Shenandoah*, 224
Waitangi, ship, capstan, *147*
Walker, William, builder of *Ambassador*, 145; of *Shamrock*, 241; of *Shun Lee*, 242
Wallace, Frederick W, author, 138, 150, 186
Walter Hamilton, brig, costs, 275
Walter Hood, ship, 159
Walters, John, 141
Walters, Samuel, artist, *165*, 175, 180-81
Wanderer, brig, costs, 276
Ward, T W, artist, 46, 69, 70, 80, *103*, 162, 254
Ward, William, owner and master, 44-45
Wardley, J R, shipowner, 225
Warren, Charles William, photographer, *2* (frontispiece)
Warren Packet, smack, costs, 275
HMS *Warrior*, armoured ship, design of, 243-44
Warrington, schooner, 198
Warrington, shipbuilding at, 198-201
Water Witch (Waterwitch), (1843), schooner, 101, 107; costs, 276
Waterman, Capt R, 124-25, 184
Waterwitch (1831), barque, *98;* hull-form, 91; opium clipper, 91, 94
Waterwitch (1834), brig, yacht, 89-90; compared with *Anonyma*, 92, 94; design, 87; half-model, 19
Waterford Line, 84, 99
Watkins, barque, *120;* compared with *Electric Telegraph*, 121, 197; described, 120-21; hull-form similar to *Acasta*, 109, 116, 120-21; lines plan, 119, 120
Watson, G C, naval architect, *238*, 238-39
Watson, William, 141
Watts, Isaac, naval architect, 243
Wave, brigantine, costs, 276
Wave Form theory, (Wave Line theory), 168-69
Wawn, T W, surveyor, 175
Waymouth, Bernard, naval architect, career, 242; designed *Thermopylae*, 242-47, 262; of clippers, 242-44; names of ships designed, 242, 262; *Thermopylae's* sail plan, 245, 247; surveyor to Lloyds Register, 242-43
Webb, Isaac, builder, 123
Webb, William H, builder of *Challenge*, 185; China packets, 123, *124;* of *Comet*, *184;* of *Helena*, 123, *123;* of *Malek-Adhel*, *88;* of *Swordfish*, 177; of *Volant*, *211*
Webster, J, shipbuilder, 209
Weedon, E, artist, *163*
Welch, J K, 251
Wesleyan Missionary Socity, 251
West Indiamen, hull proportions, 13, 32
Westacott, John, shipbuilder, 198, 263
Westacott, William, shipbuilder, 263-64
Western Isles, schooner, costs, 276
Weymouth, ship, 204
Whalsey, smack, costs, 279
Whirlwind, ship, 161
Whitcombe, Thomas, artist, *42*, 64
White, Joseph, builder of *Waterwitch*, 19, 89-91
White, J & R, 221; diagonal wood construction, and list of ships built, 23, 140, 281; diagrams, *140*
White, Thomas, jnr, shipbuilder, 89
White, W H, naval architect, 247
White Eagle, ship, *170*, career and passages, 172; compared with *Storm Cloud*, 169-72; extreme clipper, 172, 222; hull-form, 169-70, 196; listed, 134; weight of materials, 170
White Mouse, schooner, 107, 116; costs, 277
White Star, Canadian ship, 139
White Star Line (Liverpool), 190-91, 194
Whiteadder, ship, 254
Wigram's dry dock, 224
Wigram & Green, builders of *St. Helena*, 55
Wild Dayrell, schooner, 214
Wild Deer, ship, 239
Wild Duck, ship, *149*
Wild Flower, ship, 154
William and Mary, Royal yacht, 52
William Davie, ship, *227*, 262
William Fairbairn, ship, 134
William le Lacheur, ship, described, 227-28; photographed, 227-28, *229*
William Punton, brig, *112;* costs, 277; hull details, 110, 113; listed, 107; sail plan, 110, 113
Williams, Capt, 251
Willis, John, interest in composite ships, 143; names of ships owned, 254, 258; buys PS *Punjaub*, 254; cousin orders clipper, 257
Wilson, John, shipbuilder, 96
Wilson, M R, buys *Shenandoah*, 225
Windhover, ship, 239
Windlass, Armstrong Patent, 146; improvements after 1850, 146-47; in *Hurricane*, 162; indicates merchant ship, 59, 64; makers, 111, 146-47, 237; operation of, *128*, 146-47, *147*, 260
Windsor Castle, mail packet, *48*
Winefred, ship, 134
Witch of the Wave, American ship, 180
Wizard, schooner, costs, 277
Wm. Renton, incorrent spelling, 117
Wolley, Capt Thomas, 37
HMS *Wolverine*, 225
Wood, Charles, shipbilder, 165
Wood shipbuilding, American and British ships compared, 136-37; American clippers of over 1500 tons listed, 139-40; conserving timber in construction, 135-36; diagonal and experimental construction, *22;* few ships of over 1000 tons built in UK, 137-38; many ships of over 1000 tons produced in Canada, 138-39; quantities of timber used, 20; sectional drawings, *136;* shortage of grown timber affects hull design, 21-22; structural timbers, *18*, *21;* UK ships of over 1000 tons listed, 138; use of iron for structural members, 22; *see also*, Construction, Diagonal
Woodland, brig, costs, 278
Woodlark, brig, 181; correct spelling for *Woodland*, 278
Woodpecker, schooner, 142
Worcester, John R, merchant, 288
Workington, shipbuilding at, 136, 201
Workington & Harrington Shipbuilding Co, builders of *Dunmail* and *Jubilee*, 201-02
Wright, Thomas, shipbuilder, 141
Wright, W & R, shipbuilders, *192*, 192
Wylo, ship, 234; hull-form, 234

Xarifa, ex *Theresa Secunda*, schooner, 86

Yachting (American), 212
Yachts, analysed by Fincham, 73; *Anonyma*, 92; bought for opium trade, 92, 95, 209; built of iron, 122; influence on naval design, 88; plan by Hedderwick, 18; *Salamander*, 207-09; *see also* Royal Yachts, Falcon
Yang-tze, ship, 221; costs, 279; compared with

Eliza Shaw, 218
Yarborough, Lord, 71-74
Ythan, schooner, costs, 275
Young, Charles, author, 132
Young Sea-Officer's Sheet Anchor, 47
Young Lochinvar, ship, 218, 234

Zanzibar, Sultan of, 221, 225
Zephyr, barquentine, *265*
Zariza, Norwegian schooner, lines and sail plans, *210*
Ziba, jackass barque, costs, 278; described, 205; in tea trade, 221
Zinc sheathing, 132